Cognition

Cognition

The Thinking Animal

Daniel B. Willingham

University of Virginia

Prentice
Hall

Upper Saddle River, New Jersey 07458

Library of Congress Cataloging-in-Publication Data

Willingham, Daniel B.
     Cognition : the thinking animal / Daniel B. Willingham.
        p. cm.
     Includes bibliographical references and index.
     ISBN 0–13–028699–0
     1. Cognitive psychology.   I. Title.
  BF201.W56 2001
  153—dc21

                                        00–047882

VP/Editorial Director: *Laura Pearson*
Acquisitions Editor: *Jayme Heffler*
Editorial Assistant: *April Klemm*
AVP/Director of Production and Manufacturing: *Barbara Kittle*
Director of Marketing: *Beth Gillet Mejia*
Marketing Manager: *Sharon Cosgrove*
Managing Editor: *Mary Rottino*
Project Manager: *Alison Gnerre*
Production Assistant: *Elizabeth Best*
Prepress and Manufacturing Manager: *Nick Sklitsis*
Prepress and Manufacturing Buyer: *Tricia Kenny*
Interior Design: *Bruce Hobart (Pine Tree Composition)*
Line Art Manager: *Guy Ruggiero*
Art Director: *Jayne Conte*
Cover Design: *Bruce Kenselaar*
Electronic Illustrations: *Mirella Signoretto*
Director, Image Resource Center: *Melinda Reo*
Photo Research Supervisor: *Beth Boyd*
Image Permission Supervisor: *Kay Dellosa*
Photo Researcher: *Karen Pugliano*
Cover Art: *Auguste Rodin/Explorer, Paris/Superstock, Inc.*

Acknowledgments for copyrighted material may be found beginning
on p. 590, which constitutes an extension of this copyright page.

This book was set in 10/12 Trump Mediaeval by Pub-Set
and was printed by R. R. Donnelley/Harrisonburg.
The cover was printed by Phoenix.

© 2001 by Prentice-Hall, Inc.
Upper Saddle River, New Jersey 07458

Printed in the United States of America
10   9   8   7   6   5   4   3   2   1

ISBN 0-13-028699-0

Prentice-Hall International (UK) Limited, *London*
Prentice-Hall of Australia Pty. Limited, *Sydney*
Prentice-Hall Canada Inc., *Toronto*
Prentice-Hall Hispanoamericana, S.A., *Mexico*
Prentice-Hall of India Private Limited, *New Delhi*
Prentice-Hall of Japan, Inc., *Tokyo*
Pearson Education Asia Pte. Ltd., *Singapore*
Editora Prentice-Hall do Brasil, Ltda., *Rio de Janeiro*

*This book is dedicated
to my parents*

CONTENTS

3   Attention   100

4   Sensory Memory and Primary Memory   145

5 Memory Encoding   192

6   Memory Retrieval   235

7   Memory Storage   279

8 Visual Imagery   333

9 Decision Making and Deductive Reasoning   382

10 Problem Solving   436

11 Language   485

PREFACE

A long-standing goal of human enquiry is to understand ourselves. How can we characterize the human species? Here are some of the better-known proposals:

> Man is by nature a political animal—Aristotle
> Man is a noble animal—Sir Thomas Browne
> Man is a tool-using animal—Thomas Carlyle
> Man is a reasoning animal—Seneca
> Man is a social animal—Benedict Spinoza
> Man is a rational animal who always loses his temper when he is called upon to act in accordance with the dictates of reason—Oscar Wilde.

I would propose that all of these proposals are, in a sense, correct, but they are all rooted in another characteristic. We are able to act politically, to use tools effectively, to understand nobility, etc., because of our ability to think. The heart of the matter is that we are thinking animals, and it is thinking that affords these other abilities or, at least, affords our having these abilities in the manner that we do. The book you are reading is a study of cognition—of how humans think.

This book is intended for students taking their first course in cognitive psychology. No background knowledge in psychology or statistics is presupposed. As is typical of other books designed for such a course, the book is organized around the major subject areas of cognitive psychology, and most of the book can be covered over the course of a semester. Again, as is typical of cognitive psychology textbooks, the coverage begins at what may be loosely thought of as lower-level processes, and proceeds toward higher-level processes.

There are three things I would like you to know about this book: what I have done regarding it's readability, what I have done regarding pedagogy, and how I have handled the inclusion of material from cognitive neuroscience.

➤ READABILITY

I have friends throughout the country who teach introductory cognitive psychology at their college or university. None of them ever says something like, "My students are crowding office hours, calling me at home, and filling my email in-box demanding to know more, more, more cognitive psychology! They love it like a mouse loves cheese!" The comments of my friends usually run more along the lines of, "They hate the subject matter, hate the course, hate the book, hate me."

Why? I don't know, but it has been the guiding force in my writing this book. *My goal is to have a class full of students who have done the assigned reading, and who are excited by cognitive psychology.* The way to do that, I think, is to communicate what makes cognitive psychology interesting. To be honest, I've never cared much for the way that other textbooks have sought to keep students interested. The usual strategy is to include lots of "real world" examples and lots of demonstrations, usually found in little boxes that appear every few pages. This strategy seems to confirm the reader's growing suspicion that they are bored by sending the implicit message, "Yes, yes, I know this stuff is boring, but hang in there, and every few pages I'll toss in one of those boxes with a demonstration or real-world application to keep you going."

I've done three things in this book to try to arouse the reader's interest in the material:

1. I have tried to be careful about making the questions that motivate cognitive psychologists explicit. I think the questions we ask are of interest to a lot of people, but we don't always do the best job of explaining the questions in any detail. We plunge right into the answers, and the answers seem arcane and removed from anything anyone would care about. Each chapter in this book is organized around two or three straightforward questions that are easy to appreciate, and the importance of which are explained in detail.

2. To the extent possible, I have used a narrative structure. By that I mean that there are causal links within and across chapter sections, so that it makes it more clear *why* you are reading something. Nothing is more boring than a list of unconnected facts.

3. I have tried to write in a non-stilted, not-especially-academic style.

Despite the light tone, this book is not light in content. As you can see by flipping through any given chapter, I cover the major topics in each sub-area of the field. (An easy way to check the coverage is by examining the "key terms" section at the end of each chapter.) Included in the coverage of almost all of these topics are significant details from landmark experiments, including the methodology, graphs of results, and so on. Again, a lighter tone should not be interpreted as indicating lighter coverage.

➤ PEDAGOGY

Readability is fine, but the goal of a textbook is, after all, that students learn the material. Different students like and use different pedagogical features, so I've included a few different ones to help them learn.

- Brief **previews** of each section pose the broad questions and provide the broad answers contained in the section.

- **Key terms** are identified by bold-face type, and are defined immediately thereafter. They are also collected in a glossary.
- Each section closes with a series of questions. The **Stand-on-one-foot summary questions** simply ask the student to summarize what they have learned in the section they have just read. I call them stand-on-one-foot-summaries after the talmudic story of the heretic who went to great sages, asking each to summarize all of the Torah in the time that he could stand on one foot. (He finally found a willing sage in Hillel who quoted from Leviticus, "What is hateful to you, do not to others.") Thus, the idea is simply to get the reader to pause for a moment and make sure they understood the major points by summarizing what they have just read.
- The end of each section also includes questions that require considerably more thought; the student will need to apply what he or she has just learned to new situations, or to go beyond the material in some way. I call these **Questions that require two feet.** Answers to all questions are provided at the close of each chapter.
- There is a companion web site http://www.prenhall.com/willingham to accompany the text, authored by Robert Bramucci of the California State University, Fullerton. The web site includes an online study guide for students (lots of self-test questions in different formats), a recap and summary of each chapter, links to relevant sites on the internet, and more.

Another feature of this book that I think students and professors will find useful is the Appendix. This book assumes no background knowledge on the part of the student, but an appreciation of the work in cognitive psychology often requires knowledge of statistical or methodological concepts. The Appendix contains background information and explanations of several concepts (e.g., statistical significance) that may be familiar to a student who has taken other psychology courses, but that a beginning student may not know. In order to maintain the flow of the book, these explanations are collected in the Appendix.

➤ THE BRAIN

There is no doubt that the influence of neuroscience on cognitive psychology is substantial, and it is increasing. This trend poses a problem for the writers of textbooks, and the teachers of cognitive psychology courses. Cognitive neuroscience can easily fill a semester-long course, and indeed, there are stand-alone texts on the subject. Further, discussion of this work presupposes some background in neuroscience. How, then, to fairly represent the impact of cognitive neuroscience on cognitive psychology without making the course twice as long, and without setting another prerequisite for the students?

I have tried to represent the state of the field, including key findings from cognitive neuroscience, and at the same time to give the instructor some flexibility. The chapters of this book make reference to key neuroscientific studies where appropriate; there are certain findings that have had such an impact on cognitive psychology that they simply must be part of any course. I have tried to describe these findings in a way that assumes no background on the part of the student.

For the instructor who prefers a greater emphasis on cognitive neuroscience, I have included additional materials. The "Brain Interlude" that follows Chapter 1 introduces the student to the rationale behind cognitive neuroscientific studies, the methods they use, and a brief introduction to brain anatomy. Throughout the rest of the book, key studies from cognitive neuroscience are discussed in boxes set off from the main text. These experiments were selected with an eye towards exposing students to a variety of methods and some of the key issues in cognitive neuroscience. Those instructors who place less emphasis on cognitive neuroscientific approaches can, of course, instruct students to simply skip over this material.

I hope that I have written a textbook that will make students enthusiastic about this field, and will make them want to know more than they can find in this book. Hillel's answer to the impatient heretic is not always quoted in full; after providing the summary of the Torah, Hillel added, "Now go and study," acknowledging that a one-sentence summary was bound to be lacking, and that the heretic should learn more. I have not succeeded in summarizing cognitive psychology in a sentence, but I can add the entreaty; I hope that this book will serve as a starting point from which students will want to learn still more about the field.

I would greatly appreciate feedback and suggestions regarding this text. It is easiest to reach me via electronic mail: willingham@virginia.edu

► ACKNOWLEDGMENTS

Discovering what you do not know and the extent to which you must lean on others when writing a textbook is a humbling experience. This humility comes into sharp focus when writing acknowledgments. I have had to resist the urge to catalogue the many persons who were of assistance ("Mad love and a big shout-out to that guy who gave me a dime for the Xerox machine in the library!") and will try limit my thanks to those people whose contributions were quite direct.

I am very grateful to the team of people at Prentice Hall who transformed the messy sheets I sent them into the book you hold: Mary Rottino was ever vigilant as managing editor in all matters; Alison Gnerre beautifully combined the calm actions and faint air of desperation characteristic of an effective production editor; Jayne Conte and Bruce Kenselaar are responsible for the beautiful cover; and Guy Ruggiero and Mirella Signoretto remade my scribbles into the clear line art you see here. My thanks, too, to Sharon Cosgrove, marketing manager, and Ronald Fox, marketing assistant, for their work to ensure people know about the book, and to Tricia Kenny as prepress and manufacturing buyer. April Dawn Klemm was an excellent jack-of-all-trades as editorial assistant. I also thank Andy Snyder for his help in preparing the index. Eric Stano was my first editor and had much to do with shaping the book to its current form. I'm especially grateful to Jayme Heffler, who had the difficult task of stepping into the editorial process in mid-stream, a job she consistently performed with great skill, common sense, and good humor. I'm very grateful to all for their hard work.

I also offer sincere thanks to my colleagues who reviewed earlier versions of chapters: Thomas R. Alley, Clemson University; Terri Bonebright, De Pauw University; Linda S. Buyer, Governor's State University; Stephen Christman, University of Toledo; Jane Marie Clipman, Lafayette College; Peter Derks, The College of William and Mary; Bob Ferguson, Buena Vista University; Diana Heise, Millsaps College; Richard L. Marsh, University of Georgia; Danielle McNamara, Old Dominion University; Kristy A. Nielson, Marquette University; and Marilyn L. Turner, Wichita State University. Their thoughtful, careful reviews led to substantial changes in the format and the details of the book. I have reviewed textbooks for publishers and can attest to the fact that no one does it for the honorarium; it is a service to the field, and I greatly appreciate it.

I have had the remarkable good fortune to learn from and work with some great cognitive psychologists, all of whom are also gentle, warm-hearted people. My thanks to my graduate school advisors—Bill Estes, Steve Kosslyn, and Mary Jo Nissen—who were so generous with their time and wisdom. John Gabrieli has also been an enduring influence as a colleague and friend. I'm also grateful to my cognitive colleagues at the University of Virginia—Michael Kubovy, Denny Proffitt, Tim Salthouse, and Bobbie Spellman—for their helpfulness with particular questions, for their encouragement in all matters, and for making it fun to come to work.

Finally, my special thanks to my parents, who have been patient and supportive guides throughout my life. I dedicate this book to them, for the advices.

Daniel B. Willingham
University of Virginia

1

The Approach of Cognitive Psychology

Have you ever wondered how we see or how we remember things? Have you ever contemplated the strange nature of attention?

I didn't think so.

Most of the people I know do contemplate how the mind works, but only when their mind lets them down. They contemplate memory ("Why can't I find my keys?"), attention ("I *want* to find my keys, so why can't I concentrate?"), and vision ("How could I not see my keys when they were right in front of me the whole time?"). Questions such as "How does vision work?" seem somewhat interesting, but no more interesting than thousands of other questions. It's like someone asking you whether you want to know about the history of guitar making. "I don't know; maybe. Is it interesting?"

Truthfully, "How does vision work?" is a bad question because it's too general. In cognitive psychology, as in most fields, the devil is in the details, but that's where the fun is, too. Vision, attention, and memory become interesting only when you pose more specific questions about them.

This book poses questions about the mind and describes the answers cognitive psychologists have uncovered. The first thing we have to decide, then, is which questions to ask—how to get more specific than "How do we see?" You'll find that the questions one asks are deeply influenced by assumptions one makes about the mind and indeed, assumptions about what it is to be human. It seems obvious that it would be better not to make assumptions when one is just starting to study the mind. Therefore, the first question to take up is **"Why make assumptions?"** As we'll see, the answer is that it is difficult or impossible to avoid making assumptions.

If that's true, we should at least be clear about the assumptions cognitive psychologists make. If you know the assumptions, it will be clearer to you why cognitive psychologists ask the questions they do, and if you understand why they ask a particular question, it will be much easier to understand the answer. But I'm not going to start with the questions cognitive psychologists ask. The approach of cognitive psychologists was developed in part as a response to other approaches that people had tried but that seemed to have flaws. Thus we start by asking, **"How did philosophers and early psychologists study the mind?"** As you'll see, a number of different approaches have been tried in the last 2,000 years, but it was only about 100 years ago that there was a serious, systematic effort to use the scientific method to study human thought. That date is some 200 years or more after the scientific method had been applied to other domains of knowledge. Furthermore, cognitive psychology was not the first scientific approach to studying the mind; it arose in response to the flaws in other methods.

Finally, we end this chapter by asking, **"How do cognitive psychologists study the mind?"** As you'll see, the cognitive approach is informed largely by an analogy of the mind to a computer; both take in information, manipulate it, and then produce responses. The metaphor is more complicated than that, of course, and we will elaborate this metaphor later. But first, we have to start at the beginning.

➤ *WHY MAKE ASSUMPTIONS?*

> ➤ *PREVIEW* People make two types of assumptions when they study the mind. The first assumption concerns <u>what the important questions are.</u> You can't study everything at once, so you must pick some aspect of the mind as a starting point for study. What you perceive to be the starting point is biased by your assumptions about the mind. The second type of assumption concerns <u>beliefs about the mind</u> (even very general, vague beliefs) that color how you think about vision, attention, or memory before you really know anything about them. In this section we look at examples of these assumptions in the study of vision.

Two types of assumptions typically are made in studying the mind. First, you make assumptions about what aspects of the mind are important enough to explain. You can't say, for example, "I want to explain all of vision." Of course you do. But you have to start somewhere. So what aspect of vision will you tackle? The second type of assumption is more obviously an assumption in that it is something you believe (maybe for good reason, maybe not) that affects what you believe about vision before you even start trying to learn about it.

Here's an example of each type of assumption, applied to vision. We start with an assumption about what is important to explain. For most of the last 2,000 years, people interested in vision wanted to explain the conscious experience of visual perception. The thing to be explained was how we consciously perceive the qualities of an object such as its shape, size, and distance; unconscious processes involved in vision were not considered. Cognitive psychologists also seek to explain conscious visual perception, but they are more interested in the unconscious processes that eventually lead to conscious perception. In some ways, visual information in consciousness is the endpoint of vision; it is the many steps before the endpoint that need to be explained because they are doing the work. More recently it has become obvious that some types of vision never become conscious. Some parts of the visual system help you move your body, but you are never aware of any aspect of this type of vision; I explain how this is possible in chapter 2.

The second type of assumption occurs when your beliefs influence the questions you pose when you study something. Here's an example. For a couple of centuries, one of the specific questions posed about vision was, "The lens of the eye inverts the image of the world, so that the image is projected on to the back of the eye upside down. We obviously don't see the world upside-down, so how does the image get turned back rightside-up?" (Figure 1.1).

This question was posed in 1604 after Johanes Kepler speculated that the crystalline body of the eye functions as a lens does and therefore inverts the image. (René Descartes put the idea to the test some 20 years thereafter, conducting an experiment of sorts with the eye of a bull.) This question bothered philosophers until the early 19th century, even though William Molyneux, writing in 1692, gave the correct answer to this problem: It's not really a problem. It doesn't

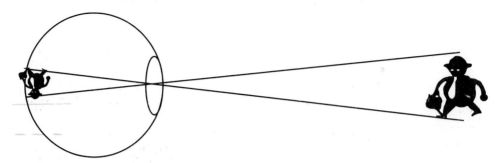

Figure 1.1. *Light falling on the eye is inverted by the lens. Therefore, the image on the retina is upside-down compared with objects in the real world.*

matter that the top of the world is represented on the bottom of the retina. But the problem of the inverted retinal image was so troubling to people that Johanes Mueller, a famous physiologist, still felt compelled to address it as late as 1826.

Why was the inversion of the retinal image so disturbing? Because of a background assumption about vision everyone was making. It seemed reasonable to assume that the conscious perception of the visual world was not in the retina but in some part of the brain. The assumption was that the retina presents an image to the part of the brain that handles conscious perception. When you are thinking that way, the back of the eye seems like a little screen on which another part of the brain watches the world go by, only the movie appears to be upside-down. So the natural question to ask is, "How does the mind perceive the world rightside-up?" This assumption is wrong-headed because it turns the conscious visual part of the brain into a little person watching the retina.

Mueller proposed instead that everything the mind perceives is a function of the state of the nerves coming into the brain (he called it the theory of specific nerve energies). In other words, perception is based solely on what the brain does. The pattern of neural activity *is* perception; perception is not the product of someone watching the pattern of neural activity. Therefore, it doesn't matter whether the top of the world is represented in the top or the bottom of the retina as long as there is a consistent relationship between what is in the world and the pattern of neural activity to which it leads. If the top of the world is always in the bottom of the retina, that's fine, but if the top of the world could be anywhere in the retina, that would be a problem.

Here's another way to think about it. As you might know, a computer graphic file is stored as a series of 1s and 0s. When they are interpreted by the software in your computer, they form an image of . . . let's say a cat. You would not expect that if you printed out the 1s and 0s on a piece of paper that they would form the image of a cat; the 1s and 0s are a different representation of the image of the cat (Figure 1.2). In the same way, the pattern of neural activity on the retina doesn't have to look like the thing it's representing.

Once you drop the belief that the pattern of neural activity on the retina must look like what is out in the world, the inverted image problem disappears. But the belief that they must look alike is hard to drop if you are assuming that the mind watches the retina.

Computer File   **Software**   **Appearance on Computer Monitor**

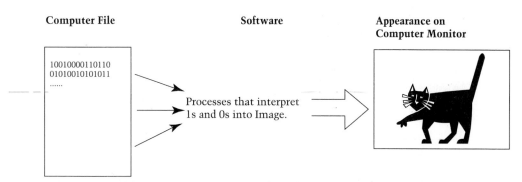

Figure 1.2. *A computer can represent the image of a cat in a format that looks nothing like a cat. The representation is interpreted by software in the computer and displayed as an image on the screen that is recognizable as a cat.*

So it sounds like assumptions get you in trouble, and what you need to do is not to make any assumptions; that way you won't start down the wrong path. It is much harder than you think not to assume anything. The tricky thing is that many of the assumptions we make are hard to spot because we take them so much for granted. Had I lived in the 17th century I don't think I would have been smarter than everyone else. I would have been scratching my head with the rest of them.

The next question we need to ask, obviously, is what sorts of assumptions cognitive psychologists make. How do they view the mind? What questions seem natural to ask if you're a cognitive psychologist? We'll get to that later in the chapter. In fact, we're not going to start our discussion with cognitive psychology. Cognitive psychology is approximately 40 years old, and people have been thinking about how the mind works for about 2,400 years. It is misleading to wrench cognitive psychology out of that historical context, because cognitive psychology evolved from that context. Many of the ideas in cognitive psychology grew out of older ideas, or in some cases in direct opposition to older ideas. So we start with the older ideas, which set the stage for cognitive psychology.

STAND-ON-ONE-FOOT QUESTION

1. What two types of assumptions usually are made when we study the mind?

QUESTION REQUIRING TWO FEET

2. When we study the mind, we can't observe it directly. We can observe what people do and we can observe the environment around them, but we can't observe thought directly. What do you think this fact will mean for theories of the mind?

➤ How Did Philosophers and Early Psychologists Study the Mind?

> ➤ PREVIEW We can identify three waves in the history of the study of the mind before the advent of cognitive psychology. In the first wave, philosophers considered the workings of the mind. They were interested primarily in the acquisition of knowledge because philosophy is the study of knowledge in all its forms. During the Renaissance many domains were studied via the scientific method. The scientific method stressed observation, not simply reason alone. The scientific method was not applied to the study of the mind until the late 19th century, however, mostly because of assumptions people held about how the mind was likely to work. This application of scientific method to the study of the mind is the second wave. Initially, psychology was largely the study of conscious experience, but it took a radical turn between 1910 and the 1920s, when consciousness was expunged and psychology became the science of overt behavior. This movement, called behaviorism, was the third wave. Behaviorism was ascendant until the late 1950s, when mental life reasserted itself as an important part of any explanation of human behavior.

In this section we cover three basic trends in the history of the study of the mind before the development of cognitive psychology. The first trend concerns the philosophical background of the study of mind. We discuss only Western philosophy because that is the philosophical tradition that influenced early psychologists and, eventually, cognitive psychologists. The second concerns the application of the scientific method to the study of the mind. The third concerns the abandonment of the study of the mind in favor of the study of behavior. We cover each trend in turn.

Philosophical Underpinnings

ANCIENT GREECE. We're going to understand the questions cognitive psychologists pose by first looking at older approaches to understanding the mind. How far back do we go? As is often the case, we go back to the ancient philosophers of Greece, approximately 2,400 years ago. They left the first written record of consistent curiosity about and speculations on the workings of the mind (although there are bits and pieces scattered through earlier documents).

Philosophy is the pursuit of knowledge in all its forms, although over time many philosophical questions have been co-opted by the sciences. Because knowledge is central to philosophy, philosophers have been especially interested in how knowledge is acquired. There are three ways of asking about how knowledge is acquired, and these three questions were later asked by cognitive psychologists.

- Perception. How do we gain access to knowledge about the world immediately around us?
- Memory. How do we retain knowledge about the world for later use?

- Nature and nurture. What is the origin of knowledge? Is knowledge gained through experience, or is it largely innate, with experience serving merely to, in some sense, release or activate knowledge we are born with?

The Greek philosophers posed questions about the mind that were relevant to their broader interests about knowledge. What sort of answers did they come up with? They weren't even close. The answers usually were incorrect both in outlook and in detail. For example, in the 5th century BC, Democritus proposed that objects emit beams of atoms in the shape of the object, and these beams go into the eye, so that the shape of the object is pictured in the eye. Aristotle agreed that the heart of perception was a matter of characteristics of an object being carried to one's body; hence, a white object makes some part of your eye white.

Okay, so their answers were not very accurate, but were they at least asking good questions? Many books will tell you that the Greeks' lasting contribution lies in the questions they raised. "They set the agenda for future philosophers and eventually for cognitive psychology," is the usual verdict. I don't think that's quite accurate, though. I think that the real contribution lay not in the specific questions but in the assumptions they made that allowed them to pose those questions. We can list three.

- The world can be understood and predicted. It is worth trying to understand how the world works because the world works in systematic, predictable ways. The alternative view is that events occur randomly or at the whim of capricious gods, which would mean that trying to predict events is hopeless.
- Humans are part of that world. Humans are not different from other entities in the world in terms of our potential to understand and predict how they operate. Humans have no special status. The alternative view is that physical objects and perhaps animals may be predictable, but humans are qualitatively different, and one can never hope to predict what humans will do or how they will think.
- Explanations should be of this world. If you are explaining an event in this world, your explanation should be composed of other events within this world. You can't invoke magical or mystical happenings. For example, Hippocrates proposed that epilepsy was a disease of the body (as other diseases were understood to be), thereby rejecting earlier views that it resulted from direct intervention of a god.

These assumptions feel so natural to us today that it is hard to remember that they are assumptions. Indeed, these three assumptions are critical to all of the sciences. Experience now tells us that these assumptions are probably helpful in trying to explain things around us; at the time the Greeks first made them, they were considered quite bold. Once you assume that the world is predictable, that we can understand it, and that humans have no special place in this world (meaning human behavior can be explained just like anything else), it is natural to take the next step and ask a few questions about how the human mind works, such as how it perceives and remembers things. Hence, it's the assumptions that are most impressive, rather than the questions or the answers that were posed.

THE DARK AND MIDDLE AGES. It is hard to find any contributions to the philosophy of mind between the times of Aristotle, who died in 322 BC, and Descartes, born at the end of the 16th century. How is this possible?

Now, it's a slight exaggeration to say that nothing of interest on this subject happened during approximately 1,900 years, but the exaggeration is no more than slight. Any advances you could point to occurred in another field that influenced philosophy of mind indirectly.

In a nutshell, people dropped some of the background assumptions that the Greeks made. By 146 BC Greece was dominated by Rome, and the Romans had a more practical mindset than the Greeks. Pursuit of knowledge for its own sake was not especially esteemed, so no one was asking where knowledge comes from, as the Greeks had. With the fall of the Roman empire in 476 AD, Europe was dominated by various Germanic peoples, usually called "barbarians." Although *barbarian* has unpleasant connotations that probably aren't fairly applied to these people, it's fair to say they were not sitting around contemplating the workings of the mind. In addition, feudalism and the decline of urbanism did little to help intellectual life. The ascendance of the Christian church around the year 400 AD did not make for a favorable climate, either. The church much preferred that one be interested in the soul, not in scholarly pursuits unrelated to theology.

You shouldn't have the impression that intellectualism was dead during this age, but it was definitely channeled in certain directions, and those directions were not towards study of the human mind.

RENAISSANCE THROUGH THE 19TH CENTURY.

The Advent of Scientific Methods. The Renaissance refers to a time in Europe (the 15th through 17th centuries, very broadly) marked by the rise of humanism, a subsequent flowering of literature and the arts, and the beginnings of modern science. Humanism is an emphasis on secular concerns and the individual (as opposed to religious concerns and the religious community). From the viewpoint of a cognitive psychologist, a critical feature of the Renaissance was the return of one of the assumptions characteristic of ancient Greece: that the world can be understood and predicted and even more, that trying to understand the world is a worthwhile pursuit. Thus the literal meaning of *Renaissance* (rebirth) is appropriate. The Renaissance also saw a birth: the birth of modern science.

What makes something scientific? We often think of science as being associated with white coats and antiseptic laboratory equipment. In fact, science is not characterized by the people who do it or by subject matter. Science is simply a *method* of finding out new things. It is a method well suited to some questions (e.g., "What does the heart do?") and poorly suited to other questions (e.g., "What makes a novel great?").

What made the scientific method new in the Renaissance was its emphasis on observation as a route to knowledge. How do you know something is true? There are two possible roads to the truth: You can sit in your armchair and reason about what you think must be true, or you can go out and observe what happens in the world. For example, you might reason that planetary orbits must be circles because a circle is a perfect shape, and it would make sense for the universe to be organized in terms of perfect shapes (Figure 1.3). Or you would get a telescope and make observations of the planets and try to figure out what shape your observations are consistent with. Before the Renaissance, people did some observation, but contemplation and logic were more often considered the best route to knowledge.

There are two things to bear in mind. First, scientists then and now use both methods; after you've gone out into the world and made your observations, you still go back to your armchair to try to make sense of it all using reason. But the key is that once you think you've made sense of it, you go back out into the world armed with new predictions (the product of your armchair reasoning), which you will test with new observations. The second thing to bear in mind is that just because you're observing doesn't mean that you won't make (occasionally colossal) mistakes. Aristotle concluded that the mind must be located in the heart, not the brain, based on the observation that people sometimes survived severe injury to the brain, but they never survived serious injury to the heart.

Renaissance scientists made mistakes of interpretation (like Aristotle and like scientists today), but they were sound in their emphasis on observation. The power of understanding nature through observation had a number of dramatic successes during the Renaissance: Copernicus's assertion that the earth revolves around the sun and not vice versa; Galileo's formulation of the law relating distance, time and speed of free-falling bodies; Isaac Newton's assertion that gravity rules heavenly bodies and the humble apple; and William Harvey's assertion that blood circulates and that the heart functions as a pump. All of these advances were triumphs of the observational method as a path to knowledge.

Why Didn't Psychology Start Until 1879? Science really started moving in the 17th century. Advances were made in astronomy, physics, chemistry, and biology. Why did it take another 200 years for scientists to start studying the mind using the scientific method? You might be tempted to think that it was an equipment problem; they needed computers, sophisticated timing devices,

Figure 1.3. *The two main methods of inquiry: reasoning and observation.*

and so forth. . . forget it. A world of experiments on the workings of the mind can be done with a deck of playing cards (invented in about the 10th century).

No, the problem was still one of assumptions. The Renaissance brought back two of the assumptions that the Greeks made: that the world can be understood and predicted and that explanations should be of this world (i.e., you can't invoke ghosts or gods in your explanations). But their third assumption—that humans have no special status—was very, very hard to bring back. When you think about it for a moment, it is easy to see why.

Suppose you assume that humans have no special status in the world, in that human behavior is predictable, just as the behavior of physical bodies (such as a falling apple) is predictable. Humans are more complex, obviously, but they are still predictable. What does being predictable imply? It implies that the mind follows a set of rules. When you're in Situation A, your mind follows Rule 1; when you're in Situation B, it follows Rule 2; and so on. In saying that behavior is predictable, we are essentially saying, "It is possible to have a complete understanding of human behavior such that I can know what a person will do before he or she does it." This view is called **deterministic.**

The alternative is a **nondeterministic** view. This view says, "No, there is something else that guides our thoughts and determines our actions. Call it a soul, if you like. It's the working of this other agent that gives us free will. We are free to act as we please, so you will never be able to predict another person's behavior accurately."

If you take a nondeterministic view—if you believe that we have free will—studying the mind seems futile. Psychology tries to understand why people act as they do. But if they act as they do because of the vagaries of free will, which is by definition not bound by rules, how will psychologists ever understand human behavior? They won't.

Most people of that time probably assumed that free will existed and that although the scientific method might tell us a lot about the behavior of inanimate bodies such as planets and falling rocks, humans are wholly different, and the scientific method simply can't be applied to us. The very idea of applying the scientific method to studying the mind probably seemed as ridiculous to them as it would seem to you if I suggested that we apply the scientific method to evaluating literature.

The foregoing discussion does not mean that scientists believe that there is no such thing as a soul or that there is no such thing as free will. Whether there is a soul is a question that science is not well suited to answer. Many scientists believe that humans have a soul and have free will. However, one can't use these concepts in scientific theories and explanations of human behavior. That's not because they don't exist; it's because they are not understood in a scientific sense, so they don't mesh well with other concepts that are defined as scientists define concepts.

The great philosopher Immanuel Kant put up another roadblock to a science of the mind, but of a different sort. He concluded that mental processes take place in time, but they do not take up any space. Because they don't take up space, they can't be measured. Therefore you cannot apply the scientific method to mental processes. Many people were persuaded by this argument and concluded that there was no point in trying to use the scientific method to understand mental processes.

In short, there was no science of the mind during the Renaissance because of background assumptions, this time the assumption that the scientific method wouldn't work on the mind because the mind is inherently unpredictable. But the Renaissance was not devoid of smart people contemplating the workings of the human mind. Philosophers were still hard at work. So what were they doing? In the 300 years or so between Descartes and the beginnings of scientific psychology, a number of different topics were being debated. It is fair to say that many of the topics they took up were rooted in one question: Where does knowledge come from? Like the Greeks, Renaissance philosophers were interested in memory and perception, but these interests often were offshoots of the question of the origin of knowledge.

On the Origin of Knowledge. Descartes usually is credited with the first modern extended treatment of philosophy of mind, written in the early 17th century. He set forth a fairly moderate view on the origin of knowledge. He said that there are ideas that come from experience as well as innate ideas (i.e., those that everyone is born with). The position that ideas are innate came to be known as **nativist** because ideas were seen as native to every human. Another group of philosophers who came to be known as **empiricists** (Thomas Hobbes, John Locke, George Berkeley) argued that all of our knowledge comes from experience impinging on an impressionable mind. Later empiricists (David Hume, James Mill, John Stuart Mill) argued that the mind is more active in learning from experience, whereas the earlier empiricists had painted a picture of a rather passive mind being shaped by experience.

Gottfried Leibniz, in a direct response to Locke (but published much later), wrote that innate ideas are very important. He believed that experience serves only to liberate ideas that were in the mind already, presumably because one is born with such knowledge.

Immanuel Kant offered a compromise between nativist and empiricist views that was similar in spirit to Descartes's view, arguing that experience is the teacher, but *how* we experience things depends on native categories. For example, our perception of time and space does not depend on experience. You are born with the ability to perceive them; you don't need to be exposed to time and space, compared to the way you *do* need to be exposed to English in order to learn it. Furthermore, how you perceive time and space does not depend on your experience. All humans experience time and space the same way because they are human.

Nativist and empiricist views had been set forth by the Greeks, most forcefully by Plato and Epicurus, respectively, but philosophers in the Renaissance and beyond furthered these views, considered new arguments, and formulated compromise positions.

Perception. Descartes discussed perception for the reasons the Greeks did: to understand where knowledge comes from. Other philosophers, notably George Berkeley, discussed perception as part of the empiricist versus nativist argument. Recall that Descartes said that some ideas are inborn or innate.

Among these are the nature of our perceptual experience, such as how we perceive space and motion. Berkeley was an extreme empiricist, and in *An Essay Towards a New Theory of Vision*, he set out to show that even basic perceptual experience is learned. Berkeley pointed out that the three dimensions of space are projected onto a two-dimensional surface—the retina—and that it is therefore not possible to perceive space directly. Rather, he argued, we *learn* to perceive distance. Visual cues to distance become associated with another sensation: touch (in which he included the sensation of walking, and how far you walk tells you distance information). One learns that if you can't see the details of something (e.g., you can't make out individual leaves on a tree), it will take more walking to get to the object than if you can see the details (e.g., you can see individual leaves on a tree). Thus, experience is critical in all aspects of mental life. Even something that feels as natural as the perception of space actually requires experience. Berkeley discussed some cues to the perception of distance that are still thought to be important today, but he discussed them to emphasize that even something as natural as perceiving distance is learned, and hence that there are no native, inborn ideas.

Memory. The empiricists were also associationists. Associationism holds that knowledge originates from simple information from the senses and that this sensory information can be combined into more complex ideas. You know what an apple looks like because you have seen an apple before. But some complex ideas, such as the concept "democracy," clearly are not sensations. So where does this sort of knowledge come from? A complex idea such as "democracy" is the product of a number of simpler ideas that are stuck together (i.e., associated). Things become associated if they have occurred at or near each other in time in the past.

Aristotle described the process of association, and he proposed several principles or rules by which associations are formed; ideas would be associated if they were similar, or if they were very dissimilar, or if they were contiguous in space or time. All of the empiricists (Hobbes, Locke, Berkeley, Hume, James Mill, and John Stuart Mill, to name the best known) agreed that contiguity was important. Things that happen in the same place or at the same time will be associated. If a clown appears every time you go to a particular shopping mall, you'll come to expect to see the clown when you enter the mall. Experimental work in the 20th century showed that they were correct in stressing time as a critical factor in associations. Locke and Hobbes were also correct when they stressed that repeating an association would make it easier to learn, and Locke added the (mostly correct) idea that learning associations also depends on whether they lead to pleasure or pain.

Associationism can serve not only as a theory of memory but also as a theory of the moment-to-moment flow of consciousness. Consciousness is sometimes likened to a stream in that it is always moving, always flowing. But the metaphor is not quite right because, unlike in a stream, it's not obvious what the next thought in consciousness will be. What will you be thinking of in a moment? The associationist's answer is "something that is associated with what you are thinking of now."

SUMMARY. Naturally, I've hardly scratched the surface of the thought of Renaissance and post-Renaissance philosophers. What's important to know is what they were trying to do. For the most part, they were arguing about the origin of knowledge. Renaissance philosophers also made observation part of their method, although they rarely conducted experiments as such. In a famous demonstration, Locke pointed out that if you put one hand in warm water and the other in cold, and then put both hands in tepid water, the tepid water feels hot to one hand and cold to the other. Locke was making a point about different types of perception but what's of interest here is that Locke thought it was important to support his assertion with an observation of the world. Why did Locke feel that such real-world demonstrations were important to supporting his point? We might infer that he felt that way because of the success of scientific method in other fields.

It is also worth noting that many Renaissance philosophers borrowed metaphors from other sciences in discussing the mind. Locke talked about consciousness as a chemical compound, perhaps because he had been at Oxford University, where Robert Boyle had demonstrated the principle of chemical compounds being composed of elements. John Stuart Mill also used the chemistry analogy. Hobbes was influenced by Galileo's movement studies and believed that thought was motion of the nervous system. Hume also discussed Newton and the possibility of finding basic laws of thought to correspond to the basic laws of motion.

Thus, in their use of scientific metaphors and their increasing use of observation in the world to support their ideas, we can see the creeping influence of the scientific method on Renaissance philosophers.

The Beginnings of Modern Psychology

What we saw in the last section is that the intellectual apparatus was in place to start a science of the human mind as early as the 17th or 18th century, but people's background assumptions about the nature of the human mind led them to conclude that it wasn't even worth trying to apply the scientific method. All that was needed, therefore, was for someone to give it a try and have a little success, and they would have launched a new science.

Wilhelm Wundt usually gets credit for founding modern psychology in 1879. He was not the first to publish a scientific psychological work, actually. For example, in 1860 Gustav Fechner published *Elements of Psychophysics* (Fechner, 1860), in which he sought to tie together the physical and psychological realms. He showed that it is possible to investigate the threshold at which someone can just detect that a very weak stimulus (e.g., a very soft tone) is present. A few years earlier, Ernst Weber had described methods of addressing a similar problem: How physically different must two stimuli be for them to be perceived as different? These were the first demonstrations that it was possible to use the scientific method to answer questions about how the mind works—in this case, how things are perceived. Why, then, aren't Fechner and Weber called the first psychologists?

WHY WUNDT GETS CREDIT.   The reason you usually hear is that Wundt was the first to establish a laboratory devoted to psychology. It's not actually true. Wundt started his lab in 1879 at the University of Leipzig. William James started a lab in 1875 at Harvard. But James apparently used it only for demonstrations in teaching, so that lab is deemed not to count. Actually, the year doesn't matter so much because Wundt founded the discipline of psychology not because he started a lab but because he did what was necessary to get the science going.

Imagine for a moment that you have decided to invent a new scientific field. For example, suppose you think the field of ethics needs your help. There is little agreement about what is ethical and what isn't. You feel that if only people would apply the scientific method to the study of ethics, we would eventually home in on the one true set of ethical principles that all humans should use to guide their concepts of right and wrong. You're going to start the field of ethicology. How will you launch your new science? Well, you'll need to

- Start journals devoted to ethicology to show that the field is making progress
- Train a lot of students so that they can go out and teach ethicology
- Write a textbook of ethicology to make it easier to teach others
- Organize symposia on ethicology to gain publicity
- Try to get universities to organize departments of ethicology
- Spend a fair amount of time persuading people that the whole enterprise is possible because initially they'll think it's a crock.

Wundt did all these things for psychology. The idea of studying the mind using scientific method seemed as improbable to a lot of people in the late 19th century as studying ethics using the scientific method does right now.

Another important thing you must do if you are starting a science is to define its domain. What does the science seek to explain? There were two slightly different answers to this question around the turn of the century. Wundt was inspired by the success of chemistry. The periodic table had just been worked out, and Wundt thought it was a realistic and worthwhile goal to try to work out a periodic table of the mind. What are the basic elements of consciousness, out of which more complex thoughts are constructed? Although Wundt later denied the chemistry analogy, his writings are suffused with the idea. This viewpoint came to be known as **structuralism** because the goal was to describe the structures that make up thought. (We can recognize the associationism of Locke and others in this idea of simple concepts combining.)

Meanwhile, William James, the one who started the laboratory that didn't count, was inspired by developments in evolutionary theory. A guiding principle for James was that mental processes must have a purpose, they must be *for* something. This viewpoint came to be known as **functionalism** because the emphasis was not on mental structures, but on the function of mental processes.

The emphasis on what was to be explained differed between Wundt and James, but there was a common thread. Both sought to explain how thought worked, and for them thought was pretty much synonymous with consciousness.

Structuralism and functionalism had different ways of framing this question, however, and they had different methods of gathering evidence. Wundt championed a method called **introspectionism.** Introspectionism was a method of studying thought processes in which people tried to follow their own thought processes, usually as they performed some simple task such as listening to a metronome. The trick was that such introspection was said to require training. You couldn't just listen to the metronome. Someone more experienced than you had to help you learn the right way to listen. Then that person would tell you what you should be experiencing. If that sounds odd to you, it should. This method turned out to be a big problem. Because people were trained to report what they were thinking about, the trainer played too big a role in shaping what people said they experienced. So five different people may have had five different reports of what they experienced when they looked at an apple, but after they had been trained they would all report the same experience, which was pretty much whatever the trainer thought they should say. I'm making the problem a bit extreme to illustrate the point, but that is the heart of it.

James also used introspection but of a different sort. He followed his own mental processes as a way of learning about them, but he was much less dogmatic about how introspection should be done. He frowned on dogma in psychology, and he had a healthy respect for objective experiments that didn't rely on introspection. He actually disliked doing them himself, but he knew that the results of objective experiments are important.

Perhaps because he later lost interest in psychology, or perhaps because James's distaste for dogma was not conducive to starting a movement in the field, functionalism never became a prominent school of psychology. Still, James has had a more lasting impact on experimental psychology than any other turn-of-the-century figure. His *Principles of Psychology* (James, 1890), is still a source of ideas for cognitive psychologists.

Wundt's legacy is quite different. Although he worked out a detailed theory of psychology and published prolifically, little of his thinking remains influential. Still, he is duly credited with starting the field, and because he trained so many students, many of today's psychologists can trace their academic lineage to Wundt (including me; I was a student of W. K. Estes, who was a student of B. F. Skinner, who was a student of E. G. Boring, who was a student of E. Titchener, who was a student of Wundt).

The Response: Behaviorism

There was one big problem with Wundt's introspectionism; it didn't work. There was the problem of training people to introspect—a problem of the method they used—and there were other methodological problems. A more basic problem was that the introspectionists didn't come up with any interesting results. In the end, you can make all the arguments you want for why your method is the best, but if you don't learn something using the method, the whole enterprise begins to look silly. Between 1879 and 1913, the introspectionists had little they could point to.

In 1913, John Watson published his paper titled "Psychology as the Behaviorist Views It." The first paragraph of that paper is remarkable enough that it must be read in the original:

> Psychology as the behaviorist views it is a purely objective experimental branch of natural science. Its theoretical goal is the prediction and control of behavior. Introspection forms no essential part of its methods, nor is the scientific value of its data dependent upon the readiness with which they lend themselves to interpretation in terms of consciousness.

Watson was throwing down the gauntlet, calling for a complete shift in psychology. By 1913 psychology was a full-fledged science. Wundt had trained many students, and they in turn had started psychology departments all over the world. Most of them remained introspectionists of one sort or another. They were the establishment of psychology in 1913. Watson was challenging the assumptions of this establishment. We can list four basic principles of **behaviorism** that Watson set down.

- Psychologists should focus only on that which is observable.
- Psychologists should explain behavior, not thought or consciousness.
- Theories should be simple.
- The overarching goal of psychology is to break behavior down into irreducible constructs.

FOCUS ON OBSERVABLE EVENTS.   Watson was emphasizing that objective measurement is crucial, and introspection obviously can't be measured objectively. If you were introspecting in front of a metronome, you could say that you're thinking about anything and I couldn't prove you wrong.

EXPLAIN BEHAVIOR.   Because objective measurement was so important, Watson maintained that consciousness was not a suitable subject for psychology. The subject matter of psychology should be behavior, not the contents of consciousness. Watson was saying that the subject matter of the science should change.

THEORIES SHOULD BE SIMPLE.   Everyone agreed on this point; it's a basic principle of scientific method. Watson raised the issue because the psychological theories of the time (which we haven't gone into in any detail, and won't) were getting very convoluted.

BREAK BEHAVIOR DOWN.   Again, this was not revolutionary; everyone agreed that the point of science is to discover the basic units of the field. Structuralists had been trying to find the basic building blocks of consciousness. Watson suggested instead that the search be for the basic building blocks of behavior. (Watson's candidate for the basic building block was the conditioned reflex).

Backtrack just a second. We said that renaissance philosophers were concerned primarily with the origin of knowledge, and they addressed questions of memory and perception as part of that issue. The introspectionists were not really concerned with the origin of knowledge but instead were trying to explain the workings of the mind. What did they mean by *mind?* They meant *conscious thought*. Recall that Wundt was trying to do mental chemistry, to figure out the basic elements that compose consciousness.

Watson was saying, "Throw the mind out the window." Remember that Kant said, "You can't measure mental processes, so applying scientific methods to them is impossible." Watson agreed with him! He was saying that introspectionism hadn't made progress because trying to deal with mental processes was hopeless. Instead, we should redefine psychology: It should no longer be a science of mental processes but a science of behavior. The Gordian knot of psychology was this: How can we explain the workings of mental processes, which are so complicated and elusive? Watson cut the Gordian knot by declaring that mental processes were irrelevant. Behavior should be the subject matter of psychology. This point of view had to be pretty tempting. Many of the problems that stumped researchers of the mind for centuries simply disappeared. We don't study thought; we study behavior.

And psychologists went for behaviorism. It's fair to say that behaviorism was the dominant point of view in America by the 1920s and that that dominance lasted until the 1950s (Gardner, 1985). It wasn't just a matter of expedience. Behaviorism offered the interesting results that introspectionism lacked, and it looked as if behaviorism had a great deal of promise. Ultimately behaviorism was found lacking, and it was replaced by cognitive psychology. Before I explain what went wrong with behaviorism, let me tell you why it was looking good for a while.

Behaviorism's Success

The philosophy underlying behaviorism was appealing because it was so straightforward. It seems very hard-nosed and scientific to emphasize behavior because it is observable: Everyone can agree on what a person does, but it is much more difficult to say anything about a person's mental processes (Figure 1.4). Everyone can agree that Joe hit Bill, but it's much harder to agree on what Joe's thoughts were when he hit Bill: Was he angry or frustrated, or had Joe just had a bad day?

Behaviorism also seemed to offer a very promising start on the framework of a grand theory of behavior. Behaviorism, like almost every other science, sought to simplify complex subject matter by finding basic, irreducible units. Chemistry has the elements, biology has the cell, physics has the atom, psychology has . . . what? Behaviorists proposed that the basic unit of behavior is the **reflex.** A reflex is an automatic action by the body that occurs when a particular stimulus is perceived in the environment.

You are born with many reflexes. If you touch something hot, you will jerk your hand away. You don't need to learn that reflex; you're born with it. Other reflexes are learned. For example, if every day I ring a bell and then give you a sour ball, in time the sound of the bell will elicit the responses usually elicited by the sour ball (e.g., salivation).

That sounds like Pavlov's dog. Yes. It is. Watson proposed that the basic unit of behavior might be the conditioned reflex, as described by Pavlov. Some

Figure 1.4. *It is difficult to agree on what a rat is doing if you try to guess the rat's internal states; it's much easier to agree on the rat's behavior. The same is true of humans.*

reflexes are innate (e.g., withdrawing your hand from pain) and others are the product of experience (e.g., salivating when you hear a bell). These learned reflexes are called **conditioned reflexes.** The training procedure (and the resultant learning) that produces conditioned reflexes is called **classical conditioning** (Figure 1.5).

Classical conditioning begins with an **unconditioned stimulus**, which elicits an **unconditioned response.** *Unconditioned* means that the animal comes to the experiment with the predisposition to respond in a particular way. Food is an unconditioned stimulus leading to the unconditioned response of salivation because before the experiment is conducted, the unconditioned stimulus (food) leads to the unconditioned response (salivation). The **conditioned stimulus** is one to which the animal shows little or no response (e.g., a bell). If you ring a bell, a dog might turn toward the sound, but that's about it, and if you ring the bell a few times, the dog stops turning its head.

If you pair the conditioned stimulus (bell) with the unconditioned stimulus (food) enough times, the conditioned stimulus (bell) comes to elicit a **conditioned response.** The conditioned response is similar to (but not always identical to) the unconditioned response. In this case, the conditioned response would be salivation, but the animal might not salivate as much.

The idea that the conditioned reflex might be the building block of all thought and behavior sounds reminiscent of the empiricist philosophers: simple

Before training	Training	After training
Bell → no response Food → salivation	Bell, followed by food.	Bell → salivation

Figure 1.5. *Pavlov's classical conditioning procedure.*

associations build up to produce more complex thoughts. The new addition was that it was possible to do experiments to test these concepts. The basic idea was very old. Aristotle talked about the fact that if two things happen at the same time often enough (such as a bell and being fed) they become associated. And anyone who has a cat knows this principle; your cat comes running when it hears the can opener (Figure 1.6). Same as Pavlov's set up, really. The sound of the opener is like the bell ringing, and the cat food is like the dry meat powder Pavlov used in his experiment. And if the sound (bell or can opener) is followed by the food enough times, the animal prepares to eat the food when it hears the sound: The dog salivates, the cat approaches the food. It seems a little odd that Pavlov became famous for this.

The difference between Pavlov and my casual observations of my cat is that Pavlov was able to be very specific about how the learning takes place and therefore could speculate about the mechanism. Pavlov performed a simple surgery so that one of the dog's salivary glands was on the outside of its cheek, and the number of drops of saliva it secreted could be measured accurately. Thus he could get a precise measure of how much the dog salivated, which in this case is essentially a measure of the dog's expectation of being fed. Having this good experimental setup allowed Pavlov to ask other questions: How many times must the bell and food be paired for the animal to learn? What happens if I ring a different bell? What happens if sometimes I ring the bell and don't provide food? How about if I ring the bell and give a different type of food?

Being able to ask (and answer) such specific questions allowed behaviorists to start thinking about a very general theory of behavior, with the conditioned reflex at its center.

It wasn't long before people noticed that the conditioned reflex can't account for all of behavior. In the conditioned reflex, two stimuli are presented to the animal, and the animal responds to stimuli, but animals also can actively do things that have important consequences. For example, suppose you try a new Chinese restaurant in town, and the food is awful. You figure that they may have had a bad night, or that you ordered something that happened to be bad, so you try again. Again, it's awful. So you don't go back. This experience obviously entails learning, but it is not classical conditioning. You actively made a choice (you went to the restaurant) and your choice had consequences (you got a lousy meal). The consequences of your choice influence the likelihood that you will make the same choice again. This type of learning is called operant conditioning. **Operant conditioning** occurs when the animal actively makes a response (the operant) and the probability of making that response in the future changes, based on the consequences the animal encounters. Operant

Before training	Training	After training
Can opener → no response	Sound of can opener,	Sound of can
Smell Food → approach food source	followed by food.	opener → approach

Figure 1.6.   *You probably have noticed this naturally occurring classical conditioning if you have a cat. So why aren't you famous, like Pavlov?*

conditioning was seen to be different from classical conditioning. In classical conditioning a neutral stimulus (e.g., a bell) comes to have meaning. In operant conditioning, an initially neutral response (e.g., selecting a particular restaurant) comes to have meaning.

Edward Thorndike did some work in this vein in the early 20th century (Thorndike, 1911). He put a cat in a slatted box. The box had a door operated by a lever inside the box. Thorndike timed how long it took the cat to make its escape over a number of trials and found a very systematic learning curve. Based on this and other experiments, Thorndike proposed the law of effect, which basically said that if you do something and good consequences follow, you're more likely to do it again, whereas if bad consequences follow, you're less likely to do it again. Still, it wasn't until the 1930s that the importance of this type of learning was fully appreciated, largely through the work of B. F. Skinner (e.g., Skinner, 1938).

But here the story gets longer, and I want to push ahead to cognitive psychology. Suffice to say that from the 1920s until the early 1960s virtually all experimental psychologists in America were behaviorists. Behaviorism dominated American psychology because, to a large extent, it worked. Behaviorists could make many good predictions about behavior. Most of their experiments were with animals, but that didn't worry people too much. From the behaviorist perspective, behavior was mostly the product of what had happened to you, meaning what sorts of conditioned reflexes you had acquired through the environment and what sorts of behaviors had been rewarded or punished over the course of your lifetime. It was therefore difficult to conduct experiments on humans because the experimenter had no way of knowing what their history was and therefore what they already knew coming into the experiment. But you could raise an animal from birth and know exactly what its history was. So everyone used animals. But were animals really like people? Well, behaviorists figured that humans were much more complex, but the basic laws of learning probably were the same. They also noted that every science starts with simple situations. When Galileo wanted to investigate how objects move, he started with spheres rolling down planes, not leaves in a high wind. Once you understand the simple situation you can move on to more complex situations.

Behaviorism showed that in some situations it had useful applications to human learning. In some clinical settings, techniques derived from operant conditioning have been applied to disruptive or learning-disabled patients with good results. There was much effort in the 1950s and 1960s to use behaviorist principles to improve teaching in the schools, but it didn't meet with much success (mostly because the students complained that the programs were boring; some problems are not so easily solved).

In the late 1950s behaviorism began to crumble. There were a number of contributors, but they fall into two categories. (1) People started to doubt that behaviorism could do what it had promised. (2) It became obvious that eliminating any discussion of mental processes from psychology was hurting more than it was helping. The replacement was cognitive psychology, and so our story begins.

STAND-ON-ONE-FOOT QUESTIONS

3. *Why was scientific method not applied to the human mind before the 19th century?*
4. *What psychological questions did philosophers address during the Renaissance?*
5. *What change did scientific psychology undergo in terms of what it sought to explain?*

QUESTIONS REQUIRING TWO FEET

6. *One of the assumptions that the Greeks made was that explanations for events in the world should be "of this world." In other words, there is not much point in proposing explanations of observable events in terms of unobservable forces precisely because they cannot be observed. To what extent do you think people you know hold this assumption?*
7. *Behaviorism swept away the introspective method. But should people's introspections be of any interest to psychology?*

➤ HOW DO COGNITIVE PSYCHOLOGISTS STUDY THE MIND?

> ➤ PREVIEW The impetus for a new way to study the mind came from several sources. From within psychology, there was increasing dissatisfaction with the behaviorist position because it seemed unable to account for some important human behaviors (e.g., language). From outside psychology, other fields (artificial intelligence and neuroscience) seemed to make great use of abstract constructs—hypothetical representations and processes—in accounting for intelligent behavior, although these were anathema to behaviorists. In moving away from behaviorism, cognitive psychologists needed to move toward something, and artificial intelligence researchers offered a ready model. One could conceive of the human mind as similar in some respects to a computer. Both manipulated information as a way of generating intelligent behavior. This computer metaphor has remained influential to this day, although it can be taken too literally. In the last part of this section, I show you an example of how a cognitive psychologist would analyze one very simple bit of behavior: answering the question "What is your home town?"

What Behaviorism Couldn't Do

One small bump in the road for behaviorism came as early as World War II. The armed forces became interested in problems of human performance. Human performance simply refers to what humans can do well and what they can't. A great deal of military equipment was operated by humans, and when humans made mistakes, the results could be catastrophic. For example, people had to sit in front of radar screens trying to sort out what the little green lights meant; some meant enemy planes, some didn't, and it was not easy to differentiate them. Obviously a mistake by the person in front of the screen was very, very costly. The army quickly found out that radar operators occasionally made mistakes, no matter how much training they had undergone. You couldn't make a radar operator perfect. So the army wanted to know (and in a hurry) why there was a limit to human performance: How come you could only get very good, and not perfect? Behaviorists were supposed to be the experts on behavior, but they had little to say on this topic. Behaviorism could explain how certain things are learned (if you start with no knowledge, you can get better) but it didn't have much to say about the endpoint of learning (why you don't eventually get perfect). This limitation wasn't a problem for behaviorism, exactly, but it did make clear that there were some things behaviorism couldn't explain.

Much more serious were problems raised in the 1950s. Behaviorism was perceived by psychologists as proposing that the experiences of an animal during its lifetime completely determined its behavior—in other words, that the animal's genetic inheritance counted for nothing and that what the animal did was a function of what it had been rewarded and punished for doing. Strictly speaking, that is not what behaviorism proposed, and indeed such a proposal could only be called silly. Obviously it is easy to train a pigeon to peck something, and it is very difficult train a rat to peck something, and the predisposition to peck or not peck is a product of the animal's genetic inheritance. But it is true that behaviorists did not emphasize the possibility of important genetic contributions to behavior. Almost everything they studied was the learning that took place during the lifetime of the animal, and so it seemed as though they were saying that when an animal is born it is a clean slate, a blank tablet, waiting to be written on by the environment.

In the 1950s a number of important papers were published in ethology showing that the clean slate idea could not be true. Ethologists do not study animals in laboratory settings; they go into the wild and study animals in their natural habitat. Ethologists described what they called fixed-action patterns. **Fixed-action patterns** are complex behaviors that the animal engages in with very little opportunity for practice or reward. For example, the male stickleback fish engages in a very stereotyped series of mating behaviors, including establishing a territory, building a nest, luring a female into the nest (with seductive wagging motions) and inducing the female to lay eggs in the nest by prodding her tail (Tinbergen, 1952). Behaviorist accounts do not offer a ready explanation for such stereotyped, complex behaviors. According to behaviorist principles, such behaviors should require more practice and should require reward.

Another dramatic finding from ethology was that of a critical period. A **critical period** is a window of time during which an organism is primed to learn some particular information. If the organism doesn't learn the information within the time defined by the critical period, it may be difficult or impossible to learn the information. For example, there is a critical period during which baby chicks (and geese, ducks, and some other birds) learn who their mother is (Hess, 1958). The first large object chicks see during this time period is taken to be the mother, and chicks follow the object around thereafter. If a few days pass and the chicks don't see a large object, the learning is more difficult to obtain. If the first object that chicks see is a large ethologist (e.g., Konrad Lorenz,

Photo 1.1. *Konrad Lorenz with ducklings.*

as shown with goslings) then Konrad Lorenz is taken to be Mom. (For a recent review of this work, see Bolhuis & Honey, 1998.)

As with fixed-action patterns, the results supporting critical periods make it seem likely that the nervous system is not a learning machine that responds only to whether reward or punishment follows an action. Rather, organisms seem to come into the world with a nervous system that is primed to learn particular things; it is part of their genetic heritage. This explanation sounds obvious, but did not fit into the behaviorist theory in any obvious way.

So the first problem was that it appeared that behaviorism could not account for some elements of animal behavior. The second problem was that people started to get uneasy about whether behaviorism could account for human behavior.

Failures of Behaviorism to Account for Human Behavior

The study of language was a dark cloud looming on the behaviorist horizon almost since the beginnings of the behaviorist movement. Keep in mind that behaviorists conducted almost all their experiments on animals. They were essentially offering a promissory note: "All this work with animals will apply to humans; don't worry." Some people did worry, and their chief worry was that behaviorist principles derived from experiments with animals would not be able to account for language because language is uniquely human. B. F. Skinner recounts in his autobiography that he had such a discussion with the great philosopher Alfred North Whitehead when Skinner was a newly minted Ph.D. in the mid-1930s.

> Here was an opportunity which I could not overlook to strike a blow for the cause, and I began to set forth the principal arguments of behaviorism with enthusiasm. Professor Whitehead was equally in earnest—not in defending his own position, but in trying to understand what I was saying and (I suppose) to discover how I could possibly bring myself to say it. Eventually we took the following stand. He agreed that science might be successful in accounting for human behavior provided one made an exception of *verbal* behavior. Here, he insisted, something else must be at work. He brought the discussion to a close with a friendly challenge: "Let me see you," he said "account for my behavior as I sit here saying, 'no black scorpion is falling upon this table.' "
>
> The next morning I drew up the outline of a book on verbal behavior. (Skinner, 1984, pp. 149–150, emphasis original)

Skinner may have outlined the book the next morning, but it was not until 1957 that he published the final work, a book called *Verbal Behavior* (Skinner, 1957). His analysis of language was straightforward behaviorism. How does a child learn language? Through reward in the environment. The infant learns that saying "Da" elicits excitement from the parents, which is very rewarding. But the parents get used to the child saying "Da," and soon the child must produce a more complex utterance, such as "Dad," to be rewarded. Through reward, the child learns ever more complex utterances. The analysis was more sophisticated than that, but it did not stray far from the behaviorist line.

Two years after Skinner's book was published, a review came out that soon attracted more attention than the book, although the review was not published in a major journal (Chomsky, 1959). It was written by a young linguist named Noam Chomsky, and the review can be summarized this way: "Not only is Skinner's account wrong, but a behaviorist explanation cannot, in principle, ever account for language." Chomsky made many points, most of which argued in one way or another that Skinner had grossly underestimated the complexity of language. I will mention just two of those arguments here. First, Chomsky attacked Skinner's account of the scorpion-on-the-table problem. To account for why one utters a remark at any given time, Skinner could only say that the behavior was under stimulus control, meaning that some subtle property of the stimulus (combined with your history) had elicited this verbal response from you. Chomsky pointed out that this explanation is really no explanation at all. If you see a painting and say "Dutch," it is presumably due to some subtle property of the painting. But you might just as well have said "Stinks," "Nice," or "Too much red." And in each case, Skinner could only say that, because of the comment you made, he must infer that that particular aspect of the stimulus (stinkiness, niceness, redness) was controlling your behavior. That is no explanation.

A second important point Chomsky made was that language is **generative**, meaning that you can create novel sentences. Behaviorism is great for describing why you do something again if you've already done it (you were rewarded last time), but it's not nearly as good at describing why you do something novel, such as utter a sentence you've never said before. And the ability to generate novel utterances is the heart of language. We seldom say the same thing twice in just the same way.

Indeed, how is it that you can say or comprehend a series of words you've never said or heard before, such as "Banana peels have nothing to do with success as a cab driver?" How do you get the grammar right? Now it's tempting, very tempting to say "Well, there are *rules* for what makes a sentence grammatical. It's like the formula for a line: $y = mx + b$. You put in values for m, which is the slope, and for b, which is where the line runs into the y-axis, and you have described a line. In the same way, there might be abstract formulas you use to construct a sentence. You plug in the ideas for the things you want to say, and the formulas turn your ideas into a grammatical sentence." A lot of people thought something like this must be right, which was a big blow against behaviorism. Starting in the 1950s and 1960s more psychologists of language proposed such sets of rules (called grammars) and left behaviorist accounts behind.

Could the behaviorists have backpedaled a bit? They could have said, "Okay, maybe we can't account for language. But we can account for all the rest of human behavior, and all of animal behavior." It is true that a theory doesn't always have to account for everything. But it was too late for such modesty. Behaviorist psychologists had for years been pitching their theory as the Theory of Everything; all behavior, animal and human, would eventually be swallowed by behaviorist theory, so behaviorists could not retreat. Indeed, in his review Chomsky quotes this line from *Verbal Behavior:* "The results [of this experimental work] have been surprisingly free of species restrictions. Recent work has shown that the methods can be extended to human behavior without serious modification." Many psychologists ended up convinced that the results of animal experiments did *not* extend well to human linguistic abilities. The result was that a lot psychologists, not just those who studied language, were shaken by Chomsky's argument. If behaviorism can't account for language, who knows what else it will fail on?

The impression that behaviorist principles couldn't give a complete account of human behavior was reinforced by studies of memory. Here's an example from a study by Weston Bousfield (1953). Suppose I give you a list of words to remember:

lion, onion, Bill, firefighter, carrot, zebra, John, clerk, Tim, nurse, cow

Ten minutes later I ask you to recall the words. Most people do not recall the words in the order they heard them. They recall all of one category (e.g., animals), then all of another category (e.g., names), and so on. How can this result be explained? When participants are asked what they are doing in such studies, they say they are using a retrieval strategy: They know that one animal will make them think of other animals, so it's easiest to recall all the animals at once. A behaviorist would shrink from the term *strategy* because a strategy is not observable. But people clearly reorganize the order of the words, and they say they are doing that reorganization to remember them better. Can we ignore what the people say they are doing? At the very least, we can't ignore the fact that people reorganize the word order—that's observable behavior—so how can we account for it? Behaviorism dictated that you shouldn't talk about a person's plans, goals, or strategies in accounting for what they do. But talking about strategy seemed to be a big help in understanding what people did in memory studies such as this one.

Behaviorism was not going to provide a framework in which to use constructs such as "grammars" or "strategies." But if behaviorism were abandoned, what would take its place? A replacement was found through analogy of the human mind to a computer.

The Computer Metaphor and Information Processing

Metaphors are very important in the study of the mind (Daugman, 1990). No one knows what the mind is or how it works, so people often say "I think the mind is like. . . ." For example, Descartes was impressed by animated statues he saw in the gardens at the chateau of Saint-Germain-en-Laye, outside Paris. As a visitor strolled through the gardens he or she stepped on hidden plates that set the statues in motion. In one, Perseus descended from the ceiling of a grotto and slew a dragon that rose from the water. The system animating the statues was based on hydraulics—water moving through hidden pipes—and Descartes proposed a hydraulic system of nerve function (Descartes, 1664/1972).

In the 19th century many researchers (e.g., von Helmholtz, 1910/1962) likened the brain to a telephone switchboard; the criss-crossing pattern of connectivity of neurons is reminiscent of an enormous switching station. And Donald Hebb (1949) proposed a model of neural functioning in the late 1940s that had the mark of solenoids and capacitors.

In the 1950s a new metaphor became available. Early computers did little more than crunch numbers, but artificial intelligence researchers realized that computers solved these number-crunching problems with symbols. The number "8" was not physically realized with eight pieces of something in the computer, the way an abacus represents "8" with eight beads. The computer uses a binary code in which 0-1-1 might mean "8," but 0-1-1 is just a symbol. 0-1-1 could represent "bird" or "twiddling thumbs." So artificial intelligence researchers began speculating on what a computer might be capable of if the symbols it used (e.g., 0-1-1) were to represent something other than numbers.

Naturally, when 0-1-1 means "8" and the goal is to get a computer to crunch numbers, you have certain expectations about what you're going to do with 0-1-1 and other numbers. You want to be able to add them, subtract them, and so forth, and you expect that the basic laws of addition will be built in to the computer. For example, the order in which numbers are added by the computer shouldn't matter: 8 + 3 = 11 and 3 + 8 = 11. Thus, a computer uses representations (such as 0-1-1) and processes that do things to the representations such as addition and subtraction. A **representation** is a symbol (e.g., 0-1-1) for an entity in the real world (e.g., "8"). A **process** manipulates representations in some way.

That's clear enough for computers. What if you can think of humans that way? Suppose humans are sort of like computers in that they use representations and processes? If we think of humans as processors of information, it sets up new questions for the study of the mind. What we want to know about humans is (1) what kind of symbols or representations humans use and (2) what processes humans use to manipulate those representations.

Here's another way to use the computer metaphor. Computers have hardware and software. The hardware is the actual physical piece of machinery (the central processing unit, the hard drive, the memory, and so on). The software is the set of instructions that tells the hardware what to do. Why not think of humans that way? Some people study the brain, and that's fine—they are studying the hardware. Cognitive psychologists study the software. It's possible to study the software divorced from the hardware. How many computer programmers know precisely what the electronics of the computer are doing? A computer program in the language C++ will run (with minor adjustments) on a PC or a Macintosh or a NeXT or a SUN; the guts of the machines might be doing very different things, but at another level of description the computers are doing the same thing. To continue the metaphor, you could say that behaviorists wanted to talk only about what was observable—what was seen on the screen of the computer and what was typed on the keyboard—and therefore were missing most of the interesting stuff.

This metaphor proved very powerful and became known as **information processing.** Information processing is an approach to studying the human mind that is characterized by these assumptions:

- Humans are processors of information, just as computers are processors of information. The processing of information supports human thought and behavior.
- Representations of objects, events, and processes that operate on these representations underlie information processing.
- Information processing typically occurs within largely isolated modules, which are organized in stages of processing. Thus, one module receives information from another module, performs an operation on the information, and passes the information on to another module.

I provide an example of this information processing perspective toward the end of this chapter. For now, just keep in mind that humans were seen to take in information from the environment (e.g., see things, hear things), transform that information (e.g., interpret what they saw in light of what was in memory), and then emit more information (e.g., utter a sentence such as "Look at those birds!"). Psychologists were hypothesizing that just as you enter information into a computer, whereupon the computer uses processes and representations to add 4 and 4, humans can take in information and then use processes and representations identify birds and remark on them.

The Behaviorist Response

The idea that you could propose hypothetical representations and processes seemed very powerful to a lot of psychologists. We've already mentioned the case of language, in which something like sentence grammars seemed an absolute necessity to account for people's ability to generate novel sentences; grammars are an example of a representation. Here's another domain of behavior in which hypothetical processes and representations seemed potentially useful.

People have noticed that it seems easy to keep a little bit of information in mind for a short time (about 30 seconds). You might look up a telephone number and cross the room to the phone, repeating the number to yourself. You dial the number, and then it is gone from your memory. If you are interrupted as you cross the room and stop repeating the number for 2 minutes, you'll have to look it up again. That's a little odd. Clearly, you usually remember things for longer than 30 seconds. How come you remember the phone number only for that long?

Here's an account you might give for that. You might say that there are two types of memory: a long-term memory, which can keep memories for years, and a short-term memory, which is used to maintain information for 30 seconds or so. A short-term memory is useful because it is hard to get material into long-term memory, and you don't always need to remember things for years; you won't need to remember the phone number of the pizza place 20 years from now. Sometimes you just need to remember something briefly. So it's hard to get information into long-term memory, but once it's in there it stays for years; it's easy to get information into short-term memory, but it stays around only for a minute.

Short-term memory could be said to contain representations; just as a computer has a representation (0-1-1) for the concept "8," your mind has a way to represent "8." Furthermore, short-term memory would also use processes that manipulate representations. For example, if you wanted to remember "8" for several minutes, a process would continually refresh the concept "8" so that it remains accessible.

A behaviorist would say that's garbage. "Where exactly is this mystical representation of '8'? I don't see it." The response is that short-term memory is an abstract construct. An **abstract construct** is a theoretical set of processes (e.g., refresh) and representations (e.g., 8) that you think are useful in explaining some data. Any abstract construct you propose is therefore a mini-theory. It is a proposal about the way the mind operates.

A behaviorist would say that by proposing an abstract construct (short-term memory), you are not doing what you should be doing; namely, accounting for the person's behavior. Instead, you're making up things that are supposedly in the person's head. This practice is wrong because

- It's circular. You're taking the behavior (people easily recall information for 30 seconds) and then sticking the behavior in the head in the form of an abstract construct. "People remember things for 30 seconds because they have a memory system designed to remember things for 30 seconds." You haven't explained anything by doing that.
- You are taking attention from the important issues. Remember, psychology is a science of behavior, not of thought.
- It is impossible to verify because it's not observable. There is no way to confirm whether short-term memory exists because short-term memory

can't be seen, or touched, or measured in any way. Therefore, you are dragging us back to the days of the introspectionists.

It was very hard for psychologists to shake the idea that if they talked about representations and processes, then they were not being scientific. They needed support for the idea that abstract constructs could be scientifically useful. Such support came from two fields: computer science and neuroscience.

Abstract Constructs in Other Fields

It looked as if the information processing perspective might be very useful in accounting for human thought, but there was still the issue of whether you were being scientific if you used abstract constructs. In both computer science and neuroscience researchers were using abstract constructs with abandon and with no apparent loss of rigor.

ARTIFICIAL INTELLIGENCE.   Artificial intelligence is the pursuit of intelligent behavior by a computer. The idea is to get a computer to produce output that would be considered intelligent if a human did it. Most researchers consider that the program that gets the computer to complete a task can be considered a theory of how the human mind completes the task. Thus, artificial intelligence researchers are proposing theories of how the mind operates. And these theories rely completely on abstract constructs. The programs propose that certain information is in memory and that this information can be combined or used in specific ways, according to a set of rules, and that these rules and the information in memory drive behavior.

Here's an example. In the mid-1950s Allen Newell and Herb Simon developed a program that proved theorems in formal logic (Newell & Simon, 1956). The program worked by starting with a list of axioms—statements that it could take as true—and a list of rules for how the axioms could be combined. The program also remembered proofs that it had already discovered so that they could be used as needed. The program had a number of strategies it used to discover proofs; for example, sometimes it tried working backwards by starting with the conclusion and trying to get back to the initial premises.

Three things are critical about this program and what it represents. First, the behavior the program produced was quite impressive. Until that time, behaviorists could more easily ignore artificial intelligence because the artificial intelligence programs didn't do anything sophisticated. Behaviorists could say, "Computers are nothing but fancy adding machines. What they are capable of is not really behavior." But here was a program constructing logical proofs; that certainly sounds like sophisticated behavior.

Second, Newell and Simon were not simply saying "Look, we can get a computer to do something that looks like thought; isn't that neat?" To this, a behaviorist might say "So what? You programmed the computer to solve proofs, and it solves proofs. *You* are the intelligent agent, because you programmed the computer." But Newell and Simon were saying that the method the computer used to solve the problem was like the method humans used.

They provided evidence for this by asking people to prove the theorems and to describe what they were doing as they did it. People reported strategies similar to those the program used (such as working backwards).

The third important thing about the program is that it used abstract constructs. You can't see or touch the strategies that the program used. The usual response of behaviorists to a theory that entailed strategies was, "That's not scientific. You can't observe strategies." But there was nothing unscientific or mystical about the program. The artificial intelligence researcher could say "I'm being quite specific about what I mean by 'strategy.' Look, there's the strategy right there in the program, and here are the rules describing when the strategy is invoked."

NEUROSCIENCE.   One way to be specific about an abstract construct is to make a computer model of it. A second way is to tie it to a brain structure. It's one thing to say, "Suppose there were a short-term memory system." It's something else again to say "Suppose there were a short-term memory system in the dorsolateral frontal cortex of the brain." In the second case, it feels as if you've found the abstract construct you're proposing.

Finding things in the brain has been pursued since the 19th century, but it's a difficult proposition. The way you typically do this is by examining people with brain damage caused by stroke, tumor, or disease. Some of these people have quite specific cognitive problems. For example, suppose you find a patient whose cognitive functioning is completely normal in every respect but who has no short-term memory—he can't keep a phone number in mind for 30 seconds. If you know where the brain damage is, you might infer that you know where short-term memory is. If this patient has damage to brain area X and no longer has short-term memory, then brain area X must support short-term memory, right?

Right, up to a point. That thinking can lead to mistakes, but for the most part that assumption is an adequate starting point. The problem is, how do you know which part of the brain is damaged? In the 1970s in vivo imaging techniques were developed so that you could look at the brain in a living person without hurting the patient. But before that you had to wait for the patient to die and then look at their brain directly during an autopsy. Thus, these new imaging techniques obviously greatly facilitated this neuroscientific work.

There is another way to know where the brain damage is; you'll know where the damage is if there is a medical reason to perform an operation to remove part of the brain. If a surgeon must go in and remove some tissue (to remove a tumor, for example), you know exactly where the brain damage is: the surgeon caused it. In the late 1950s and early 1960s there were a few cases in which dramatic and important things were learned about cognition.

Perhaps the most famous patient of this sort is H.M. (Corkin, 1984). H.M. (he is known by his initials only, to protect his privacy) had epilepsy that was unresponsive to even very high dosages of antiepileptic medication. His seizures were frequent and severe and were so debilitating that he could not continue in school. In such cases, surgery may be appropriate. Seizures usually have a focus, meaning that they start in one part of the brain and then spread. If you can take out that part of the brain that is the focus, the seizures may never get going at all.

H.M. underwent surgery in 1957 in which a number of structures near the center of his brain were removed. At that time, the best knowledge about the function of these structures was that they were important to one's sense of smell. So it was thought that H.M. probably would lose his sense of smell, but that seemed a small price to pay to eliminate the seizures.

Unfortunately, H.M. lost his ability to form new memories. His short-term memory is fine: He can remember a phone number for 30 seconds just as you or I can. His long-term memory is fine, too; if you ask him about events that happened before his surgery, he can remember his friends in high school, what was happening in the world in the early 1950s, and so on. What he can't do is form new long-term memories. Thus, H.M. has learned almost nothing new since 1957. He does not know who the president is now or what year it is. He wouldn't recognize the term *Watergate* or know that the Berlin wall has fallen. You could spend an hour with H.M. and have a very pleasant conversation with him, then leave the room for 2 minutes, and upon your return H.M. would not remember having met you.

The point here is that data from H.M. provided dramatic evidence in favor of using an abstract construct such as short-term memory in a theory of how memory works: "There is short-term memory and long-term memory. H.M. tells us that the hippocampus and other structures that he lost are important for transferring information from short-term memory into long-term memory. But those structures don't support short-term or long-term memory themselves because those are fine in H.M. So now we need to find which parts of the brain support those other functions."

Suppose now that you're not a neurologist but an experimental psychologist interested in learning and memory. On one hand, the behaviorists are saying "You can't use terms such as *short-term memory.* They are not rigorous because they refer to things that cannot be observed." On the other hand are findings such as those from H.M. that strongly suggest that the concept of short-term memory would be useful. What would you do?

So What, Finally, Is the Cognitive Perspective?

What I've told you so far is that

- Behaviorism couldn't account for all the data, especially in studies of language and memory.
- It looked as if abstract constructs would help account for the data.
- Neuroscientists and artificial intelligence researchers provided examples of how abstract constructs could be used effectively in a scientific way.
- The interaction of representations and the processes that manipulate them can be likened to the workings of a computer.

This brief overview also makes it obvious what the assumptions of the cognitive perspective are. The chief assumption is that there are representations,

and processes that operate on them. Another assumption is that we can discover what these processes and representations are. There is currently no way
to observe these processes directly. We infer the existence of these processes
based on people's behavior. For the moment, let's just say that the assumptions
of the cognitive perspective look fairly reasonable, but we should never forget
that they are assumptions, and we shouldn't smugly think that we have at last
found the True Path (for a recent perspective on the use of representations in cognitive theory, see Markman & Dietrich, 2000).

So that's the approach and the assumptions behind it. How is it applied?
Here's the way a cognitive psychologist would think about a problem.

Suppose you and I meet at a party and we make the usual small talk:

YOU: So how's it going, or something?
ME: All right. Where are you from?
YOU: Pittsburgh. How's your research going?
ME: Uhh . . . you don't really care, do you?
YOU: No, that was me being polite. I'm going to go to the bar now.

Take one little part of that interchange. I ask where you're from. You answer.
It takes you perhaps half a second, but consider all that had to happen during
that half a second. My question "Where are you from?" comes to you as a series
of sounds. First, these sounds must be interpreted as speech. Speech interpretation, it turns out, is not trivial. Take just one component of speech interpretation:
figuring out where the boundaries of words are. How do you know where the
boundaries of words are? You'd think that there are pauses between them—little breaks where there is no sound—but that's not the case. There are little breaks
when people talk, but they don't correspond to the boundaries of words. So the
first thing that must be done is to figure out the words of the sentence.

Then you have to assemble the words into something with meaning. Here
is a small example of why that is complex. "Where are you from?" in this context is innocuous, but the same utterance could mean something very different
in another context. For example, if I said, "Where are *you* from?" right after
you spilled your drink all over yourself, it would probably be an expression of
scorn, not a polite pleasantry.

Once you know what I'm asking, you have to find the answer in memory.
Your memory is loaded with information: what a snowflake looks like, what oat-
meal is, the lyrics of many songs you hate but can't forget, where Brazil is located, and so on. Among all the mountains of stuff in your memory, how are you
able to reach in and almost instantly pluck out exactly the right piece of information and ignore everything else?

Once you have the right piece of information ("Pittsburgh") you have to
decide what to do with it. I've asked you where you're from and you've retrieved
the answer, but are you going to answer my question? Not necessarily. You may
think I have something against Pittsburgh, so you would be reluctant to tell
me you're from there. You may know that I love Pittsburgh, and telling me
you're from there will set off a 20-minute soliloquy on the poetry of the three

rivers, and you'd rather avoid that. You are constantly making social and practical decisions about what to say and what not to say.

Suppose you decide to go ahead and say "Pittsburgh." You still have to decide *how* to say it. You could say "Pittsburgh," or "I'm from Pittsburgh," or "Pittsburgh, PA," or "I hail from Pittsburgh," or "Pittsburgh—what's it to you?" The possibilities are endless. The decision is pretty straightforward because you'll probably just answer the question with the single piece of information I requested. But in general, every time you say something there is more than one way to phrase it, and you have to select which of the many ways you are going to use.

Now suppose you know you're just going to say "Pittsburgh." You have to send the proper commands to the muscles of the lips, tongue, velum, and so on, to form the word. This is a problem of motor control: getting the muscles to do the right thing. Here again, the problem is that you have many choices. You can say "Pittsburgh" in a variety of ways, if you care to: with an English accent, or with long, drawn-out vowels, as though you had a pipe clenched in your teeth; how do you pick which way to say it? This is a specific example of a very general problem in motor control that is easier to understand if you think about reaching for something rather than thinking about speech. If you reach for a cup, how do you select the trajectory your hand should take? You could reach overhand or underhand, you could make your hand swoop, you could move quickly or slowly; how do you decide how to reach for it? The question seems silly because the answer seems quite clear: You pick the shortest trajectory to save energy. Fine. But what's meant by "shortest?" You're probably thinking of "shortest" as a straight line between your hand and the cup. But another way to think of "shortest" is to make the movement so that your joints move as little as possible. It turns out that's a different "shortest" than making a straight line between your hand and the cup.

Just as there are an infinite number of ways to pick up a cup (and it's not obvious which is the "right" way), there are an infinite number of ways to say "Pittsburgh."

Here's the point. I ask you what your hometown is, and in less than a second you say "Pittsburgh." But an amazing amount of cognition (unconscious, of course) had to happen in that brief second (Figure 1.7). You perceived what I said, looked up the answer in memory, and so on. And each of these processes looks pretty amazing just on its own.

This example provides a rough summary of how cognitive psychologists think about problems. They look at cognitive tasks and try to figure out which processes are absolutely necessary to getting the task accomplished. Cognitive psychologists tend to think of mental work being performed in stages (e.g., speech perception, memory, decision making, motor control), and any one psychologist usually studies just one of these stages. Each stage is so complex that it's enough of a challenge to understand just one. In trying to characterize these stages, cognitive psychologists devise theories in terms of abstract constructs: hypothetical representations and processes that operate on those representations.

That's the overview of the cognitive perspective. I've tried to give a sense of how cognitive psychologists think about problems. The remainder of the book describes the answers cognitive psychologists have proposed. As described

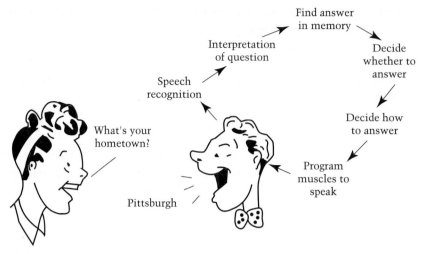

Figure 1.7. *The processes that might be involved in answering the simple question, "What's your hometown?"*

earlier, cognitive psychologists tend to think in terms of stages of information processing: First, information from the environment is perceived, then memory is contacted, and so on. This book follows that stage theory in presenting one cognitive process in each chapter. We begin with the question of how one knows what is in the environment: how we perceive.

STAND-ON-ONE-FOOT QUESTIONS

8. What problems led to a decline in the influence of behaviorism?
9. What is information processing?
10. How did cognitive psychologists respond to the protests of behaviorists that references to abstract representations and processes were not scientific?

QUESTIONS THAT REQUIRE TWO FEET

11. Do you think some of the things humans learn might be subject to critical periods?
12. At the start of this chapter I mentioned that most of the people I know tend to notice the workings of their mind only when it fails. How often do you think that your mind fails, relative to the number of times it succeeds in carrying out a cognitive process?
13. The "What's your hometown?" example emphasized that many cognitive processes are involved in performing what seems to be a simple cognitive task. The basic approach was to figure out processes that had to occur to make the behavior happen. Would that approach apply equally well to the subcomponents we identified (e.g., identifying words in the sentence, finding the answer in memory)?

KEY TERMS

deterministic	reflex	fixed-action patterns
nondeterministic	conditioned reflex	critical period
nativist	classical conditioning	generative
empiricist	unconditioned stimulus	representation
structuralism	unconditioned response	process
functionalism	conditioned stimulus	information processing
introspection	conditioned response	abstract construct
behaviorism	operant conditioning	

Interlude:
The Brain

We've just gotten started; why are we almost immediately stopping for this interlude about the brain? At one level the answer may seem quite obvious: We're studying the mind, so it seems clear that some knowledge of the brain would be useful.

This conclusion is not as obvious as it first might seem. Many researchers believe that one can study the mind separately from the brain. To continue the metaphor from chapter 1, one could maintain that it is possible to study the software separately from the hardware. Until the mid-1980s most cognitive psychology textbooks contained little information about the brain, and that choice accurately reflected the research strategy of the field. There were researchers who studied the relationship of the mind and the brain, but their fields remained separate from cognitive psychology.

Neuropsychologists did give the cognitive viewpoint an initial boost, as described in chapter 1, but neuropsychology as a whole was more clinically oriented (i.e., concerned with the treatment of brain-damaged patients) and less concerned with basic research in how the mind works. Other researchers study the brain and behavior primarily in animals, and many of the questions they pursue are separate from the concerns of cognitive psychologists.

Today, cognitive psychology is greatly informed by neuropsychology. This change has its roots in the mid-1970s, when tools to examine the human brain became available. The information about the brain that has proven most useful to cognitive psychologists is that of **localization.** Localization means finding a location in the brain that supports a particular cognitive process or function. We alluded to this goal in chapter 1. Cognitive psychology seeks to describe the representations the brain uses and the processes that manipulate those representations. The assumption is that one should be able to find evidence that these hypothetical processes and representations are localized in the brain. For example, if we propose that people use visual images to solve certain problems, we should be able to find a location in the brain that seems to be the storehouse for images, or we should find part of the brain that supports a process that manipulates the images (e.g., rotates them or makes them larger or smaller).

How could you find evidence of localization? Two families of methods have been used. The logic of each is fairly straightforward:

> If brain area X supports cognitive function Y, then damage to area X will lead to an impairment in tasks that require function Y. For example, if the temporal cortex of the brain supports the storage of mental images, then damage to the temporal cortex should lead to impairment in the use of mental images.

> If brain area X supports cognitive function Y, then area X will be active when function Y is engaged. For example, if the temporal cortex of the brain supports the storage of mental images, then the temporal cortex should be active when people use visual images.

These principles seem straightforward enough, and the principles dictate the tools we need. For the first method we need some method of knowing where there is brain damage. For the second method we need some way of measuring brain activity. We'll examine each in turn.

➤ WHERE IS THE DAMAGE?

Damage to the brain can result from a stroke, an infection, resection to relieve epilepsy or a tumor, or a degenerative disease such as Alzheimer's disease, to name a few sources of damage. Examining patients who have some damage to the brain and using that information to infer the function of different parts of the brain has a long history of success. In the early 1860s Paul Broca reported the case of a patient who had damage to the left frontal lobe and had a problem in speech limited to production: The patient could understand language (as long as the grammar was simple) but could produce speech only very poorly. A few years later, Carl Wernike reported the case of a patient who had damage to a different part of the brain; this patient could not understand speech, and although he could speak fluently, what he said was not sensible. These results caused a sensation because they clearly indicated that one could assign different functions to different parts of the brain. (People assumed these areas handled production and perception of speech, respectively. That characterization turned out to be oversimplified.)

The difficulty in the 1860s and the century that followed was that no technology could localize brain damage adequately. Note that the inference takes this form:

> If the patient cannot understand language, and the patient has damage to ventral lateral frontal cortex, then the ventral lateral frontal cortex supports language.

To get to the conclusion, you need to know the location of the damage, and there were few ways to do that. One method was to wait until the patient died and then physically inspect the brain to see where the damage was. That's not very satisfactory simply because you might have to wait decades until the patient dies; it so happened that Broca's patient died young, because of an infection. Another method was to restrict your attention to the small population of cases in which the location of the damage was known because it was the result of brain surgery. But that is a very restrictive strategy because most brain damage is the consequence of stroke, not surgery, so you won't get to examine many people.

Much better would be a method by which one could see the brain damage without invading the patient's skull. Why not take an X ray of the brain? X-ray images show internal structure, but the problem is that they compress the three-dimensional brain into a two-dimensional image. The resulting image not only loses volumetric information, it's a big blur.

The solution is **computerized axial tomography** (commonly called CAT scan). This scan still uses X-ray technology but allows one to see three-dimensional structure in the following way. The patient lies on a gurney with his or her head in the center of a large doughnut-shaped structure. Around the perimeter of the doughnut are X-ray sources and X-ray detectors. The X rays pass through the patient's head; some of the X rays are absorbed by the various structures in the head (skull, blood, brain structures, etc.) and some pass all the way through to the X-ray detector on the other side; the denser a structure is, the more of the X ray it absorbs.

The detector on the other side of the X-ray source can tell you how much of the X ray has gotten through the head, but what absorbed some of the X rays along the way, and where was it? You are left with the average density of the brain for all the tissue in a line drawn from the generator to the detector. The following diagram shows a simple analogy using visible light instead of X rays and tinted glass instead of tissue density. Suppose that each square represents a cube of glass. We know that the cubes are tinted and range from clear, to gray, to dark black. Suppose we shine a flashlight through the cubes. We can say that the light is of intensity 20 (in arbitrary units), a clear cube absorbs 0 units, and a black one absorbs 20 units. After the flashlight has shined through the cubes, we might find that the remaining light is of intensity 17, but we can't work backward from that to determine the tint of each cube; many configurations of tinted cubes would yield light of intensity 17.

$$20 \quad \rightarrow \quad \boxed{?} \quad \boxed{?} \quad \boxed{?} \quad 17$$

Suppose now that there is an array of 9 glass cubes, and we know the intensity of light going into each row and column (20) and the surviving intensity after the light shines through each row and column, shown at left. Can we derive the value of each individual cube?

	20	20	20				20	20	20	
	↓	↓	↓				↓	↓	↓	
20 →	□	□	□	17		20 →	1	2	0	17
20 →	□	□	□	8		20 →	4	3	5	8
20 →	□	□	□	17		20 →	1	2	0	17
	14	13	15				14	13	15	

As shown in the diagram on the right, we can derive the values for each cube. If we just look at an individual row (e.g., the top row), all we know is that the three cubes combined to absorb three units of light, but we don't know which cube absorbed how much. But if we look at all of the rows and columns simultaneously, it constrains the possible values that each cube can take, and we can home in on a unique solution.

That is what a CAT scan does. It uses multiple X-ray sources and detectors, as shown in Figure I.1. Each detector tells you the density of the tissue in a single line, but if you combine the densities along intersecting lines, you can derive the density for a single point.

In the cube example, one can tinker with the numbers and come up with the values for each cube. In a CAT scan, one is dealing with thousands of values,

X-Ray Source

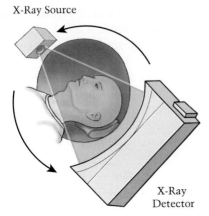

X-Ray
Detector

Figure I.1. *Computerized axial tomography.*

so the calculations are performed by a computer. The resulting values represent the density of a cube of tissue about 1 cm^3 in size; if there are differences within that centimeter, you won't see them because the image just gives you the average density value within that block of tissue. A CAT scan provides a huge three-dimensional map of values; a sculpture of 1-cm^3 blocks of density values. They usually are presented in two-dimensional slices.

What good are density values? The tissues of interest vary in density. Bone is very dense, blood is not dense at all, and neurons (the stuff we care about) are of intermediate density. This technique allows one to see tumors, which differ from surrounding healthy tissue in density, and to see the result of stroke. And so we can localize damage to the brain (at least some types of damage) without opening the patient's head.

A second method that uses similar logic but a different technique is magnetic resonance imaging (MRI). MRI provides much better resolution than CAT; the individual cube in the sculpture may be as small as 1 mm^3. MRI again uses a doughnut-shaped structure with detectors in the perimeter, and again the final map is one of densities, but the principle is not X-ray detection. Instead, MRI exploits a magnetic principle of molecules. Atoms with an unequal number of protons and neutrons spin. MRI is calibrated to detect the behavior of hydrogen atoms, which are plentiful in organic matter. In their normal state, hydrogen atoms spin around an axis, and these axes are oriented randomly. The MRI machine generates a very strong magnetic field, which causes all the hydrogen atoms to orient their axes parallel to the magnetic field. A second magnetic wave is then applied. This second wave is tuned to make only certain atoms spin, or resonate (just as only sound waves of correct frequency make a tuning fork resonate). The concentration of the hydrogen can be read from the intensity of the resonance. (Localizing these intensity values actually requires a third signal, but you get the idea.)

Recall why these methods are of interest. We are interested in localizing function. One way to do that is to apply the principle that if brain area X is damaged, and cognitive function Y is lost, then brain area X supports brain area Y. These methods allow us to make confident statements about the first part of the equation, i.e., which part of the brain is damaged.

➤ WHERE IS THE ACTIVATION?

A different approach is to measure ongoing activity in the brain as an organism engages in a behavior. This measurement contributes toward our second method of localizing cognitive function in the brain: If brain area X supports function Y, then activity should be observed in area X when function Y is engaged.

How does one know when part of the brain is active? Different methods measure different properties of brain activity. To understand the most commonly used measures of brain activity, you need to know a bit about the basics of brain activity.

As you may know, the cells in the brain that support cognition are called **neurons.** There are approximately 10^{12} neurons in the brain (that's a thousand billion), and these neurons are connected with one another, meaning that one neuron can tell another neuron that it is firing. If enough of a neuron's neighbors are active, that indicates to an individual neuron that it too should be active, and it will, in turn, communicate this activity to its neighbors.

This communication process is chemical; neurons communicate by releasing chemicals that influence neighboring neurons. At the same time, the event is electrical because the effect of the chemicals is to change the neighboring neuron's membrane so that electrically charged ions can pass through it. Under normal circumstances, there are more negative ions inside the neuron's membrane than in the fluid surrounding the neural membrane; thus the charge across the membrane is about -70 mV. When a neuron fires, the membrane allows positively charged ions to rush into the neuron, changing the membrane potential to $+40$ mV. Thus, the chemical influence of neighboring neurons causes a chemical change in the neural membrane, which results in an electrical change in the neuron.

The firing of a neuron has two important characteristics for our present discussion. First, it is an all-or-none event. The neuron fires if the influence of its neighbors reaches some threshold. Although the response seems just to be on or off, the neuron can communicate a degree of activity by the frequency of firing (in other words, how many of these firings occur per second). The second important property of neural firing is that it's an electrical event. That means that, if we can measure electrical activity in the brain we can measure the activity of neurons.

Neuroscientists have two chief ways to eavesdrop on the electrical conversations of neurons. The first is **single-cell recordings.** As the term implies, this technique records the activity of an individual neuron: It records the number of times per second that an individual neuron fires. Single-cell recording studies are almost always performed on animal subjects. The animal undergoes a surgery in which a small hole is drilled in the skull, and a plastic anchoring device is attached. An electrode probe can be placed through the anchoring device and directly into the desired part of the brain. The brain does not have pain receptors, so the probe does not hurt the animal. The probe is insulated, except for the tip, so the probe's tip can record electrical activity, specifically neural firings.

The basic technique in single-cell recording is to have the animal engage in some behavior while the researcher records from a brain area of interest. Hence, one might record from a cortical area and have a monkey make a reaching movement. A particular neuron fires when the monkey reaches in a particular direction but does not fire when the monkey reaches in another direction. By having the monkey engage in many different behaviors, the researcher can investigate the precise conditions under which the neuron fires. By finding an association between a neuron's activity and the behavior, one can begin to get clues about what the neuron contributes to behavior.

The second method, most often used with humans, is an **electroencephalogram** (EEG). During an EEG electrodes are placed over the participant's scalp. Each electrode reads the electrical activity of the neurons below it. (The electrical activity is very weak, of course, so the signal must be greatly amplified.) Usually 12 to 64 electrodes are used to cover the surface of the head, so each electrode records the summed activity of millions of neurons. Furthermore, the skull and protective tissue covering the brain are fairly good insulators, which diffuses the electrical signal. Thus, the ability of EEG to localize activity is not as good as that of other methods. One advantage of EEG is that it can provide very precise temporal information, that is, information about *when* neural activity takes place. In fact, EEG can provide information about when neurons fire that is accurate to 0.001 s.

EEG actually is used in a slightly different way than we've described so far. If you simply put electrodes on a person's head, what you would see is not a flat line (representing no electrical activity) and then some activity once he or she does some task. Instead, you would see a wavy line all the time, representing continuous activity. The problem is that neurons have resting potentials, which means that they are always firing at some rather slow pace (just how quickly or slowly depends on the type of neuron). Thus, because each electrode summarizes millions of neurons, each of which are always slightly active, the summation shows a lot of irregular activity. To get around this problem, researchers use a technique called **event-related potentials** (ERPs). In this technique the researcher administers tens or hundreds of trials that are similar to one another and average all of the squiggly EEG waves from each of these trials (Figure I.2).

The resulting average wave is smooth. Researchers often compare two types of ERPs that are similar but vary on one dimension. For example, a researcher studying memory might compare ERPs when the participant successfully recalled a word with ERPs when the participant couldn't recall a word. Suppose there were 64 electrodes on the scalp. The researcher could compare the ERPs for these two conditions (recall vs. no recall) at each of the 64 electrodes. There probably will be no difference in the ERPs of these two types of trials at most of the electrodes; the electrode sites that do show a difference are the ones that help the researcher localize successful recall in the brain.

Again, EEG is not a very good technique for spatial localization, but it is good for temporal resolution. EEG may tell you only that a difference in successful

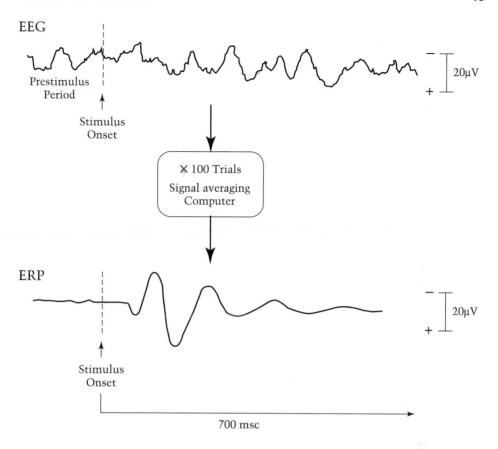

EEG

Prestimulus
Period

Stimulus
Onset

20μV

× 100 Trials

Signal averaging
Computer

ERP

Stimulus
Onset

20μV

700 msc

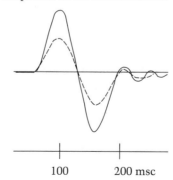

N1 Amplitude Effect With Attention

100   200 msc

Figure I.2. *Comparison of electroencephalogram (EEG) and event-related potential (ERP)*
waves.

and unsuccessful retrieval appears in the ERP of the right frontal lobe, which is
pretty vague, but the technique could tell you very precisely at what time you
start to see a difference in successful and unsuccessful recall. More researchers

are starting to use EEG in combination with other techniques so that they can get information about activity that is precise both in terms of when it occurs and where it occurs.

The two most important methods of localizing human brain activity more accurately are **positron emission tomography** (PET) and **functional magnetic resonance imaging** (fMRI). Single-cell recording and EEG are both electrical measures and therefore measure a direct product of neural activity. PET and fMRI measure brain activity indirectly. These methods detect changes in metabolism or in blood flow in the brain. The assumption (which appears to be well founded) is that metabolism follows brain activity; when the brain is more active, it demands more glucose, which is the sugar the brain uses for energy. Another assumption is that if a particular part of the brain needs more glucose, the vascular system will shunt more blood to that part of brain to satisfy the need. Therefore, functional imaging techniques measure the blood flow in the brain and thereby measure neural activity indirectly.

PET measures blood flow in this way. A very small amount of a radioactive tracer with a short half-life is injected. The tracer begins to decay immediately. As it decays, it emits positrons. Each positron immediately collides with a nearby electron and is destroyed. In so doing, two gamma rays are generated, which move away from the collision in exactly opposite directions. All this is happening while the patient's head is in (you guessed it) a large-doughnut shaped device that detects gamma rays. The detector can determine where the gamma rays originated. More gamma rays means more positrons, which means more radioactive isotope, which means more blood, which means more neural activity. Although this pattern of inference might seem tortuous, it is well founded.

fMRI works in a manner similar to MRI. (The type we've already discussed sometimes is called structural MRI to emphasize that it reveals neural structure but not activity). fMRI takes advantage of the magnetic properties of hemoglobin. Hemoglobin carries oxygen to neurons. When the oxygen is absorbed, the hemoglobin no longer carries the oxygen, so we can refer to blood as being oxygenated or deoxygenated. Oxygenated blood has magnetic properties, but deoxygenated blood does not. fMRI techniques calculate a ratio of oxygenated to deoxygenated blood in a local area. You would think that an active area would have mostly deoxygenated blood because the brain has absorbed all of the oxygen. Actually, the opposite is true; active areas have lots of oxygenated blood because when part of the brain is active, the vascular system overcompensates and floods that part of the brain with oxygenated blood.

➤ THE BEHAVIORAL SIDE OF THE EQUATION

Recall that there are two inferences we would like to be able to make that will help us localize cognitive function in the brain:

If brain area X supports cognitive function Y, then damage to area X will lead to an impairment in tasks that require function Y.

If brain area X supports cognitive function Y, then area X will be active when function Y is engaged.

In the previous section we discussed ways of figuring out how we know whether area X is impaired (for lesion studies) and whether area X is active. We have not yet discussed how to isolate cognitive function Y. We now turn our attention to this problem.

Lesion Studies

Suppose you have localized the brain damage in a particular patient. Now you want to discover which cognitive process is damaged in this patient. This is not a trivial problem. For example, in chapter 1 we mentioned patient H.M., who has very severe amnesia; he cannot learn new information. Suppose you had just conducted the first study of patient H.M.: You read a list of words aloud to him and asked him 5 min later to recall the list, and he was unable to remember any of the words. You are tempted to conclude that H.M.'s memory is impaired. But how do you know it's his memory that is causing the problem? Suppose it's a problem of attention, and he ignored the words you read? Suppose it's a problem of language: His memory is fine, but he didn't understand the words?

How do you get around this problem? Well, for the specific example we just gave, you could ask H.M. to immediately repeat back the words you mention so you know he's paying attention, and you could test his language ability in other ways to make sure he can understand the words in the memory task. Basically, that's what you do in all lesion experiments. When you administer a task, usually there are many potential reasons someone could be impaired on the task, so you have to administer other tasks to narrow down the possible reasons for the impairment.

You also have to keep in mind that the brain damage may not neatly knock out one cognitive function. The part of the brain that is damaged by a stroke or tumor does not depend on the cognitive organization of the brain. A stroke may kill parts of several areas, each of which supports a different cognitive function, leaving the patient partially impaired on a large number of cognitive tasks.

Imaging Studies

PET and fMRI studies also demand that one isolate a cognitive function. PET and fMRI measure brain activity, but the problem is that much of the brain is active much of the time. If you wanted to know which part of the brain is involved in reading a word, for example, you can't simply put people in a scanner and have them read. Instead, you must administer at least two (and possibly several) tasks that are very similar to one another but differ in the particular function you want to study. The participant would perform each of the conditions.

For example, you might conduct a study like this one

Condition	Description	Hypothetical Processes Involved
1	See fixation point	Attention
2	See random letter strings	Attention + vision
3	Read words	Attention + vision + reading
4	Say related word	Attention + vision + reading + memory

For each task, we have a set of cognitive processes that we think are needed to accomplish the task. We can take a PET scan showing the brain areas that are active for Condition 2 and subtract the activation from Condition 1, and that should subtract out the activations caused by attention, leaving us with just the activations caused by the visual processes engaged when the participant looks at letters. We can do similar subtractions to isolate other cognitive processes because each successive condition adds one cognitive process. Other techniques in fMRI do not use subtractions per se, but they still make use of task comparisons like this one.

➤ PROBLEMS AND LIMITATIONS

Let's summarize what we've said so far. Our ultimate goal is to gain support for hypothetical cognitive processes and representations. One way to do that is to localize these processes or representations in the brain. We do that by two sets of inferences:

> If brain area X is damaged and cognitive function Y is impaired, then X supports Y.
> If brain area X is active while cognitive function Y is performed, then X supports Y.

So far we have discussed how you know when X is damaged (localizing lesion) and how you know when X is active (single-cell recordings and imaging techniques). We've also discussed how you can isolate a function, Y.

Unfortunately, the inferences we've discussed are not quite as straightforward as we would like. You may or may not have noticed that the ordering of these if–then statements actually was reversed when we first mentioned them. They were:

> If brain area X supports cognitive function Y, then damage to X will impair Y.
> If brain area X supports cognitive function Y, then engaging Y will lead to activity in X.

These statements are true, but that does not mean the reversed statements we've been working with must be true. If you know that P leads to Q, that does not mean that Q leads to P. For example, it is true that if you drink beer, you must be 21. That doesn't mean that if you are 21, you must drink beer; you can drink soft drinks, beer, or whatever you want. Have a look at this table to appreciate the problem:

Rule	Valid Deduction	Invalid Deduction
Beer drinkers must be at least 21 years old.	Given: That person is drinking beer. Conclude: That person must be at least 21.	Given: That person is at least 21. Conclude: That person must be drinking beer.
If the hippocampus supports memory, then damage to the hippocampus will impair memory.	Given: The hippocampus supports memory. Conclude: Damage to the hippocampus will impair memory.	Given: The hippocampus is damaged and memory is impaired. Conclude: The hippocampus must support memory.

The problem is that the evidence we've been talking about gathering is the type that leads us to the invalid deduction. It might be true that brain area X supports function Y, just as the 21-year-old might be drinking beer, but there are other possibilities. What are these other possibilities? The other possibilities vary, depending on the type of study under discussion.

In lesion studies, one may actually fail to see cognitive impairment. If a cognitive process is lost, the brain may find a new way to support the behavior that the missing process used to support. Another possibility is that the patient may notice that he or she can no longer perform certain tasks as effectively as he or she used to do and adopt new strategies for these tasks to minimize his or her reliance on the missing cognitive process. Area X may support function Y, there can be damage to area X, and yet you don't observe any deficit.

Another possible source of error in lesion studies is that one assigns a cognitive function to a particular brain area that has been lesioned, but it is not the brain area itself that supported the function; rather, fibers connecting two brain areas passed through the area that was lesioned, and it was the loss of this connection that caused the observed loss of function.

Another problem lies in the very heart of the logic of interpreting lesion studies. Consider this metaphor. Suppose you remove a transistor from a radio, with the result that the radio squawks. You cannot conclude that the transistor was a squawk-suppressor. Similarly, damage to area X leading to loss of function Y does not allow the conclusion that X supports Y. Just as the interactions among the components of a radio are complex and loss does not provide a clear window to function, we can expect the interactions of the components of the brain to be complex.

Functional imaging studies have different problems of interpretation. One potential problem is that of correlated activity. Functional scans show all of the brain's activity associated with a particular cognitive function. Some of that activity may be associated reliably with the function—every time you perform the function you get the activity—but the brain area showing the activity is not absolutely crucial to getting the function done. For example, frontal cortical areas reliably show robust activation in memory studies, but if that cortex is damaged or missing, patients do not show a devastating loss of memory.

Another problem in interpreting imaging studies lies in the task analysis. Recall that each participant would perform several tasks, each task adding one cognitive process. If the tasks are not analyzed correctly, the whole enterprise falls apart. But there's an even more subtle problem. What if adding one process changes the other processes? For example, we said that in one condition the participant might look at letter strings (which requires vision and attention), and in another condition the participant might look at words (which requires vision, attention, and reading). But what if looking at words requires attention in a different way, or in a different amount, than looking at letter strings? If that's true, then when the researcher does the subtraction, the activity associated with reading hasn't really been isolated because the attention processes in the two tasks weren't equivalent, so the subtraction didn't remove the activation caused by attention. The assumption that one can selectively add cognitive processes without changing the other cognitive processes is called the **assumption of pure insertion.**

What do we do about all these problems? The answer is that we don't rely on any one method; we try to use all of the methods simultaneously, and if they all point to the same answer, that greatly increases our confidence that we have successfully localized a cognitive process. Notice that each method has its drawbacks, but these drawbacks differ. For example, we said that patients with a lesion might find another way to perform a task, and we said that functional imaging might indicate activity in a brain area that is not absolutely crucial for a cognitive process. These drawbacks are mirror images of one another; lesion studies might tell you which brain areas are absolutely essential for a cognitive process but might miss areas typically associated with a process, whereas imaging studies show you all areas associated with a cognitive process but don't tell you which areas are crucial for getting the job done. The strengths and weaknesses of different techniques complement one another. The strategy of using multiple techniques to address the same question usually is called using **converging operations.** If different methods converge on one answer, our confidence that the answer is correct greatly increases.

➤ COGNITIVE NEUROPSYCHOLOGY

The mapping of cognitive processes to brain structures is proceeding at a very rapid rate, particularly because of ever-improving methods and wider availability of fMRI. This poses a problem for the writer of a textbook. Just how much cognitive neuropsychology should be included in a cognitive psychology textbook? The truth is that it should be a separate course. Medical students take a semester-long course in brain anatomy alone, so trying to add cognitive neuropsychology—which requires some knowledge of brain anatomy—to a cognitive psychology course does not allow thorough coverage. Nevertheless, to get a representative view of what's happening in the field, you have to have at least a taste for this type of work. Therefore, I've included two or three key studies from cognitive neuropsychology in each chapter. These studies are plainly set off in boxes, but they complement the cognitive work you'll read about. Other studies from neuroscience are so integral to cognitive psychology that they are not set off in boxes but are simply part of the text. My hope is that these studies will help you appreciate how cognitive neuropsychology complements the work of cognitive psychologists and encourage you to learn more about the field.

➤ THE FIVE-MINUTE BRAIN ANATOMY LESSON

The first thing you need to know is how to refer to directions in the brain; one often talks about the position of structures relative to other structures. Also, many structures are large enough that one might want to refer to only part of the structure; it's tiresome to refer to "the part of the thalamus that's closer to the top of the head and toward the back of the head." As shown Figure I.3, toward the top of the head is called **dorsal,** toward the bottom of the head is **ventral,** toward the front of the head is **anterior** or **rostral,** toward the back of the head is **posterior** or **caudal,** toward the middle of the head is **medial,** and toward the side of the head is **lateral.** Thus, we could replace the cumbersome phrase "the part of the thalamus that's closer to the top of the head and toward the back of the head" with "dorsal posterior thalamus."

The major structures of the central nervous system are shown in Figure I.4.

The **spinal cord** collects somatosensory information (i.e., information about pressure, temperature, pain, etc.) and sends motor information to the muscles, both the muscles that move the body and the muscles that move internal organs. The **medulla oblongata,** or simply the medulla, contains nuclei that support

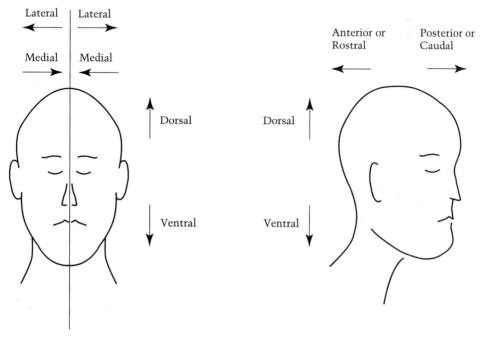

Figure I.3. *Directional descriptors of brain anatomy.*

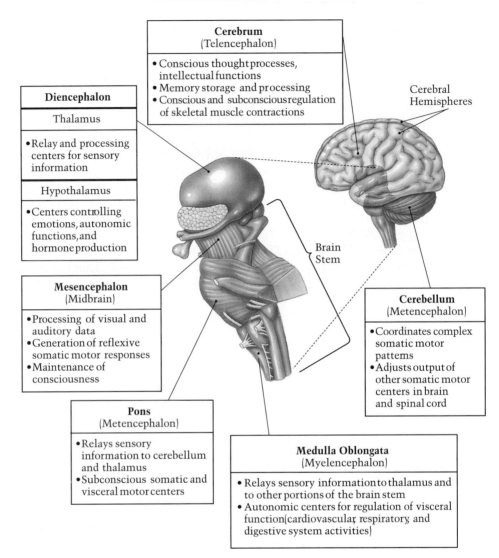

Cerebrum
(Telencephalon)

• Conscious thought processes, intellectual functions
• Memory storage and processing
• Conscious and subconscious regulation of skeletal muscle contractions

Cerebral Hemispheres

Diencephalon

Thalamus

• Relay and processing centers for sensory information

Hypothalamus

• Centers controlling emotions, autonomic functions, and hormone production

Brain Stem

Mesencephalon
(Midbrain)

• Processing of visual and auditory data
• Generation of reflexive somatic motor responses
• Maintenance of consciousness

Cerebellum
(Metencephalon)

• Coordinates complex somatic motor patterns
• Adjusts output of other somatic motor centers in brain and spinal cord

Pons
(Metencephalon)

• Relays sensory information to cerebellum and thalamus
• Subconscious somatic and visceral motor centers

Medulla Oblongata
(Myelencephalon)

• Relays sensory information to thalamus and to other portions of the brain stem
• Autonomic centers for regulation of visceral function (cardiovascular, respiratory, and digestive system activities)

Figure I.4. *Basic brain structures and their functions.*

basic functions, such as respiration and cardiovascular function, and nuclei that regulate activation and general alertness throughout the brain. It relays certain sensory information to the thalamus. The **pons** also contains nuclei that regulate arousal (and sleep), and it serves as a pathway from fibers going from higher brain regions to the cerebellum.

The **cerebellum** is the large structure in the posterior and ventral part of the brain. The cerebellum is split into two hemispheres; indeed, all of the structures mentioned as we continue our discussion will be duplicated on the left and right sides of the brain. The cerebellum receives multiple sources of information—visuospatial, auditory, vestibular, and motor—and sends projections out to higher motor centers. The cerebellum clearly plays an important role in

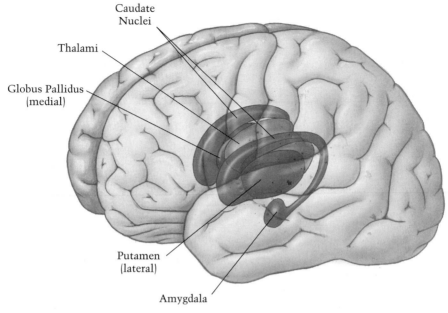

Caudate
Nuclei

Thalami

Globus Pallidus
(medial)

Putamen
(lateral)

Amygdala

Figure I.5. *The basal ganglia.*

motor behavior, but in the last decade it has become increasingly clear that it plays a role in other cognitive functions as well.

The **midbrain** is a catch-all term for a number of structures, including the superior and infererior colliculus, which are important in generating eye movements; the reticular formation, which is important in sleep and arousal; the red nucleus and substantia nigra, which are important in movement; and other nuclei.

The **diencephalon** is medial to the striatum, and so is not visible in the figure. The diencephalon is composed of two structures: the **thalamus** and the **hypothalamus.** The dorsal part of the thalamus is the site to which all sensory information (except olfaction) first projects. From the dorsal thalamus the information is sent to the cortex. The ventral thalamus receives inputs from a variety of areas, many of which are concerned with movement, and it projects primarily to motor centers. The hypothalamus is a tiny but vital structure that controls the authonomic nervous system and endocrine system and thus is crucial for survival functions, including attack, escape from threat, feeding, and reproduction.

The **basal ganglia** are a group of structures concerned with movement and, to some extent, with higher cognitive function (Figure I.5). They are located lateral and somewhat superior to the diencephalon, and include the **caudate,** the lentiform nucleus (which is composed of the **putamen** and **globus pallidus**), the **subthalamic nucleus,** the **substantia nigra,** and the amygdaloid body, or **amygdala.**

The limbic system is a group of interconnected structures that are concerned with memory and emotion. They include the **hippocampus,** the amygdala,

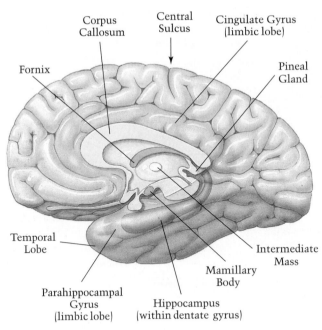

Corpus
Callosum

Central
Sulcus

Cingulate Gyrus
(limbic lobe)

Fornix

Pineal
Gland

Temporal
Lobe

Intermediate
Mass

Mamillary
Body

Parahippocampal
Gyrus
(limbic lobe)

Hippocampus
(within dentate gyrus)

Figure I.6. *The limbic system.*

the mammillary bodies, and some of the more medial areas of the cerebral cortex, as shown in the Figure I.6.

The cerebral cortex is the layer of cells that covers the outside of the brain. This cell layer is quite thin (about 3 mm) but the sheet is about 2.5 ft². That large sheet is crumpled to fit into the skull, hence the wrinkled appearance of the brain. The valleys are called **sulci** (singular, sulcus) and the hills are called **gyri** (singular, gyrus).

Researchers refer to different areas of cortex in several ways. First, the cerebral cortex is divided into four lobes, as shown in Figure I.7. The central sulcus divides the frontal lobe and the parietal lobe. The lateral fissure divides the frontal lobe and the temporal lobe. The occipital lobe is at the most posterior point in the brain (indeed, much of the occipital lobe is tucked out of sight in the medial walls of each hemisphere of the brain). Researchers often refer to parts of the cortex by a location within one of the four lobes (e.g., "dorsolateral frontal cortex").

Researchers also refer to cortical regions by their known functions. A few parts of the cortex are well enough understood that they can be referred to in this way. For example, the gyrus just anterior to the central sulcus often is called the primary motor cortex because it sends substantial input to the spinal cord and clearly controls movement. The gyrus just posterior to the central sulcus often is called the primary somatosensory cortex because it is clearly implicated in the reception of somatosensory information. The most posterior part of the occipital lobe may be called the primary visual cortex.

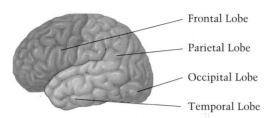

Figure I.7. *The four lobes of the cerebral cortex.*

Frontal Lobe

Parietal Lobe

Occipital Lobe

Temporal Lobe

If you didn't know this material before reading it, I am sure it seems utterly overwhelming. What we've discussed here is just a pitiful scratch on the surface; neuroanatomy is a subject to which many people devote their entire lives, and one can easily fill a semester-long course just on the basics. Still, you should take heart. Armed with even the minimal knowledge represented here, you will be in a position to appreciate that different cognitive functions can be localized to different parts of the brain. For our purposes, understanding brain anatomy is in service of understanding cognition.

Throughout this book you will see boxes that highlight key experiments and findings from neuroscience that have informed cognitive psychology. It is my hope that the bare-bones coverage offered here will encourage you to pursue cognitive neuroscience in more depth.

KEY TERMS

localization

computerized axial tomography (CAT)

neurons

single-cell recordings

electroencephalogram (EEG)

event-related potentials (ERPs)

positron emission tomography (PET)

functional magnetic resonance imaging (fMRI)

assumption of pure insertion

converging operations

dorsal

ventral

anterior

rostral

posterior

caudal

medial

lateral

spinal cord

medulla oblongata

pons

cerebellum

midbrain

diencephalon

thalamus

hypothalamus

basal ganglia

caudate

putamen

globus pallidus

subthalamic nucleus

substantia nigra

amygdala

hippocampus

sulei

gyri

2

Visual Perception

Of all the cognitive functions your brain performs, vision is both the most remarkable and the most difficult to appreciate. It is difficult to appreciate vision precisely because it is so marvelous; vision works so efficiently, so effortlessly, that you have no clue what it is doing or how difficult its task is. Consider this: $8 buys a calculator that can perform long division far more quickly and accurately than any human and can do many algebraic functions that 99% of the population can't do. For $50 you can buy a computer program that can beat 99% of the population in chess, and the very best chess player in the world is a computer program. Yet there is no computer that can drive a truck. Why not? It's clear that a robot could turn a steering wheel and press an accelerator; the problem is that there is no computer that can rapidly perceive the road, other cars, pedestrians, and so on.

This example should tell you one thing: Vision is hard. The first question we'll take up is, **"What makes visual perception hard?"** We can't simply ask, "How do humans see?" That question is not specific enough. We need to know why it's hard to see—what specific problems must be solved for vision to work—before we can start to think about how the human visual system might solve those problems. As we'll see, vision is hard because the pattern of light that falls on your retina is consistent with many different scenes out in the world; the problem is figuring out which scene is actually out in the world. Here's a very simplified version of this problem. What is the object depicted in Figure 2.1?

You probably said that this object is a square, but it could be a cube (or a number of other solids) seen edge-on. Thus, even this simple picture is consistent with more than one object in the world, and knowing the object's identity for certain is impossible.

You may well be protesting, "Dan, we're all very impressed by your square, but the fact is that we *do* see, and we usually see accurately." That's true, and we could add to your observation that vision happens effortlessly. When you walk into a room, you immediately perceive the objects that are in the room, their relative positions, their colors, their textures, whether they are moving, and so on. Indeed, everyone would agree on these properties, just as everyone agrees that Figure 2.1 depicts a square. Why does everyone agree if vision is impossible? Vision is impossible in that all stimuli are inherently ambiguous. The fact that we all see a square in Figure 2.1 tells us that the perceptual system somehow resolves the ambiguities inherent in a two-dimensional representation. The second question we will take up is, **"How does the visual system resolve ambiguities?"**

The answer is that your perceptual system makes assumptions about the way objects in the world usually look, and those assumptions make vision possible by resolving the ambiguity of figures such as the square. For example, one assumption the visual system makes is that objects are unlikely to be oriented at improbable angles. Thus, there are many ways in which a cube could be oriented

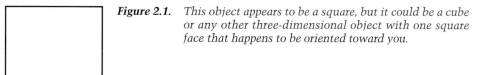

Figure 2.1. *This object appears to be a square, but it could be a cube or any other three-dimensional object with one square face that happens to be oriented toward you.*

in space, but very few of those orientations of the cube leave just one face of the cube visible to the observer. It would be phenomenal luck if the cube happened to be oriented that way, rather like seeing a coin that just happens to be edge-on so that it looks like a line. Such orientations are so rare that your visual system assumes that they don't happen. Figure 2.1 is much more likely to be a square than a just-happens-to-be-oriented-that-way cube, so the visual system gambles that it's a square. We'll talk about other assumptions the visual system makes.

Okay, we can see. But why? What is vision for? Broadly speaking, vision serves two goals. First, vision allows you to know the qualities of objects at a distance (how big is it, is it moving, and does it have large pointy teeth?). This knowledge helps you behave in appropriate ways (attack small edible-looking things, flee from large aggressive-looking things). The "at a distance" feature is helpful because you can evaluate what something is without having to walk up and touch it. The second feature of vision is that it serves action, meaning that you know where things are so that you can move around effectively (e.g., pounce with accuracy on the small edible-looking thing or skirt immovable objects as you're fleeing from the aggressive-looking thing). So briefly put, the function of visual perception is to (1) identify objects and (2) help us navigate in the world. **How do we identify objects, and how does vision help us navigate?** As we'll see, these two functions actually are handled by separate parts of the brain. Here's what that means. When you see a coffee cup and reach for it, how do you know where it is? Your introspection is that you are able to reach accurately for the cup because you have a conscious awareness of where the cup is; you consciously know where the cup is, and it's this conscious knowledge that allows you to direct your hand to the cup. That introspection is wrong. Your conscious awareness of the cup's location is calculated by a separate cognitive system from the one that guides your hand to a location for reaching. The two systems usually are both correct about the location of the cup, so it feels as though the conscious feeling guides your hand, but it doesn't. I'll explain how that's possible later in the chapter.

➤ WHAT MAKES VISUAL PERCEPTION HARD?

➤ PREVIEW As we've just discussed, visual perception is very difficult, but it's not easy to appreciate how difficult it is because our cognitive systems are so good at it. In this section we examine more closely what makes visual perception hard. The heart of the difficulty lies in the fact that there are number of indeterminisms in what we see, meaning that the image falling on the retina does not fully determine what is in the world. For example, size and distance are indeterminate; if the image of something is small, the object in the world might be small, or it might be very far way. Other indeterminisms we'll discuss include shape and orientation (if you see what looks like an ellipse, what's in the world might really be an ellipse, or it might be a circle that is turned slightly to the side) and light source, reflectance, and shadow (what appears to be a gray object might really be a white object viewed in dim light or a black object viewed in bright light).

The chief problem the visual system faces usually is called the **inverse optics problem.** The inverse optics problem is the problem of recovering three-dimensional shape (as objects in the world have) from a two-dimensional projection (such as the projection on the retina). The problem is that when you have a two-dimensional projection in hand, there is an infinite number of three-dimensional objects that can give rise to a two-dimensional projection. The result of the inverse optics problem is that it is impossible to tell what is out in the world based solely on the information source available to us—neural impulses in the retina of the eye—because the world is three-dimensional and the pattern of activity in the retina is two-dimensional.

That explanation is a little abstract. Let's start this way. Suppose you are a painter and I'm a sculptor. You decide you want to paint a picture of the groovy sculpture I've made.

Now suppose you don't know how to paint at all. What could you do? You could put my sculpture on a table and put a pane of glass in front of it and simply trace the sculpture (and background) that you see through the glass, as shown in Figure 2.2.

That would work marvelously as long as you made sure that you didn't move your head. If you moved your head—for example, if you leaned way over

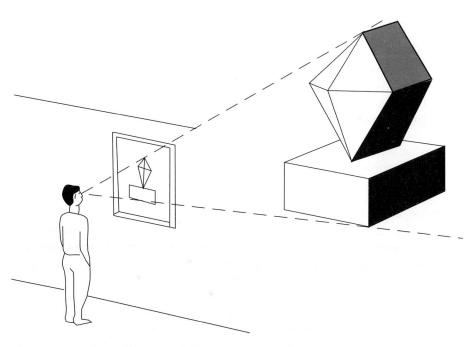

Figure 2.2. A three-dimensional object seen from a single perspective creates a unique two-dimensional projection. This two-dimensional projection is consistent with an infinite number of three-dimensional objects, however. In this figure, the observer sees the sculpture so that it looks like a kite on a rectangle rather than a diamond on a box.

to the right—the location of the sculpture would move relative to the glass, so the painting would be ruined. But if you stick with one point of view (i.e., don't move your head) you can turn a three-dimensional scene into a two-dimensional scene, and there is only one way the painting can turn out. You could get a new painter to come in, and as long as the position of the sculpture, the glass, and the painter were the same, the paintings would be identical. There is a single mapping of the three-dimensional scene into two dimensions.

Now suppose that I leave and you're showing someone the two-dimensional painting on the pane of glass. From that painting, could the person know what the sculpture looks like? Could he or she reconstruct the three-dimensional scene? No, because an infinite number of possible scenes are consistent with any two-dimensional picture. That's the inverse optics problem, and that's the problem your visual system constantly faces: how to divine the three-dimensional shape of objects based on a two-dimensional representation. In the case of the visual system, the two-dimensional representation is the pattern of light on the retina.

Bearing in mind that one of the functions of vision is to know about the properties of objects, we can be more specific about the properties of objects that we might want to know about and how the inverse optics problem creates difficulties. The example of the sculpture concerns shape; one can't know the shape of an object based on its two-dimensional projection because as the orientation of the object changes, the two-dimensional projection changes. This is exactly the problem your visual system faces. The two-dimensional representation is not painted on a window; it's painted on your retina. Your retina is two-dimensional, and recovering three-dimensional information about objects in the world poses the same problems as described in the painted window example. So one indeterminacy the visual system must solve is **shape and orientation.**

A second thing we want to know about an object is its surface features: what color it is, how dark or light it is, and so on. Shape can distinguish a cherry from rabbit droppings, but it is color, not shape, that will tell us whether the cherry is ripe and whether it is the genuine article or wax.

We run into a problem in trying to determine an object's color and brightness because the only source of information you have about surface features is the light reflected from the object. The technical term for the amount of light your eye receives is **luminance.** Three different factors contribute to luminance: the amount of illumination (e.g., a 100-watt lightbulb, a 25-watt lightbulb, the sun), the reflectance of the object (e.g., is it white, black, gray) and whether the object is in shadow. Here's an example of how these three factors combine: a piece of coal viewed in bright sunlight actually has higher luminance than a snowball viewed in candlelight. Nevertheless, the coal looks black and the snowball looks white. How does the visual system unravel the three factors that contribute to luminance so that it gets the reflectance of objects right? Here's another example. Look at the Mach card in Figure 2.3. What does it look like?

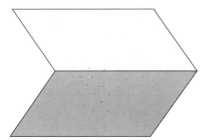

Figure 2.3. *A Mach card. The gray part of the figure could be gray because the surface of the object depicted is gray, or it could be gray because the surface is white but it is in shadow.*

This figure could depict an arrow-shaped stimulus that is white on top and gray on the bottom. Or it could be open book, face-down, illuminated from the top, so that the bottom is in shadow.

Thus a second indeterminacy is **light source, reflectance, and shadow.**

Object size and distance also are indeterminate from a two-dimensional representation. Bear in mind that everything you know about objects in the world comes from the image that the object projects onto the retina. Larger objects project larger images onto the retina. But the size of the retinal projection depends on both the size of the object and the distance between the object and the observer. If you see a square that appears quite small, is it truly a small square, or is it actually a large square that is far away? Thus a third indeterminacy is **size and distance.**

Another example of the tradeoff between object size and distance may be seen in the sun and the moon. Although the moon is much smaller than the sun, it is also much closer. It so happens that these two factors balance out nearly perfectly, so that the sun and moon project the same sized image on the retina and thus they appear to be the same size when viewed from the earth. That's why the moon just about covers the sun during a full eclipse. The moon would not appear to be the same size as the sun from a vantage point nearer or farther than the earth (e.g., on Jupiter). A more radical example of the tradeoff of object size and distance in determining the size of a retinal image can be observed; the tip of your thumb, when held at arm's length, projects about the same size retinal image as the sun or the moon; close one eye and your thumb's tip will just about block out the moon.

In summary, the main things you would want to know about an object—its shape, the color and brightness of its surface, its size, its distance—are indeterminate from the information that is available to the retina. That's why vision is hard. So how in the world are we able to see?

STAND-ON-ONE-FOOT QUESTION

1. Name the three indeterminacies that make visual perception difficult.

BOX 2.1. IS FACE PERCEPTION SPECIAL?

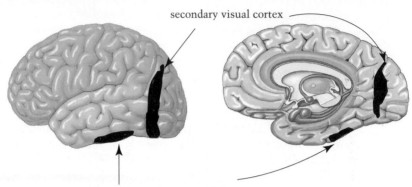

secondary visual cortex

ventral temporal lobe

In this section we're emphasizing that perceptual problems are hard. But at least one problem doesn't seem so difficult: recognizing faces. People are good at recognizing faces, considering that they differ only in subtle ways. They all have two eyes, a nose, a mouth, and so on, yet people can differentiate them at a glance. One might guess that there could be a special perceptual process for identifying faces. Given the importance of social relations in our species, one might propose that evolutionary pressures have favored a special perceptual mechanism for identifying faces.

One bit of evidence supporting the idea of a special perceptual process is the existence of a syndrome that selectively affects a patient's ability to recognize faces. The syndrome is called **prosopagnosia.** Patients have no difficulty recognizing common objects, but they cannot recognize familiar faces, including the faces of family or even themselves. Once a familiar person speaks, the patient can recognize the person by his or her voice, and the patient may be able to recognize someone by a distinctive feature (e.g., a prominent mustache). Patients with prosopagnosia typically have suffered bilateral damage to the secondary visual areas and the ventral temporal lobe.

The fact that there can be selective deficit of face recognition but normal recognition of other objects seems to be strong evidence that face recognition is supported by fundamentally different processes than object recognition. However, it should be noted that there is an important difference between recognizing an object and recognizing a face. When one recognizes an object (e.g., a car) one simply identifies the class of object, and one is not asked to differentiate individuals (e.g., is that a Chrysler or a Ford?). In face recognition, one is always asked to recognize an individual. Thus, the problem for prosopagnosic patients may be in recognizing individuals, not in recognizing faces per se.

The evidence on this proposal is mixed. On one hand, Jane McNeil and Elizabeth Warrington (1993) presented an interesting case study of a sheep farmer (W.J.) who was prosopagnosia. W.J. was shown a series of photos either of unfamiliar sheep or of unfamiliar faces and was then given a recognition test. He successfully recognized 81% of the sheep but only 50% of the faces. Other sheep farmers could recognize 89% of the faces and performed a bit worse than W.J. in recognizing sheep, averaging 69%. These data indicate that it is possible to have

(Continued)

intact memory for complex stimuli (such as the faces of individual sheep) and yet to be impaired in recognizing human faces.

Other data indicate that faces are *not* special. Functional imaging studies have emphasized the importance of the fusiform gyrus (located in the ventral temporal lobe) in face recognition, so that the area sometimes is referred to as specialized for face perception. Isabel Gauthier and her colleagues (1999) sought to show that this area is specialized not for face perception but for visual expertise. The researchers used stimuli called Greebles, which are meaningless but complex figures. Greebles are difficult to differentiate at first, but recognition improves with practice.

Figure B2.1. *Two fairly similar Greebles.*

The researchers were especially interested in what parts of the brain were associated with improvement. They found that the fusiform gyrus was a key area showing activation associated with increasing expertise, thus lending support to the idea that the fusiform gyrus may not necessarily be a "face area" per se but rather is associated with visual expertise.

In the end, the question "Are faces special?" still does not have a complete answer. It's possible that W.J. was using a different strategy to recognize the sheep, such as relying on specific markings (the sheep version of a prominent mustache), so that experiment may not be definitive. On the other hand, perhaps faces really are special, and the Greeble experiment shows only that if you give people this odd task, they recruit the brain processes that normally handle face processing to complete the task. Whether faces are special is as yet unsettled.

QUESTIONS THAT REQUIRE TWO FEET

2. *Size and distance are indeterminate, so if you see a small car, for example, you can't know whether it is a big car far away or a small car close by. Yet you seem to have no problem figuring that out. Why?*

3. *As mentioned in this section, the apparent size of the tip of your thumb when held at arm's length is about the same size as the moon, viewed from the earth, as Tom Hanks showed us in the movie* Apollo 13. *Would it work the same way if you stood on the moon and looke at the earth?*

➤ HOW ARE THESE AMBIGUITIES RESOLVED?

➤ PREVIEW In the previous section we discussed what makes visual perception difficult, and the answer was that a number of visual features are inherently ambiguous. In this section we discuss how these features are interpreted accurately (usually). The answer is that the visual system makes assumptions that resolve the ambiguities. Certain conjunctions of lines are assumed to be caused by corners of objects, and other conjunctions are assumed to be caused by one object lying in front of the other. Other assumptions are made about the color of objects and typical ambient lighting. Size and distance usually are resolved because the environment is rich in cues to distance (for example, if an object partially covers another it must be in front of it). In this section we also examine a whole different perspective on vision. Ecological psychologists propose that all of these problems and ambiguities may be more in the minds of psychologists than in the visual fields of observers. They propose that the environment actually provides a variety of cues that make the job of vision much simpler than it first appears. We examine the sorts of cues they claim people use.

The short answer to the question "How are these ambiguities resolved?" is that these insoluble problems become solvable if you are willing to make assumptions. That's what your visual system does. It makes assumptions about the nature of objects in the world and how they are illuminated. You should note that these assumptions are unconscious. You are not aware of making them, nor should you think that there is some intelligent part of your brain, outside your awareness, making executive decisions about assumptions. You can build assumptions into the way systems are engineered. For example, many cameras are designed with the assumption that pictures will be shot in daylight.

The assumptions built into your visual system allow the solution of these insoluble problems, but they do not guarantee a correct solution. Indeed, if you know these assumptions, you can use them wisely to create two-dimensional paintings that look compellingly three-dimensional or use them perversely and induce the visual system to make errors; that's what visual illusions are. The main point is that vision does not tell you what objects are out in the world. Visual perception is a construction. It is not a representation of exactly what is in the world, it is a representation of what is probably in the world. We'll go through the key properties of objects—shape, surface, size, and distance—one by one.

Shape

Likelihood Principle.   Let's start with the square. Why do you call it a square and not a cube? Your visual system is sensitive to what sorts of objects are likely to have projected a particular image onto your retina. Yes, it could be a cube, but think of all the different angles at which a cube could be positioned—just rotate a cube in three dimensions: How many views of a cube are there that look like a square? And keep in mind that it's the position of the cube relative to you that matters because if you move a bit, you would see one of the sides of the cube and realize that it's not a square. Thus, there are many ways to view a cube and only a very small fraction of those views makes it look like a square. So your visual system assumes that what you're seeing is actually a square. Herman von Helmholtz (1910/1962), one of the first giants of vision research, called this the **likelihood principle.** This principle has been important in many modern theories of vision, although as some researchers have pointed out, it's hard to distinguish whether the visual system interprets stimuli using likelihood as the guide or simplicity, meaning that you interpret ambiguous figures in the simplest way possible (Chater, 1996; Pomerantz & Kubovy, 1986).

We can state generally that the likelihood principle means that a two-dimensional straight line will be interpreted as being straight in three dimensions and lines that appear parallel in two dimensions will be interpreted as parallel in three dimensions. Again, from most vantage points, lines that are truly parallel (or nearly so) in three-dimensional space will appear that way in a two-dimensional representation, whatever your viewing angle. (Although this principle doesn't work once the lines get very long, it works for short lines, such as those that define the edges of objects.) To see that this is true, take out your wallet or a pen or anything with more or less parallel edges. Focus on the opposing, nearly parallel edges of the object. Rotate the object around, and you'll note that the edges remain parallel even as the angle of viewing changes.

Perkins's Laws.   Lines are thought to be very important in visual perception because edges are defined by lines, and edges tell us the shapes of objects. Not all lines in the world are parallel, of course. Lines often intersect, and the interpretation of the intersections is critical for organizing the perception of objects. There are three types of intersections possible: Y intersections (largest angle > 180 degrees), arrows (largest angle < 180 degrees), and T intersections (largest angle = 180). As shown in Figure 2.4, these angles tend to indicate different things. Y intersections and arrows tend to indicate corners of three-dimensional solids, whereas T intersections tend to indicate places where one object occludes (blocks one's view of) another object.

It turns out that not just any arrow or Y intersection will do. Perkins (1972) proposed that for Y intersections to appear as a corner of a rectangular solid, each of the three angles must be 90 degrees or greater. In an arrow intersection, each angle must be less than 90 degrees and they must sum to more than 90 degrees. This set of rules summarizing how the visual systems interprets angles is called **Perkins's laws.**

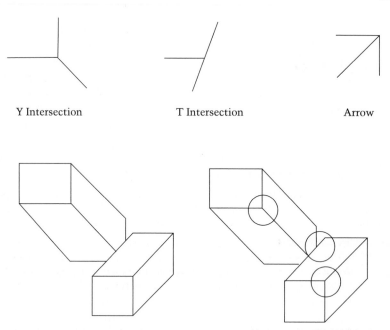

Y Intersection   T Intersection   Arrow

Figure 2.4.   *The top part of the figure shows examples of line intersections seen in visual scenes. At the bottom are two solids showing examples of these line intersections.*

Have a look at the shape on the left in Figure 2.5.

This impossible figure provides an example of the importance of the likelihood principle and the operation of Perkins's laws. Each corner of the triangle is interpretable and looks fine, but when you try to put the whole thing together, there's a problem. Let's focus first on the top corner of the figure on the right, which is the same as the one on the left, but I've labeled some lines and intersections. The lines a, b, and c are parallel in the two-dimensional picture. Thus, they are interpreted as being parallel in three dimensions. The intersections that are circled are T intersections and are thus interpreted as reflecting occlusion; the face denoted by lines e and f are in front of the end of the face denoted by the lines c and b. There are two arrow intersections in the figure, surrounded by squares. They are interpreted as being corners of rectangular solids. The one odd intersection is the T intersection, surrounded by the triangle in the figure on the right. Normally T intersections indicate occlusion, but in this case it is at the edge of the object, so it doesn't.

This interpretation is internally consistent for this one part of the figure, but this interpretation also specifies that the object is three-dimensional. Each point of the triangle appears to be composed of two rectangular solids, joined at an angle, and the angle would bring the arm up out of the picture plane. If you follow each angle at each point successively, you realize the figure is impossible.

Is there any experimental evidence that Perkins's laws are important to the visual system? Enns and Rensink (1991) provided evidence that conformity to Perkins's laws may be deeply embedded in visual processing. They showed

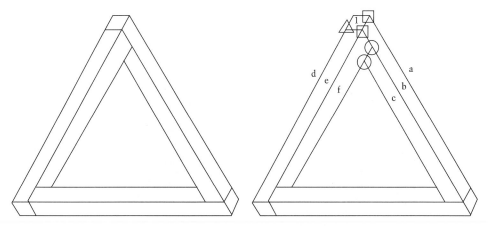

Figure 2.5. *An impossible figure is shown at the left. The intersecting lines at each corner of the triangle indicate an object that is perfectly possible but also indicate that the two bars joined at the corner are not in the same plane. The angles dictated by the three corners, taken together, make the figure impossible.*

participants fields of objects with arrow or Y junctions, and participants had to find a single target that was the same as the others but rotated 180 degrees.

When the stimuli conformed to Perkins's laws and indicated depth unambiguously, the target seemed to pop out from among the distractors. **Pop-out in a visual search task means that the participant can spot the target immediately even if there are many nontarget stimuli.** A hallmark of pop-out is that participants are equally fast in finding the target if there are a few nontargets present or if there are many nontargets present.

Pop-out is taken as evidence for a fundamental property of the visual system. When you get pop out, it must mean that the visual system is evaluating all stimuli present for this particular feature at the same time; otherwise, the number of stimuli present in the field would slow down the search. If all stimuli are evaluated for this feature simultaneously, this feature is presumably quite important to visual perception. Thus, a feature that leads to pop-out is taken as evidence that the feature is important to vision. (We'll talk about pop-out more in Chapter 3 when we discuss attention.)

Brightness Perception

When there is a change in luminance (the amount of light reflecting from an object and hitting your retina) it could result from a number of factors. For example, look at the cylinder in Figure 2.6. It looks as if it is uniformly colored and there is a light shining on it from the right because it is brighter on the right than on the left. That's because surfaces that are perpendicular to a light source are bright, whereas parallel surfaces are dim. However, it is possible that the cylinder is under several floodlights, so that all parts of it are illuminated equally, but it is colored lighter gray on the right and darker on the left.

Figure 2.6.   *The three factors that contribute to luminance: light source,
shading, and shadow.*

It is possible, but unlikely. Changes in the luminance can come from shadows, different illumination sources (as on a stage, where different lights from different angles may shine on an actor), and variations in the color or brightness of the object itself. The visual system makes several simple assumptions to clarify the ambiguity.

First, the visual system assumes that surfaces are uniformly colored. That's why shading makes such a difference in the three-dimensional quality of a painting. The shading is assumed by the visual system to reflect shadows caused by hills and valleys in the surface of an object, not sudden changes in the brightness of the object itself. That is also why the full moon looks so flat: It is uniformly bright. The moon is uniformly bright because it is full of craters and hills. When the light of the sun strikes this surface, it hits surfaces at many angles, so light reflects off these surfaces at many angles. Thus light from the moon is light that has been reflected from all angles, and that is true from every part of the moon. Thus, the brightness is even across the entire full moon and it therefore looks like a disk, not a sphere.

The second assumption is that gradual changes in brightness are caused by shadows. Shadows have fuzzy edges. Changes in the reflectance of a surface typically do not. Hence, in Figure 2.6 it is easy to distinguish the change in brightness caused by the cylinder's shadow from the change in brightness caused by the light and dark square of the checkerboard; the shadow has fuzzy borders; in this case, you can also see the object that cast the shadow.

Nevertheless, there is still ambiguity in decoding information that comes from shape. Look again at the Mach card in Figure 2.3. It is interpretable in two ways; it could be a book that is open with its spine toward you, with a light source from above or it could be a book that is open and facing you, with a light source from below. In interpreting shading information, the visual system

Photo 2.1. *Light sources are assumed to come from above, so this appears to be an indentation or crater. See what happens to the figure if you turn the book upside-down.*

assumes that light comes from above an object—a sensible assumption because vision evolved in a world where light almost always comes from the sun. The assumption that light comes from above is what makes the crater look concave; turn this book upside-down and see what happens when the pattern of shading changes.

It is also interesting to note that many women use this assumption of the visual system when they apply makeup. Blush typically is applied just under the cheekbone. That creates what appears to be a shadow—remember, the visual system assumes that surfaces (including cheeks) are uniformly colored—so the darker patch is assumed to be a shadow caused by a prominent cheekbone.

The final thing to know about brightness and shading is how the visual system treats complex scenes like the checkerboard in Figure 2.6. Believe it or not, the white squares that are in the shadow are exactly the same shade of gray as the dark squares that are not in shadow. How is that possible? Here's what the visual system does in these situations. The visual system uses **local contrast** to evaluate the likely shade of each square. Local contrast means that the perceived surface lightness depends on the ratios of lightness of areas that are next to one another and are in the same plane. Squares that are surrounded by darker squares (in shadow or not) are considered to be light. The fact that the boundaries of the squares are sharp also helps the visual system to determine that the boundaries between them are likely to be created by paint, not shadows, because shadows have fuzzy edges. Thus, the checkerboard is easy to interpret as being a field with light and dark squares, all of which are the same color. Hence, the light squares look light, even when they are in shadow.

The fact that you don't perceive the similarity of brightness between the light squares that are in shadow and the dark checks that are in full light may seem like a failing. But as Edward Adelson (1998), who designed this illusion, points out, it does not reflect a failing of the visual system but rather a success. Your visual system does not need to assess the absolute brightness of regions of space. It needs to interpret complex scenes into simple, meaningful components, such as "checkerboard with uniform dark and light patches, partly in shadow."

A more formal experiment demonstrating the importance of local contrast was conducted by Alan Gilchrist (1997). Gilchrist used a three-dimensional visual stimulus shown in Figure 2.7.

There were horizontal and vertical surfaces, some painted white and some painted black, labeled "W" and "B" in the figure. There was a lightbulb above the stimulus so that the horizontal part of the stimulus got lots of light and the vertical part got much less. Participants viewed the stimulus **monocularly**—that is, with just one eye—and through a peephole. The one-eyed viewing and the peephole restricted their viewpoint so that the stimulus looked flat, like a painting hanging on a wall. From the participant's perspective it looked like the figure

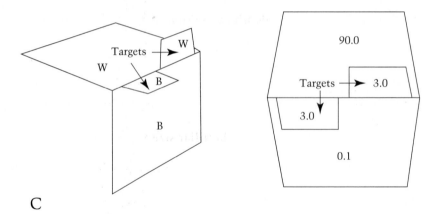

Target	Median Observer Match	
	Monocular	Binocular
Upper Tab	3.75	8.0
Lower Tab	7.75	3.0

Figure 2.7. *At top left is shown the actual stimulus participants viewed. At top right is the stimulus as it appeared when viewed with one eye. Because it was viewed with one eye, it looked like a flat surface. The numbers indicate the amount of light reflected from each surface. At the bottom are the participants' brightness ratings.*

at the top right. The numbers show the actual luminance of each part of the figure. The two tabs had equal luminance (3.0 foot-lamberts) because the upper tab was white but got little light, and the lower black tab got a lot of light.

The tabs did not look equal to participants, even though they had equal luminances. At the bottom of the figure you can see the brightness ratings participants gave to the tabs. The upper tab looked much darker than the lower tab. Why? Because it was surrounded by the much darker field that appeared to be in the same plane. If the lower tab and the field that seemed to surround it were in the same plane, they must have been hit by the same amount of illumination. Because the tab appeared much brighter than the surrounding field, it must have a lighter surface.

This effect went away completely when the participants viewed the stimulus **binocularly,** that is, with two eyes. Under those circumstances, the participants could see that the tabs were not in the same plane, which meant they could be illuminated differently; obviously, if two surfaces are at right angles (like the front of a desk and the top of a desk) then they are likely to receive different amounts of illumination from a single light source. When they were viewed binocularly, the brightness judgments for the tabs reversed.

Why can people see that the stimulus is not flat, once they view it with two eyes? That involves depth perception, which we turn to now.

Distance and Size

Size and distance trade off. Thus, when an object is far away it appears small, and when it is near it seems large. How can we disambiguate size and distance?

One obvious answer is that experience tells us the size of object; this cue to the size of an object is called **familiar size.** When we see a car, we assume it is the size of a normal car, even if it is far away and therefore appears small. Similarly, people should be people-sized, houses house-sized, and so forth. We don't often see an object that we've never encountered before and thus have no clue as to what the size it is likely to be.

Bill Epstein (1965) showed the importance (and the limits) of familiar size as a cue to distance. He took photographs of a dime, a quarter, and a half-dollar, and then made each photograph the same size: the size of a quarter. Epstein mounted the photographs on black rods and placed them an equal distance from the observer. The room was darkened, and the photographs were illuminated with a spotlight. The participants had to view them monocularly. The participants thought the photographs were real coins, and because they appeared to be the same size, participants judged them to be different distances away; a real dime would have to be closer than the half-dollar for them to appear to be the same size.

Thus, familiar size can influence one's perception of size and distance. But Epstein's results changed completely when people viewed the stimuli binocularly. Then people saw the stimuli as they actually were: equidistant and of equal size. Why did binocular viewing make a difference? Remember that binocular viewing changed participants' perception of Gilchrist's stimulus; binocular viewing allowed participants to see that the stimulus was actually three-dimensional, not a flat surface. What does binocular viewing add?

Two important cues to depth rely on binocular vision. One is **convergence,** which refers to the fact that as an object gets closer, your eyes cross more and more to gaze at it. As you might know, you point your eyes at an object so that the light reflecting from the object falls on the center of the retina, called the fovea. The fovea is the part of the retina that is the most accurate in seeing small details. Because your eyes are some distance apart, when objects are fairly close to you, your eyes start to cross to keep the image on the fovea of each eye. Convergence is useful as a cue to distance only when objects are fairly close, however. For objects that are moderately far away (say, more than 20 feet), the eyes are nearly parallel, so convergence is not a useful cue to distance.

Stereopsis is a more important binocular cue to distance. This cue is rooted in the fact that the eyes are located in different places and therefore get slightly different views of an object. This fact can easily be appreciated by simply holding one finger in front of your face and rapidly opening and closing your left and right eye, alternately. Doing so makes your finger seem to change positions. This difference in view of the left and right eye is called **binocular parallax.**

Look first at the left part of Figure 2.8. Both eyes are rotated so that points A and B fall on the center of the retina (the fovea). Note that the left and right eye receive different views of points A and B. To the left eye the points appear closer together than they appear to the right eye, which is easy to appreciate if you compare the size of the angles created by A and B with each eye. Now look at the right side of the figure. The difference between the views of the two eyes is not as extreme; the angles are closer to being the same.

Thus, the disparity between the views of the left and right eyes is larger for objects that are closer; for a distant star, the left and right eye get the same view. The visual system uses the difference between the left and right eye to figure out how far away an object must be to produce a given disparity. Thus, if there is a tree in the left and right retina and the tree is in roughly the same place on the left and right retina, that means the tree is quite distant. If there is a dog on the left and right retina but its position is very different in each, then the dog is close by. Stereopsis is the principle behind the Viewmaster toy. The Viewmaster presents slightly different views of the same scene to each eye. The disparity is interpreted by the visual system to be caused by differing distances of the objects. The view of an animal might be very different in each scene, so the animal appears to be nearby, whereas the view of a mountain is nearly identical in the two scenes, so the mountain looks far away.

Binocular parallax probably is the reason some of the effects we've been discussing work only if the stimulus is viewed monocularly. Binocular parallax obviously can't be a cue to distance if there is only one retinal image. So in Gilchrist's experiment on brightness perception, the illusion depended on participants perceiving the stimulus as a flat plane and therefore all parts of the stimulus receiving equivalent illumination, but the illusion of flatness disappeared when the participants viewed the stimulus binocularly. In Epstein's experiment with the coins, two cues to distance—binocular parallax and familiar size—were pitted against one another, with binocular parallax the clear winner.

The power of binocular parallax as a cue to depth can be observed from **random dot stereograms,** developed by Bela Julesz (1971). These patterns are

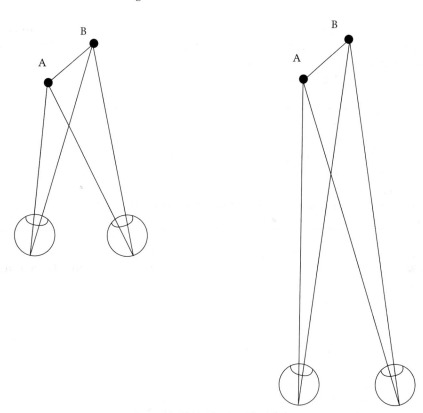

Figure 2.8. *The left and right eye get different views of objects, and this differ-*
ence is greater when the observer is closer to the object. In the left-
hand figure, the distance between A and B seems larger to the right
eye than to the left eye. The greater distance is apparent from the
greater angle of the two lines going to the right eye. The difference
between the left eye and right eye is not as great in the figure on the
right, where the distance between observer and object is greater.

constructed by taking a grid (perhaps 100 × 100) and randomly coloring each
square white or black. Then you take the grid and duplicate it. In this identical grid, you define a square in the center (perhaps 10 × 10) and move it to the
right one space. (Now you've got a blank column on the left; you fill those 10
spaces randomly with white or black.) So what you're left with is two grids
that are identical, but a square region in the center is moved over one space in
one of the grids. A simple version of this figure is shown in Figure 2.9.

Thus, if you present the left grid to the left eye and the right grid to the
right eye (like viewing them through a Viewmaster), there is a disparity in what
each eye sees at the center of the grid. The final perception is of a square in the
center, floating above the rest of the image.

Here's what makes this finding amazing. For stereopsis to work, you have
to perceive that the same object is on each retina but in different places on the
retina. Suppose you are seeing a snowman in a large field of snow, as shown in
the left part of Figure 2.10. In that case, it is not hard to see that the snowman

Figure 2.9.   *A 9 × 9 grid shows how a random dot stereogram is created. The two grids are identical with one exception. The centered 3 × 3 section of the grid on the left (outlined in gray) has been moved one square over in the grid on the right. The resulting three blank squares are filled in randomly.*

is in a different position on the retina in the left and right eye. But look at the example on the right. Here we have some pieces of coal at different distances in a field of snow. To figure out the disparity between the images of different pieces of coal, you have to know which dot in the left retina goes with which dot in the right retina; that's the only way to figure out how disparate their positions are. But how do you match up the dots?

This is called the **correspondence problem,** and it gets worse as objects in the visual field become harder to distinguish. The problem reaches peak difficulty in the random dot stereogram because the elements to be matched up are simply identical black dots and there are hundreds of them. Furthermore, in the real world you would have other cues to distance to help you (e.g., you

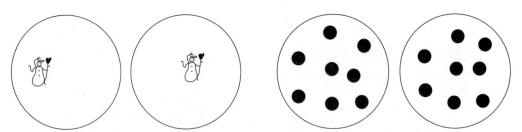

Figure 2.10.   *The two circles at left indicate the left and right retinas as one looks at a snowman in a field of snow. It is easy to find the snowman in each retina because it is unique, and it is therefore easy to calculate how different the location of the snowman is on each retina. At right, one might be looking at pieces of coal in a field of snow. To calculate the retinal disparity, one needs to know which piece of coal in the right retina matches which piece of coal in the left retina, but the pieces of coal are very similar, making this matchup (the correspondence problem) difficult.*

would know that a person was far away because she was small). In the random dot stereogram there are no cues to depth except binocular parallax. Despite the difficulty of the problem, the visual system does solve it—random dot stereograms do show depth—which was Julesz's point in devising them. Precisely how the visual system does it is not known, however. A number of theories have been offered, but they are beyond the scope of this book. For our purposes, it is noteworthy that depth can be perceived in random dot stereograms because it indicates that the visual system is very good in using binocular disparity as a cue to distance.

There are a number of other distance cues, often called pictorial cues. **Pictorial cues** can lend depth to two-dimensional pictures, whereas stereopsis and convergence rely on the physiology of the visual system. Many of these cues are used in a well-known painting by Jean-François Millet, *The Gleaners.*

One such cue is **occlusion.** An object that is in front of another will partly overlap it. In the painting, the image of the central figure overlaps the figure on the left. That is possible only if she is in front of the figure on the left. Occlusion is a useful cue even with figures that are unfamiliar because the perceptual system assumes that figures usually are closed; that is, if you see part of an object,

Photo 2.2. *Jean-François Millet's painting* The Gleaners *uses many pictorial depth cues.*

the rest of it is there, occluded by the other object. If you look at two overlapping circles, for example, you'd see one complete circle and an arc.

Your perceptual system assumes that it's two circles, one in front of the other, because for it to be a circle and an arc it would have to be the case that the arc just happens to be nuzzled right up against the circle so that there is no space between them, which is very unlikely. This assumption is another instance of the likelihood principle because it's much more likely to be two overlapping circles than it is to be a circle and an arc, perfectly aligned.

The texture on the ground of *The Gleaners* also is a good cue to distance called **texture gradient.** In the foreground, individual stalks of cut wheat are visible, but higher in the picture plane they are not. When things are closer, you can make out more detail, so this tells us that the bottom of the picture is closer in space to the viewer. It is possible, of course, that the background is not farther—it's just that there are no individual stalks of wheat in those regions—but again, the visual system assumes that surfaces (in this case, the surface of the field) are uniform, so the lack of detail higher in the picture plain is interpreted as indicating distance.

This picture also gives some sense of **linear perspective.** Linear perspective refers to the fact that lines that are parallel in three-dimensional space converge in two-dimensional space if you extend them far enough; the farther the distance, the closer they are to converging. This is easiest to imagine if you keep things in a plane. If you draw parallel lines on the floor, as the floor gets farther away the lines appear to converge. For example, the sides of the road appear to get closer together as they get farther away as shown in Figure 2.11 at left. It is less obvious from our everyday experience but equally true of parallel lines in three dimensions, as shown in Figure 2.11 at right.

There is subtle linear perspective in *The Gleaners* as well. You can see some lines or shadows on the field to the left of the leftmost figure and to the right of the rightmost figure. As in Figure 2.11, these lines converge toward a vanishing point on the horizon.

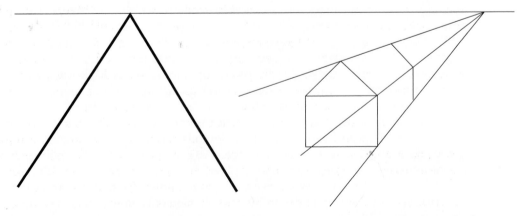

Figure 2.11. *Linear perspective. At left, two parallel lines in a plane (the sides of a road) converge in the far distance. At right, the three parallel sides of a house converge in the distance.*

The **relative height** of objects also is a cue to distance. The rightmost figure in the painting appears closer than the others not because she occludes anyone but because she is lower in the visual field. To her right is a figure on horseback. This figure is very high in the visual field, indicating great distance, which is reinforced by the very small size. This is not a microscopic horse hovering over her shoulder.

The final distance cue use in the painting is **atmospheric perspective.** Objects in the distance look indistinct and often have a hazy, bluish appearance. The air is full of dust and water particles. Dust and water particles scatter light, so if you view an object that is far away, more of the light reflected from the object is scattered by the time it hits your eye. The image of these distant objects is blurred because much of the light has been scattered.

In summary, there are a great many cues to distance. It's true that size and distance trade off—an object that appears small may be small or it may simply be far away—but distance usually should be discernible from one of these cues, and knowing distance should help disambiguate size.

Top-Down Influences in Vision

Let me summarize what I've said so far. Visual processing is very difficult because the two-dimensional image on the retina underspecifies what the three-dimensional world looks like. You can't tell what the shape of an object is from the retinal projection because shape and orientation trade off, you can't tell the size or distance of an object because these two factors trade off, and you can't tell whether an object is white, gray or black because differences in shading could result from the object shading, lighting, or shadows. Then I said that all these problems can be solved if you're willing to make a few assumptions, and we went through what these assumptions might be and what cues in the environment help you solve the problems.

You may or may not have noticed that the information discussed so far seems to flow in one direction; you start with the raw information from the environment, and from that you construct a percept of what is in the world. This sort of processing is called **bottom-up processing.** Bottom-up processing refers to beginning with raw, unprocessed sensory information and building toward more conceptual representations. Our discussion up until now has discussed only bottom-up processing, but these processes can't handle all of vision alone. For example, you may have seen stimuli like those shown in Figure 2.12.

How can the mind arrive at different interpretations of the final two characters of the lines in Figure 2.12? This demonstration seems to argue for **top-down processing.** Top-down processing refers to conceptual knowledge influencing the processing or interpretation of lower-level perceptual processes; if you're reading the second line in the figure, the conceptual knowledge that you are reading letters leads you to interpret the ambiguous characters as more letters to complete the word "this."

With impoverished perceptual information, you can still figure out what something is if you have good conceptual information. For example, suppose I

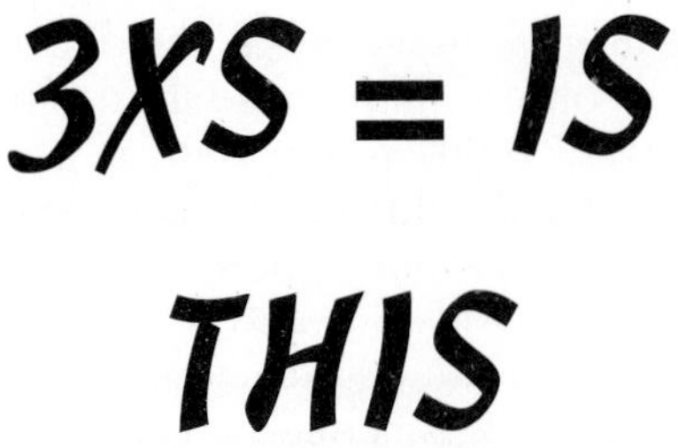

3XS = IS
THIS

Figure 2.12. Note that the final two characters are identical in the first line and the second line, but they are interpreted differently because of the surrounding context.

show you Figure 2.13, and I tell you that it is a new alphabet, but an impoverished one. It doesn't show complete letters; it just tells you whether a letter goes below the line you're writing on (e.g., *g, y, j*), above the line (e.g., *h, l, k*), or within the line (e.g., *e, a, s*). All letters are lowercase. Figure 2.13 shows a four-word phrase written in this impoverished alphabet. See whether you can identify it.

Now suppose I give you some conceptual information: I tell you that the phrase is the title of a classic movie. Most people find that the conceptual information makes an otherwise impossible perceptual task possible. With good conceptual information, you can make up for the impoverished perceptual information. But is this really changing the way you see the stimulus? Not really. It's affecting your guesses about what the stimulus is supposed to represent. So the question is whether people actually use conceptual information when they see. (The movie, by the way, is *Gone With the Wind*.)

The answer is that people do use conceptual information when they see, up to a point. There have been several experiments showing the effects of conceptual information on vision. In a classic experiment on this topic, Stephen Palmer presented participants with complex scenes.

Participants were given 2 s to look at the scene—plenty of time to figure out that it was a kitchen (or whatever was depicted). Next, one of three objects was flashed within the scene very briefly. In the case of the kitchen scene, it was either a contextually appropriate object (bread), a similarly shaped contextually inappropriate object (a mailbox), or an object that didn't fit the context and wasn't shaped like the target object. The objects were flashed for just 65 ms. Participants correctly identified the contextually appropriate object 80% of the time but were

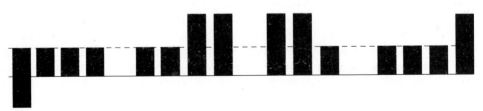

Figure 2.13. Four-word phrase in an alphabet that doesn't depict details of letters; for each letter it shows only whether the letter goes above or below the line. Without any conceptual information, it's hard to know what is spelled; with conceptual information, top-down processing helps you identify what is spelled.

right only 40% of the time for the other objects. Similar effects have been demonstrated by Irving Biederman using different paradigms (Biederman, 1981).

Of course, you would recognize the mailbox eventually, even when it is out of context. However, there are some instances in which you can't identify an object without the context.

For example, the shape third from the right at the bottom of Figure 2.14 could be a letter "C," a hook, or a sideways hill. There's really no telling. Once it is seen in context, as at the top of the figure, it is perfectly recognizable, but in isolation none of the parts are identifiable.

Here's the question. We've been assuming that processing is mostly bottom-up, meaning that you'd look at this figure and identify the nose, then the ear, then the eye, and so on, and then put all the pieces together and figure out that it's a face. On the other hand, we've just said that you can't figure out that it's a nose (or ear, or whatever) until you know that it's part of a face. Palmer called this situation the **parsing paradox.** Parsing means figuring out what the pieces of a larger whole are. Thus the parsing paradox is the apparent impossibility of identifying the face in Figure 2.14 until you know it has a nose, a mouth, and so on. But you can't identify the nose, mouth, and so on, until you know it's a face.

Palmer suggested that the resolution to the parsing paradox is that you do both top-down and bottom-up processing simultaneously, and each type of processing helps the other, as shown in Figure 2.15.

There is obviously a role for top-down processes in visual perception: Vision operates more quickly when contextually consistent information is perceived, and

Figure 2.14. *This figure is easy to recognize when the parts are seen together (in a sensible spatial arrangement) but is composed of parts that are difficult to recognize alone.*

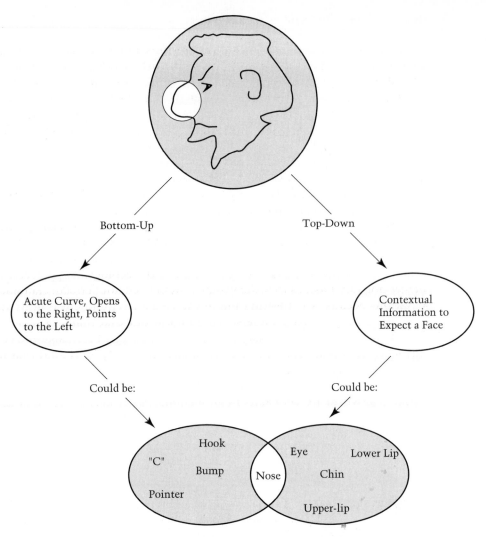

Figure 2.15. *We can use top-down and bottom-up processing simultaneously to identify objects.*

ambiguous stimuli are perceived in a way that is consistent with context. But top-down processes must take a back seat to bottom-up processes. When something appears in the environment that is completely out of context (e.g., a chimp typing at a computer), you may be slower to perceive it because it is out of context, but you do perceive it.

An Alternative Point of View: The Ecological Approach to Visual Perception

There is a second point of view on the whole problem of vision. This point of view contends that the way I posed the problem of vision in the beginning of the chapter is flat out wrong. (I heard you sigh). Up until now we have been discussing what is often called the **computational approach.** It is called the computational approach because it assumes that the information in the environment is impoverished—all that the retina has to work with is a series of lines—and therefore the visual system must do a great deal of computing to recover the three-dimensional shapes and movements of the environment.

The second perspective usually is called the **ecological approach,** and J. J. Gibson (1979) generally is considered the founder. Gibson's point was this. Researchers emphasize that vision is hard, but the reason vision looks so hard is that psychologists have done a terrible job of describing the environment. According to Gibson, the environment has a variety of cues in it that specify what is out in the world, but psychologists act as though the environment were composed of nothing but lines. Then they say, "Because the retina has no information except lines, it's going to be really tough for the visual system to get an accurate representation of what's in the world." Gibson replied, "It wouldn't be so tough if you recognized that there is much more information in the world that we can take advantage of." In summary, the ecological approach to visual perception emphasizes that the visual system need not perform elaborate computations because the information in the visual environment is quite rich.

An ecological psychologist would point out that many of the problems raised earlier in this chapter seldom exist in the real world. Take the very first example, in which I showed you the square and then pointed out that it could be a cube. I said that there is no way to determine whether it is a square or a cube. That's true, if I forbid you from moving your head. The fact is that objects in the real world are very seldom ambiguous, partly because most of them are familiar and partly because you can move your head.

So the ecological point of view holds that vision often isn't as hard as it seems because there is much richer information in the environment than you would first guess. I'll give you two examples of these sorts of information sources.

OBJECT SIZE. Size and distance trade off, right? So suppose I am in a desert with very few cues to distance and I see an unfamiliar object (or a familiar object that can take many different sizes, such as a tree). How can I figure out its size?

The approach we've been using up until now would say that because it's an unfamiliar object I'd have to first figure out about how far away it is. I could do that from stereopsis. Then I'd note how big the retinal image is (i.e., how big it looks) and work back to how big the actual object is, based on its distance.

Other researchers (Mark, 1987; Rogers, 1996; Warren, 1984) pointed out that much better size information was already in the environment. The horizon line intersects with an object at the **eyeheight** of the observer (i.e., at the height of the observer's eyes). I'm about 6 ft tall, so my eyeheight is around 5 ft 6 in. Therefore, the horizon intersects with the object at 5 ft 6 in. The horizon intersects with the object at about half of its height (Figure 2.16), so the object is around 11 ft tall. Simple.

There is evidence that people use this eyeheight metric. Maryjane Wraga (1999a, 1999b) showed people different-sized steps, and they were to judge the height of each step relative to a standard rod (was the step taller or shorter than the rod?). The tricky part of the experiment was how she manipulated eyeheight. The participants viewed the steps from another room through a small

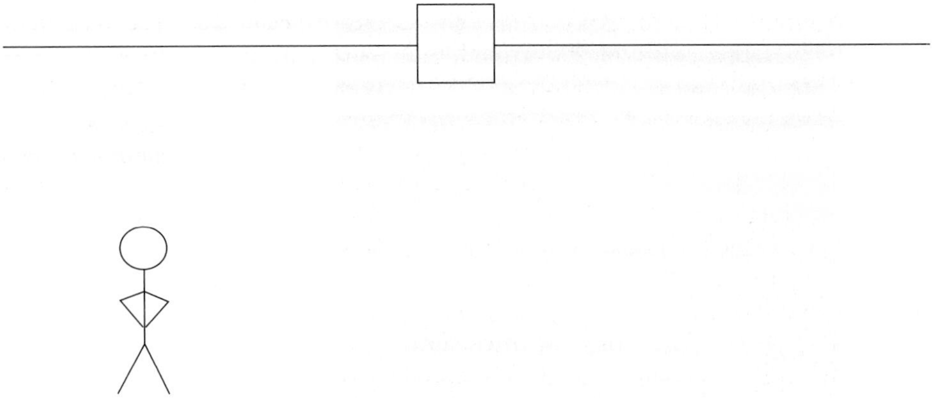

Figure 2.16. *The author evaluating the height of an object by using the intersection of the horizon with the object.*

window. On some of the trials, the floor of this other room was about 6.5 in. higher than the floor on which they were standing. This difference is small enough that participants didn't notice something funny about the floor in the other room. Still, participants judge their eyeheight relative to where they think the floor is, so the false floor effectively changes their eyeheight. (The manner in which Wraga and others hypothesized the eyeheight information is used actually is more complicated than this, but the principle is the same.) The results showed that the false floor did affect size judgments: Participants judged steps to be about an inch shorter when the floor was raised.

In another study Marco Bertamini, Tyrone Yang, and Dennis Proffitt (1998) provided evidence that people use eyeheight information indoors. If you're in a hallway, for example, you can't explicitly see the horizon, of course, but you get a strong sense of linear perspective from the walls, ceiling, and floor, and the vanishing point of these lines is where the horizon would be. The vanishing point is the point where all of these lines meet. We can call that a virtual horizon.

The experimenters asked participants to judge which of two poles was taller. The task was more difficult than it sounds because the poles were positioned nearer to or farther from the participant. Some pairs of poles were tall (100% of the participant's eyeheight) and some were short (60% of the participant's eyeheight), and participants made their judgments either standing up or sitting down. The experimenters found that participants were more accurate in judging which pole was taller when the poles were near their eyeheight. Thus, participants were more accurate in judging the tall poles when they were standing but more accurate in judging the short poles when they were sitting. That indicates that when eyeheight information is available, people use it in making size judgments.

Eyeheight information also is used in the entertainment industry. Things look bigger when your eyeheight is made artificially lower. You might note this next time you are at the movies. When a director wants to make someone look taller (a hero more impressive or a monster scarier) the director will shoot that person with the camera held not at eye level, but at perhaps waist level, effectively

Photo 2.3. *The Terminator is shot with the camera low to the ground. We assume that the camera is at our eyeheight, so the Terminator appears taller and more intimidating.*

lowering the eyeheight of the moviegoer and thereby making the subject of the shot seem taller.

DISTANCE FOR NAVIGATION. Suppose you're playing left field in a baseball game and someone hits a ball your way. How do you get to the right position to catch it? Common sense dictates that you calculate the trajectory of the ball, judge where it is going to land, and run to that spot—you run under the ball. That seems to be consistent with the computational approach described earlier in the chapter. It would take a fair amount of calculating: You have to figure out the ball's trajectory very quickly, extend that trajectory to make a prediction about where the ball is going to land, and run to that spot. The problem is that fly balls often don't follow a perfect parabolic trajectory because of the spin of the ball, gusts of wind, and other factors.

Michael McBeath, Dennis Shaffer, and Mary Kaiser (1995) provided evidence that you don't catch a fly ball by calculating a trajectory. What you appear to do is run so that the trajectory of the ball looks like a straight line in two dimensions. Imagine that you're standing in left field, and the batter at home plate hits the ball. Imagine that you're seeing a two-dimensional picture; the ball goes upward in the picture and to the left or right. If you run at a speed and in a direction that make the ball travel in what appears to you to be a straight line (in this picture) you will run directly to the spot where the ball will land. The details of the geometry are a bit complex, but the basic point is quite simple. It's a beautiful example of the ecological approach. At first glance, the problem (running to catch a fly ball) looks very complex and it seems as if the visual system would need to do some quite sophisticated calculations to solve it. But it turns out that a simple cue in the environment can be used instead.

It's nice to know that the strategy can work, but do people actually use it? The researchers conducted two experiments to address this question. First, they mounted a video camera on the shoulder of an outfielder and had him catch fly balls. Analysis of the videotape showed that for successful catches, the ball traveled in a straight line from the fielder's point of view.

In a second experiment, the researchers mounted a camera above the playing field and recorded how the fielder ran when catching fly balls. Seventy-one percent of the running paths showed the curvature predicted by the model, and 75% showed changes in speed predicted by the model. Other models of catching (that we haven't described in detail because they are a bit complex) predict constant running speed, which was observed on only 3% of the trials.

In summary, the ecological approach holds that most vision researchers make the problem of visual perception more difficult than it actually is. Once you fully describe all of the rich sources of information available in the environment, they argue, many of the problems of visual perception disappear. Are they right?

To a point, I think the answer must be yes. Ecological psychologists have made this point in the experiments described above, and in others. Still, one shouldn't think of computational researchers and ecological researchers as two warring camps. It is not difficult to find common ground between them; even the most determined ecological researchers admit that the perceptual system must do *some* processing on the information in the environment, and even the most determined computational researchers admit that the environment may contain subtle sources of information that the visual system can use. Thus, the difference between the perspectives may best be thought of as one of emphasis.

STAND-ON-ONE-FOOT QUESTIONS

4. How do Perkins's laws help to identify objects?
5. What assumptions does the visual system make about luminance?
6. Why are random dot stereograms interesting?
7. Summarize the differences between the computational and the ecologic points of view.

QUESTIONS THAT REQUIRE TWO FEET

8. I was once on a hill overlooking San Francisco on a brilliantly clear day, and the city was laid out before me. I had a very odd depth perception; the city looked like a small model, seen at about 30 feet, rather than a full-size city seen at a distance. Why?
9. Can you think of a way to use what you know about perceived size and eyeheight to improve your relationship with toddlers?

➤ *WHAT IS VISUAL PERCEPTION FOR?*

> ➤ PREVIEW In this section we discuss the two major functions of vision: helping
> you to know what objects are in the world and helping you to navigate (i.e., to
> move around). For objects to be recognized, there must be some representation
> in memory of what the object looks like; how else can you know that a car is a
> car? But a car looks very different from the front, back, or side. Does that mean
> you need three mental representations to be sure you can recognize it from each
> perspective? One group of theories holds that you have a single mental repre-
> sentation of a car that is a suitable representation for the car viewed from any
> angle. Another group of theories proposes that you keep several representations
> of each object in memory. We discuss the merits of each of these ideas. We also
> discuss navigation and focus on the difference between conscious visual percep-
> tion and visual perception that supports navigation. This work is fairly recent,
> but there is a growing consensus that there are two separate sets of visual
> processes. One set supports our conscious perception of where things are and
> what objects are out in the world. Another set of processes is privileged to the
> motor system: They help you move, but you can't get conscious access to their
> contents. Most the time these two sets of processes are in accord. They can be
> made to disagree, however, and those instances constitute some of the evidence
> that they are separate.

We've discussed why visual perception is difficult and some of the ways in
which the perceptual system overcomes the difficulties, but we haven't really
moved much beyond the attributes of objects: their size, shape, distance, and so
on. Object attributes are not the end of perceptual processing because only occasionally do you want information about a single attribute (e.g., scanning a
parking lot for the color red when trying to locate your car). More often, we
combine attributes in the visual field to achieve one of two goals: We want to
know the identity of objects around us, and we want to know their locations.
Knowing an object's identity is helpful so that you know what you want to do
to it: If it's an apple, eat it; if it's a stapler, squeeze it; if it's a book of "Shoe"
comic strips, ignore it. Knowing an object's location is helpful so that you will
know how to do what you want to do with it: where it is relative to you, where
the best place to grasp it is, whether there are obstacles in the way should you
decide to grasp it, and so on.

It turns out that the perceptual system has separated these two problems.
One system is responsible for figuring out what an object is. Another system is
responsible for figuring out the object's properties (e.g., size, orientation) that are
important for interacting with it. Object identity has been much more thoroughly studied, so we can say more about how that might work. Only fairly recently have people concluded that the visual action system is separate from the
object identity system, so most of our discussion focuses on how researchers
came to draw that conclusion.

Identifying Objects

In the previous sections we discussed how you can know the attributes of objects within your field of view (e.g., their distance, size, brightness). In this section we focus on how you identify what those objects are. Shape is the most obvious characteristic we use to identify objects. For example, a banana is easy to recognize because of its shape. But other properties can be helpful, too. For example, you can identify the handle on a chest of drawers by its location, even if it has a very unusual shape. A piece of cheese and a brick may have similar shapes, but they are distinguishable based on their color and texture. Thus, the first thing we should realize is that many cues contribute to visual object recognition. Most researchers have focused on shape, however, probably because it is the most reliable cue to object identity. You are able to identify objects even when they are in a grossly unexpected location; if an elephant were walking on your bedroom ceiling, you'd identify it quickly. You can also identify an object even it has the wrong texture or color; make the elephant on your ceiling pink and highly polished, and you'd still identify it as an elephant. Other cues are not as definitive to object identity as shape is. For example, if you were at the zoo and saw a large, gray, wrinkled animal shaped like a camel standing among the elephants, you'd call it a funny camel, not a funny elephant. Shape dominates.

Object identification has many difficult problems associated with it. We'll talk about just one, but it's probably the core issue: What does the memory representation look like that supports object identification? Suppose you successfully recognize that an animal is a cat—now, we're not talking about a specific cat here, we just mean that you know it's a cat and not a fox or a squirrel or a muffler. Some information in memory must enable you to identify what the object is. You have to have some information stored about what cats look like. What kind of information is it?

There are two families of answers to this question. The first is that the representation in memory is specific to your viewpoint. "Specific to your viewpoint" means that you store how the object looks *to you*. You don't store the object's structure as it actually is, necessarily; you store it the way it looks to you, the way light reflecting from the object falls on your retina. This is called a **viewer-centered representation** because the representation of the object is relative to how the viewer sees it. The second family of theories claims that you store how the object looks independent of any particular viewpoint. This is called an **object-centered representation** because the locations of the object's parts are relative to the object, not relative to the viewer. So a viewer-centered representation might contain the information that a jet plane's nose is to the left of its tail. That's true from one viewer's perspective, but that representation won't work if the plane is turned around or if the viewer is looking at the plane from the front. The object-centered representation locates object parts relative to other object parts; thus, it would contain the information that the plane's nose is attached to the fuselage.

For both families of theories, a key problem is dealing with rotated objects. You never know in what orientation you'll see a cat; it might be running, climbing a tree, or curled up by a fire. Think of what an odd profile a cat has when it is curled up by a fire. The object-centered theories say "Right, that's just why you need an object-centered theory. The representation in memory can't be specific to one viewpoint because you never know in what orientation you'll see the object; you need to represent the locations of the object parts relative to themselves." This claim seems self-evident, and everything we've gone over in this chapter seems to support the idea that much of vision is an effort to recover the three-dimensional shape of objects independent of the particular view you happen to take. As we'll see, however, the viewer-centered theories have a response.

Older Theories

A first pass at a theory of object recognition is the template theory. This theory proposes that we recognize objects by comparing the retinal image to a template in memory. A **template** is a representation of an object that is viewer centered, and it is basically a picture of what the object is supposed to look like, with a label attached. Thus, you compare the image of what you see with all your templates, and if a template matches what you see, you've identified the object.

There are many problems with this model. The easiest one to appreciate is depicted in Figure 2.17.

If the armadillo turns a bit, it won't match the template, so you'd need another template to match that view of the armadillo, and so on. You would need way too many templates. The truth is that no one ever took the template-matching idea very seriously, but it remains popular as a whipping boy, especially in cognitive psychology textbooks.

Template matching does have some practical uses, however. Vending machines that take dollar bills use template matching to evaluate whether what you put in is really a dollar. You can see how the fatal flaw in template matching is avoided. You must put the dollar bill in the machine at a particular orientation; the problem of identifying an object that happens to be turned at a slightly different angle is gone because the machine constrains the angle at which it can "see" the bill.

Feature-matching theories were a response to the problems of template-matching theories. Feature-matching theories still used a viewer-centered representation, but they got around many of the problems of template theories by proposing **critical features** of stimuli. Features are parts of a stimulus (e.g., the letter *T* could be defined as having two features: a horizontal line and a vertical line). Critical features are invariant to transformations; if you change the object in some way (e.g., make it larger) the critical features don't change.

So a template theory said that the memory representation that allowed you to recognize the letter *A* was a picture of the letter *A*. Feature-matching theories said that the representation was a set of features. Thus, if you see a left-slanted line, a right-slanted line, and a horizontal line, there's a good chance that it's an *A*. You can think of a set of features as being a set of lines and curves out of which you could create letters, as shown in Figure 2.18.

Feature theories have several important advantages over template theories. First, letters can still be recognized even under different transformations. For example, all uppercase *A*s share the same set of critical features. Although

Figure 2.17. *In the top figure, the observer recognizes the armadillo because it matches his armadillo template. If the same armadillo is turned 180 degrees, the observer cannot identify it because it no longer matches the template.*

they may vary in size, and some have extra, noncritical features (e.g., serifs) most capital *A*s have two diagonal lines and a horizontal line. Another nice aspect of the theory is that it appears to be consistent with known neurophysiology. David Hubel and Torsten Wiesel (see Hubel & Wiesel, 1979, for a review) won the Nobel prize for their groundbreaking work showing that cells in early visual cortical areas seemed to code lines at different orientations. These cells seemed to correspond well to feature detectors in the feature theory.

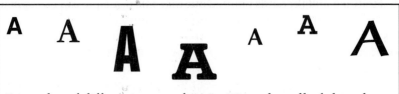

Examples of different types of "A"s. Note that all of them have two diagonal lines and a horizontal line.

Figure 2.18. *Feature set of letters.*

There are problems with the feature theory, however. For example, a sideways letter *R* is not hard for people to identify, although it has none of the critical features of an upright *R*. Furthermore, it is hard to see how feature theories can account for the perception of natural objects. Researchers built feature theories that could recognize letters of the alphabet. It's fairly obvious what the features of a letter are, but what are the features of a dog? Can you develop a theory of how a dog would be "broken down" into features?[1]

OBJECT-CENTERED THEORIES. Feature-matching theories failed because they could not recognize rotated letters (and presumably other rotated objects) and because there was no obvious way in which they could be extended to more natural objects. The solutions to these problems were to make the representations object centered rather than viewer centered and to show that natural objects can be broken down into features.

Here's the object-centered idea. You can recognize a sideways *R* even though it's rotated. Rotated relative to what? It's rotated relative to the viewer. But the parts of the *R* are not rotated relative to one another. If your frame of reference is the object, then everything is just fine: All parts are where they are supposed to be *relative to one another*. Thus, when you are looking at a dog, you shouldn't look for the parts relative to where you are (e.g., you shouldn't look for a head at the top, feet at the bottom). You should look at the dog's parts relative to its other parts (e.g., a head connected to a neck, feet connected to legs, tail connected to the back). The relationships between the parts cannot change whether the dog is facing left or right, whether it is running or curled up.

But using this representation of parts relative to one another relies on being able to recognize the parts. How do you do that? How do you "decompose" a dog into parts?

Donald Hoffman and Whitman Richards (1984) pointed out that a perceptual principle first noted in the 1930s could be applicable to this problem. The principle is called **good continuation;** it means that the visual system prefers to interpret lines as continuing along the path they have been following rather than abruptly changing direction. It is illustrated in the left panel of Figure 2.19.

You can see that good continuation is a variant of the maximum likelihood principle. It's much more likely that these are two crossed lines (for which there are an infinite number of ways that you would get a crossing similar to this one) than that the figure represents two acute angles, just touching (for which there are few ways to get a figure like this one).

Hoffman and Richards pointed out that this principle can be applied to three-dimensional objects. In the right panel of Figure 2.19, it is unlikely that a single

[1]You may wonder why everyone based their theories on letters of the alphabet. There were actually good reasons for this. First, people wanted to make their theories comparable to one another. If I have a theory that recognizes letters, and you have one that recognizes faces, how can we compare the theories to see which one is better? Letters gave everyone a standard stimulus set to work with. Second, letter recognition was an important applied problem. There are obvious uses to devising a machine that can recognize letters of different fonts and sizes; perhaps such a machine eventually would be able to recognize more complex images.

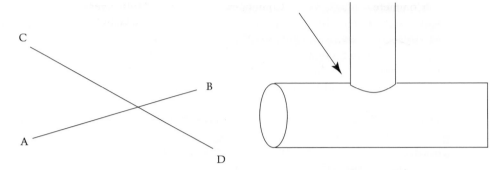

Figure 2.19.   *The principle of good continuation is illustrated at left. The visual system sees this figure as two overlapping lines,* AB *and* CD, *rather than two angles,* AC *and* BD. *The figure on the right shows how good continuation can be used to divide objects into parts. The sudden discontinuity in the edge of the object (indicated by the arrow) makes for poor continuation. Therefore, this location is seen as the place where two parts of the object are joined.*

object would make a radical turn at the point marked by the arrow. Instead, it is more likely that this radical turn is caused by the junction of two separate parts. The authors speculated that part boundaries are signaled by edges that subtend convex angles. Indeed, if you ask participants to mark the boundary of two parts, they select the point of maximum curvature. The objects in Figure 2.18 are simple cylinders, but the principle works equally well with a dog's leg and body.

Thus we may have the two principles we need to rescue a feature theory. We can solve the rotation problem if we make the representation object-centered instead of viewer-centered; we make the representation a collection of parts with their positions defined relative to one another rather than relative to our point of view. Furthermore, it looks as though we can decompose even natural objects such as dogs into component parts.

Several feature theories in this spirit have been offered. An influential feature theory was proposed by Irving Biederman (1987). He argued that object recognition is supported by a set of 36 shapes he called geons. These 36 geons operate like letters of the alphabet; complex objects can be built from these simple shapes, as shown Figure 2.20.

A strength of the theory is that the geons have properties that make them easy to distinguish from one another. For example, if you're looking at a cylinder you can almost always see two parallel edges and an ellipse, whatever the angle from which your seeing it; a cone shows two convergent edges and an ellipse, the geon called a brick shows three parallel edges, and so on.

There is also some evidence that the integrity of geons is important to vision. Biederman (1987) showed participants pictures of objects constructed from geons, similar to those in Figure 2.20. The pictures were degraded in one

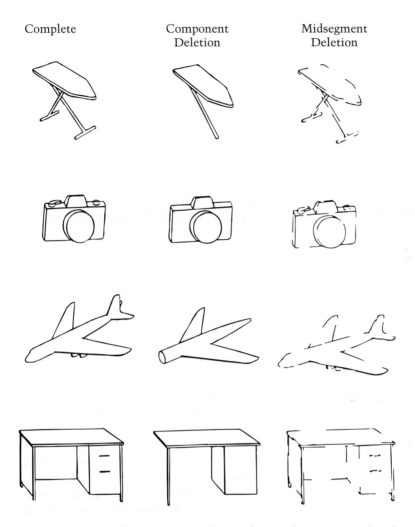

Complete   Component   Midsegment
                   Deletion   Deletion

Figure 2.20. *Examples of common objects that can be constructed with the geons proposed in Biederman's theory and two ways of degrading the figure.*

of two ways: Either he removed entire geons or he removed the equivalent length of line segments but did so across several geons. Then he flashed the degraded pictures very rapidly on a computer screen and asked participants to identify them. He found that if the picture appeared for just 65 ms, participants made more mistakes when all of the geons were degraded than when a single geon was missing. Biederman argued that this result showed that the remaining geons were sufficient to determine the object's identity, but if all geons were degraded, many of the geons could not be identified, so the object could not be identified.

Although the Biederman model is appealing, not all evidence supports it. For example Carolyn Cave and Stephen Kosslyn (1993) used a task quite similar to that used by Biederman but somewhat longer exposure times, and they found no difference in participants' ability to identify objects separated into "good" parts (as dictated by the geon theory) or objects simply chopped up any old way.

Furthermore, there are still some objects for which it is not clear how they would be represented in terms of geons. Some objects don't have obvious parts, but their single part does not look like a geon (e.g., a loaf of bread). Other common objects have parts, but the parts don't look like any of the geons (e.g., a shoe). The theory cannot readily account for the recognition of such objects.

VIEWER-CENTERED THEORIES.   It seems that object-centered theories would almost have to be right. If the representation is based on the viewer's location, you would need a different representation each time the viewer moved (or the object moved). Thus, you might need 360 different representations for each object, one for each degree the object can be rotated.

An alternative could postulate that you rotate the image of the object you see to fit your mental representation. Thus, a sideways R would be mentally rotated until it was in its normal orientation, and then it would match your viewer-centered memory representation of an R. The problem with this approach is that it assumes you know how to transform the object so that it matches the representation in memory. Should you rotate it clockwise, counterclockwise, or in depth? It seems that you would need to know what you were looking for before you could know how to transform it, but if you know what you're looking for, then you've already identified it and there is no need to rotate it.

There are technical solutions to this problem (Ullman & Basri, 1991) but they are beyond the scope of this book. In any event, a better solution appears to be a compromise between having 46 million representations and having just one. You store multiple viewer-centered representations of objects (perhaps about 40) and then apply some transformations.

There is evidence supporting this theory. The evidence works on this logic: The multiple-views theory predicts that you store representations of what an object looks like from a particular point of view. Naturally, if you have seen an object from only one point of view, you will have only one representation of that object. So what do you do if you see it from a different point of view? As we said, you rotate your image of the object until it matches the representation. That process of rotating the object takes time. Therefore, if you present the letter R rotated 90 degrees from its typical orientation, it should take longer to recognize than if you present R in its typical orientation. Note that the viewer-independent theory predicts that the orientation of the object shouldn't matter.

Numerous experiments have shown that orientation matters a great deal. Some of the most influential experiments were conducted by Roger Shepard and Lynn Cooper (summarized in Shepard & Cooper, 1986). They often used letters of the alphabet as stimuli; people had to judge whether the letter was mirror-reversed or in its normal orientation.

The more the object has been rotated from the normal orientation (upright), the longer it takes people to recognize the object. In fact, there is a very

orderly relationship between how far the object has been rotated from the upright and how long it takes people to recognize the object. That finding makes
it sound as if people imagine the object rotating in space until they imagine it
upright, whereupon they can recognize it. How do you know which way and
how far to rotate the letter so that it is upright? Shepard and Cooper argued that
you can identify the letter even when it is rotated—that's how you figure out
where the top of the letter is—and then you rotate it so that it is upright, and
then you can figure out whether the letter is mirror-reversed. So they were arguing that your memory representation is object centered; the orientation of
the letter doesn't matter when you're trying to identify it.

But letters may not be ideal stimuli for this sort of experiment because
there's no telling how many letters people have seen at different angles. What
would happen if you used unfamiliar stimuli instead of letters? What would
happen if you let people see just one orientation of the stimulus? How about several orientations? The answer is that people seem to form a representation for
each of the orientations with which they have a lot of experience. Michael Tarr
(1995) showed participants slides of objects made out of cubes; the objects could
look quite different from one viewpoint or another, as shown in Figure 2.21.

Tarr trained participants to recognize different objects. The objects were
always presented from the same point of view. Later he presented them from a
novel point of view to see whether participants could recognize them. Participants could, but the more the object was rotated from the view participants

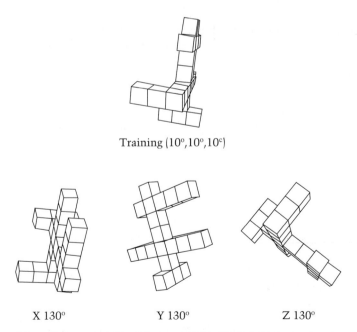

Training (10°,10°,10ᶜ)

X 130°   Y 130°   Z 130°

Figure 2.21.   *Stimuli of the sort used in Tarr's (1995) experiment.*
The top figure shows a stimulus participants might
see at training; the bottom figures show three ro-
tations of this figure in three different planes.

had seen it in during training, the longer it took them to recognize the object. It was as if participants' memory of what the object looked like was rather two-dimensional—they knew what the object looked like from one point of view—and identifying the object from another point of view required mentally rotating the stimulus. In another experiment, Tarr presented objects from several points of view during training. In that case, the time it took people to recognize the object was consistent with their imagining the object rotating to the nearest position they had seen during training.

Does this mean that the multiple-view researchers are returning to a template theory in which a nearly infinite number of templates is needed to recognize objects as they rotate through minute angles? Clearly not. Multiple-view theories acknowledge that some process must be available to regularize the image of the object, but that problem becomes much easier to deal with if you allow that six or eight views of a complex object may be stored; the image one sees will never be too far from one of the stored images.

So which is correct: decompositions in parts (object centered) or viewer centered? There is no firm answer at this point. A number of researchers have suggested that the mind may use two methods of recognition, one using each basic approach (Cooper, Schachter, Ballesteros, & Moore, 1992; Farah, 1990; Jolicoeur, 1990, Tarr & Pinker, 1990). The decomposition-into-parts approach may work well to distinguish between a car and a truck, for example, but it can't make finer-grained distinctions, such as between a Ford and a Chrysler. The decomposition-into-parts idea seems to work well for objects that have some tell-tale geons that make it easy to identify the object no matter what the orientation. The multiple-view approach seems to retain more information about details and thus may be effective for recognizing objects that don't have tell-tale parts and for distinguishing between closely related objects, such as different varieties of cars.

Navigation

The second function of vision is to help you move around in the world. When you reach out to grab a coffee cup, how do you know where the cup is? Just speaking intuitively, how would you say you know where it is? If you're like me, the core of your answer is that you are aware of where the cup is. You are conscious of the cup's location, and you guide your hand to that location. Strangely enough, recent evidence indicates that your conscious awareness of the cup's location is *not* important in guiding your hand. There is another visual system of which you are unconscious that operates in parallel with the conscious one, and that drives movements.

This evidence is fairly recent. A key finding came from visual researchers examining the primate brain. Leslie Ungerleider and Mortimer Mishkin (1982) proposed that there are two visual pathways in the brain: One pathway figures out *what* objects are, and the other figures out *where* objects are. They proposed this hypothesis based on brain anatomy and then tested it in monkeys. They had two tests: one of object identity and one of object location. The object identity test is called **nonmatching to sample.** Here's what happens. A sliding door rises, and the monkey sees an object. The monkey knocks the object aside, and under the object is a reward (e.g., a peanut). Then the door goes down and comes back up, and the monkey sees two objects: the one it just saw and a new object. If the monkey knocks aside the new object, it will find another peanut reward. If it knocks aside the object it just saw, it gets nothing. That's how the task got its name: The first object is the sample, and because the monkey is supposed to pick the other object, it's called nonmatching to sample. Note that the monkey doesn't need to know anything about object location to perform the task well; all it needs to know is the identity of the object it just saw.

The other task is the **landmark** task. In this task, the monkey sees two trapdoors in front of it. Under each trapdoor is a well. One well contains a peanut reward and the other well is empty. There is a landmark telling the monkey which is the right trapdoor to choose. The landmark is a cylinder, and the monkey should simply choose the trapdoor closer to the cylinder. Thus, for this task object identity is irrelevant; the monkey merely needs to know where in space the trapdoors and the cylinder are.

Ungerleider and Mishkin administered these tasks to some monkeys, and with sufficient training the monkeys got very good at each task. Next, the researchers lesioned (i.e., cut out) part of the monkeys' brains. One group of monkeys had part of the temporal lobe removed (that's near the side and toward the bottom of the brain), and the other group had part of the parietal lobe removed (that's near the back and toward the top). The results were dramatic. The group with the temporal lobe lesion were fine on the landmark task but could no longer do the nonmatching to sample task. The group with the parietal lesion showed just the opposite pattern of results. Ungerleider and Mishkin interpreted their results as showing that there are two streams of processing in the visual system: one that identifies objects and one that figures out where objects are located. They called these streams of processing the "what" and the "where" streams. The hypothesis that the visual system is separated into these two streams can be called the **what/where hypothesis.**

This result was very influential in visual research. There have always been one or two oddities in this interpretation, however. For example, how can all the spatial information be separate from the processes that identify objects? Don't you need to know where an object's parts are to identify it?

Those findings have been reinterpreted in an interesting and convincing way. Melvyn Goodale and David Milner (1992) suggested that it is better to think of them as "what" and "how" streams (which we'll call the **what/how hypothesis**). They argue that spatial information is present in both streams, the difference being the function of the spatial information. The "what" stream in the temporal lobe identifies objects, and it's associated with consciousness. The end product of this processing stream is your conscious perception of where objects are, what they are, their colors, and so on. The "how" stream handles information that helps you to move. Thus, the "how" stream knows the shape of objects so that you can grasp them effectively, it knows the location of objects so that you can reach to the right spot, and so on. But all of this knowledge is unconscious. Most of the time there would be no way of knowing that there are two such visual streams because they are in agreement. But Angela Haffenden and Melvyn Goodale (1998) have shown that under some circumstances you can fool one system and not the other.

For example, consider the visual illusion shown in Figure 2.22, which you've probably seen before.

When asked to compare the sizes of the circles in the center of the figures at the left and right, most people say that the one on the left appears larger, although they are actually the same size. Fine. That is an illusion of the "what" system because it is associated with consciousness. Is the "how" system fooled? The answer is no. Haffenden and Milner conducted an experiment with disks like poker chips in which they showed people displays like that in Figure 2.22. They asked participants to judge the size of the center circle by showing its size using their index fingers and thumbs. The experimenters attached infrared light–emitting diodes (IREDs) to the participant's wrist, index finger, and thumb, and with a series of cameras they could get very accurate measurements of how far apart the finger and thumb were. As expected, people estimated the circle on the left to be bigger. However, when the experimenters asked participants to pick up the poker chips in the middle, the illusion didn't hold. When you reach for an object such as a poker chip, you prepare your index finger and thumb to make the grab as your arm is moving your hand into position. The bigger the object, the further apart your index finger and thumb will be as you're reaching— it's called "grip size." They found that participants' grip size didn't differ for the left and right circles, even though the one on the left appeared bigger to participants. That result indicates that the conscious "what" system (which judges how big the objects look) is susceptible to this illusion, but the unconscious "how" system (that supports reaching) is not susceptible to it.

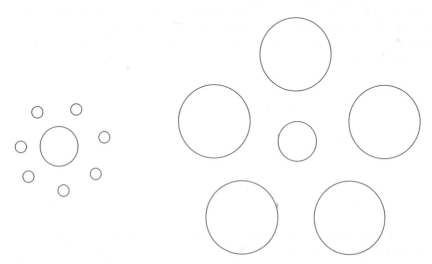

Figure 2.22.   *In this familiar visual illusion, the center circle at the left appears bigger than the center circle at the right. This illusion applies only to conscious visual perception, however. Visual perception that is used to drive motor behavior (such as reaching) is not susceptible to the illusion.*

You might think, "Well, maybe grip size doesn't differ much because the objects don't look *that* different." The experimenters did a very clever follow-up experiment. They told participants, "Okay, the one on the left looks bigger to you? I've got a bunch of poker chips here that vary just a bit in size, so I'll replace the one on the left with a smaller chip, and we'll keep adjusting the one on the left until it looks just the same as the one on the right." The experimenter adjusted the chip on the left until the participant said it was just the same as the chip on the right. On average, the chips had to be 2.44 mm different for them to look the same size. Then the participant was asked, as before, to show the size of each chip with index finger and thumb and to reach for each chip. The interesting finding is that participants had a smaller grip size when reaching for the chip on left than the one on the right. To make the two chips look the same, you have to counteract the illusion, so the chip on the left is smaller than the one on the right. The conscious "what" system doesn't detect the difference in size because it is fooled by the illusion created by the surrounding circles. The unconscious "how" system is not fooled by the illusion, and grip size is appropriate for each object.

Here's another example of the difference between the "what" system and "how" system. Think about the steepest hill you've ever had to drive on. How steep was it, in terms of degrees (i.e., a flat road would be 0 degrees, and a vertical cliff would be 90 degrees)? Most people guess that the steepest hill they've ever seen might be 45 or 50 degrees. In fact, the steepest hill in San Francisco (a city renowned for its steep hills) is only 18.5 degrees. In my home state of Virginia, no public street can have a hill steeper than 9 degrees, by law. What's going on here? Why do people overestimate? It's not just that people have bad memories. People overestimate steepness when they are right in front of the hill, not just when they are trying to remember it. Furthermore, it's not simply the case that people don't know what 50 degrees is. If you hand people a pair of calipers and ask them to set them at the angle of the hill, they create an angle very similar to the angle they give as a verbal estimate (Proffitt, Bhalla, Gossweiler, & Midgett, 1995).

Here's an interesting question. If people think a hill is 50 degrees when it's actually 8 degrees, how do they step accurately? If you misperceive the hill to be much steeper than it really is, why is it that you don't fall down when you try to climb it? Anyone who has walked up or down a staircase in the dark knows the price you pay if you think a step is present if one actually isn't; you need to know where you're going to step. So if you misperceive the angle, how do you step accurately?

The mystery is resolved if you think that the conscious "what" system is different from the unconscious "how" system. The conscious "what" system generates the perception that results in the overestimation of the steepness of the hill, but that doesn't mean that the unconscious "how" system has to overestimate as well, and it's the "how" system that generates the spatial information used for stepping. Denny Proffitt and his colleagues (1995) tested this hypothesis by having 300 people make judgments about the steepness of nine different hills found around the campus of the University of Virginia. Participants gave two estimates of the hill's steepness via the conscious

BOX 2.2. FUNCTIONAL IMAGING EVIDENCE BEARING ON THE REPRESENTATION OF SPACE IN THE TEMPORAL LOBE

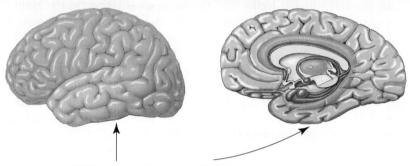

PPA on Ventral aspect (underside)
of temporal lobe

We have discussed two conceptions of the separate visual streams: "What/where" and "what/how." Although both distinctions propose that the ventral stream is the "what" stream, meaning that it is concerned with object identity, the two distinctions differ a bit in what they propose that "what" stream calculates. Underleider and Mishkin (1982) downplayed the role of spatial information in the ventral stream because that was the province of the dorsal stream. Goodale and Milner (1992) argued that there is spatial information in both streams, but they are put to different uses. In the ventral stream spatial information provides explicit information about the layout of objects in space, whereas in the dorsal stream spatial information tells you about the objects' positions in service of acting on those objects.

Neuroimaging data from Russell Epstein and Nancy Kanwisher is relevant to this debate. They report that the ventral stream contains an area that is maximally sensitive to places (i.e., to the spatial aspect of local environments). This area is part of the parahippocampal gyrus called the PPA. The parahippocampal gyrus is a cortical area on the most ventral aspect of the temporal lobe.

Epstein and Kanwisher presented slides to participants while their brains were scanned using functional magnetic resonance imaging. Figure B2.2 shows the percentage change in response of the PPA.

As shown in the figure, the PPA is maximally active to slides that depict spatial layouts. The "outdoor scenes" slides were shots taken around the university campus where the study was conducted and would be familiar spatial layouts to the participants.

These data are consistent with data from patients who have lesions that include this area, who show a deficit called topgraphic amnesia. Such patients find it hard to navigate in unfamiliar environments. The data from the Epstein and Kanwisher study are especially important in showing that a part of the cortex is devoted to evaluating the spatial layout of the local environment because the PPA is so small that lesions including only this area are quite rare. These data indicate that the ventral stream of visual processing does include the evaluation of spatial information in at least some contexts.

(Continued)

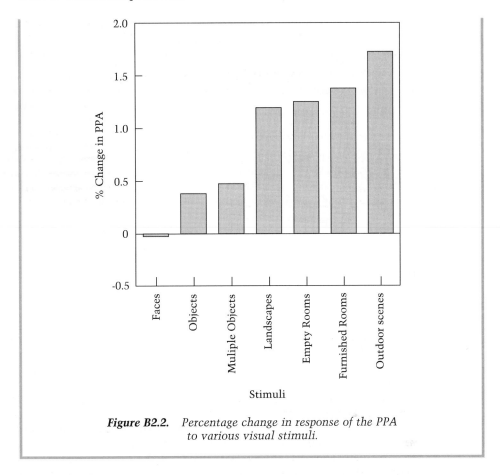

Figure B2.2. *Percentage change in response of the PPA to various visual stimuli.*

percept. They verbally judged the steepness of the hill in degrees, and they judged the steepness of the hill by adjusting a little picture of a hill to make it as steep as the hill in front of them. By both of these measures, participants overestimated the steepness of the hills, as shown in Figure 2.23. They also made a judgment via the unconscious "how" system. In this measure, participants placed their palms flat on a small board mounted on a tripod. They were asked to adjust the board so that it was parallel to the hill in front of them. Participants were not allowed to look at the board or their hand while they made this judgment; they just looked at the hill. Then the experimenters looked at the angle to which participants had set the board to see whether it matched the angle of the hill. The researchers found that participants' estimates of the hill by the palm board measure were quite accurate, as shown in Figure 2.23. They interpreted this as showing that the action system knows the actual angle of the hill, so the action system can accurately judge the angle of the hill either for stepping or for the palm board judgment.

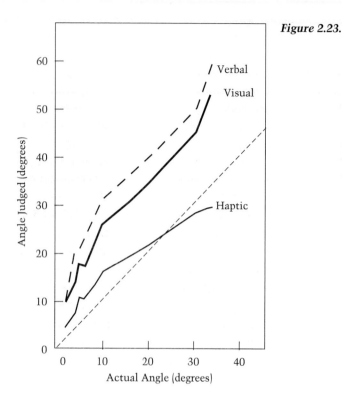

Figure 2.23. *Graph showing judgments of the steepness of nine hills compared with the actual steepness. Perfectly accurate judgments would fall on the dotted line. When participants used the palm board to estimate the hills' steepness, they were much more accurate than when they gave verbal estimates or adjusted a picture of a hill visually.*

Stand-on-One-Foot Questions

10. What are the two basic ideas about how objects are represented?
11. Name two types of evidence that "what" and "how" are represented separately.

Questions That Require Two Feet

12. Why do you suppose hills look so much steeper than they are? (Hint: consider how much harder it is to climb an eight-degree hill than a four-degree hill).
13. Are there some objects that you almost always see in the same orientation? Do you think that your mental representation of such objects might reflect that select experience?

KEY TERMS

inverse optics problem

shape and orientation
  indeterminacy

luminance

light source,
  reflectance, and
  shadow
  indeterminacy

size and distance
  indeterminacy

prosopagnosia

likelihood principle

Perkins's laws

pop-out

local contrast

monocularly

binocularly

familiar size

convergence

stereopsis

binocular parallax

random dot
  stereograms

correspondence
  problem

pictorial cues

occlusion

texture gradient

linear perspective

relative height

atmospheric
  perspective

bottom-up processing

top-down processing

parsing paradox

computational
  approach

ecological approach

eyeheight

viewer-centered
  representation

object-centered
  representation

template

critical features

good continuation

nonmatching to
  sample

landmark

what/where hypothesis

what/how hypothesis

3

Attention

Suppose I ask you to walk the length of a balance beam. You, game stranger that you are, do so. Then I ask you to walk it again but this time to simultaneously sing "Yankee Doodle." You walk and sing. Then I tell you that this is a special balance beam, sections of which can be heated or cooled, and as you walk its length (barefoot) I'd like you to say whether the section you've just stepped on is hot or cold. You'll still be singing, so just interrupt the song when necessary. You perform that task. Then I ask you to do it again, but as you walk along, I'll squirt different scents at you with an atomizer, and as you're walking, singing, and distinguishing hot from cold you should also remember the scents I squirt because you'll have to recite them after you've finished walking the beam.

Clearly, you can walk, sing, sniff, or feel temperature without trouble, but doing all of them simultaneously is hard. You're going to start walking and singing more slowly as I add tasks, and you're going to start making errors. Why? The short and obvious answer is that you can't pay attention to all of those tasks at the same time. But what is attention? In one of his more oft-quoted passages, William James commented, "everyone knows what attention is." More than 100 years later, a leading attention researcher commented, "No one knows what attention is" (Pashler, 1998, p. 1). Of course, James meant that everyone has an intuitive sense of what is meant by attention; Pashler meant that we don't have a good scientific understanding (or even definition) of attention.

In this book **attention** can be understood to mean the mechanism for continued cognitive processing. Simply put, when you "pay attention" to a painting, for example, you are engaging a mechanism that allows cognitive processing of the painting (e.g., noting what it depicts, what colors are used, its style, and so on). Note that the definition posits a mechanism for *continued* cognitive processing; it presumes that some preliminary cognitive processing takes place with or without attention and that attention affords still further processing. For example, we might guess that the cognitive system would identify the object on the wall as a painting even if you were not paying attention to it when you walked in the room. Attention (and the continued cognitive processing it brings about) would be necessary to identify what the painting depicted, whether the artist was known to you, and so on. This definition of attention as continued cognitive processing is applicable not just to perception but to action as well; we speak of paying attention to tasks such as driving, building a model airplane, or walking on a balance beam.

This simple definition of attention brings to the fore two properties of attention from our everyday experience. If attention is the mechanism by which continued cognitive processing takes place, we might guess that attention is **limited.** That simply means that continued cognitive processing cannot occur for all available stimuli simultaneously. In the first part of this chapter we consider in some detail the question, "In what way is attention limited?" The simple definitions we have been working with make attention seem like mental fuel that makes continued cognitive processing occur; you've only got so much fuel to expend, so if you expend it on one cognitive process, there is necessarily less for other processes. We know people can't do many things simultaneously, so it seems that something like this mental fuel idea must be right. As we'll see, although this metaphor is intuitively appealing, the predictions it suggests are more difficult to prove than you might guess. Nevertheless, it is clear that attention is limited in some way.

The second property of attention we can note from everyday experience is that attention is **selective.** *Selective* simply means that you can expend this mental fuel on (i.e., pay attention to) one or another cognitive process as you see fit. The very fact that attention is limited means that it must be selective.

What happens to the cognitive processes you select not to give very much attention? That's pretty obvious: Those processes don't get done. If you don't pay attention to singing, you don't sing. This point becomes less obvious when you think about perception, however. Consider this. The perceptual apparatus is always working, but you are not always aware of all the information that the perceptual apparatus processes. For example, you are probably seated as you read this, which means that there is pressure from the chair on your butt. You probably weren't aware of this pressure until you read the previous sentence, although you *could* have been aware of it at any time because the sensation was always there. There is also likely to be some noise wherever you are (the hum of a heater, the buzz of a florescent light) that you were similarly unaware of. These stimuli were there all along, too, of course. So why weren't you aware of them? You weren't aware of them because of the limited nature of attention— you can't focus on the buzzing of the lights and on reading this text—and you selected the text as the focus of attention.

Now let's go back to the question we were discussing before. If you're thinking about doing two things (e.g., walking and singing) but attention limits you to doing one of them, it's obvious that the other simply doesn't get done. But what happens to the perceptions that you don't attend to? If you're not selecting to attend to the buzzing lights, are those sounds completely closed off from the cognitive system, or are they processed to a certain extent but just don't enter awareness, or what? What is the fate of sensory stimuli that are not selected to receive attention? The answer is that the fate of these stimuli depends on just how you choose to direct attention. You may direct attention in such a way that those to-be-ignored stimuli are still processed a fair amount, as when much of your attention is directed to the book you are reading, but you are still listening to a television to determine the outcome of a vital episode of *Green Acres.* Other times you really try to shut out all distractions, as when you're attempting to read your cognitive psychology textbook and to ignore your roommate's annoying baby-talk phone conversation with his girlfriend. As we'll see, you have some control over how tight the selection of attention is, but even when you're doing your best to focus attention, the to-be-ignored material is still processed to some extent.

The final question we will pose concerns selection. Although people can select to what they want to direct attention, they are not always successful in attending only to things that they want to attend to. Selection fails. Why does selection fail? As we'll see, this problem has not been studied closely, but we can make two generalizations. First, any stimulus with an abrupt onset tends to capture attention, such as a sudden movement or a sudden noise. Second, you will attend to anything that you are specifically asked not to think about. If I say, "Whatever you do, don't think about a white bear," you're going to think about a white bear, at least for a little while. This irritating effect may tell us something interesting about mental control. Attention may also fail when one is trying to maintain attention for a long time in a situation where little happens. Such situations are called vigilance tasks, and although they have important applications in the military and in industry, they are still poorly understood.

➤ IN WHAT WAY IS ATTENTION LIMITED?

> ➤ PREVIEW Our introspection indicates that we have a limited amount of attention and that this attention may be expended on cognitive processing. Psychologists have examined different aspects of this intuitive sense of attention's limits. We can list five predictions based on this simple intuition:
>
> - Attention can be distributed to more than one task at a time.
> - Performing more than one task does not change how each task is performed.
> - A particular task always requires a particular amount of attention.
> - Attention can be distributed between tasks as the person sees fit.
> - Tasks require less attention with practice.
>
> In this section we go over evidence indicating that we cannot support the first three statements; that doesn't necessarily mean that they are wrong, but we can't definitively conclude that they are correct, either. There is better evidence that the last two statements are correct.

We began this chapter by likening attention to mental fuel that makes continued cognitive processing possible. This definition is close to the way researchers thought of attention when they first started considering its limited nature (Bryan & Harter, 1897) and has been central to more recent formulations as well (Kahneman, 1973; Moray, 1967). What can we say about the particular way in which attention is limited?

We can elaborate this simple definition into a list of predictions about the properties that attention might have that would be consistent with limited capacity and with our own experience. Our own introspection makes it feel as if attention is limited, but you can do more than one task at a time, if you want; it just means that you might not do one of the tasks as well. I can walk on the balance beam and sing, but my singing might not be quite as good as if I were just standing. Here are five predictions about the limited nature of attention.

- Attention can be distributed to more than one task at a time; that is, it is possible to perform more than one task in parallel.
- Performing more than one task does not change how each individual task is performed. In other words, if you're walking a balance beam, adding a second task (e.g., singing) might make the walking less effective,

but it does not mean that you'll start walking the beam in a fundamentally different way.

- The performance of a particular task requires a particular amount of attention. This amount of attention is consistent across situations and does not change depending on other tasks that are being performed.
- When tasks vie for attentional resources, the person can allocate attention to each task in the proportions that he or she sees fit. Thus, if you are walking the balance beam and singing, you can allocate a lot of attention to the beam to ensure that you don't fall and not worry so much about how well you sing. On the other hand, you may choose to attend to your singing to ensure excellent phrasing and expression and not worry so much if you fall off the beam now and again.
- With sufficient practice, a task will come to demand fewer attentional resources.

These five assumptions sound reasonable and fit with our everyday experience, but the fact is that we cannot be sure that the first three are true. On the other hand, there is evidence that the final two are true. Let's look at these assumptions in more detail.

Parallel Performance

It seems obvious that it is possible to perform more than one task in parallel. After all, you frequently do two things at once: talk to a friend while you drive, listen to music while you read, walk and chew gum. To investigate attention in these situations in the laboratory, researchers use a **dual task paradigm,** which is simply a situation in which the participant must perform two tasks at once. A good way to learn about the limited nature of attention is to give the cognitive system too much to do and then observe the consequences. Here's the key question about parallel performance: How do you know that you're really doing these tasks in parallel and not by switching attention rapidly between the two tasks? Couldn't I take a step on the balance beam, then sing a phrase of the song, then take another step, and so on, and do it so smoothly and seamlessly that it seems as if I'm doing the two tasks at the same time?

Researchers have tried to get around this problem by using **continuous tasks** rather than **discrete tasks.** A discrete task uses trials with identifiable beginnings and endings, and there is usually a pause between the end of one trial and the beginning of the next trial. For example, in a simple response time task a stimulus is presented (e.g., a light appears on a computer monitor or a tone sounds), whereupon the participant is to respond, usually by pressing a button.

The participant's job is simply to push the button as quickly as possible when the stimulus occurs. Note the **response to stimulus interval** in Figure 3.1, which is the period of time after the participant has responded but before the next stimulus has appeared. During this period the participant waits for the next stimulus to appear and could easily switch attention to some other task. Even if you make the next stimulus appear immediately after a response, the participant

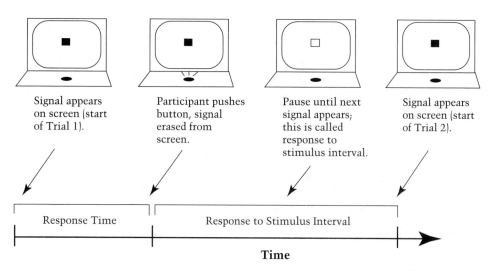

Figure 3.1. *Simple response time task with a visual signal and a button-press response.*

can simply switch attention to the other task at this point, effectively taking a break from this task.

Continuous tasks, on the other hand, use a continuous stream of stimuli and often demand a continuous stream of responses. An example would be a pursuit tracking task in which a target moves on a computer screen and the participant must chase the target with the cursor, controlled by a joystick. Performance is measured as the distance between the cursor and target. The target it always moving, so it would seem that even a momentary lapse of attention would make performance suffer. Another continuous task is touch typing. You can obtain precise measures of a participants' typing speed in words per minute, and then add a second task to be performed simultaneously. Presumably, the second task should require attention to be divided. This paradigm has been used on several occasions. For example, in one experiment it was shown that a skilled typist could recite nursery rhymes aloud while typing with only a 10% loss of typing speed compared to her speed when she typed alone (Shaffer, 1975). This study was meant to show that typing required very little attention for a highly skilled typist.

The problem with such evidence is that it is probably possible to switch attention between two tasks even if one of them is a continuous task. The task may be continuous, but the participant need not treat it as if it were continuous (Broadbent, 1982; Welford, 1980). Take touch-typing as an example. Experienced typists often report that once they've seen a word, they don't really need to think about the word as they type it, and a number of studies indicate that that is true. It seems that meaningful material that is to be typed is perceived in chunks, not letter by letter. The details would take us too far afield right now (Salthouse, 1984, provides a readable introduction). The main point is that just because the hands are typing at a steady rate doesn't mean that attentional resources are needed at a steady rate. In the case of typing, it seems likely that attention is needed in bursts; a burst of attention might be needed to read a word and then very little attention would be needed to type the word.

Thus, using dual task paradigms does not seem to guarantee evidence that one can share attentional resources between tasks. No matter how much it looks as if the participant is dividing attention between two tasks, it will remain possible that the participant is rapidly switching attention between the tasks.

Changes in Task Performance

The second property of attention listed above is that adding a second task doesn't change the way the first task is performed; the second task simply demands attentional resources. At least in some situations, this assumption is known to be false.

Here's a recent example of how this assumption can lead researchers astray. In the original experiment (Nissen & Bullemer, 1987) participants performed a primary task (button pushing) and the experimenters added a secondary task (counting tones) to distract them. It turned out that the secondary task actually changed the way participants performed the primary task.

In the button-pressing task, the participant saw four squares on the screen, arrayed in a horizontal line (Figure 3.2). There were four buttons on a keyboard, arrayed horizontally, in front of the participant. On each trial, one of the squares was filled and the participant had to push the button directly below the filled square, whereupon it was extinguished, there was a brief pause, and a new square was filled.

One thing was tricky about this task. The participant was not told that the stimuli appeared in a repeating sequence. The sequence was 10 units long, and nothing marked where it began or ended, so most participants thought that the stimuli appeared in random locations; they didn't notice the repeating sequence.

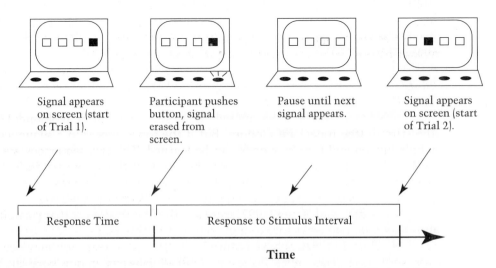

Figure 3.2. *Choice response time task with a visual signal and a button-press response.*

Nevertheless, participants learned the sequence even though they remained unaware of it. You can tell that they learned the sequence from their response times. Participants responded more and more quickly when the stimuli were sequenced. But when the stimuli started to appear randomly, their response times slowed down again. When asked what the sequence was at the end of the experiment, participants couldn't say; they never noticed that a sequence was there (see also Willingham, Nissen & Bullemer, 1989).

This experiment showed that you can get learning (as measured by response time) in the absence of awareness (because if you ask participants what the sequence is, they don't know). Next, the experimenters wanted to know whether this type of unconscious learning demands attention. (It's well established that conscious learning requires attention.) So they added a secondary task that would presumably demand some attention to see whether that affected learning. The secondary task was tone counting; on each trial, right after the participant pushed the button, a high-pitched or low-pitched tone sounded. The participant was supposed to keep track of how many of the tones were high-pitched. Every 100 trials there was a rest break, and the participant was asked to report how many of the trials in that block had been high-pitched. Nissen and Bullemer reported that the secondary task eliminated learning in the button-pressing task. They interpreted this result as indicating that the unconscious learning of the sequence in the button-pressing task demands attention, and a number of studies followed, designed to investigate the effect of attention on this type of learning.

Notice the assumption here; Nissen and Bullemer had a primary task (sequence learning in the button-pushing task) and they were interested in whether the unconscious learning in the task demanded attention. So they added a secondary task (tone counting) which they assumed would demand attentional resources but would not interact with the primary task.

That assumption proved incorrect. Volker Schmidtke and Herbert Heuer (1997) conducted a simple experiment: What happens if the tones in the secondary task are sequenced? Nissen and Bullemer had used random tones (half high, half low, but not in any particular sequence). Schmidtke and Heuer showed that if you use a sequence of tones, learning on the button-pushing task is much greater than if the tones are random, as shown in Figure 3.3.

Why is learning better in the button-pressing task if the tones are in a sequence? Because the button-pressing and tone counting tasks are *not* independent. Essentially, the mind tries to make a single sequence out of the button pushes and tones. If the tones are random, a sequence cannot be found: Half of the stimuli (the tones) are random. But if the tones appear in a sequence, the whole button and tone sequence can be learned. The two sequences are integrated. The cognitive system cannot "know" that the secondary task is supposed to be a mere distraction. Whatever process does the unconscious learning does not separate tones and button pushes. It combines everything.

Schmidtke and Heuer (1997) were not the first to suggest that participants may integrate two tasks into a single task. I gave this example because it is particularly clear, but others have pointed out that task integration may occur. In fact, some researchers have suggested that task integration may be at the heart of many apparent attention effects. Elizabeth Spelke, Bill Hirst, and Ulric Neisser

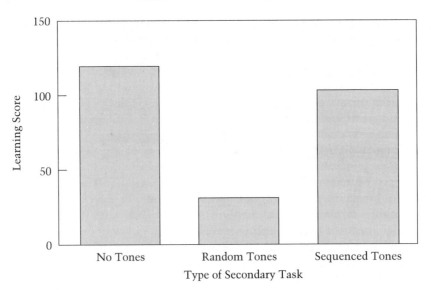

Figure 3.3.   *Results of Schmidtke and Heuer's (1997) experiment. As Nissen and Bullemer (1987) reported, they observed robust sequence learning without a secondary task and little learning with a secondary task using random tones, but they also observed robust learning when the tones were sequenced. The learning score is the difference in response times when participants responded to the sequenced and random stimuli; a higher score means faster responses to the sequence, which means more sequence knowledge.*

(1976) argued that when people improve their ability to do two tasks at once, we usually think it is because the participant has become skilled at the individual tasks and that the tasks are therefore less demanding of attention. Spelke et al. suggested instead that participants become skilled in knowing how to combine the two tasks. To prove their point, they had participants learn to do two rather difficult tasks simultaneously. First, participants were given a reading test. The experimenters tested how quickly each participant could read and how good his or her comprehension was. Then they added a secondary task. The experimenters read words aloud to participants and asked them to write down the words—to take dictation. As you would expect, when this secondary task was added, participants' reading speed and comprehension suffered greatly. Participants practiced doing the two tasks simultaneously in 1-hr sessions each weekday for 6 weeks, after which time taking dictation did not detract from their reading. Participants didn't have much knowledge of the words they were writing, but with still more practice, participants eventually were able to simultaneously read and take dictation while understanding what they were writing. In another study Hirst et al. (1980) replicated this experiment using short sentences in the dictation task. In both papers, the authors argued that participants had "restructured" the task; in other words, they had learned how to combine the tasks so that both could be performed at once. It is not clear what "restructuring" means for these tasks (it's a little clearer in the case of the Schmidtke and Heuer study described earlier), but the point is that the researchers were arguing that a key component of dual task situations is that the participant may end up combining two tasks into one.

Consistent Attention Requirements

This assumption states that if we try to perform more than one task at a time, these two tasks vie for attentional resources. This account seems straightforward, but there is a problem. It seems to predict that one particular task takes up a particular amount of attention (i.e., it requires a certain amount of attentional "fuel") regardless of the other demands on the attention. This assumption appears to be incorrect.

Suppose you have four tasks, which you ask people to perform in various combinations:

Task A: Generate a mental image of your room.
Task B: Sing the "Star-Spangled Banner."
Task C: Play a video game.
Task D: Remember a list of six words.

You find that participants can generate a mental image of their bedroom (task A) and simultaneously sing the "Star-Spangled Banner" (task B) with little apparent cost to the imaging. However, if they are imaging and then start playing the video game (task C), there is a cost to the imagery task. Therefore, the attentional cost of the video game seems to be greater than that of the singing (C > B).

But now suppose participants must remember the list of six words (task D), and you find that adding the video game (task C) causes little cost to remembering the words, but the singing (task B) causes a high cost. Now it appears that the attentional cost of the singing is greater than the video game (B > C). In short, you can't evaluate the attentional demands of a task by pairing it with a secondary task; the attentional demands of a task look different depending on the task you pair it with. One cannot say that a task has some hallmark amount of attention that it demands, independent of other tasks.

MULTIPLE RESOURCE THEORIES. Imagining your room and playing a video game simultaneously can't be done because you don't have enough attention. So why can you play the game and sing at the same time? One answer would be that there are different types of attention. This is called a **multiple resources** approach to attention (Navon & Gopher, 1979; Norman & Bobrow, 1975). Just as the name implies, the idea is that you have several independent pools of attention, not one general pool. Each works just as we described for the more general attention resource idea, but there are thought to be several types of attention, each specific to particular types of task.

What characterizes these separate attentional pools? In other words, how do they differ? In one of the early articles taking the multiple resources approach, David Navon and Daniel Gopher cited research indicating a separation based on sensory modality (e.g., vision, hearing). They cited an article by Lee

Brooks (1968) showing that if you were trying to recall a sentence, a simultaneous vocal task was much more disruptive than a simultaneous spatial task. But if you were trying to recall the shape of a line diagram, a simultaneous vocal task was less disruptive than a spatial task. Such results make it seem that there could be separate attentional pools for visuospatial processing and for auditory processing or, more simply put, for vision and for hearing.

Later research indicated that idea probably wasn't right, though. Jon Driver and Charles Spence (1994) showed that there are links between attention in vision and attention in hearing. Participants in their experiment had speakers to their left and right. On each trial a different three-word triplet came out of the left and right speakers. Participants were to repeat the triplet from the left or right speaker. They were told before each trial which speaker they should attend to. On some trials they also had visual information. They saw a person speaking the words they were to repeat. The tricky part was that the visual information was presented either over the same speaker that had the auditory information they were supposed to repeat or over the other speaker; thus the visual information could be either consistent or inconsistent with the information coming over the auditory channel on the same side.

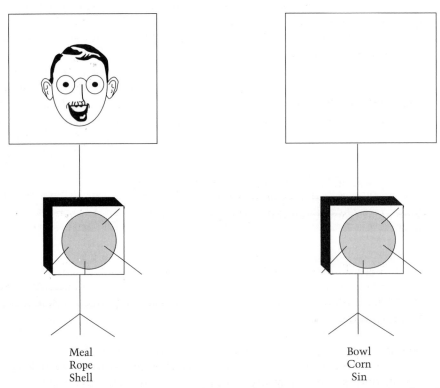

Meal   Bowl
Rope   Corn
Shell   Sin

Figure 3.4.   *Basic setup for Driver and Spence's (1994) experiment. Participants heard different groups of three words coming from speakers on their left and right and had to repeat the words from one speaker. A person on the screen mouthed the target words on either the same side as or the opposite side from the auditory information.*

The results of Driver and Spence's experiment indicated that auditory and visual information are not completely separate. When the visual information was presented on the side consistent with the auditory information, people got about 68% of the words correct; when it was not, they got about 52% correct. Thus, auditory and visual attention do seem to be tied together because you can't allocate visual and auditory attention to different locations in space without cost. Nevertheless, it is true that an auditory task will tend to interfere with another auditory task more than with a visual task. Thus, the final word seems to be that there is some division along modality lines, but the Driver and Spence study indicates that there are not completely separate pools of attention.

Chris Wickens (1984, 1992) suggested a different way of splitting up attention in a multiple resource theory. He suggested that three dimensions of tasks are relevant to attention. The first is which *stage of processing* the task emphasizes; for perceptual tasks the hard part is perceiving the stimulus, whereas for response tasks the hard part of the task is selecting the right response. Second, what *code of processing* does the task use: verbal or spatial? Third, what are the *modalities of input and output:* the input might be visual or auditory; the output might be spoken or manual. Wickens argued that there might be separate attentional resource pools for each combination of these dimensions. In other words, a task in which you searched for a visual target would be a perceptual task with visual input, and that would call on a particular pool of attentional resources. Different tasks have different properties, so there would be eight separate pools of attention in all.

The idea that there are separate pools of attention seems intuitively appealing. Unfortunately, it has proven difficult to specify how different tasks would call on these different hypothetical pools. For a theory to be useful, it must be predictive; in other words, we must be able to analyze two tasks and judge how similar they are in terms of the demands they would place on the different attentional pools. That has been one of the chief criticisms of the multiple resources theory; it's not clear how many of these attentional pools there are supposed to be nor how they are related to tasks.

A second criticism of multiple resource theories is that it is hard to tell them apart from structural explanations of task interference. We turn to structural explanations next.

STRUCTURAL EXPLANATIONS. You could also describe the different patterns of interference as a structural problem rather than a problem of attention. Suppose you have a structure in the mind that is necessary to perform visual tasks, a sort of screen in the mind where the conscious experience of vision happens. You can have only one thing on this screen at a time, so you can't do two visual tasks at the same time (e.g., play a video game and generate a mental image of your room). Attention might work just as we described it before—there is a single type of attention that is a multipurpose resource that is allocated to different tasks—but attention is not the reason you can't play the game and imagine your room at the same time. It's a limitation in the workspace that handles visual tasks. This is a **structural explanation** because it posits that interference between two tasks is caused by competition for mental structures, not for attentional resources.

It is easy to make an educated guess as to which structures would be involved in performance limitations. If two tasks require the same perceptual modality (e.g., they are both visual tasks), then there will be more interference than if they are in different perceptual modalities. Similarly, if they both require the same output modality (e.g., arm movements), there will be more interference than if they call for different responses (e.g., one arm movement and one vocal response).

Alan Welford (1952) and more recently Hal Pashler (1998) pointed out a less obvious structural explanation for performance limitations. They suggested that there may be a response selection bottleneck. Here's what that means. It is proposed that three basic processes are necessary for performing any task, even a very simple task such as pushing a button when you see a light come on. The three processes are perception (seeing the light), **response selection** (choosing the response of pushing the button), and response production (generating the muscle commands that moves your finger). Welford and Pashler suggested that you can select only one action at a time; you might be able to perceive two stimuli simultaneously and generate two movements simultaneously, but you can't select two actions simultaneously.

As evidence for the performance bottleneck, Pashler points to the psychological refractory period. A refractory period refers to difficulty in initiating an action immediately after completing a similar action. The term comes for neurophysiology; after a neuron fires, it has a higher threshold for firing again. The brief time during which it has a higher threshold is called a refractory period. (The analogy is not altogether appropriate for the task in psychology, however, because it refers to a slowing in doing two tasks simultaneously, not one after the other.) The **psychological refractory period** is a period of time after one response is selected during which a second response cannot be selected.

For example, suppose that a light sometimes appears on the left side of a computer screen, and when it does you are to push a button with your left hand. When a tone sounds, you are to depress a pedal with your foot. Suppose we find that it takes you about 500 ms to press the foot pedal once you hear the tone. Now suppose that I flash the light and then sound the tone a mere 50 ms after the light comes on. You will be slower to depress the pedal in this case. The reason is shown schematically in Figure 3.5.

select's bottleneck

Stimulus 1 is presented and then Stimulus 2 is presented while Stimulus 1 is still being perceived. Once Stimulus 1 is perceived, response selection for Stimulus 1 is initiated, but note that when perception of Stimulus 2 is complete, the response for Stimulus 2 is not initiated; it cannot be started until response selection for Stimulus 1 is complete. That is the selection bottleneck.

The effect of the bottleneck is fairly sizable—your response time to the tone might be 700 ms instead of 500 ms. According to Figure 3.5, if response selection for Stimulus 1 were completed by the time Stimulus 2 was presented (in other words, Stimulus 2 is moved to the right in the figure), there should be no bottleneck. That prediction is true; as the interval between the first and second stimulus increases, the response time to the second stimulus gets shorter.

The psychological refractory effect is obtained with many different types of stimuli and responses, even if the second response is an eye movement (Pashler,

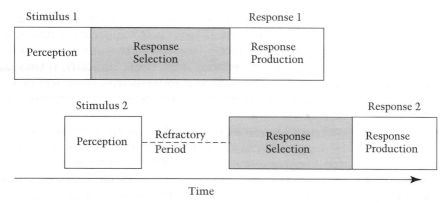

Figure 3.5. *Graphic representation of the refractory period. Time moves from left to right. The response selection for Stimulus 2 cannot begin until the response selection for Stimulus 1 is completed; that is the source of the refractory effect.*

Carrier, & Hoffman, 1993) or a foot movement (Osman & Moore, 1993; see Pashler, 1998, for a review.) This result is important because it shows that you can get interference even from extremely simple tasks (not just from tasks that demand a lot of attention) and tasks that don't share obvious structural demands (not just tasks that are both visual, for example). Think of it this way. If the tasks were more complex—say, riding a bicycle and working math problems—you would interpret interference between them in terms of attention. Naturally you're slower to work math problems if you're simultaneously riding a bicycle: They both demand attention! But in the example just described we are talking about very simple tasks that should take very little attention. Surely you have enough attention to do them simultaneously. So why does the first task affect performance of the second?

If there is an output bottleneck, you might think, "Heck, maybe we don't need this idea of attentional capacity in the first place. Maybe *all* of the problems we see when people try to do two tasks at once are due to output bottleneck problems. The problem is not capacity sharing, it's the crowding of outputs." That can't be the whole story, though, because there seem to be capacity limitations even when no output is required; for example, people can't attend to many different types of sensory inputs. Nevertheless, this evidence of an output bottleneck raises the possibility that at least some of what we thought were effects of limited attention actually have nothing to do with attention.

Summary of Difficulties

For more than 100 years, researchers have held that attention is limited; one can't attend to all available sensations simultaneously, nor can one perform multiple tasks without some performance cost. Still, it has proven quite difficult to get more specific about exactly what it means for attention to be limited. In this section we've listed three predictions about attention's limited nature that turn out to be difficult to prove. First, people should be able to split their limited attentional capacity beween several tasks in parallel, but it is difficult to prove that participants don't quickly switch attention between tasks instead of doing them in parallel. The second prediction is that performing more than one task at a time doesn't change the way individual tasks are performed; in other words, you perform Task A the same way by itself as you do when you perform Task A together with Task B. That prediction seems to be wrong at least some of the time. The third prediction is that tasks require a particular amount of attention, and that amount of attention does not vary depending on the other tasks you are performing. However, it seems that some tasks may change when you perform them at the same time as another task. This change makes it very difficult to characterize how the task taps attentional resources because it is hard to pin down exactly what the task is.

Most researchers believe that it is useful to think of attention as limited, but it has proven frustratingly difficult to be specific about how it is limited. It seems that the simple idea of an undifferentiated pool of attentional resources cannot be right, but a satisfactory alternative has not been outlined.

Do not despair. Two other properties of attention have been studied in detail and we have a better understanding about them. One is that we can allocate attention to different tasks as we see fit, and the second is that attentional demands appear to shrink as we practice a task.

Allocation of Attention

Another assumption about the limited nature of attention is that it can be allocated as one sees fit; when tasks compete for attentional resources, you can allocate more or less attention to a task according to your goals. For example, suppose you are driving and simultaneously talking to a friend; suddenly it begins to rain quite hard, making it difficult to see. You would probably allocate more attention to driving the car and less to the conversation.

The assumption that you can allocate attention in this manner is supported by controlled laboratory studies. George Sperling and Melvin Melchner (1978) showed participants arrays of letters. A set of four letters (inner set) was surrounded by a set of 16 letters (outer set). The arrays flashed by, one at a time, on a computer screen. Each appeared for just 240 ms, and the number of arrays that flashed by on each trial varied. Participants knew that two digits would appear in the arrays sometime during the trial, and they were to report the identity and location of the two digits. On some trials they were told to allocate 90% of their attention to the inner set of four letters; on other trials they were to allocate 90% of their attention to the outer set of letters, and on other trials they were to attend to the inner and outer arrays equally. Figure 3.6 shows the probability of correctly detecting a target in the outer set on the x-axis and the probability of detecting a target from the inner set on the y-axis.

Each circle represents a mean of 30 to 60 trials, and the tail of each circle indicates the instructions: straight down = 90% outside, left = 90% inside, diagonal = equal to outside and inside. The graph shows the data for just one participant, but these data are quite typical. The important point is that when

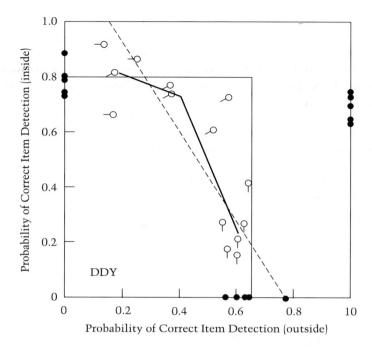

Figure 3.6.   *Graph from Sperling and Melchner (1978) showing data for a single participant. Each dot is a mean based on 30 to 60 trials. On the x-axis is the probability of detecting a letter on the outside of the stimulus; the y-axis shows the probability of detecting a letter on the inside of the stimulus. The tail of each dot shows the instructions for the trials: A downward tail means participants attended to outer letters, leftward means they attended to inner letters, and a diagonal tail means they attended to inner and outer letters equally. The data show that on trials when participants were to attend to the outer circle (tails down), the probability of identifying the outer letters was high and the probability of identifying the inner letters was low. The probabilities were reversed when participants were to attend to the inner letters (leftward-tail dots), and the probabilities were intermediate when participants were to attend to inner and outer letters equally. The results suggest that participants can direct attention as they see fit.*

participants are told to attend mostly to the outside, they get most of the targets appearing on the outside, and the same is true when they direct attention to the inside. Participants can indeed allocate attention as they see fit, and that allocation is reflected in task performance (see also Gopher, Brickner, & Navon, 1982).

Reduction in Attention Demands with Practice: Automaticity

Another strong assumption we would make is that the attentional demand of a task goes down as it is practiced. When you first learn to drive a car, it seems to tax all of your attentional resources: watching for oncoming cars, making sure that the car is in the center of your lane, checking your mirrors, checking your speed, monitoring how much pressure you are applying to the gas pedal, and watching the road signs. With enough practice, however, each of these tasks becomes **automatic;** automatic tasks take few or no attentional resources, and automatic processes happen without intention. Let's take a moment to describe what that means.

That a task takes few or no attentional resources obviously means that the task makes little demand of attention. That implies that you should be able to perform several automatic tasks at once, and indeed, an experienced driver thinks nothing of driving while simultaneously eating, talking to a friend, and listening to the radio—an accomplished task, if not attractive to watch.

That an automatic process happens without intention means that it occurs whether you want it to or not. If certain conditions are present in the environment, the automatic process occurs. Continuing the driving example, on occasion a passenger in my car will slam his or her foot against the floorboard in a vain effort to stop my car. I always inform such passengers that their foot motion is perfectly understandable; the proper stimulus was present in the environment (danger) to bring about an action (braking) even though the action is futile.

How do we know that automaticity has these two characteristics (requires little or no attention, happens without intention)? First let's consider whether automatic processes really don't require attention.

AUTOMATICITY AND ATTENTION. In a classic experiment on the training of automaticity, Walter Schneider and Richard Shiffrin (1977) used a visual search task to show the reduced attentional demand of automatic processes. On each trial, participants were given a memory set (e.g., the letters "A" and "J"), and they were to search the upcoming stimuli and report whether any of the characters in the memory set appeared on that trial. Participants then saw a series of cards with letters and numbers on them, and they had to judge whether a member of the memory set had appeared on one of the cards. The memory set items are called **targets** and the nontarget items on the cards are called **distractors.** Twenty of these cards flipped by on each trial, and each card was presented only briefly, on some trials as briefly as 40 ms. On each trial a new memory set and a new set of cards were used (Figure 3.7).

What does this task have to do with attention? We're discussing automatic processes, and in this case the process is visual search: The participant looks for the target among all the stimuli on the cards. One can use this task to examine automaticity because if the visual search is automatic, the participant ought to be

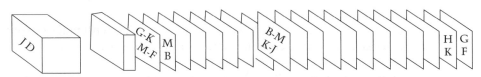

Figure 3.7. *Sample trial from Schneider and Shiffrin's (1977) task, showing cards that flashed in front of participants. The block at the far left represents that memory set.*

able to carry out visual search on lots of elements simultaneously because searching each element takes no attention. Therefore, the number of characters on each card shouldn't matter; if there are four characters on each card you'll still be able to do the visual search as effectively as if there is one character on each card.

The first experiment examined two conditions: consistent mapping and varied mapping. In the consistent mapping condition, the target was always a letter, and the distractors were always numbers (or vice versa). *Consistent* refers to the fact that a target on one trial could not be a distractor on another trial. In the varied mapping condition, the targets and distractors were of the same type, so a target on one trial might be a distractor on another trial.

The results showed that when a consistent mapping was used, visual search was automatic. Search was equally fast and accurate when there was one character on each frame or when there were two or four. It also didn't matter how long each card was presented (40, 80, or 120 ms). Furthermore, in the consistent mapping condition, participants reported experiencing pop-out. Pop-out is a description of the participant's subjective experience in this task; if the target is present, it seems to jump off the card and is therefore very easy to spot. Participants in this task say that they feel as if they hardly need to search under these conditions because they know that the target will pop out of the background.

It was quite a different story in the varied mapping condition, however. In that condition, faster presentation rates and more distractors really hurt performance. As you would expect, there was no pop-out in this condition (Figure 3.8). This experiment shows that visual search is automatic if you are dealing with letters and numbers, but participants already had a great deal of experience with these categories when they started the experiment. Can you start with unfamiliar categories and observe automaticity develop during the course of an experiment?

In a second article, Shiffrin and Schneider (1977) attempted to observe this process in the laboratory. They used the same visual search task, but only letters were used as targets and distractors. In this experiment, "categorical" meant that the memory set was selected from among the same set of letters on each trial. For example, the memory set would be selected from the letters {GMFP} and the distractors would be selected from {CNHD}. For the "mixed" condition the memory set and the distractors could be selected from any of the following letters: {RVJZBWTX}. Each participant alternated blocks of trials using the categorical and mixed stimuli. They performed 24 1-hr sessions, for a total of 9,216 trials (4,608 of each type of mapping).

Automaticity developed only if the target set was selected from the same set of letters on each trial (i.e., in the categorical mapping condition). If a letter could be a target on one trial and then a distractor on the next trial, automaticity never developed (Figure 3.9).

Thus, there appears to be good evidence that, with practice, tasks become less demanding of attention. The exact mechanism by which this happens remains unclear. Some researchers have suggested that with practice some of the intermediate steps in a complex series of processes are eliminated (Anderson, 1993; Newell & Rosenbloom, 1981).

Gordon Logan (1988) suggested a quite different account of automaticity, based on memory. Logan suggested that increasing facility with well-practiced

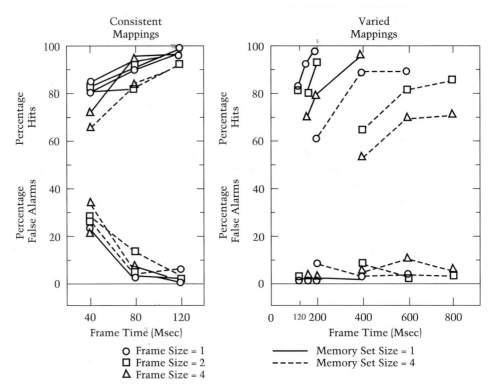

Figure 3.8. *The graph on the left shows performance for consistent mappings, and that on the right shows performance for varied mappings. Hits are successfully finding the target when it is present; false alarms are reporting that the target is present when it is not. Three factors are represented on the graph: how long each card was shown (frame time), size of the memory set, and number of characters on each card (frame size). When the mapping is consistent, none of these factors influences performance; visual search is equally good unless frame time is very short (40 ms). For varied mappings, all three factors influence performance, indicating that this sort of search is not automatic.*

tasks may reflect an increasing role of memory. For example, if I ask you how many letters are in the word *quotidian*, you would have to spell it to yourself and count the letters. If I asked you the same question 2 minutes later, you wouldn't go through the same processes; you'd remember what you said 2 minutes ago and you'd say it again. Logan suggested that memory may play just such a role in automaticity. In every task, memory competes with slower processes that actually calculate an answer to the task at hand. With more practice, you have more answers in memory, making it increasingly likely that on any given trial you can use an answer from memory and not need to do the calculation.

AUTOMATICITY AND INTENTION.   There is also evidence that automatic processes happen beyond one's control, but these data must be interpreted cautiously. The evidence in favor of this view comes from a couple of visual search tasks. One is the Stroop (1935) effect, which you have probably seen before. In this task you are asked to name the ink colors of a series of words. The ink color

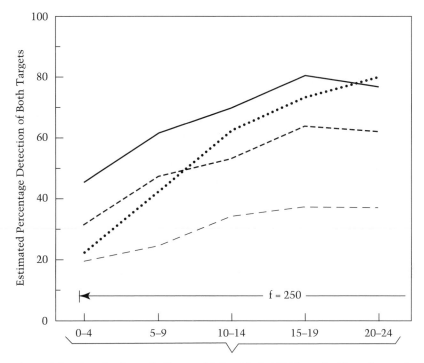

Figure 3.9.   *Results from Shiffrin and Schneider's (1977) study. Note that in the early session, participants were always more likely to find the target when there were two targets (M = 2) than when there were four targets (M = 4), and that was equally true in the categorical and mixed conditions. By the end of the training, participants were equally good when M = 2 and M = 4 but only for the categorical condition. In the mixed condition, participants were much better at detecting the target when there were fewer stimuli on each card.*

names conflict with the words that the ink spells out (e.g., the word *RED* is written in blue ink). The appropriate response would be "blue" but the fact that the ink forms the word *RED* causes interference. People are slower and less accurate in naming the ink colors than when they form unrelated words such as *RUT.* This effect can be taken as evidence that reading is an automatic process. In this case, you actually want *not* to read the word *RED* but reading it seems unavoidable, and because the word *RED* conflicts with the correct response, there is interference.

Another task supporting the involuntariness of automatic processes is the **flanker effect.** In the **flanker task** the participant is asked to respond to a stimulus presented in the center of the screen and to ignore any other stimuli that appear. The participant is shown exactly where the centrally presented stimulus will appear (usually via a crosshair that appears before the target), but some other stimuli appear near the target (i.e., they flank the target).

The effect of the flankers can be observed when participants are asked to read the target word aloud; in that case, participants begin reading slightly faster if the flankers are semantically related to the target word (i.e., if they are related in terms of their meaning). Mark Dallas and Philip Merikle (1976) showed this effect clearly. On each trial participants saw a card with two letter strings: a target word that participants were to read (e.g. "table"), and then either a semantically related word (e.g., "chair") an unrelated word (e.g., "night"), or a nonword letter string (e.g., "lhesl"). There was a cue 250 ms before the stimuli appeared telling the participant where the to-be-reported word was going to appear. They were told to simply ignore the other stimulus. Participants were equally fast when the flanker was an unrelated word or nonword (about 510 ms) but they were faster when the flanker was semantically related to the target (480 ms). The flanker effect also is observed when the task is to name the semantic category of the target rather than to read the target aloud. Categorization judgments also are faster if the flankers are examples of the same semantic category as the target (Shaffer & LaBerge, 1979). These flanker experiments seem to support the hypothesis that reading is obligatory, at least under the conditions in this experiment. If a word appears in a location to which you are attending, you seem to process it for meaning.

That leads us to a final point to consider: What conditions make reading (or any other cognitive process) obligatory? It seems unlikely that the stimulus conditions that elicit the automatic response are very broad. For example, seeing a red traffic light does not always cause you to make a braking motion with your foot. If you're walking when you see the light, it leads to a different response, namely, to stop walking. It's clear that we must be careful in describing the stimuli in the environment that trigger an automatic response, but this issue has not been explored in much detail yet.

STAND-ON-ONE-FOOT QUESTIONS

1. *Can people divide attention between more than one task? How is this known?*
2. *The dual task paradigm often is used to investigate the limited nature of attention. Describe two consequences of adding a second task that make data from the dual task paradigm difficult to interpret.*
3. *Is a structural explanation of interference the same thing as an attentional explanation?*

QUESTIONS THAT REQUIRE TWO FEET

4. *Some people can read while music is playing as long as it's instrumental music; if the music has words, they find it distracting. Why might that be?*
5. *I recently heard a comic remark that he thought it was funny that people turn the radio off when they are looking for a house number in a strange neighborhood. What theory of attention is this comedian adhering to?*
6. *Do you think it's safe to talk on cellular phones while driving?*

➤ *What Is the Fate of Sensory Stimuli That Are Not Selected to Receive Attention?*

> ➤ *PREVIEW* We attend to only a subset of the stimuli that are out in the world. What happens to the other stimuli? They must be processed and identified to at least some extent; how else would you know when to redirect attention to these other stimuli? In this section we discuss just how much processing is performed on these unattended stimuli. It seems that the physical characteristics of unattended stimuli are identified (e.g., color and shape of visual stimuli, loudness and pitch of auditory stimuli), but little information about their meaning is processed. We also look at how selection operates. What does attention focus on? Does it focus on objects or regions of space? And how does selection operate? Does it actually select things to process, or does it filter out the to-be-ignored things, leaving only the target? The answer is that it seems to select objects, not space, and it seems to do so by actively drawing attention to the target, not by ignoring the nontarget objects.

In the last section we discussed the limited nature of attention. You can't attend to everything simultaneously. In this section we consider a consequence of attention's being limited; because it is limited it must also be selective, and if you select some things to attend to, you will necessarily not be selecting others. What happens to the sensory stimuli that are not selected?

That question may strike you as odd. Who cares what happens to unattended stimuli? It's actually an important question. Consider this. What if you're attending to one stimulus and another stimulus in the environment becomes more important for you to attend to? For example, you're sitting in the library, attending to the book you're reading (*Anna Karenina*) when suddenly someone shouts "IS THAT A FIRE???!!" That would be a good moment to disengage attention from the novel and direct attention to whatever has made someone shout. If there were absolutely no processing of stimuli that you were ignoring, you wouldn't even know that someone had shouted.

Indeed, you know that attention can be diverted in this way, which indicates that there must be *some* processing of material that you are ignoring. That's why the definition of attention is that it's the mechanism for *continued* cognitive processing; everything is processed to some extent, and attention affords continued processing. The question we're taking up in this section is, "How much processing occurs in the absence of attention?" Most of this work has concerned the amount of perceptual processing that occurs on stimuli that are not attended.

We have to start our discussion of this problem by outlining an assumption. It's probably a justifiable assumption, but we should be explicit about it anyway. The assumption is that perception follows a processing course like that in Figure 3.10.

It is assumed that the physical characteristics of a stimulus are processed first. For example, for visual information that would be shape, color, spatial location, and so on. For auditory information it would be loudness, pitch, spatial location, and so on. After you know the physical characteristics, more processing

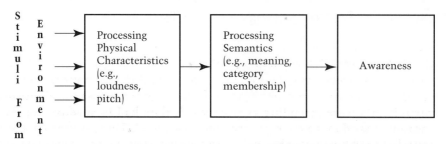

Figure 3.10. *Simple diagram showing the assumed order in which sensory stimuli are processed.*

is necessary to figure out what the object is and therefore its meaning (that shiny red blob is an apple, which means that it is edible, it has seeds, it is a member of the category "fruit," and so on).

There is a great deal of sensory information bombarding us at any given moment (e.g., sights, sounds, smells) represented at the left of the figure, but at the other end of the processing stream only a fraction of that information enters awareness. One hypothesis is that attention acts as a filter, stopping most of the information before it reaches awareness. The attentional filter stops the processing of most sensory information but allows continued processing (and eventual entry to awareness) of only the sensory information to which we are attending. We could posit that *all* the information is processed at least a bit; otherwise, how would we know when something interesting happens to which we're not attending (like someone yelling "IS THAT A FIRE?" while you're attending to *Anna Karenina*)? You have to be processing things that are not currently in awareness and evaluating them so that you can decide whether they are more worthy of attention than what you are currently attending to. The question we're posing is, "How much processing does *everything* get (including the stuff you're currently ignoring)?"

Theories about how attention acts as a filter fall into two categories: **early filter** theories and **late filter** theories. These terms refer to where the filter operates in the processing stream depicted in Figure 3.10. An early filter means that the filter is located early in the processing stream, usually right after the sensory characteristics are processed; thus, according to early filter theories, all stimuli are processed so that their sensory characteristics are determined, and then they hit the filter. Most stimuli are not processed past that point, but the filter allows through whichever stimuli are being attended to.

According to a late filter theory, the filter occurs later in the processing stream. All stimuli are processed to determine their physical characteristics and their semantic characteristics, and only then do the stimuli hit the filter; only the stimuli that are attended to go on to enter awareness. You can see that the key difference between these theories is the location of the filter. So what is the evidence for each?

Early Filter Theories

One of the first studies relevant to this question was performed by Colin Cherry (1953) using the **dichotic listening** task. In this task, participants listened to material on headphones. Each earpiece played a different message, and participants were asked to pay attention to just one of the messages. To ensure that participants were attending as instructed, they had to **shadow** the message, meaning that they had to repeat the message aloud. Thus, as they were shadowing what they heard over the right earpiece, another message was playing in the left earpiece. Later, participants were asked to report what they knew about the message from the unattended ear. Participants were terrible at reporting what the unattended message was. In fact, Cherry found that participants didn't even notice if the unattended message switched into another language or if the message was played backwards. Participants *did* notice if the unattended speech turned into a pure tone or if the gender of the speaker changed.

Cherry concluded that unattended speech is not analyzed to a semantic level—that is, it is not analyzed for meaning. He concluded that unattended speech is analyzed for its physical characteristics, such as pitch and loudness. Thus, if you're focussing attention on the message in the left ear, you don't know anything about the meaning of what's coming in the right ear. But you know its physical characteristics, so you can tell when it becomes grossly different from speech (like a pure tone) or when the pitch changes (because the gender of the speaker had changed). A dramatic example of the extent to which people don't know the meaning of unattended speech was provided by Moray (1959), who played the same word list for participants in the unattended ear 35 times. On a later recognition test of the words, participants were at chance.

Donald Broadbent (1958) was one of the first to propose a theory incorporating an early attentional filter. Broadbent suggested that information comes into a very brief sensory store (discussed in chapter 4) in which its physical characteristics are ascertained. The filter occurs just after this sensory store, and only a small portion of this information makes it to the next stage, which is primary memory. Primary memory is associated with awareness, and it is where meaning is assigned to stimuli (primary memory is also discussed in chapter 4).

Let's focus on this bit about physical characteristics. The idea is that all stimuli are analyzed for their physical characteristics, but only a limited number (those to which you attend) are also analyzed for their semantic content. Recall that unattended stimuli must be processed in case something more important is happening to which you're not attending. Thus, if someone shouted "FIRE" in a crowded party, you would switch attention because loudness is a physical characteristic. The loudness of the unattended message would make you shift attention from the conversation you were having to the source of the voice. But presumably if someone merely said "fire," you wouldn't hear it because the word doesn't stand out from any other of the stimuli coming in to the system. On the other had, if the party had only women at it and a man said "fire," it would stand out because men's voices are lower in pitch, and hence you might switch attention to it. For that matter, anything the man said would stand out because of its lower pitch.

Late Filter Theories

To summarize, Broadbent thought that all incoming stimuli are analyzed in terms of their physical characteristics. If the physical characteristics of a stimulus make it seem worthy of attention, you could switch attention to it, but if it differs only in terms of meaning, you'd never know that because unattended messages aren't processed for meaning. This proposal sounds reasonable, but your own experience might show you a difficulty with this theory. Sometimes you're at a crowded party, and you overhear your name being mentioned in another conversation. I've observed the phenomenon not only with my name but with other stimuli that are relevant to me. For example, I'll be at a booth in a restaurant talking with friends and I'll suddenly notice that the people in the next booth are talking about psychology. Just as my name pops into awareness if it is uttered within my hearing, words such as "cognitive" and "psychology" have a similar effect.

In these examples, it was the semantic content, or *meaning* of the unattended words, that caused attention to be shifted to them, which is not in line with Broadbent's and Cherry's proposal. This effect has been tested in the laboratory using the dichotic listening task. While participants shadowed a message in one ear, some material played in the unattended ear, and then the message "Dan Willingham, stop shadowing now." Moray (1959) found that participants sometimes (but not always) noticed their own name on the unattended channel. Only 33% showed the effect, although these data are a little hard to interpret because Moray didn't test very many people; 4 out of 12 participants tested noticed their name.

Noelle Wood and Nelson Cowan (1995) replicated Moray's experiment, and found the same results; 9 out of 26 (about 35%) participants noticed their own name on the unattended channel, and 0 out of 26 noticed hearing someone else's name. Does this result mean that the unattended message was processed semantically (i.e., for meaning), or does it mean that one-third of the participants didn't really follow the experimenter's instructions? Maybe they did the shadowing task, but they also switched attention to the other channel every now and then to see what was happening there? This possibility seems likely, because when Wood and Cowan told people that they should be ready for new instructions during the task, 80% detected their name. It seems likely that the increase resulted from more participants sampling the channel they were not supposed to attend to, looking for the new instructions.

Other data seem to be consistent with the idea that messages in the unattended ear are processed for meaning, however. Treisman (1960) performed a rather clever study. She had the message in the attended and the unattended ear switch in midstream. The left ear might have heard "If you're creaming butter and *piccolos, clarinets, and tubas, seldom play solos.*" Meanwhile the right ear would hear "*Many orchestral instruments, such as* sugar, it's a good idea to use a low mixer speed." Participants were supposed to shadow the right ear, but their shadowing jumped to the other ear when the semantic sense of the message started coming from the other earpiece. This effect was noted for 15 out of 18 participants. Still, they would shadow the wrong ear only for one or two words, and then they would switch back to the correct ear. Interestingly, none of the participants noticed that they had done so; they all thought they had consistently shadowed the correct ear.

Treisman also varied the sensibility of the passages that participants were shadowing. Some of the passages were easy-to-follow stories, and other passages were statistical approximations of English; that is, the sentences contained words in proportions that approximated English, but the sentences were not sensible. Treisman found that participants did not switch their shadowing for these passages. She reasoned that the filter does a fairly effective job—participants for the most part remain unaware of the unattended message—but it must be true that the unattended message is processed for meaning to some extent because whether or not a word gets through seems to depend on its contextual appropriateness. If a word that is highly probable (given the semantic context) appears on the unattended channel and an improbable word appears on the attended channel, the filter allows the probable word to get through. Treisman proposed that the filter must be sensitive to context and allows highly probable or appropriate words to pass on to awareness. She also proposed that certain words (e.g., one's own name or danger signals such as someone calling out "Fire!") will always be considered contextually relevant and will pass through the filter on to awareness.

These results led some researchers to propose late filter theories, suggesting that the filter occurs late in processing (Deutsch & Deutsch, 1963; Norman, 1968). Specifically, these theorists proposed that all inputs are processed not only for their physical characteristics but also for their semantic meaning. Attention determines what will enter awareness, but the decision of what will enter consciousness can be made on physical characteristics (e.g., attend to this thing because it's loud) or on semantic characteristics (e.g., attend to this thing because its meaning is important).

Late filter theories gained support from studies using **indirect measures** of semantic processing. An indirect measure is one in which you infer something about cognition based on how the participant performs a task rather than asking him or her a question about the processing of interest. For example, if you want to know whether a participant processed material on the unattended channel in a dichotic listening task, a **direct measure** would be simply to ask, "What did you hear on the other channel?" An indirect measure would be to give the participant some other task to do and see whether the way that task is performed is influenced by the material on the unattended channel.

In one of the better-known studies in this vein (Corteen & Wood, 1972) the indirect measure was **galvanic skin response** (GSR). It is a measure of how sweaty your palms are. Your palms are always a little bit moist, but the sweat evaporates quickly; when you are nervous, there is more sweat. GSR is an accurate measure of how sweaty your palm is. Two leads are placed on your palm. One sends out a very mild electric pulse, and the other reads electric activity.

Skin is a poor conductor of electricity, but water (including sweat) is a terrific conductor of electricity. The more sweat present on your hand, the more current the second lead will pick up. Again, to clarify the distinction between direct and indirect tests, a direct test of nervousness would be to simply ask participants how nervous they felt; GSR is an indirect test.

In Corteen and Wood's study, participants were first exposed to a training session in which they heard some words and occasionally received a mild electric shock. The shock was administered every time one of three city names was mentioned. Soon, participants came to expect the shock when they heard one of the city names, as measured by GSR. They got nervous in anticipation of the shock, and that nervousness was apparent on the GSR measure.

In the second phase of the experiment participants performed a dichotic listening task, shadowing an irrelevant message coming into their right ear. In the left ear they heard lists of words that included the city names that had been paired with shock, some new city names, and some irrelevant nouns. No shocks were administered during this part of the experiment. Participants could say little or nothing about the material that had been presented to the unattended channel. The GSR told a different story, however. Participants showed the GSR response 38% of the time to the old city names, 23% of the time to new city names, and just 10% of the time to new nouns. Thus, these results seemed to show that even if people were unaware of the words on the unattended channel, these words were being analyzed for meaning unconsciously.

This study was fairly influential but was later shown to have problems. First, it wasn't so easy to replicate (Wardlaw & Kroll, 1976). To replicate a study simply means to do it over again to be sure you get the same results. Psychologists consider replication to be quite important because if an effect is real, it should be reproducible. If you're not familiar with the importance of replication, you might have a look at the Appendix.

Second, Michael Dawson and Anne Schell (1982) showed that although the effect might be replicable, it might not be caused by semantic processing of the unattended channel but by shifts of attention during the task. They tried much harder than previous experimenters had to measure when participants shifted attention to the channel they were supposed to be ignoring. For example, the experimenters assumed that participants attended to the wrong channel when they made a mistake in shadowing or when they reported having become aware of a word on the to-be-ignored channel. When the researchers eliminated all the trials on which participants might have switched attention to the to-be-ignored channel, the main effect of interest—heightened GSR to the city names on the unattended channel—was greatly reduced. It didn't disappear completely, but it was not nearly as robust as it had looked before.

A different indirect measure was used by Eric Eich (1984). Eich had participants shadow one ear while word pairs were presented to the unattended ear. Each word pair included a homophone (a word that can have two meanings but sound the same, such as *fare* and *fair*). If one of these words is spoken in isolation, you can't know whether the person is saying *fare* or *fair* because they sound the same. In Eich's experiment, the other word of the pair disambiguated the homophone, making it clear which word was meant. For example, a word pair might have been *taxi fare.* Later, participants were asked which words they remembered from the unattended channel, and their memory was very poor. Next they were given an indirect test of their memory for the word pairs. The indirect test was simply a spelling test. The experimenter said a word aloud, and the participant had to spell it. Some of the words on the spelling test were the homophones that had been on the unattended channel. The measure of interest was whether participants used the spelling consistent with the disambiguating context. In other words, participants might spell *f-a-r-e* more often than *f-a-i-r* because they heard *taxi,* which biases one meaning to the sound *fare.* Eich reported that, indeed, participants who heard *taxi* more often used the spelling *fare* than participants who had not heard *taxi,* indicating that these unattended words were processed for meaning.

Noelle Wood and her colleagues (1997) replicated Eich's effect using the homophones, and the effect replicated nicely. But they were worried about one aspect of the procedure. Participants were shadowing text that was presented at 85 words per minute, whereas a rate of 120–150 words per minute would be more typical of real speech. Perhaps participants were able to switch attention between the two channels because the shadowing they were doing was not so demanding. So Wood and colleagues conducted the experiment again, using a faster presentation rate. This time there was *no* evidence that participants' spelling of the homophones was biased, indicating that the earlier results showing a late filter may have resulted from participants' successfully shifting attention from one channel to another.

Movable Filter

In sum, it's not clear that all information is analyzed in terms of its semantic content every time. You could easily account for all the data with an early filter model, such as that proposed by Broadbent, allowing that sometimes the focus of attention will lapse and participants will attend to material that they are supposed to be ignoring. You could even propose that the attentional system is biased to do exactly that. It is prudent to constantly monitor the environment around you so the attentional system might be biased *not* to maintain attention to one location, as dichotic listening tasks demand.

One possibility is that you can control the filter to be either early or late, depending on your needs, a point made forcefully by Michael Posner and Charles Snyder (1975). One can choose to allocate attention *completely* to some material, or to allocate attention *mostly* to the material, while periodically switching attention to other material. Unattended stimuli would always be analyzed for physical characteristics. The filter is not fixed to be early or late: It's movable.

Some data are consistent with that suggestion. William Johnston and Steven Heinz (1978) had participants listen to two word lists over headphones. Each list was spoken simultaneously, and both lists were presented to both ears. Participants were told to shadow, but some participants were instructed to shadow based on the physical characteristic of the words; they were to shadow the words spoken by a man, so the participant could attend to the pitch of the word to select which one to shadow. Other participants were asked to shadow based on the semantic content of the words; they were to shadow the word that described an occupation (e.g., *teacher*). While they were doing the shadowing task, all participants also performed a secondary task. They were to watch a computer screen, on which a light would occasionally appear. They were to press a button as quickly as possible when the light appeared. This secondary task provides an indirect measure of how attention demanding the shadowing task is. The more attention that the shadowing task took, the less attention would be available to be directed to the screen to watch for the light.

The results showed that response times to the light were longer when participants had to shadow based on the semantic content of the words rather than their physical characteristic (482 vs. 433 ms). Furthermore, participants made more shadowing errors when they shadowed based on semantic content rather than physical characteristic (20.5% errors vs. 5.3% errors). This experiment indicates that participants are capable of processing words at a semantic level as they perform a secondary task, but there is a higher attentional cost to doing so relative to processing only at a physical level; shadowing performance is worse, and performance on the secondary task is worse.

Thus the available evidence seems to indicate that all stimuli are analyzed at a physical level, and further processing demands some attentional resources. The decision to expend these resources depends on the circumstances. The likelihood that an unattended sound enters awareness depends on how you choose to allocate attentional resources, which depends on the situation. It seems that there is a fixed filter—and it seems to be early—but you can allocate your attentional resources so that it's more like having a late filter by frequently sampling other perceptual channels.

What Is Selected?

When we talk about attention being selective, we should pause to ask, "What does it select?" Until the early 1980s many researchers felt that attention was like a spotlight (Norman, 1968; Posner, Snyder, & Davidson, 1980), a beam of enhanced perceptual processing that one could point to locations in space; objects falling within the attentional spotlight were subject to more perceptual processing. Thus, attention was thought to select spatial locations; you point the spotlight of attention to a location in space. Today, it seems much more likely that attention selects objects, not spatial locations.

There are two predictions one would make using the beam metaphor that seem not to be true. First, if attention worked like a beam, then the amount of time it takes to shift attention from location to another should be proportional to the distance attention must travel. Second, experiments were conducted that directly compared whether attention was directed to spatial locations or to objects, and objects won out. Here's how these two points were made.

If the beam idea were right, it should take a longer time to move the attentional beam a greater distance, but that appears not to be true. Ho-Wan Kwak,

Dale Dagenbach, and Howard Egeth (1991; see also Sagi & Julesz, 1985) tested this prediction by asking participants to judge whether two simple stimuli (T or L) were the same or different. Participants looked at a crosshair fixation point in the center of the screen. Then two letters appeared on the screen some distance from one another for just 150 ms. Participants were asked to make a same or different judgment as quickly as possible. The results showed that the time it took to make the judgment did not vary as the distance between the letters changed, as shown in Figure 3.11. These data make it seem that attention can move ballistically from one location to another and does not sweep along in space, as a beam would.

George Sperling and Erich Weichselgartner (1995) reported that when one moves attention, it is not disrupted by intervening "obstacles." If attention were a beam, one might expect that when sweeping from one location to another, attention might be captured by an intervening object. Sperling and Weichselgartner showed that that is not the case, again implying that attention jumps from one discrete location to another.

In their procedure, the participant first saw a fixation dot at the center of the screen, and he or she pressed a button when ready to begin. Then digits started appearing at the center of the screen very rapidly (10 per second). At the same time, letters started appearing to the left of the digits so that they were not adjacent but could be perceived. Letters also appeared at a rate of 10 per second. The participant was to keep his or her eyes on the digits but to focus attention

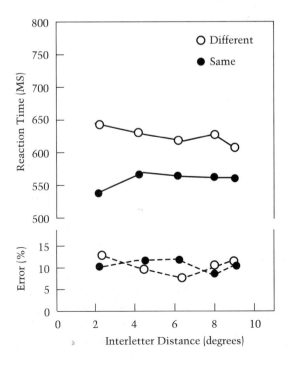

Figure 3.11. *Figure from Kwak et al. (1991) showing that the distance between two stimuli does not affect performance in terms of response times or errors. "Different" and "Same" refer to whether the stimuli were the same or different.*

on the letters. (It's possible to keep your eyes on one thing but to focus attention on another. Try it.) When the letter "C" appeared, the participant was to shift attention to the digits and to report the first four digits perceived. It's possible to measure how quickly the participant shifted attention by noting the first digit he or she reported.

The interesting manipulation was that on some trials nonalphanumeric characters (e.g., #, &, @, *) appeared between the letters and digits. The question of interest is whether these stimuli would slow the shift of attention as it moved from the letters to the digits. If attention moves as a beam, one might expect that being dragged over these flashing stimuli might slow the movement of attention, whereas if attention simply jumps from one location to another, the intervening characters should not matter. The results showed that response times averaged 374 ms without the intervening characters and 383 ms with the intervening characters, a difference that was not statistically significant. Thus, the data are consistent with the idea that attention jumps from one location to another.

Other results directly support the idea that attention selects objects, not space. One source of evidence is the fact that you can have two overlapping objects in a single spatial location, and participants can selectively attend to just one of them. One example of this phenomenon is an experiment by Ulric Neisser and Robert Becklen (1975). They had participants watch a video monitor with two different videos superimposed into one image. One video was of two people playing a hand-slapping game, and the other was of three people playing a ball-catching game. Participants were to attend to one video or the other, and they had to indicate when certain key events happened in the video they were watching (e.g., when the ball was thrown). Thus the task was a bit like a visual version of dichotic listening with shadowing. Neisser and Becklen found that participants knew very little about the unattended video, similar to the results from dichotic listening studies. Participants find it easy to attend to just one object of two, even if they are in overlapping spatial locations. If attention were directed by spatial location, that should not be possible (or at least it should not be so easy).

Here's another source of evidence that attention is object based. If attention were directed to space, you would expect that attention is focused in the center of the beam, and the farther an object is from the center, the less attention it gets. If two object parts are equidistant from the center of the beam, they get equal amounts of attention. For example, if your attention is focused on Judy's face, each of her hands would be getting an equal amount of attention because they are equidistant from the focus of attention. Now suppose that Judy has one hand behind her back, and Sherry is standing next to her, and that Sherry's left hand is the same distance from Judy's face as Judy's right hand is. The spatial theory of attention would predict that Sherry's hand and Judy's hand would get equal amounts of attention because they are equidistant from the focus of attention. The object view of attention would predict that Judy's hand will get more attention. By looking at Judy's face, you select an object (Judy) for attention, and all the parts of the object therefore get more attention.

BOX 3.1. NEURAL EVIDENCE FOR SELECTION OF OBJECTS BY ATTENTION

Attention enhances perceptual processing, but of what? Does it enhance the processing of a location in space or does it enhance the processing of an object? Kathleen O'Craven, Paul Downing, and Nancy Kanwisher (1999) collected evidence using functional magnetic resonance imaging that indicates that attention selects objects for processing, not a location in space.

The researchers had participants view stimuli of a semitransparent face superimposed on a house, with one moving and the other not. Participants were to attend to the house, the face, or the motion. The parts of the brain that respond to each of these stimuli are well established: Faces generate activity in the fusiform face area, places generate activity in the parahippocampal place area, and motion generates activity in area MT.

If attention operates through the enhanced processing of a location in space, all three of the target visual areas should more active because all three attributes are in the same location. On the other hand, if attention operates through the selection of an attribute (face, place, or motion), one should see activity localized to the brain area that supports perception of that attribute, even though the other attributes overlap in space.

The results showed selective activation of the brain area supporting perception of the attended attribute. In other words, when they attended to the face the face area was active, but not the place area or motion area, and so on.

The results for motion actually were somewhat more complicated, but they are complicated in a way that provides a great test of the object theory of attention. The theory predicts that you select an object for attention, and that should mean that you select the entire object, including all its attributes. That means that if you are told to attend to the face and the face is moving, you can't help but process the motion because motion is an attribute of the face. This prediction was also confirmed in the study: If you attend to an object, you process all attributes of the object.

This study provides compelling neural evidence supporting the behavioral evidence that attention selects objects for processing, not areas in space.

Gordon Baylis and Jon Driver (1993) tested this hypothesis. They showed that it is harder to judge the relative distance of two corners when the corners were parts of different objects than when they were parts of the same object.

On each trial participants saw a figure similar to Figure 3.12. They were to determine which vertex was higher, the one on the left or on the right. Some participants were told to examine the white parts of the figure to make these judgments. For these participants the figure on the left would entail comparing parts (i.e., the angles) of a single object, but the figure on the right would require comparing parts of two separate objects. Other participants were told to compare the angles of the black part of the figure; for these participants, the figure on the left required comparing parts of two objects, and the figure on the right just one. Thus, Baylis and Driver were able to use the exact same

Figure 3.12. *Stimuli of the sort used in Baylis and Driver's (1993) experiment.*

stimulus for each condition; they got participants to interpret the figure as depicting one or two objects by using different instructions. The results showed that participants were reliably slower in making the judgment (by about 30 ms) when the instruction led them to compare the angles of two objects rather than one object. Again, this result is consistent with the idea of attention being focused on objects, not regions of space.

The evidence that attention selects objects, not locations in space, appears compelling. But how exactly does selection operate?

How Does Selection Operate?

The process by which attention selects some objects for further processing has been studied most thoroughly in visual search paradigms. In these paradigms, the participant searches a large array of characters for one particular character. To get a feel for these paradigms, have a look at the three arrays in Figure 3.13. In each case, you are to find the large letter *Q* in the array.

It probably seemed easy to you to find the large *Q* in the first two arrays and more difficult in the third one. Note that in the first array, a single feature of the *Q*—its size—differentiated it from the other letters present. In the second array there was again a single feature—the diagonal line that differentiates a *Q* from an *O*—that made the target different than the other letters. In the third array, however, there was no single feature to differentiate the targets and

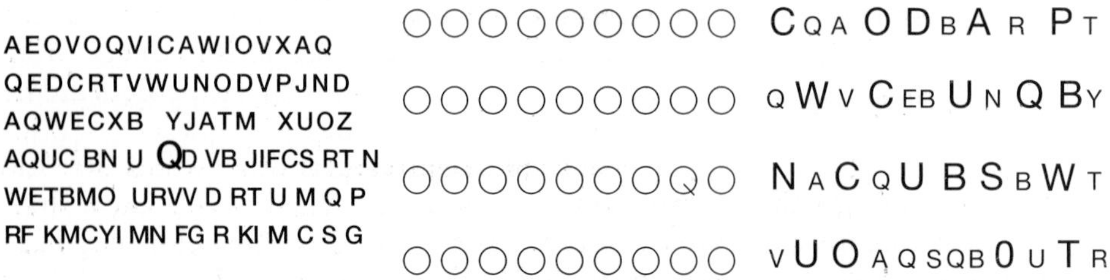
AEOVOQVICAWIOVXAQ
QEDCRTVWUNODVPJND
AQWECXB YJATM XUOZ
AQUC BN U QD VB JIFCS RT N
WETBMO URVV D RT U M Q P
RF KMCYI MN FG R KI M C S G
OOOOOOOOOO
OOOOOOOOOO
OOOOOOOOQO
OOOOOOOOOO
CQA O DBA R PT
QWV CEB UN Q BY
NACQU B SBWT
VUO AQSQB0 UTR

Figure 3.13. *Stimulus arrays of the sort used by Treisman and Gelade (1980). In each array, the target is a large Q. In the left and center arrays, the target is easy to find because a single dimension differentiates the targets from distractors. In the right array, more than one dimension is necessary to distinguish the target from distractors. The left and center arrays yield automatic searches and pop out; the right array does not.*

distractors. These two types of searches are called disjunctive and conjunctive. A **disjunctive search** is one in which the target differs from the distractors on just one feature, as in the two arrays on the left. In a **conjunctive search** a conjunction of features differentiates the target from the distractors. There are shapes that match the target, and sizes that match the target, but there is only one combination (i.e., conjunction) of shape and size that match the target. Visual search experiments have been done with many different features such as different shapes, sizes, colors, textures, and spatial orientations (see Treisman & Gormican, 1988, for a review).

When you do this sort of search task, it certainly feels as though the arrays on the left are easier, and laboratory experiments confirm this feeling. The major finding is that disjunctive searches are parallel, whereas conjunctive searches are serial. A **parallel search** is one in which all elements in the array are processed simultaneously. A **serial search** is one in which the elements of the array are evaluated one at a time.

The critical finding from laboratory experiments is this: If you increase the number of elements in the array, it does not affect the reaction time to find the target in the disjunctive search, but it increases the search time in the conjunctive search. The disjunctive search is parallel—each element is evaluated simultaneously—so increasing the number of items to be evaluated does not increase the total search time. The conjunctive search is serial—you check each element one by one—so increasing the number of items increases the search time. You will locate the target, on average, after checking half of the items in the array. (Note that this key measure of the effect of adding distractors is the same that was used in the Shiffrin and Schneider, 1977, studies of automaticity).

Indeed, people report the pop-out effect for disjunctive searches. They feel as though they don't even need to search for the target; the target seems to attract their attention, seeming to pop out of the array. We discuss this idea of targets attracting attention in the next section.

The importance of the difference between disjunctive and conjunctive searches was emphasized by Anne Treisman and Garry Gelade (1980). They proposed that the perceptual system is organized as a series of feature maps: a map for color, a map for shapes, a map for textures, a map for distances, and so on. Each map contains information about the locations in the environment of that one feature. The color map tells you where different colors are in the environment, the shape map tells you where different shapes are, and so on. The contents of these maps are loaded **preattentively.** In other words, attention is not needed to get the information on these maps. Thus, if you know that you are searching for a red target, you need only examine the color map because the colors of all the objects in the field are on that map. That's why you can do a parallel search for an object defined by a single feature; each feature is loaded on a map in parallel.

A conjunctive search, however, requires information from two maps. If you're searching for the letter Q, as in Figure 3.13, you look for a diagonal line on the shape map and find that there are many of them, and you look at the size map for a large letter, and find that there are many of those. So you need to compare the contents of both maps. Treisman and Gelade suggest that comparing the contents of maps requires attention. Attention binds features together into objects. (For other points of view on this question, see Kubovy, Cohen, & Hollier, 1999).

Thus, when you're searching for a target that is defined by a single feature, (e.g., scanning a busy street for bright yellow when you want to hail a cab), it seems that you can simply examine the color map, and attention is drawn to the appropriate color. But is attention drawn to the right color, or does attention filter out all the inappropriate colors? An experiment by Shui-I Shih and George Sperling (1996) indicates that when you search for a feature such as a color, the feature draws attention to the right stimulus rather than filtering out the wrong stimuli.

Participants in their experiment saw a series of arrays of letters flashed on a screen. A single digit appeared in one of the arrays, and participants were to find the digit. The interesting part of the experiment was that alternating arrays within a trial varied on a feature; for example, the first array would have large letters, the next array would have small letters, the next large, and so on. So in a single trial, a participant might see a series of arrays like that shown in Figure 3.14.

Shih and Sperling asked what happens if you *tell* participants that the target (the digit) will appear in an array with large characters. Does that help? If visual search operates by filtering out objects with the undesired feature, then it should be easier to spot the target because you don't waste any attention on the arrays with small letters. But that doesn't happen. Telling participants that the target will be among the large characters doesn't help them to spot it. Furthermore, if you occasionally misinform the participant and say it will be among the large characters when it actually is among the small characters, it doesn't hurt their performance either.

In their second experiment, the target differed from the surrounding distractors on one dimension within an array (e.g., the target was small whereas the other characters in the array were large). With this small change, informing the participants about the critical feature had a big impact on performance. Shih and Sperling interpreted their results as showing that the critical feature can draw attention to a correct stimulus, but it cannot filter out incorrect stimuli. To put it colloquially, when you are searching for a taxi, it's not that you ignore everything that is not yellow and then are left attending to the one yellow thing in the street; rather, your attention is drawn to the yellow thing.

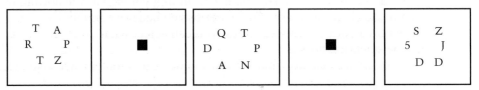

Figure 3.14.   *Trial sequence in Shih and Sperling's (1996) task.*

STAND-ON-ONE-FOOT QUESTIONS

7. In the final analysis, is the filter early or late?
8. What does selective visual attention select?
9. Summarize when a visual search is easy and when it's hard.

QUESTIONS THAT REQUIRE TWO FEET

10. In many horror movies, the heroine calmly continues taking her shower and doesn't notice the scuffling sounds made by the clodhopper shoes of the zombie carrying the axe. How is this a problem of attention?
11. Based on the discussion presented here, can you think of a situation from your own experience indicating that attention is directed to objects, not spatial locations?

➤ WHY DOES SELECTION FAIL?

> ➤ PREVIEW You can't always keep attention just where you want it. Attention wanders. When does selection not work as we desire? In the first section we consider what sorts of stimuli capture attention. As we'll see, stimuli that appear abruptly in the periphery tend to capture attention. Another type of stimulus that was hypothesized to capture attention is the feature singleton, a stimulus that has one feature that no other stimulus has (e.g., a red thing amid a field of green things). Oddly enough, the latest data make it appear that feature singletons capture attention only if you are specifically told to ignore them; if the singleton is not mentioned, it seems not to capture attention. This paradoxical effect—warnings to ignore stimuli make people think about them—has been noted in other situations. Finally, we discuss people's ability to maintain attention when distracting stimuli do not appear, but the targets do not appear often either. This ability is called vigilance.

In the last section we made it sound as though the selective aspect of attention is wholly under our conscious control. A moment's reflection will tell you that is not so. It would be marvelous if attentional selection were so simple; you would say to yourself, "I'm going to attend to this book chapter for the next hour," and you would do so, instead of finding yourself at the bottom of a page in a reverie about the marvelous spareribs you had last summer when you spilled sauce down your bathing suit. Yes, you can select what you want to attend to, but the selection does not last as long as you'd like it to. Attention wanders. In this section we discuss what's known about this problem. We also discuss an even more diabolical effect. When you badly want *not* to attend to something, it is very difficult to keep that something outside of attention.

Stimuli That Capture Attention

Why is it so hard to ignore someone near you in a movie theater rattling a candy wrapper? You can selectively attend to things, right? It's not as if the candy wrapper is so loud that it drowns out the movie soundtrack. So what's up?

Certain types of stimuli grab attention. One type of stimulus that seems to have this effect is a stimulus with a sudden onset in the periphery. This finding certainly makes sense intuitively; if there is a sudden noise or flash of light, it is probably worth investigating what it is. If it's off to the side of you, you need to move attention to determine what it is.

Careful laboratory experiments confirm this impression. John Jonides (1980) gave participants a letter search task. On each trial participants first focused on a crosshair at the center of the screen. Then eight letters appeared in a circle around the crosshair, and participants were supposed to look for the letter *R* or *L*. Each letter was far enough away from the crosshair that attention had to be moved to be able to identify it. On some trials, an arrow appeared near one of the eight positions, indicating that it was very likely that the target would appear in that position. Participants were much faster in finding the target when they had that cue. On other trials, the arrow appeared at the center of the screen, near the crosshair, but it pointed toward the screen position in which the target was likely to appear. That cue also helped participants find the target much faster.

Now things get interesting. Jonides made participants keep a seven-digit number in mind while they did the same task. He did that to occupy attention, and it led to a very different pattern of results. If the arrow appeared in the center and pointed out to the position where the target was likely to appear, participants showed no benefit compared to when they didn't get the cue. In other words, when their attention was occupied by maintaining the seven-digit number, they couldn't also use the arrow cue. But when the cue appeared out in the periphery, the seven-digit number made no difference.

Jonides argued that you can move attention in two ways. You can select a spot you want to attend to, and move attention there, as when you see the arrow at the center of the screen, and you know you're supposed to move attention to the location it points to. Moving attention that way requires attentional capacity. But if something appears in the periphery (such as the arrow), you don't need any attentional capacity to move attention there; the move happens automatically.

In a second experiment Jonides told participants that the cue would appear but that they should ignore it because it wouldn't help them find the target. (Jonides changed the task so that the cue appeared in random locations and didn't predict where the target would appear.) He found that when the cue appeared at the center of the screen, participants could ignore the cue; they were about as fast in searching for the target with or without the cue. When the cue appeared in the periphery, however, they could not ignore it. Participants were slower in finding the target when the cue didn't match the target location than when the cue did match the target location. (Remember that the cue appeared in a random location, so occasionally it matched the target location by chance.) Thus, Jonides showed that a cue with a sudden onset in the periphery captures attention, and (1) doesn't require any attentional resources to do so, and (2) does so even if the participant doesn't want attention to move.

This finding makes sense, but when you think about it, it seems that things are *always* popping into the periphery. As you walk down the street, dogs, cars, people, birds, and other objects come into your field of view, often from the periphery. You're not constantly cringing and cowering before these new stimuli until you establish that they are not a threat. It seems likely that the extent to which attention is captured by new stimuli in the periphery depends on the setting (in some settings you are used to new things appearing in the periphery) and on the extent to which these new things appear to be threatening. Some evidence supports this position. Bruce Warner and his colleagues (Warner, Juola, & Koshino, 1990) reported that a moderate amount of practice in a task like the one Jonides (1981) used weakens the effect; participants get better at ignoring the peripheral cue if they want to do so. Less is known about these attentional effects than one would hope. Part of the problem is that if you really want to do the experiment right, you can test each participant only one time because you'd like the stimulus that appears in the periphery to be a surprise. Obviously, after the experimenter has had a clown jump out of the closet and do a Bronx cheer on Trial 1, the participants are going to be suspicious that they are in for further surprises.

Feature Singletons

You may have noticed a potential problem in the idea that the abrupt onset of stimuli in the periphery captures attention. Mightn't it be the case that these new stimuli are often feature singletons? A **feature singleton** is an object that has a feature that no other stimulus in the field has; we saw examples of feature singletons earlier in the chapter (one large letter among small letters or a diagonal straight line amid a field of curved lines). We saw before that singletons seemed to draw attention. Maybe it is the status of the new objects being a singleton that draws attention.

A number of investigators have questioned whether singletons draw attention, and the answer seems to be that they draw attention if you're trying to ignore them, and they don't draw attention if you're not trying to ignore them. That seems a little strange.

Bradley Gibson and Yuhong Jiang (1998) performed a very well controlled study to examine whether a singleton drew attention when participants were not expecting it (when they didn't know that a singleton was going to appear). Participants performed a letter search task. On each trial eight letters arranged in a circular pattern appeared for just 86 ms. The participant was supposed to judge whether or not an *H* or a *U* had appeared. Participants performed 192 trials of this task, and with practice their accuracy improved, on average, to about 75%. On the 193rd trial, a target letter appeared, but this time it was filled in red. All the other letters were filled in white, as they had been before, so the target was a feature singleton. If singletons draw attention, one would expect that participants should be very accurate in judging that the target was present on this trial, but they weren't: 78% of the participants saw the target, about what they had been averaging. Just to show that the feature singleton could be useful to participants if they were expecting it, the researchers administered another 192 trials in which the target was a red singleton, and participants' accuracy averaged 90% or better on these trials.

This result is a bit surprising because some studies seemed to show that feature singletons *do* capture attention (e.g., Pashler, 1988), but these studies were conducted a bit differently from Gibson and Jiang's study. These other studies always had participants searching for a target defined on one dimension (e.g., brightness), and on some trials one of the other stimuli would be a singleton on some other feature (e.g., it would be a different color than the other stimuli). Participants were told that they were to attend to only one stimulus feature, but the irrelevant feature nevertheless influenced performance. In other words, participants knew that a singleton would appear and were told to ignore it; under those conditions, participants couldn't ignore it.

For example, Jan Theeuwes and Remca Burger (1998) showed participants a stimulus field of five letters, and participants were to search for the letter *R*. On control trials all the letters were red, but on some trials the target was green, and on other trials one of the distractor letters was green. The experimenters reported that response times averaged about 620 ms when all stimuli were red, about 650 ms when the target was green, and about 690 ms when one distractor was green. Thus, the singleton clearly influenced performance. It may seem odd that participants were slower when the target was a singleton (compared to when all the stimuli were red), but bear in mind that participants were specifically told to ignore color, so that may have been the source of the effect.

The upshot seems to be that singletons don't attract attention if one is not told anything about them, but if one is specifically told to ignore the singleton's dimension (e.g., to ignore color), then the singleton perversely *does* attract attention. This bizarre effect may be a special case of a more general effect; trying not to think of something very often makes us think of it. These are often called ironic processes of mental control.

Ironic Process of Mental Control

Suppose I tell you, "For the next 5 minutes I'd like for you not to think about a white bear. Think about whatever you like, but try *not* to think about a white bear." You know what's going to happen: It's going to be very difficult not to think about a white bear. Dan Wegner and his colleagues (Wegner, Schneider, Carter, & White, 1987) performed this procedure in the laboratory. They simply asked participants to "think aloud" for 5 min. First participants thought aloud *without* the instruction to avoid thinking about white bears, and, not surprisingly, they very seldom mentioned white bears. But then participants were asked to think aloud again, and this time they were told not to think about white bears. White bear thoughts intruded approximately seven times during the 5-min period. This effect diminished over the course of the 5-min period; on average people reported thinking about white bears approximately 4.5 times in the first minute, but then only 1 time in the second minute, and a bit less than 1 time in each minute thereafter.

Wegner (1994) proposed a theory of mental control that explains this and related phenomena. It's a theory of how we attempt to control the content of our mental events, which simply means controlling what we think about. The theory assumes that there are two processes by which you seek to control the contents of your mental events. The **operating process** seeks mental contents that are consistent with what you want to think about; for example, if you set as your goal not to think about a white bear, the operating process will search for distractions from that thought. The **monitoring process** searches for mental contents that are inconsistent with what you want to think about. For example, if you're trying not to think about white bears, it searches for mental contents about white bears and related matters. The purpose of this monitoring process is to serve as a warning system that you are about to fail in your desired mental control.

A key assumption of the theory is that the operating process demands attentional resources, but the monitoring process does not. Thus, if attentional resources are scarce (because you are thinking of something else, or you're under stress), the operating process can't do its job of searching for the appropriate mental contents. The monitoring process can, however, because it doesn't require attention. Because the operating process isn't generating appropriate thoughts, the monitoring process often finds inappropriate thoughts and brings them to awareness to alert the system that these inappropriate thoughts are present. That process, in effect, *generates* the unwanted thoughts.

Wegner and Ralph Erber (1992) conducted a straightforward test of these predictions. Participants were asked not to think about a target word, such as *house.* Then they were asked to say the first word that came to mind when they heard a word the experimenter read. The experimenter might read the word *adult* and the participant had to say the first word that came to mind (e.g., *child*). Some of the words the experimenters read were unrelated to the target word that participants were not to think about, but others were semantically associated to it (e.g., *home*). Under normal circumstances, participants had no problem inhibiting the word *house* as a response. But under time pressure, it was a different story. When participants were given a deadline so that they had to produce the response quickly, they often blurted out *house* and in fact they gave *house* as a response more often than participants who were never told not to think about it. Under time pressure, telling people not to think about *house* actually resulted in a higher frequency of responding *house* than among people who were not told to suppress the thought.

Wegner and his collaborators showed that this phenomenon is quite general. The study just described shows that if you try not to think about something, you'll think about it if you're under mental load. Wegner and others have also shown that if you are trying to concentrate on something, you get greater accessibility of irrelevant thoughts if you're under mental load. If you try to relax you'll become more aroused, and if you try to go to sleep you'll become more wakeful if you're under mental load. They've even shown that if you try to forget while under mental load, you'll remember (see Wegner, 1994, for reviews of these studies).

Keep in mind that these ironic effects occur only under mental load; under normal circumstances mental control works pretty well. Only when your attentional capacity is reduced (e.g., you're distracted, tired, drunk) are these ironic effects observed. Thus, how do you avoid ironic mental effects and keep your thoughts in line? The best advice is to pick your moment wisely. Trying to control your thoughts when your attentional capacity is low is likely to be ineffective and is likely to produce ironic effects.

This section has discussed situations in which you select something for attention automatically or you might be unsuccessful in controlling what attention selects. Does this mean that we are never able to mentally stick with a task? Of course not. One's ability to focus attention on one object or task is a special ability, called vigilance, to which we now turn.

Maintaining Attention: Vigilance

Vigilance is simply one's ability to maintain attention, usually in a search task. Vigilance tasks are defined by the fact that you need to maintain attention in one location for an extended period of time and by the fact that there are stretches of time in which nothing happens. Driving, for example, is not a vigilance task, because you're continually making adjustments of speed and direction. A quality control inspector, on the other hand, engages in a vigilance task; he or she sits and watches the factory's product go by on a conveyer belt. Almost every item is the same, and the inspector must maintain attention on the passing items to spot the occasional one that was not produced correctly.

Vigilance tasks assumed great practical importance during World War II, when it was discovered that radar and sonar operators got worse at detecting enemy craft as their shifts wore on. In fact, they got worse at a surprisingly fast rate: over the course of 30 min or so.

The first thing you should know about vigilance tasks is that it's not as easy as you might think to measure someone's performance on a vigilance task. How would you tell whether a sonar operator is doing a good job? Presumably, he or she should not miss reporting a ship when a ship is really out there. But suppose the operator simply calls out, "There's a ship!" all the time. He or she wouldn't miss any ships but would constantly cause false alarms. Another person might be very conservative in calling something a ship, so that if he or she said, "There's a ship" you could be sure that there was, but this person would often fail to identify a ship when there really was one out there. Thus, different people have different criteria in a task like this.

In fact, one person could adopt different strategies. I might say to you, "Whatever you do, don't let a ship get by; whatever looks like it *could* be a ship, call it a ship," or I might say, "Whatever you do, don't say you see a ship if it's not really a ship." Your absolute sensitivity in detecting ships doesn't change, obviously, but the type of mistakes you make may change, depending on your strategy. It turns out that there is a way to analyze these two factors

BOX 3.2. VIGILANCE AND LATERALITY

Suppose you have people perform a vigilance task while they are in a functional imaging scanner. What parts of the brain are active?

Jonathan Lewin and his colleagues (1996) performed that experiment. They had participants watch a black computer with a dim spot at the center. At random times the spot became still dimmer, and participants were to count the number of times that occurred. The experiments reported widespread activity in the frontal and parietal lobes, but interestingly there was much more activity in the right hemisphere than in the left.

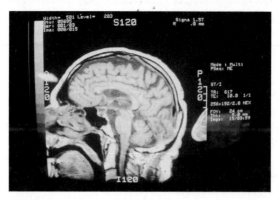

Figure B3.2.

Another key finding about laterality of attention comes from patients who suffer from hemineglect. These patients have suffered lesions to the right parietal lobe, and the syndrome leads them to ignore the left side of space. These patients ignore stimuli on the left side of the world, usually split along the midline of their body (if they move their body, parts of the world that they ignored come under attention). The modality of the information is irrelevant (e.g., whether it is visual, tactile, or auditory). Patients fail to notice stimuli on the ignored side of space (e.g., if they are given a picture to describe) and in severe cases may eat food only on the right side of the plate, or even dress only half of their body. Attention can be dragged to the ignored side of space, for example by a loud noise or flash of light on the ignored side.

One oddity of hemineglect is that it almost always affects the left side of space (because of a lesion to the right parietal area). Damage to the left parietal area seldom leads to neglect of the right side of space. Why? One interpretation might be that the left parietal lobe is less important to attention than the right parietal lobe; if the left parietal lobe is damaged, the more important right parietal lobe can handle attention for both sides of space. If the right parietal lobe is lost, however, the left parietal lobe can support attention in right side of space, but it cannot cover the function that the right parietal lobe used to do (i.e., the left side of space). This interpretation of the relative importance of the two hemispheres for sustained attention matches the fMRI results described earlier. Why the brain is organized this way is not understood.

separately: We can separate **sensitivity,** which is your absolute ability to detect ships, from **bias,** which is a measure of whether you are liberal or conservative in saying that you see a ship. The method of separating sensitivity from bias is called **signal detection theory** and it is described in the Appendix. For now, what you need to know is that vigilance is measured in terms of sensitivity, not bias. People's sensitivity in a vigilance task drops over the first 30 minutes or so.

Why does sensitivity decrease? The first thing you would think is, "Well, people get bored," but there are many other possibilities. It could be that overall alertness drops if you do the same thing for a while. It could be that motivation drops: You just don't care as much. It could be a process of habituation; it's a general principle that if you are exposed to the same stimulus again and again, you get used to it, and its stimulus qualities don't seem to have the same force they have the first time you are exposed to them. Think about eating a really spicy dish; the first mouthful tastes like fire, but as you eat more you habituate to the heat, and mouthfuls toward the bottom of the bowl don't seem to have the same bite as that first taste.

These are all marvelous ideas, but none of them can be the whole story because the extent to which sensitivity drops depends on the specific task participants do. In fact, for some tasks, sensitivity doesn't drop. Raja Parasuraman and Roy Davies (1977) suggested that sensitivity drops for just one type of task: successive tasks with high event rates. Successive tasks are those in which there is some standard you are supposed to keep in memory, and then on each trial a stimulus comes up and you must compare the stimulus to the standard. For example, you have been trained to know what a ship looks like on a radar scope, and you must keep that image in memory and compare it to the different images that come up on the radar scope. In a simultaneous task, on the other hand, you need not keep anything in memory because the stimuli you are to compare are presented simultaneously. The other quality a vigilance task must have to show the drop in sensitivity is a high event rate. That simply means that stimuli must appear frequently (Parasuraman and Davies said about 24 stimuli per minute or more). If either of these conditions is not met (i.e., if stimuli are simultaneous or if there is a low event rate), there is no drop in the sensitivity.

So it seems as though these conditions should be a good clue as to why sensitivity drops in some vigilance tasks; it might have something to do with memory. But no. Harry Koelega and his colleagues (Koelega, Brinkman, Hendriks, & Verbaten, 1989) suggested that another factor determines whether sensitivity drops: whether the task is sensory or cognitive. They suggested that sensitivity drops for sensory tasks (in which you have to evaluate brightness, color, or some other perceptual attribute), but sensitivity is stable or even increases for cognitive tasks; by *cognitive tasks* they simply meant identifying stimuli by their meaning (e.g., letters or numbers).

sensory *simultaneous* *successive*

cognitive

Judi See and her colleagues (See, Howe, Warm, & Dember, 1995) performed a meta-analysis to examine this question more carefully. A meta-analysis is a statistical technique that allows you to combine the results of many studies, even though they use different methods. The advantages of doing that are a little complicated; suffice to say that it gives you a better view of what is likely to be true, just as it is better to ask 1,000 people rather than 10 people whom they are going to vote for if you're trying to predict the outcome of a national election. The results of the analysis by See and colleagues made the story that much more complicated. Whether the task is sensory or cognitive does make a difference. For sensory tasks, sensitivity gets worse for simultaneous tasks and better for successive tasks. For cognitive tasks, it's just the opposite; sensitivity gets better for simultaneous tasks and worse for sensory tasks.

Why is that true? No one seems to have a clear idea of what's going on here. All we know is that vigilance is more complicated than we would like. Other factors may well play some role in the sensitivity drop, but even with all of these factors we can't predict with confidence whether a new vigilance task that has never been tried before will show a sensitivity drop. That's just saying that we can't predict how people will do on a task; that's not even trying to understand *why* they perform as they do. Thus, vigilance is a very important task because it is a part of many military and manufacturing jobs, but we know very little about it.

STAND-ON-ONE-FOOT QUESTIONS

12. What sorts of stimuli capture attention?
13. What is at the heart of ironic processes of mental control, according to Wegner's model?

QUESTIONS THAT REQUIRE TWO FEET

14. Suppose your friend had an ugly breakup with his girlfriend, and he finds he can't stop thinking about her. Try as he might not to think about her, he just can't stop. What would you advise him to do?
15. Apply the terminology from signal detection theory to car alarms and comment on the effectiveness of car alarms.
16. Some radar operators sit in deep silos watching radar scopes that monitor whether someone is sending a nuclear missile our way. Comment on the likely effectiveness of those radar operators and suggest ways to make them more effective.

Key Terms

attention
limited
selective
dual task procedure
continuous task
discrete task
response to stimulus
   interval
multiple resources
structural explanation
response selection
psychological
   refractory period

automatic process
target
distractor
pop-out
flanker effect
flanker task
early filter
late filter
dichotic listening
shadow
indirect measure
direct measure
galvanic skin response (GSR)

disjunctive search
conjunctive search
parallel search
serial search
preattentively
feature singleton
operating process
monitoring process
vigilance
sensitivity
signal detection
   theory
bias

4

Sensory Memory and Primary Memory

It is natural to think of memory as a storehouse—a repository for facts, rather like a library. To some extent, psychologists think of memory in that way, too, but as we'll see in later chapters, psychologists also think of memory as changes to the processes that use those facts. If you use the storehouse metaphor, it is natural to ask how new memories enter the storehouse. We address that question in chapter 5. In this chapter, we consider what happens to memories before they enter the storehouse. Psychologists refer to the storehouse as **secondary memory.** Secondary memory is the repository of information that is available to the cognitive system, but the information in secondary memory is not readily available for use by cognitive processes. For information to be used by cognitive processes, it must go from secondary memory to **primary memory.** Primary memory is a hypothetical buffer in which information can be briefly held; held for perhaps 30 seconds, if nothing is done to maintain it. For example, if I asked you "What color are polar bears?," the answer "white" would be in secondary memory, but this fact would not be available to cognitive processes (such as answering my question) until the information was retrieved from secondary memory and put into primary memory. Once it was in primary memory it would be available to the processes that construct the sentence to answer my question. Thus primary memory serves as a staging ground for thought. In addition, primary memory serves as a temporary buffer in which one can hold information. If you and I were in the grocery store and I asked you to get chocolate, bread, and margarine while I shopped for other things, you would maintain these three items in primary memory. This information needs to be maintained only briefly while the items are hunted down, so there is no need to enter them in secondary memory. Thus, primary memory both retrieves information from secondary memory, and takes in information from the environment, either for temporary maintenance, or possibly for entry into secondary memory.

If this description is accurate, we might first want to know how material gets from the environment into primary memory. The answer to that question turns out to be a bit complicated. When material in the environment is perceived it goes through another buffer (i.e., another memory system) before it ever gets to primary memory. This memory system is called **sensory memory.** Our first question, therefore, must be, **What is sensory memory?** As we'll see, sensory memory has a very large capacity—a great deal of information can rush into sensory memory simultaneously—but sensory memory is very short lived, lasting no more than a second.

Once we have some understanding of sensory memory, we'll be in a better position to consider primary memory. A key question that we would like answered is, **What are the characteristics of primary memory?** Researchers became interested in primary memory because it appeared to be fundamentally different from secondary memory. These differences should be reflected in characteristics of primary memory. We discuss three characteristics: how forgetting occurs in primary memory, how memories are represented, and the capacity of primary memory. As we'll see, it initially appeared that primary memory was easy to characterize on these dimensions, but it later turned out that primary memory was more complex than researchers had first appreciated.

Finally, we consider the question, **How does primary memory work?** In the second section we characterize primary memory, and in the third section we discuss two models of primary memory. The short-term memory model eventually was shown to be incorrect in several important ways, but it continues to be so important to cognitive psychology that some familiarity with it is necessary. The working memory model has been quite successful in accounting for a great deal of data. We close this chapter with some examples of how working memory contributes to cognitive processing.

➤ WHAT IS SENSORY MEMORY?

> ➤ PREVIEW The seeds of the study of sensory memory were planted by the introspectionists. Recall that they were interested in the contents of consciousness, and they were therefore interested in how much information could rush into consciousness in a brief exposure. They determined that people could perceive four or five complex stimuli (such as letters) in a very brief exposure. Participants in their experiments often reported that they felt as though they had perceived more letters but forgot some of them even as they were reporting the others. It was not until 1960 that psychologist George Sperling showed conclusively that many more stimuli are actually perceived but only four or five are reported because the remainder are forgotten. Sperling proposed the existence of a memory system that can hold a large number of items, but only for a second or so. In this section we consider the characteristics of sensory memory: how much information it can hold, the type of information it holds, how forgetting occurs, and so on. Later work showed that there is a comparable buffer for the auditory system that holds information for approximately one fourth of a second.

How much information can one take in simultaneously (i.e., perceive in an instant)? This question has been of interest since psychology's earliest days, and if you think back to chapter 1 and recall the program of the introspectionists, it makes sense that they would be interested in this question. Remember that they were trying to develop a mental chemistry for consciousness. Thus it was important to them to know how much information could get into consciousness at once. They called this measure the **span of apprehension.** Studies of the span of apprehension paved the way for the study of sensory memory because even though researchers were trying to study a purely perceptual process—how much information could be perceived in a very brief exposure—it seemed that memory processes nevertheless were involved in the tasks they used. We begin by briefly reviewing the span of apprehension studies, which will help you to understand why the first sensory memory studies were conducted.

Early Span of Apprehension Studies

An early study of the span of apprehension was conducted by Stanley Jevons (1871), a logician. Jevons took a small cup, dipped it into a bowl of black beans, and then tossed the beans onto a black tray, on which there was a small white box. Some of the black beans fell in the white box and some on the black tray. All of this Jevons did while looking elsewhere, so he had no idea how many beans would fall in the white box. Then Jevons glanced down at the box and estimated without hesitating how many beans were in the box. Then he counted them to see how close he was. He did this 1,027 times, and he found that if there were 3 or 4 beans, his instant estimate was always correct. With 5 beans he was still very good, but not perfect (about 95%). His accuracy dropped as the number of beans increased, so that if there were 15 beans, he was correct a little less than 20% of the time (Figure 4.1).

Jevon's Estimate	Actual Numbers												
	3	4	5	6	7	8	9	10	11	12	13	14	15
3	23												
4		65											
5			102	7									
6			4	120	18								
7			1	20	113	30	2						
8					25	76	24	6	1				
9						28	76	37	11	1			
10						1	18	46	19	4			
11							2	16	26	17	7	2	
12								2	12	19	11	3	2
13										3	6	3	2
14										1	1	4	6
15											1	2	2
Totals	23	65	107	147	156	135	122	107	69	45	26	14	11

Figure 4.1. *Results of Jevons's (1871) experiment.*

So what is Jevons's span of apprehension? You can see that it's difficult to come up with a number because his accuracy varied. If you think that his span is the maximum number of beans he could perceive reliably without error, his span is 4 because he began to make mistakes when there were 5 beans or more. That estimate seems a bit conservative, considering he was 95% correct when there were 5. On the other hand, you wouldn't want to say his span is 15 because he was right less than one fifth of the time when there were that many beans. The usual strategy in these situations is to take the 50% mark, where the participant was right half the time and wrong half the time. In Jevons's case, that put the span of apprehension at 9.

Naturally, Jevons's laboratory conditions could not be everything one would desire for such an experiment. The chief problem was that he had to rely on "a momentary glance" as his exposure to the stimuli, and it's possible that the duration of his momentary glance varied. Perhaps without meaning to, he glanced a little longer when there were a lot of beans in the box, for example. More sophisticated equipment became available by the 1920s that allowed precise timing of the exposure of visual stimuli. One such device is a tachistoscope, which uses a shutter like that of a camera to allow the participant to see the stimulus for a precise amount of time. Today such experiments are conducted on computers. A number of experimenters conducted span of apprehension experiments with better-controlled exposure durations (and substituting black dots on a white card for the beans). Their estimates of the span of apprehension were quite close to Jevons's; they averaged around 8.4, but the value varied between participants (Fernberger, 1921; Oberly, 1924; Glanville & Dallenbach, 1929).

These experimenters improved on one problem—controlling the duration of stimulus presentation—but there was another problem that they could not solve. They knew that they were not measuring the span of apprehension directly. They were measuring the span of what participants could apprehend *and* report, not simply what they could apprehend. For example, Douglas Glanville and Karl Dallenbach (1929) reported that some of their participants said that as they were reporting some stimuli, they were forgetting the others. One participant said, "Do not think that the judgment is often made during the exposure except when figures are few in number, or patterns are familiar. Otherwise I have meaning of pattern left from exposure and from that I figure out the number of forms on the card" (p. 220). A very popular textbook of the time (Woodworth, 1938) concluded that the span of apprehension must be somewhat higher than measurements showed, but how much higher was not known.

Sperling's Partial Report Procedure

It wasn't until 1960 that a better method of testing the span of apprehension was devised. George Sperling came up with the **partial report procedure** for the experiments in his Ph.D. dissertation. The partial report procedure gets around this problem of people forgetting some stimuli as they are reporting others. Sperling showed people an array of numbers and letters like this:

A	4	Q	I
B	9	6	Z
4	N	7	L

Actually, Sperling varied the number of items in an array: 12 was the largest number of items participants saw. Participants saw a display like this for 50 ms, and then had to report as much of it as they could. Sperling found that if the array had 4 items or fewer, participants got them all correct. If it had between 5 to 12 stimuli, they still got 4 items correct, on average. The span of apprehension is lower in this experiment than in Jevons's because Sperling used more complex stimuli that must be named (letters and numbers) rather than simple stimuli that are simply counted (dots, or beans in Jevons's case). As in earlier experiments, Sperling's participants said that they could see more items than 4, but forgot them quickly.

Sperling called that condition of the experiment full report, in which participants were supposed to report all the stimuli that they saw, and so far there is nothing new; participants reported about 33% of a 12-item array. The second condition was called partial report, and it worked as follows. Participants saw the display for 50 ms, as before. Then they heard a tone at one of three pitches: high, medium, or low. The pitch of the tone was a cue for which row of the display the participant was to report; participants didn't have to report the whole array, only the cued row. When the partial report procedure was used, participants got, on average, 3 items from the desired row correct. This result doesn't seem so exciting, but participants did not know which row they would have to report because the tone was random each time. Sperling reasoned that participants must have been equally prepared to report any of the three rows because they couldn't know which row they would have to report. It's the same logic that is used in classroom testing: A professor can't test students on all of the material that they are supposed to know, so the exam contains a subset of the material, and the professor assumes that students' performance on this subset of the material is a reasonable estimate of their knowledge of all the material. Therefore, Sperling figured that the percentage of the row participants got correct was a good estimate of their knowledge of the entire array. Participants got an average of 3 items correct (75% of the row) when the partial report procedure was used, so Sperling inferred that they knew 75% of the full array, or 9 items. So full report indicates that the span of apprehension is 4 items, but the partial report procedure indicates that it is 9 items.

If that were true, it would mean that participants perceive much of the array (about 75%), but they lose that information very quickly, either because it decays as soon as the stimulus is gone or because interference results from reporting the other items. Sperling tried another experiment in which he showed participants the array and then waited 1 s before presenting the tone that told participants which row to report. Now the partial report advantage was gone: participants averaged only 1 item (25%) out of the desired row, indicating that they

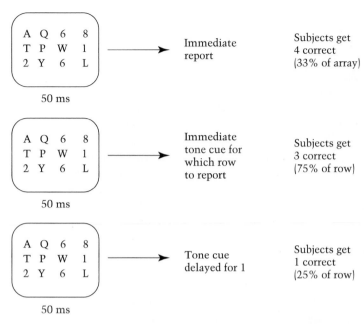

Figure 4.2. *The design and representative results of Sperling's (1960) experiment. Note that the partial report procedure (center) indicates that much of the array is perceived, but if the cue in the partial report procedure is delayed 1 s (bottom), much of the information from the array is lost.*

could report about 4 items out of the array, and 4 items is what they got in full report (Figure 4.2). Thus, it looks as if the material was lost through decay, not interference from report.

Sperling interpreted his results this way. He argued that when the array of stimuli is presented it enters **sensory memory.** Sensory memory has a large capacity, so it can hold all of the array, but the contents of sensory memory decays rapidly. The participant therefore rushes to report the contents of sensory memory, but even as he or she is reporting some letters, the others are fading, so that by the time the participant has reported 4 letters, the contents of sensory memory have faded altogether. (As a point of terminology, Sperling's term **sensory memory** later came to refer to any of a number of very short-term sensory buffers, including a visual buffer, an auditory buffer, and possibly others. The term *iconic memory* came to refer to the visual buffer, and we will follow that terminology here.)

Was it really accurate for Sperling to call this a type of memory? Couldn't we simply be dealing with visual afterimages?

ICONIC MEMORY VERSUS VISUAL AFTERIMAGES. Everyone is familiar with **visual afterimages:** If you stare at something for a while and then stare at a white wall, you will see an image of the thing you stared at. Figure 4.3 shows a

Figure 4.3.   *Stare at the center of the figure for about 30 seconds and then look at a white wall. You should observe a strong afterimage of a bearded man resembling Jesus. The visual aftereffect is real enough. It is not, however, "miraculous" as it is sometimes described to be, nor is it the source of iconic memory.*

picture that is widely disseminated on the Internet, and is sometimes presented as "miraculous."

Is iconic memory just a visual afterimage? No, visual afterimages are something else. Visual afterimages are retinal effects, meaning that they occur because of processes in the retina. Visual afterimages occur when some neurons in the retina essentially get "tired." If you keep your eye fixated on one location, light keeps hitting the same retinal cells with the same pattern of light. The neurons that are consistently hit by light slow their rate of response. The retina organizes these lower-level cells in functional pairs. Red is paired with green, and blue is paired with yellow.[1] Thus, if you stare at green circle for a long time, the neurons that respond to green light start to respond less and less vigorously. These green neurons are paired with red neurons, and because the green neurons are not firing at all, the red neurons are firing more by comparison. That's why visual afterimages are the opposite color of the stimulus that caused the afterimage.

[1]There are only three types of color receptors in cone cells, not four, but this is how it ends up working.

If iconic memory effects depended on visual afterimages, what would happen if you conducted a typical iconic memory experiment but used color patches as stimuli instead of letters? If the participants performed the task by using a retinal afterimage, they should report the colors incorrectly. But that doesn't happen. William Banks and Grayson Barber (1977) conducted an iconic memory experiment, closely following the method Sperling used, but their stimuli were color patches rather than letters. Participants saw three rows of four color patches flashed for 50 ms, and after a brief delay (0, 100, 250, 500, or 1,000 ms) they heard a high, medium, or low tone as a signal to report one row of colors (red, orange, green, blue, purple, or pink). The experimenters observed the partial report effect. Participants reported about 2.5 colors on average during full report, but the partial report procedure indicated that just over 5 colors were available in iconic memory.

Again, the accurate use of color information indicates that participants were not using an afterimage to perform this task, and we therefore infer that visual afterimages do not support iconic memory effects in other experiments.

We can fairly call iconic memory a type of memory, albeit a very brief one. We turn now to experiments that have explored the characteristics of iconic memory.

LARGE CAPACITY.   It's possible that iconic memory maintains most of what the perceptual system is presented with. It is certainly true that under some conditions, the capacity of iconic memory can be quite large, but the capacity definitely depends on the conditions. For example, Emanuel Averbach and George Sperling (1961) presented their participants with arrays of 18 characters and varied whether the participant saw a dark field or a light field before and after the letters. The results of this simple manipulation were dramatic.

Using the dark prefields and postfields has a huge effect on iconic memory. When the fields are dark iconic memory has a bigger capacity and it also lasts much longer: The icon is still available after a 2-s delay, whereas the icon is gone after 0.5 s with bright prefields and postfields. The bottom line is that the capacity of iconic memory can be large—it is 17 letters at the briefest delay with the dark fields—but the size and duration depend heavily on the details of experimental situation.

SPONTANEOUS DECAY AND POTENTIAL TO BE ERASED.   We've described the loss of information from iconic memory as one of spontaneous decay: Even if the participant does nothing and is looking at a simple white (or black) field, the contents of iconic memory will degrade. That finding is clear enough from Sperling's original experiments. The experimenter can also erase the icon; the technical term is to **mask** the icon, which means to present some random visual stimuli. The random visual material replaces the material currently in iconic memory.

In the early 1960s a number of studies showed that the partial report advantage disappears if the stimulus array is followed by a mask, consistent with the idea that the mask erases the contents of iconic memory (see Breitmeyer & Ganz, 1976, and Turvey, 1973, for reviews).

BRIEF DURATION.   As has been emphasized in our description of these experiments, iconic memory can hold a lot of information, but the memory is short-lived, perhaps as short as 500 ms and typically no longer than 1 s, depending on the experimental situation. But even under optimal circumstances, iconic memory lasts no more than 5 seconds, a far cry from other types of memory, which can last your entire lifetime.

REPRESENTATION.   Iconic memory initially was thought to be a rather literal representation of the physical characteristics of the stimuli. In other words, if the stimulus *A* is in iconic memory, there is no information about whether *A* is a number or a letter; iconic memory stores the physical shape of the stimulus, but nothing about what it means. It seemed that only physical characteristics were effective partial report cues. For example, Sperling's initial experiments used the physical location of the stimulus (top, middle, or bottom row) as the cueing characteristic, and that yielded a partial report effect. Other physical characteristics of stimuli seemed to yield cueing effects as well, such as the size of stimuli, where participants were directed to report either large or small stimuli (Von Wright, 1968). But when information about stimulus category was used ("report only the letters, not the digits") a partial report effect was not found (e.g., Sperling, 1960). Apparently one can't select material from iconic memory based on the category to which it belongs, so researchers concluded that iconic memory must not include categorical information.

During the late 1960s iconic memory seemed to fit rather neatly into the idea of how visual information is processed. The idea was that the perceptual system analyzes the basic forms of visual information and then passes it to iconic memory. Iconic memory can hold a lot of visual information, but the information is unprocessed. That means it contains only physical information about the appearance of objects but nothing about their meaning. Because the icon fades quickly, it is necessary to quickly get it into a more stable form that won't fade. One does that by focusing attention to some of the information in iconic memory, but it's impossible to focus attention to all of it. The information that is attended to is put into primary memory (at the time called short-term memory), where it will not fade so quickly. Once the material is in short-term memory, one has information about what the stimulus means, not simply how it looks. For example, the information that the stimulus form *B* is a letter becomes available. This view is summarized in Figure 4.4, and it does indeed hold together rather well. As new data came in, this neat picture became more complicated.

Further Work

The model in Figure 4.4 is useful, but further work elaborated and improved our understanding of some of the details of iconic memory. In particular, ideas about the mechanisms of decay and about the possibility of semantic representation in iconic memory were changed.

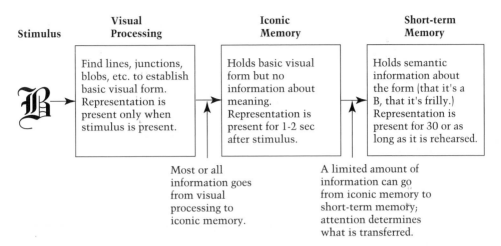

Figure 4.4. *This summary of the relationship of iconic memory to visual processing and to short-term memory was developed in the late 1960s. With two exceptions, it is still representative of current thought. The exceptions are that researchers now believe that iconic memory may hold some semantic information. Also, there is good evidence that the icon begins to fade at the appearance of the visual stimulus, not at its offset.*

It has become clear that iconic memory does not decay in the manner it was originally thought to. You would think that the icon would start to decay as soon as the stimulus disappears and that if the stimulus is visible for a longer time, it will have no effect on the decay of the icon or that, if anything, seeing the stimulus for a long time will make the icon decay a little more slowly. In fact, however, if you present the stimulus for a longer time, the icon seems to last a shorter time.

Vincent DiLollo (1980) demonstrated this effect in a compelling way. In this experiment participants knew that the basic stimulus was an array of 25 dots. They first saw 12 dots on a field for 10 to 200 ms. After a brief delay (10 ms) they saw another stimulus with 12 dots for 10 ms; thus, they saw a total of 24 dots out of the 25-dot array, and their task was to say which dot was missing. All that varied in the experiment was the duration of the first array. Surprisingly, errors increased when the first stimulus was presented for a longer time, as shown in Figure 4.5.

In a second experiment, Di Lollo presented a pattern mask (similar to the one shown in Figure 4.5) for a variable duration, and immediately thereafter a letter of the alphabet appeared for 20 ms. The participant's job was to identify which letter it was. Increasing the duration of the mask had the opposite effect than it did in the previous experiment: Participants were more accurate with increased duration of the first stimulus. Di Lollo interpreted the data this way. In the first experiment, iconic memory for the first stimulus was helpful; you needed to know where the dots were in both the first stimulus and the second stimulus to locate the missing dot. In the second experiment, iconic memory for the first stimulus hurt, rather than helped. The first stimulus was a confusing pattern mask.

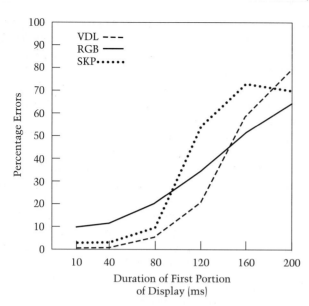

The surprising fact in both experiments was that the duration of the first stimulus had any effect at all. Researchers had been thinking that iconic memory was some effect of stimulation persisting in the visual system; thus, whenever the stimulus in the environment disappears, iconic memory begins to decay. In both of Di Lollo's experiments, however, it appeared that iconic memory began to fade when the stimulus first appeared, not when it was extinguished. Di Lollo suggested that iconic memory is based on perceptual processes that start when the stimulus is first presented. Whether that is the mechanism or not, it is true that iconic memory is sensitive to how long the stimulus has been present, not just how long it has been gone.

A second elaboration of the iconic memory concept came from experiments indicating that iconic memory does not code only the physical characteristics of stimuli. Philip Merikle (1980) pointed out that there is reason to be uneasy with such a conceptualization of iconic memory. The idea is that you get material into short-term memory by attending to material that is in iconic memory. But you don't know the meaning of what is in iconic memory—you know only what it looks like—so you have to decide where to direct attention without knowing the meaning of any of the things you might attend to.

Several experimental findings pose problems for the idea of an iconic store that contains no semantic information. First, consider the **flanker effect.** In one flanker experiment Geoffrey Underwood (1976) asked participants to identify simple line drawings copied from children's books (e.g., a bird, boat, or lemon). On some trials, a word was presented to the right of the drawing. Some of the words were semantically related to the drawing (for example, the word *juice* next to the drawing of the lemon) and some were not (for example, the word *nurse* next to the lemon), and some stimuli were nonword letter strings (e.g., the letter string *brape* next to the lemon). Participants were directed to ignore the words, but the words nevertheless influenced their performance. Participants took about 590 ms to name the line drawing in all conditions except the one with the semantically related words, in which they took an average of 617 ms. This slowing may have been caused by competition for naming between two closely related words. Whatever the source of the slowing, the result indicates that words participants try to ignore nevertheless affect performance, and this effect is based on meaning; therefore, this experiment indicates that information about meaning might be present in iconic memory.

Thus, these studies indicate that iconic memory does contain semantic information. Nevertheless, you'll recall that Sperling's original studies found that semantic cues yielded partial cueing effects, which are the hallmark of iconic memory. Later attempts to find partial cueing effects in iconic memory were only modestly successful (Merikle, 1980).

So in the end, does iconic memory contain semantic information? Researchers have not yet found a clear answer to this question, and the reasons for that may be inherent in iconic memory itself. It need not be the case that semantic content is either completely present or completely absent in iconic memory. The mixture of results we've seen on this topic may reflect the fact that semantic information is graded, or partly available in iconic memory.

What Is Iconic Memory For?

Ralph Haber (1983) presented a rather broadly based attack on the very idea of iconic memory. Haber argued that iconic memory doesn't *do* anything. We're constantly moving our eyes around, so a new stimulus is constantly knocking out the contents of iconic memory.

One idea about the use of iconic memory was that it is useful in exactly that way: It helps us keep a stable percept of the world, despite the fact that we're always moving our eyes. Haber argued that few data supported that idea, and later work showed that Haber was right: Iconic memory does not seem to be useful in maintaining stability when we make eye movements. For example, David Irwin, Steve Yantis, and John Jonides (1983) used Di Lollo's paradigm to examine this question. In their version of the task, participants saw 12 dots from a 5 × 5 matrix of dots, and then another 12 dots, and they were to say which single dot was missing from the matrix. The first matrix was shown to one side or the other of the center of the screen, and participants were to be looking at the center of the screen when it appeared. They were then to make an eye movement to the place at which the first matrix had appeared, whereupon the second matrix appeared at that location (Figure 4.6).

So the first array of dots appeared to one side or the other when participants were looking at the central fixation mark. Thus, the first array did not hit the fovea. The second array of dots did hit the fovea because participants had made an eye movement to the location of the first array. If iconic memory is useful for integrating information across eye movements, the fact that participants made an eye movement between the two arrays should not affect task performance because iconic memory should preserve the first array during the eye movement.

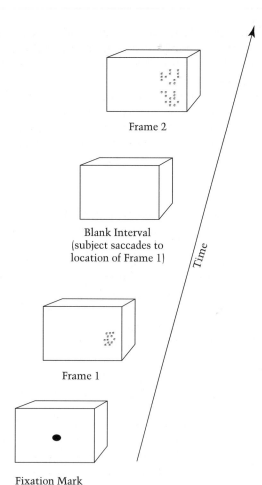

Figure 4.6. *Sequence of events in Irwin, Yantis, and Jonides's (1983) study of visual integration across saccades.*

The results showed that participants were completely at chance in locating the missing dot, indicating that iconic memory is not useful for integrating information across saccades. (Very similar results were reported by Rayner & Pollatsek, 1983. For a complete review of this work, see Irwin, 1993.)

If iconic memory is not useful for maintaining the constancy of the world across eye movements, what is it for? Haber suggested that about the only time iconic memory would be useful is if you're trying to read at night during an electrical storm.

Haber pronounced the icon dead (and urged authors to expunge it from textbooks), but researchers thought the announcement premature. Geoff Loftus (1983) argued that the apparent applicability of research to the real world is not an appropriate criterion. Loftus rightly pointed out that experiments under the rigorous control necessary to draw firm scientific conclusions may not bear much surface resemblance to the real world but that control is what makes the conclusions possible. There are no cyclotrons in nature, but they are crucial to our understanding of subatomic particles.

Most researchers agree with Loftus. It is true that we do not currently know what iconic memory does for the cognitive system. Nevertheless, the effects are robust and reproducible and thus provide important clues about how the visual system and primary memory interact. Therefore, it seems premature to ignore the work that has helped us understand these effects. Research on iconic memory has slowed a bit in the last 10 years, but it is still active, with researchers investigating issues such as whether iconic memory is actually composed of two separate aspects (Cowan, 1995) or not (Massaro & Loftus, 1996).

Echoic Memory

Echoic memory, quite simply, is the auditory version of iconic memory. (Again, *sensory memory* is a more general term. Iconic and echoic are both forms of sensory memory.)

There is good evidence for some storage of sound in the very short term. One source of evidence comes from masking experiments. These are conceptually similar to the masking experiments we discussed for vision. For example, Dominic Massaro (1970) had participants listen to a tone, which they were simply to identify as high or low in pitch. The task was made difficult by the presence of a masking tone (of random pitch) that followed the target tone. If the delay between the target and mask was rather long (350 ms), participants averaged about 90% correct, but if the mask followed the target without delay, participants averaged just 60% correct. Thus, just as visual stimuli can be masked, so can auditory stimuli.

As the interval between the target and the mask increases, the negative effect of the mask decreases, presumably because the auditory system has had more time to process the stimulus and get it into a more stable state (e.g., to transfer it to primary memory). Once the delay between the stimulus and the tone reaches 250 ms, the mask doesn't matter any more; it doesn't have any effect, presumably because 250 ms is how long it takes to get the target safely out of echoic memory and into primary memory. We can tentatively place the duration of echoic memory at 250 ms (Cowan, 1987).

This short duration of echoic memory is consistent with estimates from another task. If echoic memory makes auditory information available for a short time after the stimulus is no longer present, then people should overestimate the duration of very short sounds because the sound appears to persist after the actual stimulus has stopped. Robert Efron (1970a, 1970b) showed that this effect happens. He let participants control when a light came on and asked them to time the onset of the light with the offset of a sound. By that measure, participants consistently perceived a sound of 30 ms to last about 130 ms; in fact, 130 ms was their estimate for all sounds that lasted between 30 and 130 ms.

It appears that the auditory system keeps information around in some form rather briefly (250 ms or less), but other effects indicate that information can stick around much longer. For example, consider an experience you probably have had. A friend is speaking to you and you're daydreaming about something else. Suddenly you notice that your friend has stopped speaking, which indicates that it must be your turn to say something. You say, "What?" No

BOX 4.1. TRACKING AUDITORY SENSORY MEMORY

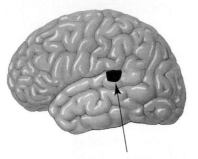 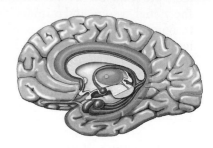

primary auditory cortex

Where does sensory memory come from? In one experiment Zhong-lin Lu and colleagues (Lu, Williamson, & Kaufman, 1992) gathered evidence that auditory sensory memory can be viewed as the lifetime of neural activity in primary auditory cortext.

Here's the behavioral task they used. Participants heard a test tone and then some time later (as little as 0.8 s or as much as 8 s) they heard a probe tone. They were to compare the two tones for loudness, pressing one of two buttons to say which tone was louder. Participants performed a total of 6,000 (!) such trials. Human performance on this task is well established. Performance gets worse as the delay between the test and the probe increases, and performance gets worse in a consistent way. As the delay after the test tone increases, people remember the loudness of the test tone as being average: If the test tone was loud, as time passes participants remember it as quieter, and if the test tone was quiet, as time passes they remember it as being louder. As they forget the test tone, their memory of what it probably sounded like drifts toward the average loudness of tones over the whole experiment.

The experimenters recorded activity in primary auditory cortex using magnetoencephalography (MEG). MEG is similar to electroencephalography (EEG) in that one records the activity of cortical neurons by placing recorders outside the skull, but MEG relies on magnetic properties of neural firing, whereas EEG relies on electrical properties. Like EEG, MEG provides mediocre spatial resolution but excellent temporal resolution.

The researchers examined the magnetic fields generated by the test tones and plotted the growth of the field over time. Using complex curve-fitting techniques they could estimate the amplitude of the curve, the lifetime of the field, and when it began to decay. In essence these are measures of when the neural signal begins to dissipate and how long it takes to dissipate.

The researchers used the participants' behavioral data to estimate how the echoic memory for the tone loudness lasted. Figure B4.1 shows these two values plotted against one another on a single graph. The experimenters tested four participants, and each dot represents data from one participant: Open squares represent trials in which the probe was louder than the test, and closed squares represent trials in which the test was louder than the probe. The important aspect

(Continued)

of the graph is the strong linearity of the data: A longer lifetime of activity in the neural trace meant a longer lifetime for the memory of the tone.

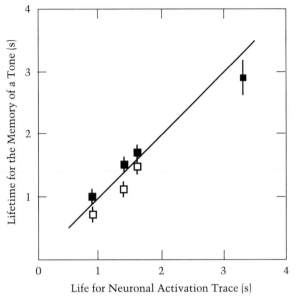

Figure B4.1. *Figure from Lu, Williamson, and Kaufman (1992) plotting neuronal activation against echoic memory of tone loudness.*

These data represent evidence that memory of the loudness of sounds over the course of several seconds is supported by transient activity in primary auditory cortex.

sooner is the word out of your mouth than you know what your friend just said. Because you were not attending to your friend's voice, what he or she said was not in primary memory. You realized you had to answer but didn't know what was said, so you said, "What?" But immediately thereafter you went to echoic memory, and the last few seconds of what your friend said was still there.

More formal data confirm this effect. Sam Glucksberg and George Cowen (1970) tested it this way. Participants wore headphones, and they heard different messages coming in through each earpiece. Participants had to shadow the message from one of the earpieces (i.e., they had to say aloud what they heard through that earpiece), and they were to ignore the other. Every now and then a light appeared, and participants were to say whether a digit had just been presented to the unattended earpiece. Obviously the idea is that when participants saw the light they would consult echoic memory to see whether a digit from the unattended earpiece was stored there. Participants were quite good at this task if the delay between the digit and the light was brief (300 ms): They got about

25% correct. As the delay lengthened they were worse: After 2.3 s they were at about 11%, and by 5.3 s the unattended items were lost. Still, there is a measurable effect of echoic memory a full 2 s after presentation of the digit.

Another effect indicating a longer estimate of echoic memory's duration is the **auditory suffix effect,** which indicates that echoic memory might be as long as 4 s. The auditory suffix effect takes a bit of explaining. Suppose I give you a list of 12 words to remember, and the way I present them is to read them aloud at a rate of say, 1 per second. Immediately, I ask you to recall the words. I can plot the probability of your getting a word correct by the **serial position** of the word; serial position refers to its position in the list, whether it's first, second, last, or whatever. An idealized serial position curve appears in Figure 4.7.

We'll talk about other features of the serial position curve in another chapter, but for the moment, just notice that the probability that participants will correctly recall the last word presented is very high. You can sort of imagine this: I'm reading a list of words to you, and I say, "Table, . . . carrot, . . . shoe," and then you're supposed to recall. "Shoe" naturally will be very fresh in your mind. One interpretation of "fresh in your mind" is that the last word is in echoic memory. Thus, when it's time to recall the words, you quickly report the word that's in echoic memory because it will fade fast. Robert Crowder (1967) reported that if the final item on the list is followed by another not-to-be-remembered word (a suffix), it dramatically reduces recall of the final word. In these experiments the suffix often is the word "ready" or "zero," and participants are told that they need not remember this word, but it is simply a cue that

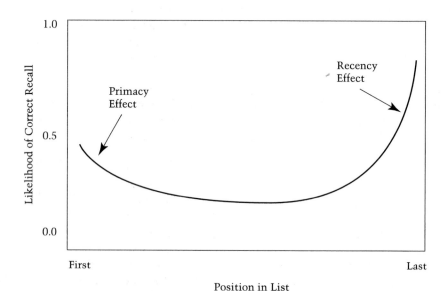

Figure 4.7.   *An idealized serial position curve representing recall of a list of items. Stimuli at the beginning of the list usually are remembered well (primary effect), as are stimuli at the end of the list (recency effect). Memory is worst for items in the middle of the list.*

they should start recalling the words on the list. Other participants heard a buzzer as their signal to begin recalling the list words.

The suffix has quite an impact on the recall of the final to-be-remembered word. The interpretation is that the suffix knocks the last to-be-remembered word out of echoic memory. Successful recall of the final word goes from about 95% when the buzzer signals recall to less than 40% when the suffix signals recall.

There are a number of interesting investigations of the suffix effect regarding its locus and so forth, but for the moment I want to emphasize its timing. The suffix has less of an effect as time passes, and is reduced (but not completely gone) if it is administered 2 s after the final word of the list. That makes it seem that echoic memory probably lasts a second or two, not the 250 ms that the other experiments seemed to indicate.

So how long does echoic memory last? The most likely interpretation is that the 250 ms estimate is correct, but this interpretation relies on the assumption that echoic memory is precategorical (i.e., does not contain semantic information). The suffix effect does seem to rely on semantic information, so if we are willing to assume that echoic memory should not contain semantic information, we would conclude that the suffix effect does not reflect the workings of echoic memory and therefore that our estimate of echoic memory's duration should be based on the other tasks.

There have been several clever studies indicating that the suffix effect relies on the meaning of the suffix. One was conducted by Ian Neath, Aimee Suprenant, and Robert Crowder (1993). Participants were told that they would hear a series of word lists that they were to repeat back. Half the participants were told that at the end of each list they would hear an animal noise, which was the signal that they should begin reporting the words, and that is what they heard— a recording of a real animal noise (dog or cow). The other participants were told that they would hear a person making an animal noise (saying "woof" or "moo"), and that was the signal to begin reporting. The critical stimulus was a third noise. This was a person imitating a sheep, and both groups heard the identical noise; half the participants thought it was a recording of a sheep, and half thought it was a person imitating a sheep. Surprisingly, the size of the suffix effect depended on whether participants thought they were hearing a real animal noise or a person making an animal noise. When participants thought it was a sheep, they remembered the final word on the list about 25% of the time. When they thought it was a person imitating a sheep, they remembered the final word on the list about 55% of the time (see Ayres, Jonides, Reitman, Egan, & Howard, 1979, for a similar effect). This result tells us that the suffix effect is not based simply on the similarity of the suffix and whatever was in echoic memory; it is strongly influenced by participants' interpretation of what they hear.

Given that the auditory suffix effect is not precategorical and that the auditory suffix effect yields an estimate of a rather long echoic memory storage time (2 s or so, as opposed to the 250 ms that other measures indicate), it seems reasonable to assume that the auditory suffix effect is not an effect of echoic memory. You should note, however, that this logic turns on our accepting that iconic memory is precategorical, and we don't know that with certainty. Indeed, we are not completely certain that iconic memory is precategorical.

Nevertheless, if the suffix effect does not result from echoic memory, there is an alternative interpretation; it may reflect the operation of a component of primary memory called the articulatory store. That interpretation fits within a particular theory of primary memory called working memory, and we'll get to it later in the chapter.

STAND-ON-ONE-FOOT QUESTIONS

1. *What is the point of the partial report procedure?*
2. *What are the characteristics of sensory memory?*
3. *Is sensory memory precategorical?*

QUESTIONS THAT REQUIRE TWO FEET

4. *Haber argued that there seems to be no function for iconic memory. Can you think of a time that you use iconic memory, however briefly? (Hint: think of the movies.)*
5. *In the "miraculous Jesus" afterimage shown in Figure 4.3, the picture you stare at is full of splotches and imperfections. How come Jesus doesn't look leprous in the afterimage?*

➤ WHAT ARE THE CHARACTERISTICS OF PRIMARY MEMORY?

➤ *PREVIEW* It has long been noted that it is possible to hold some information in mind for a brief period of time. For example if a friend mentions five things he or she needs from the grocery store, you can repeat them back immediately. In the late 1950s researchers began to think that such brief memories might be supported by a separate memory system. In this section we summarize what is known about three characteristics of primary memory: the source of forgetting, the format in which the information is coded, and amount of information that can be held (i.e., the capacity of the system). Both interference and decay appear to contribute to forgetting in primary memory. Primary memory can code material in terms of sound (acoustically), in terms of meaning (semantically), or in terms of visual appearance (visuospatially). In terms of capacity, about 2 s of acoustic material can be coded in primary memory, but the capacity in the other modalities depends on the specific material being used.

Impetus to Study Primary Memory

In this section we characterize primary memory on three dimensions: how material is lost from primary memory, how it codes material, and how much material it can hold. This work began in the late 1950s. In the late 1950s three articles were published, all considered classics today, that energized psychologists to study primary memory. The concept of a primary memory separate from secondary memory had been around since the late 19th century, but there had not been a great deal of research on the topic. These new articles triggered an avalanche of research activity during the 1960s, and primary memory remains a vibrant research topic today. Let's take a moment to consider what excited researchers so much in the 1960s; it was this excitement that led to the research we discuss in this section.

You may remember from chapter 1 that cognitive psychology was born in the late 1950s; that's when people were starting to conclude that the behaviorist approach to psychology wasn't going to work and that descriptions of hypothetical representations and processes in the mind were needed in order to explain human behavior. One of the important thinkers of that time was Donald Broadbent. Broadbent (1958) likened humans to an information processing system, perhaps similar to electronic information processing systems, and he is credited with being the first psychologist to propose a model that charted the flow of information through the mind. According to Broadbent, the flow of information starts with a large-capacity sensory memory (Broadbent called it the S system), after which information is filtered (i.e., much of it is lost) and then enters primary memory (Broadbent called it the P system). Information in primary memory is associated with consciousness, and this information fades if it is not actively rehearsed. Furthermore, information can enter primary memory not only from sensory memory but from secondary memory. Broadbent's particular model was less important than the fact that he put a distinction between primary and secondary memory at the heart of his information processing model.

A second influential article came from George Miller (1956). Miller's article emphasized two points. First, Miller stated that there seemed to be a fundamental limit or bottleneck in the human information processing system. Miller pointed out that across a number of tasks, the number seven kept popping up as a limit on human performance. The article was really about this limit to information processing, but it is almost always cited for its inclusion of the primary memory limit (as measured by the **digit span task**) of seven items, plus or minus two. Miller's second point was that there had to be a way around this limitation, and Miller suggested that one way was chunking. A **chunk** is a unit of knowledge that is decomposable into smaller units. Chunking is finding a way to treat several units as one unit, such as treating the letters *B, L, U,* and *E* not as four separate letters but as one word. Thus by chunking, one can include more information within the limited primary memory system; you can keep only seven letters in primary memory, or you can keep seven words containing many more than seven letters.

These articles by Broadbent and by Miller convinced researchers that primary memory was important to study. The third important paper gave researchers a method by which to study it. It was two papers, actually. Similar findings were published almost at the same time from two different laboratories: John Brown's (1958) in England and Lloyd Peterson and Margaret Jean Peterson's (1959) in the United States. The task they used is somewhat similar, so it is called the Brown–Peterson task. Both Brown and the Petersons were trying to gather evidence that primary memory was fundamentally different from secondary memory. It's not enough just to say, "There are two kinds of memory." You have to demonstrate that primary and secondary memory are different. One way that you could provide evidence of separate systems is to show that the two hypothetical systems operate differently. Brown and the Petersons sought to show that primary and secondary memory differed in the mechanism by which forgetting occurs. People were fairly sure that forgetting in secondary memory is caused mostly by interference, meaning that when you forget, the information is still in memory, but you can't get to it because other information in memory is interfering. Brown and the Petersons set out to show that forgetting in primary memory is caused mostly by decay, meaning that the information simply disintegrates.

Brown and the Petersons showed that participants forget even a very small amount of information over a very short delay if they are distracted. The task worked like this. The participant heard a trigram of three consonants (e.g., "TPW") and then a three-digit number ("529"). The participant's task was to immediately start counting backward by threes, beginning with the three digit number ("529, 526, 523 . . ."). After some delay (between 0 and 18 s) the experimenter stopped the participant's counting and asked him or her to report what the three consonants were. The point of the backwards counting was to prevent the participant from rehearsing the letters.

Naturally, three letters are well within the primary memory capacity of most participants, so when the delay was 0, participants were nearly 100% correct. But if the participant counted backwards for 18 s, recall dropped to around 10% (Figure 4.8). This result was rather surprising. How could you forget a simple thing like three letters in just 18 s? These results generally were interpreted as showing that information was lost from primary memory by decay. For information to stay in primary memory, it must be rehearsed actively. Researchers concluded that forgetting in primary memory was caused by decay. It was already generally believed that secondary memory forgetting was caused by interference.

These results were enough to convince many researchers that primary and secondary memory were fundamentally different. They therefore set about trying to characterize primary memory.

How Forgetting Occurs

The original experiments by Brown and by Peterson and Peterson were interpreted as showing that forgetting in primary memory occurs through decay. Further work showed that this conclusion was premature. Interference also contributes to forgetting in primary memory; in fact, it probably contributes to forgetting more than decay does.

There are actually two types of interference: proactive and retroactive. It turns out that both have an effect on primary memory, but we need to take a moment to define these terms.

Proactive interference occurs when older learning interferes with new learning. For example, suppose that you're trying to learn some French vocabulary words. Look at the two schedules in Figure 4.9.

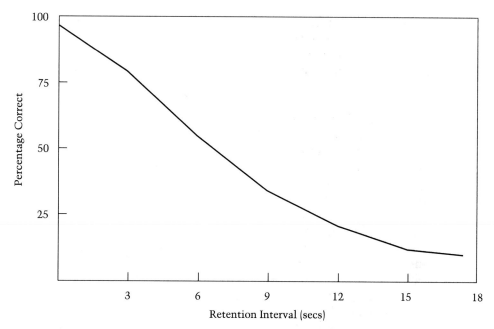

Figure 4.8.   *Results from Peterson and Peterson's (1959) study showing forgetting of very little information (three letters) after a very brief delay (18 s) if participants are distracted.*

In both cases, you study French vocabulary for an hour, and then take a test, but in one case you've just finished studying Spanish. You are likely to remember less French if you've just finished studying Spanish. That is proactive interference: Earlier learning interferes with new learning.

In **retroactive interference,** later learning interferes with earlier learning, as shown in Figure 4.10.

In this case, studying Spanish comes after the learning we are concerned with (French), so we would say that there is retroactive interference from learning Spanish. (Naturally, there is also proactive interference from the French learning on the Spanish learning in this case.)

Both proactive and retroactive interference are greater if the material studied is more similar. Thus, interference would be pretty bad if you were studying French and Spanish but not as bad if you were studying French and geometry.

8 am	9 am	10 am
Study	Study	Take
Spanish	French	French
Vocabulary	Vocabulary	Test
	Study	Take
Sleep	French	French
	Vocabulary	Test

Figure 4.9.   *If we compared performance on the French test, the people in the top row would show proactive interference compared to the people in the bottom row.*

8 am	9 am	10 am
Study French Vocabulary	Study Spanish Vocabulary	Take French Test
Study French Vocabulary	Sleep	Take French Test

Figure 4.10. *If we compared performance on the French test, the people in the top row should show retroactive interference compared to the people in the bottom row.*

Because similarity matters for the severity of proactive interference, we might expect that proactive interference could be strong in the Brown–Peterson paradigm. After all, participants have to remember consonant trigrams on each trial, and consonant trigrams are very similar to each other. Peterson and Peterson specifically addressed the issue of proactive interference by comparing recall performance in the early part of their experiment with performance late in their experiment. If proactive interference were having an effect, recall should have been worse late in the experiment, but it wasn't.

However, it turns out that proactive interference operates very quickly in this task. Peterson and Peterson should have looked at trial by trial performance instead of collapsing their data into "early" and "late." Geoffrey Keppel and Benton Underwood (1962) examined performance on the Brown–Peterson paradigm and found that even with an 18-s delay, participants average 95% correct on the first trial. On the second trial they average about 70% correct, on the third they are down to 55%, and by the sixth they are down to 40% correct. If forgetting in primary memory were caused simply by decay, there would be no reason for performance to be so good on the first trial with an 18-s delay.

Primary memory in the Brown–Peterson paradigm also is susceptible to retroactive interference. Judith Reitman (1971) found a clever way to demonstrate this fact. She reasoned that retroactive interference increases as the similarity of the new material to the old material increases. For example, there would be considerable retroactive interference if you first studied baseball statistics and then studied football statistics, but there would be much less if you first studied baseball statistics and then studied dance steps.

Reitman used the Brown–Peterson paradigm and had participants do one of two tasks during the delay. Either they had to listen to white noise (which sounds like a fan running) and try to detect a tone amid the noise, or they had to listen to a series of syllables ("doh") and detect when a target syllable "toh" appeared amidst the "doh"s. Because the to-be-remembered material was nouns, if primary memory is susceptible to interference, the "toh–doh" task should interfere more because it's verbal. That's exactly what Reitman found. People performing the tone detection distractor task averaged 92% correct recall of consonant trigrams, but people performing the "toh–doh" distractor task averaged 77% correct. That's not a huge effect, but if forgetting in primary memory were caused only by decay, there should have been no difference between the two distracting tasks because both prevented rehearsal.

What about decay? Just because there is interference doesn't rule out the possibility that there is also decay. It's certainly possible, but it's a rather difficult problem to study. If you want to test decay but avoid any possibility of proactive interference, you can test each participant only one time. On the second trial, there could be proactive interference from the first trial. You would therefore need to test hundreds of participants with one trial each to complete an experiment.

That's exactly what Alan Baddeley and Denise Scott (1971) did. They set up a camper in the middle of the University of Sussex campus and offered to donate a small sum of money to charity for each person who took part in their very brief experiment. The experimenters gave participants three, five, or seven digits to remember and then distracted them by having them copy dictated letters for 0, 3, 6, 9, 18, or 36 s. Some participants performed just one trial, whereas others performed many trials (the way the experiment is usually conducted), which allows proactive interference. Those data are shown at the left of Figure 4.11. The graph at the right is based on trials in which each participant performed only one trial, so that there is no opportunity for proactive interference. As you can see, the delay does have some effect, even when participants are tested only

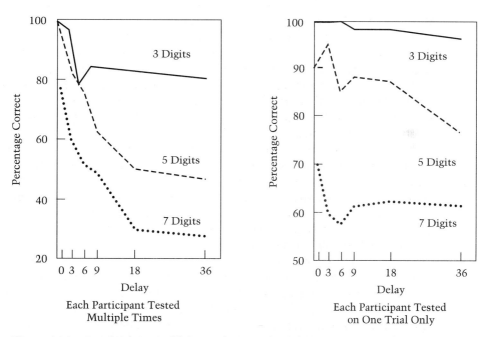

Figure 4.11. *Results from Baddeley and Scott's (1971) investigation of decay in primary memory. The graph on the left shows data from participants who were tested on multiple trials; proactive interference therefore could contribute to forgetting. The data show the usual drop in performance as the delay increases. The graph on the right shows data from participants who were tested on only one trial, so there was no opportunity for proactive interference. Note that as the delay increases, performance drops, indicating that proactive interference is not the only source of forgetting in primary memory.*

once (and therefore proactive interference is impossible). This is shown by the fact that recall drops as the delay increases. Recall drops for the three-digit and five-digit sequences, but not the seven-digit sequences.

Comparing the rate of decline as the delay increases shows that proactive interference is a big contributor to forgetting in this paradigm—the rate of decrease is much greater for the curves on the left—but when there is no opportunity for proactive interference, forgetting still occurs with a delay. This forgetting probably is caused by decay.

Thus, the final word on forgetting in primary memory is that interference and decay both contribute to forgetting.

Representation

At this point it appears that material can be coded in primary memory in a least three ways: visuospatially, acoustically (i.e., in terms of sound), and semantically (i.e., in terms of meaning). It took researchers a while to uncover these different codes, however.

Early research in primary memory seemed to indicate that everything was coded acoustically, and the type of coding was pointed to as a difference between primary and secondary memory: primary memory seemed to use an acoustic code, whereas secondary memory used a semantic code. As we'll see, that conclusion that these codes were unique to each memory system was premature, but the early work did establish that primary memory used an acoustic code at least some of the time. Alan Baddeley (1966) conducted a convincing experiment on this point. To get a feel for how it worked, try to remember two types of lists Baddeley gave to his participants. Read the following list aloud, look away from the page, and see whether you can recall it immediately.

MAD, MAN, MAT, CAP, CAD, CAN, CAT, CAP

That probably seemed pretty hard. Now try to do the same thing with a second set of words:

BIG, LONG, BROAD, GREAT, HIGH, TALL, LARGE, WIDE

And finally, try it with a third list of words:

COW, DAY, BAR, FEW, HOT, PEN, SUP, PIT

As you probably noticed, the first list contained words that sounded the same. In Baddeley's experiment, participants tried to remember short lists of five words drawn from the lists shown here, and they had 24 five-word lists from each of these master lists. When the words all sounded the same, participants could produce only 9.6% of the sequences perfectly. When the words were semantically similar (as in the second list), they could produce an average of 71.0% of the lists perfectly. When the words were neither acoustically nor semantically similar (third list), participants could produce 82.1% of the lists perfectly. Thus, there is a small cost to semantic similarity but a huge cost to performance when the words all sound the same. Baddeley concluded from this result that the words had been coded acoustically in primary memory.

The conclusion that an acoustic code was important in primary memory was especially strengthened by findings showing that if the experimenter presented words visually (e.g., written words), participants would automatically recode the words into an acoustic code. Conrad (1964) showed this in an ingenious experiment. He presented a series of six letters one at a time on a screen at a rate of one letter every 0.75 s. After the six letters appeared, participants were to write them down on an answer sheet, guessing if necessary. One twist was that only a subset of the letters of the alphabet were used: B, C, P, T, V, F, M, N, S, and X. Conrad was interested in what sorts of errors people made. If they didn't remember B, for example, would they just randomly put in one of the other nine letters? No. The errors people made were quite systematic, and they were based on the sound of the letters; making such errors is called the **acoustic confusion effect.**

For example, when M was presented in the stimulus, when people made an error they were very likely to recall it as N, which sounds like M, rather than recalling X or V, both of which look a bit like M but don't sound like it. To quantify this point, Conrad had participants read these 10 letters slowly into a tape recorder. Then other participants listened to the tapes, but with white noise (static) overlaid on the tape, so that the letters were difficult to understand. Conrad developed another confusion matrix for listening confusions, similar to the one described earlier for short-term recall confusions. He found that the pattern of confusions was quite similar. If people misheard M they usually mistook it for N. The important point of this experiment is that presentation of the stimuli was visual, but the recall confusions were based on sound. Thus, it seemed quite likely that participants spontaneously recoded the material from a visual to an acoustic code in primary memory.

Nevertheless, people do not use only an acoustic code in primary memory. Here is an example of when one might want to maintain some visuospatial information. Suppose I said to you, "I'd like you to imagine a 4 × 4 matrix of squares because that might help you in this next task. Suppose the upper right-hand cell is the starting square, and in that square, I'd like you to put a 1. In the next square down, put a 2. In the next square to the left, put a 3. In the next square to the left, put a 4." And so on. Then I ask you to reproduce my instructions to you. Almost everyone reports that they attempt this primary memory task using a spatial code.

One source of evidence that people code this information spatially comes from interference experiments. What would happen if one asked a participant to perform some sort of spatial task at the same time as the matrix task? Alan Baddeley and his colleagues (Baddeley, Grant, Wight, & Thomson, 1975) asked participants to do this primary memory matrix task while performing a pursuit tracking task in which they had to follow a little spot of light with a hand-held stylus. As you might expect, having to do this spatial tracking task played havoc with their primary memory in the matrix task. Performance went from an average of a little over two errors without the tracking task to about nine errors with the tracking task. How do we know that it was the spatial nature of each task that interfered with the other? The experimenters administered a second version of the matrix task that was not visuospatial, by replacing the words *left, right, up,* and *down* with *good, bad, slow,* and *quick*. The sentences become a little odd ("In the next square to the quick put a 2"), but that doesn't matter: The participant's job was to report back what the instructions were, sensible or not. In this version of the task participants didn't use a spatial coding scheme, and the tracking task had no effect on their performance; they made an average of about two errors, whether or not they had to do the tracking task at the same time. Again, the point of these experiments is to show that there is a visuospatial medium in which to maintain information for short periods of time.

The third type of code people use in primary memory is a semantic code: They can maintain information in primary memory about what things mean. A particular task paradigm has been used frequently to investigate semantic codes in primary memory. It's called release from proactive interference. We discussed proactive interference earlier in the chapter; proactive interference occurs when information learned earlier interferes with the learning of new information. Proactive interference is observed in the Brown–Peterson task by the fact that performance in remembering the letter trigrams decreases over trials. **Release from proactive interference** refers to the fact that the proactive interference dissipates if one changes the stimulus materials. For example, Delos Wickens and his associates (Wickens, Dalezman, & Eggemeier, 1976) used the standard Brown–Peterson paradigm, but instead of consonant trigrams, participants were to remember fruits (e.g., apple, pear, orange). All the participants performed three trials with fruits as stimuli, and on the fourth trial, different groups of participants received different stimuli. One group (the control group) received fruits as the stimuli again. Another group heard vegetables, another heard flowers, a fourth group heard meats, and a final group heard three professions as stimuli. As shown in Figure 4.12, there was considerable difference in the performance on the final trial.

Notice that the group that continued to hear the fruits performed the worst; they continued on the downward trend caused by proactive interference. The other groups showed varying amounts of release from proactive interference; the most dramatic improvement came from participants whose stimuli were professions, which are arguably the most different from fruits. This experiment constitutes evidence that primary memory codes semantics or meaning. If primary memory had not coded semantic content, the change in semantic content on the fourth trial would make no difference in performance.

In sum, there is evidence of at least three different types of codes in primary memory: acoustic, visuospatial, and semantic.

Capacity

How much information can primary memory hold? You may have heard the number seven mentioned as the capacity of primary memory. Around the turn of the century, researchers began to use the digit span task to measure the capacity of primary memory. In this task, the experimenter reads aloud a series of digits at a rate of one digit per second. The participant must repeat back the

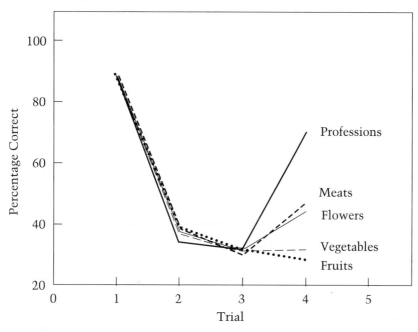

Figure 4.12. *Results from Wickens et al. (1976). All five groups used the Brown–Peterson paradigm for the first three trials with fruits as stimuli. Notice how performance declined because of proactive interference. On the fourth trial the stimuli changed for four of the groups. Notice that performance increased when the meaning of the stimuli changed. The reduction in proactive interference with the change in stimuli is called release from proactive interference.*

digits in the correct order. The experimenter increases the number of digits until the participant cannot repeat them back without error. Most adults can reproduce about seven digits. Average digit span often is described as "seven plus or minus two" to reflect the fact that people's performance varies, but most of us can recall between five and nine digits. Thus, an early view was that the capacity of primary memory was about seven. But we've just finished saying that primary memory can hold different codes. Might it not be the case that the capacity depends on the code? That does appear to be true. The capacity of the acoustic code seems best described in terms of time; the capacity is basically as much material as you can say to yourself in about 2 s. For the semantic code, the capacity is best described in terms of chunks, and the capacity of the visuo-spatial code has not been well described yet. We discuss each in turn.

An important clue to the capacity of the acoustic code comes from the **word length effect.** Participants can remember more words in a primary memory task if the words are short than if they are long. This effect was demonstrated by Alan Baddeley, Neil Thomson, and Mary Buchanan (1975). They gave participants a simple short-term memory task—listen to country names and repeat them back—and found that participants averaged 83% correct if the names were short (Chad, Cuba) but only 56% if the names were long (Somaliland, Australia).

To be certain that it was really the amount of time it takes to say the words and not some other factor that led to the differences, they conducted another experiment in which all words were matched in terms of the number of syllables and the number of phonemes. A phoneme is the smallest unit of speech sound (e.g., the sounds "buh" and "pa" are phonemes). For example, both "coerce" and "wicket" both have two syllables and they both have five phonemes, but it takes the average speaker about 0.8 s to say "coerce" and only 0.5 s to say "wicket." Comparing lists of short-to-say and long-to-say words, the experimenters found that participants got 61.6% of the long words correct and 72.2% of the short words correct.

What is the capacity of primary memory when a semantic code is used? In 1974, Herb Simon published an article on the capacity of primary memory. Simon tested his own primary memory using stimulus materials of different lengths. Simon found that he could remember about seven one- or two-syllable words but only six three-syllable words. He then tested his primary memory capacity using brief phrases with which he was familiar with such as "Milky Way" and "Lincoln's Gettysburg Address." Simon found he could remember about four of these phrases on average. Finally, he tried some long phrases, such as "Four score and seven years ago" or "To be or not to be, that is the question," and found he could remember three long phrases. These data are summarized in Figure 4.13.

What do these results tell us about the capacity of primary memory? Note that Simon could recall fewer three-syllable words than one-syllable words. This result is in line with the word length effect reported by Baddeley. But note that when words were knit into familiar phrases, Simon could maintain 22 words in primary memory. That seems too many words keep on his 2-s tape loop, and it indicates that these phrases were represented in terms of their semantic content.

Simon emphasized the importance of chunking in the capacity of primary memory. He could maintain more syllables in primary memory as the syllables were organized into chunks of greater size. Note that chunking rests on a semantic representation. Chunks typically are held together through the semantic relationships between their constituents. This is easy to appreciate in the stimuli that Simon used. The two-word idioms and the eight-word phrases have coherence as chunks because of the semantic relationship of the words. These semantic relationships are derived from secondary memory. Simon was

Size of Item	Syllables	Words	Chunks	Syllables Per Chunk
1-syllable	7	7	7	1.0
2-syllable	14	7	7	2.0
3-syllable	18	6	6	3.0
2-word	22	9	4	5.5
8-word	26	22	3	8.7

Figure 4.13.   *Results from Simon (1974). Simon tested just one participant (himself), but the results are representative. There are two important points to note. First, the capacity of primary memory when measured in syllables or words varies quite a lot, but it varies much less when measured in chunks, indicating that chunks is the right way to measure memory. Second, the amount of information per chunk makes a difference in capacity; as the number of syllables per chunk increases, the number of chunks recalled decreases.*

able to treat "Four score and seven years ago" as an effective chunk because he was familiar with that phrase; it was already in secondary memory. Thus, the capacity of primary memory when using a semantic code depends on the stimuli, specifically how easily they can be chunked. How easily they can be chunked depends, in part, on what is already in secondary memory.

What is the capacity of primary memory when a visuospatial code is used? A problem in measuring visuospatial capacity is the possibility that participants will recode the visuospatial materials to a verbal code. Researchers have tried to use materials that are not readily codable auditorily. In the Corsi block task (Milner, 1971), participants see nine black cubes, mounted on a black board. The cubes are arranged randomly (not in an array), which makes it more difficult for the participant to simply label them with numbers. The participant sits across a table from the experimenter. The experimenter taps some number of cubes in succession. The participant must then tap the same cubes in the same order. Thus, the task is quite similar to a digit span task but uses visuospatial stimuli. Neuropsychological tests show that patients with profound damage on auditory tests of primary memory nevertheless perform normally on this visuospatial test (Basso, Spinnler, Vallar, & Zanobio, 1982). Experiments with healthy young participants show that visuospatial span measured with this task consistently indicates a span of about six items (e.g., Sagar, Sullivan, Gabrieli, Corkin, & Growdon, 1988).

It seems likely that visuo-spatial information could also be susceptible to chunking. For example, suppose that I showed you nine lines and asked you to remember them. The two shapes in Figure 4.14 show the same nine lines, but they differ in their arrangement, and clearly, the one on the left would be easier to chunk and remember. Thus, it seems likely that one can chunk visuospatial information. Note that this sort of chunking is not based on semantic relationships but rather on spatial relationships, so it differs from the chunking Simon (1974) described. In chapter 8 we discuss visual imagery, which is closely related to visuospatial primary memory, and we'll have more to say about capacity limitations and chunking of spatial information in imagery.

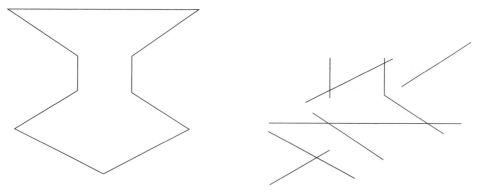

Figure 4.14. *Two figures, both containing the same nine-line segments. Clearly the figure on the left would be easier to remember because the lines can be chunked, based on their spatial relationships.*

In summary, the capacity of primary memory varies, depending on the code one uses. When an acoustic code is used, the capacity is limited by time (approximately 2 s). When the code is semantic, the capacity is flexible because meaningful units (chunks) can be unpacked. When the code is visuospatial there is again the possibility of chunking, and thus the limitation depends to a certain extent on the materials to be remembered.

In this section we have discussed three characteristics of primary memory: how forgetting occurs, the codes that are used, and the capacity. In the next section we discuss models of primary memory and how primary memory is used in cognition.

STAND-ON-ONE-FOOT QUESTIONS

6. What are the three representations in which primary memory may code material?

7. Why does forgetting occur in primary memory? Define each of the mechanisms you list.

8. Is it accurate to say that the capacity of primary memory is seven plus or minus two items?

QUESTIONS THAT REQUIRE TWO FEET

9. Baddeley and Scott offered evidence that forgetting in primary memory occurs even if you exclude the possibility of proactive interference by administering only one trial to each participant. Can you argue that there actually may have been proactive interference at work in this experiment?

10. In this section we discussed proactive and retroactive interference. (The example was studying French and studying Spanish.) Given that you must study more than one subject, it seems as though there is always going to be proactive or retroactive interference. What is the best way to minimize the effects of interference?

➤ HOW DOES PRIMARY MEMORY WORK?

➤ PREVIEW In this section we discuss two specific models of primary memory and discuss how primary memory contributes to cognition. One model (the modal model) is an amalgam of many closely related models proposed in the 1960s. It is now known to be incorrect in its details, but it has been so influential that it is important to be familiar with it. The second model is the working memory model, currently thought to be quite accurate in describing primary memory. We go on to discuss how primary memory contributes to cognition. One set of results examines how primary memory contributes to the recall of long lists of words. We also discuss working memory's contribution to general intelligence, reading, and the decline in cognition associated with aging.

Models of Primary Memory

The most important model of primary memory is Baddeley's working memory model (Baddeley, 1986; Baddeley & Hitch, 1974). Most researchers agree that this model provides a very good account of all of the data we've discussed in this chapter; indeed, much of it was collected to test the model. Another model, the short-term memory model, was so important in the late 1960s and early 1970s that a cognitive psychologist must be familiar with it. For that matter, the model was so important that the terms "short-term memory" and "long-term memory" seeped into popular culture. You may well already be familiar with those terms. Thus, although some aspects of the model are now known to be incorrect, we'll take a quick look at it.

SHORT-TERM MEMORY AND THE MODAL MODEL.   During the mid-1960s through the early 1970s a number of models of human memory were proposed that used the sensory, short-term, and long-term systems. The models had so many features in common that Bennet Murdock (1974) pointed out that one could construct a fairly clear description of memory simply by listing the properties that these models shared. He called it a **modal model,** after the statistical measure, the mode. The mode of a group of numbers is the number that occurs most often. This was not a criticism of memory theory at the time; Murdock was pointing out that there was general agreement among many researchers on the basic architecture of memory. The modal model is depicted in Figure 4.15. Some of the important models in this vein were proposed by Waugh and Norman (1965) and Atkinson and Shiffrin (1968).

The modal model emphasizes the flow of information through the cognitive system. Information enters from the senses to sensory memory. There may be sensory memory for each of the senses (e.g., olfaction and gustation), but we know that there is at least iconic and echoic memory. Some of the information is lost

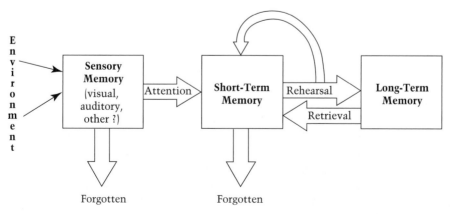

Figure 4.15.   *The modal model, showing sensory, short-term, and long-term memories and their interactions.*

from sensory memory, and some is passed on to short-term memory. Whatever you pay attention to in iconic memory is passed on to sensory memory.

Information in short-term memory decays after approximately 30 s if it is not rehearsed. If it is rehearsed, it can be maintained indefinitely. The amount of processing in short-term memory determines the likelihood that information will enter long-term memory; information that is processed longer in short-term memory is more likely to be encoded (passed on) to long-term memory. Individual models varied on exactly what sort of processing in short-term memory was likely to lead to entry into long-term memory.

Information can also enter short-term memory from long-term memory. Because short-term memory is the site of consciousness, this makes sense. The fact that you like maple syrup on pancakes but prefer lingonberry jam is in long-term memory but not short-term memory. When I ask, "What do you like on pancakes?" this fact is retrieved from long-term memory and enters short-term memory.

Finally, there is no arrow indicating forgetting from long-term memory. That's because forgetting from long-term memory was thought to occur via interference, not decay.

The modal model was shown to be incomplete or inaccurate in several ways. The description of rehearsal (the process by which material is transferred from short-term to long-term memory) was incomplete. It was proposed that short-term memory used only an acoustic code and that long-term memory used only a semantic code. It was also proposed that forgetting in short-term memory occurred primarily through decay.

Despite these inaccuracies, the very broad architecture of the modal model—sensory memory feeding into primary memory, which feeds into secondary memory—remains influential today. Nevertheless, as a model of primary memory it is lacking.

Working Memory

The basic architecture of working memory (Baddeley, 1986; Baddeley & Hitch, 1974) is fairly simple. There is a central executive and two slave systems: the phonological loop and the visuospatial sketchpad, as shown in Figure 4.16. Note

Figure 4.16. *Schematic showing the three basic components of working memory. Note that the central executive communicates with the other two components, which do not communicate with one another. The central executive controls the activity of the other two components.*

BOX 4.2. THE NEURAL BASIS OF WORKING MEMORY

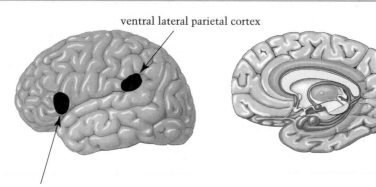

ventral lateral parietal cortex

Broca's Area

The phonological loop is said to have two components: the phonological store and an articulatory control process that "writes" material onto the phonological store. Eraldo Paulesu and his colleagues (Paulesu, Frith, & Frackowiak, 1993) conducted a study using positron emission tomography (PET) to localize the contributions of brain areas to these hypothetical processes.

Remember that PET studies often use a subtraction technique in which the activity associated with one task is subtracted from the activity associated with a closely related task. In this study, one task consisted of letters being presented on a screen to be remembered. Note that even though the letters were presented visually, participants have a bias to recode visual stimuli into an auditory code. In another task, participants were shown letters and asked to judge whether the letters rhymed (e.g., *Z* and *C*) or did not (e.g., *Z* and *K*).

The researchers reasoned that the memory task required participants to analyze the letters visually, translate the letters into sounds, rehearse them subvocally, and enter them in the phonological store. The rhyming task (because it requires an analysis of sound) uses these same processes except for entry to the phonological store; that is not required because participants are not asked to remember the letters, just to make the rhyming judgment. When the activations for the rhyming task were subtracted from the activations for the memory task, the researchers observed activation primarily in ventral lateral parietal cortex, an area strongly associated with language processing.

In another experiment, the researchers asked participants in both conditions to do a working memory task. In one condition the stimuli were English letters, as before, but in the other condition they were Korean letters. The participants did not speak Korean and could not recode the letters into auditory codes to be rehearsed via the articulatory control process. A subtraction of the activation from the two tasks showed that the English-letters condition led to significantly more activation in Broca's area, an area known to be crucial to the motor planning of speech.

In sum, this experiment successfully isolated the phonological store and the articulatory process that writes material to the phonological store.

that this figure shows only working memory, not its relationship to sensory or secondary memory.

The slave systems are storage buffers, and they are called slave systems because they do the central executive's bidding. The phonological loop allows the rehearsal of auditory information, and the visuospatial sketchpad allows the rehearsal of visual information. The central executive is in charge. It resolves conflicts over what cognitive process should happen next, it selects strategies for solving problems, and it coordinates information from multiple sources.

There are two differences between working memory and short-term memory that you can notice immediately. The first is the obvious inclusion of processes that are in service of cognition, not just in service of briefly maintaining information. Again, that reflects the idea that primary memory is a workspace as well as a short-term storage location. Second, note that there are separate storage locations for auditory information (phonological loop) and visual information (visuospatial sketch pad).

The **phonological loop** has two components: the phonological store and the articulatory control process. The **phonological store** can store about 2 s of auditory information. It is like a little tape loop lasting 2 s on which one can write auditory information. Information can enter the phonological store from the environment (e.g., I say a list of words aloud that I want you to remember). Information can also be entered into the phonological store via the second subcomponent of the phonological loop. The **articulatory control process** allows you to write information into the phonological store via articulation; it is literally the process of talking to yourself. Thus you would use the articulatory control process if I presented a written list of words to remember, and you wanted to keep them in the phonological store. The articulatory control process would recode the written words into an auditory code. The articulatory control process can also be used to refresh information that is already in the phonological store to keep it from fading.

In summary, auditory material can be stored on something similar to a 2-s tape loop. Material from the environment goes directly to the tape loop, or one can put material on the tape loop by subvocally rehearsing it (i.e., by talking to oneself). How is it known that articulation is involved?

One source of evidence for the articulatory nature of the phonological loop comes from **articulatory suppression** studies. The articulatory control process that writes material to the phonological loop is supposed to be very similar to speech. Therefore, you shouldn't be able to use it while you're speaking. If you're talking out loud, you can't put anything on your tape loop because the articulatory process is already busy. So suppose an experimenter made a participant talk while he or she performed a standard primary memory task. The experimenter wouldn't want the participant to have to think of what to say because that would require attention, so the participant might just say "blahblahblahblah" aloud while viewing words on a screen to be remembered. How would the participant approach this memory task? The words can't be coded acoustically because the articulatory control process is busy, so he or she would have to find some other way to code the words.

If the participant is not coding the words in terms of sound, that means that the acoustic confusion effect should disappear. You'll recall that it's hard to remember a list of words that sound alike (*mad, man, mat*). That effect does indeed disappear if your participants are made to say "blahblahblah" while they code the words. Participants remember words that sound alike (*man, mad, mat*) as well as they remember words that don't (*pit, sup, bar*) if they are saying "blahblahblah" aloud. That's because speaking aloud occupies the articulatory control process, forcing them to code the words in some way other than acoustically, so they are not susceptible to the acoustic confusion effect (Baddeley, Lewis, & Vallar, 1984).

You might wonder whether the effect is caused by the attentional requirements of saying "blahblahblah," even though it might seem that saying such a simple syllable repetitively would not demand much attention. The experimenters compared articulatory suppression with another simple task that did not require articulation: finger tapping. With that secondary task, they found that the acoustic confusion effect was still present.

Even though simple articulation will get material into the phonological store, simply listening to material, even if you are not trying to remember it, guarantees that the material will get into the phonological store. This is called **obligatory access** of the phonological store. For example, Herbert Colle and Alan Welsh (1976) tested their participants' memories for visually presented strings of letters with a short delay, either in silence or while listening to a tape of a foreign language they did not know. (It was a passage from *A Hunger Artist* by Kafka, in the original German.) Colle and Welsh found that there was significant interference from the speech; errors increased an average of 12%. The interpretation is that speech sounds gain obligatory access to the phonological store, even if you're trying to ignore them, and interfere with memory for the to-be-remembered consonant strings. (Many of us discover this obligatory access on our own; a 9-year-old might love to shout random numbers at a friend who is trying to remember a telephone number and to watch the friend sigh and return to the phone book to look up the number again.)

This obligatory access may well be the key to the suffix effect. You'll recall that this effect occurs when an extra not-to-be-remembered word is added to a word list and affects memory performance for the last word on the list. This effect was attributed to echoic memory, even though the suffix effect lasts several seconds, and other measures of echoic memory indicate that it lasts no longer than 250 ms. It may be that the suffix effect results from the workings of the phonological loop, not echoic memory.

The **visuospatial sketchpad** is conceived of as a visual analog to the phonological loop. It is a medium in which to keep visual or spatial information active. Earlier in this chapter we discussed evidence that people maintain spatial information in primary memory. (Remember the matrix task with sentences such as, "In the next square to the left put a 3.")

Baddeley proposed that spatial information (where things are) and visual information (what they look like) are separable in the visuospatial sketchpad. Remember that when we discussed perception in chapter 2, we discussed evidence that visual and spatial information might be handled separately in perception, so it might well be that they are also separate in the visuospatial sketchpad.

BOX 4.3. THE LOSS OF THE PHONOLOGICAL STORE

Baddeley's theory of working memory predicts that one should occasionally observe patients who have had a stroke resulting in a selective loss of the phonological store.

Giuseppe Vallar and Alan Baddeley (1984) examined one such patient, P.V. P.V. showed impaired performance on primary memory tasks that would typically rely on the phonological loop, such as remembering a sequence of letters that were read aloud to her. P.V. could remember only two or three letters and could reliably repeat back a sentence of just 6 words; normal performance would yield approximately seven letters and a sentence of approximately 16 words. P.V. performed markedly better if the letters were presented visually, so she seems to have adopted the strategy of maintaining the letters in a visual code. Neurologically intact participants usually recode these visual stimuli into an auditory code. Despite her poor performance in auditory primary memory tasks, P.V. was able to speak at a normal rate. Thus she seems to have had a selective deficit of the phonological store, but the articulatory control process was largely intact.

Aside from being unable to perform auditory short-term memory tasks, are there cognitive consequences of having lost the phonological store? Despite the fact that she could not repeat back all but the shortest sentences, P.V.'s use of language was normal in many respects. She could read individual words normally, she could discriminate speech sounds normally (e.g., "ba" vs. "da"), and she made rhyme judgments correctly. P.V. could also use syntax properly in simple sentence. For example, if shown a picture of a cat chasing a boy, she correctly selected the sentence, "The cat chased the boy," and rejected the sentence, "The boy chased the cat." When the sentences were longer, P.V. began to make errors, but only if understanding the sentences relied on keeping syntax in mind; if the semantics of the sentence could provide a guide, P.V. was unimpaired. For example, consider these sentences:

(A) Lettuce is the kind of person that one rarely meets in a schoolroom.
(B) The world divides the equator into two hemispheres, the northern and the southern.

Sentence A has been changed semantically: Lettuce is not a kind of person, obviously. Sentence B has been changed syntactically: The words *world* and *equator* have been reversed. P.V. had no difficulty rejecting sentences that were changed semantically (26 of 28 correct) but was impaired in rejecting sentences that had been changed syntactically (17 of 28 correct).

This experiment provides an important clue as to why we have a phonological store. Some sentences may have a complex syntax, and it may be difficult or impossible to unravel the syntax until one has heard much or all of the sentence. The phonological store allows the listener to maintain complex sentences in working memory so that the processes that decode syntax can get access to the entire sentence simultaneously instead of trying to decode the sentence word by word as it is perceived.

It's not easy to separate visual and spatial aspects of stimuli, but Baddeley and Lieberman (1980) came up with a clever way to do it. They had participants sit in a darkened room, blindfolded. There was a pendulum swinging before the participant, and on the bob of the pendulum was a little speaker emitting a tone (so the participant could figure out where the bob was). The participant had a flashlight, and the task was to shine the flashlight on the bob of the pendulum, which had a photocell on it, wired to change the pitch of the tone that the participant heard, thus providing feedback that the participant was tracking the pendulum successfully with the flashlight. If that doesn't sound difficult enough, the participant had to do the matrix task described earlier while doing this tracking task. The experimenters found that performance on the matrix task was compromised by this spatial (but not visual) tracking task. Other participants had to perform a visual (but not spatial) task. They compared patches of light and had to say which was brighter. This task did not affect performance on the matrix task much. Thus, we can say that the visuospatial aspect of primary memory may have dissociable spatial and visual components. As we'll see in chapter 8, a good deal of evidence has been collected showing that visual imagery can be primarily visual (what things look like) or spatial (where things are). There is less evidence on the separability of these two components in primary memory, but the existing evidence is consistent with that separation.

The **central executive** plays the role of cognitive supervisor and scheduler, integrating information from multiple sources and making decisions about strategies to be used on tasks. Less work has been directed toward elucidating the central executive. Baddeley (1996) commented that in some ways this research strategy could be compared to undertaking an analysis of *Hamlet* and spending all of one's energy on Polonius and ignoring Hamlet. By this Baddeley meant that the central executive is the most interesting part of working memory because its responsibilities are so great; it coordinates many cognitive activities. Baddeley commented that he chose to study the other components of working memory because they seemed more tractable, but he has turned his attention increasingly toward the central executive in recent years.

Baddeley has suggested that a model of attention proposed by Donald Norman and Tim Shallice (1986) may be a good starting point as a model for the operation of the central executive (Figure 4.17). In their model, there are two methods by which one coordinates cognitive activity (specifically, how one decides what action to take next). One method is based primarily on secondary memory, and it applies to situations in which an action is automatic. When the right stimuli are in the environment, they can trigger an action plan that is typically undertaken given those stimuli. For example, I don't need to plan to wash my hair when I get in the shower each morning; once I'm standing there under the water, I start washing my hair. Of course, at times there may be stimuli in the environment that would set up conflicting plans of action. Driving is an automatic process for many people, and steering the car so that it stays on the road is one automatic component of driving. The stimulus of the car beginning to edge toward the side of the road automatically triggers the behavior of making a corrective movement of the steering wheel.

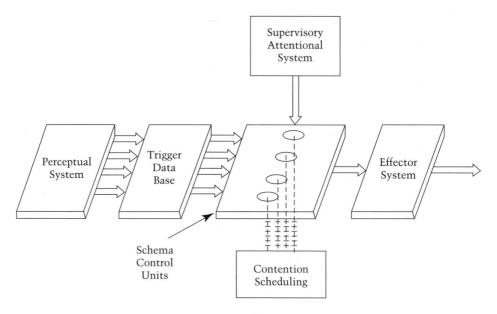

Figure 4.17.   *The Norman and Shallice (1986) model of attention.*

For many of us, eating is also largely automatic. Presented with a plate of French fries and ketchup, I can dip and eat fairly automatically. So if I'm driving and a friend in the passenger seat has some fries, why don't I automatically start eating her fries and end up sated but with my car in a ditch? The answer is that there is a process of **contention scheduling.** This simply means that there are rules by which the relative importance of two tasks can be compared and one of the tasks selected at the expense of the other. Such comparisons are made automatically and outside of awareness.

The second process of selection is the **supervisory attentional system (SAS).** The SAS is called on when one of several conditions is present: a task must be planned; the automatic processes appear to be having negative or unexpected consequences; a new, unfamiliar action must be taken; or a strong habit must be suppressed.

The model is too complex to go into much detail here, but a few interesting phenomena can be described. Donald Norman (1981) has been especially interested in action slips, in which you engage in a habitual response when it's inappropriate. You have doubtless had the experience of leaving a friend's house and driving to your home when you had meant to go to the store, or of getting 90% undressed before you realize you meant only to change your pants. In each case, you begin an action program (driving along a specific route, getting undressed) that must be altered midway through its usual course (turn toward the store instead of your house, stop undressing after you've taken off your pants), but this correction entails the action of the SAS. If the SAS is busy with other cognitive problems, the action plan will run on unimpeded, leaving you shirtless as well as pantless.

Experimental evidence supports this relationship between automatic schemata and the SAS. To study this relationship Baddeley (1966) developed the random letter generation task in which participants were simply asked to produce random letter strings. They were warned that they should not produce letter strings that spelled words (*CAT*) or acronyms (*NCAA, CBS*) and that they should try to mention all of the letters in the alphabet equally often. Participants had to produce letters at one of four rates: one letter every 0.5 s, 1 s, 2 s, or 4 s. The pace was set by a metronome. After the first 20 letters or so the task becomes quite difficult.

The interesting finding was that as the pace of production increased, participants produced more nonrandom letter strings. The relationship is quite orderly, with logarithmic increases in letter production speed being related to linear increases stereotyped responses.

Within the Norman and Shallice model we would say that letter retrieval is rather automatic, so that if you say "C" and then "B," you are more likely to follow with "S" than with something else. Therefore the SAS is constantly having to monitor output to ensure that this doesn't happen and to intervene when it is about to. As the pace increases, the SAS simply can't keep up, and more and more stereotyped responses slip by.

It may seem that the working memory model is not that impressive. It sounds as though it simply brings together or summarizes what we already know about primary memory. The fact is that much of what we know about primary memory is known because of the predictions of the working memory model, not the other way around. I presented all of the findings first and the model second because it's easier to understand that way. It was not the case that the working memory model summarized a bunch of facts that were already well known.

Primary Memory Contributions to Secondary Memory Tasks

In the next two sections we discuss how working memory contributes to cognition. In this section we talk about how primary memory has been helpful in accounting for experimental results from the often-used task of remembering a list of words. Most of this work was conducted in the 1960s, before the working memory model was proposed, so I use the more general term *primary memory* in this section, but working memory accounts for the findings equally well.

In the usual version of the task used in these experiments, the participant hears perhaps 16 words and immediately tries to recall them. Look at Figure 4.7, which shows an idealized serial position curve: a graph of the proportion of words correctly recalled on the *y*-axis and each word's position in a list on the *x*-axis. We've already discussed the fact that accuracy for the very last item on the list usually is good, probably because that last word is recalled from sensory memory.

You'll also note that accuracy is pretty good for the last few words in the list. That's called the **recency effect.** The last few words are still in primary memory when it is time to recall, so one's accuracy is very high for those words. You'll also note that the first few words on the list are remembered better than the words in the middle. This is called the **primacy effect.** The primacy effect occurs because the first words are more likely to enter secondary memory because you have more opportunity to rehearse them. We discuss rehearsal in chapter 5, but the point is easy to appreciate. Just consider that one method of rehearsal is to say each word to yourself. When you hear the first word, you begin to rehearse it ("bottle, bottle, bottle . . ."), and when you hear the second word you start saying both of them ("bottle habit, bottle habit, bottle habit . . ."), and so on. If participants are asked to rehearse out loud, this sort of repetition is what they actually do (Rundus & Atkinson, 1970). By the time the sixth word comes in, it can't be rehearsed much because the participant is trying to rehearse all of the words he or she has heard.

Here's a bit of evidence that the recency effect is caused by retrieval from primary memory. If it is, the recency effect should disappear if there is a filled delay after the last word on the list (as in the Brown–Peterson task). Murray Glanzer and Anita Cunitz (1966) conducted such an experiment. They gave participants lists of 15 words. Some participants recalled immediately after seeing the list, but others had to count backward for either 10 s or 30 s after seeing the list. The results are shown in Figure 4.18 and as you can see, when there was a filled delay after the list, memory for the final words was poor, but memory for the words early in the list was not affected.

In another experiment Glanzer and Cunitz tried to show that the primacy effect can be made more robust. They varied the amount of time between words: The words were presented at a rate of one per second, one every 2 s, or one every 3 s. The idea is that the slower rate should provide more opportunity for rehearsal of the early items, so the primacy effect should be stronger. The recency

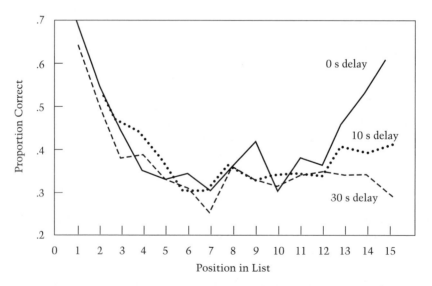

Figure 4.18.   *Results of Glanzer and Cunitz's (1966) experiment, showing that asking participants to count for 10 to 30 s after presentation of a list of to-be-remembered words affects their ability to recall words at the end of the list but not the beginning of the list. This result supports the idea that the recency effect is supported by primary memory.*

effect should be unchanged, however, because it relies on primary memory. Their results were broadly consistent with their predictions, although the advantage conferred on the primacy effect was not all that dramatic.

We initially outlined two important functions of primary memory: maintaining information over a brief period of time and providing a workspace for cognition. The contribution of primary memory to secondary memory tasks falls somewhere between these two functions; it is a contribution to cognition, but it uses primary memory specifically in its brief storage role. In the next section I review data that are more obviously examples of how primary memory serves as a workspace for cognition, and these data fit much more closely with working memory as a model of how primary memory operates.

Working Memory as a Workspace

A fair amount of work has been directed toward the role of working memory in cognition. Unlike the work examining the relationship of primary memory to secondary memory, this work has been more specifically within the scope of the working memory model. We review a few highlights here.

The phonological loop appears to be important in acquiring new vocabulary terms. In a number of studies (for a review see Baddeley, Gathercole, & Papagno, 1998) researchers have looked at the relationship between the size of the phonological loop and the number of words in the vocabulary of children in the early and middle childhood years. The size of the phonological loop is measured by digit span and by asking the children to repeat nonwords such as *loddernaypish*, which presumably can be repeated only if the child successfully maintains in the phonological loop the sounds that the experimenter utters. Vocabulary size correlates with digit span and correlates even better with nonword repetition: the correlations are on the order of .35–.60. (That's a big correlation.)

You might wonder whether this correlation is caused by a general effect of intelligence; maybe smart kids happen to have big vocabularies and also big phonological loops, but the big vocabulary wasn't *caused* by the big phonological loop. There is a statistical procedure called a semipartial correlation with which you can remove the effect of another variable (such as intelligence, in this case). Intelligence was measured by Raven's Progressive Matrices, a standard intelligence test that minimizes the contribution of verbal ability because it uses only figures. An example of a problem from the test is shown in Figure 4.19.

EXAMPLE FROM RAVEN'S PROGRESSIVE MATRICES INTELLIGENCE TEST. The test taker is to select which of the 8 figures at the bottom correctly fills the blank in the matrix at the top. Having a big vocabulary doesn't give you an edge on Raven's test. When you remove intelligence from the equation, the size of the correlation drops only slightly, down to around .30–.50.

Baddeley and his colleagues argued that the phonological loop is important for maintaining the sound of the word while more permanent long-term memory representations are being constructed. They argue that it is for that function that the phonological loop evolved. It is seldom useful to keep 2 s of speech available just so you can repeat it moments later. The real function of the phonological

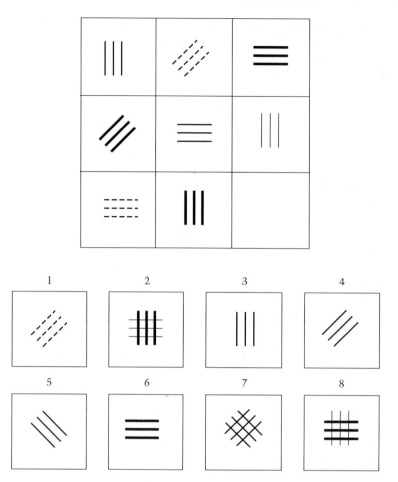

Figure 4.19. *Sample problem from Raven's Progressive Matrices intelligence test.*

loop, Baddeley and colleagues maintained, is to keep the sound of new vocabulary words around so that long-term memory representations of the sound can be developed.

Another example of working memory's role in cognition comes from an influential study by Meredyth Daneman and Patricia Carpenter (1980). They devised a task in which the participant must simultaneously manipulate and store information. In their task the participant hears a sentence (e.g., "The boy asked the bishop for the ball") followed by a question (e.g., "Who asked?"), which the participant must answer. Then another sentence is read and question about it asked, and so on. After, say, four such questions, the participant must recite the last word of each of the four sentences; thus, participants have to keep the last word of the sentences in mind while trying to listen to the new sentences and answer questions about them. The experimenter varies the number of sentences, and the final measure of working memory span is the greatest number of sentences in which the participant can answer all of the questions correctly and recite the last word of each sentence correctly. This measure of working memory span is an extremely good predictor (correlation = .72) of reading comprehension in college students.

You might think that this is because both tests require comprehension. Maybe it's not the working memory requirement of the sentence task that's critical but simply that it requires understanding sentences (as reading comprehension obviously does). But other research has shown that a working memory measure that uses math problems is an equally good predictor of reading comprehension (Turner & Engle, 1989). The interpretation of this high correlation is that working memory often is important in comprehending sentences during reading. This is especially apparent in sentences such as "The package dropped from the airplane reached the ground safely" (Fodor, 1995). In sentences like these, the grammatical structure of the sentence fools the reader. One thinks that "dropped" is the main verb of the sentence (as it would be in "The package dropped from the airplane safely"). In fact "dropped" must be interpreted as part of an adjectival phrase; "dropped from the airplane" tells you which package is being discussed. In such sentences, it is not until late in the sentence that you realize that you had misinterpreted the grammatical role of some of the words. Thus, if this material is still in working memory, you can reinterpret the early part of the sentence. If it's not in working memory, you must reread it. Thus, this is an example of a sentence in which a good working memory span might help reading comprehension. (This type of sentence is discussed further in chapter 12.)

A final example of the centrality of working memory in all varieties of cognition can be taken from the study of older participants in whom working memory is compromised. Older adults are somewhat impaired on many different reasoning tasks, such as the letter sets task in which the participant is asked to figure out which set of letters doesn't fit with the others in a stimulus like this:

NOPQ   DEFL   ABCD   HIJK   UVWX

Older adults also are impaired in other reasoning tasks, such as Raven's Progressive Matrices intelligence test mentioned earlier, and syllogistic reasoning (see Salthouse, 1992, for a review), which are the tasks in which you get two premises ("All As are Bs," "All Bs are Cs) and a conclusion ("All As are Cs") and you must evaluate the truth of the conclusion.

It turns out that age is not as good a predictor of performance on these tasks as working memory is. In other words, older participants are bad at these tasks because their working memory capability has gone down, not simply because they are old. You can tell this is true by looking at old people who happen to have a good working memory and young people who happen to have a poor working memory; given a reasoning task, who will do well and who will do poorly? Working memory, not age, determines performance. As I mentioned before, there is a statistical way to remove the effect of a variable from a correlation. There is a strong correlation between age and performance on Raven's Progressive Matrices Task (see Figure 4.20). The relationship between age and performance on this intelligence test ($r = .57$). That correlation drops

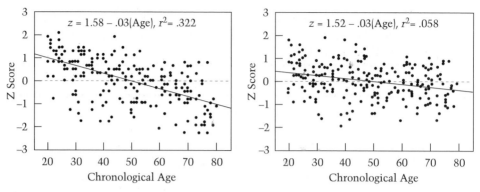

Figure 4.20. *Relationship between age and performance on Raven's Progressive Matrices Intelligence test.*

($r = .24$) once you statistically remove the effect of working memory. In other words, it's the decline in working memory with aging that drives the decline in scores on Raven's test (Salthouse, 1993).[2]

STAND-ON-ONE-FOOT QUESTIONS

11. *What is the difference between the terms primary memory, short-term memory, and working memory?*
12. *Describe the components of the phonological loop and how they operate.*
13. *We discussed three sources of evidence that working memory has an impact on other cognitive processes. Name at least two of them.*

QUESTIONS THAT REQUIRE TWO FEET

14. *Service people often thank me after they have done me a favor. For example, I will walk into a department store and ask someone at the perfume counter where the men's shoe department is, and she'll say, "Go to the back of the store in the left corner, past lingerie. Take the elevator to the fifth floor, walk straight ahead and turn right at the topcoats, and it's right there. Have a nice day and thank you for shopping with us." What's wrong with adding this last sentence?*

[2]Salthouse thinks there is a more fundamental mental process called processing speed. He has argued that the real problem in aging is a decline in processing speed and that the decline in processing speed is behind the decline in working memory capacity. Processing speed is defined simply as the speed with which cognitive processes operate, and Salthouse has interesting ways of measuring them (see Salthouse, 1996, for a review).

15. *Suppose that someone had brain damage that left him or her with almost no articulatory loop; his or her digit span was one or two items instead of the usual seven. How good would you predict the person's long-term memory to be?*

KEY TERMS

span of apprehension

partial report
  procedure

sensory memory

iconic memory

visual afterimages

mask

flanker effect

echoic memory

auditory suffix effect

serial position

digit span task

chunk

proactive interference

retroactive
  interference

acoustic confusion
  effect

release from proactive
  interference

word length effect

modal model

phonological loop

phonological store

articulatory control
  process

articulatory
  suppression

obligatory access

visuospatial sketchpad

central executive

contention scheduling

supervisory attentional
  system (SAS)

recency effect

primacy effect

5

Memory Encoding

In many ways, life would be so much simpler if memory were dictated by one's intention to remember—in other words, if you remembered the things you wanted to remember and forgot the things you wanted to forget. For example, you always want to remember people's names, so why can't you do it? Every time I go to a party, something like this happens. I'm introduced to someone new and I think to myself, "Must remember her name. That's Lisa." Five minutes later we're joined by someone else, and I can't remember whether I've been talking to Lisa, Bettina, Helga, or Jojo. So I can't introduce her to the new person who just joined us and I fall back on the lame "Uh, do you guys know each other?" (Then I'm embarrassed about having forgotten Lisa's name, so I don't even take advantage of the opportunity to really hear it again when they introduce themselves.)

Similarly, we all have things we'd like to forget. I could live the rest of my life quite happily without the memory of certain moments at junior high dances, but those memories seem branded in my brain, and they pop into consciousness, unbidden, usually at moments when I would pay cash money for them to lie dormant.

In chapter 4 we were thinking of primary memory as a gateway to the storehouse of memory. It's always possible that I wasn't really paying attention when Lisa first said her name—I was thinking that my shirt was wrinkled, or I was wondering whether I had something in my teeth—and I never really had "Lisa" in primary memory. But let's assume for the moment I did. Why didn't it get into secondary memory, even though I wanted it to? Apparently something is not guaranteed to go into secondary memory just because you want it to. What determines whether something will be entered into the memory storehouse? **What determines what we encode in memory?** Researchers have examined a number of different factors, such as whether the material engenders emotion or how often the material is repeated. It turns out that whether something is stored depends on what you do with it; roughly speaking, if you think about something hard, and seem to use it, the mind figures that you may need to use this material again, and so it is stored. A precise definition of what it means to "think about something hard" turns out to be tricky; we discuss some of the possibilities in this chapter.

This answer leads naturally to a second question: If whether you remember something depends on how you think about it, what determines how you think about it? **Why do we encode things as we do?** The answer is that how you think about something depends, in large measure, on what you already know about it (your prior knowledge). To take an extreme example, suppose you overheard someone in a restaurant say, "Zut! Qu'est-ce que cet petit singe a laissé dans ma chaussure?"[1] If you don't speak French, you might think, "Oh, someone over there is speaking a foreign language," and you'd probably forget the incident. If you did speak French you would probably be rather curious to know what was happening at that other table and would think about the incident a lot. Prior knowledge is crucial to how you process new experiences and therefore to the likelihood that you will remember them later.

The third question one might ask about encoding is whether encoding is the endpoint of the memory process. **What happens after we encode something?** Does

---

[1]"Hey! What did that little monkey leave in my shoe?"

the memory just sit quietly in its own private corner of the storehouse, waiting until it is called upon? The answer is "no." As you no doubt know, forgetting occurs—memories fade—which would make us suspicious that something is happening inside the storehouse. I discuss forgetting in chapter 6, when we talk about memory retrieval. In this chapter, an odd and mysterious process called consolidation is discussed. It's a process whereby, without being encoded again, memories in the storehouse become stronger and more stable as time passes.

➤ WHAT DETERMINES WHAT WE ENCODE IN MEMORY?

> ➤ PREVIEW In the first part of this section we discuss four factors that researchers have examined as possible influences on encoding: whether the material brings an emotional response, how often the material is repeated; whether you relate the material to other things you already know, and how much effort you expend thinking about the material. It turns out that the third of these factors—the extent to which you relate the material to things you already know—is the most important factor in encoding.
>
> In the second part of this section we explore this factor in more detail. The description of this factor probably sounds a bit vague to you, and getting a clear definition has been a problem. We also discuss the relationship between what you think about at encoding and what you think about at retrieval. The match between the two turns out to be important to memory.

Factor 1: Emotion Engendered by the Material

If you tried to think of factors that might influence memory, a starting point might be to speculate that something will get into secondary memory if it is important to you. "Important to you" might mean emotionally significant. As we'll see in this section, emotion has some influence on memory, there is no doubt about it, but the effect is not huge. Another lesson to be drawn from this area is that certain questions (such as whether emotion affects memory) are difficult to answer because it is difficult to set up an effective experiment; we spend a fair amount of time in this section detailing the difficulties in conducting this research.

LABORATORY STUDIES OF EMOTION AND MEMORY. Suppose that emotion does make things more memorable. That would fit with my junior high dance trauma. But perhaps that sort of memory is fairly unusual; maybe most people's memories from childhood aren't particularly emotional.

Research by David Rubin and Marc Kozin (1984) indicates that many childhood memories are emotional. They asked people to report their clearest memories from childhood. People tended to describe birthdays, car accidents, early romantic experiences, and other experiences that are likely to have high emotional content. Nevertheless, such evidence is not really airtight. Something other than emotionality could make such events unusually memorable. For example, my junior high dance memories (I'm obsessing, I know) may be memorable because people kept reminding me about the events leading to the memories. The fact that the events were traumatic didn't make the memories special, but it did make the events worth repeating over and over, and it was the repetition that made the events memorable.

The difficulty is that if when one studies real-life events such as birthdays or early romantic experiences, the experimenter has no control over how emotional the memories are, how often they are repeated, or any other characteristics because the experimenter didn't set up the events. Maybe birthdays are well remembered not because they are emotional but because they are distinctive; it's one day out of the year on which you are the center of attention, which is rare for a kid.

Another way to do a study is for the experimenter to create the events; that way the experimenter can control their emotionality, how much they are repeated, and so on. That procedure allows the experimenter to make stronger conclusions about the role of emotion and other factors. Here's why. When you study real-life events such as humiliation at a dance, you are studying things as they already exist; thus, if the dance is an emotional experience and it's one that people talk about a lot, then you're studying people's memory of an event that was emotional and was repeated a lot. But you don't want to know the effect of an event being emotional and talked about a lot; you just want to know about emotion. The heart of the problem is that you have no control over what people do in this situation. If they want to talk about the dance humiliation, they will.

A number of studies have sought to examine the effect of emotion on memory by conducting experiments in the laboratory that compare emotional and nonemotional materials. By conducting an experiment in the laboratory, the experimenter has much better control over what people think about and how often they think about it, unlike real-world situations. What the experimenter wants to do is compare people's memory of stimuli when the stimuli lead to strong emotion with their memory of the same stimuli when they do not lead to strong emotion; the experimenter wants everything to be the same except the emotion. That way it's certain that any difference in the memorability of the stimuli is caused by the emotion, not some other characteristics of the stimuli. But how can exactly the same set of materials be emotional for one group of participants and nonemotional for the other?

This problem is very difficult. For example, Alafair Burke, Friderike Heuer, and Daniel Reisberg (1992) used a slide show in which the emotional and unemotional stimuli were not identical but were designed to be similar. They showed participants a brief slide show about a boy visiting his father at work. At the start and end of the slide show, identical slides were used; the slides in the middle differed in the two conditions. In the emotional condition, the father was a surgeon and participants saw graphic slides of surgery. In the nonemotional condition, the father was an auto mechanic, and participants saw slides of the father working on a car. The surgery slides were better remembered, and the surgery slides surely engendered more emotion than the car slides, but it's possible that they differed in other ways (distinctiveness or complexity, for example). The experimenters did their best to match the slides from the two conditions, but it's impossible to *know* whether the slides differed only in the amount of emotion they engendered.

Larry Cahill and Jim McGaugh (1995) took a clever approach to this problem. They used the surgery slides from the emotional condition Burke et al. (1992) used. For the nonemotional condition, Cahill and McGaugh used the same slides but created a different story to go with the slides: They said the boy visited his father and the hospital personnel happened to be practicing emergency procedures at that time. In one of the critical slides, participants in the emotional condition were told that they were seeing a slide of the boy after surgeons had reattached his feet to his legs. Participants in the nonemotional condition were told that they were seeing an actor made up to look injured.

Two weeks later participants returned, expecting to see another set of slides, but instead they took a test of their memory of the first set of slides. (Participants were first asked whether they had expected a memory test, even though they had been told about it, to ensure that participants hadn't been rehearsing the material. All participants said that they hadn't expected the test.) In the first test, participants were asked to recall as much of the story as they could, both the general story line and specific details. Their responses were tape recorded so that they could be scored later. The scorers judged that a specific slide was remembered if the participant mentioned a piece of information that could be known only from having seen the slide and not from the story or from one of the other slides.

Figure 5.1 shows the results. The story was divided into three phases for analysis. The first phase (three slides) and third phase (four slides) depicted the

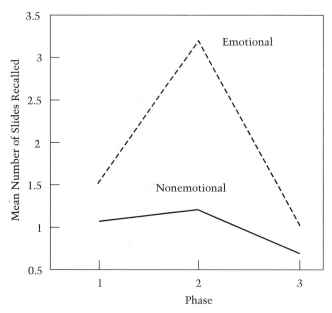

Figure 5.1. *Data from Cahill and McGaugh's (1995) experiment. The slide show participants saw was divided into three phases. All participants saw the same set of slides, but some heard a story about the slides that made the slides during Phase 2 much more emotional. These participants remembered the Phase 2 slides better on a later test.*

BOX 5.1. EMOTIONAL PROCESSING AND RECALL OF EMOTIONAL INFORMATION

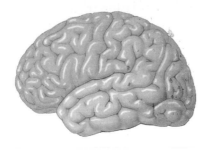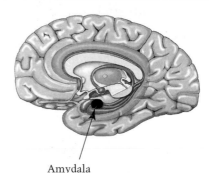

Amydala

Larry Cahill and his colleagues have shown that an emotional experience is more memorable than one that is not emotional. In this experiment, they showed that if one examines just emotionally charged stimuli, the degree to which participants respond emotionally to the stimuli predicts how well those stimuli will be remembered later (Cahill et al., 1996).

Cahill and his colleagues showed participants two videos, separated by several days. Each video contained 12 video clips that another group of participants had previously rated as either emotional events (e.g., violent crime) or unemotional events (e.g., a court proceeding). Participants viewed these clips while their brains were imaged using positron emission tomography (PET). Three weeks later they returned and were asked to recall all of the film clips.

As predicted, participants recalled more of the emotional film clips than the neutral film clips, replicating previous work in this area. Even more interesting were the results of the PET imaging analysis compared with the behavioral data. The researchers found a very strong relationship between the amount of activity in the right amygdala as participants watched the emotional film session and the number of clips that they recalled. This relationship does not mean that the amygdala is important for memory per se, however. Right amygdala activation observed during the neutral film sessions was unrelated to the number of neutral films recalled. Indeed, the amygdala is known from other work to be involved in evaluating stimuli for emotional content, especially fear and disgust. Thus, the amygdala appears to modulate memory based on its evaluation of the emotional significance of an event. The amygdala appears to evaluate only fearful and disgusting events. Other brain areas evaluate the significance of other types of emotional events, and they may modulate memory on the basis of those evaluations.

arrival and departure from the hospital, respectively. The second phase comprised five slides and showed the graphic surgery slides. As the graph shows, memory is equivalent in the two groups during the first and third phases, which were unemotional for both groups. Memory of the slides is the same during these phases, but it is much better for the emotional group only during the second phase. (It looks as if memory is slightly better for the emotional group in the first and third phases as well. Although the average recall is a bit higher, the difference is not **statistically significant.** The concept of statistical significance is very important in interpreting results from experiments. (If you're not familiar with it, see the explanation in the Appendix.)

This study does an excellent job of isolating the effect of emotion from other possible characteristics of stimuli, and it shows quite convincingly that emotion does make things more memorable.

We might wonder, however, about the strength of the emotion in this experiment, and indeed, the strength of emotion in any experiment. Seeing slides of surgery is upsetting, to be sure, but events that touch us as individuals are likely to be more upsetting (Eich & Macaulay, 2000). Would the effect of emotion on memory be stronger if we were examining events that affected the participants more than a slide show? We know it's difficult to study memory for events such as birthdays and first dates, but perhaps we're missing something important by ignoring them.

In fact, there is a rich literature on people's memories of highly emotional events that happen outside the laboratory. This literature initially led to the conclusion that this level of emotion had a profound impact on people's memories— so profound that a special memory process was proposed to be engaged during moments of great emotion. Later experiments indicated that that probably was not true, but the impact of these studies was great, so they are worth reviewing.

FLASHBULB MEMORIES.   If you want to study highly emotional events, you can't do so in the laboratory. It's simply not ethical to make people feel extremes of emotion by telling them that they are the lucky millionth participant to be tested in the laboratory and that at the end of the experiment they will be presented with a Ferrari. It would be ethical if you gave them the Ferrari, I suppose, but the billionnaire eccentric enough to support this experiment has not yet stepped forward. Thus, if you want to study the effect of high levels of emotion, you must study events that occur naturally in people's lives.

We've already discussed the fact that each memory is unique; I might remember my birthday well, but how comparable is that to your birthday? Each person's life events are different and carry different amounts of emotion and have other characteristics that differ. Does a single emotional event ever happen to a large group of people? Such events do happen, as when something tragic is covered in the national news, such as the death of a beloved public figure, and researchers have studied people's memories of such events.

Roger Brown and James Kulik (1977) were the first to conduct such a study. They asked participants to remember where they were when they heard that president John Kennedy had been assassinated. They found that participants reported surprisingly detailed memories; participants were confident that they could remember details such as what they were wearing, exactly where they were, who told them, the words that were used, and so on. Brown and Kulik called them **flashbulb memories.** A flashbulb memory is a very rich, very detailed memory that is encoded when something that is emotionally intense happens to you. Flashbulb memories have three special characteristics, according to Brown and Kulik: they are very complete, they are accurate, and they are immune to forgetting.

Brown and Kulik suggested that a special memory process is responsible for flashbulb memories. In times of great emotional duress, there is a "NOW PRINT" process that takes a memorial "snapshot" of whatever is happening at the moment of great duress. This process operates only when emotion is very high.

This all sounds pretty reasonable. The problem is that it is very difficult to assess whether people's flashbulb memories are accurate. Perhaps people want to think that they would remember highly emotional situations, and that means they set a low criterion for how confident they have to be before they think it's a memory. In other words, they want to believe that they remember hearing about Kennedy being shot, so any vague thing that they sort of remember is accepted as being a real memory. How could we check that possibility? Ideally, you'd like to compare people's memory of how they heard about Kennedy's assassination right after they heard the news with their memory a year or so later. That way, you could test whether flashbulb memories are accurate and immune to forgetting.

Michael McCloskey, Cynthia Wible, and Neal Cohen (1988) found a way to conduct such an experiment. When the space shuttle *Challenger* exploded, they realized that this event could cause flashbulb memories. Three days after the *Challenger* exploded, they administered a questionnaire to 45 people asking where they were when they heard the news, who told them, and so on. About 9 months later they tracked down 27 of the original 45 and gave them the questionnaire again. Flashbulb memories are supposed to be detailed, accurate, and immune to forgetting, so the second report should have looked quite a lot like the first. Twenty of the 27 participants gave more general answers than they had the first time, and 7 gave more specific answers. In addition, 7 of the reports were inconsistent across the two occasions (a participant may have said he or she was sitting at a desk on the first questionnaire, whereas on the second questionnaire the person said he or she was walking down the hall). McCloskey et al. concluded that there is no need to postulate a special mechanism (such as the "NOW PRINT" mechanism) to account for flashbulb memories. We may remember some events quite well—note that in the McCloskey et al. experiment, none of the reports were hugely different the second time—but flashbulb memories don't seem to have the special properties they were first thought to have. They are not complete, accurate, and immune to forgetting.

It may be fitting to close this discussion with a story about flashbulb memories told by Ulric Neisser, often considered the father of cognitive psychology. He reports that he had a flashbulb memory of hearing the news that Pearl Harbor had been bombed. He was listening to a baseball game on the radio when an announcer interrupted the game with the news. Neisser remembered where he was sitting, what the announcer said, and so forth. Only years later did he realize that it was extremely unlikely that he was listening to a baseball game because Pearl Harbor was bombed on December 7th, and baseball isn't played in December.

So what's the upshot on emotion and memory? There is good evidence that the emotionality of an event does affect how memorable it is, but there is not good evidence that a special mechanism takes over for flashbulb memories.

Furthermore, we know that emotion can't be the only factor determining whether you remember something. You remember plenty of things that are not emotional. You probably felt no great passion when you learned the Pythagorean theorem, but you memorized it nonetheless. In fact, many things you remember are not only nonemotional but completely pointless. "Gimme a break, gimme a break, break me off a piece of that Kit Kat bar"—I don't particularly like or hate that ad, but I remember it. Why? Not because it's emotional, but probably because I've seen it hundreds of times. Now we're back to repetition. Although repetition may not be behind the superior memory of emotional events over nonemotional events, does repetition affect memory on its own?

Factor 2: Repetition of the Material

Suppose that the likelihood that something makes it into the memory storehouse is based on how often you see it. Stimuli in the environment that are repeated a lot should be remembered. But consider this: You think you know what a penny looks like, right? Can you say, with confidence, right now, which way Lincoln faces? Try it. Where is the date written on a penny? Does the phrase "In God We Trust" appear on the front of a penny?

Raymond Nickerson and Marilyn Adams (1979) showed 36 college students the 15 versions of a penny as shown in Figure 5.2. Participants were asked to select which penny was most likely the right one and then to rate the other drawings as (1) "could easily be right, if my choice proves wrong;" (2) "might possibly be right, if my choice proves wrong;" or (3) "definitely not correct."

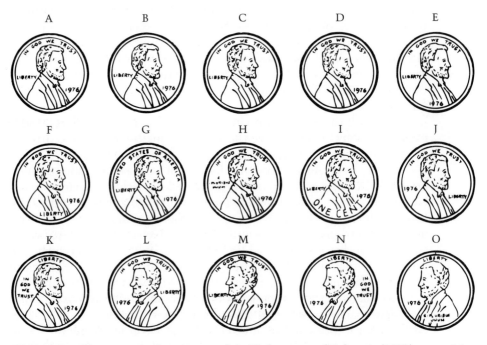

Figure 5.2. *Fifteen penny drawings used in Nickerson and Adams's (1979) recognition memory test.*

Less than half of the participants (15 of the 36) correctly picked A. Twelve thought it could easily be right, 4 thought it might be, and 5 were sure it was wrong. Pennies E, G, and J were popular choices.

In another experiment, Nickerson and Adams found that people's memory for a penny was still worse if they were asked to draw the penny from scratch instead of picking it out of a lineup. For example, 90% forgot to put the word "Liberty" on the penny, and half of the participants had Lincoln's head facing the wrong way. Why? Obviously the participants had seen thousands of pennies in their lifetimes. Shouldn't they at least have known which way Lincoln was facing and be absolutely 100% confident that they knew it? We have all seen thousands of pennies, but you seldom, if ever, really notice which way Lincoln is facing, what's written on it, or any of the other details. When you are looking through your handful of change in search of a penny, what you're thinking is, "I need the brown one." Pennies are distinguished from other coins by color, not by the way Lincoln is facing. Dimes are the small ones, not the one with Roosevelt on them, quarters are the big ones, and nickels are the biggish ones with smooth edges. You have had thousands of exposures to pennies but each exposure amounted to little more than, "Oh good, I've got a brown one, so I won't get four brown ones in change."

Nickerson and Adams's (1979) experiment gives us an important clue to memory. Sheer repetition of a stimulus in the environment won't necessarily lead to its being encoded in memory because presenting the stimulus does not guarantee that the participant will think about (or even notice) all aspects of the stimulus; participants note the color and size of pennies and little else, so that's the information about pennies that ends up in secondary memory. What gets into secondary memory is what you think about. Thus when we speculate that "repetition" is important for memory, it may be that repeated thought about the object is crucial to encoding the object into memory, not repeated exposure to the object.

But what does it mean to think about something a lot? One way to define that would be to say that you think about something a lot if it stays in primary memory a long time.

Fergus Craik and Michael Watkins (1973) conducted an experiment to determine whether keeping a word in primary memory for a longer time made it more likely that the word would be encoded into secondary memory. They told participants that they were going to hear a list of words and that they were to remember the last word on this list that began with a particular letter (e.g., g). Participants didn't know when the last g-word would appear, so they always had to keep in mind the last g-word that they had heard. The smart strategy would be to listen to the words and silently rehearse the most recent g-word until another g-word came up and then silently rehearse that one. So the list might be "radio, giraffe, nurse, game, dog, nutcracker, hotel, squirrel, giant, rake, stapler." Presumably the participant would rehearse "giraffe" until he or she heard "game" and then rehearse that until he or she heard "giant." Note that how long the participant would rehearse a word would depend on how many non–g-words intervene until the next g-word. Thus, "giraffe" would be rehearsed less than "game." By systematically varying how much participants rehearsed each word, Craik and Watkins varied how long participants kept each word in primary memory, so if time in primary memory is crucial to encoding, we should see systematic differences in later memory of the g-words.

Participants heard 27 such lists, each with 21 words. After the last of these lists, Craik and Watkins asked participants to recall every single g-word they had heard in the experiment. This test was unexpected, so naturally participants' recall was poor, but the important thing is that how long a g-word had been in primary memory (i.e., how long they had rehearsed it) had no effect on participants' long-term memory of that g-word.

Clearly, the amount of time a word resides in primary memory, which is the same as how much time you spend thinking about the word, is not the critical determinant in whether the word is encoded.

Factor 3: Depth, or Thinking About the Meaning of the Material

Craik and Watkins showed that time in primary memory is not the key to "thinking a lot" about something. Indeed, Craik argued that the distinction between primary and secondary memory was overemphasized. Craik and Robert

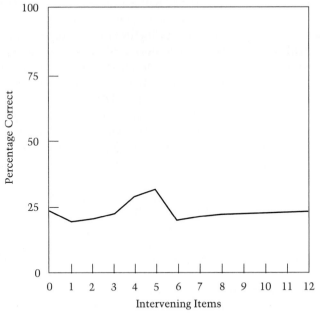

Figure 5.3. *Craik and Watkins (1973) had participants listen to a series of words, only some of which they were supposed to attend to. They could thus get participants to keep words in primary memory for different lengths of time by varying the number of to-be-ignored items intervening between the to-be-attended items. The length of time a word was in primary memory had no effect on how well participants remembered it on a later test.*

Lockhart (1972) proposed an alternative called the **levels of processing framework.** This framework for understanding memory proposes that the most important factor determining whether something will be remembered is the **depth of processing.** Depth, according to Craik and Lockhart, refers to greater degrees of semantic involvement, and semantic involvement means thinking about what the word means and how its meaning relates to other words. Thus **deep processing** involves thinking about the word's meaning. For example, if you answered the question, "What do you think of when I say the word *rose?*" you would be engaged in deep processing of the word. My question would force you to think about what the word means and what the concept *rose* is associated with in your memory. You might think that a rose is a flower of romance, that roses are fairly expensive, that they are found in formal gardens, that they have thorns, that they have a nice scent, and so on. All of these thoughts are concerned with what the concept *rose* means. **Shallow processing** refers to thinking about surface characteristics of the stimulus. For example, if you answered the question, "How many syllables are in the word *rose?*" you would be engaged in shallow processing. This questions does not encourage you to think about anything related to the meaning of the concept behind the word; it encourages you to think about the physical properties of the word itself. Another question that would encourage shallow processing would be, "How many vowels are there in the word *rose?*" or, "Is the word *rose* printed in uppercase or lowercase letters?"

As implied by the term *level of processing,* we don't categorize processing simply as deep or shallow; there can be degrees of depth of processing as well. At least that is supposed to be true in theory. As we'll see in a moment, specifying slightly deeper or shallower processing has proven difficult, and that's a weakness of the framework.

In an experiment, depth of processing can be manipulated by having the participant answer a question about a word. The following table lists four levels of processing that are progressively deeper. This table comes from a series of experiments by Craik and Endel Tulving (1975), who sought to gather evidence for the levels of processing framework set out by Craik and Lockhart. As you can see, the question the participant must answer about the stimulus word

Level of Processing	Question the Participant Must Answer	Sample Stimulus for Which Participant Answers "Yes"	Sample Stimulus for Which Participant Answers "No"
Structural	Is the word in capital letters?	TABLE	Table
Phonemic	Does the word rhyme with *weight?*	Crate	Market
Category	Is the word a type of fish?	Shark	Heaven
Sentence	"He met a ____ in the street."	Friend	Cloud

would lead the participant to think about different properties of the word (e.g., what the printed version looks like or what it sounds like).

Depth of processing has a huge effect on people's ability to remember under most testing conditions (but not all, as we'll see later). Figure 5.4 is a graph based on an experiment reported by Craik and Tulving (1975) using the four levels of processing shown in the preceding table. Participants were told that the experiment was one of perceptual processing, not memory. On each trial of the experiment, participants heard a question such as, "Does the word rhyme with *cake?*" Participants saw a word flashed in a tachistoscope for 200 ms and then had to answer the question as quickly as possible by pressing one of two buttons to indicate "yes" or "no." Participants performed 40 such trials and after a brief rest were presented with a surprise recognition test. The experimenters didn't want participants to actively try to remember the words because then participants would bring their own strategies to the task, and Craik and Tulving wanted to control the type of processing the participants did. Participants' performance on the recognition test is shown in Figure 5.4.

The levels of processing framework holds that deeper processing leads to better memory. At first it might seem that doing the deep processing is just harder. Maybe your memory is better simply because you put more work into it in the first place. But Craik and Tulving (1975) tested that possibility by conducting an experiment in which the shallow processing condition was very difficult. Before each word was presented the participants saw something like

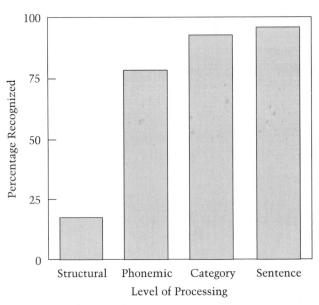

Figure 5.4.   *The basic levels of processing effect, showing that words that are processed more deeply are better remembered than words that are processssed more shallowly.*

"CVCCVC" (where "C" meant consonant and "V" meant vowel). Then they saw a word (e.g., *WITCH*). Participants had to say whether the word had the pattern of vowels and consonants specified by the first stimulus. This task was difficult; it took participants much longer to answer this shallow processing task than to perform the deep processing task (the sentence task). Nevertheless, shallow-processed words were recognized 57% of the time on a later test and deep-processed words were recognized 82% of the time. So deeper-processed words are not better remembered simply because deep processing takes more effort.

A number of researchers besides Craik and Lockhart (1972) touched on notions similar to levels of processing, but these researchers focused more on different types of rehearsal. Many distinguished two types of rehearsal (Cooper & Pantle, 1967; Craik & Watkins, 1973; Woodward, Bjork & Jongeward, 1973) most commonly called **elaborative** and **maintenance rehearsal.** In elaborative rehearsal one connects new material to things already in secondary memory, and that is proposed to be good for memory. In maintenance rehearsal, one just keeps repeating material to oneself again and again (today we would say keeping it in the articulatory loop of working memory), and that doesn't make it likely that it will get into secondary memory. For example, in the g-word experiment, participants were just doing maintenance rehearsal, so they remembered few of the words.

Craik and Lockhart's (1972) distinction of shallow versus deep processing goes further than the elaborative versus maintenance distinction in a couple of ways. First, shallow processing may include thinking about the physical characteristics of the stimuli, not just repeating them to oneself over and over again. Second, the levels of processing framework emphasizes that memory is a function of the processing of the material; whether one is trying to remember the material is unimportant. Notice that elaborative and maintenance rehearsal are types of rehearsal, implying that one is trying to remember. Levels of processing explicitly says that effort to learn is irrelevant. Is that really true? We noted at the beginning of the chapter that wanting to remember something doesn't guarantee that you'll remember it (if it did, you'd remember everyone's name at a party because you want to remember them) but is it true that intention to learn has no effect on memory at all?

Factor 4: Effort to Learn the Material

In the previous section, the research indicated that depth of processing contributes to better memory because it makes you focus on the semantic content of material (i.e., its meaning), not because it is more effortful to do deep processing.

Perhaps we should not dismiss effort as a possible influence on encoding. Certainly, some teachers believe that effort to remember is important; why else would they exhort students, "Remember this!" We need to examine research that has looked directly at the effect of effort to learn on memory.

Research on levels of processing was crucial in showing that memory is not affected by effort to learn. Most of these studies used what are called incidental memory tests. An **incidental memory test** is one in which the participants are not expressly told that their memory will be tested later; rather, they are just told to do something to the words (such as answer a question about them). Then later they get a surprise memory test. If the experimenter tells the participants that their memory will be tested later, it's an **intentional memory test.** For an intentional memory test, the researcher assumes that participants will engage in some processing that the participants believe will be effective for memory.

In depth of processing experiments, researchers used incidental tests because they wanted to see the effect of different types of processing on the words (deep vs. shallow), and they didn't want the participants dreaming up their own sort of processing to do on the words, which they might do in an effort to remember them for an upcoming test. The experimenters wanted control over the processing that participants did.

Suppose we wanted to test the effect of the participants' expectation of a later memory test. We could simply tell half the participants that they will later be tested and not tell the other half. Thomas Hyde and James Jenkins (1973) conducted exactly that study. In their study, participants saw a list of 24 words, one at a time, for 3 s each. Participants were to perform one of two tasks for each word that they saw: They were to determine whether the word contained the letter *a* or *q* (shallow task) or to rate the pleasantness of the word (deep task). "Pleasantness" simply means that if the word makes you think of pleasant things (e.g., "daisy") you give it a high rating, and if it makes you think of unpleasant things (e.g., "grave") you give it a low rating. Half the participants doing the deep processing and half the participants doing the shallow processing were additionally told that their memory of the words would be tested later (intentional condition); the remaining participants were not told about the upcoming memory test (incidental condition).

The results showed that whether the test was incidental made no difference in participants' performance on the memory test, as shown in the Figure 5.5.

Wanting to remember something doesn't help your memory. All that matters to your memory is whether you do the deep or the shallow processing.

At the beginning of the chapter we said that intention to learn was not a guarantee that you'd remember something. That might be true, yet it could still be possible that wanting to remember it would have some effect (make it more likely that you'd remember it), even if it wasn't a guarantee. The Hyde and Jenkins (1973) study shows that intention to learn has no effect at all. Depth of processing is all that matters.

Interim Summary

We've discussed four factors that researchers have examined closely for their effect on memory: emotion, repetition, depth of processing, and effort. The overall conclusion is that repetition and effort have minimal if any effect, emotion has a moderate effect, and depth of processing has a substantial effect. But you may have sensed a problem. The definition of depth—"greater degree of semantic involvement"—sounds rather vague. Many researchers, though impressed by the impact depth seemed to have on later memory, were nevertheless concerned by the difficulty of pinning down exactly what "depth" means. In the sections that

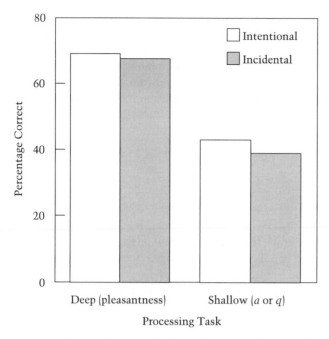

Figure 5.5. *Results from Hyde and Jenkins's (1973) study showing that intention to learn had no impact on learning. The experiment also showed the typical depth of processing effect.*

follow, we'll talk about efforts to define depth more precisely. First we'll talk about elaboration, which also seems to influence memory and yet does not seem to contribute to depth. Second, we'll talk about criticisms of the theory behind the depth of processing approach. Many of these criticisms centered on problems in defining depth. In the final two sections we'll talk about how encoding and retrieval are related and the difficulty in assessing the effect of encoding on memory without simultaneously considering how people retrieve memories.

Depth and Elaboration

The original idea in the levels of processing framework was that deep encoding was simply encoding that makes you think about the semantic content of the word. For example, in Craik and Tulving's (1975) experiment discussed earlier, the deepest processing condition was the sentence condition in which the participant saw a sentence frame ("I met a _____ in the street") followed by a word (*CLOUD*), with the task of saying whether the word fit the sentence frame. That task was thought to lead to deep processing because the participant had to consider the meaning of the word to answer the question.

But is it true that any task that makes you consider the meaning of the word will lead to equally good memory? Craik and Tulving (1975) examined that question in another experiment by varying the complexity of the sentence frame. In that experiment some sentence frames were simple ("She cooked the _____ ."), some were medium ("The _____ frightened the children."), and some were complex ("The great bird swooped down and carried off the struggling _____ ."). Craik and Tulving found that more complex sentence frames led to better memory for the words; indeed, participants remembered twice as many words that fit into the complex sentence frames (about 80% on a cued recall test) than words that fit into the simple sentence frames (about 40% recalled).

The more complex sentence frames could be said to lead to more elaborative rehearsal; the participant would be led to connect the target word to more words in memory. Recall that we introduced the concept of elaboration earlier. Other researchers (Cooper & Pantle, 1967; Craik & Watkins, 1973; Woodward, Bjork, & Jongeward, 1973) argued for an important distinction between elaborative and maintenance rehearsal, but we said earlier that depth of processing seemed a better way to conceptualize memory because the elaborative versus maintenance distinction made no predictions about what would happen when participants paid attention to physical characteristics of the words and also seemed to imply that for material to be remembered, it was necessary to actively rehearse it (i.e., as though you were expecting a memory test), and we know that intention doesn't matter for memory. Nevertheless, it seemed that level of processing was too simple a concept if you just thought that "deep" processing meant processing semantic content. Elaboration helps beyond processing for meaning.

Nevertheless, one has to be a careful about drawing conclusions too quickly about elaborative processing; it turns out that elaborative processing does not always add to deep processing to make encoding more likely. Simply adding more information that one might connect to things in secondary memory doesn't always work. The elaborations have to be relevant to what you're trying to remember.

Gary Bradshaw and John Anderson (1982) examined whether any sort of elaboration helped memory or whether the elaborations had to be relevant to the to-be-remembered material. They read people facts about famous people (e.g., "Newton became emotionally unstable and insecure when he was a child."). Some people also heard what the effects of this fact were on Newton ("Newton became irrationally paranoid when challenged by colleagues. Newton had a nervous breakdown when his mother died."). Other people heard more facts about Newton, but they were unrelated to the fact that he had problems as a child ("Newton was appointed Warden of the London mint. Newton went to Trinity College in Cambridge."). On a later test, 38% of the people who had only heard the single fact about his childhood remembered that fact, and 32% of the people who heard the extra, irrelevant facts remembered the fact about his childhood. But 61% of the people who heard the *effects* of the fact remembered it. This experiment makes a point that is easy to understand but is also easy to miss. You can't just say that deep encoding is still better if you elaborate on it by providing more information. The "more information" must be relevant to what you're trying to remember.

Problems With the Levels of Processing Theory

Even though deep processing really helps you remember, there are problems with the levels of processing theory. The first problem is that it's not really clear what is meant by the deepness of the levels. In some cases it is hard to know whether one level is deeper than another. For example, suppose I ask you to make a rhyming judgment on each word that I say. A stimulus example might be, "Rhymes with *cake?* LAKE." (And you say, "yes."). In another condition of the experiment other participants have to say whether the voice they hear saying the word is that of a man or a woman. Both of those tasks entail shallow processing, but which is more shallow? Memory performance for the rhyme people and the voice people won't be exactly the same. One group will do better, even if it's only slightly better, presumably because they were doing slightly deeper processing. I should be able to say which of these two tasks leads to deeper processing. Can't I just test a bunch of people and see which group does better and then say, "Okay, that's the deeper processing condition?" No, I can't do that. That's a **circular theory.** A circular theory is one in which term A is used to define term B, and then term B is used to define term A.

> ME: Deeper processing leads to better memory.
>
> ALERT CRITIC: How do you know when people are doing deep processing?
>
> ME: When their memory is better.

The levels of processing framework was never specified in enough detail so that you could confidently specify the depth or shallowness of every processing task.

There was a second problem, and that was that the levels of processing theory didn't say much about the importance of memory retrieval. It turns out that you can't look at encoding in isolation; you have to consider how it is tested. That point was made in the context of the transfer appropriate processing framework, so we turn to that point next.

Match Between Encoding and Retrieval: Transfer Appropriate Processing

Does deeper processing during encoding always lead to better memory? As we have discussed the idea so far, it sounds as if the answer should be "Yes." The way we've discussed depth of processing, we've made it sound as if depth functions by making it more likely that information gets into secondary memory or by making its representation stronger in some way. This way of discussing memory ignores what might be happening at retrieval.

The mental processes at retrieval turn out to be important to memory, and they cannot be ignored when we're thinking about encoding. Donald Morris, John Bransford, and Jeffrey Franks (1977) showed this in a simple but ingenious experiment in which they varied not only encoding processes (as in a typical depth experiment) but processes at retrieval (Figure 5.6). In their experiment

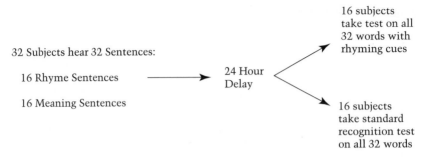

Figure 5.6. *Design of Morris, Bransford, and Franks's (1977) study.*

participants heard words and were asked to do one of two tasks. Some participants answered a rhyming question, as described earlier ("_____ rhymes with *eagle*. LEGAL."). The other participants answered a sentence frame question in which they needed to think about what the word means to determine whether it would fit the sentence frame. ("I met a _____ in the street. CLOUD."). Thus, the rhyme condition was a standard shallow task and the sentence frame was a deep task.

Each participant got one of two tests of his or her memory. One was a standard recognition test: Participants heard a list of words read to them and had to say which ones they had heard before. As shown in Figure 5.7, Morris et al. got the usual depth of processing effect when participants took this test. Other participants were not given a recognition test. They were given a cued recall test, which means that they had to try to remember the words, given a list of cues. Some of these cues rhymed with a word on the original list. For example, if one of the words had been *legal*, the word *regal* might have been on the list of cues. These rhyming cues were different from the ones participants heard the first time they saw the words.

As shown in Figure 5.7, when memory was tested with rhyming cues, the usual depth effect reversed: The people who did the supposedly shallow rhyme task remembered more than the people who did the supposedly deep sentence frame task. This result seems obvious once someone tells you about it, but it wasn't at all obvious at the time. Who would have thought you could get the levels of processing effect to reverse by changing the test? Most people were thinking that depth of encoding had its effect by making the memory representation stronger in some way, which would mean that memory would be better for any type of test.

It's not enough to just come up with that interesting result, though. It's much better if you can interpret why you got it, and Morris et al. had an interesting explanation for the reversal of the depth of processing effect. They proposed that whether you remember something depends not on the depth of encoding but rather on the extent to which there is a match between processes engaged at encoding and processes engaged at retrieval. Suppose you are in a memory experiment, and you are presented with a word (e.g., *bone*). You are going to think about *bone* in some way, and there must be particular processes in the mind

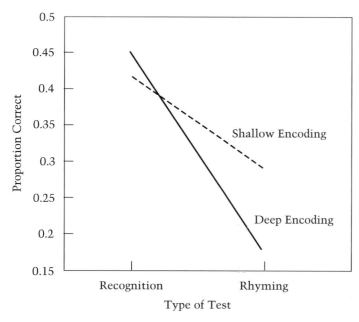

Figure 5.7. *Results of Morris, Bransford, and Franks's (1977) experiment showing that it's not just the depth of processing
at encoding that's important; the match between the
encoding task and the retrieval test also is important.*

that enable you to do that thinking. For example, if you are asked what *bone*
makes you think of, there are processes that search your memory to find concepts
associated with the concept *bone,* and perhaps you think of a skeleton. Morris,
Bransford, and Franks emphasized the importance of the memory search
processes that help you come up with the associated concept *skeleton.* They argued that if those same processes were used at retrieval, you would be very likely
to remember the original word *bone.* If other processes were engaged when you
were trying to retrieve the word, you would be less likely to remember it. For example, if at retrieval you were encouraged to think of words that sound like
phone, you would be less likely to remember the word *bone,* because you had
used different processes at encoding (you used processes that helped you think
of the associate *skeleton*).

The general hypothesis is that when processes used to think about words
are the same at encoding and retrieval, then memory will be successful; when
the processes used to think about words are different at encoding and retrieval,
then memory will not be successful. This hypothesis is known as **transfer appropriate processing.** Thus one type of encoding (e.g., deep processing) is not inherently better than another, according to the hypothesis.

The idea of transfer appropriate processing seems to explain the general pattern of results we have discussed. Unfortunately, it has the same problem that
the levels of processing idea has: circularity. Memory should be better when the
same processes are engaged at encoding and at retrieval, but how do you know
whether the processes are the same or different? Keep in mind that there is no

BOX 5.2. WHAT IS REMEMBERED, WHAT IS FORGOTTEN?

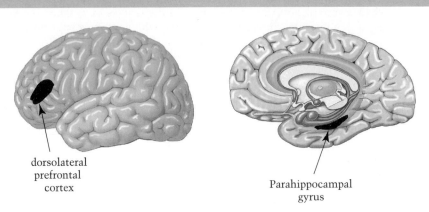

dorsolateral
prefrontal
cortex

Parahippocampal
gyrus

Is it possible to peek at the brain, observe its activity during encoding, and, based on the activity, predict whether the item is likely to be remembered or forgotten? Two research groups have done just that: Jim Brewer and his associates at Stanford and Anthony Wagner and his associates at Harvard (Brewer, Zhou, Desmond, Glover, & Gabrieli, 1998; Wagner et al., 1998). I'm presenting these studies together because they were conducted in a similar manner, drew similar conclusions, and appeared back-to-back in the same journal.

Both studies used incidental encoding, meaning participants did not know that their memory would be tested later. Participants lay in a scanner and made judgments about pictures (in Brewer et al.) or words (in Wagner et al.). The researchers used event-related functional magnetic resonance imaging, which allows assessment of brain activity in a very short time window (as short as several seconds) so the researchers could determine the amount of brain activity in the few seconds after each stimulus was presented. Later participants in both studies took a recognition test for the material, and each participant's performance on each stimulus was categorized as being remembered well, remembered weakly, or forgotten. The researchers then examined the activity measures of different parts of the brain taken at encoding to see whether activity at encoding differed for items that would later be remembered or forgotten.

Both studies drew similar conclusions. The right dorsolateral prefrontal cortex and bilateral parahippocampal cortex showed more activity for items that would eventually be remembered than for items that would eventually be forgotten. When the stimuli were words (Wagner et al.) the activity was restricted to left parahippocampal cortex, probably because the left hemisphere plays the predominant role in language processing, but when the stimuli were pictures (Brewer et al.) the activity in the parahippocampal cortex was bilateral, perhaps because pictures were coded both visually and in terms of verbal labels. The difference in laterality was extended to the frontal activations, with Brewer reporting predominantly right prefrontal activation and Wagner reporting predominantly left.

Previous research had shown that the parahippocampal cortex is active when a new stimulus appears, but it was not known whether this activity reflected encoding processes (which might be strongest for unfamiliar items) or

(Continued)

whether the parahippocampal cortex was some sort of "novelty detector" that alerted other areas that a stimulus was unfamiliar and therefore might be worthy of close attention. All of the stimuli in the studies by Wagner and Brewer were equally novel. The differences in activity, which are correlated with participant's eventual memory performance, show that the parahippocampal cortex and the prefrontal cortex are crucial in memory encoding.

way of directly observing cognitive processes. You can observe tasks and then make educated guesses about what sorts of cognitive processes would be engaged to perform those tasks. Thus, the only way to make a judgment about the similarity of cognitive processes during encoding and retrieval is to make the reasonable guess that the greater the similarity of the tasks at encoding and retrieval, the greater the similarity of the cognitive processes used to do those tasks. But there is no way to objectively measure how similar tasks are.

In some cases it seems like a safe bet that two tasks must require fairly different processes (e.g., the cognitive processes required for thinking of a word that rhymes with *bone* and the processes required for thinking of a word related to *bone*). But we don't have an objective way to measure similarity for processes. For example, suppose I think of a third task: judging how many syllables there are in the word *bone.* Is that task more similar to thinking about a word that rhymes with *bone* or to thinking of a word related to *bone?* There is no way to tell, so if I give the count-the-syllables task to all my participants at encoding and then give half of them a standard recognition test and half of them the rhyming cues test, there is no way to know which group will do better. As with the levels of processing framework, a theory must be able to make predictions for it to be useful.

So does transfer appropriate processing replace the idea of depth? Only in a sense. The transfer appropriate processing idea forces us to realize that there are interactions between encoding and retrieval, and the depth of processing framework was predicated on the idea that you could simply make a better memory in the storehouse, one that would be better however it was retrieved. In that sense, transfer appropriate processing is more accurate.

Nevertheless, depth is important because deeper encoding does lead to better recall under most of the conditions in which you'd usually test memory. That's important simply as a practical matter. It tells us that if you want to remember something, deep encoding is the way to go, even if the theory behind the principle isn't completely adequate. It's also important to our attempts to develop theories of memory. Even if the depth idea as articulated is not an adequate theory, the deep encoding still has a profound impact on memory under most circumstances, and that fact must be explained.

Match Between Encoding and Retrieval: Physical Environment

In the previous section we saw that memory is better when you think about material in the same way at encoding and retrieval; that is, the processes engaged in thinking about the material are the same at encoding and retrieval. Can we extend this idea to physical context? Is memory better if the physical context is the same at encoding and retrieval? For example, if you learn some material in one room (e.g., a dormitory room), will you be unable to remember it when you are tested in another room (e.g., a lecture hall)? Obviously not, but is it possible that you won't be able to remember it as well? If memory is better when cognitive processes match at encoding and retrieval, does that mean memory is better if the physical environment matches too? The answer is, "Just a little." Such effects of the physical environment are called **context effects,** and a number of researchers have tried experiments to observe context effects. Some have gone to pretty extreme lengths to try to get the effect.

Duncan Godden and Alan Baddeley (1975) had participants encode and retrieve information either under water or on dry land. Participants were members of a diving club, and they were outfitted with special apparatus so that they could hear words read to them under water and with special boards so that they could write down the words they remembered while under water. Then they heard and recalled word lists either under water or on dry land, or they switched between under water and dry land between encoding and retrieval. (There was a 4-min delay for everyone between encoding and retrieval so that people who were switching would have time to make the change.) The results showed that memory was about 40% better in the same context. To be certain that it was the different context and not the disruptive effect of switching that affected memory, Godden and Baddeley conducted a second experiment in which participants encoded and retrieved words on dry land, but during the 4-min delay half of the participants had to jump in the water, swim a bit, and dive down 20 feet before exiting the water and trying to recall the words. This extra, possibly disruptive activity had no effect on memory, indicating that in the first experiment it was the change in context that was affecting memory, not the disruption of switching contexts.

So there is an effect of physical context on memory, but memory is seldom tested under water. Can you get a context effect under conditions more similar to what most people experience? Steven Smith, Arthur Glenberg, and Robert Bjork (1978) had college students study lists of words presented on slides in a windowless room off campus with the experimenter neatly dressed in a tie and jacket. On a second day they studied another word list that was read aloud this time, in a room on campus with windows, and the experimenter was dressed sloppily. On a third day, they were asked to remember both lists in one or the other context. The experimenters reported that memory was somewhat better if the context matched between encoding and retrieval (59% correct) than if it didn't match (46% correct). So with a pretty extreme change (room, experimenter, words heard vs. seen) they found a modest effect.

I've mentioned two studies that show that memory is somewhat better when the physical environment is the same during encoding and retrieval. Nevertheless, I want to emphasize that the effect probably is small. Other experimenters (e.g., Fernandez & Glenberg, 1985) have tried to get an effect of physical context on memory and have gotten nothing. Furthermore, when experimenters go to extreme changes in context (as in the diving study) they get measurable but fairly modest changes in memory.

As a practical matter, one might wonder whether there is an effect (even a small one) of universities shuffling classes around at exam time. At some schools it is common for examinations to be administered in a room different from the one in which lectures took place. William Saufley, Sandra Otaka, and Joseph Bavaresco (1985) recorded over a number of years whether test grades were higher when students took the exam in the same room that the lecture was in than when they took the exam in a different room. This study was conducted at the University of California at Berkeley, where it was routine for a group of students to go to another room to take a midterm or final exam to relieve over-crowding. The students who were to take the exam in another room were selected randomly from the class list (the typical procedure for most classes). In general, these were large lecture courses, so the same-room condition was a large auditorium and the changed-room condition usually was a smaller class-room or auditorium. The experimenters collected data from 12 different exams in seven different college courses. The changed room had no effect on scores in any of the 12 exams; across the 12 exams, the average number of points obtained was 61.1 for the same context and 61.2 for the different context. (That sound you just heard was a collective sigh from registrars around the country.)

Conclusion

As you can tell, we don't yet have a complete answer to the question, "What determines what we encode in memory?" But we have made some progress. We know that repetition and effort to learn do not affect memory. Emotion has some effect. Depth has an effect, but cannot be viewed in isolation and that's another thing that we've learned (we can't look only at the processing that happens during encoding). We have to look at how memory is tested at retrieval and, even more importantly, at the match between encoding and retrieval processes.

Thus it sounds as though the storehouse metaphor wasn't appropriate. It sounds as if processing is what really matters, not a representation entering a storehouse. Actually, both processes and representations are important. The processing you do determines what sort of representation will be stored (e.g., if you are asked to think of a rhyme, the sound of the word is stored; if you are asked to rate the word's likeability, the meaning is stored). Doing the same sort of processing at retrieval makes it more likely that you will recover the stored memory; if the sound of a word was stored at encoding, you're best off thinking about the sound at retrieval. So representations are stored, as the storehouse metaphor suggests, but processing is important both in determining what sort of representation will be stored and in making it likely that you will be able to retrieve the stored memory.

It's also interesting to consider the way our memory is set up from a practical point of view. Clearly, not everything the mind experiences is stored equally well in memory; on what basis does the mind store things? Your memory system appears to be designed in such a way that it helps you to do the same thing (i.e., engage the same processes and therefore think about material in the same way) at a later time. That is a conservative and perhaps wise way for the memory system to place its bets; whatever one has thought about before is the thing that one probably will have to think about again, so memory is set up to make it easy to engage the same cognitive processes a second time.

STAND-ON-ONE-FOOT QUESTIONS

1. *What factors affect encoding?*
2. *What are the problems with the levels of processing framework?*

QUESTIONS THAT REQUIRE TWO FEET

3. *Suppose a friend knows that you're taking a cognitive psychology class and asks for your advice on how to study for exams. What would you say? Would your advice be any different to someone who wants to remember people's names at parties?*
4. *Many people say that very emotional events are well remembered (as in flashbulb memories), but other people refer to very emotional events as not being well remembered at all (e.g., they will say that their wedding day was "just a blur"). What explanation might you give?*
5. *Why do you suppose that you remember some advertisements well and others not so well?*

➤ ## WHY DO WE ENCODE THINGS AS WE DO?

> ➤ PREVIEW One of the important conclusions from the previous section was that encoding is determined by how the participant processes the material (i.e., what the participant thinks about). In this section we pose the question "What determines how the participant thinks about the material?"
>
> The answer to this question is quite simple. The way participants process material depends largely on what they already know about it. In this section, we discuss three ways that this prior knowledge affects encoding: Prior information reduces what you have to remember, it guides your interpretation of details, and it makes unusual things stand out.

Encoding alone does not determine memory—you also have to look at retrieval processes to predict whether something is going to be remembered—but memory does start with encoding. In the experiments described in the previous section, participants usually were told how to process the material at encoding. What do participants do with material when they are not told what to do? This question takes us back to the beginning of the chapter and the penny example. Recall that if you want to know what people will remember, you can't look at the stimulus; you have to look at what people think about when they see the stimulus. Thus memory depends, at least in part, on encoding, and encoding depends on what people think when they see a stimulus. What determines what they think when they see a stimulus (or hear it, or whatever)?

What they think about depends on what they already know about it. Here is a classic example. John Bransford and Marcia Johnson (1972) read this paragraph to participants:

> The procedure is actually quite simple. First you arrange items into different groups. Of course one pile may be sufficient depending on how much there is to do. If you have to go somewhere else due to lack of facilities that is the next step; otherwise, you are pretty well set. It is important not to overdo things. That is, it is better to do too few things at once than too many. In the short run this may not seem important but complications can easily arise. A mistake can be expensive as well. At first, the whole procedure will seem complicated. Soon, however, it will become just another facet of life. It is difficult to foresee any end to the necessity for this task in the immediate future, but then, one can never tell. After the procedure is completed one arranges the materials into different groups again. Then they can be put into their appropriate places. Eventually they will be used once more and the whole cycle will have to be repeated. However, that is part of life.

This paragraph doesn't make much sense, and, not surprisingly, participants remembered very little of it. But some participants were given a title of the story before reading it, and they performed much better. The title is "Washing Clothes." Read the story again now that you know the title and you'll see that it makes much more sense. If you are given the title of the story after reading it, it doesn't help. You have to the know the title in advance.

Why is the story easier to remember if you know the title? Knowing the title allows the story to interact with things that are already in memory. As we pointed out in the last section, what you remember depends on what you think about at encoding, and what you think about at encoding depends on what you already know. The way you experience things is shaped by what's already in your secondary memory. Memories are always popping out of the storehouse and into working memory when they are related to something you're already thinking about.

When you are reading something, things in your memory that are related to it can come into awareness more easily and shape how you think about what you're thinking about. Hence, when you know the title is "Washing Clothes" and you read "First you arrange items into different groups," it readily comes to mind that this vague sentence refers to sorting clothing by color. The prior knowledge (about washing clothes) shapes ongoing processing (reading).

We can point to three effects of previous knowledge on the way things are encoded into memory. Prior knowledge reduces what you have to remember, guides your interpretation of ambiguous details, and makes unusual things stand out.

Prior Knowledge Reduces What You Have to Remember

As discussed in chapter 4, a chunk is a unit of knowledge that has subcomponents; the subcomponents are related to one another (often semantically related) and they often occur together, so it is possible to think of these subcomponents as a single unit, or chunk. The term *chunking* also refers to the process of creating a chunk. Suppose I ask you to memorize some letters (Bower & Springston, 1970). I read them aloud to you, pausing for 1 s where you see a space:

       FB   ICB   SNC   AAP   BS

You'd remember some of the letters, perhaps all, but it would take some effort. Think how much easier it would be if I gave you exactly the same list of letters but I paused in different places:

       FBI   CBS   NCAA   PBS

Why is this list easier? Because the letters form familiar groups, or chunks. We discussed chunking in chapter 4, and we said that you can keep more information in working memory if you organize information into larger chunks. In this example, both lists are organized into chunks by the pauses between some of the letters, but note that for the second list the chunks derive meaning from prior knowledge. You already know these letters as groups, so the second list essentially has four things in it to remember. What are presented as individual items *might* be encodable as a single, higher-order unit if you have the right background knowledge.

William Chase and Herb Simon (1973) conducted a series of interesting experiments in the early 1970s pointing out the importance of background knowledge in chunking. These experiments tested participants who had a lot of background knowledge in chess. The memory task was fairly simple. Participants were shown a chessboard with a bunch of pieces on it; the pieces were set in such a way that it looked like the middle of an ongoing game. Participants viewed the board for just 5 s, and then the board was taken away. After some delay, participants were handed an empty chessboard and the pieces and were asked to replace as many of the pieces as they could. The non–chess expert got 8 or 10 of 32 pieces correct. The chess masters got nearly all of them right every time. Why? Chess masters have much more background knowledge. When they look at a chessboard, it looks to them like the second version of the letter task (FBI, CBS, NCAA, PBS). I look at the board and think, "Okay, the horsey is over there, and the pointy-headed guy is next to him." The chess expert glances at the board and thinks, "Queen's gambit declined, 12 moves in, but white has castled early." The chess expert has knowledge in memory that allows him or her to chunk numerous piece positions, remembering the whole board in three or four chunks. I, on the other hand, have to remember the board piece by piece because I can't condense multiple-piece positions into one chunk. When it's time to recall, the chess expert can unpack each chunk into its constituents to replace the pieces appropriately.

How can we be certain that it's really the chess experts' background knowledge that makes the difference? Maybe they are just smarter. Or perhaps they have superior memories, and that's what made them chess experts in the first place. When the experimenters placed the pieces on the board randomly instead of placing the pieces to simulate the middle of an ongoing game, the chess experts' advantage disappeared. Their extensive experience with chess was rendered irrelevant when the pieces were placed randomly, and it was their prior experience that allowed them to create chunks.

Chase and Simon had another way of testing whether chunking made the difference in this experiment. They reasoned that if participants were really recalling chunks from memory, there would be differences in the times between putting the pieces down. For example, a chunk might be "three pawns in front of the castle." Chase and Simon expected that the participants would put down those three pawns rapidly, and then there would be a pause while the participants recalled the next chunk from memory. Chase and Simon defined a pause of 2 s or longer as indicating that a new chunk was being recalled. As expected, they found that the chunk size (number of pieces put down) for chess experts was bigger than that of novices.

Chase and Simon performed a second experiment in which they asked participants to reproduce a chessboard that was in plain sight. They videotaped participants' responses, and the key measure was how often participants had to look back at the sample board before returning to the board on which they were reproducing the sample. They found that chess experts and novices had equivalent chunk sizes; they both looked at the sample board equally often. The difference was that the chess experts needed to merely glance at the sample board to pick up a chunk of information, whereas the novices had to study the sample board longer to get the same amount of information. That finding indicates that the experts were able to rely on prior knowledge to identify a chunk rapidly. The novices had to develop a chunk as they looked at the sample board.

Prior Knowledge Guides Your Interpretation of Details

Prior knowledge makes things easier to remember by reducing how much you must remember, and that happens through chunking. Prior knowledge also guides what details you are likely to pick out of a complex story or scene to think about. You are likely to notice the details relating to things you already know about. For example, I am sort of interested in theater; I like going to plays and reading them. I went to see a play called *Voir Dire,* which is about a jury's deliberations, with a friend of mine who is an attorney. At the end of the play, there was a lot of overlap in what we remembered about it, but there were some interesting differences as well. She remembered a lot of the legal details—mostly things the playwright had gotten wrong or things she was impressed to see he had gotten right—whereas I remembered moments in the play that I perceived to be turns in dramatic tension and resolution of tension. I'm not an attorney, so I have no background knowledge about legal matters and was oblivious to the happenings in the play that she noticed. Prior knowledge guides what details of an event you attend to and think about and therefore which details end up in secondary memory. How does that work?

Sometimes, the prior knowledge that is applied at encoding is an isolated fact; for example, knowing the abbreviation *FBI* allows you to treat the three letters as a single chunk. Other times, the prior knowledge is best thought of as a set of related facts; the facts come in a packet, so to speak. Such a packet of information is called a **schema.** There have been a number of different definitions of a schema since Sir Frederic Bartlett (1932) first introduced the idea, but the different definitions agree on certain points. A schema is a memory representation containing general information about an object or an event. A schema represents what is generally true of the situation or event; it represents not a single event but a type of event. Furthermore, the facts within a single schema are related to one another. These two aspects of a schema are especially important: It is general, and it contains information about related facts.

For example, a schema for the concept *dog* would include the information that it typically has four legs, is friendly, is furry, and so on. These characteristics are generally true, but each one need not be true. For example, if you met a three-legged dog you would still think of it as a dog. Similarly, a hairless chihuahua is not furry, but you still think of it as a dog. However, if one of these pieces of information is not specified, then you assume that the **default value** of the schema is true. A default value for a particular piece of information is the value that would normally be true, and thus that you assume is true, unless you are told otherwise. For example, there could be part of the *dog* schema that specifies the number of legs. If I simply tell you that I got a dog, it is unlikely that I will tell you that the dog has four legs; nevertheless, you will assume that it has four legs because that is the default value for "number of legs." Naturally, I could tell you that I got a dog and that it has three legs, in which case you would change the value of "number of legs" to three for the representation of my particular dog. But the default value for "number of legs" in the *dog* schema would still be four.

The fact that these bits of information are related means that as soon as you think about a dog, all of these characteristics become more available. For example, suppose that I said, "I just got a puppy, which probably wasn't such a great idea, because my landlord just put in new carpeting." What does getting a puppy have to do with carpeting? As soon as I say "puppy," the knowledge becomes available that puppies aren't housebroken and often pee indoors. When I say "landlord," information in the *landlord* schema becomes available, including the information that landlords typically are concerned that damage will be done to rented apartments. Thus, understanding this sentence seems effortless, but it turns on having the right information in memory. I don't have to explicitly say, "I'm worried this puppy will pee on the carpet because that's what puppies do, which will ruin the carpets, which will make the landlord angry because the carpets belong to him." The background information stored in schemas allows the listener to make these inferences from the minimal information in the sentence.

Schemas not only help us make inferences but also help us to interpret ambiguous details. Returning to the "Washing Clothes" story presented earlier in the chapter, we would say that the prior knowledge of the theme of the story (as provided by the title) activates a schema for the steps in washing clothes. This background knowledge helps to guide the interpretation of ambiguous sentences such as "First you arrange items into different groups" and "If you have to go somewhere else due to lack of facilities that is the next step," which without the schema would be meaningless.

This hypothesis—that schemas help to guide the interpretation of ambiguous details—has led to important work on prejudice. You can think of stereotypes as being schemas for groups of people. Does the schema idea apply to sterotypes of people?

It seems to in at least some cases. Andrew Sagar and Janet Schofield (1980) read brief stories to sixth-grade boys, accompanied by pictures. The stories described an act that prior testing had shown was believable to sixth-grade students and somewhat ambiguous as to whether it was aggressive or benign. Here's an example of such a story:

> Mark was sitting at his desk, working on his social studies assignment, when David started poking him in the back with the eraser end of his pencil. Mark just kept on working. David kept poking him for a while, and then he finally stopped.

The picture that accompanied each story showed each child as either white or black. Participants were asked to rate whether they thought the act was mean and threatening and then to rate whether they thought it was playful and friendly. When the possible aggressor was black, his act was rated as more mean and threatening than when he was white (8.70 vs. 7.83 on the rating scales); when the possible aggressor was white, his act as rated as more friendly and playful than when he was black (6.81 vs. 6.49). The authors interpreted these data as showing that the students had schemas of "black students" in their memories that included the idea that they were likely to be aggressive, so the ambiguous action was interpreted as aggressive.

In the previous examples, we talked about situations in which schemas influence the interpretation of ambiguous details, but schemas can influence encoding even if none of the details are ambiguous. If a schema becomes active, it can guide to which details one pays attention. John Anderson and James Pichert (1978) examined this idea. In their experiment, participants read a story about what two boys did when they stayed home from school. Just before reading it, participants were given the idea that they should read the story from the perspective of a crook thinking about robbing the apartment or from the perspective of a person thinking of buying the home; thus the experimenters activated either a "burglar" schema or a "homebuyer" schema. After a 12-min delay, participants were asked to remember everything they could about the story. As expected, the details that participants attended to and remembered were those consistent with the activated schema: They remembered 64% of the items that were consistent with the activated schema and 50% of the items that were consistent with the other schema. For example, participants who took on the perspective of a burglar at the second recall attempt were more likely to remember objects that were easy to remove from the house rather than things that would be important to a homebuyer, such as a large yard.

Prior Knowledge Makes Unusual Things Stand Out

One effect of prior knowledge is that you often know what usually happens in a given situation, and you expect that these things will happen. That means that when something unexpected happens in a given situation, it stands out. For example, if you went to a restaurant and the waitress handed you a menu, that would not stand out (and would not be especially memorable) because that's what usually happens when you go to a restaurant. However, if the waitress didn't give you a menu but instead took you back to the kitchen so that you could view all of the dishes and pick out what appealed to you, that would stand out because it violates your expectations of what happens in a restaurant (and it would be memorable). That happened to me in a restaurant about 12 years ago, and I still remember it well. (I requested a large fish I noticed in the corner of the kitchen, obviously just caught. She told me it was inedible, and I didn't ask what it was doing there.)

There has been a lot of research on people's knowledge of what usually happens in a common situations such as visiting a restaurant. Roger Schank and R. P. Abelson (1977), two computer scientists, proposed that such knowledge about common situations is encoded in knowledge structures called **scripts.** A script is particular type of schema. It is a schema for a series of events. For example, you probably have scripts in memory for routine events such as "going to a restaurant," "getting up in the morning," or "visiting a doctor." If you were asked to, you could generate a list fairly quickly as to what each of these events entails.

It turns out that there is fairly good agreement among people as to what sort of events are part of such scripts, at least within the culture of American college students. Gordon Bower, John Black, and Terrence Turner (1979) asked 161 students to describe what happens in one of these scenarios. One set of instructions read,

> "Write a list of instructions describing what people generally do when they go to a lecture in a course. We are interested in the common actions of a routine lecture stereotype. Start the list with arriving at the lecture and end it with leaving after the lecture. Include about 20 actions or events and put them in the order in which they would occur.

Bower et al. (1979) found quite good agreement among the components that each student listed for these events. For example, among the 33 participants who described the restaurant script, a total of 730 actions were listed, and only 4 of those were unique. In other words, for almost every action a participant listed, another participant had listed that action as well. For the most part, each participant listed some actions that many other participants listed, some that most wrote, and some that only a few other participants wrote. Table 5.1 lists the actions associated with the scripts, showing which were listed by most participants, fewer participants, and the fewest participants (the statistical details of how the cutoffs were established need not concern us here).

We're talking in this section about the influence of prior knowledge on memory, and interesting things happen when experimenters give participants

Table 5.1   Empirical Script Norms at Three Agreement Levels

Going to a Restaurant	Attending a Lecture	Getting Up	Grocery Shopping	Visiting a Doctor
Open door	ENTER ROOM	*Wake up*	ENTER STORE	*Enter office*
Enter	*Look for friends*	Turn off alarm	GET CART	CHECK IN WITH RECEPTIONIST
Give reservation name	FIND SEAT	Lie in bed	Take out list	SIT DOWN
Wait to be seated	SIT DOWN	Stretch	Look at list	Wait
Go to table	Settle belongings	GET UP	Go to first aisle	Look at other people
BE SEATED	TAKE OUT NOTEBOOK	Make bed	*Go up and down aisles*	READ MAGAZINE
Order drinks	*Look at other students*	*Go to bathroom*	PICK OUT ITEMS	*Name called*
Put napkins on lap	*Talk*	Use toilet	Compare prices	Follow nurse
LOOK AT MENU	Look at professor	*Take shower*	Put items in cart	*Enter exam room*
Discuss menu	LISTEN TO PROFESSOR	*Wash face*	Get meat	Undress
ORDER MEAL	TAKE NOTES	Shave	Look for items forgotten	*Sit on table*
Talk	CHECK TIME	DRESS	Talk to other shoppers	Talk to nurse
Drink water	Ask questions	Go to kitchen	Go to checkout counters	NURSE TESTS
Eat salad or soup	Change position in seat	Fix breakfast	*Find fastest line*	Wait
Meal arrives	Daydream	EAT BREAKFAST	WAIT IN LINE	Doctor enters
EAT FOOD	Look at other students	BRUSH TEETH	*Put food on belt*	Doctor greets
Finish meal	Take more notes	Read paper	Read magazines	Talk to doctor about problem
Order dessert	*Close notebook*	*Comb hair*	WATCH CASHIER RING UP	Doctor asks questions
Eat dessert	*Gather belongings*	*Get books*	PAY CASHIER	DOCTOR EXAMINES
Ask for bill	Stand up	Look in mirror	*Watch bag boy*	Get dressed
Bill arrives	Talk	Get coat	Cart bags out	Get medicine
PAY BILL	LEAVE	LEAVE HOUSE	Load bags into car	Make another appointment
Leave tip			LEAVE STORE	LEAVE OFFICE
Get coats				
LEAVE				

Items in all capital letters were mentioned by the most subjects, items in italics by fewer subjects, and items in lowercase letters by the fewest subjects.

a story to remember that is similar to a script. Here's an example of a story that closely follows a "taking a cab" script. (It also happens to be true.)

> I got off a plane in Boston. I walked through the terminal to baggage claim. I waited a while, my bags came down the little chute, and I took them outside to the cab stand. A cab pulled up and the cabbie put my bags in the trunk. I got in the cab and said "165 Charles Street, please." The cabbie drove about 10 minutes, then handed me a map and in a Boston accent asked me to find Charles Street for him. I found Charles Street on the map, and told the cabbie a major street that was near Charles. The cabbie dropped me at my destination and helped me get my bags out of the trunk, and I paid the fare.

The cabbie asking for my help in finding the destination is not part of the typical script for this scenario. If I tested your memory for this story a week later, you would probably remember this detail because it violates the script, just as the waitress taking me back to the kitchen to choose my meal violates the script of going to a restaurant.

As it turns out, only details that are not part of the script *and* are relevant to the goals of the script will be remembered. Thus, in the "taking a cab ride" script the cabbie is supposed to know the way to the destination, and it makes a material difference in what happens in the script that the cabbie doesn't know the way. Another detail that is not part of the script is that the cabbie has a Boston accent. That detail is irrelevant to the script, however, so it is less likely to be remembered. Bower et al. (1979) formulated these hypotheses about scripts and confirmed them. Participants had very good memory for things that are inconsistent with the script, but only if they are relevant to the goals of the script. In their study, participants remembered 53% of the script violations, 38% of the regular parts of the script, and 32% of the irrelevant information.

This phenomenon has been best-studied in the case of scripts, but it probably applies to other types of information as well. For example, do you remember the translation of the French sentence that appeared near the beginning of this chapter? It was "Hey! What did that little monkey leave in my shoe?" This sentence does not fit the schema for a textbook very well and is therefore likely to be remembered.

STAND-ON-ONE-FOOT QUESTIONS

6. How does prior knowledge affect encoding?

QUESTIONS THAT REQUIRE TWO FEET

7. Think of an area in which you have expertise. Is your memory for material related to that area superior to that of your friends who do not have that expertise?

8. *What do you think the schema for the concept "librarian" might look like? How about the schema for the concept "engineer?" Does the fact that you can generate these schemas make you think that you are prejudiced?*

9. *Can you think of a way to chunk the material in this section of the chapter?*

10. *Suppose you had a good deal of prior knowledge about a particular topic. Would that make deep processing easier or more difficult?*

➤ WHAT HAPPENS AFTER WE ENCODE SOMETHING?

> ➤ *PREVIEW* In the first part of this chapter, we saw that whether something is encoded into memory depends on how you process it. In the second part, we saw that how you process it depends on how it relates to things you already know. The third question we address in this chapter is, "What happens after we encode something?" The metaphor of a storehouse implies that the memories would sit quietly until they are needed, whereupon they are pulled out of the storehouse. On the other hand, intuition tells us that we forget material as time passes, so we might expect that memories become degraded over time, perhaps decaying spontaneously. In fact, research over the last 20 years has shown that the neither of these is true. Memories that are encoded are not fully formed when they enter long-term memory. They are in a fragile state and are easily disrupted. As time passes they become more stable and less easily disrupted. The idea that memories become more stable over time certainly runs counter to the obvious fact that as time passes we forget. In this section, we follow the research trail that led to this conclusion.

Retrograde and Anterograde Amnesia

Much of the evidence for the process of consolidation is neuropsychological, so we need to start with people who have amnesia. There are actually two kinds of amnesia: **retrograde amnesia** and **anterograde amnesia** (Figure 5.8). If you suffer from retrograde amnesia, you lose memories that were encoded before some insult to the brain (often a blow to the head). If you suffer from anterograde amnesia, you cannot learn new things, but old memories are largely (but not completely) intact. The manner in which old memories are still affected in anterograde amnesia is quite important, and we discuss it later in the chapter.

Retrograde amnesia is characterized by a loss of the memories laid down before the injury to the brain. It rarely happens that the amnesia is so severe that the person loses *all* autobiographical information and does not know his or her own name or any details about his or her personal past. (Retrograde amnesia of this extreme severity is an absolute public health menace on soap operas, where each character seems to get it at least once in the course of his or her lifetime.) The severity of retrograde amnesia varies, but typically patients have a patchy memory for the past and, as you would expect, things that are more important and things that were likely to be processed deeply will be better remembered than minor details. For example, the person would be more likely to remember

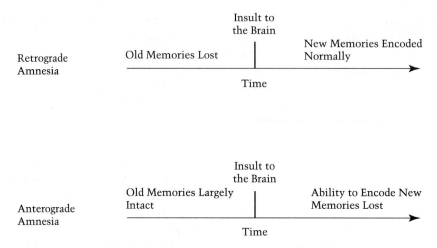

Figure 5.8. *Retrograde amnesia affects memories encoded before an insult to the brain, and anterograde amnesia affects memories encoded after an insult to the brain.*

that Ronald Reagan was president than that James Watt was in Reagan's cabinet. The ability to lay down new memories is intact in patients with retrograde amnesia, so learning about the triumphs and woes of the current president will not pose a problem.

Anterograde amnesia rarely results from a blow to the head; it is usually the consequence of a stroke to particular structures of the brain (the medial temporal lobe or diencephalon) or neurological disease (such as Alzheimer's disease) that affects those structures. Anterograde amnesia is characterized by difficulty in storing new memories. Thus, a patient who has had anterograde amnesia since 1971 might not know who is president; if you ask the patient, "Who is the president?" he or she probably will say "Nixon" because he was president at the time of the brain injury. Nor could the patient describe for you a conversation he or she had 5 min earlier. New memories simply do not enter the storehouse. Patients with anterograde amnesia have nearly intact memories from before their brain injury, but they do have a bit of retrograde amnesia.

The trail that ended in the theory of consolidation began with retrograde amnesia, specifically with a puzzling finding. Retrograde amnesia shows a **temporal gradient.** A temporal gradient means that memories from the more recent past are affected more than memories that happened a longer time ago. The things that happened just before the brain injury seem much more difficult to remember than things that happened years and years before the injury for a patient with retrograde amnesia.

You may be able to confirm this temporal gradient if you or someone you know has suffered a fairly severe blow to the head. You can probably remember events from the third grade about as well as you did before the accident, but you probably do not remember the accident itself, and you may not remember the events leading up to the accident, or perhaps even the entire day of the accident. When Princess Diana died in 1997, the exact circumstances of her death were not known because there seemed to be no eyewitnesses. The exception was her bodyguard, but he was severely injured in the accident and couldn't speak. A number of media commentators at the time mentioned that once he recovered, more would be known about the accident, but it turned out that he had little or no memory of the accident because of the blow to the head he received during the accident.

Two characteristics of retrograde amnesia are really important. First, a severe insult to the brain can result in the loss of memories going back for as long as 10 or 15 years. Second, the memory loss is temporally graded. We'll get to the interpretation of these characteristics of retrograde amnesia in a moment, but first we have to discuss the temporal gradient in a bit more detail.

Proving That There Is a Temporal Gradient

Proving that there is a temporal gradient in retrograde amnesia turns out to be tricky. For example, suppose you're a psychologist and a neurologist walks into your office with a patient. The neurologist says "This is Ms. Diacamĭglu. . . ." Okay, bad example, the neurologist says "This is Ms. Smith. She's been in a car accident and has suffered a head injury. I'd like to know whether her memory for things that happened a year ago is better or worse than her memory for things 10 years ago." Then the neurologist leaves you with Ms. Smith. What are you going to do?

The way psychologists usually test memory is to present some material to the participant, wait a while, and then say, "Hey, tell me that stuff I told you a while back." But we didn't know 10 years ago that Ms. Smith was going to need to have her memory tested today. One way around this problem is to test her memory for things we can reasonably assume she had an opportunity to learn 10 years ago. Suppose that we test her memory for news events from 10 years ago. Almost everyone is exposed to newspapers and television, so we can take events from 10 years ago and events from a year ago and compare her memory for each.

That's more or less the way it is done. One test that uses this principle is the famous faces test (Albert, Butters, & Levin, 1979). The participant is shown pictures of famous people and is asked to provide the name of the person shown.

The pictures are categorized by decade; thus the picture of Lyndon Johnson is considered a measure of one's memory for the 1960s because that's when Johnson's picture was in the news most. Farah Fawcett is a famous face from the 1970s, Mary Lou Retton is from the 1980s, and so on.

This is all well and good, but isn't it a problem that Lyndon Johnson was not in the news only during the 1960s and Babe Ruth was in the news not just in the 1930s? Ms. Smith may recognize Babe Ruth's picture although she was born in 1961, so in what sense are we testing memory for the 1930s by testing whether people recognize Babe Ruth's picture? Keep in mind what we're trying to do. We're trying to compare the durability of memories that were encoded at different times. It's not good to test Ms. Smith's memory for the 1960s by showing her a picture of Lyndon Johnson if she also saw pictures of Johnson during

Photo 5.1.   *Pictures from the famous faces test.*

the 1970s, 1980s, and 1990s. That way you're testing a memory that is a combination from four decades. What we want is a memory that Ms. Smith encoded at one time and then never encoded again.

The famous faces test works pretty well, and it is often used to test retrograde amnesia today, even though it has that conceptual problem. Another test that was important in demonstrating to researchers' satisfaction that the temporal gradient exists was developed by Larry Squire and his colleagues at the

University of California, San Diego (Squire, Slater, & Chace, 1975; Squire & Cohen, 1979). They gave people tests of information about television shows that were on for one season and were then canceled. The logic is this: A TV show is advertised, so everyone has a pretty good chance of encoding the name of the show. But once the show is canceled, you are very unlikely to encode the name of the show again because no one ever talks about it. So the memory for a TV show's name may be encoded over the course of 1 year and then never rehearsed again, unlike Babe Ruth's picture.

Squire and colleagues used a clever method to make that point. They gave their TV show name test to some people who had been out of the country for a year. These people did fine on the test except for the year they were out of the country. For that year, they were absolutely terrible. Obviously, if you're out of the country you have no opportunity to see advertising for new American TV shows, and if you don't encode the show names during that year, you will never encode them. When you come back and say, "Hey, I just had a great year in Paris! What'd I miss?" your friends don't say, "Well, there was this show called *Dan Willingham, Live!* but it wasn't very good, so it got canceled." Testing for the information about TV shows that were on for one season and then canceled is a good way to test for memories that were encoded during one year and very unlikely to be encoded again later.

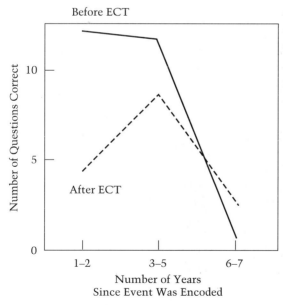

Figure 5.9. *Results from Squire, Slater, and Chace (1975) showing that patients who had retrograde amnesia caused by electroconvulsive therapy (ECT) show a temporal gradient to their memory loss.* Temporal gradient *means that recent memories (1–2 years ago) are more affected than remote memories (6–7 years ago).*

BOX 5.3. DIRECT EVIDENCE OF CHANGES IN MEMORY ACROSS TIME

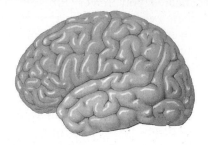 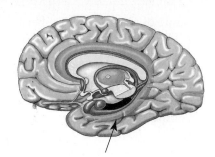

hippocampus

An important claim in our understanding of memory formation is that the role of the hippocampus is time limited. In other words, the hippocampus is very important in the formation of memories, but its importance decreases with time because memories come to depend on other brain structures. Most of the evidence supporting this contention comes from retrograde amnesia, specifically from the temporal gradient of retrograde amnesia. These data are always collected in the same fashion; they concern memories in which the hippocampus was intact at the time of encoding but is missing at the time of retrieval. Thus these studies tell us something about what the brain does when there is no hippocampus, but can we extend these results to a healthy brain? Is it true that the hippocampus contributes little or nothing to the retrieval of old memories if it is healthy and intact?

Bruno Bontempi and his colleagues (Bontempi, Laurent-Demir, Destrade, & Jaffard, 1999) examined this question in mice. They used a tracing method that is conceptually similar to positron emission tomography: The mouse is injected with glucose that is labeled with a tracer. The parts of the brain that are most active demand the most glucose, so that the brain can later be inspected to see where most of the tracer has collected.

All of the mice were trained in a spatial learning task. The task is called a radial arm maze. It has eight long arms radiating from a central hub. The ends of the arms might or might not be baited with a food reward. In this experiment the same three arms were always baited and the other five were not. The measure of learning is the number of unbaited arms the mouse enters; this number decreases with training because the mouse learns that some arms have no food in them, and it does not make pointless trips down those arms.

After training all the mice to learn this task, the researchers retested them either 5 days after training or 25 days after training. The mice showed dramatic differences in hippocampal activity; the rats trained 5 days ago showed substantially more activity in the hippocampus and related structures, including the subiculum and entorhinal cortex (a cortical area that projects directly to the hippocampus). Although the 25-day mice still performed the spatial task well, they

(Continued)

did not show activity in these areas. Where was the memory? Compared to the 5-day mice, they showed more activity in cortical areas, especially the frontal cortex, anterior cingulate, and temporal cortex.

These data strongly support the inferences made based on human lesion studies. Initially, the hippocampus contributes not only to the encoding but also to the recall of memories. As time passes, these memories are consolidated and the hippocampus does not support these memories; rather, they are supported by cortical areas.

Squire and Cohen (1979) gave different versions of the test to people before and after they underwent electroconvulsive therapy (ECT) for depression. ECT leads to retrograde amnesia, just as a blow to the head does. The researchers observed a temporal gradient to the retrograde amnesia; participants were better at remembering TV shows from 5 years ago than from last year. Thus, even though it is difficult to test, we can be pretty sure that there is a temporal gradient to retrograde amnesia.

I should mention what is meant by "their memory is better for older material." It's not better in absolute terms: After ECT participants remember more about the shows from 1–2 years ago than they do about the shows from 6–7 years ago, just as they did before ECT. Everyone remembers old events worse because of forgetting. The point is that retrograde amnesia caused by ECT affects recent memories much more than more remote memories.

Consolidation

How can we interpret this temporal gradient? What memory process has been affected? Getting a bump on the head clearly doesn't affect one's ability to encode new memories because patients with retrograde amnesia are able to learn new things. (Being unable to encode new things is characteristic of anterograde amnesia.) And it doesn't affect the processes by which one retrieves old memories. If it did, you would have trouble retrieving all memories, not just those from before the accident. It seems likely instead that it affects memories that are already stored. But what about the temporal gradient? Why aren't all memories affected equally?

Here's a way to think about what a blow to the head might do. Suppose it sort of scrambles the stored memories, shaking them around so that they might become loaded with static or even become meaningless noise. But again, if that happened, why should there be a temporal gradient? Now suppose that memories initially are fragile, open to disruption. Just a little shaking will tear the web on which these memories are built. Older memories are much more stable, much more resistant to accident.

Donald Hebb (1949) was one of the first researchers to propose a neuro-physiological account of a two-stage process of memory storage, although the general idea goes back to the early part of this century (Muller & Pilzecker, 1900, cited in Squire, 1987). Hebb proposed that memory initially is encoded as a pattern of activity in existing neural circuits; later, the actual physical connections between neurons changes to reflect the storage of a memory. Thus memories become more stable over time as their representation becomes physically reflected in the brain, according to Hebb.

The hypothetical process by which memories become more stable is called **consolidation.** Consolidation is proposed to operate continually on all memories in the brain, making them more stable and less open to disruption. Thus, a blow to the head will disrupt newer memories, which have had little time to be consolidated, but will have less effect on older memories, which have had more time to become consolidated. That would account for the temporal gradient.

Is there any evidence besides the temporal gradient in retrograde amnesia for a process such as consolidation? Yes. We said at the beginning of this section that anterograde amnesics, who cannot learn new material, also have some retrograde amnesia. In fact, all patients with anterograde amnesia also have retrograde amnesia. This fact makes perfect sense if consolidation is actually the same process as that which encodes new memories. This process is damaged in patients with anterograde amnesia so that they cannot encode new memories and old memories that were in the midst of being consolidated receive no further consolidation, resulting in some retrograde in amnesia.

This account seems to make sense, but two of its implications are a bit perplexing. The first concerns the extent of retrograde amnesia. The idea is that people who have anterograde amnesia also have retrograde amnesia because the consolidation process has been lost. The retrograde amnesia of these patients extends at least 3 years. That implies that consolidation takes at least 3 years to complete. The second implication is that consolidation occurs for all memories, whether you think about them or not. It's pretty easy to imagine memories getting more and more stable if you continually recall them: Each time you remember something, the memory becomes stronger in some way. But results from studies using the TV test are good evidence that you need not think about the material again for it to be consolidated. The participants were not thinking about the names of those single-season TV shows, yet they were being consolidated.

Taken together, these implications mean all memories are continually being made more stable (i.e., consolidated), they are all being consolidated at the same time, and that this goes on for years. Furthermore, none of these memories have to be recalled for them to be consolidated.

I have provided the barest summary of the research on consolidation, which has been studied extensively in animals (for a review, see Izquierdo & Medina, 1997).

What Does Consolidation Mean for Memory?

A dominant theme in work on the biology of memory has been that the formation of memories does not stop with encoding. A chain of neurobiological events is initiated by the encoding of memory that may go on for weeks, months, or years. For example, David Marr (1971) suggested that memory is initially stored in the hippocampus (a small structure in the center of the brain) during the day and that at night the hippocampus "plays back" the memories to the cortex (the outer covering of the brain), which is the eventual permanent storage site of memories. Closely related ideas have been pursued by a number of researchers (e.g., Alvarez & Squire, 1994; Buzsaki, 1989).

Interestingly, this principle has had less impact on cognitive psychology than one might think. It seems to represent an important problem for cognitive psychologists: What is the nature of the initial encoding, and how does that encoding change over time? Although formal models of memory based on neurophysiology have incorporated this principle (e.g., McClelland, McNaughton, & O'Reilly, 1995), there has been no systematic effort by cognitive psychologists to understand at a cognitive level the process of consolidation. However, it seems that a full understanding of encoding will be impossible without some account of consolidation.

We began this chapter with an idea that seemed reasonable enough: What you do at the time of encoding determines, in part, the likelihood that a memory will be available later to be retrieved. Two themes have emerged in our discussion. First, researchers have identified some factors at encoding that are very important for the longevity of a memory and others that are not important. Second, a memory's life does not end once it makes it into the memory storehouse. After it is in the storehouse, it will be consolidated, and the likelihood that it will come out of the storehouse at the appropriate time depends on the retrieval processes. We turn next to these processes of retrieval.

STAND-ON-ONE-FOOT QUESTION

11. What is consolidation, and why is it thought to exist?

QUESTIONS THAT REQUIRE TWO FEET

12. Suppose Marr (1971) was right and that consolidation occurs at night, when the hippocampus "plays back" memories to the cortex. Does this suggest a way that you could disrupt someone's memory, were you that kind of devious person?

13. *Can you think of a way in which consolidation could be integrated into the general cognitive framework separating working memory and long-term memory?*

KEY TERMS

statistically significant
flashbulb memories
levels of processing
    framework
depth of processing
deep processing
shallow processing
elaborative rehearsal

maintenance rehearsal
incidental memory
    test
intentional memory
    test
circular theory
transfer appropriate
    processing

context effect
schema
default value
script
retrograde amnesia
anterograde amnesia
temporal gradient
consolidation

6

Memory Retrieval

In chapter 5 we discussed why some material ends up in the memory storehouse and some doesn't. In this chapter we discuss how you get information out of the storehouse.

The storehouse metaphor leads naturally to several questions. First, if something is in the storehouse, is it guaranteed that you can get it out? A moment's reflection will tell you that the answer is "no." We've all had the frustrating experience in which you *know* you know a piece of information, but you can't quite get the piece of information itself. "You know, that actress, that pretty one with the funny first name. She was in *Ghost,* she used to be married to that guy, the guy from all the action movies. Not Julia Roberts. YES, Demi Moore!" In such cases, retrieval of the memory clearly is the problem; it was encoded, it is stored in memory, but you have problems getting it out of the storehouse (i.e., retrieving it). To put it another way, **"How come sometimes we can retrieve a memory and other times we can't retrieve the same memory?"** Based on what you learned in chapter 5, you probably won't be surprised to learn that whether you successfully retrieve a memory depends on the cues available at the time of retrieval.

Other times, your experience seems to indicate that cues will not help; the memory is simply lost. You *know* you used to know something, but you are equally certain that you've forgotten it now. Perhaps you've had this experience in looking over old high school tests: You're looking through an old desk drawer and you come across a bunch of geometry problems, all worked out in your handwriting, and you think, "I can't believe I ever knew this stuff." In cases like this, it doesn't feel to you as if there is a retrieval problem and that if you were given enough time or better cues you'd eventually be able to retrieve the memory. Rather, it feels as if the memory of how to do those geometry problems is simply gone. Why do some memories become simply irretrievable; that is, **"Why do we forget?"** The answer to this question turns out to be a bit mysterious. The idea that memories simply fade away with time corresponds to our everyday experience, but that idea is difficult to prove. It is more certain that new things you learn can interfere with things that you already know and that that can cause forgetting.

➤ *How Come Sometimes We Can Retrieve a Memory and Other Times We Can't Retrieve the Same Memory?*

> ➤ PREVIEW In discussing retrieval of memories, we must first realize that there are different ways of measuring memory. One measure of memory may indicate that you don't remember something, whereas another indicates that you do. That's one reason that sometimes the same memory can or cannot be retrieved: You test your memory differently. It thus appears that some measures of memory are more sensitive than others, meaning that they are better able to detect memories that are poorly represented in the storehouse. In fact, a more crucial factor in retrieval is the match between encoding and retrieval. Different measures of memory appear more sensitive because they typically provide different cues at retrieval. Just as encoding is affected by prior knowledge, so is retrieval.

It might seem that once a memory makes it into the storehouse, it should be yours for the asking; you should be able to retrieve it whenever you care to. As you know, memory doesn't work this way. Sometimes you try to remember Demi Moore's name and it pops right out of the storehouse. Other times you can't quite get it. But the fact is, you can get it. Once someone provides the name "Demi Moore" you immediately recognize that it is correct (and you confidently reject "Julia Roberts" as incorrect). The fact is that there are different ways to retrieve memories (i.e., to measure whether a person remembers something), and the way you measure memory has a big impact on whether it appears that a piece of information is in the storehouse. I say "appears" because the only way to know whether something is in memory is if the person can produce the information from memory, and whether he or she can do that depends on how memory is measured.

Measures of Memory

Before we can talk about the details of retrieval, we need to be more precise about the different ways in which one can measure memory. When you want to test someone's memory for some material, you can use different types of tests. In a **free recall** test, the experimenter says little more than, "Tell me what you remember." For example, if you were taking an exam for an American history class, you may have spent 2 weeks studying the Civil War, and an exam question might simply say, "In two pages, provide a summary of what you have learned about the Civil War." Such a question would be a free recall test. In a **cued recall** test the experimenter adds some hints, or cues, about the material you're supposed to remember. The cues might be some words that are semantically related (for the history test, the question might include the hint "Think about the coastline" to prompt you to write about the blockade of southern ports). The cues might also be based on sound (e.g., a clumsy clue like "Don't forget to discuss the battle that rhymes with 'Bettysburg' "). In a **recognition** test the experimenter provides the actual to-be-remembered material (called targets) along with some other material (called **distractors, foils,** or **lures**), and the participant must pick out the targets from among the distractors. This sort of memory test is used in a multiple choice exam:

> In which battle was Stonewall Jackson mortally wounded?
>
> a. Chancellorsville
> b. Gettysburg
> c. Bull Run
> d. Battle of the Bulge

In a **savings in relearning** test, the experimenter asks the participant to learn some material (e.g., the names and dates of each major Civil War battle) to a particular criterion (e.g., until he or she can recite the list perfectly two times in a row). The number of practice trials it takes to reach the criterion is recorded. At retrieval, the experimenter simply asks the participant to learn the same material to the same criterion a second time. If the participant can reach the criterion in fewer trials, that represents savings in relearning—the participant learns the material faster the second time—which presumably results from some residual memory of the earlier experience.

It's important to take note of these different ways of measuring memory because the type of test that the experimenter gives to a participant can make it appear as if he or she does or does not have the material stored in memory. For example, people often fail to remember a particular fact on a free recall test but then successfully remember it on a recognition test. This happens pretty often, actually. Someone asks you something like, "What's the name of the battle in which General Custer was killed?" and you say, "I can't think of it now, but I'd know it if I saw it." You're claiming that you could recognize the information even though you can't recall it. It seems that one type of memory test can be easier than another; in this case, recognition may be easier than recall.

In general, free recall is the most difficult memory task, followed by cued recall, then recognition. (Savings in relearning is still easier but is used much less often.) In this case, "easy" or "difficult" refers to the likelihood that you will successfully retrieve the material you encoded. In general, people are extremely good at recognition. Roger Shepard (1967) offered a compelling demonstration of the power of recognition memory. In one experiment, he had people read 540 single words. Half were words that you commonly see, such as *child* or *office,* and half were unusual words such as *ferrule* and *wattled.* Each participant could go through the words at his or her own pace. Immediately after seeing the 540 words, the participant took a recognition test: 60 of the words were matched with 60 other words that were not on the list, and on each trial participants saw a word from the list and a new word, and they were to select the new word. The results showed excellent recognition (about 88%). In a second experiment, Shepard showed participants 612 short sentences such as "A dead dog is no use for hunting ducks" or "The colt reared and threw the sick rider." Again, the 612 stimuli were followed immediately by a test, this time of 68 test pairs, and again participants performed very well, averaging 89% correct. Two heroic participants (who happened to be friends of the experimenter) read twice the number of sentences, 1,024, and their recognition scores were almost the same, 88%.

In a final experiment, Shepard used colored pictures cut from magazines. Thirty-four participants viewed 612 such pictures, again at their own pace (participants viewed the pictures for an average of 5.9 s each). Again they took a test immediately of 68 pairs. This time, Shepard also included tests after various delays. Four participants returned after 2 h, 3 days, 7 days, or 120 days. The results are shown in Figure 6.1.

What's most impressive about these data is how good participants are at recognition memory. It's pretty hard to get performance above 60% if you measure memory via free recall, even after only a short delay. But recognition memory is much better.

In truth, it's hard to compare recognition and free recall directly because the difficulty of a recognition task depends on the number of distractors (i.e., the other choices on the test) and how similar they are to the target. For example, I may say, "Here, remember this stimulus" and show you a slide with the word *Boat* written on it. Then an hour later I give you one of four tests, each of which

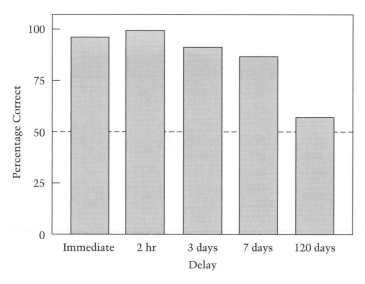

Figure 6.1.   *Results from Shepard's (1967) recognition experiment
using colored pictures. Recognition was close to perfect,
even though participants had seen 612 pictures, and
performance decreased slowly; after 7 days, participants
still recognized the pictures with 87% accuracy, and
after 4 months they were still above chance, although
they saw each picture for an average of just 6 s. The dotted line represents chance performance (i.e., guessing).*

has the target (*Boat*) and one distractor, and you have to choose which stimulus you saw (a or b). Figure 6.2 lists four possible tests.

In Test 1, you can select *Boat* with confidence only if you remember that
the first letter was capitalized at encoding; remembering that you saw the word
boat isn't enough. In Test 4, remembering the word *boat* is more than enough.
All you have to remember is that you saw a word, not a picture, and you'll get
the right answer. Clearly, the likelihood that you will correctly recognize an
item depends on the other stimuli from which you are choosing. The same logic
applies to a cued recall test. Your success on a cued recall test depends on the
usefulness of the available cues.

Thus the first conclusion we can draw is that it is very hard to fix memory performance on some absolute scale. You can't say "After a delay of 2 minutes, performance on a recognition memory test will be at about 90%." Under
most circumstances, recognition performance is quite good, as shown in Shepard's experiment, but it's not hard to devise a difficult recognition test (like Test
1 in Figure 6.2) that would guarantee poor performance.

Although we cannot make absolute statements about performance on
recognition or cued recall tests, we can compare performance on different types
of memory tests, and that is informative to the question we are addressing in
this section: How come you can sometimes retrieve a memory and other times
you cannot retrieve the very same memory?

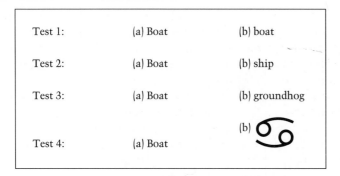

Figure 6.2.   *Four possible tests of your memory of the stimulus* Boat *in ascending order of difficulty.*

Sensitivity of Memory Measures

Although it's hard to make absolute statements about the accuracy of memory, we can say that cued recall usually is more accurate than free recall. If you can't recall something but then I give you a hint (thereby turning it into a cued recall test) you might recall it successfully. Similarly, recognition might be said to be easier than cued recall because sometimes you cannot recall something, even with hints, but you can recognize it successfully.

Another way to describe this phenomenon is to think of a memory test as a detection device designed to measure what is in a person's memory storehouse. Some memory tests are more sensitive in their ability to pick up faint or poorly represented memories. Thus we can speak of the **sensitivity** of a test as its ability to detect memories that are in the storehouse. Free recall is not a very sensitive test. For example, I might ask you, "Who starred in the movie *Ghost?*" If you said, "I don't know," I might conclude that the information is not in memory, but that conclusion could be wrong. The information might be in memory, but a free recall test is not sensitive enough to pick it up. Suppose I say, "Who starred in the movie *Ghost?* Was it Demi Moore?" and you confidently answer, "Yes." I am using a recognition test, which we could say is more sensitive than free recall because it detected that there was some information in the storehouse about this movie.

Is there any evidence beyond Demi-Moore anecdotes that these measures of memory differ in sensitivity? Yes. Recognition *usually* is more sensitive than recall, just as everyday experience indicates, and cued recall is more sensitive than free recall. As we'll see later, there are problems with the theory underlying the concept of sensitivity, but under most circumstances it's accurate to think of recognition as more sensitive than recall.

Endel Tulving and Zena Pearlstone (1966) examined the relative sensitivity of recall and cued recall. They tested 948 high school students on lists of 12, 24, or 48 items. The lists consisted of category names, followed immediately by examples of the category. For example, part of a list might be "weapons, cannon, bomb; professions, engineer, lawyer." Participants were told that the words to be remembered would be preceded by a word or phrase that described them, but that they didn't need to remember these descriptive labels. Recall occurred after a very brief delay. Some participants received a free recall test with the simple instruction to recall the words on the list. Other participants received a cued recall test. For these participants, the cues were the descriptive category labels (e.g., *weapons, professions*). In addition, participants made a second recall attempt, and this time it was a cued recall test for everyone.

Two results are important to our present discussion. First, cued recall performance was much better than free recall performance. The size of this advantage varied with list length—cued recall was more of a help when the lists were longer—but in all cases cued recall was superior. Second, remember that all participants took a second test, and it was cued recall for everyone. The participants whose first test had been free recall suddenly remembered many more words on this second test—on average about 50% more, although again the cued-recall advantage varied depending on the length of the studied list.

Tulving and Pearlstone emphasized that memories may be **available** but not **accessible.** An available memory is one that is in the memory system somewhere, but it is one that you may not have access to just now. A memory is accessible if it can be retrieved, given the current set of cues. To be honest, I find these terms a bit confusing because both *available* and *accesible* sound as if you can "get to" (retrieve) the memory. I keep them straight by thinking of available as "available in principle." The memory is available in principle, if only you had the right cues. *Accessible* means you can retrieve the memory right now, with the cues on hand. In Tulving and Pearlstone's experiment, participants failed to remember many of the words when tested via free recall. That failure of memory did not mean that the words were not available. Rather, the words were not accessible because when they were tested via cued recall, they successfully remembered them.

J. T. Hart (1965, 1967) conducted a study that was in some ways parallel to Tulving and Pearlstone's, but Hart's experiment examined free recall and recognition. Hart asked college students 50 difficult free recall questions of general knowledge, such as "What sea does West Pakistan border?" If the participant could not provide the answer, her or she tried to select the correct answer from among four alternatives (Arabian Sea, Caspian Sea, Red Sea, Black Sea). When free recall failed and participants were unable to provide an answer, they were able to recognize the correct answer about 50% of the time. Chance performance would be 25%, so people were successfully recognizing information that they could not recall.

Is recognition the most sensitive measure of memory? Turning again to our own experience, we might guess that it is not. Savings in relearning seems to be still more sensitive, as you might be able to attest if you've ever had to relearn material you thought you had forgotten. For example, when I was in high school I became nearly fluent in French, but I spoke absolutely no French thereafter. Nine years later I found I was going to Paris, and I could not recall or recognize any French vocabulary (with the exception of dialogue snippets memorized for class, with phrases such as "The Duponts will be arriving in only an hour!" and "Who is that boy in the green bathing suit?"; for a very narrow set of circumstances, I felt ready for Paris). After 5 days in France I was speaking bad but passable French. Before going to France, I knew absolutely no French, according to recognition or recall tests. That should mean there was no French in my memory storehouse, and therefore learning it should have been as difficult as it was when I first started studying French. But I relearned French vocabulary very quickly, presumably because there was a lot of knowledge in memory that recognition and recall tests simply were not sensitive enough to measure. Thus savings in relearning seems to be the most sensitive measure of memory.

Indeed, there is experimental evidence that savings in relearning is still more sensitive than recognition. Tom Nelson (1978) had participants memorize a series of number–word pairs (e.g., "43–Dog," "59–Nurse," "77–Shell"). Four weeks later he gave participants a recognition test consisting of a long list of items, some of which they had seen before ("43–Dog") and some of which they had not ("83–Coin"). Four weeks had passed since encoding, so participants recognized some of the target items, but they missed others. Immediately after this recognition test came another learning phase. Nelson constructed a new list of items for participants to memorize using items that they had just failed to recognize. Some of the items on this final list appeared just as they had on the original list ("43–Dog") and some were repairings using the words and numbers from the original list (e.g., "59–Nurse" and "77–Shell" from the old list might be recombined into "59–Shell").

Suppose a participant failed to recognize "43–Dog" and "59–Nurse." If the failure to recognize those items means that there is no memory of these items in the storehouse, then it should be equally difficult to learn "43–Dog" (unchanged item) and "59–Shell" (changed item); the participant doesn't know either one, so he or she is starting from scratch. On the other hand, if there is some residual memory for the original items in memory, then relearning the unchanged item should be easier than learning a new pairing.

Participants saw the new list just once and then took a recognition test of the new list. Participants got 34% correct on the old items (e.g., "43–Dog") and 19% correct on the new, repaired items (e.g., "59–Shell"). Thus items that one

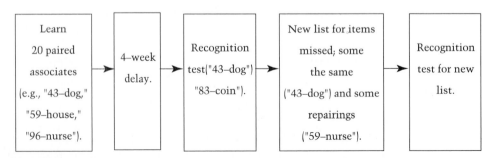

Figure 6.3. *Design of Nelson's (1978) experiment comparing the sensitivity of recognition and savings in relearning.*

fails to recognize may nevertheless remain in memory; on average, the original pairings were relearned faster, indicating that savings in relearning is a more sensitive measure of memory than recognition.

In this section we are considering why it is sometimes possible to retrieve a memory and other times impossible to retrieve the same memory. We have our first answer: Whether a memory is retrievable depends, in part, on the sensitivity of the memory test. Next we might ask why memory tests differ in their sensitivity.

Differences in Cues

Why do different measures of memory have different sensitivities? Psychologists have found it useful to think about different measures of memory in terms of the **cues** that they provide. A cue is simply some information that the experimenter gives you (or you give yourself) as a starting point for retrieval. Consider this. If I say to you, "Remember," the command makes no sense. Are you supposed to be remembering something about pickles, your second-grade teacher, or the structure of barium? You have to be told *what* you are supposed to remember. A cue provides information about what memory is to be retrieved from the storehouse. The different types of memory tests we've discussed differ in the cues that they provide.

In a free recall test, the instruction is typically "Try to recall the information I showed you earlier." Thus, the only cue you have is a bit of information about the encoding; it is understood that you are to recall information from the time and place at which the experimenter had you encode some material. This information about the time and place at which a memory was encoded is usually called the **context,** but in this case you don't even have very complete information about the context. The experimenter might have said, "Try to recall the information I showed you an hour ago, in this room we're sitting in now." Of course, even though the experimenter didn't give you that information (an hour ago, in this room) you may easily remember that, and you might use that information to help you remember the required information. Thus, you can generate your own cues to memory.

In a cued recall test the experimenter provides the context, as in a free recall test, and also adds some hints about the material. The hints might be some semantically related words ("One of the words referred to a card game") or a cue based on sound ("One of the words rhymed with *smoker*"), and so on.

In a recognition test the experimenter again provides a cue about the context ("You are to remember the material you heard earlier") but now also provides the to-be-remembered material along with some other material that was not presented at encoding. The participant's job, therefore, is simply one of matching. The participant must determine which of the stimuli go with the encoding context. See Table 6.1.

It seems that free recall, cued recall, and recognition differ in that they provide successively better cues to recall. (Savings in relearning is slightly different in that the original learning context is irrelevant; the experimenter never asks you to retrieve material from the initial encoding episode.) Perhaps if you are given

Table 6.1   Types of Memory Tests

Type of Test	Sample Instructions	Reference to Context?	Information About Target	What Must Participant Do?
Free recall	"Please remember the word list."	Yes	None	Generate the target material from the context information.
Cued recall	"Please remember the word list. One of the words was a card game."	Yes	Usually semantic (i.e., related to meaning)	Generate the target from the context information using the cue.
Recognition	"Was the word *POKER* on the list you saw before?"	Yes	Target itself	Determine whether the stimulus provided matches the context information.

more cues, you will be more likely to retrieve some information. That interpretation implies that some memories are very weak and can be detected only by a sensitive measuring device such as a recognition test, whereas other memories are strong and can be detected by a less sensitive measuring device such as a free recall test. We can call this view the **strength view of memory;** memories differ along a simple dimension of how strong they are. The sensitivity of a test is determined by the quality and quantity of cues it provides.

This view makes a lot of intuitive sense, and many psychologists thought something like this probably was right, but later experiments showed that there are problems with a strength view of memory. One clue that a simple strength view of memory won't work is that retrieval doesn't work the same way each time. For example, if someone asks you to name the three Rice Crispies guys you may draw an utter blank on one occasion, whereas other times you immediately rattle off, "Snap, Crackle, Pop." If the memory is strong, you should retrieve it every time, and if it's weak, you should fail each time; after all, the retrieval cue ("Name the Rice Crispies guys") is the same each time.

Endel Tulving (1967) emphasized this point in a classic experiment. He had people encode a list of 36 common nouns once, then make three successive attempts to recall the list, then encode it again, make three more recall attempts, and so on. Not surprisingly, people recalled more words with each successive encoding. What was more interesting is what happened when they made several recall attempts of the list. There was a fair amount of inconsistency in their recall. Over all recall attempts, participants got an average of 14.21 items correct. Of those, 3.89 (on average) were items that they had missed on the previous recall attempt. So on each recall attempt, it seems as if their recall should be improving by about 4 items. But that gain was almost perfectly offset by items they forgot. On average, 3.97 of the items they remembered on the previous trial they failed to produce on the current trial. In other words, a participant might report a word on the first test, then fail to recall it on Tests 2 and 3, then recall it again on Test 7, and so on. Tulving pointed out that this pattern of data argued against a simple strength theory of memory; there is no reason for the strength of a memory to wax and wane on successive tests.

Encoding and Retrieval Redux

The reason memories are sometimes retrieved and sometimes not may already be clear to you, based on what you read in chapter 5. We emphasized that encoding is really important, but whether a memory is retrieved ultimately depends not only on encoding but on the match between encoding and retrieval, or more precisely the match between what you think about at encoding and what you think about at retrieval. In chapter 5 we talked about why you think about what you do at encoding. (It depends on what you already know about the to-be-remembered material.) At retrieval, what you think about is greatly influenced by the cues you are given. A memory can be retrieved or not retrieved because the cues for retrieval differ on the two retrieval attempts.

In chapter 5 we saw that changing retrieval cues can have a big impact on memory. If you give rhyming cues at retrieval, that might be good or bad for memory, depending on whether you were thinking about the way the word sounded at encoding. But our discussion of retrieval in this chapter makes it sound as though this effect should be more fine grained. It seems as if retrieval cues should matter not only at a rough cut (e.g., the cues are "about meaning" or "about sound"); if retrieval cues are to influence the success of memory retrieval, it seems that the type of cues should matter in all situations, not just extreme and unusual ones such as those in which you think about the sound of the word. The type of cue should be important, even if all the cues concern meaning.

So what happens if you change the meaning of retrieval cues? Changing the meaning of a word between encoding and retrieval has a sizable effect on memory. Leah Light and Linda Carter-Sobell (1970) had participants read sentences that contained a homophone in a way that biased the meaning toward one definition. For example, participants might have seen this sentence "The harassed customer bought STRAWBERRY JAM at the supermarket." Participants were told that they would later be tested on the adjective–noun pairs signified by the underlining. At recall, participants see an adjective–noun phrase and must say whether the noun appeared in one of the sentences they saw earlier; they don't need to worry about the adjective. There were three conditions: In one, participants saw the identical phrase ("strawberry jam"), in another they saw a new adjective ("raspberry jam"), and in a third they saw a different adjective that changed the meaning of the noun ("traffic jam"). The experimenters were interested in what happens not just when the adjective changes but when the adjective actually changes the meaning of the critical noun. As shown in Figure 6.4, changing the adjective hurts recognition, but changing the adjective so that it changes the meaning of the word hurts recognition even more.

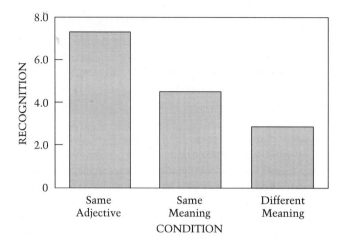

Figure 6.4. *Results from Light and Carter-Sobell's (1970) study showing that biasing the meaning of a noun at recall hurts recognition performance.*

This effect is not very surprising. One would think that you would have two separate concepts for *jam* in memory: one for the thing you spread on toast and one for the traffic tie-up. At encoding you think of one meaning, and at retrieval the cue biases you to think of the other, so you fail to recall the word. What would happen, though, if you didn't change the meaning of the word but emphasized different aspects or properties of the word?

Barclay and his colleagues (1974) pointed out that how participants think about the word *piano*, for example, would vary depending on which aspect of the concept one made participants think about. For example, what might you remember if you read "The man lifted the piano" or "The man smashed the piano?" The man might also tune, sit on, or photograph the piano, each verb biasing you to think about different properties of the same noun, *piano*.

To determine whether emphasizing a particular property of a concept influenced participants' subsequent memory for it, Barclay et al. gave 20 participants to-be-remembered words in the context of a sentence that encouraged them to think of a particular property of the word's referent. For example, a participant might hear "The man lifted the piano" or "The man tuned the piano." At recall, each participant received two cues (but not consecutively) that were pertinent to the target words. For *piano*, the cues were "something heavy" and "something with a nice sound." Each participant only heard one sentence with *piano* in it, but each participant heard both cues at recall (on separate testing occasions), so one cue was appropriate and the other inappropriate. Participants remembered an average of 4.6 words (out of 10) that were cued according to the appropriate meaning and just 1.6 words (out of 10) that were cued with the inappropriate meaning. Note that in this experiment, it was properties of an object that were changed, not the object itself. Nevertheless, there is a sizable effect of changing the cue at retrieval.

Retrieval Cues and Memory Test Sensitivity

This preceding discussion gives us a hint about what is behind the different sensitivity of different types of retrieval tests; it's not that more retrieval cues per se are better for retrieval, but that having more cues makes it more likely that one of them will match what you thought about at encoding, leading to successful retrieval.

Thus, it's not quite correct to say that one memory test is, in an absolute sense, more sensitive than another test.

If that were true, it should be possible to turn a sensitive memory test into an insensitive one by ensuring that the cues it provides don't make you think about the to-be-remembered material the same way that you did at encoding. In other words, the main reason a recognition test is more sensitive than a cued recall test is that the recognition test is more likely to make you process the material the way you did at encoding. If you set up the tests so that it's now the cued recall test that is more likely to make you think about the material as you did at encoding, than the cued recall test should be more sensitive than the recognition test.

Endel Tulving (1968) set out to show exactly that effect. Thirty-two participants were asked to learn a list of A–B paired-associates such as "TOOTH–ACHE," "AIR–PORT," and "FLOOR–SHOW." Training continued until participants could produce the B members of all 48 pairs on the list, without error, two times consecutively. Then participants were presented with a list of 96 words—the 48 B members of the pairs they had just learned and 48 foils—and they were asked to check off the words that they had just learned. None of the 32 participants could do so perfectly, and the mean number correct was 43.4. Thus on average, participants failed to recognize 4.6 items among the 48 that they could recall in a cued recall test. Tulving's point in conducting this experiment was to show that in a recognition test there are still retrieval processes at work; even though the participant is confronted with the stimulus itself, the stimulus was encoded in a particular fashion, and the way one thinks about the stimulus when it is seen alone ("PORT") may not match the way one thought about the stimulus when it was part of the paired associated task ("AIR–PORT").

Something about this task seems unfair, somehow. It feels unfair because the two words in the paired associate task actually form a compound word, and that compound word means something very different than the B member of the pair means when it is viewed alone. In a better-known paradigm, Tulving and his associate Donald Thomson (1973) used word pairs that did not form compound words.

In this experiment, participants were told that they would see word pairs, and they were to remember the words written in capital letters. There would always be an accompanying word written in lowercase letters, which might help them, but it was the words in capital letters that they would be tested on. Then participants saw a list of 24 word pairs (e.g., "glue–CHAIR," "ground–COLD," "fruit–FLOWER"). Next, participants were asked to free associate to a list of words. For each word on the list, they were to write down whatever words popped into mind (up to six words). The words on the free association test were closely associated with the to-be-remembered words from the orginal list. For example, one of the words on the free association task was "table" and participants are very likely to say "chair" in response to that cue. In fact, participants produced 74% of the to-be-remembered words when they were free associating. Then the experimenters asked participants to look over all the words they had just produced on the free recall test and to circle any that matched the to-be-remembered words. Participants recognized only 24% of the target words that they themselves had produced. Immediately after this task, participants were given the list of cues from the original to-be-remembered list (e.g., "glue ____ ," "ground ____ ," and "fruit ____"), and participants were to say which word went with each cue. Now participants were able to produce 63% of the words.

So to recap, participants first see 24 word pairs like this:

glue–CHAIR
ground–COLD
fruit–FLOWER

and they are told to remember the capitalized words. Then they see a list like this

table ____ ____ ____ ____ ____ ____
hot ____ ____ ____ ____ ____ ____
bloom ____ ____ ____ ____ ____ ____

and they are asked to write down words that each word on the list makes them think of. Next they are asked to look over the responses they've written and to circle any of the target words from the first list that they produced. Finally, they are given a cued recall test for the target words like this

glue– ____
ground– ____
fruit– ____

Tulving and Thomson called this effect **recognition failure of recallable words**—which is descriptive, if not very catchy—to emphasize that the encoding and testing conditions were set in such a way as to reverse the usual finding that recognition is superior to recall. This effect has been repeated in many, many experiments, including ones that drop the free association test, and simply administer a recognition test to participants and then a cued recall test. The results of some of the many experiments are shown in Figure 6.5, taken from a paper by Arthur Flexser and Endel Tulving (1978; see also Tulving & Wiseman, 1975). Each point on the figure represents one condition from an experiment. On the horizontal axis is the proportion of words recognized, and on the vertical axis is the proportion of words recognized *given that the word was successfully recalled.* If recognition were more sensitive (easier) than recall, then if you recall a word, you should recognize it, so the values on the vertical axis should be close to 1.0. Instead, they are quite close to the values on the horizontal axis. Put another way, the fact that a participant recalled a word tells you little about the liklihood

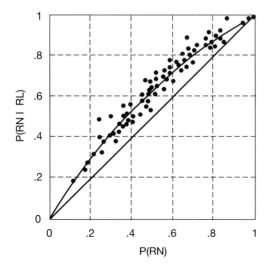

Figure 6.5. *The relationship between (P(RN|RL) and P(RN) over 89 conditions from 33 experiments. P, probability; RL, recall; RN, recognition.*

that the participant would recognize the word. If the independence between recognition and recall were perfect, the points would fall on the diagonal line. They don't—they are slightly above the diagonal, as you can see—but the data show less dependence between recognition and recall than you would think.

When you think about it, the finding is a bit bizarre: Participants can recall "CHAIR" given the cue "glue," even though 5 min earlier they had failed to pick out "CHAIR" when it was right in front of them on the page. Instead they had picked a word they had never seen. How is that possible?

There has been a good deal of debate about what is behind this phenomenon (including the idea that it was just a statistical oddity, and not of any importance; see Hintzman, 1992). At this point, the favored explanation is quite similar to the ideas we've been developing here. The secret to the recognition failure of recallable words effect lies in the lowercase cues. They are selected to be words that are *low associates* of the target words. *Low associates* means that if you ask a thousand people, "What is the first thing you think of when I say the word *chair?*" very few will say, "Glue." But a few will. It's not completely unrelated. The fact that they are not completely unrelated means that when you hear "glue" and "chair" it's not too hard to make a connection between the two words, but making the connection probably encourages you to think about "chair" in a way that you would not ordinarily think about it. For example, when you see "glue–CHAIR" it probably makes you think about the joints of a chair, which are often glued, or something similar. Now when you just see "CHAIR" in isolation, chances are that you don't think about its joints; you think about a chair as something that one can sit on, that goes with a table, and so on. So the presence of the innocent word "glue," which the experimenter says you are free to ignore, makes you think about the target in an unusual way. Then later, on the recognition test, you see "CHAIR" alone and you think about chair in the normal way—something to sit on—but that's not what you thought about at encoding. You thought about something with glued joints. So you say to yourself, "Nah, I didn't see the word *CHAIR* before. Gee, I don't know which of these three was on the list. I'll just guess." And you might guess wrong. Then later you get the recall test and see the cue "glue," and there is some chance you'll say to yourself, "Oh yeah, I thought about glue at encoding—glued joints it was. On a chair. Right, *glue* went with *CHAIR*." So this experiment shows that the match between encoding and retrieval is so important that you can actually be faced with the very stimulus you were supposed to remember and still not recognize it if you encoded the stimulus in a way that is different from the way you interpret it when you see it in a different context at retrieval.

In summary, recognition usually is a more sensitive measure of memory than recall because actually seeing the to-be-remembered material usually provides a better cue to the encoding conditions. However, if you set up a test in which a cue (such as "glue") is a better cue to the original encoding episode, then that will be the most sensitive measure of memory.

So far, so good. But this explanation doesn't make total sense. It emphasizes that different cues are behind the success or failure of retrieval attempts, but one of the examples I gave seemed to show that you can either succeed or fail in remembering something given the exact same cues; I ask you on different days, "Name the Rice Crispies guys," and one day you can do it, and another you can't. What's going on?

Well, the best guess is that it's similar to the phenomenon in recognition failure of recallable words. Someone gives you the same task—"Name the Rice Crispies guys"—but that cue won't necessarily make you think about the same things each time you hear it. One time it makes you think about the cereal itself (and that's no help), another time it makes you think about the cereal box, and you try to remember the names by scanning the mental image of the little guys to see whether their names are on their caps (they are, but maybe you can't read them), and another time the question makes you think about the television advertisement, which makes you think of the jingle, "Snap, Crackle, Pop! Rice Crispies!" and you've got it. Why does the same question make you think about the cereal, the box, or the advertisement at different times?

A reasonable guess would be that what you think about when you're given a cue is a product not only of the cue but of what you've been thinking about recently. How could you test such an idea? A natural procedure would be to make people think about some material—have them read a brief story about swimming, for example—and then a little later ask them some questions for which something about swimming would be a natural answer but not one that people would necessarily *have* to give.

John Kihlstrom (1983) devised such an experiment. He hypnotized participants and had them learn a list of 16 words. He then gave them a posthypnotic suggestion that they would forget the words. After participants were aroused from the amnesic state, they were asked to name examples of a category. For example, they might be given the category "fruit" and they might say "apple, orange, pear, banana," and so on. The interesting finding for our purposes is that having learned the item during hypnosis made it much more likely that participants would produce the item as an instance of a category. For example, having learned the word "strawberry" meant participants were likely to produce it early in their attempts to produce category instances. Of 15 possible items, participants produced 10.8, compared to an average of just 7.8 words produced by participants who had not memorized the words. This pattern was true even though participants did not consciously remember having seen the words before because of the amnesia caused by the posthypnotic suggestion. In a later study, it was shown that the same effect was found when participants were merely exposed to the words one time instead of memorizing them and when the participants had brain damage that caused the amnesia instead of hypnosis (Graf, Shimamura, & Squire, 1985).

This effect is called **priming.** Priming generally refers to the facilitation of later processing of a stimulus by prior exposure to the stimulus. In the experiment described, exposure to a word later makes you likely to think of that word a second time when you are trying to do the category exemplar task.

Priming works not only for the same word but for semantic associates. Thus, thinking about the word *Doctor* can affect how you process the word *Nurse*. This effect was demonstrated by David Meyer and Roger Schvaneveldt (1971). The task they asked participants to perform was simple. Participants saw two letter strings on a computer screen, and they were to press one button if both strings were words and another button if either string was a nonword. The experimenters were interested in how quickly participants could make this decision. The response time data are graphed in Figure 6.6.

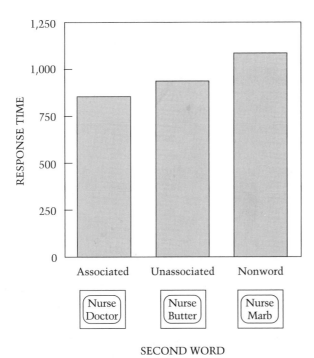

SECOND WORD

Figure 6.6. *Results of Meyer and Schvaneveldt's (1971) experiment showing that participants are faster to identify a word if they have just read a semantically related word.*

BOX 6.1. THE FRONTAL LOBE AND MEMORY RETRIEVAL

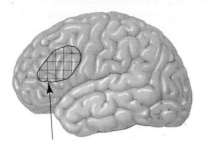 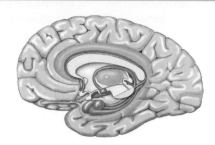

Frontal area typically
affected in a patient in
Gershberg and Shimamura's Study

One of the themes in this section is that there are different methods of measuring memory retrieval, and these different measures yield different estimates of what a person seems to remember. In other words, using one measure of memory, the person appears to have forgotten some material, but by using a different measure of memory it becomes apparent that the person remembers the material.

It is reasonable to ask whether there are separate brain areas underlying these different methods of retrieval. The answer appears to be "no." Rather, some methods of retrieval rely on extra processes, but would be going too far to call these different methods of retrieval truly separate.

Some of the more interesting research on retrieval comes from studies of patients with damage to the frontal lobes. Such patients do not have an overall difficulty in learning new material, but they do have some difficulties in retrieval. Usually they perform normally (or are minimally impaired) if their memory is tested via recognition, but they are much more impaired if they are tested with a free recall measure. Second, these patients have difficulty remembering the temporal order of events (i.e., which event came first, which came second, etc.). Third, they appear to have a particular problem with source memory (i.e., remembering not only a bit of information but where they heard the information).

What all of these deficits have in common is a reliance on memory strategies. In a recognition test, for example, the participant need only evaluate each stimulus that the experimenter has provided. In a free recall test, the experimenter provides nothing, and the participant must generate all of the materials himself or herself.

Felicia Gershberg and Art Shimamura (1995) tested the hypothesis that patients with damage to the frontal lobes have memory difficulties that are attributable to deficient strategies. In one experiment they administered five study–test trials of the same 15-item word list. Normal participants report the words in more or less the same order on each trial; it's a good strategy to do so because recalling a word probably will make you think of the next word that you reported the last time. Gershberg and Shimamura's normal participants showed those ordering effects, but the patients with damage to the frontal lobes did not. In a second experiment, participants heard lists of words that were examples of categories. Each 15-item list had three words (e.g., *car, truck, tractor*) from each of five categories (e.g., *vehicles,*

(Continued)

fruits). Normal participants will try to remember all of the vehicles, then all of the fruits, and so on. Patients with damage to the frontal lobes did not use this strategy, however, and simply remembered the words in random order. When all participants were cued with the categories, however, patients with frontal lobe damage were able to use the categories to improve their recall.

These data indicate that different types of memory measures call on different cognitive processes. Some measures of memory require that the participant adopt strategies, and these lesion studies indicate that the frontal lobe plays an important role in these strategies.

We'll discuss theories of how memory is organized that explain this phenomenon in chapter 7. For now, we're focusing on why you sometimes retrieve a memory given a cue and other times fail to retrieve it given the same cue. The answer to this puzzle seems to be that the same cue makes you think of different things at different times. The work on priming just described shows that what you've thought about recently influences what you're thinking about now, but the details of how this works are understood only for simple situations: Thinking about a word or concept makes it likely that you'll think about it again later or that you'll think about semantically related things.

Retrieval and Prior Knowledge

In chapter 5 we saw that one's prior knowledge influences how new material is processed and therefore how it is encoded. For example, if something is happening that can be described by a script (e.g., taking a cab from the airport) that is inconsistent with the script and is relevant to the goal of the script (e.g., the cabbie gets lost), that inconsistent event will be well remembered. Does prior knowledge also influence retrieval? Yes, it does, but at retrieval it influences memory of the typical events, not the atypical ones.

Suppose that you are trying to remember a story I told you last week, and you remember that it involved something about my daughter's birthday party. You have prior knowledge stored in memory about children's birthday parties that can provide retrieval cues. For example, you probably know that cake and ice cream usually are served at kids' parties, which might lead you to try to remember what sort of cake was served or whether something other than cake was served, such as an enormous chocolate chip cookie. Note that prior knowledge influences retrieval in this example. Without the prior knowledge that cake usually is served at children's birthday parties, you might have forgotten to mention the food at all. Your expectation that cake was served may be so strong that you may think to yourself, "I really don't remember cake being served, but this was a kid's birthday party, so there *had* to be cake; let me try one more time to remember what kind." In this case the retrieval cue is simply that food must have been served.

It seems to make sense that a schema could affect memory at retrieval, but how do we know that the effect of the schema actually is occurring at retrieval?

For example, here is a classic study by Sir Frederic Bartlett (1932), who first developed the idea of a schema. He read this native North American folk tale called "The War of the Ghosts" to English schoolboys.

> One night two young men from Egulac went down to the river to hunt seals, and while they were there it became foggy and calm. Then they heard war-cries, and they thought: "Maybe this is a war-party." They escaped to the shore, and hid behind a log. Now canoes came up, and they heard the noise of paddles, and saw one canoe coming up to them. There were five men in the canoe, and they said:
>
> "What do you think? We wish to take you along. We are going up the river to make war on the people." One of the young men said: "I have no arrows." "Arrows are in the canoe," they said. "I will not go along. I might be killed. My relatives do not know where I have gone. But you," he said, turning to the other, "may go with them." So one of the young men went, but the other returned home.
>
> And the warriors went on up the river to a town on the other side of Kalama. The people came down to the water, and they began to fight, and many were killed. But presently the young man heard one of the warriors say: "Quick, let us go home: that Indian has been hit." Now he thought: "Oh, they are ghosts." He did not feel sick, but they said he had been shot.
>
> So the canoes went back to Egulac, and the young man went ashore to his house, and made a fire. And he told everybody and said: "Behold I accompanied the ghosts, and we went to fight. Many of our fellows were killed, and many of those who attacked us were killed. They said I was hit, and I did not feel sick." He told it all, and then he became quiet. When the sun rose he fell down. Something black came out of his mouth. His face became contorted. The people jumped up and cried. He was dead."

Note that this story has elements that would be unfamiliar to English schoolboys in the 1930s (and probably to most American college students today). The story had cultural elements they were unfamiliar with (e.g., canoes), and the story structure itself was unfamilar; English stories typically have logical links between one event and another, whereas in this story new actions are introduced without making it clear how they relate to previous actions. Bartlett reported that when his participants tried to recall this story later, their recall was influenced by their schema of what a story is supposed to be like. They added details to put logical connections between events. They omitted other details and changed unfamiliar terms to ones they new better; Bartlett called attention to one participant who substituted the word "boat" for "canoe" when he recalled the story, and another who substituted "fishing" for "seal hunting." In fact, the particular results Bartlett reported have not always replicated that well (Roediger, Wheeler, & Rajaram, 1993), but the basic effects he reported are very well supported.

Bartlett argued that retrieval is largely a process of **reconstruction.** That means that retrieval is not simply a matter of pulling information out of the memory storehouse (which is pretty much how we've been describing it). Rather, Bartlett argued, retrieval is a process whereby you use information from the memory storehouse *and* information about the world (in the form of schemas) to reconstruct what probably happened.

This idea is supported by data from the study by Bower, Black, and Turner (1979). You'll recall that in chapter 5 we said that events that are inconsistent with the script but that are relevant to the goal of the script (e.g., the cabbie getting lost) are well remembered. Another effect that the experimenters reported is what happens if participants are asked about information that is consistent with the script but was not presented in the original story. For example, participants might read a story about going to a restaurant. The story does not mention that the patron paid the bill. After reading the story, participants were given a recognition test for sentences in the story and were asked to rate their confidence that they had seen each sentence from 1 to 7. The experimenters found that participants gave high ratings to sentences from the script that were actually contained in the story (average = 5.46) but that they also gave high ratings to actions that were consistent with the script but never mentioned in the story (average = 3.9); these ratings were much higher than the ratings they assigned to events that were not in the story but were unrelated to the script (average = 1.71). (See Table 6.2 for sample sentences.)

Thus, it appears that prior knowledge in the form of schemas influences not only encoding (remember the washing clothes example from chapter 5) but also retrieval. But how can we be certain that these effects occur at retrieval? It seems perfectly plausible that these schema effects occur at encoding; as the participant is listening to the story, he or she is changing it as it goes to make it fit his or her schema better. For example, perhaps people *infer* that Dan paid the bill when they hear the story, and they encode this inference. Then at recall, they are simply remembering the inference that they encoded; reconstruction doesn't happen at all.

James Dooling and Robert Christianson (1977) thought of a clever way to show that reconstruction can happen at recall. They asked participants to read this paragraph:

> Carol Harris was a problem child from birth. She was wild, stubborn, and violent. By the time Carol turned eight, she was still unmanageable. Her parents were very concerned about her mental health. There was no good institution for her problem in her state. Her parents finally decided to take some action. They hired a private teacher for Carol.

Table 6.2   Sample Recognition Test

Original Story	Recognition Test Sentences	Type of Sentence	Average Recognition Rating
Dan went to a restaurant. The hostess seated him. He scanned the menu. He selected what he wanted, and the waitress took his order. Dan waited for his food. The waitress brought his food. Dan ate his meal and left the restaurant.	Dan waited for his food.	Consistent with the script; in the story	5.46
	Dan paid the bill.	Consistent with the script; not in story	3.91
	The restaurant was cold.	Irrelevant to script; not in story	1.71

BOX 6.2. FUNCTIONAL IMAGING STUDIES OF THE FRONTAL LOBE AND MEMORY

We've already discussed the role of the frontal lobe in memory a couple of times. In chapter 5 I mentioned the studies by Wagner et al. (1998) and Brewer et al. (1998) showing that frontal activity at encoding predicted whether a memory would be retrieved later. Earlier in this chapter I mentioned studies of patients with frontal lobe damage that indicated that the frontal lobe was especially important for developing strategies that help memory retrieval.

You may have noticed that there is a bit of a paradox here. Lesion studies indicate that the frontal lobe is important only for strategic processes in memory because patients with frontal lobe damage are largely unimpaired on a recognition test of memory. Yet functional imaging studies give frontal cortex a starring role in memory. Recall that frontal cortex was one of two areas whose activity at encoding predicted memory at retrieval, and retrieval was measured by recognition. Indeed, almost every functional imaging study of memory shows frontal activation. Figure B6.2 shows a summary of such studies, with each circle representing the focus of activation in one study.

Why is there a discrepancy between the lesion studies (which indicate that frontal cortex is not important) and the imaging studies (which indicate that it is)?

In a review of imaging studies Randy Buckner and his colleagues (Buckner, Kelley, & Petersen, 1999) addressed this question. They suggested two possibilities. One possibility is that patients with damage to the frontal lobes have more widespread memory deficits than is commonly appreciated, but they are able to compensate for these deficits. The idea is that people can code the same stimulus in a number of different ways (e.g., verbally or pictorially), and these different encodings rely on different parts of the frontal lobe. Thus, a typical patient would

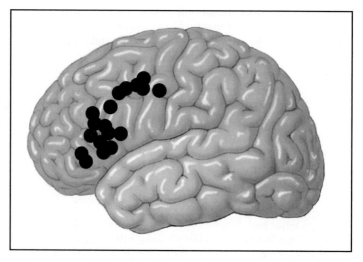

Figure B6.2. *Figure from Buckner, Kelley, and Petersen (1999) showing the focus of activation in memory studies.*

(Continued)

have damage that leads to poor encoding of one type of stimulus, but the patient usually can recode the stimulus a different way so that it relies only on the part of the frontal lobe that is intact.

A second possibility is that the researchers have been overinterpreting the imaging results. Most often when we observe activity in frontal regions it is at encoding. Buckner et al. pointed out that this activation may contribute to memory formation only in a small way and that this activity represents the cognitive processes that are active at the time of encoding (e.g., thinking about what the stimulus means) and does not represent activity that is actually forming the memory.

In the end, the disparity between the imaging results, which indicate that the frontal lobe is the star of memory formation, and the lesion studies, which indicate that it is a supporting player, remain unresolved. It is a puzzle that researchers are trying to solve.

After a 1-week delay, participants were given a recognition test for sentences; participants had to say whether each sentence was or was not in the story. The critical sentence was "She was deaf, dumb, and blind." Very few participants thought that this sentence had been part of the story. But a second group of participants underwent the same testing procedure, except that right before taking the recognition test they were told that Carol Harris was Helen Keller's real name. Many of these participants incorrectly "recognized" the critical sentence as having been in the story. This experiment shows clearly that reconstruction can take place at retrieval. There was no opportunity for the memory error to take place at encoding because participants didn't know that their background knowledge about Helen Keller would be relevant until retrieval.

Mnemonics: A Framework for Retrieval

A framework for retrieval can be a very potent aid to memory, and it is an important part of many **mnemonics** (i.e., aids to memory). Many mnemonics require that you memorize something simple, which provides effective cues to the rest of what you want to remember. I could never remember the names of all the Great Lakes until someone taught me the mnemonic *HOMES: Huron, Ontario, Michigan, Erie, Superior.* Once I have the prior knowledge *HOMES* in memory and know when to apply it, that gives me the first letter of each of the Great Lakes. The first letter is a good retrieval cue, which is itself an interesting clue. The mnemonic could use the last letter of each Great Lake: *NONER.* But imagine saying to yourself, "Which of the Great Lakes ends with *N?*" It's easier to find words in memory that start with a letter than words that end with a letter; that's a clue to what the indexing system in memory might be like, and we discuss that further in chapter 7.

Another mnemonic that was very popular when I was in college was an aid to memory for the proper consumption of alcohol. It was widely believed that if you switched from beer to whiskey in the middle of the evening you would get really sick—or maybe switching from whiskey to beer was the problem. No one could ever remember which was the dangerous order of drinking. Obviously, if you're trying to remember which is the safe order after having had a few, you are not attempting recall under optimal circumstances. Hence the mnemonic "Beer then whiskey, that's risky; whiskey then beer, never fear."

The preceding mnemonics are specific to remembering one piece of information. You can create all-purpose mnemonics on the same principle. For a general mnemonic, you first memorize something. Then, when there is new material you want to remember, you associate the new material with the stuff you've already memorized. For example, the mental walk technique (also called the method of loci) requires that you first commit to memory a mental walk with a number of points of interest, or stations, on the walk. For example, I memorized a mental walk when I lived in Williamstown, Massachusetts. The first station was my back porch, which had some rotting floorboards. Then I walked around my side yard, past a dead pear tree, which was the second station. The third station was my driveway, which needed more gravel. The walk from my house to my office had about 40 stations. If you give me a list of items to remember, such as *coffee, alligator,* and *bone,* I associate each item with a station on my walk, in order. So when you say "coffee" I try to associate that word with my first station, which is my back porch. I might imagine that as I step on the back porch, I find it is raining coffee. The next word is *alligator,* so I might imagine an enormous alligator in my dead pear tree, perhaps with a pear in its mouth. And so on. Notice that it's best to use deep encoding when using a mnemonic. Then when it's time to recall, I think "Okay, the first station was the back porch. What went with the back porch?" So each station on the walk serves as a retrieval cue for a word.

General purpose mnemonics are not very useful. First, there is always the danger of proactive interference. If you go on your mental walk frequently, you might mentally arrive at your back porch and find that it is raining coffee and also find that your rotting floorboards have been replaced by breadsticks. So which item were you trying to remember this time, and which is an association from the last mental walk? The second reason general purpose mnemonics are not so useful is that it's a lot easier to write down a shopping list than it is to go through the trouble of trying to memorize the list of items. Specific mnemonics such as HOMES are more useful because there is no chance of proactive interference and because you may find yourself wanting the information when it is inconvenient to look it up.

STAND-ON-ONE-FOOT QUESTIONS

1. *What four measures of memory are commonly used, and what does it mean to say they differ in sensitivity?*
2. *Why do different measures of memory differ in sensitivity?*
3. *Which is more important to effective retrieval: the format of the test (e.g., recognition, cued recall) or the cues the test provides?*
4. *How does prior knowledge affect retrieval?*

QUESTIONS THAT REQUIRE TWO FEET

   5. *Suppose you asked a friend to tell you what he or she was doing exactly 19 months ago. How much do you think he or she could tell you, and why?*
   6. *You probably have had the experience of walking right past a friend as though you didn't even know him or her if you were somewhere you don't typically see the friend (e.g., you see a college friend in your home town during spring break). How can the ideas discussed here explain that phenomenon?*

➤ WHY DO WE FORGET?

> ➤ *PREVIEW* There are two main theories of forgetting: decay and interference. There is little evidence supporting the idea that memories decay, but a decay theory of memory is very difficult to test. There is quite a bit more evidence for interference, and there are a couple of sources of interference, including response competition and unlearning. The idea that all forgetting is caused by interference makes it sound as if it might be true that all memories are in the storehouse and that any failure of retrieval is caused by interference, but there is no good evidence supporting that view. However, it does seem to be true that if memories are practiced enough, for all practical purposes they will never be forgotten. Finally, we consider repression as a source of forgetting. Repression is difficult to prove, but there is enough evidence in the literature to conclude that it can happen, although it is probably rare.

In the past section we discussed why something that can be retrieved sometimes is not retrieved. Other times it seems that information is lost not temporarily but permanently. It cannot be retrieved. Indeed, intuition tells us that this is the more common occurrence. Only occasionally do we say, "I'm sure I know that, but I can't think of it right now." More often we say, "I don't know. I forgot." What happens when information is forgotten?

We could imagine two basic explanations. First, the information in the storehouse might become degraded or lost. Perhaps there is a limited amount of room in the storehouse, so old, infrequently used information is ejected to make room for new information, or pehaps everything in the storehouse slowly erodes unless it is periodically refreshed in some way. A second possibility is that the information is in the storehouse, undegraded and ready to be remembered, but you can't get to it for some reason. Both of these possibilities have been suggested. The first is called decay theory, and the second is called interference theory, and we consider each in turn.

Decay Theory

The **decay theory** of forgetting proposes that memories spontaneously decay over time. Forgetting is caused by the loss of the representation supporting the memory, and this loss or degradation is simply a consequence of time. If you rehearse the memory again it will be "refreshed," but all memories are decaying, so refreshing the memory doesn't prevent decay: It simply revives the memory. I think this is the theory that would first occur to most people. The passage of time seems to be culprit in forgetting.

Indeed, a decay theory with time at its center was the first theory proposed by early cognitive psychologists. A simple version of decay theory was proposed by Thorndike (1911), the great turn-of-the-century learning theorist. He called it the law of disuse and simply proposed that if you don't use a memory, it decays. The problem with that idea is that it predicts that older memories should always be more decayed than newer memories and therefore more difficult to retrieve, and we know that that is not right because some older memories remain strong, whereas newer memories are lost. I can't recall what I had for breakfast 3 days ago, but I can still remember the name of my first-grade teacher.

Of course, you could combine decay theory with some version of a strength theory; all memories decay at a constant rate, but some start out with more strength than others (e.g., your first-grade teacher's name is quite strong), so older memories that start out with more strength could be easier to retrieve than more recent memories that started out with less strength. Until the 1930s, most psychologists thought that something like this was behind forgetting. In the last section we went over problems with a strength theory, but people didn't spot these problems until the 1960s.

Nevertheless, people rejected the strength-plus-decay theory in the 1930s because of problems in the idea of decay. The case against decay was made by John McGeogh in 1932. He pointed out that it seems natural to blame time as the great causative agent in forgetting. We forget as time passes, and one therefore thinks of the passage of time as causing the forgetting. McGeogh pointed out that that is not really an explanation, however. Time itself can't do anything; some process happening *in* time causes forgetting. He suggested the analogy of metal rusting. Metal does not rust because of time. Metal rusts because of oxidation, a process that happens *in* time. For decay to be an explanation, one must specify what the process of decay is. Naturally that process happens in time, but simply saying that memories decay because time passes is not an answer.

There is another problem with a decay theory, and it is much more serious. The decay theory is very difficult (and may be impossible) to test. Decay is supposed to occur spontaneously; as time goes on, the representation degrades, irrespective of what the cognitive system is doing. Thus, the ideal experiment would be to have people learn something, then do nothing for 8 hr (or however long), and then test their memory to see whether some of the memory decayed. That experiment cannot be conducted. You can't have people thinking about absolutely nothing for 8 hr or even for 8 s; there is a constant stream of thought, and it is known that what you think about after encoding can interfere with memory. Thus, whether there is a decay process is very hard to ascertain because if you look for decay and you observe forgetting, it is always possible that what you were really observing was the effect of interference. In sum, whether decay occurs is not known, but it is not thought to play a major role in forgetting. Quite a bit more is known about interference, however.

Interference Theory

Interference theory holds that interference causes forgetting in several different ways. One source that McGeoch and others thought was important was **response competition,** which means that an old response that is already in memory interferes with a new response you're trying to learn. In a moment I'll tell you about later work showing that it probably doesn't contribute that much to forgetting, but it's worth understanding the concept because it certainly sounds as if it ought to contribute to forgetting.

Suppose you learn a list of paired associates, such as "89–cabbage" and "72–pen." Once you've learned them pretty well, I give you a new list that consists of the same numbers, now paired with different words, such as "89–table" and "72–shovel." When you hear "89" there will be competition between the old response, "cabbage," and the new response, "table." Anyone who has changed telephone numbers is familiar with this. The new number is hard to learn because the cue, "What is your telephone number?" is strongly associated with producing the old number; you find yourself saying, "My number is 296-2—no wait, actually it's 555-2431. I'm not a nitwit, I've recently moved." Thus, it feels intuitively that response competition must be a source of forgetting.

In a classic experiment, Arthur Melton and Jean Irwin (1940) showed that response competition probably doesn't account for much interference, however. They had participants learn a list of 18 nonsense syllables. These are single-syllable stimuli that have no meaning, such as "vez." Participants practiced the list five times. On each practice run, they saw a word presented for 2 s, and participants were asked to spell the word that they thought would appear next.

Thirty minutes later participants were retested on the list. Melton and Irwin varied what different participants did during the 30 min wait. Some participants read magazines, others had to learn a second list of nonsense syllables, and the experimenters varied how much participants studied the second list (either 5, 10, 20, or 40 repetitions). The critical measure came when everyone was retested on the first list. If there is response competition, then there should be intrusions when people are retested on the first list. (An **intrusion** is simply producing the response from the second list when you're supposed to be recalling the first list. More generally, an intrusion is producing an answer that would be right in another context at the wrong time.) You would predict that they would show intrusions, based on the principle of response competition, and this does happen. You would also predict that the more they study the second list, the more intrusions there will be. This is true up to a point, but as shown in Figure 6.7, as the second list is studied more, the number of intrusions begins to drop.

On reflection, this makes sense. It's as though with increased practice you come to know the second list quite well, and when you're trying to recall the first list it's easy for you to say, "I'm thinking of 'juv' but that's a second list word and I'm supposed to be reporting first list words." But although increased practice with the second list makes the number of intrusions drop, overall forgetting of the first list increases. This finding makes it clear that response competition can't be the whole story on interference because response competition decreases with second list practice while forgetting is increasing.

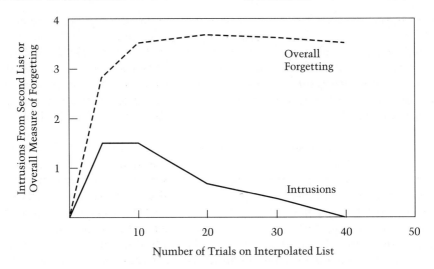

Figure 6.7.   *Graph from Melton and Irwin's experiment showing that more prac-*
tice on a second list means that you don't get more intrusions from
a second list when you later try to recall the first list. Initially there
is a rise, but then the number of intrusions falls. Nevertheless, for-
getting increases. The measure of intrusions and forgetting is a com-
plex percentage estimate designed to make these two measures
comparable on one graph.

Melton and Irwin (1940) proposed that studying the second list causes **un-**
learning of the first list. *Unlearning* means that studying new material causes forgetting of old material. Unlearning is difficult to prove: If participants fail to
recall something, how do you know that response competition is not to blame
and that the desired memory is not lying in the storehouse, ready to be retrieved?

Jean Barnes and Benton Underwood (1959) provided some evidence that unlearning can take place. They had participants learn a list of associates (this time
they were nonsense syllables paired with adjectives, such as "LUM–happy").
Once participants could recite the list perfectly one time through, they received
training on a new list that used the same nonsense syllables, but now they were
paired with new adjectives ("LUM–sleepy"). Participants received different
amounts of training on the second list (between 1 and 20 trials). On the final test,
participants saw each nonsense syllable followed by two blanks, and they were
asked to provide the appropriate response from *both* lists. This procedure was
designed to minimize response competition because participants were asked to
provide both responses. (For obscure reasons, this testing procedure is called
modified-modified free recall.) Participants were better at reporting the second list
word if they had had more practice with the second list, which is not surprising.
Furthermore, they get worse at reporting the first list word with increasing practice on the second list word. Remember, there should have been little response
competition because participants were supposed to write both associates, so confusion over which word went with which list shouldn't cause a problem. Rather,
it seems that studying the second list caused unlearning of the first list.

Or did it? Although this experiment seems to support the conclusion, Mike Anderson and Bobbie Spellman (1995) pointed out that it's possible that the second list doesn't really cause unlearning of the first. "LUM–happy" may be in memory, just as well learned as ever, but as you practice "LUM–sleepy" over and over again, this new association drowns out "LUM–happy." Here's an analogy. You're singing and I turn the radio on and keep turning up the volume; the radio doesn't make you sing any less loudly, but it makes it harder to hear your voice.

It seemed as if it was going to be very hard to distinguish unlearning from this sort of "volume" problem. Anderson and Spellman (1995) took a very clever approach to show that unlearning really does happen. They had people learn word pairs, but they used words that would already be associated in memory. Specifically, they used category names and examples of the categories in the pairs; a pair to remember might be "red–blood" (*red* refers to the category of things that are red). Suppose I ask you to study this pair. If unlearning takes place, then other things in memory that are red should be unlearned a little bit. So if I try to get you to learn "red–tomato" it will be harder because you first had to learn "red–blood," and learning that made "red–tomato" somewhat unlearned. But now we're back to the volume problem; maybe "red–tomato" is hard to learn because "red" has become so strongly associated with "blood" through my studying "red–blood."

Anderson and Spellman reasoned this way. If you study "red–blood," then "strawberry" should become harder to learn, even if "red" is not the cue. Studying "red–blood" causes unlearning in all concepts associated with "red," and that includes "strawberry," so if I try to learn "food–strawberry," that's going to be harder to learn. It's an odd prediction, but the idea is that studying "red–blood" makes it harder to learn "food–strawberry."

But wait a minute. Maybe studying "red–blood" makes it harder to learn *any* new association. Maybe you simply get tired of learning, or there is interference of learning any new pair. To test that possibility, Anderson and Spellman compared learning "food–strawberry" to learning "food–crackers." Because crackers aren't red, there should be no unlearning of "crackers" while you study "red–blood." The logic of their experiment is shown in Figure 6.8.

As the unlearning theory predicts, "food–strawberry" was harder to learn (22% correct on a later recall test) than "food–cracker" (38% correct).

This result is pretty impressive—it's an unexpected effect that the unlearning hypothesis would predict—but is it unlearning? *Unlearning* implies that the connection between the associates in the pair has gotten weaker, and we can't conclude that. It's known that these effects last at least 20 minutes (Anderson, Bjork, & Bjork, 1994), but it's not known whether it reflects a more or less *permanent* change in the memory system (which is the usual criterion for calling something memory). It may be fairer to say that this is an inhibitory effect; that is, studying the "red–blood" dampens "strawberry" but doesn't cause a permanent unlearning of the concept.

This idea that studying one concept causes inhibition (but not unlearning) in other concepts seems to have a function. Inhibition would increase gain (i.e., increase the volume of what you want to hear and decrease the volume of

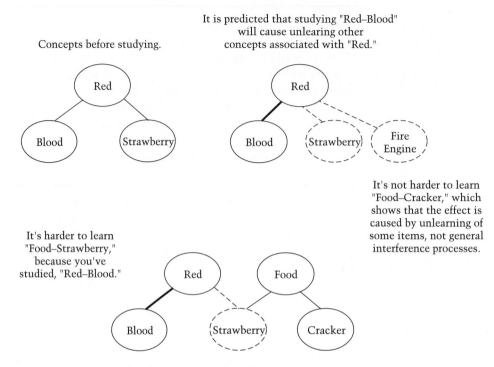

Concepts before studying.

It is predicted that studying "Red–Blood" will cause unlearing other concepts associated with "Red."

It's not harder to learn "Food–Cracker," which shows that the effect is caused by unlearning of some items, not general interference processes.

It's harder to learn "Food–Strawberry," because you've studied, "Red–Blood."

Figure 6.8.   *Logic behind Anderson and Spellman's experiments on unlearning. Dark lines mean a strong connection between the concepts caused by studying them together. Dotted lines mean unlearning.*

what you don't want to hear). The category "red" has a lot of things associated with it. Suppose that when you think of "red," red things in memory (firetruck, apple, ladybug, etc.) automatically become active. In chapter 7, we discuss that there is good evidence that such automatic activation happens. If you want to think of blood when you're given the cue "red," it may be useful to have all these other red things quiet down, so to speak.

A final idea on unlearning is rather speculative but is a lot of fun, so I'll mention it briefly. Richard Gerrig (1989) suggested that a form of unlearning may help us to enjoy movies and stories that we have seen and heard before. He pointed out that we find some stories pleasurable even when we know the ending. Why was the movie *Apollo 13* so successful? Everyone knows the astronauts are okay in the end. (Indeed, even in movies that are not based on historical fact, you often know pretty much how they are going to end. Did anyone really think Darth Vader was going to kill Luke and fly away in the *Death Star,* with Leia as his captive bride?) Gerrig suggested that when you have information that interferes with enjoying a story, you suppress this knowledge.

To test his hypothesis, Gerrig had participants read one of two short paragraphs about, for example, George Washington (Table 6.3). One paragraph simply described Washington's success in the Revolutionary War and said that his friends thought he should lead the country. Other participants saw a similar

Table 6.3   Stimulus Materials from Gerrig (1989)

No-Suspense Version
George Washington was a famous figure after the Revolutionary War.
Washington was a popular choice to lead the new country.
Few people had thought that the British could be defeated.
The success of the Revolutionary War was attributed largely to Washington.
His friends worked to convince him to go on serving his country.
Washington agreed that he had abundant experience as a leader.
Target: George Washington was elected first president of the United States.

Suspense Version
George Washington was a famous figure after the Revolutionary War.
Washington was a popular choice to lead the new country.
Washington, however, wanted to retire after the war.
The long years as general had left him tired and frail.
Washington wrote that he would be unable to accept the nomination.
Attention turned to John Adams as the next most qualified candidate.
Target: George Washington was elected first president of the United States.

paragraph, but it mentioned reasons Washington might not be president (he was in frail health, etc.). Participants read these paragraphs one sentence at a time, and toward the end they were to verify a critical sentence. In each paragraph, this sentence was, "George Washington was elected first president of the United States." Participants were slightly slower to verify that this sentence was true when the paragraph built suspense (average = 2290 ms) than when it did not build suspense (average = 2160 ms). The effect is small but reliable.

Gerrig argued that relevant information in memory can be suppressed for the sake of enjoying a story. The phrase "the suspension of disbelief" often is used in this context; when we listen to a story or watch a movie, we must be willing to forget things that we know to be true to be drawn into the world of the story. Gerrig's data indicate that this process happens, that it happens rather easily (simply by reading a sentence on a computer screen), and that this momentary forgetting has consequences for cognition; in this case, it makes you slightly slower to verify the truth of something that you know quite well to be true.

The Permanence of Memory

So far we've outlined two processes of forgetting. The first is decay, and we've said that there is not much direct evidence supporting a decay process. That doesn't mean decay doesn't happen, but we don't have evidence for it. The second process is interference, and there is certainly plenty of evidence for interference. We don't exactly understand the mechanism—it could be some response competition, it could be some unlearning, it could be other factors—but learning new material definitely interferes with old learning (that's retroactive interference), and learning new material is definitely harder if you've learned something recently (that's proactive interference).

From this summary you might conclude that forgetting is caused mostly (or exclusively) by interference. If memories do not decay, does that mean that everything that has ever happened to you is in memory? Perhaps it's all recorded in your mind, like a library of videotapes, and if you can't remember something it's not because the tape is lost but because you can't find it due to interference. This proposal seems to fit nicely with what we were talking about early in the chapter; you can appear to have forgotten something because of retrieval failure, but that retrieval failure might result from your not having the right cues. Given the right cues, it becomes apparent that you haven't forgotten at all. Hence, perhaps nothing is forgotten. Any memory is in principle retrievable if you can overcome interference effects by getting good retrieval cues. I see this idea written up in newspaper and magazine articles from time to time, usually reported as though it is fact. Most memory researchers don't think this is how things work.

First, you should note one thing. This idea is impossible to disprove. It's impossible to disprove because the basic proposition is that all memories are retrievable if you can get the right cues. So if someone can't remember something, you can always say, "Well, they just don't have the right cues yet." I can test them using a million different cues and you can always maintain that the million-and-first cue might be the right one, and they will remember. Thus, I can never state flatly that this proposal must be wrong. But I think it's unlikely to be true.

The reasons were laid out quite nicely in article by Geoff Loftus and Elizabeth Loftus (1980). They pointed out that there are three main reasons for thinking that all memories lie *somewhere* in the memory vault: spontaneous recovery, memory under hypnosis, and an interesting study by neurologist Wilder Penfield. As we'll see, there are problems with each of these sources of evidence.

SPONTANEOUS RECOVERY.   **Spontaneous recovery** is the sudden uncovering of a long-lost memory. Often there is an identifiable cue that you are quite sure has not been available that clearly led to recovery of the memory. People often report spontaneous recovery when they revisit a house they lived in as a child. They thought they remembered little of their life from that time, but once they are actually at the house, the sight of a room brings back a number of vivid memories. It's as though the cue (seeing the house again) is one end of a very fine chain, and if you pull it gently you find there are charms (memories) attached to the chain.

Many people report the spontaneous recovery of memories; it's happened to me. One obvious problem is that in many cases you don't really know whether the "recovered" memories are accurate. The people recovering the memories often believe they are accurate, but that is certainly not airtight evidence. Furthermore, even if we accept the fact that the recovered memories are accurate, the fact that some memories can be spontaneously recovered does not mean that all memories are recorded. It means that some memories that you haven't retrieved in a long time can be retrieved given the right cues.

MEMORY AND HYPNOSIS.   One sometimes hears or reads about amazing feats of memory performed under hypnosis (bricklayers accurately reporting exact descriptions of bricks they laid in walkways years ago, and so on). Again, the idea that goes along with this is that memory works like a video camera and everything is recorded, but we usually don't have access to everything that is in memory. Hypnosis supposedly bypasses the usual route and allows direct access to memory.

In a word, bunk. It is easy enough to test whether hypnosis helps memory. You have two groups of people and you give them some material to learn. You wait a while. Then you test their memory for the material, with one group under hypnosis and the other not. Many such experiments have been conducted (e.g., Lytle & Lundy, 1988; Register & Kihlstrom, 1987; for a review, see Erdelyi, 1994). In one such study, David Dinges and his colleagues (1992) showed participants 40 drawings of common objects. Participants immediately tried to remember as many as they could. One week later they returned, whereupon they again attempted to recall the drawings, half of them under hypnosis and half not. The experimenters asked the participants to try to recall the whole list five times; they wanted to give an effect of hypnosis every opportunity to become manifest. They also examined participants who were very susceptible to hypnosis and participants who were not to see whether that factor made a difference. Hypnosis did nothing to improve the accuracy of memory.

There is an advantage to memory in the procedures often used in hypnosis; you are told to relax, you are told to think carefully about what you're trying to remember, and you are asked to try to remember not just once, but a number of times. All of those things help memory, but they are all things you can do with or without hypnosis. In fact, nonhypnotized participants remembered more with repeated recall attempts. Hypnosis does not improve the accuracy of memory.

PENFIELD'S EXPERIMENTS.   Wilder Penfield (1959) reported on a rather dramatic study he performed. This procedure is a little complicated, but it's worth knowing about. Penfield's participants were people who were soon to undergo brain surgery. These people had very bad epilepsy that would not respond to medication; in such cases, surgery may be appropriate. Basically, an epileptic seizure is disorganized, out-of-control firing of neurons, and the seizure usually has a focal point, where the firing starts. If you remove the focal point (i.e., cut it out of the brain) the seizure never gets started. Obviously, this is a treatment of last resort, but it can be effective for someone whose epilepsy is disabling and will not respond to medication. One of the things the surgeon must do is ensure that in cutting out the seizure focus he or she does as little damage as possible. It's very hard to cut the brain and do no damage; the urban myth that you use only 10% of your brain is false. Nevertheless, there are better and worse parts to cut. For example, you really don't want to damage the parts that support language comprehension and production; it's known which parts do that, but it varies a bit from person to person. To figure out for an individual, Penfield stimulated the brain directly. A local anesthetic was administered in the scalp and part of the skull removed. Penfield then used a stylus that generated a very mild electrical current to stimulate different places in the patient's brain. The patient was awake during this procedure. The brain has no pain receptors; once the scalp was under a local anesthetic, this gentle stimulation didn't hurt.

The idea is that the stimulation scrambles any ongoing processing. So if you have the person talking and then stimulate spot X and he or she stops talking, it's a good bet that spot X plays some role in speech production. If you stimulate spot X and the patient continues talking as if nothing has happened, it doesn't.

On some occasions, Penfield stimulated part of the brain and the patient would say that a memory had been triggered. For example, one patient said, "Oh, a familiar memory—in an office somewhere. I could see the desks. I was there and someone was calling to me—a man leaning on a desk with a pencil in his hand" (Penfield, 1959, p. 45). Another patient reported hearing her small son, Frank, playing in the yard outside her kitchen window, as well as the typical neighborhood sounds.

If these are indeed memories, the fact that they can be produced via direct stimulation of the brain certainly fits the idea that everything is recorded in the brain but often cannot be accessed. It makes it look as if the normal route to recalling memory has been bypassed—Penfield with his stylus reached in and physically jiggled a memory loose that otherwise would have been unrecoverable.

Such results sound compelling, but there are a lot of problems in interpreting them. First, something like this happened in only a small fraction (less than 10%) of Penfield's patients, even among those who were stimulated in the part of the brain in which memories are thought to be stored (the temporal lobe). Second, those who did report it often said that the experience was not especially like a memory. For example, the woman who heard her son Frank playing in the yard was asked 10 days later whether this experience was a memory. She said, "Oh, no. It seemed more real than that" (Penfield, 1959, p. 51). Thus, it's possible that Penfield's stimulation created pictures in the person's consciousness based on things in their memories but that were not themselves an actual memory, in much the same way that dreams are constructed out of things that happened to you, but they are not exact replays of events that have happened to you. A third problem is that people who reported these memories often described viewing themselves in the scene, as though they were watching a home movie. Do you remember eating breakfast this morning? When you think about yourself eating breakfast this morning, do you see yourself at the table, as if you were someone else observing you? Probably not. You probably remember it from a first-person perspective, more like the way you experienced it. The memories Penfield elicited with his stylus in his patients tended to be like home movies, and that makes it seem likely that the memories were a **construction.** *Construction* refers to memories that feel like bonafide memories to the person experiencing them but are actually combinations of a real memory and other information, such as what the person believes probably happened.

In sum, there does not seem to be much reason to believe that everything is recorded in memory and never lost. Again, we can't prove that this is not the case. Oddly enough, the two most extreme versions of what happens in memory—everything is recorded and stays in memory, or memories are constantly decaying—are the two theories of memory that are impossible to disprove. From what we know now, however, these two theories don't seem to have much support.

PERMASTORE.   To paraphrase the well-known scatological bumper sticker, forgetting happens. But is forgetting always inevitable? We all have certain bits of information that we know so well, it is difficult to believe we could ever forget it. In *Catcher in the Rye* Holden Caufield helps a little girl adjust her skate and gets a rush of nostalgia from the feel of the skate key. He comments, "You could put a skate key in my hand in about 50 years in pitch black, and I'd still know what it is."

Recent evidence shows that Holden was right. Enough practice makes memory immune to forgetting. Harry Bahrick did a series of studies on the permanance of memory. In one study, Bahrick rounded up 733 people who had taken Spanish in high school between 1 and 50 years ago. Then he gave all of them a number of Spanish tests: vocabulary tests, comprehension tests, and so on (Figure 6.9).

Bahrick examined how much Spanish people retained as a function of how much Spanish they initially had learned. He estimated how much Spanish they had initially learned by how many courses they had taken, the level of the highest course they had taken, what their grades were in these courses, and so on. He also measured how much practice people had had with Spanish since they last took a Spanish class (whether they had visited a Spanish-speaking country, how often they estimated they were exposed to Spanish in newspapers, magazines, television, and other media, whether they had studied another Romance language, and so on).

As you can appreciate, this was a stupendously complex study to conduct, but it paid off with a very interesting result. First, as you would expect, people forget their Spanish. The forgetting is pretty rapid for the first 3–6 years, but then it more or less plateaus; there is little forgetting until about 30 years have passed. Then there is a second, more gradual drop-off until about 50 years (the last time point measured). This pattern is shown in Figure 6.10 for English–Spanish translation, but this pattern was observed for almost all the measures of Spanish that Bahrick used.

Vocabulary recognition

1. romper
   a. to roam   b. to break   c. to look   d. to roar   e. to search
2. mandar
   a. to make   b. to mend   c. to yell   d. to command   e. to arrange

Grammar recall: write the correct form of the verb given in the blank provided
1. El ____ espanol (estudiar) He studies spanish
2. Yo ____ la menor (ser) I am the youngest.

Idiom recall: write the English meaning of the Spanish idiom in the answer column
1. hace mal tiempo _____
2. en vez de _____

Figure 6.9.   *Sample questions from Bahrick (1984).*

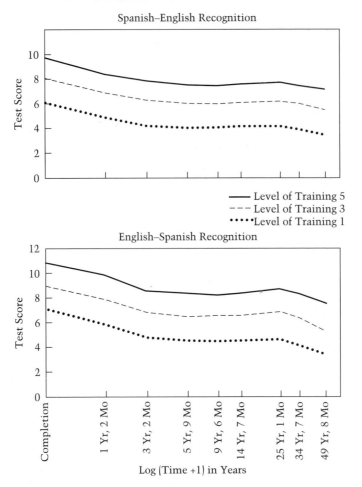

Figure 6.10.   *The effect of training level on the retention of recognition vocabulary from Bahrick (1984).*

There are two results to note here. First, for some of these participants, this knowledge of Spanish was retrievable 50 years after it was last encoded or rehearsed even if it had not been practiced at all during the intervening 50 years. For all practical purposes, we might say that this information was not going to be forgotten. Bahrick referred to memories in this not-to-be-forgotten state as being in **permastore.** Permastore is a hypothetical state of memory from which information is not lost.

Knowledge of Spanish did not end up in permastore for everyone, though. What seemed to make the difference was extended practice. The longer people had studied Spanish, the more Spanish they had in permastore. Studying Spanish for at least several years seemed to ensure that at least some of it would end up in permastore.

Whether permastore is really a form of memory, separate from secondary memory, is not known. Bahrick argues that it is separate because he notes that most of the memories have a life span of 3–6 years—after that they are forgotten—and others have a life span of 50 years or more, but no memories have a life span of 10 years or 20 years. There is no forgetting between 6 and 50 years, which indicates a transition to a different state of memory.

Other researchers, such as Ulric Neisser, think that "permastore" is just a description of secondary memories that are so well represented that they will not be forgotten, or that some of Bahrick's participants had just some vague knowledge of how the Spanish language worked, and from that they were able to generate a few correct answers on the test (Neisser, 1984). There has been little work on permastore compared to other types of memory, probably because it is so difficult to conduct studies of the sort Bahrick has done.

Forgetting Caused by Repression

Repression is the active forgetting of an episode that is very painful or emotionally charged. The person forgets the episode for the sake of self-protection: Remembering it would be too painful. The term implies some active form of dampening the memory, but this dampening process happens outside of awareness. It's not simply that you try not to think about the memory.

Repression is a difficult topic for two reasons. It is difficult to gather scientific evidence about repression, and the study of repression is itself charged with emotion.

Suppose someone comes to you and says, "I've just remembered that I had a very traumatic experience when I was 3 years old. My father sexually abused me." If you're studying repression, you need to know three things:

- Whether the event this person remembers really happened
- Whether this person really didn't remember the event from the time it happened until much later (that is, that it was really repressed)
- Whether the forgetting resulted from represssion, not some other process of forgetting

How could you verify whether the person was really abused? This crime usually is one without witnesses, and it is typically quite difficult to find corroborating evidence. Again, at the moment we're not concerned with the legal implications or the consequences of abuse to the psyche of the victim. These are very important, of course, but for the moment we're focusing on whether the mind is capable of repressing memories. And to know that, we must know that the memory is genuine.

The second concern is whether the person really had forgotten the memory of the abuse during the time he or she said it was forgotten. Strangely, people can forget that they have remembered. Jonathan Schooler, Miriam Bendiksen, and Zara Ambadar (1997) described a case in which a person's memory of a traumatic event was ambiguous. W.B., a 40-year-old woman, recounted recovering a memory of having been raped at knifepoint when she was 16. W.B. described the memory recovery as having been triggered by an encounter with a male co-worker. She commented on his advances toward a young woman, and he defended himself by saying, "She isn't exactly a virgin" (Schooler et al., 1997, p. 268). W.B. was so upset that she left the party. That night she had nightmares and awoke knowing that she had been raped. Her reaction was very emotional, and she felt shocked. This certainly sounds as though that memory had been repressed. However, in a subsequent interview, W.B. said that she hadn't necessarily forgotten the incident completely; she likened the experience to one's first day of school: "You know that the event occurred, but you don't think about it, or even remember how it was, but you know it was there" (Schooler et al., 1997, pp. 268–269). On the other hand, W.B. also firmly said that there were times that, had she been asked directly if she had ever been raped, she would have said, "No." Her ex-husband reported that several times during their marriage, W.B. had mentioned that she had been raped, but it had always been completely without emotion. W.B. had no recollection of having told her ex-husband. In sum, if a person says that he or she has completely forgotten an event for some period of time, that report cannot immediately be taken at face value.

DOES REPRESSION EXIST?   Given these three stringent criteria, is there evidence for a process of repression? The fact is that there has simply not been that much research on repression, possibly because it is difficult to study; a panel appointed by the Royal College of Psychiatrists in Britain recently concluded that "there is a vast literature [on repression] but little acceptable research" (Brandon, Boakes, Glaser, & Green, 1998, p. 296). Any conclusions we draw will therefore be rather tentative.

That said, there are several case reports and systematic studies indicating that repression does occur.

In one case report (Schooler, 1994), a 30-year-old man's memory was jogged by seeing a movie about sexual abuse. Several hours after seeing the movie, the man was lying in bed and suddenly remembered being abused by his parish priest on a camping trip when he was 11 years old. The man confronted the priest, who confessed and said that he had sought counseling after another incident with a different boy.

How common is represssion? Linda Williams (1995) interviewed 129 women who, 17 years earlier, had been admitted to a hospital emergency room because of sexual abuse. All of them were age 13 or younger at the time, and in all cases the abuse had been documented in hospital medical records. Thus, in this case there can be no doubt that abuse occurred.

The women underwent a 3-hr interview that covered many topics, including questions designed to elicit any history of sexual abuse. The interviewers knew nothing of the sexual history of the women they were interviewing. The survey showed that 75 of the women recalled the event. It is difficult to be sure of the reason for the inability to recall the event in the other 54 women; it may simply be because people often cannot remember details of their childhood well. Thus, Williams focused her analysis on the 75 participants who could remember the event.

Twelve of these 75 women reported that there had been a time in the past that they did not remember the event (i.e., that it had been repressed). Indeed,

7 of these 12 believed that their memory of the incident was still incomplete and had not been completely recovered. The women with recovered memories were on average 3 years younger than the women who had always remembered the incident.

Is it possible that some of these women therefore forgot the abuse but then later remembered it because of the vagaries of childhood memories? This may be possible for some of the participants—about half were under age 6 at the time of the abuse—but it seems unlikely to be true for all the participants.

However, it is possible that some of the women failed to report the information. This conjecture is based on the results of a study by Femina and colleagues (Femina, Yeager, & Lewis, 1990). As in the Williams study, there was independent confirmation of abuse for all of the participants. The researchers reported that a similar percentage (38%) of participants failed to report the event during interviews, indicating that they had perhaps forgotten it through repression. Unlike Williams, however, Femina et al. performed a second interview. (They were able to interview only 8 of these participants.) During the second interview, participants were told of their abuse, and all 8 admitted that they remembered the incident but had not reported it during the first interview, usually because of embarrassment.

In sum, there is probably no airtight study showing that repression can occur. This lack of evidence probably results from two factors. First, repression probably is rare. Most studies show that memory for traumatic events usually is quite vivid in both children and adults (Leopold & Dillon, 1963; Pynoos & Nader, 1989), although the memories may not be wholly accurate. Second, it is inevitably difficult to find airtight evidence because it is impossible to conduct formal experiments on repression. We can investigate life events only after they occur, and life events of course are not designed to satisfy critics' demands for neatness. Consider for a moment the conditions that must be met to convincingly demonstrate that repression has occurred.

- We must be sure the abuse occurred.
- We must be sure that the patient forgot about the abuse for some period of time.
- We must be sure that the patient does not claim to remember the abuse now merely as a result of suggestion.

Like other memory researchers (e.g., Schacter, 1996) and like a panel of experts appointed by the American Psychological Association to study the issue (Alpert et al., 1996) I believe repression occurs. Individual studies have flaws, and it is always difficult to draw broad conclusions based on case studies of individuals, but I think there is enough evidence to indicate that repression can occur. I am also confident that repression is probably fairly rare and has been overdiagnosed in recent years.

DIAGNOSIS AND OVERDIAGNOSIS OF REPRESSION.   Repression of traumatic events probably has been overdiagnosed. How do I know that? Let's start with two odd facts. Fact one: A survey of the members of the American Psychological

Association reported that 12% of the clinicians had treated patients who had been forced to participate in satanic cults. The rituals in such cults include orgies, the sacrifice of human babies, and cannibalism, all organized in a vast super-secret network. This figure closely matches figures reported by the False Memory Society, a support group for parents and others who claim to be falsely accused of sexual abuse, based on the recovery of repressed memories. Of the complaints lodged at the False Memory Society, 18% are of satanic ritual abuse. In the British False Memory Society, 8% of the accusations include satanic ritual abuse (Gudjonsson, 1997).

Fact two: This sort of activity has never been verified by law enforcement agencies, despite a number of investigations by British and American authorities (La Fontaine, 1994, cited in Brandon, Boakes, Glaser, & Green, 1998). If satanic cult activity is so widespread, why can't law enforcement agencies find any evidence that it's happening? Or to put it another way, is it more likely that these cults are very successful in remaining hidden or that these patients who believe they have participated in cult activity are mistaken?

Let's start this way. Suppose you were a therapist, and a patient you were seeing had completely repressed some memories. How would you ever know it? How could you uncover memories that the person's mind had repressed? If you simply ask the person, "Have you ever been forced to participate in satanic worship rituals?" the patient will say, "no," because he or she has repressed these memories.

One strategy open to you might be to circumvent the conscious mind and to hypnotize the patient, suggest what you think might have happened, and see whether the person verifies that it did. Or you might try to get the patient to relax, to let his or her guard down, and then get the patient to visualize things that you suspect might have happened, and then see whether it seems familiar.

These techniques—hypnosis and guided imagery—are commonly used by some therapists, and they spell big trouble for memory. Hypnosis cannot make memory more accurate, as mentioned earlier, but you can use hypnosis to plant false memories, even if that's not what you're trying to do. The typical procedure is to plant some misleading information during a hypnotic session (or during some nonhypnotic control procedure) and then to see whether participants recall the misleading information as having really happened. For example, you might say, "Do you remember a few minutes ago I asked you about your childhood? It was right after the door slammed out in the hall. Let's get back to those questions." In fact, the door never slammed, but a week later you could ask participants, "Did you hear a door slam in the hall last time you were here?" A number of studies have used such procedures and have shown that hypnotized people are susceptible to such suggestions (McConkey et al., 1990; for a review, see Lynn, Lock, Myers, & Payne, 1997). Basically, the person who has been hypnotized gets confused about what happened under hypnosis and what really happened. The same thing can happen under guided imagery.

Maryanne Garry, Charles Manning, Beth Loftus, and Steven Sherman (1996) showed the influence that imagination can have on belief. They first had participants examine a list of 40 events and rate their confidence that each event had happened to them before the age of 10 from 1 (certain it did not happen) to

8 (certain it happened). The events were things such as getting in trouble for calling 911, finding $10 in a parking lot, or accidentally putting a hand through a window. Two weeks later participants were asked to imagine that four of the events had actually happened to them. They were asked to generate a mental image of the event ("Imagine that it's after school and you are playing in the house. You hear a strange noise outside, so you run to the window to see what made the noise. As you are running your feet catch on something and you trip and fall"). Then they were asked some questions about the details of the image ("What did you trip on?"). They were then given more details to image ("As you're falling you reach out to catch yourself, and your hand goes through the window. As the window breaks you get cut and there's some blood."). This procedure was repeated for three other items and lasted about 2 min for each item.

Immediately thereafter, the experimenter pretended to panic, saying that the memory survey they had filled out 2 weeks ago had been lost and asking them to fill it out again. The measure of interest was whether participants rated the events they had just imagined happening as more likely to have really happened than they had rated them a week ago. The results showed that the confidence ratings increased for 34% of imagined items, and for 25% of not-imagined items. Thus, imagining that an event had happened increased participants' confidence that it really had happened. An increase of 9% may not seem impressive, but in statistical terms this effect was fairly substantial. (You can measure how big an effect is with a statistical measure called effect size. In this case the effect size, d, was .72, which is conventionally considered medium to large.)

Getting people to believe that they have participated in a satanic cult is a far cry from getting them to believe that they have seen a picture or heard a door slam. Is there any evidence that you can get people to believe that something traumatic happened to them? It is not ethical to try to make someone believe that they were part of a satanic cult just because you're curious to know whether you can do it. Still, the question is quite important, both for memory theory and from a practical standpoint as well.

Beth Loftus found a good compromise. She examined whether it was possible to plant a memory for an event that would have been traumatic at the time but would not be traumatic now: getting lost at age 5. Loftus interviewed pairs of participants, each including a student at the University of Washington and a relative of the student who was knowledgable about the participant's past. The relative helped construct the false memory. Participants were sent a booklet describing four events from their childhood: three true ones and the planted, false memory. Here is a sample false memory paragraph created for a 20-year-old Vietnamese-American woman:

> You, your mom, Tien, and Tuan all went to the Bremerton K-Mart. You must have been 5 years old at the time. Your mom gave each of you some money to get a blueberry Icee. You ran ahead to get into the line first, and somehow lost your way in the store. Tien found you crying to an elderly Chinese woman. You three then went together to get an Icee.

The relative provided details to make the story believable, but the basic structure was the same for each participant; getting lost in a big store at age 5, crying, being found by a helpful adult, and being reunited with the family. Participants were asked to read each of the four paragraphs and to fill in as many details as they could. If they remembered nothing, they should say so. They then mailed the booklets back to the experimenters. One to two weeks later, the participants were interviewed about the four events, and were then interviewed a second time a week or two after that. At the second interview, participants remembered 68% of the true memories, and 25% of the participants claimed to remember the false memory

The experiment provides experimental evidence for a story well known to most psychologists. The great child psychologist Jean Piaget had a false memory. He remembered an incident from childhood in which he was being taken for a walk by his nanny when two ruffians attempted to kidnap him. The nanny valiantly fought off the attackers. Piaget remembered this incident quite well but later learned that the nanny had made the whole thing up. She confessed to Piaget's parents because she felt guilty about keeping a watch she had received as a reward for her brave conduct. Piaget concluded that he must have heard the story retold by his parents and projected a memory that he believed.

Several repetitions usually is important in manufacturing false memories. What probably happens is that the person forgets the **source** of the memory (the information about how he or she learned something). Source memory often includes information about context (where and when you learned something), but it can be even more detailed. If you are with Dexter and Thalia and Thalia tells you something about social psychology, it may be important later to remember that Thalia said it, not Dexter, if she's an expert on social psychology and he isn't.

Source is important in manufacturing false memories because of the repetition of false information. With just one repetition of the false information, you may think, "I was told by my brother that I got lost, but I don't remember that." After several repetitions, you are sure that yesterday your brother said you got lost, and you are sure you knew that you got lost before he said it yesterday, but you're not sure how you knew it. You've gotten confused about whether every instance of your thinking about getting lost was suggested to you by your brother or whether only some of them were (and thus the rest are perhaps memories of getting lost).

The message to therapists is quite clear. If you hypnotize patients (which makes them suggestible) or have them do guided imagery about participation in satanic rituals, you run a real risk of making them think that whatever happened during these sessions was real. The risk increases if you do this on more than one occasion. Unfortunately, the indications are that all too many therapists use exactly these techniques. In a survery in 1994, 21% of therapists disagreed with the statement that false memories may be created during hypnosis, and 33% said that they believed that memories described while hypnotized must be true. In 1995 the American Society of Clinical Hypnosis published guidelines for the use of hypnosis in memory, including warnings about false memories. In a more recent survey of clinicians, Kathleen Palm and Pamela Gibson (1998) surveyed 300 clinicians in the state of Virginia about their use of hypnosis, among other things. Sixteen percent said they currently use hypnosis to help clients recover memories, 30% said they thought therapists should not use it, and 13% said they had recently stopped using hypnosis. Thus, the publicity and controversy surrounding recovered memories may be having some effect on the use of hypnosis.

Here's the real problem. We are fairly confident that satanic cults are few and far between, and that if someone recovers "memories" of forced participation in such cults, it is much more likely that these are manufactured memories than that these are repressed memories that are now surfacing. We are equally confident that sexual abuse of children is alarmingly widespread. So if someone recovers repressed memories of sexual abuse, how do we know whether these memories are genuine or manufactured? We don't.

We can say that, just as hypnosis and guided imagery can create false memories for satanic cult activity, they can create false memories of sexual abuse, and using these techniques to uncover repressed memories is dangerous. Unfortunately, the use of these techniques to uncover memories of sexual abuse is widespread. They became especially widespread after the success of a book, *The Courage to Heal* (Bass & Davis, 1988), which is a self-help guide for survivors of sexual abuse. The book encouraged the use of the techniques we're talking about and also encouraged the expunging of doubt about memories of the abuse. For example, one passage advises, "Often the knowledge that you were abused starts with a tiny feeling, an intuition. . . . Assume your feelings are valid," and, "Many women who were abused don't have memories and some never get any. This doesn't mean they weren't abused" (Bass & Davis, 1988). Other books also suggest that a series of interviews probably will be necessary before the patient will accept the validity of the "memories" (Frederickson, 1992; Maltz & Holman, 1986).

So what is the bottom line? Are these recovered memories valid, or are they the result of suggestion? Obviously, some memories are real and some are not, and at this point it is difficult to reliably differentiate real memories from manufactured ones if highly suggestive questioning, hypnosis, and guided imagery have been used. (Obviously the use of such techniques doesn't mean that the person was never abused. It does mean that their memories *could* be inaccurate.) The complete and utter repression of abuse appears to be rare—not impossible, but rare. It is also the case that manufactured memories do not arise out of thin air. If someone remembers abuse and they have not been prey to the sort of guiding techniques discussed here, it seems quite likely that the memories are accurate.

STAND-ON-ONE-FOOT QUESTIONS

7. Name the two main theories of forgetting, and evaluate the likelihood that each is correct.
8. Is all learning permanent, with failures of retrieval caused only by interference?
9. Can memory of traumatic events in childhood be repressed?

QUESTIONS THAT REQUIRE TWO FEET

10. *Given what you know about forgetting, how would you advise someone to schedule his or her time studying in school?*

11. *Most people have memories that they have difficulty separating from family lore. In other words, there is a story in which you star that used to seem like a bona fide memory, but now you're unsure whether you're remembering the actual event or it's just that you've been told the story so many times that you're remembering it. What might be behind this phenomenon?*

KEY TERMS

free recall

cued recall

recognition

foils, lures, distractors

savings in relearning

sensitivity

available

accessible

cues

context

strength view
  of memory

recognition failure
  of recallable words

priming

reconstruction

mnemonic

decay theory

interference theory

response competition

intrusion

unlearning

spontaneous recovery

construction

permastore

repression

source

7

Memory Storage

In the last two chapters we've covered how memories get into the storehouse and how they are retrieved from the storehouse. This final chapter on memory discusses the storehouse itself.

The first question we might consider is, **"What is in the storehouse?"** Suppose I show you a coffee cup and ask you to name it. You say, "It's a cup." I ask you how you know that and you say (after giving me a fishy look) "Well, it's got a handle, it's the right size, you could put coffee in it, so it's a cup." Then I show you one of those little cups used in Chinese restaurants and I ask you to name that. Again you say, "It's a cup." This cup has no handle, and it's much smaller, yet it's a cup. Similarly, if I showed you a cup with a small hole in it (so that it couldn't hold liquid), it would still be a cup. So when we say, "What is in the storehouse?" the provisional answer must be, "Memory representations that allow us to identify objects with different properties as nevertheless belonging to the same class." Different-looking objects are all identified as cups. As we'll see, this property of memory representations is very useful, but we still don't know exactly how these representations work.

The second question we're going to take up concerns the organization within the memory storehouse. In chapter 6 we talked about retrieval, but we skipped over a really forbidding aspect of retrieval: finding the right bit of information among the millions of things you know. We're discussing that problem here because the organization of memory is crucial to solving this retrieval problem. If you had 10,000 comic books and you wanted to be able to find any one of them quickly, what would you do? You'd organize them, of course: chronologically, by main character (Superman, Green Lantern, etc.), or by plot (superhero loses powers, world held hostage by nuclear threat, etc.). We would guess that all the information in your memory would also need a good organization system that would allow you to access material quickly. What is this organization system? **"How is memory organized?"** Again, we're not sure of the precise answer, but we do know that memory is organized around meaning.

The final question we will take up is one that psychologists did not pose in a serious way until recently: **"What else is in memory?"** The answer is that what we normally think of as memory (and what we've been discussing in the last two chapters) is just one piece of memory. **Declarative memory** is what we've been discussing in the last two chapters; it is the type of memory associated with conscious recollection. **Procedural memory,** on the other hand, is not associated with awareness. How can you remember and not be aware of it? Procedural memory is expressed as you show greater facilitation in performing skills. In this chapter we discuss how procedural memory works and how it differs from declarative memory.

➤ *WHAT IS IN THE STOREHOUSE?*

➤ *PREVIEW* In this section we take up a key problem in memory: your ability to generalize. When you see an apple, how do you know it has seeds inside? You've never seen this apple before. You know about the seeds because you generalize from other apples to this apple; in other words, you put this object in the category *apple.* Initially, researchers assumed that people categorized by using a list of properties: If it's roundish and red and has a stem, it's an apple. Each category has a set of conditions that an object must meet to be a member of the category. But some objects are more typical of a category than others. For example, an apple is a typical fruit; a raisin is not. If categorization were achieved with a list of properties, you wouldn't get typicality effects. And as we'll see, the typicality of an object affects not just how we categorize but also how we reason about and speak about that object. We'll also discuss the models that were proposed to account for these new data—prototype and exemplar models—that were based on the idea that you categorize objects not with rules but by judging their similarity to other objects of the same category. More recently, people have found problems with these models and have suggested that we sometimes use similarity, but at other times we actually may use rules, as was originally thought.

Let me describe yet another task your mind performs that sounds rather mundane but is sufficiently complex that the workings behind it have stumped cognitive psychologists for 40 years. You're walking down the street, you see a strange dog, and you say, "Hello, doggie." Now of course we don't really understand walking or talking very well, but my example was supposed to be the bit about the dog. Suppose this is a dog you've never seen before. How do you identify it as a dog, rather than a cat, a fox, or a gherkin? How can you retrieve "This is a dog" from the memory storehouse when you've never encoded this dog before?

The answer is that you are able to identify the class or category to which an object belongs, even if you've never seen that particular example of the object before. A **category** is a group of objects that have something in common. For example, *dog* is a category. An **exemplar** is an instance of a category. A particular dog that you see is an exemplar of the category *dog.* You are able to identify the novel, never-seen-before dog on the street because your experience with other dogs transfers to new dogs; this is the ability to **generalize.** To generalize means to apply information gathered from one exemplar to a different exemplar of the same category. In other words, things you know from your experience with other dogs (it eats, it breathes, it could bite you but probably won't, it smells when wet) can be applied to this new dog.

The importance of the ability to generalize is hard to overestimate. The first sentence of Ed Smith and Doug Medin's book about categorization is, "Without concepts, mental life would be chaotic" (Smith & Medin, 1981). It would be chaotic because you would approach any object you had not interacted with as though it were completely novel. "Hey, look at this furry thing. Hmm. Four legs. Wagging tail. I wonder whether it has lungs? I wonder whether it can fly?" Imagine the results if a physician showed a similar reluctance to generalize from patients seen before to new patients: "Sure, other patients with these symptoms have been cured by penicillin, but what does that tell me about this patient?"

Concepts are the mental representations that allow one to generalize. So what is a concept, and how does it allow one to generalize? We'll go through a number of different views on this topic.

The Classical View

This problem of identifying an object as a dog may not sound so hard to you. If the object has four legs and a tail, and it's furry, it's a dog. That's pretty much the **classical view of categorization,** so named because it was first articulated by Aristotle. According to the classical view, a concept is a list of necessary and sufficient conditions for membership in the concept. Remember, a concept is the mental representation of *dog* or *cake* or any class of objects. It doesn't refer to any one particular example of the object; a concept represents all the objects that can be referred to as *cake*. So the classical view is that you have a list of attributes or features; an object must have all of the attributes on the list, and having those attributes is sufficient to be an example of the concept. For example, the concept *grandmother* is composed of two conditions: female and parent of a parent. Those two conditions are necessary to be identified as a grandmother—you must have both of them to be a grandmother—and they are sufficient, meaning it does not matter what sort of other characteristics you have or do not have, you're still a grandmother if you have those two.

The nice thing about the classical view is that it seems efficient because the representation of concepts takes up so little room in memory. What we're trying to do is show how you can have a mental representation from which we can generalize, which means we have to be able to recognize a novel grandmother when we see one, and the classical view argues that any grandmother, whatever her characteristics, can be identified as a grandmother using only this short list of properties.

The earliest research on concepts took the classical view. For example, Clark Hull (1920) showed participants Chinese ideographs (Figure 7.1) one at a time and asked participants to categorize them. Each category had a single feature in common; for example, the ideographs in one category always had a large feature that looked like a check mark, but otherwise all the members of the category looked quite different. Hull didn't tell the participants anything about the stimuli, but he gave corrective feedback as participants tried to categorize them. Participants improved with practice, and Hull interpreted his results as showing that participants came to associate the key feature of the category with the appropriate category name.

In another classic study, Jerome Bruner and his colleagues (Bruner, Goodnow, & Austin, 1956) set out to show that participants learn categories not by association but by hypothesis testing. They thought that participants actively construct hypotheses about what rule might describe category membership, and then they test the rule. The experimenters used cards with four features: number of figures on the card, shape of the figures, color of the figures, and number of borders around the edge of the cards. The experimenter handed a card to the participant (e.g., a card with three black circles and two borders), telling him or her that this card is a positive instance of the category. Then the participant had to try to select another positive instance of the category from among all the possible cards, which were laid out on the table. The participant's job was to figure out what makes a card an example of the category.

Figure 7.1. *Chinese ideographs used in Hull's (1920) study of classification.*

Bruner et al. found that participants used different strategies. One strategy was focus gambling. **Focus gambling** is the strategy of generating a narrow hypothesis about the necessary and sufficient properties that define a category. For example, in the first selection, the participant might take a card with three white circles and three borders. If the participant was lucky, the experimenter would say that this too was a positive instance, and the participant would know that the two features that changed (color and number of borders) were irrelevant. If the participant was unlucky, the experimenter would say that this was not a positive instance, and the participant would not have gained as much information.

Another strategy some used was **successive scanning,** in which the participant formulated a hypothesis (e.g., black circle is the category) and make selections based on that hypothesis until it was disconfirmed, at which point the participant would generate a new hypothesis.

I've said that these experiments are examples of the classical view of categories. How so? The experimenters assumed that category membership should be set up as a list of necessary and sufficient conditions: a particular feature of an ideograph in Hull's experiment and a feature or two of the cards in Bruner et al.'s. In each case, the rest of the stimulus was irrelevant as long as it had the critical features. The problem is that many categories in the real world don't seem to work that way.

The classical view seems to work pretty well for a few real-world concepts (e.g., kinship terms such as *grandmother* or *sister*) and for terms that have been formally defined by people (legal terms such as *murderer* and mathematical terms such as *rectangle*). But there are many terms for which a list of necessary and sufficient conditions seems to be difficult to generate. This objection to the classical view was raised by philosopher Ludwig Wittgenstein (1953). His example was the concept *game.* What makes something a game? That it be a contest of some sort? No, because kids play games that aren't competitive (e.g., ring around the rosie). That it is fun? How about a professional tennis player in the Wimbledon finals who is not having fun? Is she playing a game? And some things are fun (e.g., reading a textbook) that are not games. Wittgenstein concluded that one can't come up with a list of necessary and sufficient properties to define the concept *game.* However, this may mean only that we are poor at coming up with the list of necessary and sufficient properties; it doesn't mean that the mind doesn't use such lists as the mental representation for concepts. The fact that you can't describe something doesn't mean that your mind doesn't use it. I certainly can't describe for you all the rules of English grammar, but my mind nevertheless uses these rules when I construct sentences. There are other reasons to think that the classical view of concepts is wrong, however. We turn to those reasons now.

Typicality Effects

TYPICALITY RATINGS.   Not all birds are equally "birdy." Some birds are really good examples of a bird (a real bird's bird), whereas others are pretty crummy birds. Consider the following list of birds. If I asked you to rate each bird from 1 (terrific example of a bird) to 7 (terrible example of a bird), how would you rate each one?

> Wren
> Chicken
> Robin
> Bat
> Ostrich
> Eagle

Eleanor Rosch (1973) gave participants a number of lists of nouns such as this and asked them to perform a similar task. The first thing you might note about this task is that it didn't seem stupid. One response you could give when asked to perform this task is to say, "These are all birds. What are you talking about, 'birdy birds, nonbirdy birds'—they're all birds. Except the bat." The fact is, when Rosch said "birdy birds," or "fruity fruits," or "furniturey furniture," people knew what she was talking about. Not only do people think some birds are birdier than others, but they agree on which ones are the birdy ones, as shown in Table 7.1.

You can see from the examples in Table 7.1 that this effect holds true for natural objects (such as birds) and manufactured objects (such as vehicles). Indeed, it seems that **typicality** may be found everywhere. What would you say is a more typical murder weapon: a gun or a switchblade? What is a more typical Hollywood blockbuster: *Raiders of the Lost Ark* or *Forrest Gump?*

Table 7.1 **Some Results of Rosch's (1973) Typicality Ratings**

Category	Member	Rating
Fruit	Apple	1.3
	Plum	2.3
	Pineapple	2.3
	Strawberry	2.3
	Fig	4.7
	Olive	6.2
Sport	Football	1.2
	Hockey	1.8
	Wrestling	3.0
	Archery	3.9
	Gymnastics	2.6
	Weight-lifting	4.7
Bird	Robin	1.1
	Eagle	1.2
	Wren	1.4
	Chicken	3.8
	Ostrich	3.3
	Bat	5.8
Vehicle	Car	1.0
	Boat	2.7
	Scooter	2.5
	Tricycle	3.5
	Horse	5.9
	Skis	5.7

What does this mean? It means the classical view is wrong. If the classical view were right, you would simply have a list of necessary and sufficient conditions, and if the object met them, it would be an example of the concept, and if it didn't, it wouldn't be. There wouldn't be gradations of membership in the concept. If the classical view were correct, you'd say a penguin and a robin are equally good examples of the concept *bird*.

TYPICALITY EFFECTS: CATEGORIZATION.   Ed Smith, Ed Shoben, and Lance Rips (1974) showed that people are more efficient in categorizing typical examples than atypical examples. On each trial, participants saw a word on a computer screen and had to respond as quickly as possible ("yes" or "no") as to whether the word was an example of a category. One category (*birds, insects, fruits, vegetables*) was used for each 24-trial block, and within a block half of the words fit the category and half did not. Of real interest was the variation in typicality of the objects that did fit. Some were typical instances (e.g., robin), some were medium typicality (e.g., cardinal), and some were low typicality (e.g., goose). Response times were faster for more typical examples.

This effect of typicality on categorization is also observed when participants are asked to freely generate examples of a category. In this procedure, participants are given a category and asked to come up with some number of examples of this category, perhaps seven. The experimenter then tabulates the frequency with which certain exemplars of the category are produced (Battig & Montague, 1969). The central finding is that the most frequently generated exemplars are the ones that are rated as most typical of the category. This finding holds true not only for adults but for children as young as 5 (Nelson, 1974; Rosner & Hayes, 1977). Some examples appear in Table 7.2 for the categories *fruit* and *beverage*.

TYPICALITY: LANGUAGE.   Typicality also has an impact on how we speak. Michael Kelly, Kathryn Bock, and Frank Keil (1986) found that more prototypical instances of a category are placed first in sentences. For example, a speaker would be more likely to say, "I went to the clothing store and bought a coat and a hat" than "I went to the clothing store and bought a hat and a coat." The experimenters demonstrated this effect using several different measures. In one experiment, participants were shown two sentences, one with the typical instance first and one with the typical instance second. (The order of sentences was counterbalanced, of course.) Participants were asked to judge which sentence seemed better formed, that is, which sounded better to them. Participants

Table 7.2   Frequencies With Which Items Were Listed as Category Examplars

Fruit		Beverage	
Response	Total (First)	Response	Total (First)
Apple	429 (263)	Milk	366 (89)
Orange	390 (78)	Coke	327 (202)
Pear	326 (29)	Water	295 (16)
Banana	283 (20)	Orange juice	226 (11)
Peach	249 (17)	Coffee	225 (5)
Grape	247 (8)	Tea	217 (11)
Cherry	183 (1)	Pepsi	151 (21)
Plum	167 (4)	Lemonade	119 (3)
Grapefruit	154	7-Up	105 (2)
Lemon	134 (4)	Grape juice	103 (5)
Tangerine	110	Soda	89 (40)
Apricot	102	Root beer	74 (3)
Pineapple	98	Ginger ale	73 (5)
Lime	69	Fruit juice	51 (3)
Tomato	63 (6)	Juice	48 (2)
Strawberry	58	Punch	45 (1)
Watermelon	47	Tomato juice	44
Prunes	44	Kool-Aid	40
Cantaloupe	31	Milkshake	28

selected the sentence with the typical instance first about 58% of the time, a reliable difference.

In another experiment, a new set of participants saw the same sentences and were asked to recall them after a brief delay. If the atypical instance came first in the sentence, 19% of the time participants reversed the order of the instances in their recall. If the atypical instance came second, participants reversed the order only 11% of the time.

TYPICALITY: REASONING.   Typicality also is important to how people use concepts in reasoning. Lance Rips (1975) asked people to make some inferences using either typical or atypical examples of a category as a reference point. For example, they were asked to imagine a small island on which there were only eight species of animals: sparrows, robins, eagles, hawks, ducks, geese, ostriches, and bats. Then they were told that one of the species had a contagious disease, and they were asked to estimate the probability that other animals on the island had the disease. Some participants were told that sparrows had the disease, others were told that ducks had the disease, and so on. The results showed that if a more typical bird (e.g., robin or sparrow) had the disease, it was judged that other birds probably had the disease. If an atypical species (e.g., ostrich) was described as having the disease, it was judged less likely that other species had it. The interpretation was that participants know that typical instances of a category share many properties with other members of the category. When confronted with a new feature (the disease) whose distribution is not known, participants assume that it is distributed the way other features are; if a typical instance has the feature, it's likely that the other instances of the category have the feature. If an atypical member of the category has the feature, there is less reason to assume that other members of the category will have it because atypical category members have many features that others do not.

Category Hierarchy

Another interesting aspect of categorization is that categories are nested within one another. For example, a wren is a bird, but it is also an animal because the category *bird* is nested in the category *animal,* which in turn is nested in the category *living things.* For that matter, you could also consider *wren* as a category because there are different types of wrens. House wrens and marsh wrens are members of the category *wren.* Thus, an object can be thought of as being a member of a number of different categories. What does this mean for cognition?

Eleanor Rosch and her colleagues (1976) outlined three types of category structure. **Basic level** categories are those that are most inclusive (i.e., the broadest) but members still share most of their features. For example, the category *bird* has members that for the most part share the attributes "winged," "lays eggs," "sings," and so on. A **superordinate level category** is one level more abstract than that. For example, the members of the category *animal* do not all share features: Some are winged, some are not; some have tails, some do not; some are warm blooded, some are not. **Subordinate level categories** are less abstract than basic level categories. For example, the members of the category *wrens* are all very similar; only a few features differentiate a house wren from a marsh wren. But members outside the category *wren* also share many features with members of the category. That is, there are objects outside the category *wren* that share many features with wrens; they are winged, egg laying, and so on. Examples of these levels appear in Table 7.3.

In a series of experiments, Rosch and her colleagues (Rosch et al., 1976) showed that basic level categories are the broadest categories possible that have three characteristics: They have many attributes in common, people interact with them in similar ways, and they have similar shapes. Thus, all pianos (basic level) share many attributes: They produce music, they have many keys, they are made of wood, and so on. You also interact with all pianos in similar ways (you move your fingers and hands while seated), and pianos have similar shapes. These three characteristics are not true of all musical instruments, which have different attributes, call for different movements, and have different shapes. These three characteristics are true of more specific categories such as *grand piano*, but that is not the broadest category possible that still retains these characteristics.

Rosch and her colleagues argued that the basic level category is psychologically privileged; it's the type of category we use most in thinking. For example, in one experiment participants heard an object name and then 500 ms later they saw a slide depicting an object. They were to press one button if the slide showed the object named and another button if it did not. The experimenters varied whether the object name that preceded the slide was superordinate (e.g., *fruit*), basic (*apple*), or subordinate (*delicious apple*). Half the slides depicted the named object and half did not. Participants were faster when the object name was at the basic level.

In another experiment, Rosch et al. showed that participants use the basic level when naming objects. They showed participants color photographs of objects and simply asked them to name the objects. Participants used the basic level category to name it more than 99% of the time. (In a follow-up experiment, the experimenters used a recognition test to be sure that participants actually knew the superordinate and subordinate categories for these objects; they did.)

You may have noticed an oddity about the definition of basic level categories. It seems that the definition should depend on how much you know about the objects in a category. A basic level category is defined as the broadest category in which most of the objects share most of their features. So if you knew

Table 7.3   *Examples of Nested Category Structures*

Superordinate Level	Basic Level	Subordinate	
Musical instrument	Guitar	Folk guitar	Classical guitar
	Piano	Grand piano	Upright piano
Fruit	Peach	Freestone peach	Cling peach
	Grapes	Concord grapes	Green seedless grapes
Tree	Maple	Silver maple	Sugar maple
	Birch	River birch	White birch
	Oak	White oak	Red oak

a lot about dogs, wouldn't that mean that you knew many ways in which a German shepherd differed from a beagle and therefore that you didn't think of them as being part of the same basic level category *dog?* Rather, *beagle* would be a basic level category, and different types of beagles (standard-size beagle, miniature beagle) would be the subordinate categories.

James Tanaka and Marjorie Taylor (1991) examined this issue and found support for the idea that expertise plays a role in what is defined as basic. First, they found some dog experts and bird experts and had them list features of categories: superordinate (e.g., *animal, furniture*), basic (e.g., *dog, chair*), and subordinate (e.g., *beagle, easy chair*). The critical measure was the number of new features participants listed for a category as the category became more specific. For example, the typical result is that participants will list a few features for superordinate categories (e.g., animals breathe, they have skin), many more characteristics for basic level categories (e.g., dogs have four legs, they have sharp teeth, they have paws, they are carnivores), and fewer distinguishing features for subordinate categories (e.g., beagles have curved ears). Tanaka and Taylor found exactly that pattern when participants were outside their area of expertise. But for the categories on which they were experts, they could think of more distinguishing characteristics for subordinate categories than the basic category. In other words, the dog experts know the features all dogs share, as a nonexpert does, but they also know many features of individual breeds. Each breed has so many unique features that a breed acts as a basic level category for an expert. In other studies, the experimenters showed that experts tend to use subordinate categories when naming pictures.

In a more thorough study, Kathy Johnson and Carolyn Mervis (1997) examined the effects of expertise on categorization in bird watchers. They tested novices, intermediate level experts, and advanced experts on five tasks: They generated attributes of exemplars, named exemplars, identified silhouettes, verified category membership, and visually identified birds after being primed by bird songs. The results of this extensive study are summarized in Table 7.4. Each cell shows the preferred level of category use: basic (e.g., *bird*), subordinate (*wren*), or sub-subordinate (*marsh wren*).

As can be seen in Table 7.4, novices always use the basic level. Intermediate experts use the subordinate level, and advanced experts use both the subordinate and the sub-subordinate levels. It should also be noted that the basic level never loses its privileged status on two of the tasks.

Table 7.4

Measure	Advanced Experts	Intermediate Experts	Novices
Attributes	Subordinate = basic	Subordinate = basic	Basic
Object naming	Sub-subordinate	Subordinate	Basic
Silhouette identification	Sub-subordinate	Subordinate	Basic
Category verification	Sub-subordinate = subordinate = basic	Subordinate = basic	Basic
Auditory recognition	Sub-subordinate	No effect	Basic

SUMMARY.   There are two important points to keep in mind. Typicality is important to how we use concepts. Typical examples of concepts are categorized more quickly, they are easily brought to mind as examples of the category, and we use them differently in making inferences. The level of categories also is important. It seems that the basic level holds some different status than other levels of categorization. The first point is that these facts about categorization are important and must be accounted for in a theory of categorization. The second point is that these findings indicate that the classical view of categorization cannot be a complete account of categorization. The effects indicate that categories are not represented as lists of necessary and sufficient features as the classical model maintains, but these effects alone do not tell us how categories are represented.

What might the representation of a concept look like? In the **probabilistic view of categorization,** category membership is proposed to be a matter of probability. The mind's representation of a concept is not set up to make a black-and-white judgment about category membership. Rather, an object is seen as more or less likely to be a member of a category. A central assumption is that there is no feature or group of features that is essential for category membership. Rather, each member of the category will have some but not all of the features. (For example, a given bird might have the features "sings" and "eats insects" but it doesn't have the feature "lives in trees.") There are two versions of the probabilistic view: prototype theories and exemplar theories. We discuss each in turn.

Prototypes

A crucial experiment in developing the prototype view was conducted by Mike Posner and Steve Keele (1968). Rather than using categories that their participants already knew, such as birds or furniture, they created two categories from scratch. The categories were patterns of dots, so each feature was one dot, located in a particular position. Posner and Keele created the categories by taking a random dot pattern and calling it "A" and two other random dot patterns and calling them "B" and "C" (Figure 7.2).

Those patterns were defined as the **prototypes** of each category. A prototype has all of the features that are characteristic of the category. To create examples of each category, the experimenters took the prototype (e.g., dot pattern A) and then moved each dot a bit in a random direction. That created an example of category A. Then they started over again with the prototype of category A and again moved the dots randomly—differently this time, of course. That created another example of category A. In that way, they created four examples of each category. Then they mixed the examples in random order, showed them to participants, and asked them to categorize them. Naturally, participants just guessed initially, but they got feedback as they went as to whether their categorization judgments were right or wrong, so after a while they learned to categorize correctly. They had to keep studying the list until they could categorize all 12 items correctly two times in row.

The interesting phase of the experiment came next. Participants were given a recognition test of three types of stimuli: old stimuli, which they had seen in the first phase of the experiment; new stimuli, which were novel examples of the

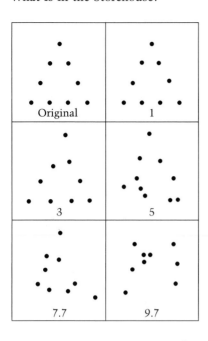

Figure 7.2. *Random dot categories of the type used by Posner and Keele (1968).*

category; and the prototypes from which the examples had been generated. They were to select the familiar member of the category from among four choices, so chance performance would be 25%. Participants got 86.0% of the old items correct and 67.4% of the new items; they remembered the items they had seen before quite well and could also recognize new members of the category. Most interesting, they got 85.1% correct on the prototypes. Participants selected the prototype, which they had never seen before, as accurately as the training items.

Most people interpreted these data as showing that the memory representation supporting categorization is an amalgamation of the examples of the category. As you see many examples of category A, you abstract the critical features of category A, and the memory representation you put in the storehouse has the most-often-occurring features of the examples of category A. It's as though you take the arithmetic average or mean of all the examples of category A that you see. Thus, what you end up storing is basically the prototype of A (and, of course, a separate representation for the prototypes of B and C). That's during the training session, where you're given feedback about which stimuli are As, Bs, and Cs.

Then at test you get a new stimulus and you're supposed to say whether it's an A or a B. So you compare the new stimulus with your stored representation of A and your stored representation of B, and you judge which one it is more similar to. That's how you categorize new stimulus. If the new stimulus is one of the prototypes, it will be an extremely good match to what is in memory because participants have been taking the average of all the different examples of category A and the average of all the different examples of category B, and because the examples were derived from small random changes to the prototype, the average and the prototype are the same thing. In a second experiment Posner and Keele (1970) showed that the prototype is still very well recognized after a 1-week delay.

Rosch and Mervis (1975) proposed a similar version of this probabilistic idea. The main difference is that whereas Posner and Keele's stimuli have continuous features (i.e., there can be infinite gradations in the distance between dots), Rosch and Mervis used stimuli with discrete features (they can take on just one of a small set of values; e.g., an animal's size might be small, medium, or large).

In Rosch and Mervis's (1975) experiment, participants saw letter strings (e.g., *JXPHM*). Categories were created by varying the likelihood that a particular letter was part of a category. For example, most of the members of category 1 might have the letter *B* but only a few members of that category had the letter *C*, and so forth. They created two categories (called 1s and 2s) with six items in each category. They varied the prototypicality of the exemplars; some exemplars had all of the common features of the category and few of the uncommon ones; some exemplars had mostly uncommon features.

During training, participants learned to distinguish 1s and 2s. They categorized each stimulus with corrective feedback until they could run through the list without making errors two times. After this training, participants were shown the members of the categories and asked to rate them for typicality, with 7 meaning highly typical and 1 meaning highly atypical. As predicted, letter strings that had lots of common features were rated as very typical (5.0), strings with fewer common features were less typical (3.4), and letter strings with lots of uncommon features were rated as atypical (2.1). The experiment also replicated Posner and Keele's results, showing in another test session that participants categorized the typical instances faster and more accurately than atypical instances.

These data seem to make it clear that people abstract the central features of examples and store the prototype. However, as pointed out by Bill Estes (1994), it has never been fleshed out in great detail exactly how a prototype is formed or what it includes. On the other hand, it is a little odd to think of people storing only the prototype. After all, I can recognize a new cat when I see it, but I also recognize specific cats, such as the orange one who has commandeered a corner of my yard for his restroom. So then you might think that both are stored. There is a representation of the prototypical cat, and alongside it are representations of all the individual cats I can identify as individuals. You could imagine that an object is first compared with different prototypes (dog, cat, raccoon, etc.) and the object is determined to be an example of whichever stored prototype it is most similar to. Next the object is compared with the individual examples of that category that I am familiar with (neighbor's cat, scary cat from across the street) to determine whether I know this particular cat.

In any event, it seemed that something like prototypes had to be part of the story to account for Posner and Keele's results; how else could you account for people's confidence that they had seen the prototype that they had never seen? Then in 1978, Doug Medin and Marguerite Schaffer showed that, surprisingly enough, prototypes are not necessary to understand categorization or typicality effects.

Exemplar Models

The fundamental point that Medin and Schaffer made was this. Results like Posner and Keele's (1968) don't necessarily indicate that a prototype is formed and then stored in memory. Posner and Keele's results indicate that abstraction takes place. The prototype model assumes that as you see each example of a category, you use that example to update your prototype and then toss out the example, as shown in Figure 7.3.

Thus, according to the prototype model the abstraction takes place at encoding. Who says it has to take place at encoding? Suppose instead that you store every experience you have with an example of a category—you store every experience you have with a dog—and then you abstract a prototypical dog only if you need it (Figure 7.4). Thus, the very same process of abstraction could take place, but it takes place at retrieval, and only if it's needed. For example, you might create a prototype if you're trying to categorize a new stimulus.

Furthermore, typicality effects work out perfectly in the exemplar model. Stored in memory are lots of examples of birds that are small, sit in branches, and go "tweet tweet," so when you see something with those characteristics and compare it with all the birds in memory, the similarity is very high; therefore, you think this object is a very birdy bird. When the animal is a flightless, 6-foot-tall thing with wings and feathers, not nearly as similar to all your stored examples of birds, you don't think that it is such a terrific example of a bird. In sum, the **exemplar model** maintains that all exemplars are stored in memory, and categorization judgments are made by judging the similarity of the new exemplar to all the old exemplars of a category.

You'll notice that the prototype and exemplar models have something important in common. In both models, similarity is the key factor in categorization.

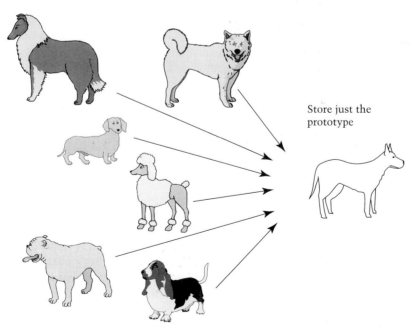

Store just the prototype

Figure 7.3. *Schematic of the prototype model. Although many types of exemplars are seen, only the prototype is stored. The prototype is updated continually as one has more experience with new exemplars.*

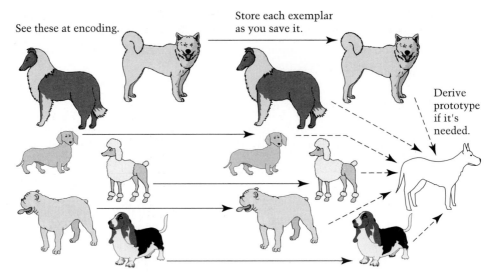

Figure 7.4.   *Schematic of the exemplar model. As each exemplar is seen, it is encoded in memory. A prototype is abstracted only when it is needed, as when a new exemplar must be categorized.*

People are thought to categorize new objects by comparing them with prototypes. If you saw an odd little animal you might determine what it was by comparing it to your prototype for *dog, cat, raccoon, fox,* and so on. Whichever prototype the new animal is most similar to, that's the category to which you would say it belongs. Similarity plays a crucial role in these models.

On the other hand, the models are very different in terms of what they propose is stored in memory. The exemplar model holds that multiple exemplars of a category are stored in memory. The prototype model holds that only the prototype is stored. Which one is right?

There is a rather sizable literature comparing exemplar models to prototype models. This literature is different from others we have discussed. The strategy is to specify the model of categorization in enough detail that you can run a computer simulation of human performance using the model. These models make specific predictions about how fast people learn categories, how fast they forget them, what transfer to new exemplars should look like, and so on. You can compare the success of exemplar and prototype models by comparing their predictions with actual human performance. If the prototype model predicts that participants will get 65% correct after 100 training trials and the exemplar model predicts it will be 72%, and humans get 71%, then obviously the exemplar model is doing a better job of predicting the data. Developing very specific models and comparing their performance with human data is a style of conducting research that is typically called mathematical psychology. In these contests, exemplar models have consistently come out ahead of prototype models (for a very thorough and readable overview, see Estes, 1994; see also Smith & Mimda, 2000).

During the late 1980s, however, more and more evidence accumulated indicating that there is more to categorization than similarity. These findings pose a problem for both exemplar and prototype models because they both are rooted solely in similarity. We turn now to these findings.

Problems With Similarity Models

A number of researchers have pointed out problems with implementing the concept of similarity. Similarity is judged by the number of features two objects share. But how do I determine the appropriate features to compare? It's almost always the case that I can select features to make any two objects look similar or dissimilar. For example, if I want an elephant and a plum to be considered similar, I could draw attention to these shared features: Both cannot perceive infrared light, both cannot jump 6 feet, both are not found on the moon, both are less than 128 years old, and so on. On the other hand, if I want an elephant and a plum to appear dissimilar, I could point out that they differ on many features: They are different weights, different sizes, different colors, and so on. The features I select determine how similar they will seem.

Other researchers have pointed out that the similarity of two objects appears to depend on the context in which they appear. Amos Tversky (1977) showed that perceived similarity does not always follow categorization. He showed participants four faces, similar to those shown in Figure 7.5.

Some participants were asked to categorize the first four faces into two groups. Participants most often made categories of AB and CD, corresponding

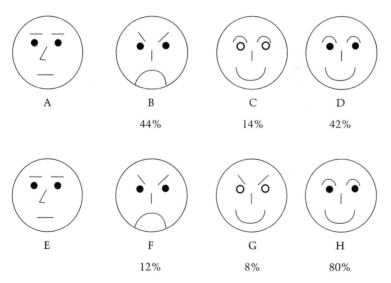

Figure 7.5. *Stimuli used in Tversky's (1977) experiment. The top row is one set of stimuli that participants saw, and the bottom row is a second set. Also shown are the percentages of participants who picked a face as being the most similar to the leftmost face in the row. Thus, the top row and the bottom row call for the same comparison but in the context of different exemplars; the context affects similarity judgments.*

BOX 7.1. FUNCTIONAL IMAGING EVIDENCE ON THE DIFFERENCE BETWEEN RULE APPLICATION AND SIMILARITY JUDGMENTS IN CATEGORIZATION

In this section we have suggested that a key function of being able to categorize objects is generalization. If you can put a novel object in a category, you have more information about it because you know that it is similar to previous members of the category you have encountered. The question is how you determine whether something is a member of a category. One view is that there is a set of rules (e.g., "people with the flu have a fever"), and you observe how many of the category criteria the new object meets. The alternative is that you evaluate the similarity of the new object to members of the category you have seen before, without applying a set of rigid rules.

In the text we discussed a task in which participants could be induced to categorize either by rules or by similarity, depending on task instructions (Allen & Brooks, 1991). Ed Smith and his colleagues (Smith, Patalano, & Jonides, 1998) administered a very similar task. The purpose was to categorize alien creatures. Some participants were given five characteristics, and if an alien had any three, it was from Venus; otherwise it was from Saturn. Other participants were not given any rules but were asked to memorize the correct categorizations for 10 animals. During the test phase, participants categorized novel animals, and brain activation was imaged with positron emission tomography.

As shown in Figure B7.1, activations in the rule condition are associated with secondary visual areas with superior parietal lobe and with premotor cortex and dorsolateral frontal cortex. This pattern of activation is readily interpretable: Participants must scan for particular visual features (secondary visual areas) to compare the features with the rule held in working memory (premotor and dorsolateral prefrontal areas). Moving attention relies on superior parietal cortex.

In the memory condition, on the other hand, the primary site of unique activation is in the occipital cortex and right cerebellum. The visual cortical activation may reflect the recovery of visual memories that were used in the memory condition, although based on other studies, some temporal lobe activation would have been sensible in that context. The cerebellar activation is difficult to interpret.

In sum, this study provides converging evidence that participants can recruit different cognitive processes to solve categorization problems, and these different processes are supported by different neural structures.

(Continued)

to smiling and nonsmiling. Nevertheless, when asked which face was most similar to A, as many participants selected D as most similar to A (42%) as picked B as most similar to A (44%). Because people had categorized A and B together, you would think that they would be judged as most similar.

Other participants were asked to categorize the second set of four faces. They tended to categorize the frowning faces (FG) and the nonfrowning faces (EH). These participants were also asked to judge which face was most similar to E.

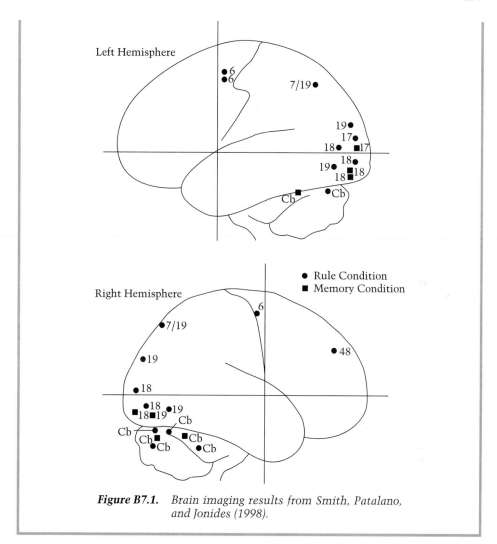

Figure B7.1. *Brain imaging results from Smith, Patalano, and Jonides (1998).*

Most selected H (80%) and many fewer selected F (12%). Note how much the similarity judgments of the first and last face changed across the two problems, even though those faces didn't change at all. The only change was in the context (i.e., in the other faces), but that influenced similarity judgments.

If there are problems with similarity, shouldn't there be problems with the categorization that we do with this flawed mechanism? Possibly. But another possibility is that we use another mechanism. A number of researchers have argued that categorization can proceed not only via similarity but via rules. Talking about categorization as being accomplished by rules can be a bit vague. After all, you could simply say that the rule for categorization is to use similarity, and there would be nothing new in the definition. For the most part, rule-based categorization is a throwback to the classical view; it is the idea that in some cases there are necessary and sufficient properties that define categories.

In a seminal study on this topic, Lance Rips (1989) had participants make categorization judgments with very little information about the object (just one feature). He also restricted the choices to two categories; one of the categories was inflexible as to the described feature and the other was not. For example, one item was this: "The object is 3 inches in diameter. Is the object a pizza or a quarter?" Most participants (63%) said it was a pizza, even though a separate group of participants had more often (70%) judged that a quarter was more similar to a 3-inch object than a pizza is. Rips argued that people are sensitive to necessary, inflexible features. A quarter must be a particular size; that feature cannot change.

This finding probably does not mean that rule-based categorization is always used. As pointed out before, rule-based categorization cannot readily account for typicality effects. Instead, it might mean that either rule-based or similarity-based categorization can be used. A study supporting that view was conducted by Scott Allen and Lee Brooks (1991). In their experiment, participants saw new creatures and were asked to categorize them as diggers or builders. Some participants were encouraged to learn the categories by memorizing exemplars and their category. Others were given a rule by which to categorize. Builders have two of the following three characteristics: long legs, angular body, and spots.

After both groups of participants learned the categories, the experimenters showed them some new exemplars. Some of the new exemplars were actually builders, but they looked very much like diggers that participants had seen during training. Participants in the memory group called them diggers 86% of the time, indicating that they were comparing the new items with remembered items from training. But those in the rule group called them diggers just 45% of the time, indicating that they were most often relying on the rule and therefore categorizing correctly. It appears that people can use either rules or similarity in categorization.

Allen and Brooks used task instructions to induce participants to categorize using either similarity or rules. People don't normally have instructions, though. So what makes people use one strategy or another?

Ed Smith and Steven Sloman (1994) argued that rules might be invoked primarily when there are no features that are characteristic of any category. For example, in Rips's (1989) study, the only feature given is diameter: The object is 3 inches. Three-inch size is not characteristic of either category. Smith and Sloman suggested that people use characteristic information when it is available, and that makes them categorize via similarity. In their study, they gave participants descriptions of objects just as Rips (1989) had done. But for some participants they added a feature that is characteristic of one category. For example, some participants were told, "The object is 3 inches in diameter. Is it a pizza or a quarter?" Others were told, "The object is 3 inches in diameter and it is silver colored. Is it a pizza or a quarter?" Note that this description contains the necessary feature (size), indicating that the object should be a pizza, but contains a feature that is highly characteristic of a quarter. The results showed that participants mostly (67%) picked *pizza* when given only the necessary feature (size), but when given both the necessary and the characteristic feature (size and color) they mostly (58%) picked *quarter*. (See also Hampton, 1995.) Studies like this one will help us unravel when people tend to use similarity and when they use rules.

Summary

The classical view of categorization was that categories were defined by a set of necessary and sufficient rules. In the 1970s, it became clear that category structure is not all-or-none, as the classical view would predict, but rather has a graded structure; some exemplars of a category are considered more typical, or better examples of the category than others are. This finding and others led to probability models of categorization, in which categorization is viewed as a matter of probability, not all-or-none. Two types of probability models were developed: prototype models (in which exemplars are abstracted into a prototype, which is stored) and exemplar models (in which all the exemplars are stored). In the late 1980s new results indicated that similarity could not account for all categorization. It seemed that rules are used to categorize at least some of the time. The latest work in this area has been directed toward determining when similarity is used and when rules are used.

STAND-ON-ONE-FOOT QUESTIONS

1. Describe the classical view of categorization. What data indicated that it could not provide a complete account of categorization?
2. List the effects of typicality on cognition.
3. What are the two main types of categorization theories that rely on similarity, and what is the key difference between them?
4. What is the final word on the difference between the rule-based view of categorization and the similarity view?

QUESTIONS THAT REQUIRE TWO FEET

5. When you heard that the exemplar model proposed that each exemplar is stored in memory and that categorization decisions are made based on the similarity of the new exemplar to groups of exemplars in memory, you may have thought of an obvious difficulty with this scheme. What logical problem seems apparent?
6. You may have noticed that newspapers (especially the more sensationalist tabloids) dearly love publishing headlines that report on a grandma doing something atypical of grandmas: "Grandma swims English Channel," "Grandma shoots intruder with Uzi." Comment on why newspapers do this, given what you've learned about categorization.

➤ How Is Memory Organized?

> ➤ PREVIEW In this section, we discuss how memory is organized. Organization is crucial because it is organization that helps you pull the right memory out of the storehouse. Our memory system does not merely allow us to find the desired memory quickly. If what is desired is not in memory, the system provides something close in meaning, or it provides material that may help you come to a reasonable guess about the information you wish you had. One early theory of memory organization, the hierarchical model, suggested that concepts were organized in a taxonomic hierarchy (e.g., *animal* above *bird, bird* above *canary*). Later models used an idea called spreading activation, whereby thinking about one concept would bring semantically related concepts to mind; for example, thinking about the concept *doctor* makes it a little more likely that you'll think of the related concept *patient*. We also discuss a variant of the spreading activation model that uses distributed representation. In some models a single concept is represented by a single unit in the model. In a distributed model one concept is represented by many units of the model; in fact, many concepts are in those units simultaneously, and which concept is represented at any moment depends on the state of the entire model. That's a little hard to grasp, so we go over it in some detail, and we discuss the advantages and disadvantages of these schemes.

The mind is faced with a formidable problem. We each have an amazing amount of material stored away in memory (although it doesn't always feel that way). For starters, most college students have a reading vocabulary of perhaps 60,000 or 70,000 words. Add to that all of your memories about what things are (a tap is for getting water), how things work (a tap should be turned), and your memory for faces (third-grade teacher), voices (Mom), music ("Mmm-Bop"), and so on. The core problem is to find useful information quickly from among these riches, and people's ability to find memories efficiently is truly amazing. Recent evidence shows that people can identify popular songs (e.g., "Macarena" or "Missing") when presented with a snippet as short as 200 ms (Schellenberg, Iverson, & McKinnon, 1999). In the last section we saw that we are unsure about how categorization operates; can we nonetheless say something about how memory is organized?

We can, but I want to start by explaining a bit about memory systems in general. This explanation will give you a better idea of what the human memory system might be doing, and it will give you a better idea of why cognitive psychologists have posed the questions they have posed.

Addressing System

As a starting point, we can think about information storage systems that we understand. Consider a library, another information storehouse. How do you find the right book in a library? Books are ordered according to the Dewey decimal system, which is a subject ordering system. That is appropriate because you almost always want to look for books according to their subject matter, not their size or color. Hence, religion is in the 200s, the arts are in the 700s, social sciences are in the 300s, and so on. But that indexing system isn't specific enough if you need a particular volume. To find a particular book, you need its unique number, which you find in a master list that has the specific numbers of all the books on it (the catalog). The system used in a library is called an **addressing system** because each entity in the storehouse has a unique address, and that address is critical for finding what you want. If the 798.30 is erased from the book or from the master list, or if the book is accidentally shelved as 898.30, no one will be able to retrieve it, or at least not quickly.

Your computer uses an addressing system that enables it to find things as needed on the hard drive (the computer's storehouse). When you create a new computer file (e.g., you write a paper for a class) and store it on the hard drive, the location of that new file is stored on a master list called a disk directory. Indeed, if the disk directory is corrupted somehow, then the computer can't find anything and you've got big problems. A computer's addressing system is somewhat different from that used in a library because the relationship between the address and the contents of the information is completely arbitrary in a computer, whereas in the library there is some correspondence between the address and the contents of the book.

We know that your mind doesn't use an addressing system because your mind behaves in ways inconsistent with one. For example, if your mind used an addressing system, the kinds of memory errors you made would be unpredictable. For example, suppose someone asked you, "Is there a good dry cleaner around here?" and you checked your master memory list and found that the answer to this question was at memory address 78342. Suppose further that your memory system made an error in one digit and looked up memory location 88342. If you used an addressing system, anything could be at that address and you might answer the dry cleaning question by saying, "Ratatouille." (If your computer looks up the wrong memory address by mistake, the material often is so different from what the program expects that the program crashes.)

Your memory system doesn't work that way, however. If you make a memory error, it tends to be a near miss: an answer that is wrong but is at least related to the right answer, such as thinking that Julia Roberts starred in *Ghost*. Usually such errors are related in terms of meaning. For example, I might ask you, "What's that thing you use on a boat to find your position; that thing you point at the sun?" You might answer "A compass," which is wrong (it's a sextant), but "compass" is close because it has something to do with finding locations (Brown & McNeill, 1966).

Content-Addressable Storage

A system that seems closer to human memory uses **content-addressable storage,** which means that the content of the memory is itself the storage address. You find a memory's location in the storehouse based on what's in the memory. Searching for a memory in a content-addressable storage system is equivalent to walking into a library and shouting out, "Okay, I need to know whether a pizza has cheese on it," whereupon the appropriate book (a cookbook, perhaps) jumps off the shelf and runs over to you on its little book-legs, presenting itself for use.

This system sounds like exactly what we need. For example, it would produce near misses; you search memory for the name of a location-finding thing (sextant) and you have a concept in memory that is pretty close in meaning: "direction-finding thing." Therefore, "direction-finding thing" (i.e., compass) pops out of the storehouse. Another good feature is that content-addressable storage systems are very fast, and the time it takes to retrieve a memory from the storehouse does not increase as you add things to the storehouse. Our memory systems also seem to work that way; as you learn more things, it doesn't take you longer to retrieve facts about the old things.

Unfortunately, the feature of this system that makes the speed possible also poses a problem. The point of the system is that you access memories based on the content. But how does the memory "know" when it is being called upon? You can set up a memory system so that each memory compares its contents with whatever is being asked for every time some memory is demanded. For the system to work, when I shout out "I need a book about pizza!" every book in the library must have the capability of knowing what I'm asking for and evaluating whether its content is a good enough match that it should jump off the shelf. Making each memory "smart" in this way is a big commitment because it takes a lot of processing resources to build it, whether you're going to design a computer memory system on this principle or whether you're speculating about how the brain works.

The human memory system has a capability beyond that of a simple content-addressable system, however. Such a system lacks an important capability of the human memory system, which is best illustrated by example. Suppose I ask you this question: "Does Leonardo DiCaprio have a large intestine?"

You would answer "yes" to this question, but why would you do so? It's likely that you've never encoded that fact, so it can't be in memory. On what basis do you give a confident "yes"?

Your "yes" is not based on a fact in memory about Leonardo DiCaprio; it is based on an inference. When you try to retrieve information that has not been encoded directly, your memory system often pulls up related information that allows you to make an inference to answer the question as follows:

FROM MEMORY: Humans have a large intestine.

FROM MEMORY: Leonardo DiCaprio is a human.

INFERENCE: Therefore, Leonardo DiCaprio has a large intestine.

The requested information is not in memory, but you do have in memory other information that can help you to answer the question, and that information is retrieved. That's why a simple content-addressable storage system can't be the whole answer; if that's how your memory worked, when I asked, "Does Leonardo DiCaprio have a large intestine," your search would come up empty; no book would jump off the shelf, so to speak, because you've never stored the information.

I just said that your memory system retrieves other information that is relevant to the question posed, and that allows you to make an inference to answer the question. So how does the memory system "know" the right information to produce?

I mentioned at the start of this section that the discussion of memory systems and their capabilities was relevant here because it was one such capability that motivated cognitive psychologists in their study of the organization of memory. This question is the one that motivated the initial work on the organization of secondary memory: What is the organization that allows not just the simple retrieval of facts but also the retrieval of relevant facts that one would not expect to necessarily be declaratively stored?

Hierarchical Theory

One of the first models to address this question came from Allan Collins and Ross Quillian (1969, 1972), and it proposed a clever solution: the **hierarchical theory.** In their model (and in many of the models that follow) memory is composed of two basic elements: nodes and links. **Nodes** represent concepts, such as *red, candy, bird, president,* and so on.

Nodes have levels of activation. **Activation** in this context means that the node has some level of energy, or excitement. These metaphors are just supposed to help you picture what is happening. In practical terms, nodes become active when the concept they represent is present in the environment. Thus, the concept *bird* might become active through my seeing a picture of a bird, seeing a real bird, or hearing or reading the word *bird,* and so on.

The second component of hierarchical networks is links. **Links** represent relationships between concepts, such as "has this property" or "is an example of." As shown in Figure 7.6, these links connect nodes and can provide property descriptions of concepts. Thus the idea that a living thing must breathe is represented in the model through a concept (*living thing*), a property (*breathe*), and a link (*must*). A small example of a hierarchical memory structure is shown in Figure 7.6.

An important characteristic of the model is **property inheritance.** As one moves down the hierarchy (e.g., from *animal* to *bird* to *chicken*), concepts inherit properties from the concepts that are higher in the hierarchy. Hence, an animal is a type of living thing, so it inherits the properties of living things. For example, chickens inherit the properties "must breathe" and "must eat" from the concept *animal* (but see also Sloman, 1998).

You'll remember that we asked earlier what happens when an inference is needed to answer a question. The inheritance of properties can be important in such situations. If I were to ask you, "Does a canary breathe?" the model predicts that you would first go to the node representing the concept *canary*. You would examine the properties associated with *canary* and you'd discover that breathing or not breathing is not part of the representation of what a canary does, so you would move up one level in the hierarchy to the concept *bird* to see whether breathing or not breathing is stored with being a bird. You'd discover

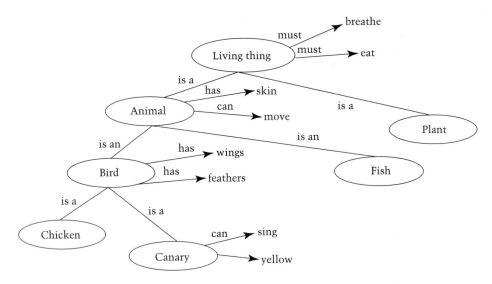

Figure 7.6. *An example of a hierarchical network described by Collins and Quillian repre-senting* animal, canary, *and* chicken, *among other concepts. There are also links such as "is a" and "has."*

it is not, and you'd continue to the concept *animal* and finally to *living thing*, where you would finally find the relevant information.

Suppose we make the simple assumption that moving up the hierarchy takes time. We would predict that each of these successive sentences would take a longer time to verify.

Collins and Quillian tested exactly that prediction simply by showing one sentence at a time on a computer screen and asking participants to push one button if the sentence was true and another if it was false. Half of the time the sentence was false (e.g., "A canary is a plant"), but the experimenters were in-terested in how long it took participants to verify the sentences when they were true. Participants' response times came out in the order that the model predicted (the numbers in parentheses are the response times to verify the sentences):

A canary is a canary (1,000 ms)
A canary is a bird (1,160 ms)
A canary is an animal (1,240 ms)

The effect worked just as well for properties:

A canary can sing (1,305 ms)
A canary has wings (1,395 ms)
A canary has skin (1,480 ms)

Thus, the findings seemed to support the model for the tricky ability we dis-cussed in regard to DiCaprio's intestine. Unfortunately, it soon became apparent that the model didn't always make the right predictions. One problem was that the hierarchy sometimes didn't seem to hold. For example, people were faster to verify the sentence "A chicken is an animal" than to verify "A chicken is a bird."

Another problem was that participants were faster to verify a sentence such as "A canary is a bird" than they were to verify "A chicken is a bird" (Rips, Shoben, & Smith, 1973). This is a typicality effect, as you may recall from the last section. Bear in mind that Collins and Quillian's model was proposed before Rosch had done most of her work outlining typicality effects.

Another problem of this model grows out of a property that initially seemed to be a strength. Looking at Figure 7.6 you'll notice that the property *has wings* is stored only once, with *bird*. Robins have wings, cardinals have wings, chickens have wings, but Collins and Quillian figured it was crazy to store the property *has wings* with every bird. It made much more sense to store the property just once, with *bird*, along with all the other properties that birds have, and then have each type of bird simply refer to the general concept *bird* if you need to know whether a particular bird has that property. This principle is called **cognitive economy.** In general cognitive economy refers to designing a cognitive system in a way that conserves resources. In this case, cognitive economy seems to dictate that you can't possibly store all of the features of every concept with the concept because there would be so much repetition. That idea seems pretty sensible, but it's not true, at least not the way Collins and Quillian implemented it. Carol Conrad (1972) gave participants a list of words and asked them to simply write down what the word made them think of. She found that participants often wrote information that was one or two levels higher in the hierarchy. For example, if you give people the word *robin, canary,* or *bluebird* they are very likely to write *flies* as one of the properties, even though *flies* is stored with the concept *bird*, not with *robin, canary,* or *bluebird*. You would predict that people would be most likely to list properties that are stored with the concept, not properties from higher up in the hierarchy. Furthermore, this result seems to directly contradict the cognitive economy idea. The property *flies* seems to be stored with all of these different birds.

Spreading Activation Theories

Collins developed a different approach to address the shortcomings of his earlier model. Allan Collins and Elizabeth Loftus (1975) proposed a **spreading activation model.** A spreading activation model is another network model, again consisting of nodes and links. The new feature of the model is that the links represent associations between concepts. Concepts are linked to (i.e., associated with) semantically related concepts. Memory is thus conceived as a vast network of linked concepts called a **semantic network.** Collins and Loftus used links that had properties such as "is a" and "has a." Later models that built on their work did not (e.g., McClelland, 1981) and I'm presenting that later model here.

Here's how a semantic network operates. As in the hierarchical network, nodes can become active, and you can think of this activity as the node having energy. Nodes become active through stimulation from the environment. Thus, the concept *president* might become active through my seeing a picture of the president or through hearing or reading the word president. Figure 7.7 shows three nodes in a memory network (I'm taking a break from canaries and chickens).

Time moves from left to right in the figure, so at left we see a node without activation, then the word *president* comes in from the environment (because someone said it, for example) and at right we see the same node, now activated, with the activation represented by the thicker border on the node.

What's new in this model is that active nodes send some of their activity to nodes to which they are linked. Hence, nodes can also become active by receiving activity from other nodes that have become active. They send a high proportion of their activation to concepts they are closely related to and a smaller proportion to concepts they are not so related to. Hence, Clinton might send a lot of activation to *White House* but less to *Congress*. This principle is shown in the right part of the figure.

We can be a bit more formal in defining the six properties of a semantic network (Rumelhart, Hinton, & McClelland, 1986):

- *A set of units.* Each unit represents a concept.
- *A state of activation.* Each unit has its own state of activation, or how much "energy" it has at a given moment.
- *An output function.* Units pass activation to one another. How much of a unit's activation it passes to its neighbors depends on two things. In many models, the link between two units has a weight. If the weight is 0.5, then whatever activation the unit tries to send down that weight will be multiplied by 0.5. If the weight is 0.75, the activation will be multiplied by 0.75, and so on. In addition, units may have output functions, which relates the current activation state of the unit to the amount of

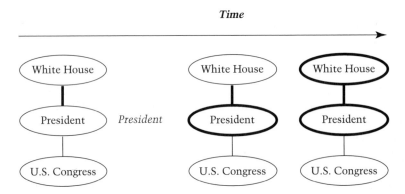

Figure 7.7. *When the word* president *is perceived in the environment (left), the corresponding concept becomes active in memory (center), and activation spreads to related concepts (right). The amount of activation depends on the weight of the link between concepts.*

activation it tries to send down its links. The output activation function may simply be to multiply the activation by 1.0 (i.e., simply send the same amount of activation down the links that the unit itself has). Other models use a threshold function, so that the unit must have a particular amount of activation or more (i.e., exceed a threshold) before it can have any influence on its neighbors.

- *A pattern of connectivity.* Units are connected to one another by links, and each link has a weight associated with it. The knowledge of the system is in these weights. The extent to which you know that birds fly depends on the strength of the link between *bird* and *flies.*
- *An activation rule.* This is a rule by which a unit integrates the activation sent to it by other units via links. If I say to you, "amber color, foamy, cold," these words are closely associated with the concept *beer.* Suppose that these three concepts (*amber color, foamy, cold*), which were activated when I said the words, send activation of 0.85, 0.48, and 0.15 to the concept *beer.* What will the activation of *beer* now be? Should we add the three, yielding 1.48? Should we find the mean, yielding 0.49? Should we allow only activations higher than 0.25 to enter our calculations and take the mean of those, yielding 0.67? The activation rule determines how the inputs should be combined.
- *Learning rule to change weights.* A semantic network cannot be static. The knowledge of the network is in weights, so there must be a mechanism to change the weights if the model is to learn. Suppose you didn't know that horses love candy peppermints. The link between *horse* and *peppermint* would be 0.0. Now that you've read that fact one time, what should the weight of that link be? There must be a rule by which the weights change. (I recently learned that horses do, by the way.)

Spreading Activation Models: An Example

We've gone over the properties of spreading activation models. To give a better sense of their strengths, let's have a look at one example that is developed in some detail (McClelland, 1981). Table 7.5 lists information about 27 men.

All the information in this list can be represented in a semantic network. A subset of the units necessary is shown in Figure 7.8. Notice that some units in the center of the network do not represent any concept. These units are important for passing activation between nodes, but a technical description of why they are needed is beyond the scope of our discussion.

This sort of model has a number of very useful characteristics. First, it obviously allows for the retrieval of properties. If you say "Lance," that word is perceived and the *Lance* node becomes active. That node passes activity to other nodes and it will lead to activity of the nodes *Jets, 20s, junior high, married,* and *burglar.*

Second, the model allows content-addressable storage. Recall that this is the very useful property discussed at the start of the chapter whereby memories are accessed not by an address but by the content of the memory. Spreading

Table 7.5   The Jets and the Sharks

Name	Gang	Age	Education	Marital Status	Occupation
Art	Jets	40s	Junior High	Single	Pusher
Al	Jets	30s	Junior High	Married	Burglar
Sam	Jets	20s	College	Single	Bookie
Clyde	Jets	40s	Junior High	Single	Bookie
Mike	Jets	30s	Junior High	Single	Bookie
Jim	Jets	20s	Junior High	Divorced	Burglar
Greg	Jets	20s	High School	Married	Pusher
John	Jets	20s	Junior High	Married	Burglar
Doug	Jets	30s	High School	Single	Bookie
Lance	Jets	20s	Junior High	Married	Burglar
George	Jets	20s	Junior High	Divorced	Burglar
Pete	Jets	20s	High School	Single	Bookie
Fred	Jets	20s	High School	Single	Pusher
Gene	Jets	20s	College	Single	Pusher
Ralph	Jets	30s	Junior High	Single	Pusher
Phil	Sharks	30s	College	Married	Pusher
Ike	Sharks	30s	Junior High	Single	Bookie
Nick	Sharks	30s	High School	Single	Pusher
Don	Sharks	30s	College	Married	Burglar
Ned	Sharks	30s	College	Married	Bookie
Karl	Sharks	40s	High School	Married	Bookie
Ken	Sharks	20s	High School	Single	Burglar
Earl	Sharks	40s	High School	Married	Burglar
Rick	Sharks	30s	High School	Divorced	Burglar
Ol	Sharks	30s	College	Married	Pusher
Neal	Sharks	30s	High School	Single	Bookie
Dave	Sharks	30s	High School	Divorced	Pusher

activation models have this property. For example, if we activated the nodes *Jets* and *40s* the activation would spread through the network and *Art* would become active. If we activated *Jets* and *30s* then the four Jets in their 30s would become active: *Al, Mike, Doug,* and *Ralph.*

Third, it is easy to see how typicality grows naturally out of the model. A concept such as *robin* will have strong links to many concepts that are in turn strongly linked to *bird* (*small, sits in trees, lays eggs*). An atypical bird such as an ostrich has many links to concepts that are weakly linked to *bird* (*large, runs fast, can't fly*). If I simply say "Bird," all the nodes that have strong links to that concept will become active. Thus, it is easy for me to describe the typical bird. Similarly, in the model in Figure 7.8, above if I say "Jet," all of the features of the prototypical Jet become active, even if no one Jet has all of the typical qualities.

Fourth, the model naturally creates *defaults*. A default is a value that a variable or an attribute takes in the absence of any other information. For example, how does a bird get around? In the absence of any other information, the

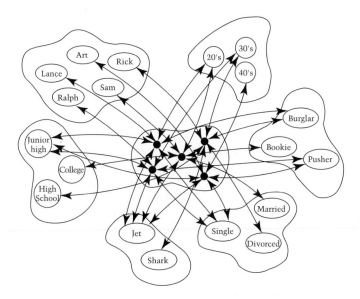

Figure 7.8. *The information from Table 7.5 presented in a network.*

default is that it flies. Default values are assigned for concepts as a natural part of the spreading activation. If you have reason to think that the object you're dealing with is a bird, then the connection between *bird* and *flies* will lead to activation in the concept *flies* unless you are specifically told that this bird does not fly.

Fifth, spreading activation models are resistant to faulty input. Suppose I said to you, "I went to a restaurant last night that was pretty good. I can't remember the name, but it was a fast-food place, and they had something called a Big Mac and the restaurant had green arches out front." You would say to me, "You mean McDonald's, but the arches are gold." Notice that you've retrieved the right memory, even though I've given you faulty information. It's easy to imagine that you could check the memory system for a description of my restaurant and find nothing; indeed, you've never heard of a restaurant matching the description I gave. But your memory system is resistant to faulty input and can come up with the right memory. Spreading activation models have this property. The properties *fast food* and *Big Mac* are so strongly linked to *McDonald's* that it is activated, despite the fact that *green arches* might inhibit its activation a bit. Once *McDonald's* is activated, that in turn activates *golden arches*, which makes me surmise that you have made an error in your description.

Evidence of Activation

There is evidence consistent with the idea that concepts in memory become active and that when the activity surpasses a threshold they enter awareness. Many paradigms demonstrate an effect called **repetition priming.** In these tasks, the participant reads a list of words. Sometime later (usually an hour) the participant performs a second task. Some of the words used in the second task are the same as the words in the original list, but the participant is not told that. Table 7.6 lists the type of tasks that researchers have used to measure priming.

In each of the tasks described in the table, participants show some bias on the task caused by the processing of the words on the original list of words they read. These repetition priming effects often are interpreted as showing that nodes representing concepts become active when participants first read the words on the list. Then, when they perform the second task an hour later, those nodes are still somewhat active, making these concepts easier to access.

Repetition priming effects indicate that activation of nodes lasts an hour or more and that this activation is measurable. Another effect, **semantic priming,** indicates that this activation passes between nodes. We discussed this effect in chapter 6. To remind you, participants performing a lexical decision task were faster to say "yes" when the two words were related (e.g., they saw *doctor* then *nurse*) than when they were not (*radio* then *nurse*; Meyer & Schvaneveldt, 1971). A straightforward interpretation is that when participants saw the word *doctor*,

Table 7.6   *Tasks Used to Measure Priming*

Task	Description	Priming Measure	Reference
Fragment completion	Participants must complete word fragments to form words. Each fragment has just one possible completion.	Number of fragments successfully completed that were on the original list versus fragments completed that were not.	Tulving, Schacter, & Stark (1982)
Stem completion	Participants must complete word stems to form a word. Each fragment has at least 10 possible completions.	Number of stems completed to make a word on the original list versus stems completed to make words not on the list.	Warrington & Weiskrantz (1968)
Category exemplar generation	Participants must name category members.	Somewhat unusual category members appear on the original list. Priming is measured by how many of these unusual members participants mention.	Graf, Shimamura, & Squire (1985)
Lexical decision	Participants see a letter string appear and they must respond with a button press as quickly as possible to indicate whether the letter string forms a word.	Priming is reflected by shorter response times to words that were on the list compared to words that were not.	Just & Carpenter (1980)

the node representing the concept became active and immediately passed activation to all semantically related concepts, including *nurse.* So when the participants read the word *nurse,* the concept representing it was already somewhat active, so it was easier to identify the word.

Criticisms of Spreading Activation

The spreading activation idea is quite popular in cognitive psychology, and the use of spreading activation is widespread in models of memory (e.g., Anderson, 1976, 1983; McClelland & Rumelhart, 1981; McNamara, 1992). Nevertheless, there are some problems with the concept of spreading activation. One problem is that spreading activation as a concept often is somewhat vague. Researchers are not always specific about exactly how one determines the location and strength of links; instead, if one item primes another, one assumes that they must be linked. But that's a circular theory.

A second problem concerns just how far activation spreads. Activation appears to spread not just one link away, but at least two and possibly three links away. For example, it has been demonstrated that the word *lion* primes the word *stripes.* Presumably, *lion* primes *tiger,* which primes *stripes.* Priming that goes through another word in this fashion is called **mediated priming** (McNamara & Healy, 1988). Some evidence indicates that mediated priming can extend through two mediators, not just one. But Roger Ratcliff and Gail McCoon (1994) pointed out a problem. Suppose that each word that is activated spreads its activation to about 20 other words; when I say "lion," about 20 words (one of them *tiger*) are activated. If each of these 20 words activates 20 other words, and they in turn activate 20 other words (which three-step priming indicates would happen), then a total of $20 \times 20 \times 20 = 8,000$ words is activated by the utterance of just one word. Because most adults have a vocabulary of about 64,000 words, that means hearing a single word activates about one eighth of all the words you know. This scheme seems to make the idea of spreading activation sort of pointless because it seems that in the course of a normal conversation most of the concepts would be active most of the time. (See Ratcliff & McKoon, 1988, for an alternative account of priming that doesn't include spreading activation, and McNamara, 1992, 1994, for a spirited defense of spreading activation.)

Distributed Representation (Parallel Distributed Processing)

The spreading activation model I've described uses nodes and links, of course, and in this model each node represents a single concept; one node represents *bird,* another node represents *cardinal,* and so on. In another class of models, a concept is represented across multiple nodes. Suppose, for example, that I have four nodes. I could make each of these nodes represent a concept: *vanilla, chocolate, strawberry,* and *coffee.* If the *vanilla* node has an activation of 1.0, then I'm thinking about vanilla, and so on, for the other nodes. That would be the one-node, one-concept scheme described earlier. But suppose I look at all four nodes simultaneously, and meaning is based on what all four nodes are doing, as shown in Figure 7.9.

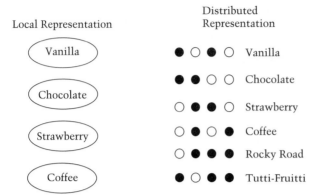

Figure 7.9. *Examples of local representations (each node represents one concept) and distributed representations (each concept is represented across multiple nodes).*

We've been talking about a **local representation.** In a local representation, a concept has a single location: It's localized in a single node, as shown at left. If that node is active, the concept is active, regardless of what any other nodes are doing. In a **distributed representation,** concepts are distributed across multiple nodes. You can't look at one node and know whether the concept *vanilla* is active. You have to look at all four nodes simultaneously. One advantage of a distributed representation is obvious: You can get more concepts into the same number of nodes with a distributed representation.

Many distributed network models have a structure that looks something like Figure 7.10.

There is a series of input nodes, some number of hidden nodes, and a series of output nodes. Suppose this were a network that identified taste. (In truth, a real model of this function would comprise hundreds or thousands of units.) The input nodes would theoretically be getting their input from the senses (taste and smell). For example, vanilla ice cream might input the values +1 0 0 +1 –1 +1 0 0 into the eight input nodes. These inputs activate the hidden units, which in turn activate the output nodes. The output nodes represent the concepts *vanilla, chocolate, strawberry,* and so on. These models often are called **parallel distributed processing (PDP)** models.

This model has all the advantages of the model using local representations and some new ones. For one, the model exhibits another very useful property of memory called **graceful degradation.** *Graceful degradation* means that if something goes wrong, the system doesn't simply shut down. Its performance gets worse, but it is still somewhat able to function. For example, if one or two of the nodes were removed from the model in Figure 7.10, the rest of the model would still function—not perfectly, because the pattern of activation would be disrupted, but it would still function because each node gets inputs from many other nodes. If just a few nodes are lost, each node still gets most of the input

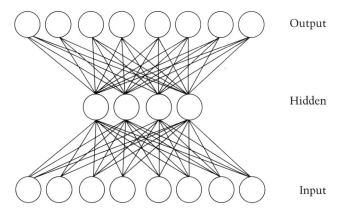

Output

Hidden

Input

Figure 7.10. *A typical network that uses a distributed representation showing nodes and links.*

that it gets when all nodes are present. Graceful degradation seems to be a property of the human memory system as well. The amount of damage to cognitive function is roughly proportional to the amount of damage to the part of the brain that supports it. Minimal damage causes minimal cognitive loss. This feature is very different from a computer's memory, where minimal damage can be catastrophic.

Another strength of these models is that they can actually learn in a convincing way. In many models using local representation, the knowledge (e.g., that birds have wings) is put into the model by the experimenter. Distributed representation models are designed to learn. They typically assume that the learner is given feedback about correctness. At the start of training, the model is assumed to know nothing, which is represented by setting all the weights of the links to values near zero. Then the researcher puts the input values corresponding to vanilla ice cream, for example, into the model. The activation works through the model, and the output nodes might take the values 0 0 0 +1 0 0 –1 0, which is not close to the correct identification of the concept *vanilla*. The model gets feedback (basically that the correct output was +1 0 0 +1 –1 +1 0 0), and the weights are changed slightly to bring the model slightly closer to producing the correct output, given that input. The rule for how the weights are changed depends on the difference between the input and the output, and the rule is the same on each trial. It may seem like cheating to you that the model is told what the correct answer is, but when you think about it, that's how it works in real life. Someone gives you ice cream and tells you, "This is vanilla." On successive trials the model would get the inputs for *chocolate, strawberry,* and all the other flavors, with feedback and weight changes on each trial. Thus, the strength of the model is that it seeks not just to show us how memories are represented after they are learned but also how memories are acquired.

An important strength of this learning process is that it automatically finds both prototypes and exceptions to prototypes. Suppose you include training of three flavors: vanilla, French vanilla, and vanilla bean.

BOX 7.2. HOW ARE CONCEPTS ORGANIZED IN THE BRAIN?

Does the organization of the brain tell us anything about how concepts are organized in the mind? Perhaps. There are two sources of evidence on this point, and they seem to conflict.

First, let's consider lesion evidence. Over the years, a number of cases have been reported of patients who have suffered strokes resulting in deficits that are specific to one narrow category of stimuli. For example, some patients have difficulty naming living things (lion, tiger, ant) but no difficulty naming other objects (book, truck, cake). Other patients show the opposite deficit. Other patients have still more specific deficits. For example, patient E.W. (Caramazza & Shelton, 1998) could name fruits and vegetables perfectly and 92% of manufactured objects (e.g., furniture, tools) but only 34% of the pictures of animals. E.W. also had difficulty distinguishing between real and unreal animals (made by combining body parts of different animals), and she had difficulty in affirming property statements about animals (e.g., that a horse has four legs). Her performance with objects other than animals was normal. One interpretation of these data is that the organization of knowledge in the brain follows the categories we use in describing the world. Just as we categorize things in the world as fruits or tools, our conceptual knowledge about these objects is organized in these categories in the brain. Thus a patient might have a stroke that affects only a small part of the brain, and it happens to knock out knowledge about a specific category of objects.

Neuroimaging evidence tells a different story, however. Alex Martin and his colleagues (Martin, Ungerleider, & Haxby, 2000) suggested that concepts in the brain are not organized by their category. Rather, different aspects of an object are located in different parts of the brain: What the object looks like is stored in one part of the brain and what it is for is in another part, for example. In one study, Martin and his colleagues (1995) showed participants an object (e.g., a wagon) and asked them to think about either its color (red) or an action appropriate to the object (pull). They found different areas of activation: color in the ventral temporal lobe and action in the left middle temporal gyrus. In each case, the stored attribute of objects was just anterior to the location that is believed to support the visual processing of the attribute.

The researchers suggested that concepts are represented as a conglomeration of semantic primitives such as form, color, characteristic motions, and ways of manipulating an object. Each concept has different attributes represented in different locations of the cortex.

Which view is correct? Are concepts organized by their category, as the lesion data suggest, or are they distributed throughout the cortex as a collection of attributes, as the functional imaging data suggest? The data do not clearly dictate that one theory or the other is correct, but it seems possible that an alternative interpretation of the lesion data may be proposed that will bring it into line with the imaging data (e.g., that the category-specific deficits are caused by a deficit in processing some attribute that many living objects happen to have, for example). None of the proposals along these lines have successfully accounted for the data, however, so how concepts are organized in the brain is still not entirely clear.

(Continued)

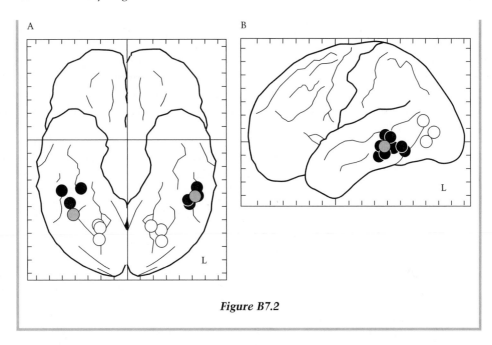

Figure B7.2

As you can see from Table 7.7, the input patterns of these three flavors are quite similar, and so is the output pattern. It seems logical that it should be harder for the model to learn to distinguish these three input–output patterns than three that are quite different. That happens, and it is perfectly appropriate, just as it would be more difficult for you to distinguish these three flavors than *vanilla, chocolate,* and *strawberry.* Now suppose that you have trained the model so that it knows these three flavors, and then you present the last flavor "bland," which is basically ice cream with no flavoring at all. What should a memory model do with this novel flavor? You might think, "Well, if you've never tasted it before, there is nothing in memory about this flavor. Therefore you should just say 'I don't know what it is.' " But that wouldn't happen. You would say, "Gee, it's not vanilla, but it sort of tastes like vanilla." That is generalization, and you'll recall that we said generalization is a key property of human memory. **Generalization** is responding to a new stimulus in the way you would respond to an old stimulus that is similar to the new one. Generalization is a natural outgrowth of this sort of model.

Table 7.7

Flavor	Input Pattern	Output Pattern
Vanilla	+1 0 0 +1 −1 +1 0 0	+1 0 0 +1 −1 +1 0 0
French vanilla	0 0 0 +1 −1 +1 0 0	+1 −1 0 +1 −1 +1 0 −1
Vanilla bean	−1 0 0 +1 −1 +1 0 0	+1 0 −1 +1 −1 +1 0 0
Bland	+1 −1 0 +1 −1 +1 0 0	+1 0 0 +1 −1 +1 −1 0

Criticisms of Parallel Distributed Processing Models

PDP models seem to be racking up all of the points. Nevertheless, there are problems with these models. One problem is that many PDP models suffer from what is called catastrophic interference. That means that if the model learns one set of associations (Set A) and then learns a different set (Set B), Set B will overwrite Set A. Set A will be completely lost from the model (McCloskey & Cohen, 1989). Set A and Set B can both be learned if the two sets are interleaved in training. The problem is observed only if you train the sets sequentially. As you know, this is not a characteristic of human memory. Researchers have come up with several suggestions to try to address the problem (Lewandowsky & Li, 1995; Sloman & Rumelhart, 1992).

A second problem is the ability of PDP models to learn rules. This problem came to the fore in an article by Steve Pinker and Alan Prince (1988) in which they criticized a well-known model developed by David Rumelhart and Jay McClelland (1987). This model sought to account for how children learn the past tense of the English language. As you may know, kids go through a period in which they add "ed" to words inappropriately. For example, a child might say, "Yesterday mom and I goed to the park." Interestingly, this period of overregularization follows a period in which the child conjugates the past tense of irregular verbs *correctly*. Initially the kids produce the correct past tense (*went*), then they make overregularization errors (*goed*), then they go back to producing the correct past tense (*went*). Many researchers have proposed that this pattern results from the child acquiring a rule about producing the past tense. Initially, the child doesn't know the rule but produces the correct past tense via memorizing the word *went* and applying it in the right situation. Then the child learns the rule "to make the past tense, add 'ed' to the infinitive of the verb." But that rule applies only to regular verbs, and the child applies it to irregular verbs such as *go*. Later, the child learns that there are exceptions to the rule, and the child memorizes these exceptions.

Rumelhart and McClelland's model produced the same pattern of output as the child does, only without any representation of a specific rule. They argued that a representation of a rule was not necessary. Pinker and Prince, in a detailed analysis of the model and of children's language learning, argued that there were many subtle aspects of children's language that the model did not account for and that these aspects required some rule-based representation. The details are beyond the scope of this chapter, but many researchers were convinced that an adequate model of children's language learning probably needs to include some representation of rules, and implementing rules in PDP models appears difficult.

So what's the final word on the organization of memory? Right now it appears that memory might be organized in some manner consistent with spreading activation, but the spreading activation hypothesis has not been immune to criticism. Until there is a preferable alternative theory, most cognitive psychologists will stick with spreading activation. As to whether the representation is local or distributed, that point is also not settled.

STAND-ON-ONE-FOOT QUESTIONS

7. Name two formidable problems that face any large memory storage device that your memory system is able to solve.
8. Name some of the advantages and disadvantages of the spreading activation model that uses a local representation.
9. What is the difference between the spreading activation models that use local representation and those that use distributed representation?

QUESTIONS THAT REQUIRE TWO FEET

10. Can you see how the spreading activation model might be related to early associationist ideas discussed in chapter 1? If not, can you see how it might be applied to the flow of consciousness?
11. Given what you know about the brain, do you think a local representation or a distributed representation is more realistic?
12. One way of measuring what concepts are connected in a spreading activation model is simply to name a word and ask people to name the first word that comes to mind. For example, what's the first word you think of when you hear "salt"? Presumably when you hear the word it is activated, and it passes its activation to concepts it is linked to. You pick the most active word as your response. Try another one. What is the first word you think of when you hear "pepper"? For "salt" the first word many people pick is "pepper," but when people hear "pepper," few of them list "salt" as the first associate. (Although you may have because I had just reminded you of the association between them.) Why should "salt" activate "pepper" but "pepper" not activate "salt"? What does this result imply for spreading activation models?

➤ WHAT ELSE IS IN MEMORY?

> ➤ PREVIEW In this section we consider what else might be in the memory storehouse. Most researchers now believe that there are many forms of memory and that the type of memory we have discussed in the last two chapters is just one form. We discuss what motivated that view; basically, it was motivated by data from amnesic patients showing that although this form of memory is impaired, many other types of memory are still intact. Initially, the proposals were for two forms of memory, but as researchers became more inquisitive about possible forms of learning and as the underlying anatomy of memory became clearer, it was determined that there are at least five forms of memory that have different anatomical bases. Oddly enough, it has been difficult to find persuasive evidence that these forms of memory are different at a cognitive level of description.

Is that it? Have we covered everything that is in the storehouse? Until about 30 years ago the answer might have been a guarded "yes." Memory research was conducted using mostly verbal materials in a laboratory setting and often tested memory for these materials over short intervals. Since that time, several important distinctions have been proposed that broadened our definition of memory. In broadening the definition of memory, a number of researchers have actually suggested that there are several types of memory—that the storehouse contains fundamentally different types of representations.

In this section we discuss how the definition of memory was broadened, and we discuss the distinctions between different types of memory systems that have been proposed.

What Are Separate Memory Systems?

The rest of this chapter often refers to separate memory systems, an idea that has received a great deal of attention in the last 20 years or so. Why is this question interesting or important? Recall that in chapter 1 we said that cognitive psychologists were interested in mental representations and the processes that operate on them. When researchers propose that there are separate memory systems, they are proposing that there is more than one type of memory representation. We can draw an analogy to your computer. A word processing program (such as WordPerfect) has a particular format in which it stores data. The Word-Perfect program is a set of processes that can work with this representation to read and modify the data in the file. The question at stake here is whether, in addition to this one set of processes and representations, there is a second, different set of processes and representations that serves memory. For example, if you have Excel on your hard drive, it uses a different format for its files. The Excel program is a different set of processes, and it uses a different type of representation. Thus the question of whether there are separate memory systems is at the very heart of cognitive psychology. It is concerned with processes and representations. How many different types are there?

Procedural and Declarative Memory

I have briefly mentioned the procedural versus declarative distinction before; declarative memory is conscious and seems to fit the storehouse metaphor. Procedural memory is unconscious and does not call to mind representations entering a storehouse, but rather, changes to the processes that use representations. Later I return to that difference, and I also discuss how they differ in terms of processes and representations, but I want to begin by telling you about the origin of the procedural versus declarative distinction.

The story begins with patient H.M. We discussed H.M. in chapter 4 as well as chapter 1. H.M. is the man who had much of his medial temporal lobe removed to relieve intractable epilepsy, a surgery that left him with a profound anterograde amnesia. Recall that anterograde amnesia means that he was unable to learn new material. By 1965 H.M.'s memory had been tested using just about every type of material you could think of: words, nonwords, rhythms, songs, faces, and so on (Corkin, 1984). In 1968 Suzanne Corkin (1968) administered a motor skill learning task to H.M. In this task, called the pursuit rotor, a target the size of a nickel rotates on a circular platter. The participant holds a stylus (sort of like a pen) in his or her hand and tries to keep the tip of the stylus on the moving target. Initially, people are pretty bad at this, keeping the stylus in contact with the target for perhaps 5 s out of a 25-s trial, but they quickly improve. Corkin reported that H.M. improved as well (i.e., he learned the skill). Interestingly, H.M. did not remember any details of the testing situation when later asked about it. He was shown the testing apparatus but didn't recognize it, and couldn't say what it was for. Yet he learned the task, as measured by his performance. This finding constitutes a partial anatomic dissociation. An **anatomic dissociation** is demonstrated when you have evidence that different tasks are supported by different parts of the brain. In this case, we can conclude that the medial temporal lobe (which is damaged in H.M.) is important for remembering the testing situation, but it is not important for motor skill learning. We can call it a partial dissociation because these data don't tell us which part of the brain is important for motor skills. We just know it's not the medial temporal lobe. One way to interpret this evidence is in terms of multiple memory systems. Perhaps motor skill learning uses different processes and representations than the type of memory that supports recognizing the testing apparatus and knowing that you've done the task before. The medial temporal lobe, which is damaged in H.M., might support this sort of recognition, but motor skill learning is supported by another part of the brain, so it is not compromised in H.M.

This finding and interpretation did not exactly rock the memory world at the time. No one really thought that learning to ride a bicycle was the same thing as memorizing the Pledge of Allegiance. People figured, "Fine, there's memory, and then there are motor skills." By "memory" people meant what is measured by recognition or free recall tests. The distinction between memory and motor skills didn't seem controversial or all that interesting.

WHAT'S MISSING?   The simple distinction got complicated in 1968 by a new finding with amnesic patients. Elizabeth Warrington and Larry Weiskrantz (1968) developed a clever task. They took 10 words (e.g., *porch*) and photographed them through different filters so that they had three incomplete versions of the word.

In this task, the participant is shown the least complete version of the word and asked to identify it. Successively more complete versions are shown until the participant can read the word. The list is then repeated in just the same manner, and the experimenter records whether the participant is able to read successively less complete versions of the words with practice. The results showed that participants do indeed improve in this way, and amnesic patients also show significant improvement, although not quite as fast. When participants were shown other incomplete words that they had not seen before, they were not especially good at them; therefore, they must have been learning something about the specific words used in training, not a general skill in reading incomplete words. Thus, amnesic patients who normally would not be able to remember a word list at all show good retention of the word list when tested via this different method.

Why? Most researchers did not interpret this finding in terms of multiple memory systems. Notice that it is perfectly possible to do so. The finding is comparable to the finding with the pursuit rotor. In each case there is a new task that amnesic patients learn normally. This new finding from Warrington and Weiskrantz was a bit more dramatic because the very same word list appears to be either remembered or not remembered by amnesic patients, depending on how they are tested.

Warrington and Weiskrantz interpreted their result in terms of a missing process in amnesia. The idea was that multiple cognitive processes are necessary for normal memory performance. Because of the brain damage they have suffered, amnesic patients are missing one of those processes. Presumably, this missing process is important for most memory tasks because amnesic patients are impaired on most memory tasks. Occasionally, we might come across a task to which this process doesn't contribute. Amnesic patients should learn such a task normally because the process they miss is not needed.

Warrington and Weiskrantz's results made it seem that amnesic patients had a problem with the process of retrieval. There was nothing special about the conditions under which the words were encoded, but the experimenters changed the retrieval process. They didn't exactly ask the participants to remember anything. They simply asked them to try to read the degraded words.

There was a fundamental difficulty with this idea, however. Amnesic patients could still retrieve material from before the onset of their amnesia. Although these patients with anterograde amnesia still had some retrograde amnesia (for reasons described in chapter 5), they were still able to retrieve plenty of memories from before the onset of their amnesia. If the damaged process were retrieval, why was the memory problem limited to material they had encoded since the onset of brain damage?

Other studies in the 1970s investigated other hypotheses about what this missing process might be. Some researchers suggested that encoding might be faulty in amnesic patients. Perhaps they consistently encode material only at a shallow level instead of encoding at a deep level, as nonamnesic participants do. Some early evidence indicated that this hypothesis might be true. Laird Cermak and Nelson Butters (1972) asked patients to remember an eight-item list; these eight items came from four categories, (e.g., *strawberry* and *pear* from the category *fruits*). Unlike controls, amnesic patients were not able to remember more items from the list when given the categories as cues. The experimenters proposed that the amnesic patients might not be encoding the material deeply (i.e., in terms of meaning). Instead, they might be encoding the material in terms of the sound of the words.

But the idea that encoding was the faulty process in amnesia was largely discounted when several studies failed to show much effect on amnesic patients' memory when they were forced to encode material deeply. Imagine three conditions in an experiment. Participants are told to encode shallowly or encode deeply or are simply told to learn the material. In the first two conditions, they are not told about an upcoming test. The idea is that normal participants, when told about an upcoming memory test, will spontaneously encode material deeply, so their performance will be the same as it is when they are forced to encode deeply. However, amnesic patients spontaneously encode shallowly when told to learn material, so if they are simply told to learn, their performance looks the same as when they encoded shallowly.

Andrew Mayes and his colleagues (Mayes, Mendell, & Neary, 1980) examined this prediction by asking amnesic patients to examine photographs of faces. In the "shallow" condition they judged whether the person had straight or curly hair, in the "deep" condition they judged whether the person appeared friendly or unfriendly, and in the "learn" condition they were simply told to study the faces for a later memory test. The data were not consistent with an encoding deficit. Amnesic patients' memory was worse in all conditions, but they showed the same advantage of deeper encoding (and disadvantage of shallow encoding) that the controls did. Thus, amnesic patients do not have a special problem with encoding.

Perhaps, then, the problem lies in forgetting. Perhaps amnesic patients show poor memory because they forget material very quickly. It's difficult to evaluate how quickly amnesic patients forget, however, because they don't remember very much in the first place. Felicia Huppert and Malcolm Piercy (1978) varied the amount of time that amnesics and controls saw the stimulus materials in an effort to equate their performance. They showed 120 colored pictures to amnesic patients and controls. Controls saw them for 1 s each, and amnesics for either 4 or 8 s. These times were selected so that everyone would have a recognition accuracy of about 75% after 10 min. Sure enough, the increased study time equated performance in the two groups at 10 min. Participants were also tested 24 hr later and a week later, and the results showed that amnesic patients did not show faster forgetting; they forgot at the same rate at which controls did.

THE MISSING PROCESS AND NEW DATA.   While researchers were trying to figure out which memory process was missing in amnesic patients, their job was becoming more difficult. Other experimenters were discovering new memory tasks that amnesic patients learned normally, despite their memory impairment. For example, Warrington and Weiskrantz (1979) reported that amnesic patients showed normal acquisition of a classically conditioned response. In this experiment, a tone was paired with a puff of air to the eye. With practice participants learned this association and blinked when the tone sounded. Amnesic patients learned as quickly as normal participants. In another experiment, participants learned to read mirror-reversed words (Cohen & Squire, 1980). The actual time it took participants to read the words aloud was measured, and amnesic patients, like controls, improved with practice. As the number of tasks that amnesic patients could learn normally grew, it became harder to think of a single process that would both account for deficit in amnesia and account for all the tasks that they were able to learn normally.

MULTIPLE MEMORY SYSTEMS PROPOSALS.   In the late 1970s and early 1980s a number of researchers proposed that there must be multiple systems of human memory (Cohen & Squire, 1980; O'Keefe & Nadel, 1978). One system supported

BOX 7.3. FUNCTIONAL IMAGING EVIDENCE OF PROCEDURAL/DECLARATIVE MEMORY

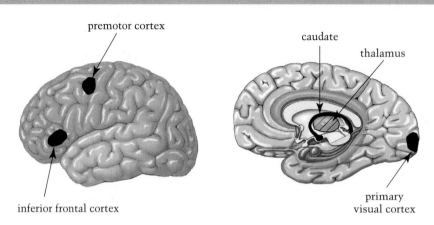

premotor cortex

caudate

thalamus

inferior frontal cortex

primary
visual cortex

Given that one sees robust differences in the ability of amnesic patients to acquire implicit and explicit memories, one would expect to see differences in functional imaging studies as well. Numerous studies have investigated the difference between implicit and explicit memory. I describe just one here.

In the text I briefly describe the serial response time task. This task can be learned either implicitly or explicitly and is therefore ideal for study in functional imaging. Four boxes on a computer monitor are arranged in a horizontal line. On each trial, an X appears in one of the boxes, the participant must press one of four response keys (also arranged in a horizontal line) as quickly as possible. The stimulus disappears, and after a very short pause (perhaps 250 ms) a new stimulus appears. The only other trick is that the stimuli appear in a repeating sequence. The sequence is 12 positions long, and nothing marks its beginning or end. Therefore, if the experimenter doesn't mention the sequence to participants, they typically don't notice it. Nevertheless, their response times to the stimuli get faster with practice and then slow again if the stimuli appear randomly; thus participants learn the sequence, as reflected in their task performance, even if they do not consciously know what the sequence was. On the other hand, if the experimenter tells participants what the sequence was and encourages them to consciously memorize it, they can do so. Thus, the same button-pressing task can lead to the development of implicit or explicit memory.

Scott Rauch and his colleagues (1995) trained participants first on the implicit version of the task and then on the explicit version while imaging in positron emission tomography. The activations when the stimuli were sequenced may be compared with activations when the stimuli appear randomly; the task is identical except for the presence of the sequence, so once the control activations are subtracted, one is left with activations caused only by knowledge of the sequence.

They reported that sequence learning in the implicit condition was associated with activation in areas known to support motor control: ventral premotor cortex, caudate, and thalamus, as well as secondary visual cortex. These activations are consistent with the idea that in the implicit condition people are learning a

(Continued)

motor skill; they are learning how to respond. Learning in the explicit condition showed a different pattern. Activity included primary visual cortex, left inferior frontal cortex, and middle temporal cortex. Rauch and his colleagues interpreted these activations as reflecting covert verbal rehearsal (hence the activity in frontal cortex reflecting working memory and temporal cortex reflecting language processes). The visual cortical activations may reflect visual imagery strategies for rehearsal.

In sum, this study shows that the same task can lead to radically different patterns of activation, reflecting the fact that something radically different is learned in the two tasks.

performance on standard recognition and recall tests. This system was severely compromised in amnesia. The other system supported performance on tasks such as motor skills, classical conditioning, and perceptual skills (such as mirror reading). These tasks were intact in amnesia because this other memory system was not damaged.

Researchers tried to characterize these different memory systems. An early and important distinction was between procedural and declarative memory (Cohen & Squire, 1980). **Procedural memory** is memory for skills and is often called "knowing how" memory. For example, if you know how to ride a bicycle, that ability is supported by procedural memory. **Declarative memory** supports memory for facts and events and is often called "knowing that" memory, such as knowing that George Washington was the first president.

These hypothetical memory systems are closely identified with the implicit versus explicit distinction, which is a distinction of tasks (Graf & Schacter, 1985). Explicit tasks are those that directly query memory (e.g., "Who was the first president?"), and usually they are supported by the declarative memory system. Implicit tasks do not directly query memory ("Here, ride this bicycle"); rather, memory is inferred from the participant's performance. Implicit tasks usually are supported by procedural memory.

So now you know why researchers proposed that there are multiple memory systems. These proposals grew out of attempts to account for the memory performance of amnesic patients. Researchers tried to maintain a single-system framework but couldn't see a way to do it, so they concluded that there must be more than one memory system.

The 1980s saw two developments of memory theory. First, researchers continued to study patients with brain damage and started to fractionate memory still further in multiple subsystems. Second, researchers began to look for evidence of multiple memory systems in neurologically intact people.

FURTHER FRACTIONATION OF MEMORY. The data from amnesic patients made it appear that declarative memory was supported by the hippocampus and other structures near the center of the brain (for a review, see Squire, 1992). But what brain structures supported procedural memory? Researchers soon discovered that different procedural tasks (classical conditioning, repetition priming, motor skill learning) were supported by different parts of the brain. There has been some disagreement over exactly how many memory systems there might be, but there is general agreement about the list provided in Table 7.8 (for a review see Gabrieli, 1998; Willingham, 1997).

As shown in Table 7.8, there is evidence for at least five memory systems. As discussed earlier, the declarative system supports conscious memory of facts and events. We've also discussed priming, which makes representations of concepts more available for use either because they have been used recently (repetition priming) or because a semantically related concept has been used recently (semantic priming). Motor skill learning is improved accuracy of movements as a consequence of practice, and is discussed in more detail in chapter 9. Classical conditioning was mentioned in chapter 1. In classical conditioning, an unconditioned stimulus (e.g., food) that elicits an unconditioned response (e.g., salivation) is paired with a conditioned stimulus (e.g., a bell) until the conditioned stimulus elicits a conditioned response (salivation). **Emotional conditioning** is a classical conditioning situation, but one of the unconditioned responses is an emotion. Fear is the emotion that has been studied most frequently. For example, participants might be shown different colored slides, and each time the slide depicts a snake, the participant is given a mild electric shock. In time, pictures of snakes will come to elicit fear.

The key thing to note at this point is the motivation for proposing separate memory systems. Again, the initial mystery was why amnesic patients are impaired at learning some memory tasks but learn others normally. The initial interpretation was that there is a single memory system but that one of the processes that contributes to memory is damaged in amnesia. This damage leaves most memory impaired, but some tasks can be learned normally even without this process. This interpretation of why amnesic patients can learn some tasks normally was abandoned because researchers could not find the

Table 7.8   Memory Systems

System	Function	Neural Substrate	Reference or Review
Declarative	Conscious memory of facts and events	Hippocampus and other structures	Squire (1992)
Priming	Brief activation of existing representation	Occipital, temporal, and frontal cortex	Schacter, Chiu, & Ochsner (1993)
Motor skill learning	Acquires new motor skills	Striatum, motor cortical areas	Willingham (1998)
Classical conditioning	Learns relationships between perceptual stimuli and motor responses	Cerebellum	Thompson (1986)
Emotional conditioning	Learns relationships between perceptual stimuli and emotional responses	Amygdala	Maren & Fanselow (1996)

missing process that could account for the pattern of learning and failure to learn observed in amnesia. Therefore, they proposed that some tasks are preserved in amnesia not because they don't need the missing process but because they rely on an altogether different memory system. This hypothesis was strengthened when the tasks that are preserved in amnesia (priming, motor skill) were susceptible to disruption if other areas of the brain were damaged. *Thus, the multiple memory systems hypothesis is rooted in anatomy.* The basic assumption is that these memory systems are different because they are localized in different parts of the brain.

Basing memory systems on anatomy seems to make sense, but one would like to see cognitive differences among memory systems as well. If declarative memory and motor skill learning are really different, this difference should be visible in behavior, not just anatomy. For example, perhaps the rate of learning should be different, or perhaps one type of learning is more flexible than the other. It turns out that differences in behavior between the putative memory systems have been harder to observe than one would think.

Support From Studies With Control Participants

How do these various memory systems differ? The most reliable difference has been in terms of awareness; this distinction separates declarative memory from all other memory systems. Declarative memory is always associated with awareness, meaning that you always are aware that you are learning something, and you are aware of what you are learning. If you learn that hydrogen has an atomic weight of 1, you are aware of having learned something, and you are aware of what you have learned. Other types of learning are not necessarily associated with awareness. For example, in a priming task you see the word stem "sta___" and you complete it to spell *stamp* in part because you saw that word an hour ago. You need not be aware of this priming effect for it to influence your behavior. Another example of this sort of unconscious learning is the serial response time task, discussed earlier. In this task there are four positions on a computer screen, arranged horizontally, and there are four response buttons. A stimulus appears at one of the four positions on the screen, and the participant must push the button directly below the stimulus. The participant is not told that the stimuli appear in a repeating sequence 12 units long. Because the sequence is pretty long and nothing marks where it begins or ends, it can seem like a continuous stream of randomly appearing stimuli. Indeed, after responding to several hundred stimuli, many participants have said that they did not notice the sequence. Yet their response times get faster with training. They know the sequence (as assessed by their responses), but they have no conscious knowledge of the sequence—in fact, they don't even consciously know that there is a sequence (Willingham, Nissen, & Bullemer, 1989).

Again, the point of all this business about awareness is that you'd like to see some difference between declarative and procedural memory, not just in terms of the brain structures that support them but in terms of how the systems seem to operate in normal participants. The fact that awareness seems to be necessary for declarative but not procedural memory is some evidence that they differ.

Unfortunately, it has been difficult to find convincing evidence of other differences. Much of the focus has concerned potential differences between declarative memory and other memory systems. For example, it was suggested that declarative learning is fast and can even occur on a single trial, whereas other types of learning (e.g., motor skills) are slow and require multiple trials (Sherry & Schacter, 1987). Such a distinction is hard to evaluate, however, because it is not clear how to equate the two tasks. If you want to compare the speed of learning a word list to the speed of learning how to ride a bicycle, how long should the word list be to make it a task of equivalent difficulty? And how much practice riding the bicycle is equivalent to, say, one reading of the word list? Such problems in comparing what may be inherently different types of memory make it difficult to evaluate claims about behavioral differences.

EPISODIC AND SEMANTIC MEMORY.   There is another distinction that is important to know about, although its status is not quite as clear as that of the systems described in Table 7.7. In 1972, Endel Tulving (1972) wrote an article pointing out that memory researchers had been ignoring a rather sizable proportion of what must be in memory. **Episodic memory** is memory associated with a particular time and place (i.e., you know when and where you acquired the material). In addition, episodic memories are associated with a this-happened-to-me feeling. There is a personal quality to the act of remembering. If I ask you, "When was the last time you bought a pair of shoes?" you would recall an episodic memory. You would have time and place information associated with this memory ("I last bought shoes at the mall, 3 weeks ago."). Part of the memory would also be the feeling that *you* did this thing. Such memories can be contrasted with **semantic memory.** Suppose I asked you, "Is a loafer a type of shoe?" You would answer, "Yes," but there is no time or place information associated with that memory, nor is there an it-happened-to-me feeling. Semantic memory sometimes is called knowledge of the world. All of your knowledge of what things are, what they look like, how they work, and so on is part of semantic memory.

In the first two sections of this chapter we discussed semantic memory. Researchers have tried to determine how semantic memory—such as your knowledge that a robin is a bird—is organized. The study of semantic memory was spurred, in part, by Tulving pointing out that everyone was ignoring it. Think about it for a moment and you'll see his point. A standard memory experiment tests episodic memory. The experimenter presents some material to the participant, there is a delay, and then there is a retention test. If the participant remembers the material, it will be an episodic memory because the participant will remember the material and will also remember the time and place it was acquired, and it will typically have an it-happened-to-me feeling. All the work on encoding and retrieval presented in the last two chapters was in this vein, whereas all the work presented in this chapter concerned semantic memory; memory was tested, but it was always memory for things such as whether a canary has wings.

Tulving (1972, 1983) argued that semantic and episodic memory differed in a number of important ways. Episodic memories are more prone to forgetting, they are more likely to contain sensory information, they are organized by time, and they take longer to remember. Semantic memories are less prone to forgetting, they contain more conceptual than sensory information, they are organized by meaning rather than time, and they are recalled more quickly.

There is some evidence supporting the semantic versus episodic distinction, most of it from neuroscience. First, there have been reports of patients who have a selective loss of episodic but not semantic memory. If episodic and semantic memory are separate systems, they might well be localized in different parts of the brain, so one would expect to see the occasional patient who happens to have had selective damage to one system or the other. Such patients are rare, but some have been identified. For example, Endel Tulving and his colleagues (Hayman, Macdonald, & Tulving, 1993; Tulving, Schacter, McLachlan, & Moscovitch, 1988) reported on a man, K.C., who suffered extensive damage to the left hemisphere and some damage to the right as a consequence of a motorcycle accident at age 30. He was unconscious for 72 hr, and in intensive care for 4 weeks. Like other amnesic patients, K.C. shows intact intellectual functioning. His ability to use language, working memory, and problem-solving skills are all intact.

K.C.'s semantic memory seems to be intact. His vocabulary appears to be of normal size, and he can provide accurate descriptions of scripts (see chapter 5) such as going to a restaurant or changing a flat tire. He can also remember technical terms associated with his job. What K.C. seems to have lost is his episodic memory. He does not remember events from his life that one would think should be quite vivid: for example, he does not remember the events surrounding a train derailment in which 240,000 people (including K.C.) had to evacuate their homes for a week, any of the circumstances of the death of his brother by drowning, or a bar fight in which his shoulder was broken.

In another remarkable report, Farena Vargha-Khadem and her associates (Vargha-Khadem et al., 1997) reported on three patients, all of whom suffered severe hippocampal damage early in life (between birth and 9 years). All three patients have terrible memory for personal episodes in their lives, yet all three have fairly normal semantic memories: They have attended mainstream schools and acquired factual knowledge about the world that is about average (or perhaps slightly below) what would be expected of people their age.

What of brain imaging studies in neurologically intact people? These studies have also provided some evidence that is consistent with the semantic versus episodic distinction. Figure 7.11 shows a summary of a eight studies examining semantic memory retrieval, and another slide summarizing activations associated with episodic memory retrieval (Buckner & Petersen, 1996). You are looking at a slice through the middle of the brain, cut parallel to the floor. The top of the figure is the front part of the head. Each circle corresponds to a spot of great activation in one study. As you can see, episodic retrieval is associated mostly with activity in the right frontal lobe, whereas semantic memory retrieval is associated with lots of activity in the left frontal lobe.

A difficulty with the interpretation of all of these studies is that episodic and semantic memories are different in more ways than the distinction proposes. Episodic and semantic memories differ in the content of the memories;

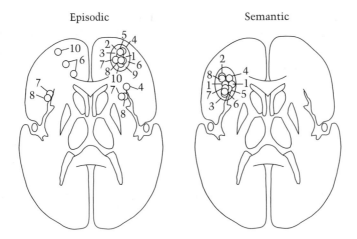

Figure 7.11. *Data from neuroimaging studies of encoding of episodic and semantic memories. Each circle represents a focal point of activation for one study. Note that semantic memory leads to activation primarily in the left hemisphere, and episodic memory leads to activation primarily in the right hemisphere.*

episodic memories are time based and autobiographical, and semantic memories are knowledge about the world. But episodic memories typically are encoded and rehearsed much less often than semantic memories. I might encode an episodic memory only once (e.g., the time I went to McDonald's and they let me try on one of the McDonald's caps) and then rehearse the memory a few times over the course of a few years when I tell the story. How many countless times have I rehearsed the semantic knowledge that a quarter is 25 cents? This difference in rehearsal makes it difficult to interpret these neurological studies as straightforward evidence supporting the episodic versus semantic distinction.

There is also a problem in distinguishing just what is episodic and what is semantic. If you tell me a new fact that I didn't know (the three main Hindu gods are Brahma, Vishnu, and Shiva), that is an episodic memory: I know when and where I acquired that memory. Suppose someone else tells me that fact tomorrow. I now have two episodic memories of this fact. If different people keep telling me that fact, at some point it will turn into a semantic memory. But at what point does it stop being an episodic memory and start being a semantic memory? The line is not clear.

Here's another problem. Suppose that, 5 years from now, the three main gods of Hinduism are firmly in semantic memory. Someone comes up to me and starts lecturing me in a very patronizing way about Hinduism. The next day I have an episodic memory of being lectured to, but embedded in that episodic memory is a semantic memory; I was annoyed that this person thought I didn't know the three main Hindu gods (which are in semantic memory). Thus most, if not all, episodic memories must have semantic memories in them in. You need semantic memory to make sense of the world. So it seems that semantic and episodic memory must be closely linked, at the very least.

Because of conceptual problems such as these, many memory researchers (Johnson & Hasher, 1987; McKoon, Ratcliff, & Dell, 1986; Richardson-Klavehn & Bjork, 1988) have argued that episodic and semantic memory are not separate memory systems (but see also Schacter & Tulving, 1994). They interpret the different anatomic bases as reflecting a few different processes at work or perhaps the difference in the amount of practice the memories have received. Indeed in some forums, Tulving (1986) has written that the distinction may be most useful for its heuristic value. In other words, the distinction helps one's thinking about memory and may help to generate interesting experiments, whether or not it turns out to be psychologically important. Indeed, you may note that this book uses the episodic versus semantic distinction in its organization. Chapters 5 and 6 (encoding and retrieval) were concerned primarily with episodic memory, and this chapter is concerned primarily with semantic memory.

CURRENT STATUS OF MEMORY SYSTEMS.   Research in the last 20 years has shown that our previous definitions of memory were too narrow because they were restricted to conscious, declarative forms of memory. Most memory theorists believe that many cognitive systems are capable of learning. For example, your visual system learns with experience, and that learning can support performance on priming tasks. Similiarly, the motor control system that allows you to move around in the world changes with experience, and those changes support motor skill learning. So you have a system that is devoted to memory—that's the declarative system, with the storehouse—but you also have other systems that are dedicated primarily to another function such as vision or movement, and these systems also have the capability to learn. The motor system can learn motor skills, the visual system can learn perceptual skills, and so on. In these forms of memory nothing is stored per se, but there are changes to the actual processes. The motor system or the visual system is changed. Declarative memory seems to fit the storehouse idea, with memory being supported by the creation and storage of new representations.

Criticism of the Multiple-System Approach

As I've presented things in this section I've made it sound as though the evidence for multiple memory systems is pretty solid (with the exception of the distinction between episodic and semantic memory), and I think that's a fair representation of the state of the field. Nevertheless, drawing the conclusion that there are separate memory systems is not straightforward, and some researchers still argue that there is not sufficient evidence to draw that conclusion (e.g., Shanks & St. John, 1994).

In this section I want to point out the difficulties in assessing whether there are multiple memory systems. Suppose I said, "There are two types of memories: memories that are about chocolate bars and memories that are not about chocolate bars." Those categories don't sound very meaningful. How could we tell whether two categories of memories are meaningful?

The question we really want answered is whether two types of memory (e.g., declarative and motor skill) are represented differently in the mind. To draw an analogy, two WordPerfect files on your computer are treated as the same by the word processing program. One file might contain information about your last summer vacation, and the other might contain a list of all the presidents you can name, but the two files are not different in a way that a cognitive psychologist would care about. But a WordPerfect file and an Excel file use different representations, and they don't work the same way. What we want to know is whether motor skills and declarative memory are different in that way.

How could you figure that out? It turns out to be very difficult. One thing you might think about doing is looking for differences in how people perform declarative memory tasks and motor skills. Suppose you set a deadline for people to respond in a memory task—basically, you force participants to respond very quickly—and you find that hurrying participants increases errors in the motor skill task, whereas it has no effect on the declarative memory task. Such a pattern of data is called a **behavioral dissociation:** One type of memory is affected by a factor (in this case, forcing people to respond quickly), whereas the other is not affected by that factor. It seems that if motor skill and declarative memory were the same thing, then they should always be affected in the same way by some factor, such as time pressure. Indeed, if you find some factor that affects one type of memory but not the other, it seems that you would be forced to conclude that the two types of memory are not the same; if they were the same, they would have to be affected the same way by any factor.

There are two difficulties in interpreting behavioral dissociations. First, there is the problem of equating the two tasks, as we noted earlier. Maybe the reason motor skills are susceptible to time pressure is that in your experiment motor skills weren't practiced as much as the declarative memory task was. How can you be sure that practice is equated in the two tasks? Even if you could solve that problem, behavioral dissociations have a second problem of interpretation. You could have two memory systems that mostly overlap, but have one process that is not in common, and that's where the factor has its effect.

In the 1980s there was a great deal of discussion about how to prove the existence of separate memory systems using behavioral evidence, and the upshot is that it's very difficult to do. The hope was that there would be some sort of signature data pattern (e.g., a behavioral dissociation) that would determine when memory systems were truly separate. That signature was never identified, if it exists.

The second way to verify that there are separate memory systems is to abandon behavior and appeal to brain anatomy. We said that declarative memories appeared to be stored in one part of the brain, whereas motor skill memories appeared to be stored in a different location, and indeed all types of memory listed in Table 7.8 have different anatomic locations. As we discussed earlier in the chapter, this is an anatomic dissociation: evidence that different types of memory are supported by different brain structures. Isn't that compelling evidence that the two types of memory are different? Yes and no. We can't be 100% sure that anatomic differences necessarily imply cognitive differences. Suppose that the representation and the processes that support motor skills and declarative memory were exactly the same, but they just happened to be localized in different parts of the brain. It would be just like having two WordPerfect files on different locations of your hard drive. There are no interesting differences between how the files work; they just happen to be localized in different places. If that were true of motor skills and declarative memory, would you still think that they are different? To a cognitive psychologist trying to figure out how the mind works, anatomic localization alone is not very interesting; we want to know how things work, not where they are. And we just finished saying that researchers can't seem to find cognitive differences between the different types of memory systems.

Most researchers (including me) don't buy this argument. Most researchers feel that cognitive differences follow anatomic specification, and if two functions are localized differently, that is probably because there are important computational differences between them. If we don't have evidence yet for these cognitive differences, it may be because we haven't been looking in the right way. Or it may be that there are real differences that we already have seen, but the difficulties in comparing different types of memory make us not trust that these differences are real (e.g., that motor skills are not readily forgotten but declarative memories are).

Coda

So the final answer I've just given you makes it sound as though the answer to the question, "Is there anything else in the storehouse?" would be as follows: "Well, not really. The storehouse contains the concepts we discussed earlier in the chapter, and there are other ways you can learn things, but it sounds as if that sort of learning is not tied to the storehouse per se. You have the ability to learn motor skills, perceptual skills, classical conditioning, and so on, but those sorts of learning seem tied to the systems that support the performance in the first place, for example, motor skill learning is tied to the motor system. And that seems different from the storehouse we've been talking about."

Good answer. But there is actually more in the storehouse than just the concepts we've discussed in this chapter. There are visual images. Demonstrating that visual images exist as a separate representation in the brain took about 10 years of concerted effort from a number of researchers and was one of the more bitter disputes in cognitive psychology. Telling this story properly requires its own chapter, which follows.

STAND-ON-ONE-FOOT QUESTIONS

13. What key feature would make potential memory systems separate?
14. What is the origin of the multiple memory systems idea?
15. What is the current count of memory systems?

QUESTIONS THAT REQUIRE TWO FEET

16. How likely does it seem to you that these separate memory systems interact in some fashion?
17. Can you think of a time during which two of your memory systems may have conflicted?

KEY TERMS

category
exemplar
generalize
concepts
classical view
   of categorization
focus gambling
successive scanning
typicality
basic level category
superordinate level
   category
subordinate level
   category
probabilistic view
   of categorization

prototypes
exemplar model
addressing system
content-addressable
   storage
hierarchical theory
nodes
activation
links
property inheritance
cognitive economy
spreading activation
   model
semantic network
defaults
repetition priming

semantic priming
mediated priming
local representation
distributed
   representation
parallel distributed
   processing (PDP)
graceful degradation
generalization
anatomic dissociation
procedural memory
declarative memory
emotional conditioning
episodic memory
semantic memory
behavioral dissociation

8

Visual Imagery

If you want to, you can imagine actor Jim Carrey walking on the moon. In fact, you can put a ponytail on Jim and make him stand on this head and plow through the lunar surface as though he were a motor boat, with his ponytail acting as a propeller. What earthly use is a cognitive ability that allows such nonsense?

The first question we take up in the study of mental imagery is, **"What purpose does visual imagery serve?"** This may seem like an odd place to start, but the function of a mental process is actually crucial to the way we study it. Our study of perception is informed by our belief that perception tells about the physical features and locations of objects. Once you know what the function of a process is, that tells you something about what the process must do; knowing its job helps you to divine the mechanisms the process might use. The function of mental imagery has been the subject of some debate, as we'll discuss in this chapter. At this point, the fairly settled view is that imagery serves a memory function, making the visual properties of objects available (under some conditions), and a problem-solving function, allowing you to try out changes in the positions of objects or your body by moving them in your mind's eye before you move them physically.

These two functions both imply that mental images are pictorial representations; that is, images are a way of representing information in the mind that is different from other representations, specifically, different from verbal representations. If you want to communicate to me the idea "the hat rack is in the parking lot" you could say those words to me, or you could show me a picture of a hat rack in a parking lot. We can propose that similar representations are used in the mind—representations that are verbal and representations that are pictorial—although as we'll see, you don't think in words or pictures, exactly.

The proposal that mental images are a different sort of representation from verbal representations got some researchers upset. Bear in mind what cognitive psychology is all about. We're trying to discern the processes and representations that the mind uses to support thinking. If everyone agrees that there are verbal representations and then someone proposes that there are also mental images, that's a rather significant addition. It requires not only a new set of representations (images) but a whole new set of processes that can operate on those representations. There's no reason to think that the processes that manipulate verbal representations can be applied to images, just as you wouldn't expect that a computer's word processing program would also be able to use files that are designed to help you perform statistics.

You may say, "Isn't it obvious that we use mental images? Maybe it's going to be complicated to propose that mental images exist, but it seems clear that we are forced to make that proposal, however inconvenient it may be, because we obviously use images when we think." If you pose the following questions to participants, they almost always report using visual imagery to solve them:

What shape are a German shepherd's ears?

Which is a darker green: A christmas tree or a frozen pea?

In which hand does the Statue of Liberty hold her torch?

How many windows are there in your house or apartment?

It's obvious that people feel that they use mental imagery, but it is not obvious that mental images actually serve a function. Remember, we first started thinking about a separate mental representation system because of the functions images serve. If you could get verbal representations to serve those same functions would you still propose that visual images are necessary? **Are visual images supported by a separate mental representation system?** The answer is "yes," but it was rather more difficult to prove than you would first think. In fact, it was not proven to the complete satisfaction of most psychologists until about 1980. We'll go over why it was so complicated to settle this question. Once that question was resolved, researchers started to take more seriously the question, **"How does visual imagery work?"** What does the representation of a visual image look like, and how does it operate? We will discuss how visual images are generated, inspected, and transformed.

➤ WHAT PURPOSE DOES VISUAL IMAGERY SERVE?

> ➤ PREVIEW In the late 19th century visual imagery was at the center of experimental psychology. Visual imagery was the main subject of introspection, and psychologists using introspectionist methods believed that visual images were a direct window to thought. When behaviorism swept introspectionism aside, visual imagery was swept aside as well. Visual imagery went largely unstudied from 1920 until 1960. In the 1960s visual imagery reentered experimental psychology, mostly through Alan Paivio's ingenious demonstrations of the importance of visual imagery to memory. This work showed not only that imagery affects memory but that imagery also serves a function related to memory: Imagery makes available for later inspection the visual properties of objects. In the early 1970s, researchers began to examine ways in which mental images could be transformed (e.g., rotated, expanded). This work made salient another function of imagery: It allows one to try out some change mentally before going to the trouble of executing the change in the real world. For example, one can mentally rotate a pile of books to see whether there is room for it on a bookshelf before going to the trouble of moving the books. In this section we follow the history of visual imagery in experimental psychology to learn how people have studied imagery, why they have studied it, and how they arrived at these two functions I have listed.

Visual images have been of interest to researchers since the beginnings of experimental psychology in the late 19th century (and of interest to philosophers for centuries before that, at least back to Plato). The same is true of memory, perception, and other cognitive processes, but there has been general agreement about the function those other processes serve in cognition. Visual perception determines the locations and some characteristics of objects in the world. Memory makes available the properties of objects that are not currently present but that you have experienced before in the same or similar objects. So what is visual imagery for? If I say, "Image a cat," and you do so, what function could that serve? Perhaps because it is not immediately obvious, the answer to this question has changed over the history of experimental psychology. The history of visual imagery research has been contentious, and I think that is true partly because people's views of imagery's function have changed. People's views of imagery's function developed, in part, as a reaction to the views that their predecessors held, so to get to the bottom of this issue we must go back to the late 19th century, to the start of experimental psychology. From there, we will see how modern research on visual imagery developed.

Imagery in Early Psychology

Recall from chapter 1 that experimental psychology began with an approach called introspectionism. The introspectionists were interested in accounting for the contents of consciousness. They sought to describe a small set of irreducible elements that could be combined to create more complex mental states. The mental states that introspectionists most often sought to explain were mental images. Thus, a mental image was generated and the observer attempted to describe the mental image in terms of its fundamental characteristics. Interestingly, no sharp distinction was drawn between generating a mental image and seeing an object. It was thought that there was simply no clear reason to distinguish between imagery and perception (Wundt, 1894). Imagery was considered tantamount to thought: You could understand thought by understanding images.

This point of view suffered a blow in what came to be called the **imageless thought controversy.** This term refers to arguments over whether it is possible to have thoughts that are not accompanied by images. This controversy was primed by a series of experiments by Sir Francis Galton (1883), who reported on fairly extensive individual differences in participants' reports of the vividness of their mental images. Galton asked participants to describe their breakfast table as it had appeared that morning. Here is part of the questionnaire he administered:

> Before addressing yourself to any of the Questions on the opposite page, think of some definite object—suppose it is your breakfast-table as you sat down to it this morning—and consider carefully the picture that rises before your mind's eye.
>
> 1. *Illumination*—Is the image dim or fairly clear? Is its brightness comparable to that of the actual scene?
> 2. *Definition*—Are all the objects pretty well defined at the same time, or is the place of sharpest definition at any one moment more contracted than it is in a real scene?
> 3. *Colouring*—Are the colours of the china, of the toast, bread-crust, mustard, meat, parsley, or whatever may have been on the table, quite distinct and natural? (Galton, 1907/1973, p. 58)

Galton collected about 100 responses. He found that some respondents rated their images as being very rich and detailed. Here are some quotations from such respondents:

> Quite comparable to the real object. I feel as though I was dazzled, e.g., when recalling the sun to my mental vision.

> I can see my breakfast-table or any equally familiar thing with my mind's eye, quite as well in all particulars as I can do if the reality is before me. (Galton, 1907/1973, p. 62)

Others claimed to have vague images that lacked detail, and still others (about 10%) claimed to have no images whatsoever. Here are some examples:

> I am very rarely able to recall any object whatever with any sort of distinctness. I seem to be almost destitute of visualizing power.
> My powers are zero. To my consciousness there is almost no association of memory with objective visual impression. I recollect the breakfast-table, but do not see it. (Galton, 1907/1973, pp. 63–64)

These results spell trouble for the introspectionist program. If imagery is more or less synonymous with thought, how are these people (who claim not to have images) thinking? These data were not taken as conclusive evidence that thought can proceed in the absence of images—after all, most people did report having images—but new results came in that seemed more troubling because they indicated that for certain types of tasks, no one reported using images.

In one study, Marbe (1901) reported that when participants were asked to hold one weight in each hand, they could readily say which was heavier, but they reported doing so without any images. In a typical introspectionist experiment, the experimenter predicted that the participant would have images that followed some progression (even if it was very rapid), which could be analyzed. However, Marbe's participants reported that the solution simply popped into consciousness. Thus, this bit of thought—determining the heavier of two weights—seemed unanalyzable using introspectionist methods.

Titchener (one of Wundt's students, and a staunch defender of introspectionist methods) had one of his students, Helen Clarke, conduct a series of experiments on problems that were supposed to yield imageless thought (Clarke, 1911). Clarke concluded that these thoughts were analyzable using introspectionist methods. Toward the close of her article she wrote, "The introspections of any one observer show different stages of clearness and intensity of imagery, which allow us to connect, by a graded series of intermediate steps, a complex of vivid and explicit imagery with a vague and condensed consciousness which we suppose to represent what is called 'imageless' thought." She concluded that Marbe (and others) had not instructed the participants in the right way, so the participants did not analyze what was in consciousness very carefully. Thoughts *were* accompanied by images, according to Clarke; there was no such thing as imageless thought. Participants who don't think they have images as they perform a task simply haven't followed their own thought processes very carefully, probably because the experimenter didn't tell them to do so.

But what does this analysis of consciousness really tell us? Isn't it possible that "proper instructions" to the participants to analyze their thoughts was tantamount to telling them what to think?

These demonstrations (and counterarguments) about imagery centered on what people thought about as they solved problems (e.g., the comparison of weights). A related problem had been pointed out by philosophers for centuries:

Some concepts are not readily describable in terms of an image. Philosopher John Locke had raised the question of how one could have an image that represents the idea of a triangle. An image can represent one individual triangle, surely, but how can you have an image of the class of triangles, because all that defines a triangle is that it be a closed figure with three straight sides? Titchener's comment on this problem ran as follows:

> My own picture of the triangle, the image that means triangle to me, is usually a fairly definite outline of the little triangular figure that stands for the word "triangle" in the geometries. But I can quite well get Locke's picture, the triangle that is no triangle and all triangles at one and the same time. It is a flashy thing, come and gone from moment to moment; it hints two or three red angles, with the red lines deepening into black, seen on a dark green ground. It is not there long enough for me to say whether the angles are joining to form the complete figure, or even whether all three of the necessary angles are given. Nevertheless, it means triangle; it is Locke's general idea of a triangle. (Titchener, 1909, pp. 17–18)

This is all well and good for Titchener, but there is obviously no way to verify whether any of it is true.

Thus, the introspectionists believed that imagery was absolutely central to psychology because all thought was accessible through images. If you wanted to know how thought worked, studying images that occurred during thought was the method of choice. The idea that some types of thoughts are not expressible as images led researchers to question the usefulness of the method, however.

The table was swept clean in 1913 when John Watson proposed that psychology shift to a behaviorist point of view. Watson wasn't interested in arguing about whether some types of thoughts were imageless. He claimed that studying the mind was going to be fruitless and that researchers should focus on behavior. You can see how effective Watson's argument might be. On one hand, different laboratories were claiming that thoughts may or may not be accompanied by images, and the difference appears to be a function of how experimenters instructed the participants. On the other hand, Titchener was contemplating generic triangles that have two or three red angles, and so on. It certainly doesn't sound very objective or scientific, and it's easy to see why Watson's manifesto fell on sympathetic ears. Thus the study of visual imagery went from being the central star of the field to being eliminated from the field.

Imagery was largely ignored by psychologists in the United States for about 50 years, until the early 1960s. The main reason for that neglect was that it was deemed impossible to study imagery objectively. By definition, images are accessible only to the person doing the imagery, so the experimenter has no choice but to take the participant's word for whatever he or she claims to be seeing. That's no way to build a science. Woodworth and Schlossberg summed up people's attitude toward the study of imagery in their very popular textbook, written in 1954:

> An outstanding characteristic of modern experimental psychology is its emphasis on objective experiments. As we have just seen, this reliance on objectivity misses

some aspects of the act of recalling. One such aspect is the presence of images, but imagery is such a fluid thing that it is very difficult to study. (Woodworth & Schlosberg, 1954, pp. 720–721)

In other words, imagery is interesting—what a pity that you can't study it.

Imagery Reenters Psychology

In 1971, Allan Paivio published a book on imagery and memory (Paivio, 1971). By that time, many psychologists were sympathetic to the idea of describing mental processes; they didn't feel that psychology must focus solely on behavior. Nevertheless, many psychologists still felt that imagery was off limits as a research topic because it was subjective and inferential. Thus, researchers were willing to take participants' verbal reports as data (e.g., verbal reports of what they remembered) and use these reports to make inferences about hypothetical cognitive structures that were verbal, but they were not willing to take these verbal reports and make inferences about hypothetical cognitive structures that might be images.

The opening chapter of Paivio's book was a refutation of this argument and other arguments proposing that imagery was impossible to study. When participants describe a memory (e.g., they describe their memory of a word list the experimenter read to them), they describe the memory in words. Researchers are willing to accept the participant's verbal description of their memory as bearing a close relationship to what the participant actually remembers. Researchers feel that participants can talk about their thoughts when their thoughts are verbal; the words participants say are not an exact reproduction of the thoughts they are having as they remember; the words they say are a model of the verbal thoughts they have. Paivio pointed out that it is just as possible to produce a verbal description of a mental image. There is no reason one should be willing to make the jump from spoken words to a mental construct such as "verbal representation" and not make the jump from spoken words to a mental construct such as "visual image representation." Paivio also pointed out that images do have a functional role. He pointed out that imageless thought is a theoretical problem only if you want to argue that all thought is based on images. Paivio didn't want to make that claim; rather, he claimed that *some* thoughts were based on images. The fact that some thoughts are imageless is not a threat to that position.

So what functional role do images play? Paivio discussed a role for imagery in memory. The memory task Paivio used most often was a paired-associate task. In this task, the experimenter presents a pair of words to the participant (e.g., "fork–tape") and later the participant must produce the word "tape" given the word "fork." Most of Paivio's experiments used verbal materials and required verbal recall. How, then, could he show that imagery played a role in memory when he used only verbal materials? Paivio used two strategies: He varied the characteristics of the stimuli, and he varied the instructions to the participant. Here's how he did it.

The characteristic of the stimuli that Paivio usually varied was the concreteness or abstractness of the word. Concrete words refer to a physical object.

Potato is a concrete word. Abstract words do not refer to a physical object (e.g., *Intellect*). Paivio (1963) reasoned that one could use imagery for concrete words but not for abstract ones. In a direct test of this hypothesis, Paivio (1965) administered a paired-associate test, varying the concreteness or abstractness of the word pairs. There are four possible combinations of concrete and abstract words in a paired-associate test: concrete–concrete, concrete–abstract, abstract–concrete, and abstract–abstract.

Memory is best when both words are concrete and is worst when both are abstract. Paivio interpreted this result as showing the effectiveness of imagery in memory. It is easy to generate images for concrete words such as *potato* but difficult to generate images for abstract words such as *justice*. We'll say more about the proposed mechanism by which imagery improves memory later.

Paivio also examined the reported use of imagery as a learning strategy. In one study (Paivio, Smythe, & Yuille, 1968) participants performed a paired-associate memory task. Then they were shown all of the word pairs, and they were asked to write a brief description of how they had tried to remember that particular pair and to classify whether their strategy had been verbal (e.g., making up a short phrase using the words) or visual (e.g. imaging a picture involving the referents of both words) or if they had used no strategy. The experimenters reported that significantly more words were remembered when participants reported that they had generated visual images rather than verbal strategies.

The same results were obtained when participants were not left to their own devices but rather were instructed to engage in a particular type of processing. Paivio and Dennis Foth (1970) gave participants a list of 30 word pairs to remember. On each trial the participant saw a word pair and was instructed to rehearse the pair either via an image (including copying the image on a piece of paper to ensure that they had created one) or via verbal mediation (including writing the phrase they had created to link the two words). Each participant performed some verbal rehearsal and some imagery rehearsal. Paivio and Foth also varied the types of word pairs: Some of the word pairs were abstract (e.g. "democracy–intellect") and some were concrete ("tree–pencil").

Their results showed that when stimuli are abstract you're better off with verbal encoding, whereas if the stimuli are concrete you're better off with imagery instructions.

To account for these data, Paivio proposed a **dual-coding hypothesis.** The dual-coding hypothesis proposes that there are two ways to represent concepts: through a mental image or through a verbal representation. Concrete concepts such as *fork* can be represented via a verbal representation that would be used in understanding and producing language, and that would be used in certain types of thinking. Concrete concepts also can be represented as visual images. Abstract concepts, on the other hand, have only one representation. For example, a concept such as *democracy* would have only a verbal representation, not a visual one (Figure 8.1). What sort of image, after all, could represent democracy? Someone voting? Someone reading a noncensored newspaper? Those are not very compelling or very specific. There might also be concepts for which

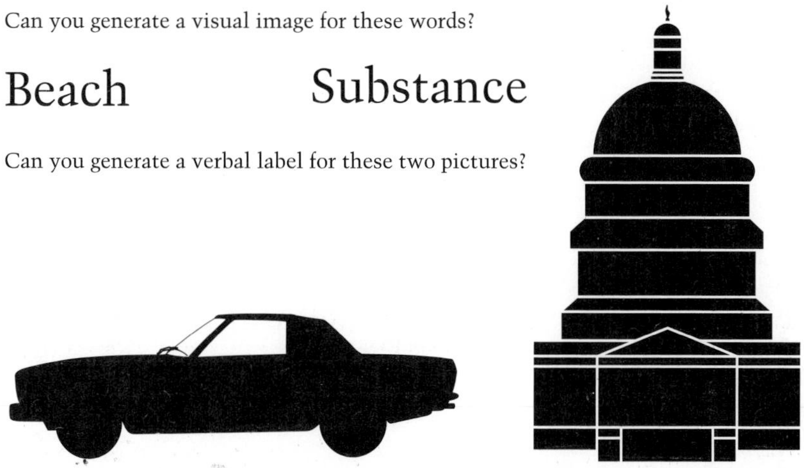

Can you generate a visual image for these words?

Beach   Substance

Can you generate a verbal label for these two pictures?

Figure 8.1.   *It's easy to generate an image of* beach, *a concrete word, but hard to generate an image of* substance. *Most people would agree that the picture on the left should be named* car, *but there would be less agreement about the picture on the right. It could be called* democracy, *or it could be* capitol *or* dome. *If the picture on the right is a bad representation of democracy, what would be a better one?*

there is a visual image but a paltry verbal description. For example, someone who knows the odd shape of a crankshaft would have a hard time describing it, although he or she could image it.

These two representations—verbal and imagery—operate in parallel, and if both are working, it is more likely that memory will be successful because if one representation can't be retrieved when you try to recall the memory, you might be able to retrieve the other one. Concrete words are easier to remember than abstract words because concrete words are more likely than abstract words to activate a representation in the imagery system. Abstract words are likely to activate only a verbal representation. Thus, concrete words are better remembered because there are two representations, and if one fails, the other representation might still be available. If the words are abstract, however, there is actually a cost to a memory strategy of generating images; abstract words don't readily lend themselves to images, so the participant must struggle to come up with an image of the words, and the image probably is ineffective because even if you remember the image, its relationship to the abstract word may not be very clear. For example, if you're trying to remember the word *miracle* you might come up with an image of the parting of the Red Sea; at retrieval you might reproduce the image but then think that you generated that image for the word *desert*, *Bible*, or *Egyptians*.

Paivio offered a specific interpretation of his dual-coding theory, depicted in Figure 8.2.

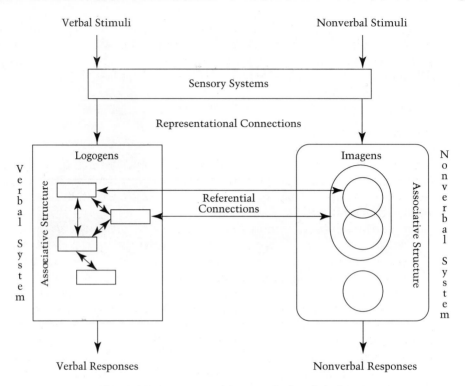

Figure 8.2.   *Diagram of Paivio's dual-coding theory.*

According to Paivio (1986), both verbal and nonverbal stimuli come in to the sensory systems; verbal stimuli tend to activate representations in the verbal system. Paivio called these representations **logogens,** a term borrowed from Morton (1969). The representations in the nonverbal system that support images are called **imagens.** Notice that imagens can be embedded within one another. For example, you might be able to generate an image of your family standing together, within which is an image of your brother; you could image your brother separately if you wanted to, and within that image you could image just his face if you wanted to. Logogens do not have this quality of one being embedded in the other. Paivio also proposed that imagens and logogens have connections. The logogen for *poodle* has a connection to the corresponding imagen. Note too (as represented in Figure 8.2) that some logogens don't have a connection to imagens. These would be abstract concepts such as *villainy* and *woe.* There are also imagens that do not have connections to logogens; these would be concepts you are familiar with but do not have a verbal representation of, such as the crease below the nose and above the lip, which most people can image but do not know the name of (it's called the filtrum).

Paivio's theory describes in considerably more detail exactly how logogens and imagens relate and why memory is better when images are used, but this story will take us too far afield into memory (see Paivio, 1986, 1991, for reviews). The key point to be made here is that Paivio showed that imagery affects memory and probably did more than any other person to bring visual imagery back within the purview of experimental psychology. Note that this work does not address directly how imagery is thought to work. It does not discuss how images are generated or transformed. Rather, it examines how imagery affects memory.

Imagery and Perception

Imagery seems to be most obviously related to perception. Although Paivio took note of this fact, his experiments were not directly addressed to the possible relationship of imagery and perception. However, other researchers examined this relationship.

In one of the better known examples, Lee Brooks (1968) used a dual task method to examine codes in primary memory. Brooks used two different types of tasks. In the verbal task, participants were given a sentence such as "A bird in the hand is not in the bush" and participants were required to identify each word as being a noun or not being a noun. Hence a correct response would be, "No, yes, no, no, yes, no, no, no, no, yes." In the imagery task, participants were asked to image a block letter (such as F) beginning in the lower left hand corner and to mentally travel around the letter clockwise, responding "yes" when a corner was at the top or bottom of the letter and "no" for other corners.

Thus the first task is largely verbal, and the second task is spatial. Brooks also had participants use either a verbal or a spatial mode of response. In the verbal mode, they were simply to say "yes" or "no" aloud. For the spatial mode, participants had a piece of paper in front of them, with rows of irregularly placed Ys and Ns, and they were to point to a letter to signify "yes" or "no."

For the sentence task (which is verbal) participants were better off responding by pointing, whereas for the letter task (which is spatial) they were better off responding verbally. This pattern of results indicates that there might be separate verbal and spatial forms of representation; you can use verbal and spatial

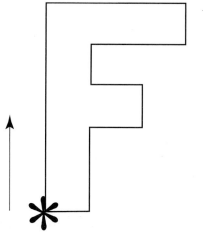

Figure 8.3. *Sample figure from Brooks (1968). Participants were shown block letters like this one. Later they were shown lowercase letters, which was a cue to image the corresponding block capital. Starting at the asterisk and working clockwise, participants were to work their way around the letter, classifying each corner: "yes" if the corner was at the top or bottom of the figure and "no" otherwise. The correct responses for this letter would be "yes, yes, yes, no, no, no, no, no, no, yes."*

BOX 8.1. THE OVERLAP OF IMAGERY AND PERCEPTUAL PROCESSES

Many researchers believe that imagery and perception overlap, and behavioral experiments were conducted to test this hypothesis (e.g., through interference paradigms). One study has examined in a very direct way the overlap in the anatomic structures that support imagery and those that support perception.

Stephen Kosslyn and his associates (Kosslyn, Thompson, & Alpert, 1997) predicted that there should be considerable overlap between perception and imagery in terms of higher-level processes, although low-level visual areas might not participate in imagery. Their research strategy was therefore quite simple: Administer a perceptual task and an imagery task that call on high-level processes while participants are in a positron emission tomography scanner and see how many brain areas overlap between the two tasks. Furthermore, they sought to make the perceptual and the imagery tasks fairly different so that any observed anatomic overlap would be all the more impressive.

The perceptual task was object naming. In one version of the task participants saw drawings of objects (e.g., a guitar, a fence) and they were to name the object. Brain activity for this task obviously would involve not only perceptual processes to identify the object but also retrieval of the name. Thus, they used a second task, which was to name objects viewed from a noncanonical position. Participants might have seen the guitar tilted from the edge and see the picket fence from above. Such objects are difficult to identify and thus require further visual processing to name. The researchers subtracted the activation from the first task (naming pictures) from the activation from the second task (naming noncanonical pictures) to yield activation that is specific to high-level perceptual processes.

For the imagery task, participants saw a lowercase letter (e.g., *f*), which they knew was a signal to generate an image of a block capital letter (e.g., *F*). Participants then saw a grid with an *X* in one square, and participants were to say whether the letter they were imaging would cover the *X*. In the baseline condition for this task, they simply responded when they saw the *X*, without having to generate an image.

When the activations for the imagery task and the perceptual task were compared, there was a good deal of overlap. A total of 21 areas were activated, and 14 of these were active in both the perceptual and the imagery tasks. Two were active in perception but not imagery, and 5 were active in imagery but not perception. The areas that both tasks activated are shown in Figure B8.1.

This study supports the conclusions from behavioral studies. There is considerable but not complete overlap in the system that supports perception and the system that supports imagery.

(Continued)

representations simultaneously and they don't interfere, but if you try to use two different verbal representations simultaneously or two different spatial representations simultaneously, they interfere.

These results can also be taken as indirect support for a relationship between perception and imagery because the letter task requires the use of imagery and is interfered with by a task that requires the use of perception (pointing).

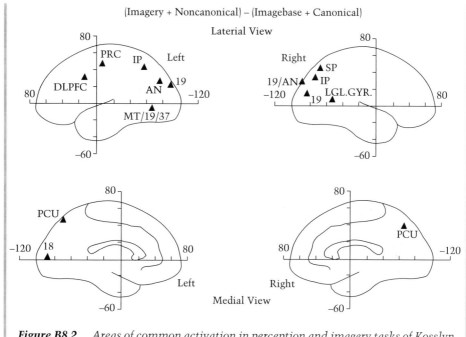

Figure B8.2. *Areas of common activation in perception and imagery tasks of Kosslyn et al. (1997). 18, 19, 37, MT, secondary visual areas; AN, angular gyrus; DLFPC, dorsolateral prefrontal cortex; IP, inferior parietal; LGL GYR, lingual gyrus; PCU, precuneus; PRC, precentral gyrus; SP, superior parietal.*

A second result truly rocked the psychological world. Roger Shepard and Jacqueline Metzler (1971) sought to examine the process by which images are transformed. They showed participants figures like that shown in Figure 8.4.

Participants were asked to evaluate whether the two pictures were of the same object but at different angles or whether the objects were different. Half of the objects depicted were different; they were mirror reflections of one another. The other half showed figures that were the same, but one picture was rotated in space relative to the other. The amount of rotation was varied. Sometimes the figures were rotated in the picture plane, and sometimes they were rotated in depth. Participants were to pull one of two levers to indicate what their decision was (same or different). Eight participants each performed 1,600 trials over the course of 8 to 10 1-hr sessions.

The interesting trials were those on which the objects were the same. Two findings stood out. First, the amount of time it took participants to make their decision was a very orderly function of the degree of rotation between the two pictures, as shown in Figure 8.5. Second, response time was the same whether the rotation was in the picture plane or in depth.

Researchers got very excited about these results for several reasons. First, the experiment opened an entirely new area of research. Until that point, most researchers had treated images as static; you imaged a tree and the tree just sat

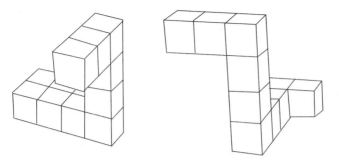

Figure 8.4.   *Figures similar to those used by Shepard and Metzler (1971).*

there. Shepard and Metzler studied how images are transformed. They studied how one could use imagery to imagine something happening. Transformation of images points up a second important function of mental imagery: It allows you to try something out mentally before you try it out physically. Will the sofa fit in the alcove? Can I reach the top shelf with this feather duster? Will this magazine

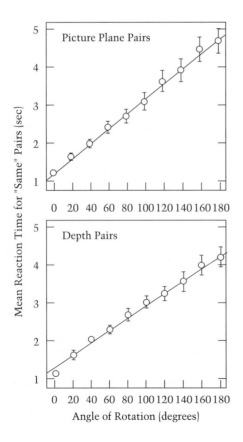

Figure 8.5.   *Results from Shepard and Metzler (1971). The graphs show the time it takes participants to respond "same." Note that the mean values form an almost perfect straight line. The lines above and below each circle are a measure of variability; the lines are very small, which means that most of the individual values are quite close to the mean. Also note that the slope of the line going through the points is the same for the picture plane pairs and the depth pairs. That indicates that the speed with which mental rotation can be performed is about the same in the picture plane and in depth.*

cover the stain on the coffee table? These are questions one might try to answer using visual imagery. This point may not seem like much to you—didn't everyone know you could do things like that with imagery? As Michael Kubovy put it, "Often, formulating something that we all know but have not been able to put into words is a major step in its own right" (Kubovy, 1983, p. 662).

Kubovy goes on to point out the great advances represented by the experimental paradigm Shepard and Metzler introduced. This was the first time that a very private, mental event (such as imaging an object rotating) could be studied experimentally, and the problems one faces in studying the transformation of images are formidable. The stimuli have to be difficult to name so that participants won't attach verbal labels to them and thus use a verbal strategy instead of imagery. At the same time, the stimuli must be easy to image. There have to be some pairs of stimuli that *don't* match (so that participants don't simply say "yes" every time without looking at the stimuli), but the nonmatches can't be so different that participants can merely note that one feature (e.g., four cubes on one end) is missing from one of the stimuli. Shepard and Metzler solved this problem by using mirror-reversed stimuli for the "no" trials. These clever aspects of the paradigm made it possible to study the transformation of images, not just static images, and so to study for the first time this second function of imagery: imaging what real objects would do if moved in a particular way.

A second reason psychologists were enthusiastic about Shepard and Metzler's results is that their data were so orderly. The graph shows a remarkably systematic relationship between the angle of rotation between the two figures and the amount of time it took people to declare that they were the same figure. The line in the figure is called a best-fitting line. That means that a straight line is drawn so that all of the circles are as close as possible to the line. In this case, the circles are incredibly close to the line. Furthermore, these circles represent averages from all of the participants tested. The little lines above and below the circles (called error bars) are a measure of how far most of the data are from the arithmetic mean (i.e., the average). The mean might be 3, but it could be that half the values are about 1 and half are about 5, leaving a mean of 3, even though none of the values that went into the mean were close to 3. The very small error bars in the figure show that most of the values were quite close to the mean.

The orderliness of this result got researchers very excited. Keep in mind that when psychologists do experiments, they are usually dealing with types of behavior that have many things determining them. For example, I might vary how many times somebody rehearses a word list, and then a day later test his or her memory for the list. How many words is someone going to remember? It depends in part on how many times he or she rehearsed the list a day earlier, but it also depends on a lot of other things, such as whether he or she paid attention the day before, whether he or she is paying attention during the test, what he or she has done in the past 24 hr, and so on. People sometimes use the term ***multiply determined*** to describe behavior, which simply means that a lot of factors contribute to behavior. That means that the data will be somewhat sloppy; my manipulation of how many times participants rehearse the word list definitely will affect their memory, but so will a lot of other things that are beyond my control. The remarkable thing about Shepard and Metzler's data is that they are not sloppy: They follow a perfect linear trend. This orderliness makes you feel that the task they used is not multiply determined. It makes it seem that the task they used depends on one process, namely a process that is affected by angle of rotation.

So what might the single process be? That's the third thing that got researchers excited about the result. An obvious candidate is mental rotation of the image. All eight of the participants in this experiment reported performing this task by mentally rotating one of the objects to see whether it could be matched to the other object. That implies that there is a representation to be rotated. Roger Shepard and Susan Chipman (1970) proposed that images are a **second-order isomorphism** to pictures, which means that the parts of images have the same functional relationship to one another that the parts of pictures have to one another. A mental image is not a picture in the head; indeed, that wouldn't make any sense because who would be looking at such a picture? But an image has some similarity to a picture because the parts of each have the same functional relationship to one another.

In sum, these data and similar experiments by Shepard and his colleagues (see Shepard & Cooper, 1982 for a review) were very influential in convincing people that it is possible (and important) to study another function of imagery: the functions afforded by the transformation of images. Furthermore, this work made real the possibility that there may be a representation system (imagery) that is qualitatively different from the verbal representation system.

We started this section by raising the question, "What is mental imagery for?" Let me summarize the progression of the answers. The introspectionists thought that imagery was a window into all thought processes and therefore put imagery at the center of their psychology. The behaviorists pointed out that imagery was unobservable, because it was completely private to the observer, and was not very relevant to the concerns of psychology because psychology was the science of behavior, not of thought. Mental imagery research then lay dormant for about 50 years, until Paivio pointed out that mental imagery is indeed important because it affects memory and speculated that imagery may be supported by a separate representation system. Shepard and others offered a way of studying mental transformations in imagery (the unobservable events that behaviorists exorcised) and offered compelling circumstantial (but not conclusive) evidence that imagery might be supported by a separate representational system.

We will return to the work of Shepard and his colleagues later in the chapter when we discuss imagery transformations. Shepard raised the possibility that images constituted a separate representation system, but he did not make it a priority to prove that this was the case. As it turns out, some people were far from convinced that this work demonstrated that visual images were important to human cognition. In the next section, we discuss a decade of research that did not address how imagery operates but rather was concerned with demonstrating that mental imagery is important to human cognition in the first place.

STAND-ON-ONE-FOOT QUESTIONS

1. *What was the imageless thought controversy, and why was it important?*
2. *In the early 1960s cognitive psychologists were still ignoring visual imagery and seemed unwilling to accept as data participants' report about what they experienced during imagery tasks. What did Paivio say about that unwillingness?*
3. *What were the two key results from the Shepard and Metzler (1971) study, and why were they so important?*

QUESTIONS THAT REQUIRE TWO FEET

4. *Do you see a problem with asking people to rate their imagery abilities, as Galton did with the "breakfast table" questionnaire?*
5. *We've discussed in detail the fact that imagery helps memory. Do you think it would help memory still more if the images were bizarre? What is your reason for your answer?*
6. *Given what we've discussed about the apparent overlap of perception and imagery, can you see any situations in which it might be downright dangerous to listen to a sporting event on the radio?*

➤ *ARE VISUAL IMAGES SUPPORTED BY A SEPARATE REPRESENTATION SYSTEM?*

➤ PREVIEW In this section we review the arguments against the idea that visual images are evidence of a separate representation system. Researchers argued that although the sensation of seeing visual images in the mind's eye might be real, that does not imply that there is a separate representation that helps cognition. They also argued that many of the results of imagery experiments could be explained by the participants' knowing what was expected of them and being willing or eager to produce the expected results. These critics argued that a separate representation system of images was not necessary to account for the data from imagery experiments; all of these data could be accounted for by verbal representations. Perhaps most troublesome of all was a logical problem: If you add extra processes to manipulate a verbal representation in the right way, you can always get it to mimic an imagery representation. In this section, we discuss how researchers of imagery met these criticisms and how they convinced cognitive psychologists that there is indeed a separate representation for visual images.

How could people think that we don't have visual images? Many of the arguments against the notion of a separate representational system of visual images have been articulated by Zenon Pylyshyn (1973, 1981). Pylyshyn offered a number of reasons researchers should exercise caution in proposing a new representational system.

The Role of Introspection: Imagery as an Epiphenomenon

It might seem obvious that we use visual imagery for some tasks. You may say "Look. You tell people to create visual images when they learn word pairs. They say they are doing it, and they can draw you a picture of the image they created. You also find that if they create a visual image they remember the word pair better than if they don't. What do you want?"

Pylyshyn didn't argue that people don't have the internal sensation of generating and manipulating visual images. That's not at issue; people have those sensations. The argument is about what those sensations mean. The fact that you feel as if you use a visual image doesn't mean that there is a representation supporting the visual image. Pylyshyn pointed out that you don't expect to be aware of which part of your brain is active when you perform a task ("Gee, why doesn't my cerebellum tingle or get warm or something while I walk?"). So why should you be aware of the representations that support cognition? According to Pylyshyn, it need not be the case that you can consciously observe the representations that support cognitive processing.

One might respond by saying that perhaps the representations supporting cognition don't *have* to be open to introspection, but they sure seem to be in this case; how else can you explain that people have these sensations of looking at visual images when they perform imagery tasks?

Again, no one is denying the reality of the sensations; it's what those sensations mean that is at issue. The sensations may be an **epiphenomenon.** An epiphenomenon is a perfectly real phenomenon that is not related to the function of the system. An epiphenomenon is a byproduct of the processes that are doing the actual work. Here's an example. I used to have an old Honda station wagon. Every time I went over 65 miles per hour the car shook. Slow down to 60, no shaking. Speed up to 70, shaking. Slow down, no shaking. From this it seems I can conclude that shaking made the car go fast. This conclusion is obviously ridiculous, but the logic is exactly the same as in the imagery case.

In the case of the car, you notice that every time you accomplish a particular type of task (going fast) you get a sensation (shaking), and you assume that the sensation causes the task to be accomplished (shaking makes the car go fast). In the case of imagery you notice that every time you accomplish a particular type of task (mental rotation) you get a sensation (it feels as if you're seeing pictures in your head), and you assume that the sensation causes the task to be accomplished (pictures in the head are solving the imagery task). The sensation of the images could be an epiphenomenon. Like the shaking of the car, the sensation of mental imagery may be perfectly real, but it's not related to the processes that are getting the work done. Sure, it feels as if we are using mental images when we do certain tasks, but the fact is that we don't know that mental images are getting the work done to perform the task.

The Metaphor Is Misleading

Pylyshyn argued that it was not clear what was meant by a visual image. How detailed was an image? If you imaged a tiger, could you count the stripes on its tail? If not, why not? He pointed out that the concept of a mental image had not been developed in enough detail to allow predictions about how imagery operated and what would happen in different types of imagery tasks.

Pylyshyn also argued that the idea of mental imagery often was used as a metaphor ("looking at a picture in the mind's eye") and that this metaphor is dangerously misleading. Who exactly is looking at a mental image? If there are pictures in the head, there must be a viewer who can see the pictures. This approach conjures up images of a **homunculus,** a small person inside of what is supposed to a model of cognition. The homunculus might be a little green person sitting at the center of the brain, pulling levers and spinning dials (and looking at visual image screens) to make thought happen. A homunculus is never a good feature to have in a model because it simply moves the problem of cognition one step farther into the mind: "Okay if there is a homunculus looking at the pictures on the visual imagery screen, I suppose we'd better get to work explaining how the homunculus' mind works." Pylyshyn claimed that if you argued for images, you were really arguing for a homunculus to sit in the mind and appreciate the visual images.

Demand Characteristics and Tacit Knowledge

The theoretical arguments (such as that imagery might be an epiphenomenon) are fine, but there were also data that had to be accounted for. If you think that people transform visual images, it's easy to account for Shepard and Metzler's results in the picture comparison task. Response times increase linearly with angle rotation because it takes longer for an image to rotate a greater distance. How do you account for these data if you don't think that performance of this task is supported by visual images?

Pylyshyn (1981) pointed out that participants could hardly fail to guess what was supposed to happen in such an experiment; rotating images a greater distance should take a longer time because rotating real objects a greater distance takes a longer time. If participants simply expect that mental imagery works the way vision works, then they can guess how the experiment will turn out. Participants in experiments are mostly nice people, and consciously or unconsciously they may try to "help" the experimenter by providing the results they think the experimenter wants. Or they may simply want to produce the kind of data they expect everyone else will produce so that they look "normal." These are called **demand characteristics.** Demand characteristics are something about the way the experiment is conducted that signals to the participant what the desired, appropriate, or expected behavior is. **Tacit knowledge** is participants' knowledge of how objects in the real world behave. According to one argument, participants use tacit knowledge to simulate real-world movement and thereby produce results in imagery experiments that match real-world phenomena (e.g., scanning longer distances takes a longer time and rotating images a greater distance takes a longer time).

Propositional Versus Analog Representation

This final objection may be the most difficult to overcome: Images simply aren't needed to account for human behavior because verbal representations take care of everything.

The verbal representation in question is a **proposition.** A proposition usually is defined as the most basic unit of meaning that has a truth value. Propositions have a particular syntax; they take the form *relation(argument)*. A relational term can be a verb, adjective, or conjunction. The arguments are nouns. For example, the proposition *red(car)* represents the idea that a particular car is red. The proposition *kicked (boy, girl)* represents the idea that the boy kicked the girl.

Images, on the other hand, often are defined as quasipictorial, meaning that they have some of the important qualities of pictures but are not themselves pictures. As noted earlier, Shepard and Chipman (1970) proposed that one of these qualities is that the parts of images have the same functional relation to one another that parts of pictures have.

Stephen Kosslyn (1980) outlined five key properties that differentiate propositions from images.

- A proposition is relational, meaning that it describes a relation of an object and a quality or of two objects. An image does not describe a particular relation. For example, an image of a ball and a box could just as easily describe "the box is under the ball" or "the ball is on the box."
- A proposition has a syntax. There is a right way and a wrong way to form a proposition. An image has no syntax.
- A proposition has a truth value. *On(ball, box)* either truly reflects the state of the world or it doesn't—not so of an image. Ludwig Wittgenstein (1953) pointed out that there is nothing about an image of a man walking up a hill that prevents you from interpreting it as an image of a man sliding down a hill backwards. The image does not make an unambiguous statement about the world.
- A proposition is abstract. The proposition makes a statement about *some* ball and *some* box. It says nothing about the relative sizes of the ball and box, about their dimensions, color, and so on. An image is necessarily specific on these points.
- An image occurs in a spatial medium, but a proposition does not. That means that images preserve geometric qualities of real objects in space. That does not mean that there must be a screen in the head. Kosslyn (1980) provided an analogy. A computer spreadsheet allows you to enter numbers into an array like the following:

X	Y			
				Z

This representation preserves geometric relations between the numbers. We can say that X is closer to Y than it is to Z. We can say that X and Y are adjacent but Z is adjacent to neither, we can talk about the angle subtended by X,Y,Z, and so on. That doesn't mean that there is a little screen in the computer's memory that physically preserves those spatial relations. The computer might do that, it might not. That's another question. The main thing is that it somehow preserves these spatial relations in the representation.

We've just been through some of the differences between images and propositions. The point is that some researchers said that a second type of representation is not needed. You can account for everything the mind does using propositions.

Here's an example. One strategy to demonstrate that images are used by the mind is to show that people's behavior during imagery tasks reflects the spatial properties of images. For example, Stephen Kosslyn (1973) published an experiment arguing that because images are inherently spatial, the use of certain features of images should be predictable. For example, if you are scanning an image to inspect it, it should take a longer time to scan between two parts of the image that are farther apart than to scan a shorter distance. Here's the experiment Kosslyn conducted. First he had participants memorize pictures of objects. They viewed a picture of each object, then closed their eyes and imaged the object. Then they opened their eyes and compared their image to the drawing and continued that practice until they reported that they had memorized the drawing. Sample drawings are shown in Figure 8.6.

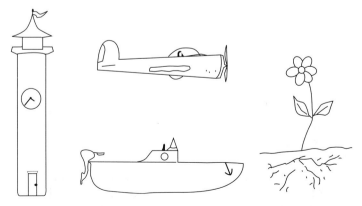

Figure 8.6. *Sample pictures from Kosslyn's (1973) experiment. Participants were asked to memorize these pictures so that they could image them later.*

In the second phase of the experiment, participants were asked to verify parts of the object. Thus, the experimenter would say, "Focus on the speedboat. Is there a propeller?" and the participant should respond "yes" to indicate that the speedboat has a propeller. (On half the trials a part would be named that was not part of the image; e.g., "Is there a mast?").

Half of the participants were asked to focus on one end of the image when they generated it. (Some focused on the left if the image was basically horizontal and the top if it was basically vertical. Others focused on the bottom or the right.)

The measure of interest was how long it took participants to respond as a function of the distance between where they were focusing and the location of the part to be verified. Participants who did not focus on a particular part of the image took about 1,500 ms to respond. (The location of the part they were asked to verify didn't affect their response time.) But the location of the part did matter if the participant had been asked to focus on a particular part of the image. Participants focusing on the left were quick to verify parts on the left (e.g., propeller), slower to verify parts near the center (e.g., porthole), and still slower to verify objects near the right (e.g., anchor). It's a bit odd that the "no focus" group is slower than any of the "focus" conditions. It may be that being asked to focus on one part of the object encouraged participants to attend to the whole image more carefully. In any event, the key result is in the focus group, and Kosslyn interpreted these results as showing that participants had to scan across the image to locate the requested part and thereby verify it. That sounds reasonable.

Kosslyn (1980) described a phone call he received from computer scientist Danny Bobrow shortly after this experiment was published. Bobrow pointed out that another, purely verbal representation would yield the same result Kosslyn reported. That representation is illustrated in Figure 8.7.

This is a propositional representation. It consists of nodes that represent object parts (e.g., *propeller*, *porthole*) and links that represent relations (e.g., *behind*, *attached to*). This representation codes the spatial relations of the parts of the speedboat in propositions, not in an inherently spatial medium such as a visual image, but if participants used this verbal representation, it would lead

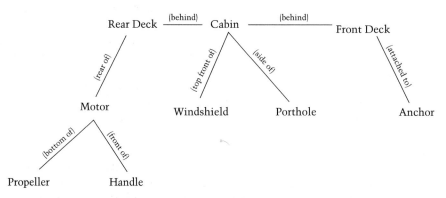

Figure 8.7. *Hypothetical propositional representation of the motor boat in Kosslyn's (1973) experiment.*

to a pattern of results that Kosslyn reported in the imagery condition. You just need to assume that it takes more time to traverse a greater number of links in the representation. For example, if you start with your attention focused on the left, you must traverse three links to get to the porthole but four links to get to the anchor. Thus, it takes longer to verify that the speedboat has an anchor than to verify that it has a porthole if you start at the motor.

Imagery Theorists Fight Back

How did imagery theorists cope with this barrage of criticism? Let's take it point by point.

IMAGERY AS EPIPHENOMENON.   There is little to say about this point. There is simply no guarantee that introspection provides any sort of a reliable guide to the representations that support a particular cognitive process, and it's true that images could be an epiphenomenon. Introspection may give you a hunch about the representations you think are involved, but hunches aren't evidence. On the other hand, this criticism doesn't prove that imagery doesn't contribute to cognition. The main barb to this criticism is that the burden of proof should be on those who want to claim that imagery does contribute. That's because a theory with just one type of representation (propositions) is more parsimonious than a theory with two representations (propositions and images). A theory is **parsimonious** if it is the simplest theory possible that still accounts for all the data. The idea that parsimony is important in scientific theory often is called **Occam's razor,** which was proposed by William of Occam, a 14th-century philosopher. He suggested that when two scientific theories account for the facts equally well, the simpler theory is the one to be preferred. Early in the imagery debate, parsimony was on the side of those who argued that imaginal representation was unnecessary. Propositions could account for how people performed imagery tasks, and a propositional theory was a simpler one because it used only one form of representation.

Although introspective hunches can't be counted as evidence, it is interesting to note that an introspective hunch first fueled Stephen Kosslyn's interest in imagery, as reported in the foreword to his 1980 book, *Image and Mind.* He was conducting an experiment on memory in which two of his participants said that the statement "A flea can bite" was false. After the experiment Kosslyn asked them why and they said things like "I couldn't see any teeth." These two participants had not been instructed to use visual imagery but apparently had been doing so. Kosslyn therefore began asking all participants about their use of imagery. When he graphed the results for imagery users and nonusers separately, he found very different patterns of results, and he began his investigations of imagery.

IMAGERY AS METAPHOR.   Pylyshyn was correct in arguing that mental imagery was misleading as a metaphor, but that was only because it had not yet been very well developed as a theory. Pylyshyn's criticisms forced imagery theorists to be more specific about what they thought imaginal representation contained and how it worked. Most researchers held to some version of a **picture theory of imagery.** The picture theory does not mean that there are literal pictures in the head, but rather that when you see an actual object it leads to a certain pattern of activation in the brain associated with the experience of seeing. A representation is stored in memory that is capable of restoring that pattern of activation, at least in part, and that is the experience of visual imagery (Bower, 1972; Hebb, 1968; Neisser, 1967, 1972). The problem is that this theory's origin is vague. Most people say that when they image a tiger, they cannot count the stripes. Why not? You might argue that images are less detailed than perception is. But if you image a die, you can count the spots. What's the difference? Kosslyn (Kosslyn & Schwartz, 1977; Kosslyn, 1980) provided one of the earlier and more notable theories of imagery that was quite specific about the representation and how it operated; it was specific enough to later be embodied in a computer simulation of imagery (Kosslyn, Flynn, Amsterdam, & Wang, 1990; Kosslyn, 1994).

DEMAND CHARACTERISTICS AND TACIT KNOWLEDGE.   The heart of this argument is that experimental results that appear to support an imagery theory (such as scanning experiments) may simply result from participants' performing tasks as they believe they are expected to perform them. Imagery researchers adopted two strategies to counter this claim. They misinformed participants about the expected results, and they performed experiments in which participants couldn't know what the expected results were.

In one set of experiments, researchers misinformed the people who tested the participants about the expected results of the experiment. It may seem surprising that they misinformed the experimenters about the results instead of misinforming the participants. There is actually a rich literature showing that an experimenter's expectations about an experiment can influence its outcome (Rosenthal, 1976). So is that behind the results in imagery? Is it the case that experimenter's expectations were subtly communicated to participants?

There is some evidence that experimenter expectations can influence the outcome of imagery experiments. For example, Margaret Intons-Peterson (1983; see also Mitchell & Richman, 1980; Richman, Mitchell, & Reznick, 1979) reported that participants responded more quickly when actually seeing stimuli (rather than imaging them) only when the person testing them expected this effect. If the experimenter didn't expect it, they were no faster. But the most important effect of scanning (scanning longer distances in an image takes a longer time) was still observed.

Pierre Jolicoeur and Kosslyn (1985) sought to test this effect more carefully. To test whether the experimenters were somehow communicating to participants what the expected results were, Jolicoeur and Kosslyn told the people testing the participants that they should expect not a linear relation between time and distance scanned but a U-shaped function. They told the people testing the participants that it's hard to differentiate objects that are fairly close together because they are chunked into one group, so the time taken to scan between objects that are close together will actually be slower than the time taken to scan objects that are a bit farther apart. Despite these instructions to the experimenters, the participants produced data showing the linear relation between distance and scanning time.

All in all, these data seem to indicate that experimenter expectations may make participants scan faster or slower, but they do not influence the basic finding that scanning longer distances take a longer time (although Goldston, Hinrichs, & Richman, 1985, reported that directly misinforming participants about the likely outcome of the experiment produced a modest difference in the relation of distance and scanning).

A second defense against the charge that participants are simply producing data that they expect to be true is to use tasks in which participants have no way of knowing what to expect. For example, if one could get participants who are imaging to fall prey to a visual illusion that they were unfamiliar with, it seems impossible that the basis of the illusion was the participant's expectations. An attempt was made to use this strategy by trying to obtain a visual illusion called the McCollough effect in imagery, but whether the effect is obtainable in imagery is debatable (Broerse & Crassini, 1980, 1981; Finke, 1981; Kunen & May, 1980, 1981).

Other data indicated that participants actually don't know what the "expected" results are in an imagery experiment. Michel Denis and Mayvonne Carfantan (1985) administered a questionnaire about imagery to 148 undergraduates taking their first course in psychology. Each of the 15 questions described a basic paradigm in the study of visual imagery and asked the participant to select the correct outcome from among several alternatives. For example, one question read,

> When people are asked to imagine an object rotating 60°, or the same object rotating 120°, which of the following is generally observed?
> If it takes a given time to imagine a 60° rotation for one object. . . .
>
> a. it takes longer to imagine a 120° rotation
> b. it takes less time to imagine a 120° rotation
> c. it takes the same time to imagine a 120° rotation
> d. can't answer

Participants correctly predicted that mental imagery was helpful to memory, spatial reasoning, and deductive reasoning. However, very few could predict the basic results that were at issue in imagery experiments (e.g., that it takes a longer time to scan longer distances). In the preceding question, only 14.9% correctly said that it takes longer to rotate the object 120°. Most thought it takes the same amount of time (40.6%). Thus it appears that participants don't have very much knowledge to go on if they want to produce the "correct" results in imagery experiments.

PROPOSITIONAL VERSUS ANALOG.   This was the most troubling issue. No one disputed that people use propositional (verbal) representations. The question was whether it was necessary to add to the cognitive system another set of representations plus all of the processes to manipulate those representations. As shown in Figure 8.7, it is possible to create networks of propositions that behave in accordance with the predictions of an imagery theory.

This point was made quite forcefully in an article by John Anderson (1978). He argued that it was impossible to select between imagery and propositions. Here's the problem. Images and propositions are different representations, but a representation by itself can't do anything, just as a file on the hard drive of your computer can't do anything by itself; it needs processes to interpret it. The simple assumption in the scanning experiment was that attention was focused on a spatial location of an image and moved around, scanning the image. You could propose a different way that attention operated on an image and come up with a completely different predicted result for the scanning experiment, even though you're still proposing that there is a mental image of a speedboat. For example, suppose you said that attention is subject to inertia when it moves: Trying to stop attention is like trying to stop a physical object, and the faster it's going, the longer it takes to stop it. Suppose that you can't "apply the brakes" to the spotlight of attention early; you can only start stopping the spotlight's movement once it passes the place you want to stop. If you make those assumptions about the process of scanning, you would predict that the relationship of scanning distance and scanning time would not be linear. The point is not whether the inertia idea seems realistic; the point is that we get two different predictions about the relationship of scanning distance and time even though we're assuming identical representations.

Anderson argued that you can't make any predictions about behavior unless you specify both the representation and the processes that act on the representation. Hence, you can't argue about propositional versus imaginal representations without specifying the processes that operate on these representations. In the speedboat example described earlier, a propositional representation, given the appropriate processes, can yield data similar to those that an image representation would yield, given a particular set of processes. Anderson argued that no matter what result came out of an experiment, you could always adjust the hypothetical processes so that a propositional representation would provide an account of the data.

So what's an imagery theorist to do?

They didn't give up, but neither did they try to prove that a propositional representation could not possibly account for the data. Instead they collected data that made it increasingly difficult to make a propositional representation plausible. The results of this research program, much of it spearheaded by Stephen Kosslyn, showed that certain tasks had properties that were very easy to account for if you posited visual images but were clumsy to account for using only propositions.

SCANNING.   You've been reading a lot about scanning, but there is one more experiment you should know about. Recall that in the scanning experiment with the speedboat there was an alternative explanation. It could be that the propositional representation was used and that it took more time to traverse a greater number of links in the representation. In a follow-up experiment, Kosslyn, Thomas Ball, and Brian Reiser (1978) used new stimulus materials to be sure that it was the distance between scanned objects that was important, not the number of parts or objects you ran across while scanning. In other words, it should still take a long time to scan a long distance, even if the distance is filled with white space. Participants were asked to memorize a map depicting a fictional island, with landmarks such as a well and a hut.

After they memorized the map participants were asked to image it and to scan between pairs of landmarks. On some occasions the second location was not one depicted on the map, although it was a plausible location, such as "beach." Participants were to focus attention on the first location and press a button when they "arrived" at the second location. They were to press another button if the second location was not on the map. The time it took for participants to "arrive" at the second location was again a linear function of distance scanned, even though there were no object parts intervening between the beginning and end points of the scan. These results confirmed that it is indeed distance that determines scanning time.

IMAGERY SCREEN SIZE.   Another prediction of the hypothesis that imagery is like perception is that imagery should be limited in its spatial extent. If you think of images as being experienced on the same screen that perception is, you'll note that the screen is of a limited extent. If you look up from this book, you can see what is in front of you but not what is behind you or what is directly on your right or left. Your field of vision covers about 120 degrees of visual angle. Visual angle is simply a measure of the apparent size of things on the retina. It's not very meaningful to measure the size of objects in inches or centimeters because how much space the object takes up on the retina depends not only on its absolute size but on its distance from the observer. As discussed in chapter 2, size and distance trade off. Thus, visual angle is a convenient way to measure the size an object projects on the retina, and the total amount of room in the visual field is 120 degrees.

The formula providing a rough estimate of visual angle is

$$\text{Visual angle (degrees)} = \frac{57.3 \times \text{Size of object}}{\text{Distance between object and observer}}$$

Kosslyn (1978) sought to show that during imagery tasks there is a limited amount of room on the screen. He told people to image an object—in some of the experiments, the objects were animals—and he told them the height and width of the object to be imaged. They were to imagine the object quite far away, and then to imagine walking slowly toward the object. They were to continue walking until the object just filled the mind's eye; if they took another step, they wouldn't be able to see the whole thing; if they took a step back they would be able to see all of the object plus some of the background. Then they were asked to judge how far away from the object they were. Kosslyn then had what he needed to estimate the visual angle of the mind's eye: the object size and the distance from the object to the observer.

The data showed an extremely orderly relationship between the size of the object and the distance at which people said the image overflowed the screen. Across seven experiments using different stimuli and instructions, the actual size of the screen varied, but it usually hovered around 30 degrees, quite a bit smaller than for perception. The important result from this series

BOX 8.2. THE VISUAL ANGLE OF THE MIND'S EYE AND AVAILABLE CORTEX

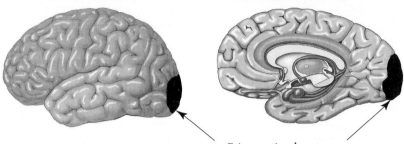

Primary visual cortex

Does imagery depend on visual experience that is strongly spatial in its representation? As described in the text, researchers tried to convince people that imagery is spatial by showing that our imagery capacity is limited in spatial extent. Indeed, one can measure the visual angle of the imagery buffer, just as one can measure the visual angle in perception. The screen size is quite a bit smaller in imagery, but there is enough consistency in the estimate to convince many people that imagery is limited in its spatial extent.

Martha Farah and her colleagues (Farah, Soso, & Dasheiff, 1992) wondered whether someone who had damage to visual cortex might have a smaller medium on which to represent visual material. One would predict that the visual buffer would depend on secondary visual cortex, so if that were damaged the visual buffer would either shrink or be absent. There are two difficulties in investigating that question. First, not everyone has vivid enough imagery abilities to answer the questions necessary to obtain an estimate of the visual angle of the mind's eye. Second, typically one sees patients with occipital lobe damage after a stroke. You could measure the visual angle of the mind's eye at that point, but you wouldn't know whether it had shrunk because of occipital lobe damage or whether it had always been that size.

Farah and her colleagues tested a 36-year-old woman (M.G.S.) who was about to undergo the removal of her right occipital lobe as a treatment for severe epilepsy; the researchers had the opportunity to test the woman before and after the operation. As expected, M.G.S. lost visual perception in the left side of space after the surgery.

To test the surgery's influence on imagery, M.G.S. was asked to image 12 objects (e.g., bicycle, watermelon, horse) and in each case to have the object move closer and closer until it was as close as possible without overflowing and then to estimate its distance. Before testing, the estimates of the visual angle of the mind's eye was about 151.7 degrees, and after the surgery it was 62.9 degrees. In another experiment, M.G.S. was asked to image a long and thin object (a ruler) at different orientations, and this experiment indicated that most of the loss was in the horizontal dimension rather than the vertical, which makes sense, given that the removal of tissue was in the right hemisphere and therefore resulted in a narrowing of the visual field horizontally.

(Continued)

It seems possible that M.G.S. could be complying with how she thought the experimenters wanted the experiment to turn out. To test this possibility, the experimenters also tested her on an imagery ability that they thought would not be impaired, but they told her that they expected it would be impaired. Thus, the instructions included the ideas that most people with the sort of brain damage she had sustained could not image color very well, and the next test would "document this deficit" in M.G.S. The imagery task was to name the colors of objects that are not usually associated with the verbal description of the object (e.g., what color is a pineapple's skin); most people report using imagery to answer these questions. Despite the strong hints that she was expected to fail on this task, M.G.S. performed very well, which indicates that her performance on other tasks is not simply caused by her being a compliant participant who aims to provide data that will satisfy researchers.

These data provide an unusual and interesting test of the hypothesis that imagery occurs in a spatially mapped representational medium that is shared with vision. When that representational medium is compromised, one observes the problem in both vision and imagery.

of experiments is the consistent finding that that the imagery screen has a limited spatial extent.

SCREEN DETAIL. Another property of the imagery concerns the amount of detail or grain participants report. If images are represented in a spatial medium, then physical features are not represented in an image if the image is made very small; if you image a tiny elephant, you may not be able to see its toenails in your mind's eye.

Kosslyn (1975, 1976) tested this prediction. He asked participants to imagine a rabbit with a fly next to it (Figure 8.8). Once they said they had the image in mind, he asked them a question about a rabbit: "Does a rabbit have a pink nose?" Another set of participants got exactly the same tasks, except that they were asked to imagine the rabbit next to an elephant.

Participants were faster in answering whether a rabbit has a pink nose when the rabbit was imaged next to a fly than when it was imaged next to an elephant. (As you would expect, this task was performed with many different animals. In fact, to be sure it was the size of the animals, not just the particular animals used, Kosslyn had participants image enormous flies and tiny elephants.) Participants' introspective reports were in line with the predictions. When asked to report a physical detail of an animal that they had imaged in a very small size, participants reported zooming in on the animal to increase its size so that they could inspect the image for the desired detail.

CONCLUSION. In this phase of the imagery debate researchers concluded that there must be a separate representation for visual images, as Paivio, Shepard, Kosslyn, and others had described. It's not that these researchers had proven conclusively that the mind had to have such a representational system. It was theoretically still possible to get along with nothing but propositions, but to

≈ 2,250 ms to answer "Does
a rabbit have a pink nose?"

≈ 2,050 ms to answer "Does
a rabbit have a pink nose?"

Figure 8.8.   *Sample illustration of what participants were supposed to image in Koss-*
lyn's (1975, 1976) experiments. In one case, they imaged a rabbit next to
an elephant, and in another they imaged a rabbit next to a fly. Partici-
pants were slower to verify that a rabbit has a pink nose in the former
than in the latter, presumably because they had to enlarge the image of
the rabbit to see its nose.

have nothing but propositions would create a cognitive theory that would be extremely unwieldy, and it would have many processes that were obviously tossed
in to account for the latest imagery results.

At the start of the imagery debate, parsimony was the main argument in
favor of the purely propositional account of imagery tasks. Propositions could
account for how people performed imagery tasks, and a propositional theory
was a simpler one because it used only one form of representations. By 1980,
however, it was parsimony that slayed the propositions-only theory. Through
the 1970s researchers reported more and more results that were easy to account
for with a simple imagery theory but were increasingly difficult to account for
with propositions alone. To keep a single system of representations (just propositions), one needed an increasingly complex set of processes to act on that simple set of representations. Thus, the simple theory was the one that proposed
that mental images are a separate type of representation.

By the early 1980s, most cognitive psychologists had made up their minds
that the evidence in favor of a representational system of mental images was
compelling. In the late 1980s and early 1990s a new tool became available that
convinced any final holdouts. Functional imaging of the brain using positron
emission tomography (PET) and functional magnetic resonance imaging (fMRI)
allows one to measure indirectly how active different parts of the brain are. The
predictions for imagery are quite clear. If you think imagery is a separate
representation that has a lot in common with perception, then you'd predict
that when participants perform imagery tasks, the part of the brain that usually handles visual tasks will be most active; that's toward the back of the
brain, in occipital cortex. On the other hand, if you think that propositions do
the work behind these imagery tasks, then you'll predict that the language

centers of the brain will be most active during imagery tasks because propositions are linguistic. The results of neuroimaging studies supported the imagery theorists' predictions.

In one study Denis Le Bihan and his colleagues (1993) used fMRI. Participants were shown a pattern and then simply waited for the next pattern or imagined the pattern they had just seen until the next pattern appeared. They found that imagery led to significant activation of primary visual cortex. Furthermore, that activation is not general to the whole brain; it's not that the whole brain is active when participants perform the task. Rather, the activation was specific to visual areas.

A number of other investigators reported activation of primary visual cortex during imagery tasks (Chen et al., 1998; Kosslyn et al., 1993; Kosslyn, Thompson, Kim, & Alpert, 1995; Kosslyn, Thompson, Kim, Rauch, & Alpert, 1996; Sabbah et al., 1995). Others have not found such activity (Charlot et al., 1992; Fletcher et al., 1995; Mellet, Tzourio, Denis, & Mazoyer, 1995; Roland, Eriksson, Stone-Elander, & Widen, 1987). The difference may lie in what the experimenters asked the participants to image. It may be that primary visual cortex is activated when detailed images are called for (Kosslyn, Sukel, & Bly, 1999), but that question remains open.

The important conclusion from the imaging work is that the activations observed are in the same brain areas that are known to support visual perception rather than areas that are known to support language (as the propositional theory of imagery would predict). John Anderson's (1978) article argued that the imagery debate was not resolvable if one simply tried to differentiate images and propositions. He argued that one must also posit the processes that operate on these representations to derive truly testable hypotheses. In that article he also mentioned the possibility that physiological data might someday resolve the question. Imaging data did just that; or rather, imaging data confirmed what most researchers already believed, based on the behavioral data.

STAND-ON-ONE-FOOT QUESTIONS

7. List the key criticisms of the idea that visual images are supported by a separate representation system.

8. What are the key differences between images and propositions?

9. How did imagery theorists respond to the criticism of the idea that visual images are supported by a separate representation system?

QUESTIONS THAT REQUIRE TWO FEET

10. In the text we discussed how a propositional representation could yield the same results as an imagery representation for visual scanning (i.e., scanning longer distances takes a longer time). Can you think of how a propositional representation could account for the

screen detail effect (in which participants report having to zoom in to see a small detail on an image)?

11. *Psychologists seemed to completely discount participants' introspections about how they perform imagery tasks; that is, even though participants are quite sure that they are creating images, their feelings that they are doing so seem to count not at all as evidence for whether images exist. Why do you think cognitive psychologists distrust participants' introspections so much?*

➤ HOW DOES VISUAL IMAGERY WORK?

> ➤ *PREVIEW* In this section we discuss how imagery works. Images are generated sequentially from parts: First one part is generated, then another part, and so on. Furthermore, evidence from neuropsychology shows that there are separate processes for the visual and spatial aspects of imagery (roughly, what the objects in the image look like and where the objects are located). Once generated, images must be actively maintained, and there is evidence that the number of objects that can be maintained in imagery is limited, although it appears that that number can be increased via chunking. Images may be inspected, apparently through processes similar to inspection processes in perception. Finally, we discuss a number of processes of image transformation, all of which indicate that images of objects transforming show many properties that physical objects show when they move (e.g., an image of a rotating object has inertia).

Remember how our discussion began. We were trying to figure out what imagery's function was. Some researchers suggested that it has a memory function (Paivio, 1971) and helps us to solve problems by imagining the outcome of moving things without actually moving them (Shepard & Cooper, 1982), whereas others suggested that may have no function and may be an epiphenomenon (Pylyshyn, 1973, 1981). There ensued about a decade of work designed to show that imagery is not an epiphenomenon but is supported by a separate representation system.

Having established that imagery is not an epiphenomenon, we can return to the question, "How does imagery work?" There are two components to this question. First, we might ask where images come from, that is, how they are generated and maintained. Second, we might ask how they are used: How are images inspected and transformed (e.g., rotated, expanded)?

Image Generation

Images are generated one part at a time. This finding is a bit surprising because it does not match our introspection. It feels as though images pop into mind all of a piece.

Before there was solid evidence that images are formed in parts, there were strong hints to that effect. In one experiment, Stephen Reed (1974) showed participants line drawings and then showed a simpler line drawing. The participant's job was to say whether the simpler drawing had been part of the complete drawing. Some of the simpler drawings constituted "good" parts of the drawing and some constituted "bad" parts. Good and bad parts were defined by Gestalt perceptual laws, which we haven't discussed, but you can get an intuitive sense of what it means from Figure 8.9. The good parts are easy to spot in the complete drawing, whereas the bad parts take a bit of effort to see.

On each trial the participant saw the complete drawing followed by a brief pause (either 1.5 or 5.5 s) and then a simpler drawing; the participant had to say whether it was a part of the just-seen drawing. Half of the time it was a part (good or bad) and half of the time it was not.

Reed reported that participants were much more accurate in making this judgment if it was a good part than if it was a bad part. The percentages of participants making accurate judgments are shown in Figure 8.9. These results can be interpreted as follows. The participant sees the complete drawing and immediately breaks the figure down into component parts (which would be "good" parts). When the figure disappears, the participant reconstructs a visual image of the figure using these parts. Thus, when a good part is presented, it's easy to verify as part of the figure because it is actually a part of the representation supporting the image. A bad part is not, so it is difficult to verify that it is part of the image.

Other evidence supporting the idea that images are composed of multiple parts comes from the long-standing finding in many studies that images of scenes with multiple objects (or of objects with multiple parts) take longer to generate than simpler scenes (Beech & Allport, 1978; Hartley, 1977; Paivio, 1975; Podgorny & Shepard, 1978; Weber & Harnish, 1974).

Kosslyn and his associates (Kosslyn, Cave, Provost, & von Gierke, 1988) examined the issue of image generation by parts using a modification of a task

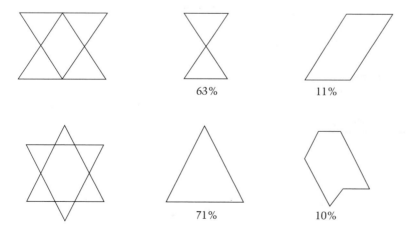

Figure 8.9. *Sample images in Reed's (1974) experiment. Percentages of participants making accurate judgments about each smaller drawing are given.*

first described by Podgorny and Shepard (1978). They first showed participants block capital letters such as that shown at the left of Figure 8.10. Participants were to familiarize themselves with these letters so that they could image them later. In the imagery task, participants were shown the lowercase version of the letter (e.g., *g*), and they knew that this meant that they were to image the uppercase block letter they had been shown earlier. Participants were shown a blank grid like the one shown in Figure 8.10, and they were told to image the letter on the grid. After a brief delay, *xs* appeared in two of the cells, and participants were to say whether the imaged letter would cover both *xs*.

An important aspect of the design is that the delay between when the lowercase cue (e.g., *g*) and the *xs* appeared was only 500 ms. Because previous estimates of the time it takes to generate images were on the order of at least 1.5 sec, participants should still be generating the image when the *xs* appeared.

The results showed that images with more parts take longer to generate than images with fewer parts. In this case, multiple-part images are letters that take many strokes to write (e.g., *G*), and images with fewer parts are letters that take fewer strokes to write (e.g., *L*). The number of strokes necessary to complete the letter varied from two to five. The response time was about 900 ms for a two-stroke letter such as *L* and about 1,200 ms for a five-stroke letter such as *G*. This extra time must be used to generate the image because, in a separate condition in which the block capital was present (and therefore imagery was unnecessary), the number of segments in the letter didn't affect judgment time.

A second feature of this experiment was that the experimenters systematically varied the locations of the *xs*. On some trials the *xs* appeared in locations that they thought would be imaged first, and on other trials the *xs* appeared in locations that they thought would be imaged last. They assumed that participants image block capitals by strokes, in the same way that they write them. Thus, the block capital *G* is imaged by first imaging the topmost horizontal bar, then the vertical bar on the left, then the bottom horizontal bar, and so on. (The experimenters verified that this is true by asking a separate group of participants to draw block capitals and observing how they wrote them.)

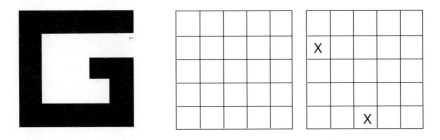

g

Figure 8.10.   *Sample block letter to be imaged (left) and the cue to image it (center) in Kosslyn et al.'s (1988) experiment. Participants were to verify whether the two xs (right) would be covered by the block capital.*

The results showed that response times were shorter when the xs were on line segments that participants tend to generate first, and response times increased if the xs were on segments that would be imaged later. Because the delay between the cue to image the letter and the xs was so short, participants' speed in responding to the xs depended on where the xs appeared. If the xs appeared in the top horizontal bar, they could respond quickly, but if the xs appeared in the small horizontal "tail" of the *G*, they were not so quick to respond. A straightforward interpretation is that when the xs appeared, the participants were in the middle of generating the image. If the xs were in the part of the image that the participant had already generated (e.g., the top horizontal), then the participant could respond quickly (about 850 ms), but if the xs were in a part that the participant had yet to image, the participant had to continue generating the image to see whether the xs would be covered, so the time to respond was longer (about 1,400 ms).

Think back to our discussion of perception in chapter 2, and you can see that this result in imagery is broadly consistent with the idea that imagery and perception overlap a good deal. (Indeed, the overlap of imagery and perceptual processes has been a theme throughout this literature; see Craver-Lemley & Reeves, 1992; Finke, 1980; Finke & Shepard, 1986; Podgorny & Shepard, 1978.) Recall that we discussed the neuroanatomic separation of object identity and spatial location in visual perception; they were called the "what" stream and the "where" stream (Ungerleider & Mishkin, 1982). From this discussion of image generation, we might speculate that the same is true of imagery. It appears that images are generated in parts, which necessarily means that the parts must be put together in the correct spatial configuration. Therefore, it seems possible that anatomically separate processes support the generation of image parts and the configuration of the parts into the correct spatial locations.

Supporting evidence can be gleaned from patients with brain damage; if a patient has selective brain damage to the "what" stream or the "where" stream, we would expect selective deficits in imagery, either in generating the parts of an image or in manipulating the spatial aspect of an image. More generally, researchers have drawn a distinction between **visual imagery** and **spatial imagery.** It's a bit confusing, because *visual imagery* is often used to describe any sort of imagery task in the visual modality. In this context, the term *visual imagery* refers to imagery tasks that emphasize what things look like. On the other hand, spatial imagery tasks require that one knows where objects or parts of objects are located in space. Table 8.1 lists some visual imagery and spatial imagery tasks. The question is whether there is any reason to believe that visual imagery and spatial imagery are anatomically separable.

Martha Farah and her associates (Farah, Hammond, Levine, & Calvanio, 1988) provided evidence supporting the anatomic separation of visual and spatial imagery, matching the "what" and "where" perceptual brain areas. They reported the case of patient L.H., who had damage to the temporal lobe, which is part of the ventral or "what" processing stream. This damage caused a perceptual deficit in L.H. called **agnosia:** He had trouble identifying objects through vision, but the difficulty was not caused by a low-level visual problem. In other words, L.H. could see lines and curves accurately, but he could not put those

Table 8.1   Visual Imagery and Spatial Imagery

Visual Imagery	Description	Spatial Imagery	Description
Animal tails	Judge whether an animal has a long tail proportional to its body size.	Letter rotation	Participant must say whether a rotated letter is mirror-reversed.
Colors	Name the color of a common object that has a characteristic color (e.g., a football).	Mental scanning	Participant judges whether an arrow, if continued, would hit one of two distant dots.
Size comparison	Compare sizes of two objects that are close in size (e.g., cigarette pack and Popsicle).	Letter corners	Classify corners of a block letter as to whether each is at the top or bottom or the middle of the letter.
State shapes	Participant hears 3 state names and must say which 2 are the most similar in shape.	State locations	Participant hears 3 state names and must say which 2 are the closest on the U.S. map.

parts together to recognize an object. For example, someone with agnosia might be able to describe an object as having five short tubes attached to a larger pocket but not recognize that the object is a glove. On the other hand, L.H. had minimal problems in visually locating objects; if you put the glove on a large desk, for example, he could easily locate it even though he couldn't identify it.

L.H. had problems with imagery tasks that mirrored his perceptual deficits. He was grossly impaired in the visual imagery tasks described in Table 8.1. L.H. performed the spatial memory tasks normally, however.

In a somewhat less detailed test of another patient, David Levine, Joshua Warach, and Martha Farah (1985) described a patient who had damage to the "where" processing stream. In terms of perception, this patient had difficulty with spatial aspects of vision (e.g., localizing objects in space) but had no problem in identifying objects based on their appearance. This patient could also describe the appearance of objects from memory using visual imagery but could not describe from memory the locations of landmarks and objects that should have been familiar to him.

Functional imaging results seem to support the data from patients with brain damage. Bessie Alivisatos and Michael Petrides (1997) used PET to image 10 participants while they performed a mirror rotation task. Participants saw a rotated letter and had to say whether it would be mirror-reversed when upright. Strong activation of the parietal cortex (dorsal stream) was associated with the mental rotation.

In another study, Emmanuel Mellet and his colleagues (Mellet, Tzourio, Denis, & Mazoyer, 1998) used a strongly visual task while imaging with PET. Participants heard concrete nouns, and they were to generate an image of the word's referent. This task led to little activation in the parietal lobe but significant activation in the temporal lobe.

In sum, there is good evidence that visual images are generated from memory representations that are used to identify objects. Furthermore, there is evidence that anatomically separate processes underlie the visual aspect of this task (recruiting the mental representation of what the object looks like) and the spatial aspect (spatially arranging and possibly transforming the parts). The anatomical separation implies that there could well be differences in the storage of visual and spatial aspects of images. These details are not yet known.

We've been talking about the processes involved in generating an image. Bear in mind that once an image is generated it does not simply remain in memory. An image must be maintained actively, and that requires attention. You can easily note this fact yourself. If you create a visual image (say, a cat running with a football in its mouth), the image disappears if you divert attention from it. An image fades very quickly and needs constant refreshing, perhaps because imagery shares processes with vision, and vision requires this fast fading so that our view of the world doesn't get confused as we move our eyes. If the image faded slowly it would be confused with the new view of the world obtained when we moved our eyes (Kosslyn, 1995).

Images are limited in that they must be refreshed continually, and they are also limited in the amount of information they can contain. Again, you can appreciate this fact intuitively, simply by imaging an object and adding objects to your image. You quickly find it difficult to keep all the objects in mind.

Nancy Kerr (1987; see also Attneave & Curlee, 1983; Cornoldi, Cortesi, & Preti, 1991) studied the capacity limitations of visual imagery. She asked participants to image a matrix of squares and to follow a pathway through the matrix. Participants saw a matrix, and the experimenters designated one square as the starting square. The picture of the matrix was then removed and the participant heard seven direction instructions (left, right, up, down, etc.), after which the matrix was shown again, and the participant was to show the current location within the matrix. The matrices varied in size, and some were two-dimensional and some were three-dimensional. As shown in Table 8.2, dimensionality had a big impact on performance. Performance was much better on a $3 \times 3 \times 4$ matrix than a 6×6 matrix, even though they had the same number of squares.

One interpretation of this result is that participants chunk spatial dimensions; it is easier to maintain an image of four 3×3 arrays than to maintain a single 6×6 array. Kerr tested this possibility in another experiment by

Table 8.2   Results of Kerr's (1987) Imagery Capacity Experiment

Matrix Size	Number of Squares	% Correct
3×3	9	99
$2 \times 2 \times 2$	8	99
6×6	36	57
$3 \times 3 \times 4$	36	79

presenting participants with an 8×8 array but instructing them to consider it as composed of four 4×4 arrays. To aid in this chunking, she added heavy lines to the 8×8 matrix so that the 4×4 arrays were apparent. As shown in Table 8.3, performance was almost the same on this 8×8 array as it was on a $4 \times 4 \times 4$ array and better than it was on an 8×8 array without instructions to chunk.

Image Inspection

What does it meant to inspect a visual image? It sounds suspiciously like one is talking about a person (make it a very small person) who inspects a literal screen in the brain. I keep emphasizing that that's not what is meant because it is so easy to misunderstand the claim. Inspecting the image means interpreting the representation that is on the visual buffer. It requires a small person no more than perception does.

Several sources of evidence help us to understand image inspection. We can define image inspection as processes one engages to better know the visual characteristics of the image. We engage similar processes in visual perception; when you're looking at a picture, you scan the picture, looking at different parts of it, and perhaps moving closer to an area to get a good look at it. It is thought that the inspection of images recruits some of the same processes that are used in inspecting the world in perception. Several sources of evidence indicate that this is true. One source of evidence is that visual perception interferes with imagery if each process attempts to inspect different objects, and the two processes complement each other if they attempt to inspect the same object.

You'll recall that in Alan Baddeley's working memory model, the visuospatial sketchpad was thought to be similar to, if not synonymous with, visual imagery. In chapter 4 we discussed a relevant experiment performed by Baddeley and his colleagues (Baddeley, Grant, Wight, & Thomson, 1975). They asked participants to remember a series of sentences such as, "In the next square down, put a 1. In the next square to the left, put a 2," and so on. Some participants were told that it might help them to remember the sentences if they imaged a 4×4 matrix and considered the upper right square as the starting square. Other participants heard sentences that made it very difficult to use an imagery strategy; the directional terms *up, down, right,* and *left* were replaced with the nonsense words *good, bad, quick* and *slow*, making odd sentences such as "In the next square bad, put a 2."

Table 8.3   *Effects of Chunking in Kerr's (1987) Experiment*

Matrix Size	Number of Squares	% Correct
8×8 without chunking	64	30
8×8 with chunking	64	53
$4 \times 4 \times 4$	64	59

At the same time participants were listening to (and trying to remember) these sentences, some of them had to perform a tracking task that was demanding of perception. They had to try to keep a hand-held stylus on a moving target. The results showed that memory for the sentences was greatly affected by the tracking task. Participants made about three errors on the sentences when they were not performing the tracking task, but they made about nine errors with the tracking task. Furthermore, the tracking task did not interfere with the sentence task when the sentences did not encourage the use of imagery; performance for these sentences was about three errors with or without tracking. That indicates that the high error rates with tracking occurred not simply because a secondary task was performed but because participants were trying to use imagery for one task (sentences) at the same time that they were trying to use perception for a different task (tracking). The interpretation of this result is that imagery and perception share resources.

Baddeley et al. showed that imagery and perception interfere if you try to do different things with them. Martha Farah (1985) showed that imagery can facilitate perception if they are doing the same thing. Participants were asked to watch a video monitor on which a box appeared for 850 ms, disappeared for 100 ms, and then reappeared for 850 ms. One of the two boxes contained a very faint letter (either an *H* or a *T*, but participants didn't know which). Participants simply had to say which of the two boxes contained the faint letter. In addition, participants were to perform this task while they imaged either an *H* or a *T*. On some trials the letter they imaged matched the faint letter on the screen, but on others it didn't. The results showed that when the imaged and perceived letters matched, participants averaged 85.3% correct, but when they did not match, participants averaged 76.8%. In a second experiment, Farah showed that the facilitation works only if the participant images the letter in the same place that it appears on the screen. This finding shows that the effect is not caused simply by thinking about the letter. Activating a secondary memory representation of the matching letter is not enough; the image and the perception share some truly visual property.

These results concerned the commonality of processes supporting imagery and perception in terms of using the image on the screen (e.g., to place the numbers in the matrix in the experiment by Baddeley et al., 1975). Another important function is to use visual imagery to construct parts mentally and see the whole that results. Several experiments have shown that participants can look at multiple geometric parts and verify whether those parts can be assembled into a whole that the experimenter specifies (e.g., Intons-Peterson, 1981; Thompson & Klatzky, 1978).

Even more striking are demonstrations by Ronald Finke and his colleagues (see Finke, 1996, for a review) that participants can use imagery to combine simple parts and then see unexpected wholes on the visual image. For example, Finke and colleagues Steven Pinker and Martha Farah (1989) showed that participants can manipulate mental images of simple figures and recognize the resulting patterns as something different from what they started out with. Here are the instructions participants heard. The first item was practice. The correct answers appear at the end of the chapter.

Practice. Imagine the letter "Q." Put the letter "O" next to it on the left. Remove the diagonal line. Now rotate the figure 90 degrees to the left. The pattern is the number 8.

1) Imagine the number "7." Make the diagonal line vertical. Move the horizontal line down to the middle of the vertical line. Now rotate the figure 90 degrees to the left. What is it?

2) Imagine the letter "B." Rotate it 90 degrees to the left. Put a triangle directly below it having the same width and pointing down. Remove the horizontal line. What is it?

3) Imagine the letter "y." Put a small circle at the bottom of it. Add a horizontal line halfway up. Now rotate the figure 180 degrees. What is it?

4) Imagine the letter "K." Place a square next to it on the left side. Put a circle inside of the square. Now rotate the figure 90 degrees to the left. What is it?

5) Imagine a plus sign. Add a vertical line on the left side. Rotate the figure 90 degrees to the right. Now remove all lines to the left of the vertical line. What is it?

6) Imagine the letter "D." Rotate it 90 degrees to the right. Put the number "4" above it. Now remove the horizontal segment of the "4" to the right of the vertical line. What is it?

The transformations were successfully carried out 58.1% of the time (so that the final image looked the way the experimenters intended). When the transformations were executed correctly, participants could identify the object that the new resulting pattern depicted 59.7% of the time. Thus, this task is not trivially easy, but it is quite possible to manipulate images, to inspect the results, and in so doing to discover a new emergent pattern.

Another aspect of image inspection is the ability to inspect different parts of an image in isolation of other parts. We have already discussed this ability earlier, when we talked about Kosslyn's (1975) results showing that participants can zoom in to parts of an image when necessary to inspect a specific subpart. For example, one might focus on a rabbit's nose to determine whether it is pink, and one might rescale the size of the image if necessary to make this determination (see also Bundesen & Larsen, 1975, for more on size rescaling).

It seems that one would need to shift attention to various locations of the visual image to inspect different parts of it. There is evidence that this attentional process has much in common with the attentional processes that support visual perception. These data come from patients with brain damage. Edoardo Bisiach and Claudio Luzzatti (1978) tested several patients with **hemispatial neglect.** These patients ignore half of the visual world (almost always the patient's left side). It is a deficit of attention, not perception. Visual perception is normal if attention can somehow be dragged over to the neglected side of the world, but under most circumstances it cannot. The patient behaves as if that side of the world does not exist. If you show the patient a painting and ask for a description, the left side will be ignored. If you ask the patient to split a candy bar down the middle, the cut will be made about three-fourths of the way to the right: The left half of the bar is ignored, so the patient divides the half that he or she sees.

Remarkably, this deficit of attention extends to visual imagery. Bisiach and Luzzatti asked the patients to go on a mental walk (i.e., to image taking a walk) around Milan, their hometown. At one point, patients were asked to walk into the Piazza del Duomo, a well-known square in Milan, and to describe what they saw. Patients described well-known landmarks, but all of them were on the right side of the piazza. Patients were then asked to continue their mental walk. Sometime later, they were asked to again enter the Piazza del Duomo and describe what they saw in their image, but this time they entered from the opposite end of the square. Patients again described only objects on the right side, but because they entered from the other side, they were now describing the objects they had previously ignored.

This result shows that they can image the whole square, but because of their attention deficit they either image just half of it at a time, or they image the whole thing but cannot direct attention to the left side of the image. In either case, the important point is that the perceptual deficit extends to imagery. The implication is that attention is directed to inspect parts of an image in the same way that attention is directed to inspect perceptual scenes.

Another interesting finding about image inspection concerns the relation of eye movements during perception of a moderately complex pattern and visual imagery of the pattern (see Stark & Ellis, 1981, for a review). Stephan Brandt and Lawrence Stark (1997) showed participants irregular checkerboard-type matrices and recorded participants' eye movements when they inspected pictures of the matrices and when they later imaged the matrices and inspected the images. The researchers found that saccades (eye movements) and fixation times (how long the eye stayed in a particular spot) were closely correlated in the perception and the imagery conditions. Figure 8.11 shows one of the checkerboard-type matrices, with the locations of eye fixations when the checkerboard was viewed and when it was imaged. Each number refers to a place where the eyes fixated.

Why would participants move their eyes when they inspect a visual image? The eyes aren't seeing anything helpful, so why move them? Eye movements are closely linked to shifts of attention; we normally move our eyes when we shift

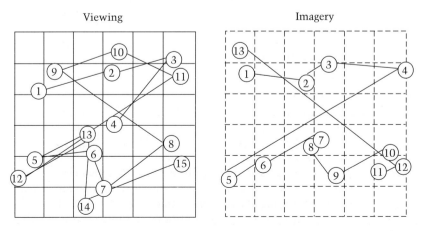

Figure 8.11. *Checkerboard-type matrix used in Brandt and Stark's (1997) eye movement experiment.*

attention. Scanning a visual image means shifting your attention to a different part of the image, so it is likely that eye movements are generated and executed simply because eye movements are so typically a part of a shift of attention.

Image Transformation

We mentioned earlier that an important purpose of image transformation is the ability to examine the consequences of physical actions before one goes to the trouble of taking the physical action. Will my car fit in that tight parking space? Is this brick the right size to prop up my sofa with the missing leg?

In the course of this chapter we have described some of the ways in which images can be transformed. A list of the transformations we have described (and some that we haven't) appears in Table 8.4.

Most of the work examining the transformation of visual images has asked participants to rotate the images. An important result of this work is the conclusion that mental image transformation faithfully reflects the physical properties of objects. Mental images in motion obey the same laws of motion that real objects do. How do we know that?

Objects in the world rotate all of a piece, that is, you don't see one part rotating, and then the next part rotating, and so on. Thus, the complexity of the object (how many parts is has) doesn't affect the ease with which we can perceive the object rotating. The same should be true of imagery. Lynn Cooper (1975) tested this hypothesis, using made-up objects with different numbers of angles, to represent different levels of object complexity. Participants first underwent training to learn the objects; they learned which orientation was to be considered standard and which was mirror reversed. In sessions 2 through 6 participants were asked to judge whether the standard or mirror-reversed figure was presented, but the figures were rotated either 0, 60, 120, or 180 degrees from the training orientation. In each session participants performed 128 trials. The critical question was whether the time it took for participants to make the rotation varied with the complexity of the object, and the answer is that it did not, as shown in Figure 8.12.

Table 8.4 Image Transformations

Transformation	Description	Citation
Rotation	Rotate the image about an axis.	Shepard & Metzler (1971)
Expansion and contraction	Expand (or shrink) an image in size.	Bundesen & Larsen (1975)
Sequenced transformation	Apply more than one spatial manipulation in a sequence.	Sekuler & Nash (1972)
Folding parts to make a whole	Move parts of an object that have limitations on how they can move to make a whole with a different shape (e.g., fold paper to make a box).	Shepard & Feng (1972)
Transforming color	Change the color of an object.	Watkins & Schiano (1982)

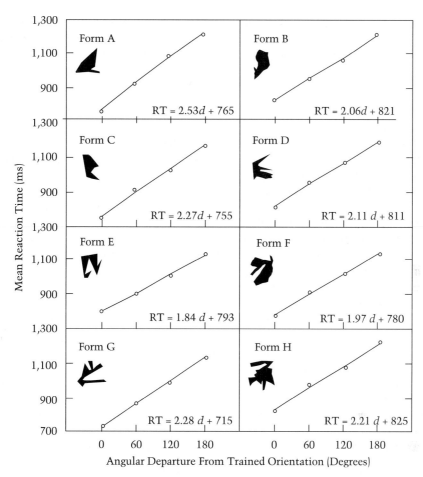

Figure 8.12. *Results of Cooper's (1975) object rotation experiment.*

The crucial part of Figure 8.12 is the slope of the lines. What you're seeing is the response times to evaluate each figure at each rotation. Each graph
shows the line that best fits the data. You can evaluate how hard it is to mentally rotate the object by measuring the slope of that line. If it's harder to rotate an object a greater distance, response times for 180 degrees will be much
higher than for 120 degrees, which will be much higher than 60 degrees, and
the slope will be quite steep. As you can see, the slopes are about the same
for all of the figures; thus, more complex figures are not more difficult to
mentally rotate. It's as easy to image a complex object rotating as a simple
one, just as it's equally easy to perceive the rotation of a complex object or a
simple object.

A second characteristic of objects in the world is that when they rotate,
they must occupy all intermediate positions on their way to their final position. Objects in the world don't jump from one position to another without
occupying intermediate positions. Therefore, one might expect that rotating
mental images would not be a series of pictures of slightly different orientations

but should be more like a movie of a smoothly moving image. Cooper (1976) tested this proposal. She used the same angular test stimuli that were used in Cooper (1975) and tested a subset of the participants who had been in that experiment. Cooper therefore knew the rate at which these participants mentally rotated images. (Obviously some participants have faster rates of rotation than others.)

At the start of each trial, the participant saw one of the stimuli, then a blank field, and then a circle, which was a signal to begin a clockwise mental rotation of the stimulus. After some time passed, a pattern was presented and participants had to determine whether it was the standard version or the mirror-reversed version of the stimulus.

There were two tricky parts of the experiment. The first was the delay between when the participant started mentally rotating the stimulus and when the test stimulus appeared. Recall that Cooper knew how fast these participants could mentally rotate these objects; she had that data from the previous experiment. Suppose, for example, that she knew that one participant could mentally rotate a particular stimulus at a rate of 1.5 degrees per millisecond. If Cooper let the participant mentally rotate the object for 80 ms and then presented the cue at 120 degrees from upright, the participant's mental rotation should be in exactly the same position as the test stimulus. You would therefore expect that response times would be quite fast for that trial. On the other hand, if she let the participant mentally rotate the stimulus for 80 ms and then presented the cue at 240 degrees, you would expect response times to be slower. That is exactly the result she found: Response times got slower relative to the position that the mental image should have been, given that the participant was mentally rotating it. The main thing this result reveals is that participants were indeed mentally rotating the objects and that Cooper's measures of how fast they could rotate them were accurate.

The second result is the important one. For this result, we're dealing only with trials on which the orientation of the test stimulus matched the orientation at which the participant should have been imaging the stimulus; in other words, Cooper timed the presentation time and the orientation of the test stimulus so that it should be right in line with where the participant's image would be. The participants had seen the stimuli at six different orientations in Cooper's 1975 experiment; these were the familiar orientations. The real question of interest here is whether, when participants claim to be mentally rotating objects, they are smoothly rotating the object through all of the intermediate positions or flipping through a series of discrete positions. Cooper assumed that if participants were flipping through a series of discrete positions, it would be the six positions with which they were familiar. Therefore, if she presented the stimulus in an unfamiliar position (say 150 degrees) the participant would be imaging the stimulus at 120 or 180 degrees (the closest familiar orientations) and would therefore take a little longer to identify it than when the stimulus was presented at one of the familiar orientations. On the other hand, if the participant wasn't flipping through the familiar orientations but imaged the stimulus smoothly rotating through all of the intermediate positions, then it shouldn't matter whether the stimulus was at a familiar or an unfamiliar orientation: The participant would be imaging the stimulus at exactly the right orientation. The results showed that participants were just as fast in responding to familiar or unfamiliar orientations, indicating that they rotated objects smoothly through all intermediate positions rather than flipping through a series of familiar pictures.

A third source of evidence that mental transformations mirror the real world is that imaging rotations takes longer if the rotation would be difficult in the real world. Parsons (1987a, 1987b) showed participants drawings of hands and asked them to judge whether it was a right or left hand. The data showed that, as with other stimuli, greater rotation took a longer time. More interesting was that it took longer to make the judgment if the rotational movement would be uncomfortable to make because of a biomechanical constraint, that is, a rotation that is uncomfortable because of the way the joint is constructed. (Parsons confirmed that certain hand rotations were uncomfortable by having participants rate the comfort of different hand positions.)

Participants saw the right hand, palm down, as the "standard" hand, and the hand was rotated through various angles. Parsons recorded the time it took respondents to judge whether the hand shown was a right or left hand. Participants were much slower to identify the hand with the thumb pointed toward the floor than the hand with the thumb pointing toward the ceiling, even though both hands were 90-degree rotations from the "standard" hand. This result indicates that participants performed this task by imagining their own hands making the required transformation, and that when your hand would be slow to assume a particular position (such as having your right thumb toward the floor) you are slow to mentally image taking that position (see also Cooper & Shepard, 1975). Again, this result is consistent with the idea that mental imagery mirrors what happens in perception.

The final bit of evidence that mental images mirror perception is that rotating images have momentum. There is no reason that an image of a rotating object shouldn't be able to stop on a dime, except that a real object doesn't do that. But how can you show that when participants imagine a rotating object, they actually imagine it rotating just a bit beyond the stopping place they might intend because of momentum? Jennifer Freyd and Ronald Finke (1984) tested this possibility as follows. They showed participants three pictures of a rectangle in successive positions of a rotation. Participants were told to remember the final picture. The experimenters then showed the participants a test picture, which they were to compare with the final to-be-remembered picture. Presumably they would compare the test picture (which was visible) with an image of the final picture. The experimenters reasoned that if rotating images have momentum, participants would likely remember the final picture as continuing the rotation slightly. Therefore, they should say that the test picture was the same as the final picture if the test actually continued the rotation slightly. That's exactly what the results showed. If the test stimulus continued the rotation, they

BOX 8.3.   DIRECT EVIDENCE FOR SMOOTH ROTATION

There has been some controversy over whether image rotation occurs smoothly—that is the object occupies all intermediate positions between the starting and ending position—or whether rotation occurs by flipping through a series of snapshots, each some distance closer to the endpoint. The behavioral data indicate that the image does occupy all of the intermediate positions, Neuroscientific data support the same conclusion.

Apostolos Georgopoulos and his colleagues (1989) trained a rhesus monkey to perform mental rotation, hard as that may be to believe. The monkey sat in a chair with a table before it. On the table were eight lights, arranged in a circle. There was also a jointed arm with a handle. At the start of each trial the monkey was to move the handle to the center of the circle of lights. Then one of the lights illuminated and the monkey moved the handle to the light to get a reward. In another condition, the monkey moved the handle not to the illuminated light but to the light that was 90 degrees counterclockwise from the illuminated light. While the monkey was performing this task, the researchers were recording from individual neurons in primary motor cortex.

The analysis of these data is a little complicated. How is a direction for movement represented? (Suppose we call movement directly away from the body 90 degrees.) It is *not* the case that a movement of 90 degrees is represented by a small pool of cells that fire when you want to move that way, and these neurons do not fire otherwise. Rather, each cell has a *preferred* direction of movement, and when you move in that direction it fires a lot; when you move in other directions it still fires, but less intensely. Thus for every movement, all cells in primary motor cortex fire, but an individual cell fires in proportion to the similarity of its preferred direction of movement to the desired direction of movement of the arm. It's as if each cell is a bidder at an auction; when some other part of the system determines that the arm should move 90 degrees, all of the cells start bidding, and the cell that likes to move 90 degrees bids the highest (i.e., fires the most). All of these "bids" can be summarized and the average bid ends up being the direction that the arm moves.

Georgopoulos and his colleagues tested what happens when they asked the monkey not to move directly to the light but instead to move to the light 90 degrees counterclockwise from the one that was illuminated. The summary of activity was calculated every 10 ms between the appearance of the light and when the monkey made the movement. The summary of activity showed that initially the neurons fired in the direction toward the light, but then the activity changed in a way consistent with a counterclockwise sweep until the selected direction was the required 90 degrees counterclockwise from the light. The researchers could see the pattern of neural activity change in time, rotating from the location of the light to the required location, as shown in Figure B8.3.

It should be noted that these recordings were taken in the primary motor cortex; thus the spatial rotation is very unlikely to be taking place in these cells. Rather, the rotation occurs elsewhere (likely parietal cortex) but rather than completing the rotation and *then* feeding the final direction for movement to

(Continued)

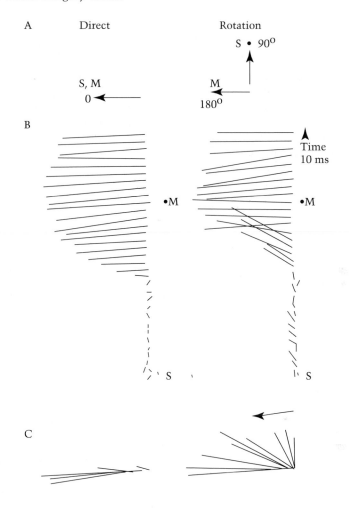

Figure B8.3

motor cortex, the cortical area that performs the rotation continually feeds the current best guess about the direction of movement to the motor cortex. By eavesdropping on the motor cortex, we have another source of solid evidence that mental rotation occurs via smooth rotation, including all of the positions between the starting and stopping points of the rotation.

made errors about 45% of the time. If the test stimulus was rotated slightly the wrong way, participants made errors only 5% of the time. Freyd and Finke interpreted these results as showing that the rotation continues to a small extent. There is momentum in the rotation of a visual image, just as there is momentum in the rotation of a real object (see also Freyd, 1987; Munger, Solberg, & Horrocks, 1999).

In summary, mental images appear to show many properties that actual physical objects do. Mental images, like real objects, rotate holistically, occupy intermediate positions as they rotate, are subject to biomechanical constraints, and have momentum. Why is this true? Why do images behave like real objects when they obviously do not need to? One possible explanation lies in a distinction first made explicit by Michael Kubovy (1983). Kubovy pointed out that when researchers talk about image transformation, they often speak as though there is a representation (e.g., a representation of an *R*) and that this representation itself rotates. Nothing in the data we've discussed necessitates this interpretation however. Instead of the representation of the object rotating, it could be that you image the object rotating. You don't form an image of an *R* and then rotate the representation of *R*. Rather, you form an image of a rotating *R*. This subtle distinction may help explain why mental images move in ways that are consistent with real objects. It seems odd that they do so because we don't expect that mental entities (such as representations) should necessarily move in the same ways that physical entities do. But this oddity is explained if you instead assume that the mental entity is not being moved at all; rather, the mental entity represents the movement of a physical entity. In that case, it makes sense that mental images move as physical objects do because they represent the physical world.

STAND-ON-ONE-FOOT QUESTIONS

12. Name the key processes involved in using visual imagery.
13. Describe the difference between visual imagery and spatial imagery and describe their anatomic locations.
14. Describe how it is known that images are generated by parts, not all at once.

QUESTIONS THAT REQUIRE TWO FEET

15. What evidence have we discussed in this chapter that is relevant to Baddeley's working memory theory?
16. Many of the functions of imagery we've described in this chapter are closely tied to imagery itself; we've talked about using transformations to imagine the outcome of moving physical objects before you move them, and we've talked about the memory function of imagery. Can you think of another cognitive process that imagery might help?
17. Evaluate the truth of this very broad characterization of visual imagery: "Visual imagery is just perception running backwards."

KEY TERMS

imageless thought controversy

concreteness or abstractness

dual-coding hypothesis

logogens

imagens

multiply determined

second-order isomorphism

epiphenomenon

homunculus

demand characteristics

tacit knowledge

proposition

image

parsimonious

Occam's razor

picture theory of imagery

visual angle

visual imagery

spatial imagery

agnosia

image inspection

hemispatial neglect

Answers to Finke, Pinker, & Farah imagery questions, p. 372: (1) the letter T; (2) heart; (3) stick figure person; (4) television; (5) letter F; (6) sailboat.

Decision Making and Deductive Reasoning

You probably don't even notice the number of decisions you make each day. Take the bus or walk? Say "hello" to the acquaintance or pretend not to see her? Paper or plastic? Similarly, you probably do not notice the frequency with which you reason deductively. I may say to you, "If we buy the soda up the street, we'll save a nickel." If you then go up the street and buy the soda, you obviously expect to save a nickel. This expectation is based on deductive reasoning, although you probably wouldn't notice that you had engaged in reasoning at all. In this chapter we examine how we make decisions and how we reason.

We consider these two topics in turn: first decision making and then deductive reasoning. We consider them in the same chapter because for both types of problems, one can derive answers that are objectively correct. As we'll see later in the chapter, one can argue about whether these "objectively correct" answers are necessarily the ones psychologists should pay attention to, but to a first degree of approximation decision making and deductive reasoning problems have clear answers. Other questions do not have such clear answers, and we consider those in chapter 11. The first question we take up in this chapter is, **"Do people consistently make optimal decisions?"** That is, if there is an objectively correct answer to a decision-making problem, do people make that decision? As we'll see, the answer often is "no." That doesn't mean that people never make optimal decisions, but it does indicate that they do not use decision rules that are designed for optimality. At least part of the reason people don't come up with these answers is that it is often too time-consuming and difficult to derive optimal answers to moderately complex questions. People need shortcuts to derive good (but not necessarily optimal) solutions, so the next question is **"What shortcuts do people use to make decisions?"** As we'll see, the most influential answer to this question is that people use what we might call reasoning shortcuts: procedures that allow one to arrive at an answer quickly and with little effort and that produce an answer that is usually correct.

In decision-making problems, a choice must be made from among two or more outcomes. In most reasoning problems, we are presented with an argument and asked what conclusion can be made, or we are asked to evaluate the validity of a conclusion that is supplied. For example, I might ask what conclusions (if any) could be drawn from these two premises.

On Thursdays, I eat melon.
Today is not Thursday.

As mentioned earlier, deductive reasoning is similar to decision making in that one can identify objectively correct answers. Deductive reasoning is different, however, in that the problems often are less complex, at least in principle. We might therefore entertain the possibility that people are optimal problem solvers in this domain (i.e., that they reason in accordance with the rules of formal logic). **Do people reason logically?** Alas, the answer is "no," as you probably already guessed. Because people use shortcuts in decision-making problems, we might guess that people use them in reasoning problems as well. To some extent that's true, but we'll also look at some models of reasoning that don't use such shortcuts, and these models seem to do a better job of accounting for people's behavior.

➤ DO PEOPLE CONSISTENTLY MAKE OPTIMAL DECISIONS?

> ➤ *PREVIEW* Decision making generally entails problems in which two (or occasionally more) options are laid before a person, and he or she must select one of the options. In such problems, one can define criteria by which some answers are better than others. One criterion is rationality, which means that my choices are internally consistent: I make choices in the same way each time. In normative models of decision making, a second criterion is added that dictates which of the choices is best. For example, a possible criterion would be to maximize financial gain. In this section we go over evidence showing that people's choices are not rational (that is, they are not consistent) and that they are not normative (that is, they do not conform to any criterion such as maximizing financial reward). This conclusion doesn't mean that people always make irrational, poor choices; it means that whatever mechanisms guide decisions are not tuned to make optimal decisions consistently. The mechanisms are guided by some other principle.

Defining decision making is a little odd, because in a way it can encompass all of human behavior. As you read this book, you are making a decision not to find a pair of scissors and cut it into very small pieces. You are also making a decision not to hunker on the floor and chatter like a squirrel, and so on. When researchers say that they study **decision making,** they usually mean a situation in which someone is presented with two or more explicit courses of action, with the requirement that they select just one.

Normative or Rational Models

Most of us would like to think of ourselves as sensible, and part of being sensible is making effective choices. There are two ways in which our choices can be effective or ineffective. First, our choices may or may not be **rational.** Rational in this sense refers to being internally consistent. For example, we might expect choices to show **transitivity.** Transitivity generally means that if some relationship holds between the first and the second of three elements, and it holds between the second and third elements, then it ought to hold between the first and third. For example, suppose I am to choose between apple pie and Bavarian cream pie. I choose the apple pie. Next, I am presented with Bavarian cream pie and chocolate cake, and I choose Bavarian cream pie. Finally, I am presented with chocolate cake and apple pie. If my choices show transitivity, I should select apple pie.

Rational choices must also be consistent; I can't say that I like classical music better than funk and I also like funk better than classical. Notice that the requirement of rationality has no bearing on the particular choices a person makes. The theory doesn't proscribe that you should like apple pie better than Bavarian cream. Rationality simply means that there is consistency across the choices that you make.

However, other theories are proscriptive, meaning that they maintain that some choices are better than others, and usually that one choice is optimal from among the possibilities; these are called **normative theories.** What makes a choice the optimal one varies with the particular theory. In **expected value** theory the optimal choice is the one that offers the largest financial payoff, taking into account the probability of the payoff. For example, suppose you were offered the following choices:

Problem 1
A) .50 chance of winning $50
B) .25 chance of winning $110

The expected value of each choice is easy to calculate: It's simply the probability of winning multiplied by the value of the prize. Thus the expected value of the first choice is .50 × $50 = $25. The expected value of the second choice is .25 × $110 = $27.50. Hence, if expected value guides people's decisions, they would always select the second choice.

In the next section we discuss in more detail how people's choices violate normative and rational models, but we can at least note here that people often make choices that are suboptimal if expected value is the guide. Anyone who buys a lottery ticket or gambles in a casino is not making choices guided by expected value. There are no bets in a casino that are not set in favor of the house (Table 9.1); hence, expected value dictates that you should make the choice of not wagering.

Setting casino games aside, it is not difficult to think of instances where expected value would not guide your choices. For example, suppose that it's 3 o'clock in the afternoon, you skipped lunch and are really hungry, and you're also broke. I offer you the choice that follows in Problem 2.

Table 9.1 *Average Return for Casino Games*

Game	Bet	Average Return (%)
Roulette	Single number	94.7
Roulette	Red or black	97.2
Blackjack	Varies	~99
Craps	Pass or don't pass	98.6
Slot machine	Nickel	84.8
Slot machine	Quarter	89.8
Baccarat	Banker	98.6
Baccarat	Player	98.2

Average return indicates the percentage of your money you can expect to recoup over an infinitely long session of betting. Odds are from Reber (1999). Roulette odds depend on the wheel, which varies by locale; odds shown are for most U.S. casinos. Odds of blackjack and baccarat depend in part on the skillfulness of choices made by the player, and on the rules, which vary slightly by locale. The return of slot machines also varies.

Problem 2
A) .85 chance of winning $8
B) .25 chance of winning $28

Expected value dictates that you should take choice B. The expected value of choice A is $6.80 and for choice B it's $7.00. But we've said that you're very hungry, and you're broke. You may well think to yourself, "I'm quite likely to get the $8, but I'm not very likely to get the $28. Although it would be nice to have the extra $20, I really want to make sure I get *some* money so that I can go to McDonald's and get something to eat." This is an example of maximizing **expected utility.** Utility is the personal value we attach to outcomes, rather than to their absolute monetary value. Eight dollars at this moment has a lot of utility to you; the extra $20 does not have sufficient utility to justify the risk of not getting the $8. Similarly, I might offer you one sandwich for a dollar or 100 sandwiches for $50. In terms of expected value, you're better off with 100 sandwiches, but what will you do with 100 sandwiches?

Here's another example of a choice that is probably guided by expected utility, not expected value.

Problem 3
A) .10 chance of winning $10 million dollars
B) .99 chance of winning $1 million dollars

Expected value dictates that you should choose A (with an expected value of $1 million) rather than B (with an expected value of $990,000). Obviously you pick B because you'd rather be pretty sure of having $1 million than be likely to have nothing, with a small chance of having $10 million; the utility of the extra $9 million is not worth the risk. Thinking of decision making that way makes problems like this more understandable:

Problem 4
A) 1.0 chance of winning $1
B) .00000014 chance of winning $3 million

This problem represents the typical odds of winning the state lottery in Virginia. You can either be certain of keeping your dollar (by not playing in the first place), or you can sacrifice your dollar to try to win $3 million, but the odds of winning are about 1 in 7 million. The expected value clearly favors keeping your dollar. The expected utility of losing $1 dollar is pretty low, and expected utility of $3 million is quite high.

Although I seldom play the lottery, I do carry insurance. Insurance is like a lottery in that it's a bad deal in terms of expected value. The insurance company runs its business and makes its profit on the difference between the premiums it takes in and the payments its doles out. The premiums I pay are doubtless more than they should be if we calculated the expected value of the insurance, based on the probability of my house burning down and the cash I would be paid should that happen. But when I consider the inconvenience of my house burning down, it's clear that the utility of that event would be hugely negative, and I'm willing to accept a choice that is not very attractive in terms of expected value to protect against this highly negative utility outcome.

Although the concept of utility (first introduced by von Neumann and Morgenstern, 1944) seems to help a great deal in understanding people's choices, it is far from sufficient to explain all choices. There are a number of cases in which people do not behave as expected utility theory would predict. In the next section, we review these findings.

Demonstrations of Human Irrationality

We can point to at least two principles that should be observed if decisions are made rationally: procedure invariance and description invariance. Description invariance means that people will consistently make the same choice irrespective of how the problem is described to them as long as the basic structure of the choices is the same. Procedure invariance means that people will consistently make the same choice irrespective of the how their preference for that choice is measured. You might ask them to choose among several alternatives, make a series of pairwise comparisons, or assign a monetary value to each choice; it shouldn't matter. Experiments have repeatedly shown that neither procedure invariance nor description invariance holds.

Here are two problems that were presented to participants in a study by Amos Tversky and Danny Kahneman (1986). They gave each problem to about 125 participants. The numbers in parentheses indicate the percentage of participants selecting each choice.

> *Problem 5a*
> Suppose I give you $300, but you must also select one of these two options:
> (72%) A) 1.0 chance of gaining $100
> (28%) B) .50 chance of gaining $200 and a .50 chance of gaining nothing

> *Problem 5b*
> Suppose I give you $500, but you must also select one of these two options:
> (36%) A) 1.0 chance of losing $100
> (64%) B) .50 chance of losing nothing and a .50 chance of losing $200

Notice that Problem 5a and Problem 5b are formally similar to one another; the monetary outcomes (once you factor in the $300 or $500 you start with) are the same, so the expected utilities should be the same, but the dominant choice nevertheless reverses. Why? The problem frame changed. A **problem frame** refers to the way that a problem is described. Problem 5a gives you a choice between gains; Problem 5b offers a choice between losses. Although the formal outcome of the two problems is the same, the description (or frame) differs, and that affects the choice that people make.

Here's another problem showing framing effects. Participants are told that a disease is expected to kill 600 people, and two programs to fight the disease are being considered. They are given the estimates of what will happen if each program is followed and must choose a program. As before, the percentage of people selecting a choice is shown in parentheses, and as in the monetary example, people are conservative when selecting between potential gains, but they take risks when they select among potential losses.

Problem 6a

(72%) A) 200 people will be saved.

(28%) B) There's a 1/3 chance that 600 people will be saved and a 2/3 chance that no people will be saved.

Problem 6b

(22%) A) 400 people will die.

(78%) B) There's a 1/3 chance that no one will die and a 2/3 chance that 600 people will die.

There is evidence that physicians make different decisions for treatments (e.g., the use of chemotherapy to treat cancer) when they are presented with death rates and when they are presented with survival rates. In general, people's assessment of risks differs depending on whether the outcome is described in terms of its costs or its benefits. People are averse to taking risks if the outcome is described positively but more willing to take risks if the outcomes are negative.

Another aspect of framing concerns **psychic budgets** (Thaler, 1980). Psychic budgets concerns how we mentally categorize money that we have spent or are contemplating spending. For example, you may not buy yourself a coat that you like because you consider it too expensive. You are putting it in the mental category "luxury" and are unwilling to allocate that sum to a luxury. Suppose your spouse suggests buying that coat as a present for you. Now the same coat at the same price is in a different mental category—"gift"—and it doesn't seem to be such a bad deal anymore, even though if you and your spouse share a checking account, the cost to you is the same.

Tversky and Kahneman (1981) offered a compelling example of this sort of psychic budgeting. They presented scenarios like these to participants.

Problem 7a

Suppose you and a friend are going to the theater. When you get to the theater you realize that somewhere on your way you've lost the tickets, which cost a total of $100. You have more than $100 cash with you. Tickets are still available at the box office. Would you buy tickets to replace those that you've lost?

Problem 7b

Suppose that you and a friend are going to the theater. When you get to the theater you realize that somewhere on our way you've lost $100 cash.

The tickets cost $100, and you can get a full refund. Would you cash in the tickets to offset the loss?

Only 46% said that they would buy a second set of tickets if they lost the set, but almost everyone would still see the play if they had lost cash. In both cases, you've lost $100 and you must decide whether to see the show. People make different decisions because Problem 7a leads you to put the $100 loss in the "ticket budget," so buying more tickets makes it seem as though the show is costing $200. The description in Problem 7b leads you to put the loss in the "bad luck budget," so to speak, so it seems irrelevant to whether you see the show.

There are several related effects. One is that the cost or gain of some part of an item is considered relative to the cost of the entire item. For example, suppose that you were buying a car for $15,000 and someone told you that you could buy an identical car for $14,975 at a dealership across town. Many people would not consider it worth the trouble to go across town to the other dealership. On the other hand, suppose you were buying a briefcase for $75 and someone told you that you could get the same briefcase for $50 across town. You might well think it was worth pursuing that deal. In each case the cost (traveling across town) and the benefit (saving $25) is the same, but the benefit is evaluated relative to the total amount spent in the purchase, not in absolute terms. Car dealers are notorious for exploiting this irregularity of human reasoning. Dealers are able to convince consumers to buy stereo systems, rustproofing, and other options that they would in other situations consider poor choices by pointing out that the option costs only a few hundred dollars, which is nothing considering that the customer is already spending $15,000.

Another related effect is that of **sunk costs.** A sunk cost is an investment that is irretrievably spent and therefore should not affect present decision making. The investment need not be of money; it could be time, emotion, and so on. Sunk costs almost always refer to an investment that, in retrospect, was spent unwisely. Consider this. Have you ever sat through a movie you weren't enjoying but were determined not to leave because you wanted to "get your money's worth"? When you think about it, you really can't get your money's worth. The movie stinks, and nothing will make it worth $8. The $8 is gone—it's a sunk cost. Whether you stay (and suffer through a bad movie) or leave (and do something more pleasurable) does not change the fact that your $8 is gone.

A related concept is **loss aversion.** *Loss aversion* refers to fact that the unpleasantness of a loss is larger than the pleasure of a similar gain. People may be more motivated to make risky choices in an effort to avoid losses because of loss aversion. In a classic study on this phenomenon Kahneman, Jack Knetsch, and Richard Thaler (1990) showed all the participants in their study a coffee mug. Half of the participants were told that the mug was theirs to keep. The other participants were simply shown the mug. Then all participants were told to assign a value to the mug. They were also told that there was a real market value to the mug, which would be revealed at the end of the experiment. If the price an individual participant assigned to the mug was higher than the market value, the participant got the mug (e.g., if I think it's worth $10 and the market price is $8, I get the mug). If the assigned price was lower, the participant got the cash. The interesting finding was that people who were initially told they were given the mug assigned much higher prices to the mug ($7.12) than people who were merely shown the mug ($3.12). This effect is caused by the way people view the transaction. The people who were shown the mug figured they were going to get a mug or some cash. The people who were told that they owned the mug viewed the transaction as their having to give up their mug (a loss) to get some cash. Because of loss aversion, people don't want to give up "their" mugs, and they demand a high price ($7.12) for doing so.

People's decisions also change when other choices are added, sometimes in unexpected ways. For example, consider Problem 8, described by Eldar Shafir and Amos Tversky (1995; see also Huber, Payne, & Puto, 1982; Tversky & Simonson, 1993).

Problem 8a
Participants were allowed to select one of two prizes:
(36%) An elegant Cross pen
(64%) $6

Problem 8b
Participants were allowed to select one of three prizes:
(46%) An elegant Cross pen
(52%) $6
(02%) An inferior pen

Note that in Problem 8b the addition of the inferior pen rendered the Cross pen more attractive; the percentage of people selecting it increased. The addition of the nonpreferred pen should not influence how one compares $6 with the Cross pen, but it does.

You'll recall that we initially said that we might test people's decisions for two types of rationality: description invariance (making the same choice irrespective of the problem description) and procedure invariance (making the same choice irrespective of the procedure by which preference is measured). The previous examples show violations of description invariance: People make different choices depending on how the problem is described. What about procedure invariance? Research has repeatedly shown that people's choices change, depending on how the choice is elicited. For example, suppose you give people a choice between these two outcomes:

Problem 9
A) 8/9 chance to win $4
B) 1/9 chance to win $40

When asked to choose directly between these choices, most people (71%) prefer Choice A. Now suppose we elicit choice another way. Suppose I ask people, "What is the minimum price at which you would sell your right to this choice? You know that you have an 8/9 chance to win $4, but I am ready to give you cash so that *I* now have an 8/9 chance to get the $4. What is the minimum amount of money I would have to give you for you to sell your right to play this game to me? And what price would you assign to Choice B?" When asked to assign prices, 67% of participants assign a higher monetary value to choice B than to choice A (Tversky, Slovic, & Kahneman, 1990).

Another example of choice varying depending on how it is measured comes from a study by Tversky, Shmuel Sattath and Paul Slovic (1988). They asked participants to select between two programs that were designed to reduce casualties caused by traffic accidents. Program X cost $55 million, and 500 casualties would be expected in the next year. Program Y cost $12 million, and 570 casualties would be expected next year. When comparing them directly, most participants selected the more expensive program that saves more lives. In another version of the problem, participants were told only the number of casualties, and they were asked to assign a price differential that would make the two programs equivalent choices. Nearly all participants assigned a price difference indicating that $43 million is too much extra to pay to save 70 lives. Again, people's decisions vary, depending on how these decisions are elicited.

Finally, consider transitivity. We would assume that if you prefer A to B and you prefer B to C, you will also prefer A to C. Not always. Tversky (1969) presented participants with five gambles, shown in Table 9.2.

Participants evaluated these gambles on wheels that were to be spun. The probability of winning was illustrated by a colored area of the wheel; if the wheel stopped in the colored area, you won the payoff, which was written on the wheel. So preference was elicited simply by picking which of two wheels you'd prefer to have spun. Participants were never told what the expected value of the gambles were, of course; it's shown here so you can see that gamble E is better than D, which is better than C, and so on. Participants started by choosing between gambles D and E. They tended to prefer D to E; even though the odds of winning are lower, the differences in the areas of the spinners seemed small to participants relative to the 25-cent increase in the payoff. Tversky found that this effect held true for all the comparisons; participants preferred gamble C to D, gamble B to C, and so on, because the slightly smaller chance of winning in each case was not as salient as the increase in the payoff. But when Tversky finally offered the choice of gambles A and E, participants preferred E. Why? Because the difference in the odds of winning was now quite apparent. Participants

Table 9.2 *Gambles Used in Tversky's (1969) Experiment*

Gamble	Odds of Winning	Payoff	Expected Value
A	7/24	5.00	1.46
B	8/24	4.75	1.48
C	9/24	4.50	1.69
D	10/24	4.25	1.77
E	11/24	4.00	1.83

preferred what looked like a much more likely chance of winning, even if the pay-off was smaller. The odds difference became salient instead of the payoff being salient. The crucial point for our present purposes is that transitivity was violated.

Thus far, we have shown that people don't make their decisions based on the principles of expected value or expected utility, and indeed that their choices vary depending on how the problem is described or how their preference is elicited. But consider this. How optimal is optimal selection, really? What I mean by that is that truly optimizing means picking the best solution of all those available. Thus, to optimize, you must either evaluate all possible options or have developed a formula that you know will provide the best solution, even if you don't evaluate all options. Either one of those may require a lot of calculation, especially for moderately complex problems. If you are choosing a car, are you going to test drive every type of car on the market? Are you going to thoroughly research the safety of each, and bargain with multiple dealers for the best price on every model before making a selection? Wouldn't those steps be necessary if you are to optimize? Getting the optimal solution may not be optimal at all in terms of the cost to you of computing it.

Herb Simon (1957) suggested that instead of optimizing, people **satisfice.** Satisficing means selecting the first choice that is above some threshold (i.e., that is satisfactory). One option would be to start generating all possible solutions and select the first solution that was satisfactory. Even better would be to start by generating solutions that are likely to be satisfactory. You can't generate all of the possibilities, so you need a shortcut that will let you generate a few that are likely to be satisfactory. What sorts of shortcuts could generate likely-to-be-satisfactory solutions? We turn now to that question.

STAND-ON-ONE-FOOT QUESTIONS

1. What is the difference between normative and rational models?
2. What is the difference between expected value and expected utility, and how are they similar?
3. How do we know that people do not make rational choices?

QUESTIONS THAT REQUIRE TWO FEET

4. Can utility theory explain why people gamble in casinos?
5. Suppose I offered you a bet where if you won, you got a nickel, but if you lost you died. Presumably I would have to give you pretty steep odds in your favor before you would accept such a bet. In fact, you might even say that you would not accept such a bet no matter what the odds are. Try rephrasing the question so that more people would accept the bet (hint: think of a situation in which people don't necessarily realize that they may be risking their lives).

➤ WHAT SHORTCUTS DO PEOPLE USE TO MAKE DECISIONS?

➤ PREVIEW Instead of making detailed calculations to select choices, people appear to use heuristics. A heuristic is a simple rule that requires little calculation and usually yields an acceptable solution. However, heuristics can lead to nonoptimal choices. We discuss three heuristics in this section: representativeness (where an event is judged to be probable if it has properties that are representative of a process or category), availability (where an event is judged to be probable if one can think of many examples of the event), and anchoring and adjustment (where the judged probability of an event is influenced by an initial estimate of its probability). In addition, we examine the sorts of information that would be informative for people to consider in making decisions that they nevertheless systematically ignore. We'll also examine another approach to choice, spearheaded by psychologist Gerd Gigerenzer. Heuristics generally deal with people's ability to estimate probabilities; Gigerenzer suggests that humans are evolutionarily prepared to think about frequencies (how often something occurs) rather than probabilities (the likelihood that something will occur). Although this approach has received a great deal of attention in recent years, its usefulness appears limited.

Most psychologists think people use heuristics as shortcuts when they make decisions. **Heuristics** are simple cognitive rules that are easy to apply and that usually yield acceptable decisions but can lead to errors. Heuristics often are called rules of thumb; they don't require much calculation (if any) and therefore are easy to apply. Heuristics usually yield acceptable decisions but may lead to disadvantageous or inconsistent decisions. A heuristic can be contrasted with an **algorithm.** An algorithm is a formula. It has the advantage of producing consistent outcomes and, if the right algorithm is selected, of producing outcomes that are optimal. The disadvantage is that the algorithm may be complex and difficult to compute. Expected value is an example of an algorithm. If you calculate the expected value of two choices, you will always end up making the same decision, no matter how the problem is described or how preferences are elicited. We've just shown that people don't use expected value or expected utility. It has been proposed that they use heuristics instead of these algorithms. So what do these heuristics look like? We'll take up a number of them in turn.

Representativeness

This heuristic is used when people are asked to judge the probability of some event occurring. **Representativeness** leads you to judge that an event is likely to belong to a category if the event has the features of the category that you strongly associate with that category or if it has features that you associate with the process that generates examples of the category. For example, consider these two descriptions from a study by Tversky and Kahneman (1983).

Problem 10

Linda is 31 years old, single, outspoken and very bright. She majored in philosophy. As a student, she was deeply concerned with issues of discrimination and social justice, and also participated in antinuclear demonstrations.

Which of these is more likely?
Linda is a bank teller.
Linda is a bank teller and is active in the feminist movement.

People think that the second statement is more likely to be true than the first, although the second statement cannot be more likely than the first. There is some probability that Linda is a bank teller, and *if* she's a bank teller, then she may or may not be a feminist as well. The odds of a conjunction of probabilities (i.e., two simultaneous probabilities) can never be higher than one of the constituent probabilities. But people erroneously select the second statement because the description of Linda is that of a stereotypical feminist. The representativeness heuristic dictates that an individual (like Linda) that has features (like deeply concerned with social justice) that people strongly associate with the category (feminist) is likely to be a member of the category.

Representativeness also can be based on the feature that is strongly associated with a process. For example, suppose I toss five pennies two times; first I obtain five heads, then I obtain two heads and three tails.

Which outcome is more likely? The answer is that both outcomes are equally likely; the probability of getting five heads is just the same as getting two heads and three tails. The second toss seems more random, however, because there is no pattern apparent in the toss. For that reason, the second toss is representative of randomness, and because you know that randomness is the process that produces patterns of coin tosses, you judge it to be more likely than the first toss.

Availability

This heuristic can be used to judge the probability of events. To use the **availability** heuristics, you simply try to call examples of the event to mind, and if many examples can be called to mind easily, you judge an event to be more probable. Tversky and Kahneman (1973) offered several examples of problems that they argued participants solved by using the availability heuristic. For example, in one they asked 152 participants whether there are more words in English that have *R* as the first letter or *R* as the third letter. The answer is that there are more with *R* as the third letter of the word, but 105 incorrectly judged that it's the first. Tversky and Kahneman argued that it is easy to think of words with *R* as the first letter but quite difficult to think of words with *R* as the third letter; the mental dictionary, or lexicon, that represents words simply is not organized in a way that lets you access words according to their third letter.

Here's another problem (Tversky & Kahneman, 1973) in which participants may use availability to make a judgment.

Problem 11

Ten people are to form committees.

How many different committees of X members can they form?

One hundred eighteen people were shown this problem, with *X* equal to some number between two and eight. As shown in Figure 9.1, as *X* increased participants' estimates of the number of committees decreased systematically, although the true value increases and then decreases. The experimenters argued that people use the availability heuristic to answer this question. It is easier to mentally generate two-person committees than six-person committees, so they assume there must be more of them.

Availability may also be the mechanism behind **illusory correlation.** Correlation refers to the degree to which two things are related. *Illusory correlation* refers to the fact that people sometimes are inaccurate in judging correlations as they occur in the real world. In particular, people have a bias to judge that events are correlated if they had a prior belief that the events go together or if the two events are natural associates. For example, I may think to myself, "You know,

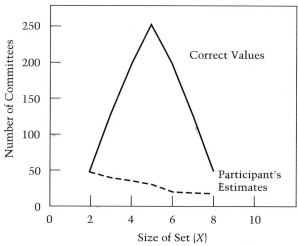

Figure 9.1. *People's estimates of the numbers of committees that can be created from a group of 10 people. The experimenters varied the size of the committees. Note that the graph for the correct values is in an inverted U shape; that's because you can create the same number of committees from two values of X that add up to 10. In other words, every time you create a two-person committee, you have also created a de facto eight-person committee (the people you excluded in creating the two-person committee). Participants' estimates systematically decrease as X increases because it is more difficult to generate committees as X increases (i.e., they are less available).*

anyone who is an actor must be a real egomaniac. How else would they have the nerve to perform in front of large groups of people?" I have the hypothesis that actors will tend to act in an egotistical way. Note that I can observe four possible types of behaviors: People can act egotistically or not, and the person I'm observing may be an actor or not. The idea is that it is more noticeable to you when people act in ways that confirm your expectations (see chapter 5). It is more memorable when an actor behaves in an egotistical way. Furthermore, if someone behaves in a way that is ambiguous—it might be egotistical, it might not—you are more likely to interpret it to be egotistical if the person is an actor than if he or she is not an actor. Meanwhile, the other three types of events (the ones that are not consistent with your hypothesis) are not noticed as much, and not remembered as well. Hence, when you think to yourself, "Is it really true that actors are egomaniacs?" you are able to think of many instances in which you observed that behavior, and because many instances are available, you judge that the general statement must be true.

A considerable amount of work indicates that people are more susceptible to illusory correlations if they get information about the events only infrequently. David Hamilton and his colleagues (Hamilton & Gifford, 1976; Hamilton, Stroessner, & Mackie, 1993; McConnell, Sherman, & Hamilton, 1994) showed that the less information you have about a group of people, the more likely it is that you will develop an illusory correlation about their behavior. In one study (Hamilton & Gifford, 1976) participants read about two imaginary groups of people: the As and the Bs. Participants saw desirable and undesirable information about the As and the Bs in equal proportions; for both the As and the Bs, two thirds of the statements were positive and one third were negative. But more information overall was presented about As than Bs: 24 statements about As were presented and 12 statements about Bs. When participants were later asked to judge the number of desirable and undesirable behaviors that were descriptive of As and Bs, participants overestimated the number of undesirable behaviors attributable to Bs.

Why do people overestimate the number of undesirable behaviors that Bs committed? Because the Bs behaviors were less frequent than the As (making B more distinctive) and undesirable behaviors were less frequent (making them more distinctive), so when B performed an undesirable behavior, it was very distinctive. The relationship to race, ethnicity, and religion in a society is obvious. Minority groups inevitably are more distinctive by virtue of their rarity relative to the majority. On the occasions when members of a minority group engage in negative behavior, it will be distinctive. Once one develops a belief that members of a particular minority group behave in this way, one is still more biased to remember these instances and to interpret ambiguous behaviors as consistent with one's belief.

Anchoring and Adjustment

The **anchoring and adjustment** heuristic is used to estimate probabilities. The person starts with an initial probability value (the anchor) by doing a partial computation of the problem or using a probability estimate that is suggested by some statement in the problem. Then the person adjusts this estimate upward or downward, based on other information in the problem. For example, Tversky and Kahneman showed people this problem and told them they would have 5 s to produce an estimate of the answer: $1 \times 2 \times 3 \times 4 \times 5 \times 6 \times 7 \times 8$. The correct answer is 40,320. The median estimate was 512. When the order of the factors was reversed $(8 \times 7 \times 6 \times 5 \times 4 \times 3 \times 2 \times 1)$ the median estimate was much higher: 2,250. The experimenters interpreted this effect by hypothesizing that participants start this problem by multiplying a few of the first numbers (anchoring) and then adjusting this initial estimate upward, based on the remaining factors. The order of the factors matters because it affects the size of the anchor. Both estimates are too low because adjustments usually are insufficient in any problem in which anchoring and adjustment is applied.

Anchoring and adjustment has been shown to influence many judgments, including preference judgments (Carlson, 1990), judgments of answers to factual questions (Tversky & Kahneman, 1974), estimates of probabilities of events such as nuclear war (Plous, 1989), and estimates of preferences of one's spouse (Davis, Hoch, & Ragsdale, 1986). In one study, anchoring and adjustment was also shown to be important in some legal settings. Gretchen Chapman and Brian Bornstein (1996) had participants read a one-page description of a personal injury suit in which a woman sued a health maintenance organization, arguing that the birth control pills prescribed for her had caused her ovarian cancer. The experimenters varied the amount of compensation the woman sought: $100, $20,000, $5 million, or $1 billion.

Participants awarded greater compensation as the amount of requested compensation increased. The researchers argued that participants used the requested amount of compensation as an anchor and then adjusted their award based on their assessment of the facts of the case.

Information That We Ignore

In the last section we discussed heuristics that can be used to make decisions. Researchers have also argued that there are certain types of information that we systematically ignore when we make decisions. Thus, these are not heuristics that are invoked, but these effects nevertheless have important consequences for decision making.

IGNORING SAMPLE SIZE.   **Sample size** is the number of things in a group that you are evaluating. For example, suppose you want to know how tall the average student at your college or university is. It's unlikely that you will measure each person; there are too many of them. Instead, you'll pick a group of people to measure. How big a group should it be? Sample size refers to the size of the group, and it turns out that whether the sample is large or small has an impact on what you're likely to find in your measurement. When a sample is large, its average value is closer to the average value of the entire group. In other words, suppose that there are 4,000 people at your school, and their average height is 67 inches. If I randomly select 100 people of the 4,000 (sample size = 100) I am more likely to find that the average height of those 100 is close to 67 inches than if my sample size is 10 people.

You can get an intuitive feel for this effect in another way. If I tossed a coin twice and it came up heads both times, you wouldn't find that very remarkable. But if I tossed a coin 50 times and it came up heads each time, you would find that remarkable to the point of being suspicious. Why? We expect that in the long run, we will have 50% heads and 50% tails. In each case, I said that I got 100% heads. But in the first case the sample size was just 2, and in the second case the sample size was 50. If you take an outcome that you know will be true in the long run (i.e., with many observations) such as seeing an average height of 67 inches or 50% heads, it's nevertheless easy to observe that outcome being violated in the short run (e.g., average height of 54 inches or 100% heads).

Sample size is important in calculating such probabilities, but people do not seem to be naturally sensitive to this information. Tversky and Kahneman (1974) gave participants this problem:

Problem 12
    A certain town is served by two hospitals. In the larger hospital about 45 babies are born each day, and in the small hospital about 15 babies are born each day. About 50% of all babies are boys. However, the exact percentage varies from day to day. Sometimes it may be higher than 50%, sometimes lower.
    For a period of 1 year, each hospital recorded the days on which more than 60 percent of the babies born were boys. Which hospital do you think recorded more such days?

    The larger hospital [21]
    The small hospital [21]
    About the same (that is, within 5% of each other) [53]

A large sample is much less likely to deviate from 50% than a small one, but people seem not to appreciate that fact. Kahneman and Tversky argue that people solve this problem by using the representativeness heuristic: Whether a particular birth is a boy or girl is random at each hospital, and because the process producing the gender is random, it seems that there is an equal chance of deviation from randomness.

IGNORING THE BASE RATE.   I'm going to introduce this example by describing the classic problem used to demonstrate it.

Problem 13
    In a certain city there are two cab companies, the Blue and the Green. In this city the Blue company owns 85% of the cabs and the Green owns 15%. A cab is involved in a hit-and-run accident. An eyewitness says she thinks it was a green cab. The eyewitness' vision is tested and it is determined that under the lighting conditions at the time of the accident, she can correctly identify the color of the cab 80% of the time. What are the odds that the hit-and-run cab was green?

Many participants judge that there is an 80% chance that it was green. In fact there is only a 40% chance that it was a green cab. Why? Think of it this way. If I told you that 80% of the cabs were blue cabs, and that there wasn't an eyewitness, what would you say the chances are that it was a blue cab? You'd say 80%, right? (Assuming the drivers of the two companies are equally safe or reckless.) In Problem 13, you still have that information (80% are blue), but now you have additional information based on the eyewitness. The eyewitness account does not invalidate the information about the percentage of cabs; that information should still be taken into account. This information is called the base rate. The **base rate** is the frequency of an event (e.g., the number of blue cabs) among a larger pool of events (e.g., the total number of cabs).

If this seems difficult to understand, consider another example. Suppose you and I are walking along the Champs Elysees in Paris one Sunday afternoon and I suddenly say, "Wow! I just saw a penguin in that cafe. Did you see it? It popped out for second and then ran back in. At least, I think it was a penguin. Call it 80% sure." What would you say the odds are that I actually saw a penguin? Even if vision tests showed that I'm 80% accurate in identifying penguins under those conditions, you'd say chances are very small that I actually saw one. You'd figure that I saw an odd dog, or a little kid or something. Why? Because with the extremely rare exception of a zoo escapee or perhaps the shooting of a television commercial, there are no penguins in Paris cafes. The base rate is extremely low.

People use base rate information unless they also get additional information. Then they usually ignore the base rate. Notice that the base rate should be ignored if the additional information you get is infallible. If the penguin is walking around the street and I have time to inspect it, watch it walk, etc., then the chances of my successfully identifying penguins goes from 80% to 100%. If the additional information is 100% accurate, the base rate becomes irrelevant.

Here's a practical and very important example of the importance of base rate information in medical decision making illustrated by David Eddy (1982). The diagnostic tests physicians use usually are imperfect. In Eddy's example, he considered mammography to detect the presence of breast cancer. Suppose 10,000 women are given a mammogram. In Eddy's problem, if a woman has cancer, the probability was .92 that the test result would be positive. If she did not have cancer, the probability was .88 that the results would be negative. The question they posed was this: "If a woman's test result comes back positive, what are the odds that she does indeed have cancer?" Not .92; again, it depends on the base rate. Consider Table 9.3, where the base rate is set at 1 woman out of 100 having cancer.

Note that a total of 100 women out of 10,000 have cancer (base rate = .01) and that of the 100 women with cancer, 90 have a positive test (.9 probability)

Table 9.3 *Fictional Mammogram Outcome for 100 Women*

	Women With Cancer	Women Without Cancer	Total
Women with positive test	90	1,200	1,290
Women with negative test	10	8,700	8,710
Total	100	9,900	10,000

and that of the 9,900 women without cancer, 8,700 have a negative test (.88 probability). So a total of 1,290 women have a positive test, but only 90 of those have cancer; if you have a positive test, the odds of having cancer is about .07.

How is this possible? It's because of the low base rate. When you have a low base rate, most of the people who show a positive test for cancer are ones who don't have it but who show a false positive. The overall low rate of cancer given a positive test comes about because of the low base rate. We assumed a low base rate of 1% because we said that these 10,000 women were selected randomly. Given that all women are encouraged to get a yearly mammogram, a low base rate among these women may not be unreasonable. The situation would be quite different if we examined a group of women who were getting a mammogram because they had some other symptom indicative of breast cancer (e.g., a lump in the breast). Then we would expect the base rate of the presence of cancer to be quite a bit higher.

REGRESSION TO THE MEAN.   Regression to the mean is a statistical concept. First I'll explain what it is, and then I'll show how it's relevant to decision making. Let's take scores on the Scholastic Aptitude Test (SAT), math and verbal combined, as an example. Suppose I know that if you took the SAT 10,000 times, your average score would be 1,200; we'll call that your "true score." There is of course no way we can know what a person's true score is because no one takes the test 10,000 or even 10 times, but for the sake of argument, assume that yours is 1,200. Now suppose you are going to take the test this Saturday. What is my best guess as to what your score will be? Twelve hundred, because the average score is, by definition, the score that is closest to all the other scores; if I'm trying to make a good guess, 1,200 is the best I can do. But will your score necessarily be exactly 1,200? No, of course not, that's your average score, not the one you get every time. It might be that the test version administered that day happens to contain a lot of questions that you know, you might be feeling really alert and confident that day, and your score might be higher than 1,200. Alternatively, the test might happen to contain a lot of items you don't know, you feel ill, and your score would be lower than 1,200.

Suppose now that the good scenario occurs and you score 1,300. If you took the test again the next Saturday, what is your score likely to be? Well, your true score is 1,200, so my best guess is that your score next Saturday will be 1,200. Your score is likely to drop.

Now here's where things get a little tricky. We don't magically know what your (or anyone's) true score on the SAT is. But suppose I meet someone who scored 1,450. It is possible that that person's true score is 1,500, he or she happened to have a bad day, and if he or she took the test again the score would probably be 1,500 (i.e., would go up a bit). It is more likely, however, that this person's true score is lower than 1,450, and that if he or she took the test again the score would go down. How do I know that the person's true score is more likely to be lower than 1,450 rather than higher than 1,450? Because there are more people with true scores of 1,450 than 1,500. As scores get very high, fewer people have them. Thus, when you meet someone with a score that is very high, it is likely that there are two reasons the score is so extreme; first, his or her true score probably is pretty high to start with, but then the person probably also had a good day when he or she took the test; scores are a combination of the true score plus some factor of luck, and someone with a really high score probably has both factors working in his or her favor to make their score high.

Here's the crucial idea. The next time the person takes the test, his or her true score will not change—that will still contribute to the new score—but there is no reason to expect that he or she necessarily will have good luck again. Thus, when someone has a very high score, you should expect that his or her score will drop the next time he or she takes the test. What we've been calling this person's "true score" is called the mean (in the sense of arithmetic average), and **regression to the mean** refers to the fact that extreme scores regress (i.e., return) to the mean the next time a score is taken.

Very few people know about this phenomenon or factor it into their evaluation of situations. Staying with the SAT for a moment, consider the effectiveness of schools that coach you to improve your score on the SAT. They often make pretty compelling claims about the improvement of students' scores after taking their course. Consider this. Who takes these courses? They are probably taken by students who took the SAT once and were dissatisfied with their score. If you take the SAT and expect to get a 1,200 but actually get a 1,300, you're not going to say to yourself, "Hmm, that score doesn't seem right. I better take the test again." You're going to smile slyly and leave well enough alone. But if you get an 1,100, you may well think, "Oh no! This is a catastrophe! I had better take a course to boost my score!" You take the course and score 1,200 the next time you take the SAT and come away satisfied that the course boosted your score 100 points. But suppose that your "true mean" was 1,200, just as you thought it was. Your score probably would have gone up 100 points even if you hadn't taken the course. This is just one reason such courses are difficult to evaluate. The people who take them typically are people who have taken the SAT, didn't do as well as they expected, and so are trying to remedy the situation. Such people probably will get higher scores if they take the test again without any other intervention because of regression to the mean.

Richard Nisbett and Lee Ross (1980) noted that regression to the mean may account for the oft-noted sophomore slump in baseball. The best first-year player in each league is named Rookie of the Year, but that person's second year, though often good, is seldom as good as the first year. Sports commentators go to some lengths to interpret this phenomenon: The pitchers learned what to throw to him, he became overconfident from all the attention, the expectations were too much for him, and so on. It may simply be regression to the mean. The person named Rookie of the Year will be the player who is both very good (has a high true mean, if you will) and happens to have a great first year because of some chance factors. The next year he will still be a good player but will not necessarily have a great year.

Kahneman and Tversky (1973) described another example from the Israeli Air Force. Pilot trainers noted that when they praised a pilot for flying well, that pilot almost always flew worse the next time. At the same time, if they criticized a pilot for flying poorly, that pilot almost always flew better the next time. They suggested to their superior officers that pilots be criticized for poor

BOX 9.1. DECISION MAKING AND EMOTION: THE SOMATIC MARKER HYPOTHESIS

You may have noticed that emotion has played no role whatever in our discussion of decision making thus far. That doesn't seem right, somehow. Many of the decisions we make have emotional consequences. If I see an attractive woman at a restaurant, I must decide whether to speak to her. No matter what my decision, there are emotional consequences: If I speak to her she'll either be friendly or not (with obvious consequences to my emotions), and if I don't speak to her, I will likely feel regret. Anthony Damasio, Dan Tranel, and their associates highlighted emotional consequences in their somatic marker theory of decision making.

A starting point of the theory was the observation of patients with damage to the medial ventral frontal cortex. These patients perform normally on standard neuropsychological tests of memory, language, intelligence, and so on. Nevertheless, they show marked changes in their personality: They don't respond normally to punishing consequences, they have an overly optimistic view of themselves and their capabilities, and they often show inappropriate emotional reactions. Furthermore, they seem incapable of making long-range plans in their own best interests. They make poor decisions in selecting friends, planning their careers, and so forth.

Damasio and Tranel suggested that these prefrontal cortical areas are important for learning associations between higher-order stimuli and the emotional consequences that follow from these stimuli. In a typical person, when the higher-order stimuli are present, the ventromedial prefrontal cortex reactivates the somatic response that the stimulus has engendered in the past. The somatic response includes feelings generated by the autonomic nervous system characteristic of emotion: a racing heart, sweaty palms, a peaceful feeling, or whatever. For example, when I see the attractive woman the ventromedial prefrontal cortex makes available all the emotional states that might result from various courses of action in this situation (e.g., nervousness in speaking to her, happiness if she seems to like me). Damasio and Tranel argued that these emotional reactions, as well as more logical, cognitive processes, help to limit the possible field of choices.

Thus patients with ventromedial frontal damage make poor decisions because they have lost the ability to make associations between complex stimuli and their consequences. In one study, Tranel tested the emotional responsiveness of ventromedial prefrontal cortical lesions to emotional stimuli. These patients were shown emotionally charged pictures such as nude people, or mutilations while their skin conductance was measured. Skin conductance is a measure of how sweaty one's palms are and therefore provides an indirect measure of emotion. Although the patients showed a normal skin conductance response to a loud noise, they showed no response to the emotionally charged pictures. Patients with damage to other cortical areas showed a normal response.

In a different task that entailed choice (Bechara, Damasio, Damasio, & Anderson, 1994) patients were to choose a card from one of four decks, A–D. They began the task with $2,000 in play money. They received $100 for selecting from decks A or B and $50 for selecting from decks C or D. Each card carried a financial penalty that varied from card to card. Unknown to the participants, the penalties

(Continued)

on the A and B deck were on average greater than the penalties in the C and D deck. In the long run, it was advantageous to select only from the C and D deck. As shown in Figure B9.1, patients with ventromedial frontal damage continued to select primarily from the A and B decks, although patients with brain damage in other regions and normal control participants learned to select primarily from the C and D decks.

Recall that these patients are intellectually intact. This study forcefully makes the point that emotion plays a role in decision making. Decisions can have positive or negative consequences. These consequences are emotional, and we learn from them, in part, because of their emotional content. Patients who do not show normal emotional responses do not make advantageous choices, at least for some tasks.

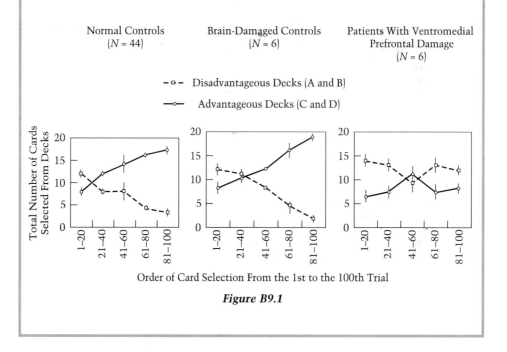

Figure B9.1

performance but not praised for good performance. By now you can see the error in this logic.

Summary

There are two main points in the preceding sections. First, people do not behave rationally when they make choices. This irrationality takes two forms. People's choices don't show procedure invariance (making the same choice no matter how preference is measured) or description invariance (making the same choice no matter how the choice is described). Second, people do not always make optimal choices of the type dictated by expected value or expected utility theory. Note that I'm not saying that people never make an optimal choice.

Rather, we're assuming that there is some set of mechanisms that guides people's choices; if the mechanisms were built to optimize, people would select optimally every time. They don't select optimally every time, so we assume that a mechanism built on a different principle guides choice. So what is it? The argument I've presented here is that people use different heuristics. Heuristics are rules that are easy to use and provide rapid answers.

It's important to emphasize that heuristics usually provide good answers. In the examples we've gone over, heuristics are made to look maladaptive or even foolish. These problems were set up to pit heuristics against expected utility or probability calculations, so the answers based on heuristics aren't optimal, but that doesn't mean that heuristics don't lead to good answers most of the time.

However, you should note that a background assumption runs through this literature; this assumption is that there is a single best decision, and that decision should be based on some assessment of probability. In the last 10 years or so some researchers have argued that people may make rational decisions that are not based on expected utility; expected utility is the wrong criterion. For that reason, many of the problems researchers have used don't ring true; they are problems that reveal little about the way humans actually reason. In the next section we discuss alternative concepts of what may drive human decision making.

Alternative Concepts of Optimality

The substance of the preceding material can be summarized succinctly. Even though people typically say that they strive to maximize their financial rewards, they do not behave in optimal ways. Rather, it seems that heuristics guide their choices. We've said little about optimality, but it's time to take a moment to consider several aspects of optimality.

Others have suggested alternative views of optimality that are pointed criticisms of the heuristics literature. Lola Lopes (1991) argued that the heuristics literature is itself biased. The problems typically offer two solutions: the statistically correct solution and the solution that will be generated if participants use heuristics, which will be incorrect. The problems are always set up so that the heuristic solution is incorrect, and Lopes argues that this results in researchers concluding that people are irrational and poor at reasoning. She even implies that researchers have a financial incentive to conclude that people are irrational; if people can't make good decisions, then perhaps there is a need for decision-making consultants to help them make better decisions, and who better to hire as a consultant than someone who studies decision making? I think that this criticism is unfair and unjustified. Kahneman and Tversky have said repeatedly that their problems are indeed designed so that people are likely to make mistakes but that that does not mean that human decision making is in general poor. Rather, researchers set up situations in which decisions might be poor so as to learn about the mechanisms that guide decisions. They draw an analogy to visual illusions that perceptual psychologists use, such as the Mueller–Lyer illusion shown in Figure 9.2. The fact that people are subject to visual illusions does not mean that their perceptual system is poor. The point

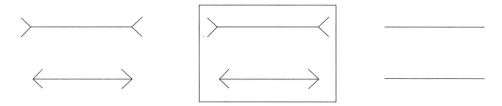

Figure 9.2. *At left is the well-known Mueller–Lyer illusion. The participant is to compare the length of the lines. The line with the outward-turning "wings" appears longer than the one with the inward-turning "wings." At center is the same illusion with a box surrounding the arrows. The box attenuates the illusion. At right are the lines without the "wings."*

of the Mueller–Lyer illusion is to figure out the properties of the perceptual system that make the illusion possible.

Lopes's point was mostly about research strategy (whether it is worth studying mostly mistakes) and the result of that research strategy (the conclusion that people are mistake-prone). A deeper theoretical criticism is that researchers have been so concerned with statistical optimality that they have ignored other factors that contribute to decision making. People make choices based on social contracts, opportunities to cheat, implications for future choices, and so on (Cosmides & Tooby, 1994, 1996; Gigerenzer & Hoffrage, 1995; Gigerenzer, Hoffrage, & Kleinboelting, 1991; Gigerenzer & Hug, 1992). Gerd Gigerenzer cited the following story (which he credited to psychologist Brendan Maher):

> A small town in Wales has a village idiot. He once was offered the choice between a pound and a shilling, and he took the shilling. People came from everywhere to witness this phenomenon. They repeatedly offered him a choice between a pound and a shilling. He always took the shilling. (Gigerenzer, 1992, p. 108)

The larger point is that many choices occur in a social context, and the social context should not be ignored. In the case of the village idiot, the individual choice is irrational by any metric, but it's the social context that guarantees the opportunity for future choices and thus makes the choice beneficial.

Early research on choice conceived of the mind as a statistician, calculating the probabilities of different rewards that might accrue from different choices. Philip Tetlock (1991, 1992) pointed out that other metaphors for choice may be more appropriate. The mind may not simply act as a statistician that calculates probabilities. It may also be a theologian protecting values and principles that are sacred, as in choosing human life over any monetary value. It may sometimes act as a politician mediating between conflicting concerns. It may sometimes act as an attorney prosecuting others who are deemed to have violated social contracts.

So how do these researchers think choices are made? First, Gigerenzer argued that psychologists make a fundamental flaw in treating probabilities as though they are equivalent to frequencies. Probabilities, Gigerenzer says, cannot be applied to single events. A probability of .5 means that an event happens half the time over a large number of trials in which the event does or does not happen. You cannot apply this probability to an individual trial and say that the probability over the long haul means that on the next trial there is a 50–50 chance that the event will occur. This point is fairly deep in statistical theory, specifically in how one should think about probabilities, and there is controversy among statisticians about which view is correct. For our purposes, Gigerenzer's key idea is that the human mind treats frequencies and probabilities differently. He argues that the mind does not work with probabilities very well. He argues that describing events in terms of their probabilities (e.g., the probability is .5 that he brought his umbrella today) is an invention that is only about 200 years old. Before that time, people described events in terms of their frequency (e.g., in the last 100 days, he's brought his umbrella 50 times). Gigerenzer makes an evolutionary argument that our minds are designed to keep track of frequencies, not probabilities. He cites work from animal researchers (e.g., Gallistel, 1990) indicating that foraging animals keep track of frequencies (e.g., of food sources) in their environment. Thus, we have a hard time reasoning and making decisions when problems are presented in terms of probabilities because our minds are not set up to deal with probabilities. By analogy, numbers can be represented as Roman numerals, but you wouldn't want to do long division that way because the representation is inappropriate for the processes you use to do long division.

The implication is that people should perform much better on choice problems if you present them in terms of frequencies instead of probabilities. Over the last 10 years, Gigerenzer has tested this hypothesis in several different paradigms. Gigerenzer and Hoffrage (1995) examined base rate neglect. They presented participants with 15 problems that had been used in the past to study base rate neglect. Participants saw the standard probability version, or they saw the problem in a frequency format. Examples follow.

Problem 14a
   Probability. The probability that a woman at age forty will get a positive mammography in routine screening is 10.3%. The probability of breast cancer *and* a positive mammography is 0.8% for a woman at age forty who participates in routine screening. A woman in this age group had a positive mammography in a routine screening. What is the probability that she actually has breast cancer? _____%.

Problem 14b
   Frequency. 103 out of every 1,000 women at age forty get a positive mammography in routine screening. 8 out of every 1,000 women at age forty who participate in routine screening have breast cancer *and* a positive mammography. Here is a new representative sample of women at age forty who got a positive mammography in routine screening. How many of these women do you expect to actually have breast cancer? _____ _____ out of _____.

Sixty participants each solved 15 problems, including this mammography problem and the cab problem described earlier. They saw each problem in either the frequency or the probability format. Participants averaged 48% correct with the frequency description and 22% correct with the probability description (see also Cosmides & Tooby, 1996; Gigerenzer, Hell, & Blank, 1988).

Why is base rate neglect apparently greater for probability than frequency information? Gigerenzer and Hoffrage argued that when one deals with frequencies it is much easier to keep track of the relevant information. They suggested a thought experiment. Imagine an experienced physician in a preliterate society. She knows of a symptom that signals a serious disease, although it is not a perfect predictor. In her lifetime she has seen 1,000 people, 10 of whom had the disease. Of those 10, 8 showed the symptom; of the 990 who did not have disease, 95 had the symptom. A new patient appears, carrying the symptom. Does the patient have the disease? Gigerenzer and Hoffrage argued that the physician can accurately assess that 8 people had the disease out of a total of 103 (i.e., 95 healthy plus 8 sick) who had the symptom. Thus the odds of this person having the disease is 8 out of 103, or a bit less than 8%. Performing this calculation is simple, given the frequency information, and guarantees that people include base rate information. Note that this problem is conceptually the same as the mammography problem, but it seems much simpler to solve.

So is frequency the answer? Do people make good choices with difficult problems as long as they are translated into frequencies? Briefly, no. A number of countercriticisms have been leveled at the work of Gigerenzer, Tooby, Cosmides, and their colleagues.

Regarding base rate neglect, Charles Lewis and Gideon Keren (1999) argued that Gigerenzer and Hoffrage's version of the problem not only changed the probability information to frequency information but it also changed statements about conditional probabilities to statements about joint probabilities. A conditional probability states the probability that one thing will happen, given that another thing is true (e.g., "If a woman has breast cancer, the probability is 80% that she will have a positive mammogram."). The standard problem format used conditional statements like these. Joint occurrence statements state conditions in which two things are known to be true. For example, "Eight of every 10 women with breast cancer will receive a positive mammography report." Lewis and Keren argued that it was the change from conditional statements to joint occurrence statements that caused the improvement in performance on these problems, not the change from probability to frequency information, as Gigerenzer and Hoffrage claimed. They conducted an experiment pitting the two principles against one another, and reported that it was joint occurrence statements that made the problems easier.

Consider also the story that Gigerenzer and Hoffrage (1995) told about the doctor in the preliterate society who keeps track of frequency information. The fact is that experiments very similar to Gigerenzer and Hoffrage's story have been conducted several times (Estes, Campbell, Hatsopoulos, & Hurwitz, 1989; Gluck & Bower, 1988; Nosofsky, Kruschke, & McKinley, 1992). In one (Estes et al., 1989) participants were shown fictitious medical charts with symptoms such as "runny nose," "fever," "rash," and "headache." Based on the presence or absence of these symptoms, participants were to say whether the patient had disease A or B, and each symptom was an imperfect predictor of the diseases (or sometimes was unrelated to the disease). At the end of the experiment, participants were asked to evaluate each symptom for its diagnosticity for each disease. The key finding was that participants didn't behave at all the way that Gigerenzer and Hoffrage's story predicted. They ignored base rates. If a runny nose was fairly diagnostic of disease A, participants said that anyone with a runny nose probably had disease A, even if disease A was quite rare.

In sum, it is almost certainly not the case that "the mind is a frequentist," as Gigerenzer has flatly stated. For one thing, the data about the importance of frequency information are mixed. However, there is a larger point to be made. It has long been known that the cognitive biases and illusions come and go in different problems. In the case of base rate neglect, the order in which information is presented is relevant (Krosnick, Li, & Lehman, 1990), and varying the base rate across questions can attenuate the effect (Bar-Hillel & Fischhoff, 1981), as can the instructions to participants (Schwarz, Strack, Hilton, & Naderer, 1991). The key question is not whether the effects we've described can be made to disappear; they surely can. The question is why they appear in the first place and what makes them go away. As Massimo Piatelli-Palmarini (1994) pointed out, the Muller–Lyer illusion can be attenuated if you put a box around the arrows, as shown in Figure 9.2. But the fact that it can be attenuated doesn't make the illusion invalid or irrelevant. For that matter, you can eliminate the illusion altogether by removing the "wings" from the lines; again, that makes the illusion no less interesting.

Kahneman and Tversky's (1996) conclusion on this matter serves well as a conclusion to this section of the chapter. They are probably not so far apart in their view from Gigerenzer and from Tooby and Cosmides as it first appears. Everyone agrees that errors are made in some problems but that these errors can be lessened with various interventions. The question is whether it is productive to study these errors as a way to understand normal human reasoning. Although we are far from a complete understanding of decision making, I think we have made clear progress.

However, decision making is not the only sort of problem with which humans are faced. Indeed, another class of problems, like decision making problems, arguably have a single answer. These problems can be analyzed using formal logic, and we start with the same question that began our discussion of decision making: Do people use these formal processes to answer such questions?

STAND-ON-ONE-FOOT QUESTIONS

6. *What are the three heuristics that people use to estimate probabilities, and how do they work?*

7. *What type of information do people typically ignore when making choices?*

8. *What is the core of Gigerenzer's argument about why the problems posed to participants in typical choice experiments are unfair and make people look stupider than they are?*

QUESTIONS THAT REQUIRE TWO FEET

9. *You should have no faith in lie detector tests because people who evaluate lie detector tests ignore the base rate of liars. Explain what this means.*

10. *Suppose you are the president of a large university. Your football team is okay, but not great; it usually wins about half of its games. One year it performs badly, obtaining a record of two wins and nine losses. You decide enough is enough and you fire the coach. The replacement coach does much better the next year, getting six wins and five losses. He asks for a raise. What do you say?*

11. *You may have noticed that it often seems as if projects take longer than you thought they were going to when you planned them. Can you apply the anchoring and adjustment heuristic to guess why your estimate often is wrong?*

➤ DO PEOPLE REASON LOGICALLY?

> ➤ PREVIEW In the first part of this chapter we saw that people don't make optimal choices. What happens when the problem they face is more obviously amenable to logical processes? In this section we start with a brief review of deductive logic, in particular as it applies to conditional statements and syllogisms, the two logical forms psychologists have examined most often. Two important conclusions from this research are that people do not use deductive logic to solve these problems and that the content of the problem has a big impact on people's success in solving it; two problems with the same logical structure may be easy or hard to solve, depending on how they are presented. At this point, people can best evaluate conditional statements that are thought of as permissions ("If you want to do A, you must do B first to be allowed to do A") or precautions ("If you want to do A, do B first as a precaution"). Broadly speaking, the same conclusions apply to people's ability to evaluate syllogisms; people are not logical, and the content of the syllogism matters, but it is harder to say what kind of form allows people to solve syllogisms successfully.

It is not an exaggeration to say that our ability to reason supports much of what we think makes our lives as humans pleasant and interesting; even the simplest actions we perform often are the end product of reasoning processes (for a broader discussion of the role of reasoning in life, see Calne, 1999). We engage these processes dozens of times each day, usually without even noticing that we are doing so. Suppose you're sitting in your room and you know that you have a class at 11:00. You check the clock and see that it is 10:50. You leave your room to go to class. We could say that that simple act has this structure:

If it's almost 11:00, I should leave for class.
It's almost 11:00.
Therefore, I should leave for class.

This example probably seems so simple as to be uninformative, and in fact people are quite good at reasoning in this sort of situation. As we will see, there are many other situations in which people do not reason quite so well.

In the first part of this chapter on choice, we noted that one could specify particular answers to choice problems that were arguably the optimal or correct choices. That is also true of deductive reasoning. In the case of deductive reasoning, these answers can be derived by formal logic. As was true with choice behavior, people do not always select this objectively correct answer; in fact, there are certain types of problems that people consistently get wrong, and they tend to make the same types of mistakes. These errors indicate that formal logic processes do not drive people's behavior. The mechanisms that do drive reasoning are under debate, and we discuss several proposals.

Formal Logic

In this chapter we're discussing **deductive reasoning.** *Deductive reasoning* refers to problems to which one can apply formal logical processes and derive an objectively correct solution. In deductive reasoning problems you begin with some number of **premises.** Premises are statements of fact that are taken to be true for the purposes of the problem. Given these premises, deductive reasoning allows you to make further statements of fact—**conclusions**—that must be true. For example, consider the following:

> Problem 15
> *Premise:*   If an election is contentious, a lot of people will turn out to vote.
> *Premise:*   This election is contentious.
> *Conclusion:*   A lot of people will turn out to vote.

Because of the structure of the two premises, the conclusion must be true. What's important in deductive reasoning is the form of the argument. You don't use deductive reasoning to ascertain the truth of the conclusion in the real world; you use deductive reasoning to determine whether the conclusion necessarily follows from the premises. For example, consider the following:

> Problem 16
> *Premise:*   If snow is black, it makes a good hiding place for coal.
> *Premise:*   Snow is black.
> *Conclusion:*   Snow makes a good hiding place for coal.

The second premise is, of course, false. Nevertheless, the argument is deductively valid, meaning that the conclusion must be true if the premises are true. It may seem silly to get excited about (or even mildly interested in) deductive reasoning if it can lead to ridiculous conclusions like this one, but bear in mind that the point is to let you know what kind of conclusions can be drawn soundly, given the evidence of what you already know. Ascertaining the accuracy of what you already know (e.g., whether snow is black) is up to you.

Inductive reasoning allows one to say that a conclusion is more likely (or less likely) to be true. It does not allow one to draw the conclusion that it must be true, the way deductive reasoning does. Consider this example:

> *Problem 17*
> *Premise:*   If I cook cabbage, then the house smells funny.
> *Premise:*   The house smells funny.
> *Conclusion:* I cooked cabbage.

This conclusion is not deductively necessary. Why? Because there could be other reasons that the house smells funny (I may have cooked brussels sprouts, I may be cat-sitting for a friend, etc.). Although the conclusion is not deductively necessary, we could inductively conclude that it is more likely that I cooked cabbage than if the premises were not true. If my house didn't smell funny after cooking cabbage (because I have a good kitchen fan) or if my house didn't smell funny now, it would certainly be less likely that I had cooked cabbage. Thus, deduction allows conclusions to be made with certainty, whereas induction allows one to change one's assessment of the probability of a conclusion being true.

How do you know when a deductive argument is valid? Deductive arguments have been studied extensively in two formats: conditional statements and syllogisms. **Conditional statements** actually have three statements. The first is a premise of the form "If p, then q." P is a condition, and Q is a consequence; if condition P is met, then consequence Q follows. The second premise makes a statement about whether P or Q is true or not true. The third is a conclusion about P or Q; if the second premise is about P, the conclusion will be about Q, and if the second premise concerns Q, the conclusion will concern P. As shown in Figure 9.3, the classic logical forms call for the conclusion to match the second premise; if you verify truth in the second premise (e.g., state that P is true in the second premise) then you verify truth in the conclusion (state that Q is true in the conclusion). If you follow the examples in Figure 9.3, it is easy to understand why some of the conclusions are valid and some are not. The first one is rather obvious: If I ate too much dessert, then I must be uncomfortably full. The next example states that I am uncomfortably full, but it doesn't necessarily follow that I must have eaten too much dessert; I might have eaten too much dinner, for example. In logical problems, the word "if" does not mean "if and only if." "If P then Q" means that P causes Q, but it does not preclude other things from causing Q. Similarly, in the third example, I didn't eat too much dessert, but it doesn't necessarily follow that I am not uncomfortably full; I might be full for other reasons. In the final example, we are told that I am not uncomfortably full; it must be true, therefore, that I did not eat too much dessert. Also shown in Figure 9.3 are the names used for these different problems. The names are derived from the conclusions. The antecedent is the first part of the conditional statement (P in this case), and the consequent is the second part of the

BOX 9.2. ARE INDUCTIVE AND DEDUCTIVE REASONING SUPPORTED BY DIFFERENT BRAIN STRUCTURES?

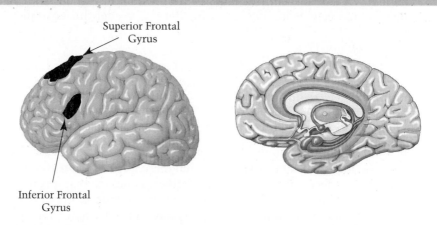

In the text we described the difference between inductive and deductive reasoning. Deductive reasoning is susceptible to the application of logical rules and allows one to draw a firm conclusion about the truth of a conclusion. Inductive reasoning allows one to say that a conclusion is likely (or unlikely) to be true but does not allow one to state that a conclusion must be true or false. Do people use qualitatively different cognitive processes for these two types of reasoning? One way to address that question is to examine the processes in functional imaging and see whether they appear to have distinct neural bases. This approach has been taken by two research groups.

Vinod Goel and his colleagues (Goel, Gold, Kapur, & Houle, 1997) presented participants with three sentences on each trial.

All Capricorns pass their exams.	Lithium is a poison.
No Aries pass their exams.	Poisons cause vomiting in monkeys.
No Aries are Capricorns.	Lithium will cause vomiting in humans.

The examples show a deductive statement set (left) and an inductive statement set (right). Participants saw one statement set and were asked to judge whether the conclusion was necessarily true or false (deductive judgment) or probably true or false (inductive judgment). In the control condition they judged in how many of the sentences people were the subject, thus forcing participants to process the meaning of the sentences. The researchers compared the activations for inductive and deductive conditions with the control.

The results showed that deductive and inductive reasoning led to different patterns of activations. Deductive reasoning was associated with activation primarily in the left inferior frontal gyrus, whereas inductive reasoning was associated with activity in broader areas of the left frontal lobe but showed much greater activity than deductive reasoning in the superior frontal gyrus.

Another study using similar techniques only partly replicated these results. Dan Osherson and his colleagues (Osherson et al., 1998) also presented sets of

(Continued)

three sentences and asked participants to judge the truth of the final statement, its likelihood, or whether the final statement contained elements not mentioned in the first two statements (control). Despite the similarity of the method, these researchers reported very different sets of activations. Deductive reasoning and inductive reasoning both were associated with activity in the supplementary motor area, bilateral cerebellum, right caudate, and left thalamus. The probability task alone was associated with activity in the cingulate gyrus and the right midfrontal gyrus, whereas the deductive reasoning task was asssociated with secondary visual cortical activity.

The difference between these two studies is disquieting. It may be a result of the differences in the control tasks they used, but it may also be a result of the very complex nature of inductive and deductive reasoning tasks. The complexity of the tasks may make it difficult to develop suitable control tasks, and also makes it more likely that participants adopt different strategies. We must wait for more data to clarify some of the discrepancies between studies before we can draw firm conclusions about differences between inductive and deductive reasoning.

conditional statement (Q in this case). You can say that the antecedent or consequent is true (called affirming), or you can say it is not true (called denying). Thus you can affirm or deny the antecedent or the consequent. The two valid forms have their own names, as shown in Figure 9.3.

The other logical form that has been studied in some detail is the **syllogism.** A syllogism, like a conditional statement, has three parts: two premises followed by a conclusion. They differ in that conditional statements include an "if–then" statement, whereas for syllogisms, all three statements are statements of fact. Here's an example:

> All computers are annoyances.
>
> A Macintosh is a computer.
>
> Therefore, a Macintosh is an annoyance.

Note that there are three terms in this syllogism (*computer, Macintosh,* and *annoyance*). In most syllogisms, one term (*computer*) occurs in both premises. That is called the middle term. The conclusion connects the other two terms. By convention, the first term in the conclusion (*Macintosh*) is called the subject and the second term (*annoyance*) is called the predicate. Thus, one could present a syllogism in eight ways, as shown in Figure 9.4.

In addition, syllogisms use some combination of four quantifiers: *all, none, some,* and *some . . . not.* For example, the first line of a syllogism could be "Some computers are not annoyances." Thus, a syllogism could be presented in eight ways, as shown in Figure 9.5, and each of the lines of the premise could use any one of four quantifiers, yielding $4 \times 4 \times 4 \times 8$, or 512, types of syllogisms.

There are too many combinations of statements to allow us to review all possible syllogisms, but a few will give you the flavor. As you can see in Figure 9.5, some are easy and others are hard. (Note: $\therefore$ stands for "therefore.")

The easiest way to evaluate the truth of a syllogism is use a Venn diagram like the ones shown in Figure 9.5. It's also important to try to falsify the syllogism.

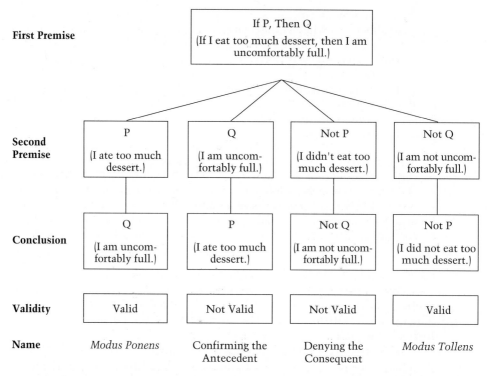

Figure 9.3.   *Figure showing the four common conditional statement forms. The first premise states a condition (if P then Q), and the second premise asserts that either P or Q is not true. Although an infinite number of invalid conclusions might be drawn from the premises, the four conclusions shown here are important enough to be considered in detail in the psychological literature.*

Many syllogisms can be true under some circumstances, but we're interested in logical imperatives: If the first two premises are true, can we conclude that the third statement must be true?

Naturally, you don't need to phrase syllogisms using just letters. For example, consider the syllogism in Problem 18.

M–P	P–M	M–P	P–M	S–M	S–M	M–S	M–S
S–M	S–M	M–S	M–S	M–P	P–M	M–P	P–M
S–P	S–P	S–P	S–P	S–P	S–P	S–P	S–P

Figure 9.4.   *The eight possible ways of presenting a syllogism. Each syllogism is a column. M, middle term (the one that appears in both premises); P, predicate (the second term in the conclusion); S, subject (the first term in the conclusion).*

All A are B.	Some A are B.	Some A are B.	All A are B.
All B are C.	Some B are C.	No B are C.	Some B are C.
∴ All A are C.	∴ Some A are C.	∴ No A are C.	∴ Some A are C.
True	False	False	False

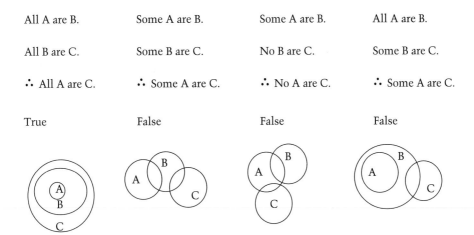

The same false syllogisms can be true under some conditions, but they are considered true only if they must always be true.

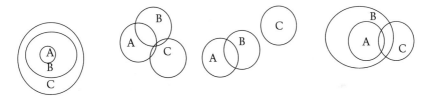

Figure 9.5. *Four sample syllogisms, one true and three false. Note that for a syllogism to be true, it must always be true. The second line of illustrations shows that many syllogisms may be true under some circumstances, but because they are not always true, they are considered false.*

Problem 18
Some cigarettes are made from tobacco products.
Some tobacco products are unhealthful.
∴ Some cigarettes are unhealthful.

This syllogism sounds like it might be true, but in fact it is false. It has the same logical structure as the second syllogism in Figure 9.5, which is also false.

As with conditional statements, the point of syllogisms is to discover how statements can be combined so that a logically valid conclusion must follow. Researchers investigating syllogistic reasoning typically provide people with a syllogism and ask them whether any conclusions can be made from the two premises, and if so what they are. In the next section, we discuss how well people do in solving both conditional and syllogistic deductive reasoning problems.

Human Success and Failure in Reasoning: Conditional Statements

It was long assumed that humans are rational, behaving according to the rules of logic. If a correct deduction can be made, humans will make it, was the thinking. This point of view originated with the ancient Greek philosophers, particularly Aristotle, and continued into the 20th century. Jean Piaget, the famous developmental psychologist, argued that the final stage of cognitive development is characterized by the use of logic. You should keep in mind that people need not be aware of the rules of logic for those rules to guide their behavior; I may speak grammatically, but that does not mean that I can consciously produce the rules of grammar, any more than I can give a precise description of the physics of bicycle riding, although my movements may conform to those physical laws when I ride one.

In the late 1960s Peter Wason (1968, 1969) devised a compelling demonstration that humans do not always reason well. He posed this problem:

> *Problem 19*
>   Figure 9.6 shows four cards. Each card has a letter on one side and a digit on the other side. You are to verify whether the following rule is true: If there is a vowel on one side, there is an even number on the other side. You should verify this rule by turning over the minimum number of cards.

Before you continue reading, think over the problem. Which cards would you turn over, and why?

Most college students (and, more generally, most people) do not answer this problem correctly. The correct answer is that you should turn over the A card and the 3 card. Most people realize that you must turn over the A card. The tricky one is that 3 card. This problem has the same form as the "If P then Q" problems discussed earlier. The cards from left to right give you the following information: P, Q, not P, and not Q. Only P and not Q allow valid deductions. To put it another way, for the card with the A you can see that because there's

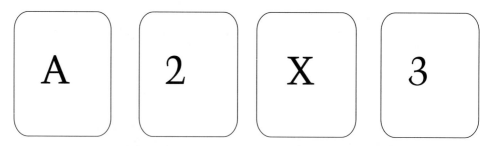

Figure 9.6.   *The Wason card selection problem. This problem embodies a conditional logic problem. The first premise is the rule "If there is a vowel, there is an even number" ("If P, then Q"). Each card is equivalent to a second premise; from left to right they are P, Q, not P, and not Q. By selecting cards to turn over, he participant is deciding which of these second premises can lead to a valid conclusion.*

a vowel on one side, there must be an even number on the other. For the card with the 2, it doesn't matter whether there is a vowel or a consonant on the other side. The X card can also have anything on the other side, but the 3 card cannot have a vowel on the other side; if it does, it disproves the rule. Across a wide variety of studies, about 15% percent of college students answer this problem correctly, although it varies a bit from study to study (for some recent examples, see Ahn & Graham, 1999; Gebauer & Laming, 1997; Oberauer, Wilhelm, & Diaz, 1999). Even students who have just finished a one-semester course in logic don't do much better (Cheng, Holyoak, Nisbett, & Oliver, 1986). These studies indicate that people do not behave in accordance with the rules of logic.

Interestingly, you can make a small change to the task and greatly improve performance. Consider the problem administered by Philip Johnson-Laird and his associates (Johnson-Laird, Legrenzi, & Legrenzi, 1972). A postal worker sorting letters must ensure that they conform to the following rule: If a letter is sealed, then it has a 50-lire stamp on it. Participants saw the back of a sealed envelope, the front of an envelope with a 50-lire stamp, the back of an unsealed envelope, and the front of an envelope with a 40-lire stamp.

Participants were much more successful with this problem: 92% got the problem correct. (In all of these card problems, I'll present the choices left to right as P, Q, not P, not Q, so the correct answers P and not Q will always be at the far right and far left.) The same participants also performed the abstract version of the task (with letters and digits) and only 29% got the problem correct. Johnson-Laird and his associates thought that it was the realism or the concreteness of the problem that made it so much easier for participants, although they admitted it was not clear why realism should make the problem easier.

Other researchers found this realism effect much more elusive, however. Ken Manktelow and John St. B. T. Evans (1979) tried a number of different concrete versions of the problem and compared performance with that on the abstract version. For example, they had participants test rules about what sort of food and drink the experimenter consumed together, such as, "If I eat haddock, then I drink gin," or, "If I eat macaroni, then I don't drink champagne." The researchers also administered the abstract version of the task to each participant. Across five experiments, the researchers observed no advantage for the more concrete version of the task; performance on both the concrete and the abstract was quite low (about 25%). Other researchers using different concrete versions of the problem also observed poor performance (Griggs, 1984; Reich & Ruth, 1982; Valentine, 1985; Yachanin, 1986).

Why were Johnson-Laird et al.'s participants able to do the postal version of the problem? Possibly because they were familiar with this postal regulation. There used to be a rule in the British postal system about the amount of postage and whether the envelope was sealed; perhaps familiarity with the rule is important. Richard Griggs and James Cox (1982) tested that hypothesis. They administered two versions of the card selection (including the postage version) and found poor performance on both of them (fewer than 20% correct) in American college students who would be unfamiliar with the postal rule. Then they administered this problem.

Problem 20

 The cards in front of you have information about four people sitting at a table. On one side of a card is a person's age and on the other side of the card is what the person is drinking. Here is a rule: If a person is drinking beer, then the person must be over 19 years of age. Select the card or cards that you definitely need to turn over to determine whether they are violating the rule.

 The first card read "Beer," the second read "22," the third read "Coke," and the fourth read "17." Participants were to enforce the rule "If a person is drinking beer, then that person must be over 19 years of age." Participants averaged 72% correct, even though none of their participants got the problem correct when they did the abstract version that uses letters and numbers. Griggs and Cox asked participants whether they were familiar with this rule, and not surprisingly almost all of them said that they were. Such results led some researchers to propose that the key aspect of this problem was its familiarity. Indeed, **case-based reasoning theories** hold that we reason about problems by remembering similar problems and how they were solved (e.g., Kolodner, 1992, 1994; see Leake, 1998, for a review; for models that are in part case based, see Anderson, 1993; Newell, 1990). Such theories typically have been implemented in artificial intelligence programs and are able to recognize problems that are similar to known problems. Indeed, Griggs and Cox (1982) reported that many more participants are able to solve a card problem with the rule, "If a person wears a blue shirt, the person must be at least 19 years old" if they have just finished the drinking rule problem.

 Note that we have presented two opposite ideas about reasoning. The first view was that humans use logical rules (such as *modus tollens*) to solve reasoning problems, and that these rules are abstract and content free. By "content free" I mean that any sort of material can be plugged into *modus tollens,* and it works equally well. Obviously, the data we've been discussing show that people cannot plug any information into an abstract *modus tollens* module in their mind; the content of the problem matters a great deal. A case-based approach is the exact opposite. At the start of the chapter we asked, "What set of rules guides our choices?" The answer, according to the case-based view, is "none." There are no rules; there are only cases that we've experienced before.

 A third approach was developed by Patricia Cheng and Keith Holyoak (1985). They suggested that there are abstract mental structures that help us reason, not simply hyperspecific memories of instances. These mental structures are **pragmatic reasoning schemas.** Pragmatic reasoning schemas are generalized sets of rules that are defined in relation to goals. They are called pragmatic because they lead to inferences that are practical in solving problems. Logical rules lead to valid, true inferences that may not be of much help. For example, the rule, "If I have a headache, I should take an aspirin" leads to the valid inference,

"If I need not take an aspirin, then I don't have a headache." This deduction is logically sound but not very practical.

Cheng and Holyoak suggested that people have abstract reasoning schemas for experiences such as permissions, obligations, and causations. The permission schema (which is most relevant to the problems we've been looking at) describes a situation in which a precondition must be satisfied before some action can be taken. The schema is composed of four if–then rules.

Rule 1: If the action is to be taken, then the precondition must be satisfied.

Rule 2: If the action is not to be taken, then the precondition need not be satisfied.

Rule 3: If the precondition is satisfied, then the action may be taken.

Rule 4: If the precondition is not satisfied, then the action must not be taken.

Once the schema is active, these rules serve as a guide to what sort of evidence (if any) is needed to evaluate whether the permission rules are being followed. If you know that someone is not taking the action (not drinking beer) then they need not satisfy the precondition (be over 19) from Rule 2; if they are taking the action, they had better have fulfilled the condition, from Rule 4.

How does the schema become active, or applied to the problem? The problem itself may be described directly as one involving permission (e.g., by use of the word "permitted" or "allowed") or by describing the problem in terms of Rule 1. For example, if I said, "To use this exercise machine, you must put on a safety harness," that would activate the permission schema because I have described an action and a precondition for that action. Prior knowledge (or cases, if you like) may be also important in activating the schema; for example, hearing a description of drinking and age or of paying tuition and attending classes would be enough to activate the permission schema to most American college students.

Cheng and Holyoak (1985) demonstrated the importance of the permission schema by varying whether they gave participants a rationale for the rule they were to evaluate in a card selection problem. They simply gave participants the standard abstract card selection task but phrased it in terms of permission; they said that to take action A, one had to have fulfilled precondition P. The cards said, "Has taken action A," "Has fulfilled precondition P," and so on. They found that 61% of college students they tested answered correctly, whereas only 19% got it right when they did not frame the problem in terms of permission. Thus, even though the materials were abstract and unfamiliar, participants were much more successful when the permission schema was activated.

A related proposal comes from Leda Cosmides and John Tooby (1992, 2000) and from Gerd Gigerenzer and his colleagues (Gigerenzer & Hug, 1992; Gigerenzer & Todd, 1999). Recall that they proposed an evolutionary account of choice behavior. They also appealed to evolutionary concerns in reasoning. They argued that humans evolved as social animals, meaning that we live in communities and have social ties that we rely on to help us survive. A social network requires that individuals either help or punish other members of the community, depending on their behavior. Cosmides and Tooby argued that this rule is so important that our cognitive systems have evolved to make the rule easy to understand. They argue that we are especially good at detecting cheaters—noting people who are violating a social contract—such as underage people drinking alcohol. Cosmides (1989) presented data indicating that performance is much better on problems when they are presented as a social contract than when they are presented simply as a rule. For example, some participants were told that in another society only men with facial tattoos were permitted to eat cassava root. Performance on a card selection task embodying this rule was poor, but it increased when participants were told that cassava root was considered an aphrodisiac, and a facial tattoo was a sign of being married.

An interesting prediction of the evolutionary perspective is that the definition of "cheater" varies, depending not on the logical structure of the problem but on your social perspective. Gerd Gigerenzer and Klaus Hug (1992) provided a compelling example of this effect. They used the rule "If a worker works on the weekend, then that person gets a day off during the week." For half of the participants, the story surrounding the rule encouraged the participant to take the role of the employer; the other half took the perspective of the worker.

Problem 21
    If an employee works during the weekend, then that person gets a day off during the week.

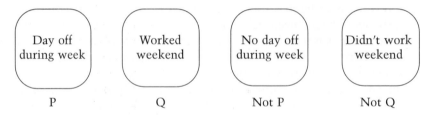

Participants who took the employers perspective tended to select P and not Q: people who took the day off during the week and people who didn't work on the weekend. The not Q card will catch workers who are trying to cheat: those who take a day off during the week but didn't work on the weekend. Participants who took the worker's perspective tended to select not P and Q. Although logically incorrect, note that these participants are still trying to catch cheaters, but this time it's the employers who might cheat. Selecting the Q card ensures that if a fellow worker worked on the weekend, then he or she will get the day off during the week, and the not P card ensures that no one who wasn't allowed to take a day off during the week had worked on the weekend. Seventy-five percent of participants in the employer condition selected P and not Q; 61% of the participants in the worker condition selected not P and Q. (See also Manktelow & Over, 1991.)

Cheng and Holyoak (1989) pointed out that catching cheaters cannot be the only mechanism used in such problems because participants sometimes are effective in solving reasoning problems that do not have the social exchange structure the evolutionary perspective posits. Participants seem to reason effectively with precaution rules as well. For example, Ken Manktelow and David Over (1990) used the rule, "If you clean up spilt blood, you must wear rubber gloves," and found that participants were quite successful in solving the problem. Other researchers have confirmed that participants perform well with permission scenarios, even when they are unfamiliar. For example Cosmides and Tooby (1992) had participants verify the rule, "If you go outside at night, you must have a volcanic rock tied around your ankle." Participants performed poorly in verifying this rule (44% correct) when they were told that they were going out at night to take out the garbage, but when the rule was presented in the context of a precaution (a society that believed that the rocks protected one from night-stalking evil spirits), performance was greatly improved (80%).

So if permission rules are as easy for people as catching cheaters, how does that fit in with the evolutionary story? Evolutionary psychologists have proposed that two separate modules may have evolved (Cosmides & Tooby, 2000): one for catching cheaters and one for dealing with precautions. Critics have charged that this proposal is post hoc (Johnson-Laird, 1999), meaning that the new module is proposed only after it becomes clear that the old module cannot accommodate the findings. If one simply created new modules whenever necessary, the theory could account for anything, but it would account for things only after the outcome was known, and it could predict nothing; that's fatal to a theory.

So in the end, what do we know about how people reason in this paradigm? We clearly know that people are not logic machines who can plug any problem into logic algorithms, with the correct answer popping out. The content of the problem matters. We also know that familiarity of the content (i.e., if the problem is about something you know) is neither necessary nor sufficient for successful reasoning. It's not necessary because we know that people can reason well about unfamiliar things (such as cassava roots and facial tattoos), and we know it's not sufficient because in some situations people reason poorly about domains they probably are somewhat familiar with (e.g., foods and drinks that go together, such as gin and haddock). The question we'd all like to know the answer to is, "What are the critical features of a problem that help people to reason well?" We've discussed evolutionary theories of permission and we've discussed pragmatic reasoning schemas as hypotheses about the key features of reasoning. Later in this chapter we discuss more general theories of reasoning that encompass conditional statements as well as other sorts of problems. But first we turn to another type of logic problem: syllogisms.

Human Success and Failure in Reasoning: Syllogisms

The first thing to know about people's ability to reason with syllogisms is that we're not very good at it. In one study that used many of the possible forms, participants got 52% correct (Dickstein, 1978; see also Johnson-Laird, 1999; Evans, Handley, Harper, & Johnson-Laird, 1999). Chance performance was 20% because they were shown five possible conclusions and were asked to select one. Why do people find syllogisms so difficult? It is not the case that people simply cannot deduce the correct implications and then make a guess. Errors on syllogisms are quite systematic (e.g., Dickstein, 1975), which indicates that people aren't guessing; rather, there is some principle guiding their choice of conclusions, but that principle leads to incorrect conclusions. Researchers have proposed several candidates for this faulty process. Note at the outset that all of the hypotheses we're about to discuss may account for the performance of people on some problems, but none of them is a complete account at all.

One type of error people make is a **conversion error** (Dickstein, 1975, 1976; Revlis, 1975). In a conversion error, the participant reverses terms that should not be reversed. The terms "no" and "some" can be reversed. If I say, "No dogs are plumbers," I can also say, "No plumbers are dogs." Similarly, "some" is reversible; if I assert, "Some knives are weapons," I can assert, "Some weapons are knives."

The terms "all" and "some . . . not" are not convertible, however. If I assert, "All canaries are birds," that does not justify asserting, "All birds are canaries." And stating, "Some mammals are not whales" does not justify saying, "Some whales are not mammals." The conversion error occurs when participants believe that they can safely convert a statement that they should not convert. For example, the syllogism "Some Cs are Bs; all As are Bs" does not have a valid conclusion. But if the person reading it converted the second premise, then you could conclude that some Cs are As, and indeed, that conclusion is a typical error that people make, possibly indicating that they convert the second premise (Evans, Newstead, & Byrne, 1993). Although conversion probably leads to some errors, it cannot be a complete account because some participants are aware that some of the quantifiers cannot be converted (Newstead & Griggs, 1983) and because participants make errors where conversion is not a potential problem.

Another problem is **conversational implicature.** This daunting term refers to the fact that syllogisms are a logical form, and they use the language of logicians, which is not always the same as everyday language, although it is easily confused with everyday language. For example, when the term "some" is used in a syllogism, it really means "at least one, and possibly all." It is perfectly appropriate to say, "Some triangles have three sides," even though all triangles have three sides. In normal usage, people say "some" to mean "more than one, but not all." Thus, when people read "some" in a syllogism they probably think of the term in its conversational sense, meaning "at least one, but not all" instead of the logical sense, "at least one, and possibly all," and indeed there is evidence that people use these conversational terms (Begg & Harris, 1982). Although these interpretations occur, analyses of the types of errors people make indicate that conversational implicature accounts for some but not many syllogistic reasoning errors.

Another important candidate source of the systematic errors people show in syllogistic reasoning is **atmosphere.** Atmosphere is created when the two premises of a syllogism are both either positive or negative or when the quantifiers (e.g., *all, none*) of the premises are the same (Woodworth & Sells, 1935). For example, consider these syllogisms:

No As are Bs	Some As are Bs
No Bs are Cs	Some Bs are Cs
No As are Cs	Some As are Cs

In both cases, the conclusion seems appropriate because it is consistent with the atmosphere created by the premises, either because they are all negative (example on left) or because they all use the same quantifier (example on right). Neither syllogism is true.

Atmosphere explains syllogistic reasoning errors quite well. It accounts for about 50% of the erroneous responses in a multiple-choice format (Dickstein, 1978) and nearly that many in an open-ended test where the participant must supply the conclusion (Johnson-Laird & Bara, 1984). Nevertheless, it is clearly not a complete explanation of syllogistic reasoning. It explains how participants approach only a subset of syllogisms. Furthermore, Johnson-Laird and Ruth Byrne (1989) suggested that the atmosphere effect may be particular to the quantifying terms used in traditional syllogisms. They reported that the atmosphere effect was greatly reduced when they substituted the word "only" for the word "all."

People may also be influenced by **prior beliefs** when they solve syllogisms. Syllogisms are supposed to be a purely logical exercise in which one evaluates the conclusion only in light of its relationship to the premises. In other words, the premises "All *As* are *Bs*" or "All dogs are cats" should contribute to one's evaluation of a syllogism in the same way. In fact, however, people are more likely to reject a syllogism as false if the conclusion is known to be false. John St. B. T. Evans and his colleagues (Evans, Barston, & Pollard, 1983; see also Newstead, Pollard, & Evans, 1992) compared these two syllogisms, which have the same form:

Problem 22

No cigarettes are inexpensive.	No addictive things are inexpensive.
Some addictive things are inexpensive.	Some cigarettes are inexpensive.
Some addictive things are not cigarettes.	Some cigarettes are not addictive.

Both syllogisms are valid, but 81% evaluated the one on the left as valid, whereas only 63% evaluated the one on the right as valid. In another example, Jane Oakhill, Phillip Johnson-Laird and Alan Garnham (1989; Oakhill & Johnson-Laird, 1985) presented participants with one of these two syllogisms:

Problem 23

All of the Frenchmen in the room are wine-drinkers.
Some of the wine-drinkers in the room are gourmets.
Some of the Frenchmen are gourmets.

All of the Frenchmen in the room are wine-drinkers.
Some of the wine-drinkers in the room are Italians.
Some of the Frenchmen in the room are Italians.

Note that these syllogisms have same form ("Italian" has replaced "gourmet" in the second syllogism). No valid conclusion can be drawn from the first two premises, but the majority of participants incorrectly accepted the conclusion in the first syllogism, whereas almost none did in the second syllogism (see also Cherubini, Garnham, & Oakhill, 1998).

In summary, we have reviewed four influences of syllogistic reasoning: conversion errors, conversational implicature, atmosphere, and prior beliefs. There is evidence that each of these can affect performance, but it should be emphasized that these effects do not overwhelm whatever other mechanisms might be at work; many participants get the problem right. Even more important is that each effect applies to only selected problems, and thus their explanatory power is limited. We cannot consider the naming of these effects to be a model of reasoning. We turn next to a discussion of more complete models of reasoning that have been proposed.

General Models of Reasoning

There are two varieties of deductive reasoning models: **syntactic models** and **semantic models.** Syntactic models of reasoning propose that deductive reasoning works as follows: We take the premises as they are given to us, and we apply rules to them in an effort to prove that a conclusion is true (or in an effort to find a conclusion that can be proven true). This process may sound like trying to solve a proof in high school geometry class, and that's not a bad analogy, although the process may well be unconscious, at least in part. The goal for researchers who develop syntactic models is to describe what these rules are. We know the rules are not simply logical rules such as *modus tollens,* so what are they? We'll discuss a syntactic model proposed by Martin Braine (1990); a very interesting syntactic model has been proposed by Lance Rips (1994), but it is a bit too complex to describe in an introductory text.

Semantic models (Johnson-Laird & Byrne, 1991; Polk & Newell, 1995) take a different approach. Whereas syntactic models seek to show that a conclusion is provable from the premises, a semantic model is based on the idea that an argument is deductively true if the conclusion is true under all conditions in which the premises are true. If the conclusion is true under all the different possible conditions that the premises are true, then we say that the argument is deductively valid.

BRAINE'S "NATURAL LOGIC" THEORY.   Martin Braine (Braine, 1990; Braine & O'Brien, 1998) suggested that humans do reason according to a set of rules, although those rules clearly are not the set of rules described by logicians. Rather, he postulated a set of simple inference schemas he called primary skills. Humans probably are born with a genetic predisposition to learn these simple reasoning schemas (for a discussion of the development of logical concepts in children, see Falmagne, 1990). They can be supplemented by reasoning strategies that people learn through experience. Some of these postulates are shown in Table 9.4.

As you can see, the inferences seem childishly simple, but that's the point. These are inferences that Braine argues humans are hard-wired to understand.

How are these inferential schemas used? Braine offered a universal reasoning program. It's a method of applying these inference schemas to derive

Table 9.4   Inference Schemas of Natural Propositional Logic

#	Schema	Example
1	p₁ p₂ pₐ	E.g., There is a cat. There is an apple/ There is a cat and an apple
2	p₁ AND p₂ AND AND p p₁ AND AND p AND ANDp₁	E.g., There is a chicken and a horse/ There is a chicken.
3	A p₁ AND (q, OR OR Q)/ (p AND p₁) OR OR (p and Q)	E.g., There is a grape, and there is a lemon or an egg/ There is a grape and a lemon, or there is a grape and an egg
4	p₁ A[p]	E.g., There is an orange. There is not an orange//INCOMPATIBLE.
5	p₁ OR ORp₁, A[p₁] AND AND F(p₁) INCOMPATIBLE	E.g., There is a dog or a tiger. There is not a dog and there is not a tiger//INCOMPATIBLE
6	INCOMPATIBLE F[F[p] # p	E.g., It is false that there is not a banana/ There is a banana.
7	IF p₁ OR OR p₁ THEN q:A	E.g., If there is either a cow or a got, then there is a pear. There is a cow/ There is a pear.
8	q p₁ OR OR p₁, F(p)	E.g., There is a strawberry or a blackberry. There is not a strawberry/ There is a blackberry.
9	p₁ OR OR p OR A or OR p₁ F[p₁ AND AND pq: p	E.g., It is false that there is both a plum and a pineapple. There is a plum/ There is not a pineapple.
10	F[p₁ AND AND p₁, AND A, AND AND p₁ p₁ OR OR p₁, IF p₁ THEN q₁, Fp₁ THEN q	E.g., There is a fox or a wolf. If there is a fox, then there is a nut/ If there is a wolf, then there is a nut// There is a nut/
11	q p₁ OR OR p₁, IF p Then q, Fp, THEN q	E.g., There is a duck or a goose. If there is a duck, then there is a plum, if there is a goose then there is a cherry// There is a plum or a cherry.
12	q, OR OR q1 IF p₁ THEN q: p	E.g., If there is a grapefruit, then there is an elephant; there is a grapefruit// There is an elephant.
13	Q Given a chain of reasoning of the form Suppose p . . . q One can conclude If p THEN q	
14	Given a chain of reasoning of the form Suppose p .... INCOMPATIBLE One can conclude F[p]	

conclusions from syllogistic reasoning problems. The program consists of two steps, a direct and an indirect. The direct step is a variant of the **British Museum algorithm,** which can be used to derive conclusions from a list of premises. The algorithm works like this:

1. Begin with a list of premises.
2. Apply the rules to the premises.
3. If new conclusions are derived from this application, add the conclusions to the list of premises.
4. If the conclusion to be proven is in the premise list, stop. Otherwise apply the list of rules again, adding new conclusions to the premise list.
5. Continue until the conclusion is proven or until no new conclusions are added to the premise list.

There are safeguards in applying these rules to prevent settling into endless loops where the same conclusions are derived from the same premises again and again. The British Museum algorithm is so named as a play on the idea that given an infinite amount of time, a chimp at a typewriter could eventually produce all the books in the British Museum. In other words, the algorithm is extremely simple, but it is also fairly stupid in the way it searches for a conclusion.

In Braine's theory, if the direct method does not work, a second, indirect method is invoked. The indirect method invokes new inference schemas that are qualitatively different from those used in direct reasoning. For example, one schema proposes a starting point for reasoning that is outside of the premises of the problem. Another schema introduces suppositions. A **supposition** is something you suppose is true and then evaluate the consequences of its being true. If the consequences of its being true are that one of the premises would have to be false, then you can conclude that the supposition was incorrect. For example:

1. If he brought a cake, we'll have dessert.
2. We're not having dessert.
3. He did bring the cake.   (a supposition)
4. We're having dessert.   (*modus ponens* applied to 1 and 3)

There is a contradiction between a premise ("We're not having dessert") and a conclusion ("We're having dessert") that was derived from a supposition. Therefore, the supposition must be wrong.

5. Therefore, he did not bring the cake.

Braine proposed that the indirect method of deduction is more difficult to use than the direct method because it is not certain that one will find the line of reasoning that will lead to a successful solution to the problem. Braine proposed that heuristics influence the choice of inference schemas in indirect reasoning.

Braine's model has had some success in accounting for the pattern of data produced by participants. As his theory predicts, if you give participants simple problems that require application of only one of the inference schemas, then almost no one errs, even children (Braine & Rumain, 1983). An example of such a problem is as follows:

Problem 24
There is a firefighter or a police officer. There is not a firefighter.
Conclude: There is a police officer.

Furthermore, there is evidence that participants' accuracy decreases on problems as the number of inference schemas necessary to solve the problem increases (Braine, Reiser, & Rumain, 1984). Many logical problems simply are too complicated for the system to handle, even when the indirect method is used. Braine and his colleagues did not propose that humans simply shut down when faced with these problems. Rather, they proposed that their model accounts only for certain types of (fairly simple) reasoning problems, and that when other problems are posed, people recruit other reasoning methods.

JOHNSON-LAIRD'S MENTAL MODELS THEORY.   Philip Johnson-Laird and his associates (Johnson-Laird, 1999; Johnson-Laird & Byrne, 1991) proposed a very different approach to reasoning. They proposed that the meaning, or semantics, of a problem is crucial to its solution. Braine's model treats the premises of a conclusion as logical statements; it is assumed that the premises you read or hear are translated directly into some format that can be plugged into the inference schemas that combine to allow inferences to be made. In the mental models theory, the meaning of the premises remain in a meaning-based format. The premises are used to construct a mental model of the situation. Each **mental model** represents a possible configuration of the world; for example, the premise on the left of Figure 9.7 might give rise to mental images on the right (which are based on mental models; we won't represent the mental models themselves for the sake of simplicity).

Mental models don't just represent the world; they can also be used for deduction because you can combine mental models. Suppose you saw the syllogism on the left of Figure 9.8 and generated the mental models on the right.

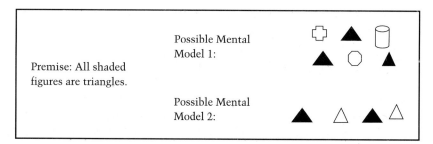

Figure 9.7.   *Mental models for the premise "All shaded figures are triangles." The mental models are presented as visual images for simplicity; true mental models are meaning-based structures that might be used to generate mental images but are not images themselves.*

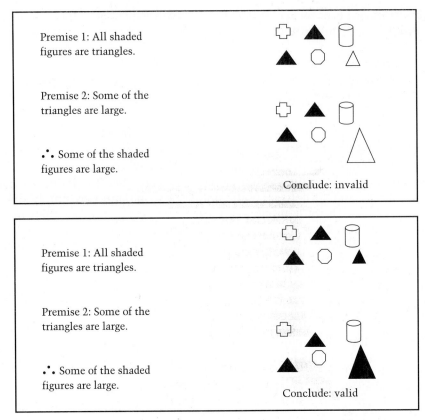

Figure 9.8. *This example shows how your mental model might change as new premises are stated and how you would use the mental model to evaluate the validity of a conclusion. Look at the top example. The first mental model is one of several possible, based on this premise. The mental model is changed when the second premise is stated. The conclusion, "Some of the shaded figures are large," is inconsistent with the mental model, so you would conclude that the syllogism is invalid. In the second example, you start with a different mental model of Premise 1. With this mental model, one ends up accepting the validity of the conclusion.*

The fact that more than one mental model can represent a premise has important implications for the way the theory works. Figure 9.8 shows two examples of mental models that might be drawn from a pair of premises. In the top example, the valid conclusion is drawn. In the bottom example, an invalid conclusion is drawn. This invalid conclusion is traceable to the image based on the mental model for the first premise. The person may have committed a conversion error, believing that because all shaded figures are triangles, it was also true that all triangles are shaded figures.

How does one avoid such errors? One must generate multiple mental models representing all possible situations, given the stated premises. Thus, one may have to keep several mental models in working memory simultaneously, corresponding to these multiple possibilities. A conclusion is possible if it is represented in one of the models; it is impossible if it is represented in none of the models, and it is necessary if it is represented in all of the models.

It sounds as if the theory predicts that one's success in reasoning depends strongly on the size of working memory. If you have a bigger working memory, you'll be able to maintain more mental models simultaneously and will therefore be able to keep track of more possible ways that premises can be interpreted. That is exactly what the theory predicts, and that prediction seems to be supported by the data; as syllogisms offer more possible interpretations, participants have a harder time evaluating their truth (Johnson-Laird, Byrne, & Schaeken, 1992).

John St. B. T. Evans and his colleagues (Evans, Handley, Harper, & Johnson-Laird, 1999) presented participants with 256 syllogisms, in each case asking them to evaluate the conclusion as necessary, possible, or impossible. The mental models theory was quite successful in predicting participants' responses. Of 36 problems whose conclusions are necessary, 18 could be solved with a single mental model and 18 required multiple models, according to a previous analysis by Johnson-Laird and Bara (1984). Evans and his colleagues found that 81% of the single-model problems were evaluated correctly, but just 59% of the multiple-model problems were.

Limitations of working memory seem only to predict that people will fail on problems that are difficult, but the types of errors that people make are systematic, beyond this failing. Johnson-Laird proposes that many errors arise from the **principle of truth,** which states that people tend to construct mental models representing only what is true and not what is false. One reason they do so is to reduce the load on working memory. For example, for the premise "There is a mailbox or a pair of glasses" they would construct three mental models (shown as sample mental images in the right part of Figure 9.9) showing the mailbox, or glasses, or both. They would not construct the mental models at left, which shows what is absent in each case.

Most of the time, failing to explicitly represent all possibilities leaves the reasoner unable to draw a conclusion. Sometimes, however, it leads systematically to an incorrect conclusion. Consider this problem regarding a hand of cards.

Problem 25
If there is a king in the hand then there is an ace in the hand, or else if there is a queen in the hand then there is an ace in the hand.
There is a king in the hand.
What, if anything, follows?

Most people believe that "There is an ace in the hand" is a valid conclusion, but that is a fallacy. You may be relieved to know that this fallacy is so powerful that when Philip Johnson-Laird first started working with this problem, he thought the computer had made an error when it reported it to be a fallacy. Why do people make this error? Johnson-Laird and Fabien Savary (1999) argue that it is because they fail to construct mental models that include what is not true. Given the premises, people construct the two mental models in Figure 9.10.

Figure 9.9.   *Mental models people construct from the statements
"If there is a king in the hand, then there is an ace in
the hand, or else if there is a queen in the hand, then
there is an ace in the hand." This model fails to capture
a key aspect of the statement: There are two conditionals in the statement, only one of which is true.*

The problem states that one of two conditional statements is true: either
(if there is a queen there is an ace) or else (if there is a king there is an ace). Each
model describes one of the two conditionals. The second premise (there is a
king) seems to pick out which of the two hands is true: It's the one with the king
in it, and that hand has an ace in it, so it seems valid to conclude that there is
an ace in the hand.

But you have to keep in mind that the conditional statements are disjunctive (i.e., they include the term *else*, meaning one is true or the other is
true). Thus, either (if there is a queen there is an ace) or (if there is a king there

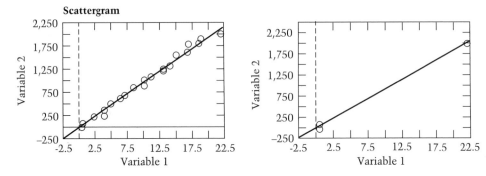

Figure 9.10.   *Graphs showing that a formula (in this case the formula for a line) may successfully describe a set of data. That a formula describes a set of data is
much more impressive in the graph on the left because there are many data
points. It's much less impressive in the graph on the right, which has just
three data points.*

is an ace). If it is true that (if there is a queen there is an ace) then it is not true that (if there is a king there is an ace). You don't know which of the two conditionals is true.

Suppose it is true that (if there is a queen there is an ace). In that case it is not true that (if there is a king there is an ace). If it is not true that (if there is a king there is an ace), then knowing that there is a king means that there is not an ace. Now suppose the other conditional is true. If it is true that (if there is a king there is an ace), then knowing that there is a king in the hand does indeed lead to the conclusion that there is an ace. Hence, you have to know which of the two conditionals is true before you can draw any conclusions about the problem.

In Johnson-Laird and Savary's (1999) Experiment 1, none of the participants got the problem correct. Performance improved to 25% when the experimenters changed the phrasing to make it more explicit to participants that only one of the two conditional statements could be true.

In sum, the mental models theory has had a lot of success. It successfully accounts for participants' responses and even predicts fallacies that people will evaluate as true. Furthermore, it can be applied not only to syllogisms (as we have discussed) but to reasoning problems such as Wason's card selection task. Nevertheless, the theory has its critics, as you would expect, some of whom are champions of other theories. A recent development has been an altogether different approach emphasizing statistical selection of choices. We complete our discussion with this model.

Rational Analysis Models

This approach to reasoning got its start from an article published by Kris Kirby in 1994. Kirby began his article with a nice thought experiment that I'll paraphrase: "If you asked me to add two and two and told me you'd give me $10 to say anything but 'four,' I'd say 'five.' It would be a mistake to conclude from my answer that I can't add." His point constitutes the heart of **rational analysis models:** When we give participants reasoning problems, they may answer on the basis of their assessment of the costs and benefits of particular answers rather than on a logical basis. That doesn't mean that they can't reason.

To put it another way, consider the drinking version of the Wason card sort, but this time with more "people" to evaluate.

Problem 26

The cards in front of you have information about six people sitting at a table. On one side of a card is a person's age and on the other side of the card is what the person is drinking. Here is a rule: If a person is drinking beer, then the person must be over 21 years of age. Select the card or cards that you definitely need to turn over to determine whether they are violating the rule.

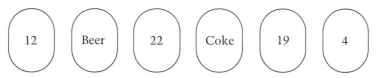

BOX 9.3. MENTAL MODELS, SPATIAL REASONING, AND BRAIN IMAGING

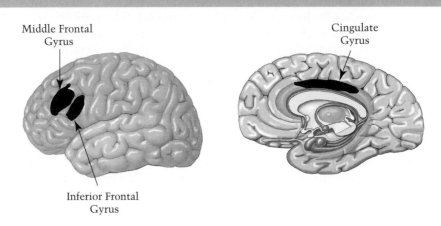

Middle Frontal Gyrus

Cingulate Gyrus

Inferior Frontal Gyrus

Johnson-Laird's mental models theory can be applied to different forms of reasoning, as described in the text. Some of the problems used are classic syllogistic forms, like the one on the left. Others are relational problems like the two shown at center and on the right.

Some officers are generals.	Officers are next to generals.	Officers are heavier than generals.
No privates are generals.	Privates are behind generals.	Generals are heavier than privates.
Some officers are not privates.	Privates are behind officers.	Privates are lighter than officers.

Introspection might indicate that you would use a spatial representation to evaluate the second set of statements because the descriptors are spatial. One could also use a spatial representation to evaluate the set on the right. Vinod Goel and his colleagues (Goel, Gold, Kapur, & Houle, 1998) asked participants to evaluate these three types of stimuli—syllogisms, spatial relational, and nonspatial relational—to examine whether parts of the brain known to be involved in spatial reasoning are activated differentially.

The results showed that there was considerable overlap in the activations associated with each condition. In all three conditions, the most active areas were the left inferior frontal gyrus, the left middle frontal gyrus, and the left cingulate gyrus. Other areas showed activity particular to individual tasks in various parts of the left temporal lobe, and for the nonspatial task, in the globus pallidus.

There are two important points in this study. The first is that the overlap in the activations for the different reasoning tasks is fairly impressive. It is not complete, but the most active areas are the same for all three problem types. Even

(Continued)

though one of the problems is explictly spatial, the other is not, and the third is at least amenable to a spatial representation. The other noteworthy feature of the activations is that none of them are in areas typically associated with spatial reasoning (i.e., right hemisphere parietal areas).

The predominance of left hemisphere activations indicates that reasoning may be largely language based, even when the contents of the reasoning problem are inherently spatial. Still, it would be wise to delay final judgment until there has been further work on this topic.

Are you really going to snatch the sippy cup from the 4-year-old and inspect it to ensure that she's not drinking beer? Kirby conducted this experiment, and he reported that 65% of participants said they would check the 4-year-old, compared to 86% who said they would check the 19-year-old (the drinking age was 21 when this experiment was conducted). Kirby could also manipulate how likely participants were to select cards by giving them slightly different cover stories. When he said that the boss gets very angry when customers are insulted by having their ID checked, only 47% checked the ID of the 12-year-old. When they were told that failing to check ID could result in the loss of the liquor license (and their job), 86% of participants checked the 12-year-old. In other experiments, Kirby used abstract versions of the card selection problem to make the same points; people are sensitive to the likelihood of gaining useful information by flipping the card, and they are sensitive to the benefit of seeking that information. You're sensitive to the likelihood that a 4-year-old is drinking beer, and you're sensitive to the costs and benefits of making that investigation. Kirby's conclusion was that some of the problems that have been used to study reasoning may not be optimal for that purpose because concerns other than reasoning go into people's answers to the problems that are posed.

A similar perspective that leads to a very different conclusion has been offered by Nick Chater and Mike Oaksford (1999; Oaksford & Chater, 1996). Oaksford and Chater used a statistical method that they claimed could evaluate the amount of information one was likely to get when each card was turned over. They assumed that people turn over cards in the Wason task that are most likely to reduce uncertainty in the problem. Kirby invoked the notion of expected utility (described earlier in this chapter) as a way of predicting which cards people will turn over. Oaksford and Chater instead argued that people calculate how much information they are likely to get from a card, and on that basis decide whether to turn it over. "Information" in their sense refers to how much uncertainty is present in the first place and how likely it is that turning over a card will reduce that uncertainty. For example, we know that 4-year-old kids almost never drink beer, so it's not very likely that we're going to learn anything by investigating the 4-year-old.

A key question in such a formulation is, "How do we know that 4-year-olds don't drink beer?" The answer is prior experience. In other words, the base rate of 4-year-olds drinking beer is extremely low. Oaksford and Chater point out that most researchers act as though the potential relationships of P and Q are equally probable in the world (i.e., that given P there is an equal likelihood of Q or not Q). That may or may not be, and the prior probabilities should be accounted for in analyzing where to seek more information. Chater and Oaksford (1999) developed a model of syllogistic reasoning in the same spirit.

Oaksford and Chater's model has received a great deal of attention. Many researchers feel that they are on the right track in emphasizing that people's main motivation in reasoning tasks may be to seek out information that will be maximally informative, not necessarily information that will lead to answers that are correct according to formal logic. Still, their model has detractors, such as those who claim that it cannot account for some data (e.g., Almor & Sloman, 1996) and those who claim that Oaksford and Chater did not measure information correctly (Laming, 1996).

Summary

We've reviewed two types of reasoning problems. Conditional reasoning problems ("If P, then Q") can be difficult or easy depending on the materials used, and we examined several theories accounting for these effects, including the evolutionary perspective and pragmatic reasoning schemas. The second type of problem was the syllogism. We reviewed four features of syllogisms (e.g., atmosphere) each of which has some effect on performance but none of which is a complete theory of reasoning. We also examined three general theories of reasoning: Braine's natural logic theory, which emphasizes simple inference schemas and a syntax by which they can be combined; Johnson-Laird's mental models theory, which emphasizes the semantic content of the premises; and Chater and Oaksford's rational analysis model, which emphasizes that people may have nonlogical reasons that motivate their choices in a reasoning problem.

In this chapter, we have been concerned with problems for which there is arguably an optimal solution. Many problems humans face do not have this structure; they are more open ended. In chapter 11 we discuss these problems.

STAND-ON-ONE-FOOT QUESTIONS

12. *What is the difference between deductive and inductive reasoning?*

13. *Is it true that familiarity is the critical feature that determines whether people will successfully evaluate a conditional statement such as the one embodied in the Wason card selection task?*

14. *What is the difference between a syntactic and a semantic model of reasoning?*

QUESTIONS THAT REQUIRE TWO FEET

15. Case-based reasoning seems to have been given little attention. How often do you think you engage in case-based reasoning?
16. We saw before that conditional statements may be hard or easy to evaluate, and we saw in this section that syllogisms may be hard or easy to evaluate. Do you see any similarities between what makes each type of problem hard or easy?
17. The rational models seem to argue that people don't actually reason in reasoning problems but rather try to maximize the amount of information they can obtain. Assuming that this result is true, does it mean that people don't reason?

KEY TERMS

decision making
rational
transitivity
normative theories
expected value
expected utility
problem frame
psychic budget
sunk costs
loss aversion
satisfice
heuristics
algorithm
representativeness
availability

illusory correlation
anchoring and
    adjustment
sample size
base rate
regression to the
    mean
deductive reasoning
premise
conclusion
inductive reasoning
conditional
    statements
syllogism
case-based reasoning
    theories

pragmatic reasoning
    schemas
conversion error
conversational
    implicature
atmosphere
prior beliefs
syntactic models
semantic models
British Museum
    algorithm
supposition
mental model
principle of truth
rational analysis
    models

10

Problem Solving

In chapter 9, we discussed decision making and reasoning. A notable feature of these kinds of problems was that they were closed-ended, meaning that there was a limited number of possible answers or that a subset of the possible answers was provided, with the person left to choose between them. In this chapter we discuss problem solving. **Problem solving** can be defined very generally as any situation in which a person has a goal that is not yet accomplished. That general definition encompasses what we called decision making in the last chapter, but when psychologists talk about problem solving they mean open-ended problems in which the person knows the goal, but there is nothing in the problem describing how to accomplish the goal.

According to this definition of *problem*—you have a goal and you have not accomplished the goal—you are faced with problems dozens of times each day. You want a pizza and you don't have one; that's a problem. You want to be outside, but you're not currently outside; that's a problem. These problems don't seem very thrilling. They are uninteresting because you have faced them (and solved them) countless times before. Your response to these problems is so automatic that it doesn't even feel like there is a problem to be solved. When you think of a problem you more likely think of something like one of those little puzzles made out of two twisted nails that you are to disentangle.

These problems—getting outside and untwisting nails—are at opposite ends of a continuum, namely, a continuum of relevant experience. The getting outside problem can be solved based on past experience. The twisted nails problem usually cannot. In the nails problem, you don't have much in memory that will help you, so you must recruit processes that will give you some guidance as to how to try to solve the problem, even though you don't have relevant experience. We could imagine that all problems will vary on this dimension (the extent to which previous experience guides us in our attempts to solve the problem).

Indeed, the ends of this continuum illustrate two main themes of problem-solving research: the importance of memory (i.e., prior experience) and the importance of more general problem-solving routines. Many problems are not at the extremes I've just described: They are neither completely familiar so that one simply needs to remember how it was solved last time, nor completely unfamiliar, so that one has no guidance from past experience. Rather, most problems are solved through a combination of memories of similar problems that might be applicable to the current problem and general purpose problem-solving strategies.

To study the general problem-solving routines, psychologists have used problems with which most people are unfamiliar to force people to rely only on these general strategies, not on memories of similar problems. Our first question is, **"How do you solve a problem if you have had no experience with similar problems?"** As we'll see, there do seem to be general-purpose strategies that people engage to deal with this sort of problem.

Again, it is not always the case that people have complete knowledge or absolutely no knowledge of a problem. Often, they have some knowledge that might be applicable to a problem. **What do you do when you have some knowledge that seems to apply to a problem but no experience with the specific problem posed?** You would think that some experience would be better than no experience. As we'll see, that's not always true. Experience with similar problems can help if you can draw an analogy between the current problem and the familiar problem, but it is difficult to draw analogies except in a few cases. Furthermore, prior knowledge can put you in a mental rut; you might approach new problems in the same way that you approached old problems, even though that approach is not appropriate.

Finally, we'll consider **what happens when people have knowledge that is relevant to a task.** As you might guess from the forgoing discussion, there are two main sources of skill in problem solving. You can be good at using the general purpose processes, or you can have lots of problem solutions in secondary memory, so that when a problem comes along, it is likely to be one that you know how to solve. It appears that both of these factors can contribute to skill, and we discuss them both.

> ## ➤ HOW DO YOU SOLVE A PROBLEM IF YOU HAVE HAD NO EXPERIENCE WITH SIMILAR PROBLEMS?

> ➤ PREVIEW The heart of problem solving is change. You are presented with a situation that is not satisfactory, and you want to change it in some way to meet a goal. The problem is that there are usually so many ways to make changes that it is unclear how to proceed. If you have experience with a problem, you can proceed as you did the last time you faced the problem. If you have no relevant experience, you are forced to fall back on general strategies that can be applied to unfamiliar problems. One—working forward—is simply to look for ways to get closer to the goal. This strategy sounds sensible, but as we'll see it is often ineffective. A second strategy is to begin at the goal and see whether you can mentally work your way back to the beginning of the problem. The third and most effective strategy is called means–ends analysis, and it provides a set of guidelines that combines working forward and backward on problems and dictates when it is effective to set subgoals that should be completed before the main goal of the problem should be tackled. We'll discuss evidence that humans use means–ends analysis on some problems.

Problem Spaces

Before we get to the particulars of how people solve unfamiliar problems, we need to discuss how psychologists think about and describe problems. Allan Newell and Herb Simon (1972) emphasized the usefulness of thinking of problems in terms of a problem space. A **problem space** can be thought of as all possible configurations a problem can take. For example, consider the classic puzzle called the Tower of Hanoi depicted in Figure 10.1.

There is a board with three pegs. There are three rings of decreasing size on the leftmost peg. The goal is to get all of the rings on the rightmost peg. There are three rules about how you can move the rings:

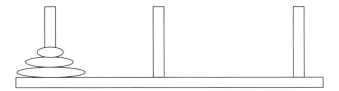

Figure 10.1.   *The Tower of Hanoi puzzle.*

- You can move only one ring at a time.
- You can move only the topmost ring on a peg.
- You cannot put a larger ring on top of a smaller ring.

The Tower of Hanoi will be used as an example several times in this chapter. You'll probably get more out of these examples if you try to work the problem yourself. Just get three coins of varying size (e.g., a quarter, a nickel, and a penny) and try the problem yourself using Figure 10.2.

The problem space for the Tower of Hanoi puzzle can be thought of as all possible positions that the puzzle board might take on. We could represent that problem space as in Figure 10.3.

Each position the puzzle can take is called a state of the problem space. More generally, a **problem state** is a particular configuration of the elements of the problem. Notice that there are links between the different states in the problem space. These links indicate the possible paths along which you can move through the problem space. You can't simply jump from one state in the problem space to another; you must move from state to state by way of the links. What determines how the states are linked? The links represent operators; an **operator** is a process one can apply to the problem to change its configuration (i.e., to change where you are in the problem space). For example, an operator in the Tower of Hanoi problem is to move a disk.

Typically, certain conditions must be met before you are allowed to apply an operator. In the Tower of Hanoi, three conditions (described in the figure)

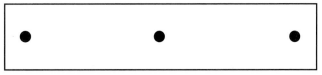

Figure 10.2.   *Use this figure as a board to work the Tower of Hanoi puzzle shown in Figure 10.1. Just put three coins of decreasing size (e.g., quarter, nickel, penny) on the leftmost dot and try to move the coins to the rightmost dot, following the rules: You can move only one coin at a time, you can move only the topmost coin on a stack, and you can't put a larger coin on top of a smaller coin. If this is puzzle seems too easy, use four coins.*

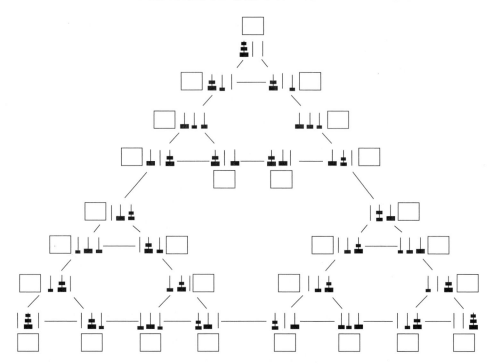

Figure 10.3. *Problem space for the Tower of Hanoi puzzle. It's easist to understand the figure by starting at the top. Notice that your choice of moves at this point is represented in the figure. Also note that you always have the option of moving backward in the space by returning to the position you just occupied.*

must be met before you can apply the operator of moving a disk. In summary, you start at one point in the problem space (all rings on the left peg), you are trying to reach another point in the problem space (all rings on the right peg), and you move through the space by applying operators.

From this conceptualization you can see that the key to problem solving is selecting the right operators. The right operators are the ones that will move you efficiently through the problem space to the goal. Obviously, if you simply move through the problem space randomly, you might accidentally end up at the goal, but you'd like to be assured that you will reach the goal. Furthermore, it would be desirable to reach the goal directly rather than via a circuitous route through the problem space. How do you select operators to ensure a reasonably direct route to the goal?

You could imagine doing a **brute force search.** In a brute force search, you examine every possible answer until you find the correct one. For example, suppose you were working a crossword puzzle and saw the letters "_ a l t" with the clue "seasoning." You could sequentially substitute each letter of letter of the alphabet ("<u>a</u> a l t," "<u>b</u> a l t," "<u>c</u> a l t") in the blank space until you got to "s" and solve it with "salt." The advantage of brute force search is that it's very simple to apply. The disadvantage is that it doesn't restrict the part of the problem space through which you search; you have to try all the possibilities. As the number of possibilities to be tried increases modestly, the number of combinations to be tried increases very rapidly. This phenomenon is called **combinatorial explosion.** For example, suppose the clue was "_ al _." You could still do a brute force search by putting "a" in the first blank space and trying the letters of the alphabet in the second blank space ("a a l a," "a a l b," "a a l c," etc.). If that doesn't work, you would try the next letter of the alphabet in the first space and the others in sequence in the second blank space ("b a l a," "b a l b," "b a l c," etc.). Notice that although we've doubled the number of blank letters, the number of states in the problem space that we must explore has much more than doubled. Specifically, if there are 26 possible letters to fill in the blanks and 2 blanks to be filled, there are 26^2 (676) possible combinations of letters in the blanks. If we add one more blank, the possibilities increase to 26^3 (17,576). Thus, it's clear that a brute force search is often impractical.

What do we use instead? It appears that people use **heuristics** to guide their search for operators that will move them through the problem space. A heuristic in problem solving means the same thing that it did in reasoning and decision making: It's a simple rule that can be applied to a complex problem. It requires minimal computation and often yields an acceptable answer but does not guarantee one.

One problem-solving heuristic is **hill climbing.** Hill climbing means that you look for an operator that will take you to a state in the problem space that appears to be closer to the goal than you are now. The heuristic is so named because you could imagine thinking of the goal of the problem state as the top of a hill. Each step you take is a change in the problem space; to decide where to step, you simply evaluate whether the step you are contemplating would take you closer to the goal.

The hill-climbing heuristic is certainly more effective than brute force—you are at least evaluating moves before you try them—but it is still applicable to a limited number of problems because many problems require that you move backward in the problem space to reach your goal. Here's what that means. Take the "hill climbing" name literally for a moment and suppose that your goal is to reach the highest point in an area. You take a few steps, the choice of each step guided by whether taking that step leads you upward, and find yourself at the top of a hill. But nearby you see a hill that is still higher than the one that you're on. Given your present position, you can't get to the top of this highest hill using the hill-climbing heuristic because any step you might take would be downhill; you have to briefly go downhill (away from the goal) to ultimately reach the goal.

One sometimes sees animals caught in a similar bind. Most people have seen a dog tied to a post, straining (and failing) to reach a ball (or a cat) that it could easily reach if it would momentarily move away from the ball so that the leash would no longer be caught on a pole. Although one might snicker about the mental superiority of our species, the fact is that humans are not indifferent to moving backward in a problem space. We can do it, obviously, or else many problems would be insoluble, but we are more likely to make errors if we must move backward, and we are slower to make these moves than hill-climbing moves. This phenomenon was demonstrated by John Thomas (1974; see also Greeno, 1974), who examined participants solving the Hobbits and Orcs problem. This problem (or one like it) probably is familiar to you. In this version the participant is told that there are three Hobbits and three Orcs on one side of a river. They all want to cross the river, but their boat can hold only one or two creatures. Orcs must never outnumber Hobbits on either side of the river because if they do, they will devour them. How can everyone get across the river safely? The problem space for this problem is depicted in Figure 10.4.

The asterisk in the figure marks the state from which participants are slow to move and from which they often make errors. If you examine that state, you can see that to move forward in the problem space (i.e., toward the goal) the

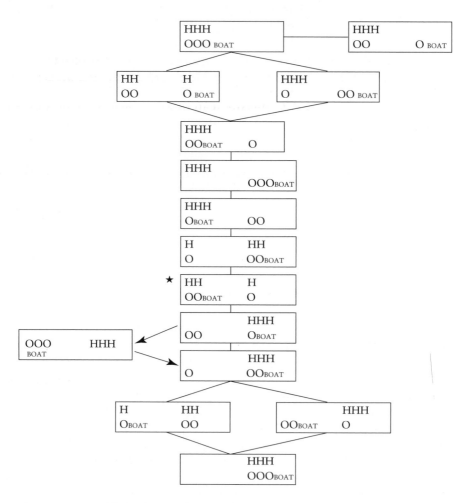

Figure 10.4. *Problem space for the Hobbit and Orcs problem. The space is fairly linear (i.e., there are few branches) because the boat greatly restricts what you can do at any point. The key thing to note is that at one point in the problem (marked by the asterisk) you have to move some creatures away from the goal shore back to the starting shore. People are slow to make that move, indicating that they are influenced by the hill-climbing heuristic.*

participant must make a move that seems to be away from the goal, specifically to take some creatures away from the goal side of the river. Thus, although humans can move away from a goal, we are reluctant to do so.

Another heuristic for moving through a problem space is **working backward.** As the name suggests, in this heuristic one begins at the goal state of the problem space and tries to work back to the starting state. This heuristic is useful when the goal state is known but the initial state is not. For example, consider the double-money problem, posed by Wayne Wickelgren (1974).

> Three people play a game in which one person loses and two people win each game. The one who loses must double the amount of money that each of the other two players has at that time. The three players agree to play three games. At the end of the three games, each player has lost one game, and each player has $8. What was the original stake of each player?

One could try to solve this problemly selecting some initial state (i.e., the stakes of the three players) and working forward, evaluating the outcome, and if the correct answer is not obtained, trying to adjust the initial state. However, it is much easier to work backward. If all three players ended with $8, after the last game the loser had doubled the money of the two winners; hence before the last game the winners must have each had $4, and the loser must have had $16. Because we know that each player won exactly once, it is easy to trace back the stakes, as shown here (in each game the asterisk indicates the loser):

Game	Player 1	Player 2	Player 3
Ending Stake	8	8	8
Stake before game 3	16*	4	4
Stake before game 2	8	14*	2
Stake before game 1	4	7	13*

As you can see, the problem is easy to solve if one works backward from the goal state to the initial state. Wickelgren argued that problems are well suited to this heuristic if the goal state is known but there are many possible initial states. If there are many possible initial states, there may not be an intelligent heuristic by which one could select an initial state (and then see whether it leads to the goal state). Working forward on problems like this has been likened to finding a needle in a haystack, but working backward on such problems is more like the needle working its way out of the haystack (Newell, Shaw, & Simon, 1962).

This game is a rather extreme example of working backward because the goal state is specified but there is no information about the starting state. Here's another example in which working backward is useful; see whether you can solve this problem by working backward.

Fifteen pennies are placed on a table in front of two players. Each player is allowed to remove at least 1 penny but not more than 5 pennies at his or her turn. The players alternate turns, each removing from 1 to 5 pennies, until one player takes the last penny on the table and thereby wins all 15 pennies. Is there a method of play that will guarantee victory? If so, what is it?

How can you solve this problem by working backward? Consider this. If you can be presented with between 1 to 5 pennies, you can take all of them and win the game. What can you do to ensure that your opponent will leave you with 1 to 5 pennies? If you leave him with 6, he'll have to leave you with 1 to 5. How can you ensure that you leave him with 6? If you are able to leave him with 12, no matter how many he takes on his turn, you'll be able to take some number that will leave him with six. Thus, if you go first in this game, you should take 3, leaving him with 12. This game provides a more realistic example of the working backward strategy because the initial state (15 pennies) is specified.

There is some evidence that people use the working backward heuristic in solving problems. Robert Rist (1989) asked 10 undergraduates taking their first computer programming course to write brief programs. Rist examined the computer code that participants wrote. (He also asked them to describe their problem-solving strategies as they worked, a technique we'll discuss shortly.) He found that when they were using unfamiliar concepts, participants often worked backward. They started by considering the answer they wanted the program to produce and then tried to deduce what they would need to do to produce that answer. For example, in one problem they were to write a program that would calculate the average daily rainfall, given the rainfall that had occurred on each of 30 days. Participants often began by deciding that if they were to find an average, an easy way to do that would be to find the total rainfall and divide by the number of days. They wrote the code that would achieve that final step in the program and then tried to figure out how to find the total rainfall.

Hill climbing and working backward have their applications, but the range of problems to which they can be applied is limited because most problems require moving both backward and forward. Indeed, Rist found that once participants had a bit of experience with a programming concept, they typically worked both backward and forward in the course of writing a program, even if it was possible to solve the problem only by working backward.

By far the most thoroughly tested and probably the most broadly applicable heuristic is **means–ends analysis.** Means–ends analysis uses a combination of forward- and backward-moving strategies. It can be summarized simply:

1. Compare the current state with the goal state. If there is no difference between them, the problem is solved.

2. If there is a difference between the current state and the goal state, set as a goal to solve that difference. If there is more than one difference, set as a goal to solve the largest difference.

3. Select an operator that will solve the difference identified in Step 2.

4. If the operator can be applied, apply it. If it cannot, set as a new goal to reach a state that would allow the application of the operator.
5. Return to step 1 with the new goal set in step 4.

Take as an example the simple act of taking a cat to the vet. Means–ends analysis would solve that problem this way:

Step 1. What is the difference between my current state (at home) and my goal state (at the vet with my cat)? The difference is one of distance.

Step 2. Set goal to reduce distance.

Step 3. What operator reduces distance?

Step 4. A car reduces distance. A condition of using a car is that it not have an uncaged cat in it.

Step 5. Set as a subgoal to make the car suitable to carry cats.

Step 1. What is the difference between my current state (no cat carrier) and my goal state (have a cat carrier)?

Step 2. Set goal to get a cat carrier.

Step 1. What has cat carriers?

Step 2. Pet stores have cat carriers. Set subgoal to be at pet store.

You get the idea. Setting new goals is the key advantage of means–ends analysis. More accurately, it's a subgoal; it's a goal in service of the larger goal of being able to apply the operator of using the car to take the cat to the vet. Setting subgoals is so important because it allows you to move away from the goal when necessary (unlike the hill-climbing heuristic), but you move away from the goal only when it is necessary—when it is in service of achieving another goal that will bring you closer to the goal state. If there is a potentially useful operator that can't be applied, the means–ends analysis heuristic tries to make it applicable. The hill-climbing heuristic abandons an operator that can't be applied immediately and seeks another method (e.g., if your car can't carry the cat, you could walk to the vet with the cat in your arms).

This example shows that problems can be described in ways that sound consistent with means–ends analysis. A more important question is whether there is evidence that people use means–ends analysis when they solve problems. Alan Newell and Herb Simon (1972) developed a computer program that solved problems by using means–ends analysis. The program was designed to be general in its applicability to a broad range of problems and so was called the **General Problem Solver.**

Newell, Simon, and their colleagues have used three methods to test whether the General Problem Solver provides an accurate description of how humans solve problems: verbal protocols, problem behavior graphs, and aggregate statistics from larger groups of participants. Here's what each of those sources of evidence means. A **verbal protocol** is a method in which one asks the participant to solve a problem and to simultaneously talk out loud, describing his or her thoughts while solving the problem. He or she is not to remain silent for more than a second or two; the experimenter prompts the participant to speak. The assumption is that the participant has conscious access to at least some of the mental processes that support solving the problem. Although this assumption is controversial (Nisbett & Wilson, 1977), Anders Ericsson and Herb Simon (1993) made an effective case that such data are useful, and indeed have proposed a model of how and when information becomes available for verbal report. Newell and Simon (1972) examined the verbal protocols of several participants who worked abstract logic problems and found an impressive degree of correspondence between the steps they reported taking as they solved the problem and the steps that the General Problem Solver took. The important finding was not so much the detailed match between participant and model but the finding that the general character of their approach was similar: Both humans and the model sought to reduce differences between their current state and the goal, and both created subgoals when an operator could not be applied that would reduce a difference.

A **problem behavior graph** is a representation of the problem space through which participants moved as they solved (or attempted to solve) a problem. Newell and Simon's problem behavior graphs consisted of rectangles, representing the cognitive state of the participant at a given moment (i.e., how far he or she had gotten in the problem), and lines connecting the states, representing changes in states. Often, a change in state came about as the participant applied an operator. Other times the participant might abandon a line of reasoning and jump to a different part of the problem or try a new strategy. Newell and Simon examined the problem behavior graphs and categorized each transition between states. They found that about 82% of the state transitions were consistent with those expected from the application of means–ends analysis. The other 18% were activities such as reviewing what had been done or trying to avoid paths through the problem space that the participant thought would be difficult.

Both of these methods entailed very detailed analysis of just a few participants. In a third method, Newell and Simon examined the data of a larger group (64 participants) who were asked to solve similar logic problems. They made the same categorization judgments of the steps taken to solve the problem, but in this case they used only the steps that were written, rather than the verbal protocols. Again, they found evidence that was broadly consistent with means–ends analysis.

These three sources of evidence were collected using the same type of problem: logical proofs. Similar methods have been applied using many other problems. Some of the problems that the General Problem Solver has solved successfully are listed in Table 10.1 (Ernst & Newell, 1969).

So far we have discussed a very specific type of problem: those in which the problem solver has no experience with the problem presented and has no experience that seems relevant to the problem. Although such problems arise periodically, it is probably more typical that you have some experience in memory that seems to apply to some aspect of the problem, even if you haven't seen this particular problem. We turn now to these problems.

Table 10.1   Problems Solved by the General Problem Solver

Problem	Description
Hobbits & Orcs	As described earlier.
Tower of Hanoi	As described earlier; the General Problem Solver was given the four-disk version.
Proving theorems from first-order predicate calculus	Logical theorems are to be proved, given a limited number of axioms and ways that the axioms can be combined.
Father and sons task	A father and his two sons want to cross a river using a boat that can hold only 200 lb. The father weighs 200 lb and each son weighs 100 lb.
Three coins puzzle	There are 3 coins. The first and third show heads, middle shows tails. A move consists of turning over 2 of the 3 coins. Make all 3 coins show the same side (heads or tails) in exactly three moves.
Parsing sentences	Finding parts of speech (e.g., noun phrases) in sentences.
Water jug task	Given a 5-gallon jug and an 8-gallon jug, how can precisely 2 gallons be put in the 5-gallon jug? The jugs are empty, but there is a tap for water and a drain for excess. (Other problems use different-sized jugs and demand different amounts of water.)
Letter series completion	Partial sequences are provided, with the goal to continue the sequence (e.g., B C B D B E B _ _).

STAND-ON-ONE-FOOT QUESTIONS

1. Why are heuristics needed for problem solving?
2. Name three heuristics for unfamiliar problems.
3. Summarize how means—ends analysis works.

QUESTIONS THAT REQUIRE TWO FEET

4. We said that the hill-climbing heuristic would not be successful in getting you to the top of the largest hill in an area if you happened to first scale a smaller hill. Could means—ends analysis get you to the top of the largest hill in the area? How would it do so?
5. Which has a bigger problem space: chess or checkers? Why? How could you shrink the problem space of either game?
6. Which of the methods we've discussed so far do you think the average person would use in trying to open a safe? Which method might a professional safecracker use?

➤   *What Do You Do When You Have Knowledge*
    That Seems to Apply to a Problem but No Experience
    With the Specific Problem?

➤ PREVIEW In the previous section we discussed problem-solving strategies that
are used for unfamiliar problems. In this section we discuss how these strategies
change if one has some relevant background knowledge. Background knowledge
may help one solve problems by allowing one to classify the problem and thereby
to see immediately the problem's underlying structure. It may also help because
sufficient knowledge means that some of the operators may be automatized, meaning that they don't demand attention, leaving attention free for unfamiliar aspects
of the problem. A third way in which background knowledge may help is if one
can draw an analogy from the present problem to a different problem that shares
the same underlying structure; however, people are not very skilled in drawing
analogies, as we'll see. We'll also discuss ways in which background knowledge can
hurt your performance, chiefly if you try to apply old knowledge to a new problem
when it just isn't applicable, a tendency that is common under certain circumstances.
Even when people make this mistake, the problem sometimes yields to repeated attempts to solve it, and we'll discuss recent work that has begun to investigate how
people are able to avoid these mental traps and go on to solve problems.

In the previous section we discussed problems that we assumed were completely unfamiliar to the solver, so we didn't have to worry about how the person's prior knowledge might affect his or her solution attempts. Now we're
ready to complicate the situation and consider what happens when we assume
that the solver has some relevant background knowledge. You would assume that
some knowledge must be better than no knowledge for solving problems. As
we'll see in this section, that is generally true, but in some situations background knowledge hurts your problem-solving efforts, and psychologists have
been especially interested in exploring those situations.

How Background Knowledge Helps

Although we'll discuss how prior knowledge can negatively affect problem solving, bear in mind that most of the time background knowledge is helpful. The
ways in which background knowledge helps are pretty straightforward in
the context of the General Problem Solver. First, if you have background knowledge of the domain, you are better able to classify the problem and therefore to
understand the problem's critical components. Recall from chapter 4 our discussion of chess masters in William Chase and Herb Simon's (1973) study. They
showed that chess masters are able to remember the positions of chess pieces very
accurately. They also showed that chess masters do so by chunking pieces into
meaningful configurations. They don't perceive 32 chess pieces; they perceive
a much smaller number of chess piece chunks, each composed of several pieces.
The perception of the board in chunks relies on prior experience: if the pieces are

arranged randomly, chess masters perceive (and remember) the board no differently than novices.

How does the perception of the board in chunks help problem solving? It greatly reduces the search space of problem solving. By perceiving configurations of pieces, the master can instantly perceive that the black queen is in jeopardy or that white is dominating the center of the board. These patterns are recognized from memory, and they provide a clear guide for how to focus problem-solving strategies to formulate the next move. Thus we can generally state that domain knowledge allows better perception of the most important part of the problem that should be addressed and thereby restricts the search to the key part of the problem space.

The second way that domain knowledge can help problem solving is by automatizing some of the problem-solving steps. One of the first (and most important) steps to automatize is what operators are available and how they move you in the problem space. For example, if you are just learning how to play chess, you must think hard about how the knight moves, how the rook moves, and the oddity that the pawns move ahead one space but can move two spaces from their starting position, take other pieces on the diagonal, and can take pieces in passing from their starting position. Until you have thoroughly learned the rules for piece movement, it is difficult to form much strategy.

Here's an example of a problem in which the rules are fairly complex, and one might imagine that the problem will be difficult to solve until one gains greater familiarity with the rules.

> In the inns of certain Himalayan villages is practiced a refined tea ceremony. The ceremony involves a host and exactly two guests, neither more nor less. When his guests have arrived and seated themselves at his table, the host performs three services for them. These services are listed in the order of the nobility the Himalayans attribute to them: stoking the fire, fanning the flames, and pouring the tea. During the ceremony, any of those present may ask another, "Honored Sir, may I perform this onerous task for you?" However, a person may request of another only the least noble of the tasks which the other is performing. Furthermore, if a person is performing any tasks, then he may not request a task that is nobler than the least noble task he is already performing. Custom requires that by the time the tea ceremony is over, all the tasks will have been transferred from the host to the most senior of the guests. How can this be accomplished?

If you're like me, you had to read this problem several times just to understand what the rules are. It's hard to even consider how to get to the goal because the operators are so complicated that they consume all of my working memory capacity.

Contemplating moves through a problem space requires working memory, and it becomes difficult to maintain the goal and the operators in working memory if the operators are not automatized so that they take little or no working memory capacity. Recall the example of taking the cat to the vet. Notice that the solution to this problem relied heavily on background knowledge, especially on knowledge of how subgoals could be achieved. When confronted with a problem of distance, we know immediately that an automobile

BOX 10.1. USING BACKGROUND KNOWLEDGE: THE ROLE OF THE FRONTAL LOBE

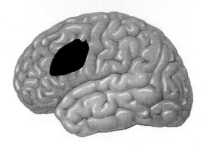 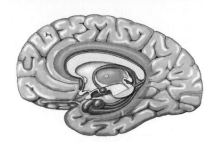

Frontal area
typically affected
in Shallice and Evans's
(1978) study

As you might expect, problem solving is hard to localize in the brain, probably because solving problems requires the contribution of multiple cortical and subcortical structures. Nevertheless, it is true that patients with lesions restricted to the frontal lobes seem to have particular difficulty in solving problems. The source of that difficulty appears to be in patient's ability to develop strategies. This problem was mentioned in the context of memory in chapter 6. In addition to difficulty in developing strategies, patients with frontal lobe lesions are impaired in divergent thinking, that is, in coming up with different ideas and not always thinking along the same paths.

The difficulty patients with frontal lobe lesions have in developing strategies can be appreciated by a simple test devised by Tim Shallice and Margaret Evans (1978). They asked participants questions to which one was very unlikely to have the answer in memory. Instead, one would need to devise a strategy by which a reasonable answer could be derived, based on information that was in memory. Here are some sample questions:

> How fast do race horses gallop?
> What is the best paid job or occupation in Britain today?
> What is the length of the average man's spine?
> How tall is the tallest building in London?
> How many camels are there in Holland?

It is not expected that anyone will be able to answer these questions accurately; the expectation is that patients with frontal lobe lesions, because they cannot devise a strategy to come up with a reasonable answer, will produce truly bizarre answers. Therefore, patients' answers were evaluated for how near or far they were from the answers of normal participants. Patients with damage to the frontal lobe were much more likely to produce bizarre answers than patients with more posterior lesions. For example, one patient said that the tallest building in London was between 18,000 and 20,000 feet, that the best-paid occupation was long-distance truck driver, and that the length of the average spine was between 4 and 5 feet.

(Continued)

Another task, the Wisconsin Card Sorting Task, tests the participant's ability to respond flexibly. The patient is given a deck of cards, each bearing some symbols. Each card has three features, including the number of symbols (one to four), the symbol type (diamond, star, plus, circle), and the symbol color (red, green, yellow, blue). The participant is asked to sort the cards into piles. The participant is not told what feature to use in sorting, but corrective feedback is provided by the experimenter, so participants usually catch on to the rule fairly quickly. The trick is that once the participant understands the rule and sorts 10 cards correctly, the experimenter changes the rule. Normal participants (and patients with nonfrontal brain lesions) quickly understand that the rule must have changed, and they set about figuring out the new rule. However, patients with frontal damage keep sorting according to the old rule. They have a great difficulty breaking free of the behavior in which they are currently engaged. This tendency is called perseveration.

You can see how these problems would affect successful completion of many different types of problems. Effective problem solving requires that one be able to develop a strategy for dealing with the problem. Furthermore, effective problem solving often requires divergent thinking; one must break free of old ways of doing things and try something new. If the old way of doing things were effective, it wouldn't be a problem! In sum, although problem solving is quite complex, we can identify two functions subserved by the frontal lobe that are important to solving many problem solving situations: strategic thinking and divergent thinking.

---

is an effective operator to reduce distance; we don't have to cast about for a solution. If we did not know that one should use a car, that subgoal might require considerable search that would occupy working memory, which might mean that other components of the problem would be lost from working memory.

You would think that having some knowledge about a problem is bound to be better than having no knowledge. In some cases familiarity does help. We think about how the various parts of a problem relate to one another and draw an analogy between those relationships and the relationships in another familiar problem that we know how to solve. For example, if you are familiar with calculating probabilities in gambling games and are confronted with a probability question in a statistics class, you may see the similarity of the statistics question to gambling questions you are familiar with and successfully solve the statistics question.

Another type of familiarity with part of a problem is not so helpful, however. Instead of being familiar with the relationships between parts of a problem, you may be familiar with the isolated components of a problem. In those situations, people often have a hard time thinking of objects outside of their normal use. A rubber dog bone is merely a toy for dogs—that's its attribute— and it won't seem to be something that could be used as a pencil eraser in a pinch. In this case, familiarity with the object hurts problem-solving performance. In this section, we'll talk about each of these ways in which familiarity with a problem can affect problem solving.

Thinking About the Relationships Between Objects in a Problem: Analogy

In the last section we looked at a problem involving a tea ceremony. Were you able to solve it? Did you notice that an analogy could be drawn between this problem and the Tower of Hanoi problem that you saw (and perhaps solved) earlier in this chapter? Figure 10.5 should make this analogy concrete.

In this section we're discussing the use of prior knowledge in the solving of problems. Here's a situation in which you thought about a problem quite recently, you were given a new problem that is directly analogous to it, yet you didn't use your knowledge of this prior problem to solve this one. How is that possible?

The first thing you should know is that this finding is common. The classic studies on analogy were conducted by Mary Gick and Keith Holyoak (1980, 1983). They used a problem originally devised by Karl Duncker (1945) called the radiation problem that reads as follows:

> Suppose you are a doctor faced with a patient who has a malignant tumor in his stomach. It is impossible to operate on the patient, but unless the tumor is destroyed the patient will die. There is a kind of ray that can be used to destroy the tumor. If the rays reach the tumor all at once at a sufficiently high intensity, the tumor will be destroyed. Unfortunately, at this intensity the healthy tissue that the rays pass through on the way to the tumor will also be destroyed. At lower intensities the rays are harmless to healthy tissue, but they will not affect the tumor either. What type of procedure might be used to destroy the tumor with the rays without destroying the healthy tissue?

Most people find this problem extremely difficult, and even if they work on it for a long time, only about 10% of participants solve it. The answer is that you could use several of the rays at low intensity and point them in such a way that they all meet at the tumor. Thus, only the tumor would be exposed to a high

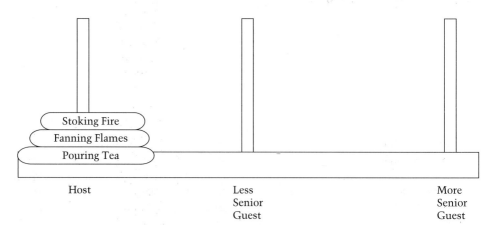

Figure 10.5. *Figure showing how the tea ceremony problem is analogous to the Tower of Hanoi problem. Did you see the analogy?*

intensity of the rays, and surrounding tissue would not be damaged. Again, this is a very difficult problem, but suppose that when you took up the radiation problem, you had just finished reading this story:

> A dictator ruled a small country from a fortress. The fortress was situated in the middle of the country and many roads radiated outward from it, like spokes on a wheel. A great general vowed to capture the fortress and free the country of the dictator. The general knew that if his entire army could attack the fortress at once it could be captured. But a spy reported that the dictator had planted mines on each of the roads. The mines were set so that small bodies of men could pass over them safely, since the dictator needed to be able to move troops and workers about, however, any large force would detonate the mines. Not only would this blow up the road, but the dictator would destroy many villages in retaliation. A full-scale direct attack on the fortress therefore seemed impossible.
>
> The general, however, was undaunted. He divided his army up into small groups and dispatched each group to the head of a different road. When all was ready he gave the signal, and each group charged down a different road. All of the small groups passed safely over the mines, and the army then attacked the fortress in full strength. In this way the general was able to capture the fortress.

Gick and Holyoak found that if participants were told that the dictator story that they had just read might help them solve the radiation problem, 100% came up with the correct solution. However, if the experimenters did not tell them to use the dictator story, only 35% of the participants solved the radiation problem. Furthermore, that estimate of 35% spontaneously using the analogous story might be high because some of these participants may have suspected that there was supposed to be some connection between the two stories, even though they were not told about it. Therefore, Gick and Holyoak conducted another study in which the dictator story was just one of three other stories participants heard before they heard the radiation problem. In that experiment, only 20% got the problem correct; thus when the connection between the radiation problem and the dictator problem was made less obvious, even fewer participants drew the analogy. Indeed, if the two stories are separated by a delay or if they are presented in different contexts, almost none of the participants use the analogy (Spencer & Weisberg, 1986).

So is it the case that people must be told to use an analogy? That doesn't seem right. Surely we spontaneously use analogy sometimes. That's true, and a critical predictor of whether people will use an analogous problem that they've seen before is whether there is surface similarity. **Surface similarity** refers to whether the problems use the same elements (e.g., tumors and rays). **Structural similarity** refers to whether the content of the problem that allows you to solve it is the same. For example, the radiation and dictator problems are structurally similar because the solution to both entails dispersing strength and focusing it only at the point to be attacked. People seem to be more sensitive to surface similarity when considering analogy. For example, Mark Keane (1987) found that 88% of his participants used analogy to solve a problem even if they had read the analogous story several days before, as long as the analogous story was extremely similar—in this case another surgery story. When the story was changed so that it still entailed rays being focused on a target, but now the target was intercontinental missiles, the use of the analogy dropped to 58%.

In another experiment emphasizing the importance of surface similarity, Miriam Bassok (1990) trained participants in some algebraic problem-solving procedures using word problems as examples. She tested whether participants could transfer the procedures from one training domain (e.g., physics) to another (e.g., finance). In an earlier experiment, Bassok and Holyoak (1989) reported very poor transfer of problem-solving procedures learned in physics to any nonphysics domain. In her 1990 study, Bassok found that transfer across domains was good as long as the new problems used variables similar to those used during training (e.g., if participants were trained on a procedure using the speed of an object and later encountered a problem using typing rate). In such cases, transfer of the learned procedure was spontaneous. If the new problem used a different type of quantity (e.g., interest accruing in a bank), transfer was not spontaneous, although with a hint that they should do so, participants could map the learned procedure onto the new problem. Thus, this study indicated that surface similarity might be important for spontaneously thinking about using an analogy, but people were still capable of using an analogous problem with no more than a general hint to do so.

From these studies it sounds as though surface similarity of problems is the key to whether participants will think of using an analogy. But other data indicate that the structural similarity of a problem plays a role as well. Keith Holyoak and Kyunghee Koh (1987; see also Ross, 1987) systematically varied structural and surface similarity of the analogous story, which was about an expensive lightbulb that needed repair. Lasers could be used to fuse the filament, but a laser of sufficiently high intensity would break the glass of the bulb. (The solution is to use multiple low-intensity lasers that focus on the filament.) To change the surface features of the story, they replaced the lasers with ultrasound waves; the experimenters argued that the lasers were more similar to the rays than the ultrasound waves were. To change the structural similarity of the analogous problem, the story was changed so that none of the several available lasers could generate a sufficiently strong ray to fuse the filament—that a strong ray would break the glass was not mentioned. Note that the solution of applying multiple low-intensity rays is still a valid solution to the problem. The difference is that the problem is structurally less similar to the radiation problem because the constraint preventing the obvious solution (using a single high-intensity ray) differs. The four possible analogous stories are depicted in Table 10.2.

In accord with previous work, the results of Holyoak and Koh's study indicated that the surface structure of the story was important to whether there was transfer. In addition, their results indicated that the presence of structural similarity also had an impact. The results are shown in Table 10.3.

When structural similarity is high, more people solve the analogous problem (72% vs. 27%) and when surface similarity is high more people solve the problem (64% vs. 35%). Thus in this study both surface and structural similarity were important. Almost all studies indicate that surface similarity is important and structural similarity is important at least under some conditions, but exactly what those conditions are is not clear yet.

Table 10.2   Four Conditions in Holyoak and Koh's (1987) Study

	High Surface Similarity	Low Surface Similarity
High structural similarity	Lasers fuse lightbulb filament; high intensity will break glass.	Ultrasound waves jar filament apart; high intensity will break glass.
Low structural similarity	Lasers fuse lightbulb filament; no one laser is powerful enough.	Ultrasound waves jar filament apart; no one ultrasound wave is powerful enough.

Thus far we have talked about analogy in terms of people's success in considering whether to use an analogous problem, and we're assuming (rightly, it seems) that if the participant considers using it, he or she will be successful in doing so. Other times, however, you have already thought of using an analogy but still have problems mapping a sample problem to the problem to be solved. For example, for students studying physics, chemistry, or statistics, having a formula to work from is not enough; they need to see sample problems that use the formula to fully understand how to use the formula. Brian Ross (1987; see also Novick & Holyoak, 1991; Ross, 1989; Chen, 1995) studied people's success in using sample problems to help them solve novel problems. In all cases, the formulas to solve the problems were available. The upshot of Ross's study was that people are strongly influenced by the surface similarity of sample problems. If the objects play different roles in the problems, people often are confused. Here's how the study worked. Participants learned mathematical principles—for example, how to calculate the probability of an occurrence over repeated trials—and read an example of the principle's application. Then they were asked to work another problem. In the new problem, the objects either did or did not correspond to the objects in the sample problem. One problem was as follows:

Study Problem: The Brite-Lite company makes all kinds of light bulbs. The red ones are hard to make. Of these bulbs, 5/7 work and 2/7 of them don't work. John has a new job in which he tests each red bulb by screwing it into a socket and seeing if it lights. What is the probability that the first red bulb to fail to light is the third one he tries?

Table 10.3   Results of Holyoak and Koh's (1987) Study

	High Surface Similarity	Low Surface Similarity	Mean
High structural similarity	88	56	72
Low structural similarity	40	13	27
Mean	64	35	

Objects Correspond Test: The Brite-Lite Company makes all kinds of light bulbs. On 5/8 of their bulbs, their name is legible, while on 3/8 it is illegible. John's job is to inspect bulbs to see if the name is illegible. What is the probability that the first bulb with an illegible name is the fourth one he tries?

Objects Don't Correspond Test: The Brite-Lite Company makes all kinds of light bulbs. On 3/8 of their bulbs, their name is legible, while on 5/8 it is illegible. John's job is to inspect bulbs to see if the name is illegible. What is the probability that the first bulb with a legible name is the fourth one he tries?

When mapping the entities in the study problem and the test problem is easy (objects correspond), 74% of participants get the test problem correct. When the mapping is difficult (objects don't correspond), only 37% solve the problem.

In summary, two processes (at least) are needed to make effective use of an analogy. It must occur to the person that an analogous problem may be helpful, and as we've seen (starting with the Gick and Holyoak study), it often does not occur to people that they can draw an analogy, even if they've seen an analogous problem recently. The second process is drawing a mapping or correspondence between the elements of the two problems. In the Gick and Holyoak problem this mapping did not seem difficult; once people were reminded to use the dictator story, they were very successful in solving the radiation problem. In other problems, however, the mapping can be difficult, as Ross demonstrated in his study.

Can one make it easier for people to draw analogies? Some researchers have suggested that with continued exposure to a type of problem, one develops an abstract schema for that type of problem (Holyoak & Thagard, 1989; Ross & Kennedy, 1990). Recall from chapter 5 that a schema is a memory representation that captures the general features of an object or event. In this case, a schema would contain the deep structure of the problem and a solution strategy that would be applicable across a variety of problems with this structure. As we discuss later in this chapter, it's certainly true that experts can readily describe the underlying structure of problems that have different surface structures. It therefore seems logical to infer that when one practices a particular type of problem (e.g., calculating conservation of energy in physics) one is building a schema that can be applied to a variety of problems in that domain.

There does seem to be evidence that practice with a class of problems promotes development of a schema that is general enough to handle problems of that class. Laura Novick and Keith Holyoak (1991) gave participants example problems that illustrated the use of algebraic procedures. Participants then tried to apply these principles to novel problems. The experimenters assessed whether applying the analogous problems to the new problems created a schema; they measured schema quality by asking participants to describe which parts of the solution procedures were common to the two problems. The experimenters found that participants with higher-quality schemas tended to show more transfer from the analogous problem. Other experiments supporting the idea of schema induction have shown that repeated solution of analogous problems makes participants better able to make inferences that would be consistent with the schema (Donnelly & McDaniel, 1993; Robins & Mayer, 1993).

One of the key themes in this section on analogy is that the mapping is important, specifically, the relational mapping between the parts of one entity and another entity. For example, if you're drawing an analogy between the solar system and an atom, then the relationships of the parts of the solar system should be similar to the relationships of the parts of the atom. The attributes of the objects are not so important in mapping the analogy. It doesn't matter that the sun is hot; what matters is how the sun relates to the planets (they rotate around it, just as electrons rotate around the nucleus of an atom).

We might ask what happens if you don't have a ready analogy. Can it happen that you don't focus on the relationships between the parts of the problem and instead focus on the attributes (e.g., if you aren't thinking about the planets revolving around the sun, will you focus on the sun's heat)? Focusing on the common attributes of objects can happen, and it can cause difficulties in problem solving when the common attributes of the object are not the ones that are critical for solving the problem. We turn our attention to these difficulties next.

Thinking About the Attributes of Individual Objects in a Problem: Functional Fixedness

Just as we began the last section with a sample problem, I'd like to start this section with a sample problem, adapted from a classic experiment by Karl Duncker (1945).

> In an empty room are a candle, some matches, and a box of tacks. The goal is to have the lit candle about 5 feet off the ground. You've tried melting some of the wax on the bottom of the candle and sticking it to the wall, but that wasn't effective. How can you get the lit candle to be 5 feet off the ground without your having to hold it there?

Could you solve the problem? The solution is to dump the tacks out of the box and tack the box to the wall. The box can then serve as a platform to support the candle.

Here's another simple problem for you. Dan and Abe played six games of chess. Dan won four and Abe won four. There were no ties. How is that possible?

The answer to that problem is that they were not playing against one another. Both of these are examples of **insight problems.** An insight problem is one in which it feels to the solver that the solution (assuming that it is solved) comes all at once, in a moment of illumination. It has long been assumed that insight problems differ from other problems in that they do not yield to an analytic approach; for example, the Hobbits and Orcs problem described earlier usually is solved step by step, through an analysis of the requirements and constraints of the problem. The candle problem requires just one thing: understanding that the box can serve as a platform. The lack of analytic procedure and the flashing, "Aha!" feeling to the solution go hand in hand. People usually report feeling stumped by an insight problem, as though they've hit a brick wall. Then they get an idea, seemingly out of nowhere, and the problem is solved.

The subjective impression I've just described may ring true to you, but do we really know that it's true? Do people feel as though they can't solve the problem and then suddenly find that they have solved it? In a word, "yes." Janet

Metcalfe and David Wiebe (1987; see also Metcalfe, 1986a; 1986b) examined this question by administering insight questions or algebra problems to their participants. Sample problems are shown in Table 10.4.

Participants were given 4 min to solve each problem. Every 15 s, they were to rate how close they thought they were to a solution (how "warm" they were getting).

The pattern of warmth ratings differed between the algebra and insight problems. For the algebra ratings, at the time of solution everyone gave a rating of 7, which makes sense because they had just solved the problem. Fifteen seconds before that, many of the ratings were still at 6 or 7; participants knew that they were getting warm. Moving backward in time, the warmth ratings for the algebra problems became more crowded toward the bottom of the scale. The ratings for the insight problems reflected a different pattern. Although participants were confident at the time of solution, just 15 s before then they are did not feel very "warm" at all. Indeed, the pattern of ratings was the same at every time interval until solution. Thus, there is good evidence that insight is a sudden solution, not incremental, and that people don't know that it's coming.

The solutions we've talked about have all been quite incremental. Means–ends analysis is a systematic working through a problem space. Applying an analogy also seems incremental: One must find the appropriate analogy, then map the new problem to the old one, then work through the old solution, and so on. How are insight problems solved, given that these incremental solutions don't seem appropriate?

We can characterize insight problems as involving an impasse; something in the description of the problem just doesn't fit, and one is tempted to say, "This problem can't be solved." When you hear that two people played six games of chess and each won four, it seems clear that that can't be right. If we accept that insight problems entail an impasse, we can ask two questions: What causes the impasse, and how is the impasse resolved?

Table 10.4   Insight and Algebra Problems Used in Metcalfe and Wiebe's (1987) Study of Insight

Sample Insight Problems	Sample Algebra Problems
A prisoner was trying to escape from a tower. He found in his cell a rope that was half long enough to permit him to reach the ground safely. He divided the rope in half and tied the two parts together and escaped. How could he have done this?	Factor: $x^2 + 6x + 9$
A landscape gardener is given instructions to plant four special trees so that each one is exactly the same distance from each of the others. How is this possible?	$(3x^2 + 2x + 10)(3x) =$
Describe how to cut a hole in a 3×5 in. card that is big enough for you to put your head through.	Solve for x: $1/5x + 10 = 25$

WHAT CAUSES THE IMPASSE IN AN INSIGHT PROBLEM?   It seems that in many insight problems, one reaches an impasse because of the way that one of the concepts in the problem is used. For example, in the candle problem, the box is coded as something that can hold tacks; it is not coded as a small bit of cardboard with a flat surface that could serve as a platform. The problem in which one is to place four trees equidistant from one another again seems impossible. People typically do not think of planting a tree on top of a hill, but nothing in the problem precludes one doing so, just as nothing precludes finding an alternative use for a box.

Thus it seems that one cause of an impasse may be that people's interpretation of concepts is biased, based on their prior experience: Trees are planted in flat gardens, boxes serve the function of holding things, and so. This phenomenon is called **functional fixedness.** Functional fixedness, as the name implies, means that one is fixated on an object serving its typical function, and one fails to think of an alternative use of the object, even though it would be quite useful in the problem.

This interpretation of the difficulty of the problem implies that if the key object is presented so that it is not so obviously typical, problem solving may be facilitated. That does seem to work. People more often solve the candle problem if the box is depicted as empty, with the tacks next to it (Adamson, 1952). In another example of this effect, Martin Scheerer presented a problem in which part of the solution required that participants tie two sticks together. People readily noticed and used a piece of string depicted as hanging from a nail in the wall, but if the piece of string was holding up a picture, it seldom occurred to them that they could use it (Scheerer, 1963).

Other times an impasse is reached not because an object is used in an atypical fashion but because the description of the problem encourages one to represent it in a way that makes its solution very difficult. An example is the problem in which one is to plant four trees equidistant from one another in a garden. One thinks of a garden as a flat (or perhaps sloped) lawn, which leads you to represent the problem as "place four points equidistant on a plane," which is impossible. Nothing in the problem says that the four points must be in a plane, but most people's concepts of gardens lead them to represent it that way.

The classic problem that is difficult because of its representation is the mutilated checkerboard problem (Figure 10.6).

Most people who try this problem start out by mentally covering the checkerboard with dominoes. This is not an effective strategy, although it is the one the phrasing of the problem encourages. In one computer simulation, it took 758,148 domino placements for the program to conclude that it couldn't be done (cited in Kaplan & Simon, 1990).

It is much more effective to use a fact that the problem description does not make reference to: Both of the removed squares are white. That means that of the remaining squares, 30 are white and 32 are black. Because each domino must cover one white square and one black square, it is impossible to cover the mutilated board with the dominoes.

In the cases I've described so far, one thinks too narrowly about the functions of the objects in the problem. You can reach an impasse in a problem not

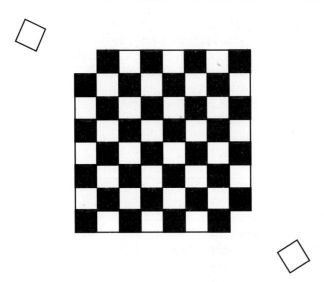

Figure 10.6. *This checkerboard has been mutilated by removing two squares. Sixty-two squares remain. If you had 31 dominoes, each of which could cover two squares, could you cover the remaining 62 squares? If so, show how it can be done; if not, prove that it cannot be done.*

only because you typically use an object in a particular way, but also because you are used to using a particular procedure to solve a problem. The classic problem in which participants become fixed in a problem solving-procedure is Luchins's water jar problem (Luchins, 1942). To measure a particular amount of water, you are provided with three measuring jars, a water tap, and a drain to pour off excess water. As an example, consider Problem 1 in Table 10.5. You could obtain the required amount (20 ounces) by filling jug A (29 ounces), then pouring off enough to fill jug B (3 ounces) three times.

All problems except 1 and 9 can be solved by filling jug B, then subtracting A, then subtracting C twice (Desired amount = B − A − 2C). Problems 7 through 11 can also be solved in a simpler way, involving only A and C (either adding or subtracting). The interesting finding is that participants who have solved Problems 2 through 6 continue to use the formula B − A − 2C for these later problems, even though it is unnecessarily complex. Not surprisingly, if you start participants immediately on Problem 7, they solve it the simpler way. Furthermore, Problem 9, which can't be solved with B − A − 2C, proves difficult for participants who have been using that formula for the other problems, even though a much simpler solution is correct. These are called **set effects;** a set effect occurs when a particular problem-solving procedure is applied based on past experience, even if it is not appropriate to the current problem.

Oddly enough, the literature on set effects and functional fixedness makes it sound as though knowledge can hurt you. If you knew nothing about what boxes usually are for, wouldn't you be more likely to use that piece of cardboard

Table 10.5 Luchins's (1942) Water Jug Problem

Problem Number	Jug A Capacity (ounces)	Jug B Capacity (ounces)	Jug C Capacity (ounces)	Required Amount (ounces)
1	29	3		20
2	21	127	33	40
3	14	163	25	99
4	18	43	10	5
5	9	42	6	21
6	20	59	4	31
7	23	49	3	20
8	15	39	3	18
9	28	76	3	25
10	18	48	4	22
11	14	36	8	6

as a platform and solve the candle problem? The idea that knowledge or expertise is behind set effects was examined in an experiment by Jennifer Wiley (1998). She administered the Remote Association Test (RAT). In this test participants read three words and must find a word that is related to all three. For example, they might read *blue, knife,* and *cottage,* in which case the answer would be *cheese,* forming *blue cheese, cheese knife,* and *cottage cheese.*

Wiley used two types of stimulus sets. For some the first word was consistent with a baseball term (baseball-consistent stimuli). An example of a baseball-consistent item would be *plate, broken,* and *rest,* which could be solved by *home* (*home plate, broken home,* and *rest home*). In other sets, the third word of the set was changed so that the baseball interpretation would no longer lead to a correct solution; an example would be *plate, broken,* and *shot,* which could be solved by *glass* (*plate glass, broken glass,* and *shot glass*). These stimuli were called baseball-misleading. A third set of neutral stimuli had nothing to do with baseball. Wiley tested participants who either had a great deal of baseball expertise or had very little. The prediction is that people with more baseball knowledge should be poorer at generating solutions on the baseball-misleading items because *plate* will make them think of *home plate* (a baseball term), and the second term (*broken*) fits *home* as well, but that last item does not. These participants will have difficulty generating other solutions, it is predicted, because their baseball expertise causes them to generate *home* for *plate.*

High-knowledge and low-knowledge participants performed comparably, except on the baseball-misleading questions. The low-knowledge participants were able to ignore any initial baseball-related responses they may have generated, but participants who knew a lot about baseball were not able to do so and often gave incorrect baseball-related responses. In a second experiment Wiley showed that even a warning to high-knowledge participants that they should not get stuck in baseball answers if they were inappropriate had little effect.

Bear in mind that in most cases, being an expert helps you solve problems, as we discuss later in the chapter. In this case, being an expert was detrimental only because the task was designed to make expertise ineffective. The interesting point of this study, I think, is that it is a more transparent version of how set effects usually work. Set effects and functional fixedness occur because we are all experts, so to speak, in mundane things such as what a box is for; a box is for holding things, such as tacks. It is difficult *not* to apply this expertise when we see the box full of tacks, just as it is difficult for the baseball players not to apply their expertise to the baseball-misleading questions on the RAT in Wiley's experiment.

How Is the Impasse Resolved?   We've gone on at some length about how an impasse is created in these problems, but some people solve them, so we must consider how the impasse is resolved. If it finally occurs to you to dump the tacks out and use the box as a platform, why did that occur to you? And why did that occur to you after 15 min of thinking, and not after 15 s of thinking?

The insight problems we've been discussing were first proposed by Gestalt psychologists. Gestalt psychologists are best known for their work in perception. A key point they made was that perception of a figure often is determined by the relationship between the components of the figure. (You may recall that in chapter 2 we discussed the Gestalt principle of good continuation in our discussion of vision.) The Gestaltists emphasized that the same figure may be perceived in more than one way. For example, in the well-known Necker cube (Figure 10.7), your perception of the cube's structure flips between two stable organizations. Gestalt psychologists suggested that a similar process was at work in insight problems (e.g., Kohler, 1929). They called it **restructuring.** In restructuring, one perceives a whole that had not been seen before. The relationship of the elements of the problem change, just at the relationship of the lines making up the cube change; the lines themselves do not change, but your interpretation of how they relate to one another changes. In problem solving, suddenly the box is not related to the tacks as a container; it is thought of as something that the tacks can stick on the wall. The processes that support this restructuring were thought to be unconscious.

An interesting finding indicated that the restructuring actually is not so sudden; the feeling of insight might be sudden, but it is preceded by some cognitive process that is more gradual. Kenneth Bowers and his colleagues (Bowers, Regehr, Balthazard, & Parker, 1990) gave participants a variant of the RAT described earlier. In their version, participants saw two sets of words, such as the following:

Figure 10.7.   *A Necker cube. The perceptual organization of the cube is unstable, so it flips between two interpretations. Simply staring at the figure for several seconds usually will make your perception of the figure change.*

PLAYING	STILL
CREDIT	PAGES
REPORT	MUSIC

For one of the word sets, a single unnamed word could make noun phrases of each presented word. In this case, it's the first set, and the word is *card,* yielding *playing card, credit card,* and *report card.* The words in the other set were selected randomly, and there was no single word to unify them. Every 8 s the participants made a judgment about which was the coherent triad of words. They had to make this judgment even if they hadn't found a solution; they were to simply make a guess based on any hunch that they had, and they were asked to rate their confidence about their judgment. The findings showed that when participants thought they were merely guessing about which was the coherent triad, they did indeed perform at chance. When they started having some confidence in their judgments (even though they still had not solved the triad), they were correct about 60% of the time. In other words, when people had a hunch or an intuition about which was the coherent triad, their intuitions were better than chance predictors.

Bowers et al.'s study indicates that people have meaningful intuitions before they solve a problem, even though the eventual solution of the problem might feel like a sudden insight. Can it be shown that something like restructuring is happening to support these intuitions? Francis Durso and his colleagues (Durso, Rea, & Dayton, 1994) found a way to measure restructuring in a rather open-ended problem, and they too found that the change came slowly and started before participants were aware of it. They gave participants this puzzle: "A man walks into a bar and asks for a glass of water. The bartender points a shotgun at the man. The man says 'thank you' and walks out." Participants were asked to figure out what piece of information was missing that would make the story sensible. Participants were allowed to ask the experimenter yes–no questions to help them get to the answer. Half of the participants could not solve the puzzle and half solved it. (The solution is that the man wanted the water because he had the hiccups, but the bartender cured him by scaring him with the shotgun.)

The experimenters asked participants to rate the relatedness of pairs of words in the puzzle. Some were relevant to the puzzle (e.g., *man, bartender*), some were relevant to the solution (e.g., *surprise, remedy*), and some were objects one would find in a bar (e.g., *TV, pretzels*). Participants rated 91 possible combinations of 14 words. The experimenters used the relatedness ratings to construct graphs of relatedness (using a technique called pathfinder scaling). The graphs of people who solved the puzzle and people who could not solve the puzzle are shown in Figure 10.8.

The boldface box shows the concept that is the focal point of the graph (i.e., the concept with the shortest distance to other concepts). As you can see, the central concept for solvers was "relieved," whereas for nonsolvers it was "bartender." The people who couldn't solve the puzzle focused on the bartender pulling out the shotgun; those who could solve it focused on what drew the story together, namely the relieving effect of the shotgun.

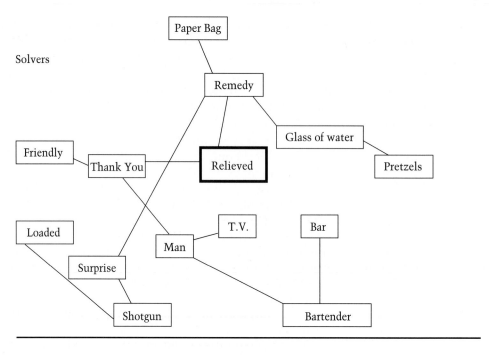

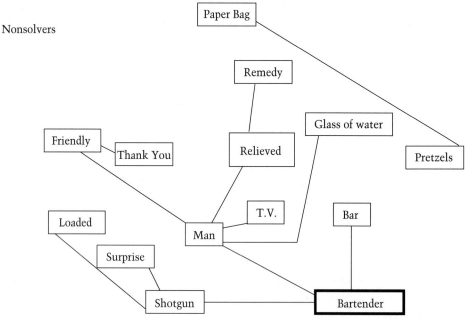

Figure 10.8. *Pathfinder graph representing participants' mental representations of concepts in the bartender–shotgun problem used by Durso et al. (1994). Compare the differences in the representation of those who solved the puzzle and those who did not. The boldface box is the representation with the shortest distance to other concepts.*

In a second experiment, the experimenters took these same measures as a second group of participants were attempting to solve the puzzle. The authors took their results from experiment 1 and derived three categories of word pairs, based on the relatedness judgments: related words were those that were connected in all pathfinder graphs, and unrelated words were those that were connected in none of the pathfinder graphs. Insight words were those that were connected in the pathfinder graphs of the people who had solved the problem but not the graphs of the people who didn't solve the problem. The experimenters collected ratings of related, unrelated, and insight word pairs (plus some filler word pairs) as participants worked on the problem.

The average similarity of word pairs stayed the same for related and unrelated words, but it increased for the insight word pairs. Even more interesting, these words started to seem related before the participant had solved the puzzle! Thus, restructuring was taking place before the participant successfully solved the problem. Although the experimenters did not take measures of how "warm" the participants thought they were getting, it is interesting to speculate that this restructuring takes place without the participant recognizing that he or she is getting closer to the solution.

So we have seen that impasses are broken as people restructure the problem, and that this restructuring takes place slowly, and outside awareness. Can we take this discussion one step further and speculate on what causes the restructuring? Gunter Knoblich and his colleagues (Knoblich, Ohlsson, Haider, & Rhemius, 1999) suggested a framework for thinking about how impasses are broken in insight problems. They agreed that impasses occur because there is a constraint in the way in which the problem solver uses a concept (e.g., a box must be used as a container). They suggested that one way you can solve insight problems is by relaxing these constraints; in other words, you begin to entertain the notion that a box need not be used as a container. They proposed that repeated failure on a problem automatically leads one to relax constraints. One first relaxes constraints that are narrow in scope, and if that doesn't lead to a solution, one moves on to broader constraints.

Knoblich et al. also suggested a second response to repeated failure to solve a problem. They argued that we tend to perceive the world in familiar chunks. Recall from chapter 4 that a chunk is a unit of knowledge that can be decomposed into smaller units. If a problem cannot be solved, Knoblich argued, one automatically decomposes these chunks and regroups the components into new configurations.

To test these predictions, Knoblich and his associates asked participants to solve matchstick arithmetic problems. These problems show roman numerals composed of matchsticks that describe an arithmetic relation (Figure 10.9). The goal is to make the relation true by moving a single matchstick. A move consists of moving, rotating or sliding a stick. A slanted stick cannot be interpreted as vertical, nor vertical as slanted. A stick cannot be discarded.

The first problem can be transformed into the equation VI = III + III. That one is pretty straightforward. The second problem is more difficult. You can change the plus sign to an equal sign, leaving III = III = III.

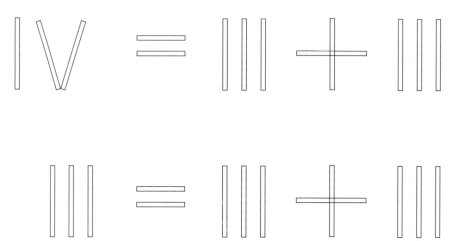

Figure 10.9.   *Two matchstick arithmetic problems. The goal is to move a single*
matchstick to make the expression valid.

The authors argued that to solve matchstick arithmetic problems, people
must relax constraints they have learned in school about math. Examples of
such constraints are that tautological statements (e.g., X = X) are not useful and
that making a change to one side of an equation requires a corresponding change
to the other side of the equation. Furthermore, people must decompose chunks
because the solution to the problem entails decomposing numerals or arithmetic symbols; for example, you must be able to see that you can remove one
matchstick from VII and get VI.

The authors tested how quickly participants could solve matchstick arithmetic problems, varying which type of constraint needed to be relaxed or which
chunk needed to be decomposed. They argued that composite numerals (e.g., VI)
are easy to decompose because they are composed of meaningful chunks (e.g.,
V and I), whereas decomposing a noncomposite numeral (e.g., changing V to an
X) would be harder. They also offered a hierarchy of the difficulty of relaxing constraints, for example that it is easier to change a number (e.g., VII to VI) than to
make an equation into a tautology (e.g., III = III = III).

The results were broadly consistent with the authors' predictions. If the
solution to the problem required relaxing a broader constraint or decomposing
noncomposite numerals, participants took longer to solve it and were more
often unable to solve it.

Knoblich et al.'s account of insight problems is appealing because of its
applicability to a wide range of problems. Functional fixedness proposes that an
impasse occurs because the problem solution requires that an object be used in
an unusual way, but the unusual use cannot be generated because the typical
use is retrieved from memory time and again. The functional fixedness idea
cannot account for the difficulty of matchstick arithmetic problems, and certainly not for differences in their difficulty. Although little research has been directed toward the ideas of constraint relaxation and chunk decomposition, the
approach appears promising (see also Sternberg & Davidson, 1995, for a number of different views of insight).

PRIOR KNOWLEDGE IN OTHER SYSTEMS.   We seemed to have dropped altogether our discussion of problem spaces and the General Problem Solver. What happened? Is this approach incompatible with insight problems, or indeed with problems in which the participant has some knowledge relevant to the problem but has not solved this particular problem before? As a matter of fact, the proponents of these models have applied them successfully to situations in which the problem solver has relevant prior knowledge, but it has usually been in situations in which the person has a great deal of knowledge—in other words, when he or she is an expert in a particular domain. We discuss those studies in the next section.

Regarding insight, Craig Kaplan and Herb Simon (1990) examined the mutilated checkerboard problem, which we discussed earlier. This problem certainly seems like one that is not well suited to the metaphor of a search space. Think for a moment about how you would describe the problem in terms of a search space.

It seems that the typical participant would set up a search space in which the states were the checkerboard covered by various numbers of dominoes. The available operators are the placing and removing of an individual domino, and those operators move you around the space. As we discussed earlier, that search space is so vast that it is almost impossible to explore all of it, so it is almost impossible to be sure that there is not a way to cover all the squares. What's needed is to get out of that search space.

Kaplan and Simon suggested that one can think of a space of different problem representations, just as one thinks of a space of different problem states. We might call this a metaspace; it's a space of problem representations, and each of those representations has its own space of problem states. In the mutilated checkerboard, the phrasing of the problem or the participant's background knowledge might bias them to represent the problem in a particular way when they first hear it. If the search through that space is unproductive, they might start searching for another representation. But how does one generate other representations of the problem?

Kaplan and Simon suggested that there are four heuristics one can use for changing the representation. One is features of the problem. If the relevant information is highlighted in the description of the problem, it is more likely that the person will include that information in his or her representation. A second source of constraint is hints from the experimenter. The experimenter might tell the participant which features of the problem are especially important, thereby explicitly encouraging the participant to include those features in his or her representation. The third source of constraint is the participant's background knowledge; the participant may have beliefs about what sort of representation will be useful. This background knowledge may not necessarily be useful. Kaplan and Simon told the story of a chemical engineering graduate student who spent 18 hours on the mutilated checkerboard problem, most of it in the unsuccessful application of mathematical approaches. His strong background in mathematics may have led him to believe that the solution could be found through this approach. The final constraint on finding a new representation is the use of heuristics. One heuristic in which they were particularly interested was noticing invariants. An invariant is some feature of the problem that appears repeatedly in failed solutions. For example, in the mutilated checkerboard problem, one might notice that the two final squares that can't be covered are always black, leading one to think about the importance of color in the problem representation.

Kaplan and Simon examined some of these constraints on search. They assumed that the best representation for solving this problem is to consider pairs of checkerboard squares, and in one experiment they varied the problem to change how likely participants were to represent the squares in terms of pairs. In one condition, the board was completely blank; in one the squares were colored black and pink, in one the words *black* and *pink* were written in alternating squares, and in one the words *bread* and *butter* were written in alternating squares. These four conditions were designed to be successively more likely to lead the participants to represent that problem in terms of pairs of squares.

In addition, participants who failed to solve the problem received a succession of cues, one delivered approximately every 10 min. The first hint was that the problem was impossible and that they should search for a new "trick" way of thinking about the problem. The second hint was that they should think about pairs of squares. The third hint was to count the different types of squares.

There were three results I'll emphasize. First, the different representations of the problem did affect the time to solve the problem, as shown in Table 10.6. As the experimenters predicted, varying the initial representation affected how likely participants were to think of the problem in terms of the pairs of squares, and that in turn was associated with how quickly people solved the problem.

Their results also showed that hints effectively constrain the search for a representation of the problem. The hint that the participant should think in terms of pairs of squares was especially effective; although the blank condition was much harder than the other conditions, this hint was a great leveler. What made one representation better than another was the likelihood that it would lead the solver to think in terms of pairs. Once the hint made all participants think in terms of pairs, that advantage almost disappeared, and indeed, most participants solved the problem soon after that hint.

Table 10.6   Variations of the Mutilated Checkerboard

Condition	Time to First Mention Pairs (s)	Time to Declare Impossible (s)	Time to Proof (s)
Blank	1,980	828	2,242
Color	1,265	672	1,375
Black and pink	904	639	1,378
Bread and butter	342	483	995

The final important finding was that participants noticed features of their attempted solutions that kept popping up. Examination of the participants' comments as they worked on the problem showed that 88% commented on the fact that covering the squares failed, and 75% commented that a domino covers two different squares (e.g. *bread* and *butter*). If participants had not already received the hint, noticing this invariant was associated with solving the problem sooner.

Kaplan and Simon's analysis of the mutilated checkerboard problem is compelling but may not be applicable to all the problems we've discussed here. The approach strongly assumes that the important processes involved in problem solving are accessible to consciousness. Some of the data we've reviewed in this section indicate that for at least some problems, the problem space changes outside of the participants' awareness until they have solved the problem, at which point they perceive that the problem space has been restructured. Is one of these approaches better than the other, or are there different classes of problem to which each is more fitting? We don't know the answer to that question yet.

In this section we have examined what happens when one has some knowledge that is relevant to a problem, but not extensive knowledge. We have emphasized situations in which that partial knowledge is detrimental to problem solving. Again, I should emphasize that such situations are rare; psychologists engineer problems to have this characteristic because they help us understand how people solve problems, just as psychologists interested in visual perception design visual illusions.

With that in mind, we're ready to move on to our next topic. What happens when you have knowledge that is relevant to a task?

STAND-ON-ONE-FOOT QUESTIONS

7. Name the two ways in which background knowledge can aid problem solving.
8. What seems to be the main reason that people are not better in using analogies to solve problems?
9. How are set effects and functional fixedness similar?

QUESTIONS THAT REQUIRE TWO FEET

10. You may have heard this advice when you couldn't solve a problem: "Stop thinking about it and come back to it." Given what you know about how impasses are broken in insight problems, do you think the advice might be sound?
11. Do any of the phenomena we've discussed in this section seem to bear on creativity? Can you think of any ways you could encourage creative behavior in yourself or others?

➤ WHAT MAKES PEOPLE GOOD AT SOLVING PROBLEMS?

> ➤ *PREVIEW* In this section we first consider how expert problem solvers differ from novice problem solvers. The most important difference seems to be that experts have much more knowledge about the domain. Surprisingly, they don't seem to differ so much in terms of processes they use to select operators; their expertise is a function of applying those operators to a better part of the problem space. We also consider how one acquires expertise. There is no great secret; a great deal of practice is crucial to expertise. Although there is much support for the idea that certain talents (e.g., intelligence as measured by intelligence tests) are largely innate, how such innate talents contribute to expertise is not yet clear. Finally, we consider how nonexperts can be better problem solvers. One factor that seems to predict success in solving problems is working memory capacity (over which one has little control), but a second factor is the effective setting of subgoals, which may be open to practice.

In the past two sections we often focused on the difficulties of problem solving: What you do when you do not have experience that is relevant to a problem, and how your prior experience can lead you astray. In this section we turn our attention to successful problem solving. We first consider the nature of expertise. By characterizing the differences between expert problem solvers and novices, we hope to better understand why experts are so successful in solving problems. Then we discuss whether one can extrapolate the basic findings about experts to novices to see whether the things that give experts their advantage can be applied in some way to novices so that they can improve their problem solving. We begin by considering the nature of expertise.

How Do Experts Differ From Novices?

By definition, an expert is someone who is very, very good at solving problems in a particular domain, such as chess, physics, or baking. Some of the earliest and most influential work on expertise examined chess masters (De Groot, 1946/1978). Chess is an excellent domain in which to study expertise because it has a large number of possible moves, allowing high levels of expertise (as opposed to, say, tic-tac-toe, where it is easy to become an expert), but at the same time the game is bounded, so comparing performance among players is straightforward; it is not so easy to compare the expertise of two bakers. In fact, chess masters are an ideal group to study because their expertise is verified through tournaments that have a standard scoring system by which players can be compared.

Based on our previous discussion of problem solving, we might expect two differences between experts and novices: Experts might have more knowledge about the domain, and experts might be better at selecting operators to move through the problem space. It turns out that there is excellent evidence for the first of these proposals (more knowledge) but mixed evidence for the second (better operators).

William Chase and Herb Simon, following up on classic experiments by Adrianus De Groot (1946/1978), reported that chess masters have extensive knowledge of game positions. Recall that we discussed these results in chapter 5. Chess experts can remember nearly perfectly all of the positions of the pieces after just a brief exposure to the board. However, experts perform about as well as novices if the chess pieces are not in a midgame position but are arranged randomly. The importance of the midgame position indicates that masters rely on their stored memory of previous games in performing this working memory task. Novices and masters both remember the same number of chunks of information from the chess board, but for a novice, a single piece is a chunk of information, whereas for a master a group of chess pieces is a chunk. For example, a master might perceive a rook, king, and three pawns in the corner of the board as a chunk: the standard position of these pieces after a player has castled. It is estimated that chess masters may have as many as 50,000 chess patterns stored in secondary memory (Gobet & Simon, 1998; Simon & Gilmartin, 1973). That experts have a large number of patterns stored in secondary memory has been verified in other domains such as bridge, electronic circuit design, and computer programming.

Experts not only have a more information stored in secondary memory than novices do, but also organize the information differently. For example, Micheline Chi and her colleagues (Chi, Feltovich, & Glaser, 1981) asked participants to sort physics problems depicted on cards. Physics novices tended to sort cards based on the surface features of the problem, such as the objects used in the problem; for example, all the problems that concerned inclined planes might be grouped together. Physics experts classified problems based on the physical law that applied to the problem; for example, all problems concerning conservation of motion might be classified together. These results have been extended to other domains, such as computer programming problems, and objects such as rice bowls and pictures of dinosaurs (Bedard & Chi, 1992).

Experts' secondary memory is more extensively interconnected than that of novices, and it is interconnected in ways that are consistent with their expertise. For example, a study by Frank Hassebrock and his colleagues (Hassebrock et al., 1993) examined the memory of participants at three levels of expertise (novice, trainee, and expert) for information about a medical case. All participants were asked to diagnose the case and then to recall the information presented in the case. Initially, all participants remembered about the same amount. One week later, however, those with more medical expertise remembered less of the case overall.

A more fine-grained analysis of the recall data showed that participants with more expertise remembered a greater proportion of the information that was critical in making a diagnosis. Furthermore, their memory recall was structured similarly to their diagnosis; they remembered information in the same order that they had used it when making a diagnosis. This study shows that new memories within their domains of expertise are influenced by the organization of existing memories in that domain.

There is very good evidence that experts have more domain-relevant information stored in memory and that this information is stored differently.

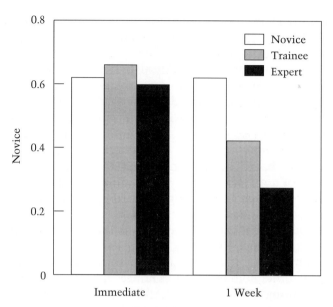

Figure 10.10. *Data from Hassebrock et al.'s (1993) study showing that experts remember fewer of the details from a medical case than novices do after a 1-week delay. More detailed analysis showed that the experts remembered the details that were important for diagnosis and little else.*

How about the processes (i.e., operators) that move one through a problem space? Do experts engage different problem solving strategies than novices do? Early research indicated that they do (Larkin, McDermott, Simon, & Simon, 1980; Simon & Simon, 1978). For example, in one study (Larkin et al., 1980) participants were asked to solve physics problems and to talk aloud about their strategies as they did so. It appeared that novices most often worked backward. They identified the variable requested in the problem and then tried to think of a formula that would yield that variable. Once they had that, they considered what variables in that formula were as yet unknown and tried to generate formulas that could give them those values. Experts, on the other hand, seemed to examine the problem and then solve it starting at the beginning of that chain of inference as though they could look ahead and see the entire solution path.

More recent evidence has questioned this distinction in processing between novices and experts (Zajchowski & Martin, 1993, cited in Clarke & Lamberts, 1997). In one study (Priest & Lindsay, 1992), the experimenters sought to test a larger group of participants than had been tested in the typical experiment, and they also sought to use some measure other than talking-aloud verbal protocols to assess whether people were working forward or backward. Therefore, they tested 79 participants and asked them to write out all the equations and formulas they used as they solved problems. One measure of reasoning is the order in which formulas appeared in the solution. The results showed that there was no difference between experts and novices in terms of how they worked the problems; both groups used primarily forward reasoning.

Not only is there apparently little difference in the procedures that experts and novices apply to problems, it has also been suggested that these processes are not very important in expertise. Indeed, in his original studies of chess expertise, De Groot claimed that top-level masters and expert players search the problem space equally deeply; however, the best players are able to restrict their search to branches of the tree that are much more productive (i.e., that lead to better moves). In another study, Fernand Gobet (1994, cited in Gobet & Simon, 1996) found that masters do search the problem space more deeply than amateur players. Thus, it may be that early in training some of the acquisition of chess expertise results from improved or deeper search but that this source of improvement is quickly exhausted, and further improvement results from increasing the memory database of chess positions.

The relative unimportance of search processes in very high level chess is supported by a study by Fernand Gobet and Herb Simon (1996). They examined the play (via nine published matches) of the world's highest-ranked chess player, Gary Kasparov, under two conditions: when he played a single opponent in a tournament and when he played four to eight opponents simultaneously in exhibitions. In these games Kasparov was limited to an average of 3 min for each round (i.e., one move against each of his four to eight opponents). However, his opponents had 3 min to make each of their moves. All told, then, his opponents in these simultaneous matches had full tournament time to make their moves, whereas Kasparov had one fourth to one eight of tournament time to make his moves.

As mentioned earlier, the skill of all chess players is ranked on a common scale, so it is easy to compare Kasparov's performance when he had full tournament time for each move with his performance when his time was severely restricted. The upshot of that analysis showed that Kasparov's play suffered surprisingly little from the time restriction. The authors argued that the severe time restriction meant that Kasparov had little time to look ahead; the fact that his play did not deteriorate dramatically indicates that looking ahead is much less important than the processes of recognition memory. Recognition memory allowed Kasparov to identify cues to weaknesses in his opponent's position.

How Do You Get to Be an Expert?

We've discussed how experts differ from novices—they differ chiefly in their amount of knowledge about the domain—but we haven't discussed how one gets to be an expert. The evidence points to two factors that you probably can name. To become an expert, you need to practice a great deal, and to reach great heights of proficiency you probably need some inherent talent as well. Although this chapter is about problem solving, much of the interesting work on expertise comes from other domains (such as athletics and music), so this section cites that literature as well. As far as we know, generalizations can be made from the development of expertise in those domains to the development of expertise in problem solving.

The importance of deliberate practice has been emphasized by Anders Ericsson (Ericsson, Krampe, & Tesch-Roemer, 1993). Ericsson defines **practice** as having the following the characteristics:

- The subject must be motivated.
- The task must be at the appropriate level, neither too easy so that the person can perform it effortlessly nor too difficult so that the person cannot perform it.
- There must be immediate corrective feedback (e.g., high-level chess players study games published in newspapers, try to anticipate the next move of each player, and then check to see whether they have anticipated correctly).
- It involves the repetition of the same or similar tasks.

These characteristics distinguish practice from play (in which the purpose is to derive pleasure) and from performance (in which the purpose is to give pleasure to others).

One must not only practice, but practice extensively to become an expert. A number of authors have referred to a **ten-year rule:** It takes about a decade of intense practice to reach the upper levels of expertise. Herb Simon and William Chase (1973) noted that the ten-year rule seemed to apply to chess expertise, and since that time it has been applied to a number of other domains, including musical composition (Hayes, 1981), musical performance (Sosniak, 1985), mathematics (Gustin, 1985), tennis (Monsaas, 1985), long-distance running (Wallingford, 1975), livestock evaluation (Phelps & Shanteau, 1978), radiographic diagnosis (Lesgold, 1984), and medical diagnosis (Patel & Groen, 1991).

All these studies examined people who had already achieved expertise in their respective fields and then determined how long they had been practicing; the figure was always 10 years or more. Another approach to determining the importance of practice is to examine people who are trying to be experts and to see whether those who are practicing more now seem to be making better progress toward expertise. That was the approach taken by Ericsson and his colleagues (1993). The experimenters studied violinists at a music academy. Some were studying to be music teachers, so although they were competent players, they had no aspirations to become professionals. Other students were studying in the hopes of professional careers. Of these, the professors at the academy nominated a group of 10 students who were most likely to succeed as soloists. Ten other violin students were selected who, although very good, were not quite at that level. The experimenters then had the three groups of participants (music teachers, good violinists, and best violinists) keep diaries of their practice schedules (and other activities) and to estimate the number of hours that they had practiced at different ages. Figure 10.11 shows the estimated accumulated amount of practice over the years.

As you can see in Figure 10.11, the best violists practice more than the good violinists, who (not surprisingly) practiced more than the aspiring music teachers. Keep in mind that these are self-report data, meaning that participants told the experimenters how much they practiced, so these numbers may reflect

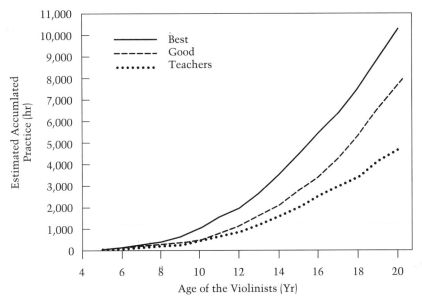

Figure 10.11. *Graph from Ericsson et al. (1996) showing the cumulative amount of practice by two groups of aspiring musical performers (expert violinists and good violinists) and those who planned to teach music.*

the amount of practice they aspired to rather than actually executed. Still, the results are noteworthy, especially given that one could propose that the best violinists would be the ones with the most innate talent and they would not need to practice as much as the other groups.

Based on interviews with experts from a variety of fields, Benjamin Bloom (1985) proposed that there is some consistency in the development of children who become eminent in a field. In the first stage, the child becomes exposed to the domain under playful conditions. The child shows interest and shows promise relative to other children. In the second stage the parents arrange for instruction with a teacher or coach who works well with children. The importance of practice and a regular schedule of practice is emphasized. During this stage the parents show a great deal of enthusiasm and support for the activity, providing a series of teachers of increasing expertise and increasing the financial commitment (which can be great). In the third stage (usually in the mid-teens) a decision is made to commit to the activity full time, and to seek out the very best teaching and training conditions, which often means that the child must leave home. Nearly all students who eventually achieve greatness have a teacher at this stage who has reached the top level of the field. In the fourth and final stage, the student has absorbed most or all of what their teachers can offer and begins to make their own innovations in the domain.

What about talent? Thus far, we've emphasized practice, practice, practice; doesn't the raw material with which one starts have some impact on success? Interestingly, some researchers argue that talent has little to do with success; it's practice that really matters. It is certainly true that some aspects of performance are clearly attributable to practice. As we've discussed, chess experts can remember chess positions so well not because they have superior working memory capacity but because they have studied chess positions. But what about perfect pitch (the ability to name tones accurately), which professional musicians are more likely to have? Isn't perfect pitch something you're born with? Ericsson (1996) suggested that perfect pitch can be acquired at an early age (Takeuchi & Hulse, 1993) and indeed suggests that other apparently innate factors (such as strength, speed, and aerobic capacity) are the product of training.

I think that is taking the influence of practice too far. Returning to problem solving for a moment, there is a great deal of evidence that certain types of talent are at least in part, innate (i.e., that you are born with them). The best known of these is intelligence, at least as measured by standard intelligence tests. How can you tell whether someone is smart because they were born smart or because the person has done things that made them smart? Tom Bouchard and Matt McGue (1981) examined identical twins who were raised apart. Because they are identical twins, they have the same genetic inheritance, but because they were raised apart (usually because they were adopted by different families), their life experiences could be quite different. McGue and Bouchard reported that the intelligence test scores of identical twins reared apart were more similar than the scores of fraternal twins (who don't have identical genes) reared apart.

What does that mean for problem solving? Well, intelligence usually is measured by intelligence quotient (IQ) tests. These tests are designed to predict how people will perform in academic settings. Although it is debatable just how general this definition of intelligence is, it is true that higher intelligence test scores are associated with better performance on certain types of problems that we have been discussing. On the other hand, it has been shown that chess grand masters do not have especially high IQs and, in a quite different domain, that IQ is unrelated to the ability to handicap horse races (Ceci & Liker, 1986). One possible way to accommodate these seemingly conflicting data is to propose that factors such as general intelligence may play a role in the early development of a skill, but with increasing levels of proficiency the contribution of intelligence decreases and the importance of practice increases.

What Makes Nonexperts Good at Solving Problems?

In this section we are discussing what makes people good at solving problems, but thus far we have focused on experts. Suppose you don't want to be an expert (e.g., you're not willing to commit the next 10 years to practice), but you'd like to improve your problem solving. What makes people more effective problem solvers?

Working memory seems to make an important contribution to problem solving. A prominent role for working memory in problem solving is sensible in light of the framework discussed early in this chapter: using operators to move through a problem space. Several things must be kept in working memory simultaneously if one is to use means–ends analysis, for example: the current subgoal, the operator one is trying to apply, and the conditions of that operator. Perhaps more importantly, one must shuttle a lot of information between working memory and secondary memory; as a subgoal is achieved one must retrieve the next goal, one must search secondary memory for appropriate operators, and so on.

Kenneth Kotovsky and his colleagues (Kotovsky, Hayes, & Simon, 1985; Kotovsky & Simon, 1990) argued for the importance of working memory in problem solving. They administered different isomorphs of the Tower of Hanoi problem to participants. An **isomorph** is a problem with a different cover story but with a problem space of the same size, number of branches, and minimum solution path. Here is one such isomorph:

> Three five-handed extraterrestrial monsters were holding three crystal globes. Because of the quantum mechanical peculiarities of their neighborhood, both monsters and globes come in exactly three sizes with no others permitted: small, medium, and large. The small monster was holding the medium-sized globe; the medium-sized monster was holding the large globe; and the large monster was holding the small globe. Because this situation offended their keenly developed sense of symmetry, they proceeded to shrink and expand the globes so that each monster would have a globe proportionate to its own size.
>
> Monster etiquette complicated the solution of the problem because it requires the following:
>
>> Only one globe may be changed at a time.
>>
>> If two globes have the same size, only the globe held by the larger monster may be changed.
>>
>> A globe may not be changed to the same size as the globe of the larger monster.
>>
>> By what sequence of changes could the monsters have solved this problem?

You can see that this problem is isomorphic to the Tower of Hanoi problem discussed earlier. People found this version of the problem extremely difficult, however. Why? Kotovsky and his colleagues argued that the problem is one of working memory. The rules are complicated. There is no physical realization of the problem (i.e., a board with pegs), so you have to remember where you are in the problem space (in this case, which monster is holding which globe). Just thinking about the rules and imagining the monsters uses up most people's working memory capacity, so they have nothing left over to work the problem. In other work it has been shown that people are less successful in solving syllogisms if the premises are given orally rather than in writing, presumably because maintaining the premises in working memory reduces the capacity to manipulate them to evaluate the syllogism (Gilhooly, Logie, Wetherick, & Wynn, 1993). A somewhat similar approach was taken in a study by Pierre Barrouillet (1996), who examined working memory contributions to transitive inference by varying the amount of irrelevant information that appeared

BOX 10.2. FUNCTIONAL IMAGING OF PROBLEM SOLVING AND WORKING MEMORY

Premotor cortex

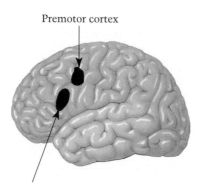

Inferior temporal gyrus

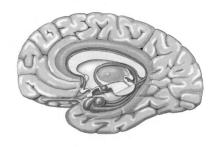

Is it possible to obtain functional images of complex problem solving? It may seem like an extremely difficult exercise because one would expect that even moderately difficult problems will lead to widespread brain activation. Nevertheless, several studies have successfully localized at least some of the processes associated with problem solving.

In one such study Vivek Prabhakaran and his colleagues (Prabhakaran et al., 1997) had participants solve problems from Raven's progressive matrices test (Raven, 1976). This test measures intelligence and is known to predict performance on a wide variety of reasoning tasks. In this test participants are shown a pattern of stimuli and must select a stimulus (from eight choices) that completes the pattern.

The figure also shows the control tasks that Prabhakaran used. The top problem is a match problem, in which participants merely select the response choice that matches the bottom right pattern in the larger figure. This control task demands visual processing of the stimuli but few logical or problem solving patterns. The middle problem is a figural problem in which participants must select the response alternative that completes the pattern. In figural problems, the principle guiding the correct choice was an increase of size, position, or number and demanded primarily visuospatial analysis, but it did demand more than a simple matching process. The bottom problem in the figure is from Raven's progressive matrices test, and you can see it demands the use of a logical rule, not simply one based on the visual properties of successive stimuli.

(Continued)

The figural task was associated with more activation than the match condition, and this increased activation was primarily in the right hemisphere. In particular, the right middle gyrus was especially active, as were the anterior cingulate, superior and inferior parietal gyri, inferior temporal gyrus, and precuneus. Activation was also observed in the left parietal lobe. Thus, most of these activations appear in the right hemisphere, which makes sense because the right hemisphere is especially important for processing spatial information.

When the analytic task was compared with the figural task, significant activation was observed in the frontal lobe, in both the inferior frontal gyri and the premotor areas. In addition, there was greater activity in the left hemisphere in parts of the parietal temporal and occipital lobes. Most regions activated by the analytic task were activated by the figural task, but the activity was stronger for the analytic than the figural.

Most dramatic are the frontal activations, especially because these are the exact regions that are active during working memory tasks. As noted in the text, cognitive researchers have highlighted the importance of working memory capacity in problem solving. The study by Prabhakaran et al. provides converging evidence by showing that brain structures associated with working memory are strongly active during problem-solving tasks.

between key statements that could be used to make inferences. He reported that increasing the number of irrelevant statements increased erroneous inferences, presumably because of the difficulty of maintaining the statements for a longer time in working memory.

Other studies have examined the role of working memory and problem solving by using **dual task paradigms.** In a dual task paradigm, one examines performance of a task under two conditions: when the task is performed in isolation and when the task is performed simultaneously with a second task. The second task is designed to occupy working memory, so if the first task does not require working memory, it should be performed equally well alone or with the second task.

Louise Phillips and her colleagues (Phillips, Wynn, Gilhooly, Della Sala, & Logie, 1999) examined the Tower of London task using a dual task paradigm (Figure 10.12). The Tower of London is similar to the Tower of Hanoi and was named after its better-known cousin (Shallice, 1982). In the Tower of London, colored disks (or beads) must be moved from an initial state to a goal state that is depicted on a card. Only one disk may be moved at a time, and the participant is instructed to plan the whole sequence of moves before executing the sequence.

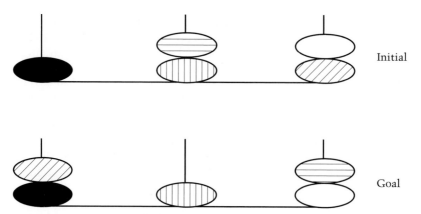

Figure 10.12. *Tower of London problem. The problem is composed of three pegs*
with some number of colored disks (here distinguished by pat-
terns). The participant is shown the puzzle with the disks in a
particular configuration, is shown a goal state on a card, and must
move the disks so that the puzzle matches the card. The disks
must be moved one at a time, and the participant is asked to plan
the entire sequence mentally before beginning to move the disks.

Participants typically perform several versions of the task with different
initial and goal states. The problems vary in terms of the minimum number of
moves required for solution, from 3 to 11. This task has typically been taken as
a measure of problem solving, especially of the ability to plan in problem solving, because one is supposed to plan the whole solution before making the first
move (Lezak, 1995; Owen, 1997; Shallice, 1982).

The secondary task that Phillips and her colleagues (1999) used was a random number generation task in which participants were asked to say digits
aloud in time to a metronome beat. The digits were to be random, with no discernible order (e.g., 123, 654, or 246 would be obviously ordered and thus forbidden). This task is fairly difficult. Indeed, simultaneously performing this
task was detrimental to performance on the Tower of London. Participants performing only the Tower of London task made an average of approximately five
excess moves during the task, whereas participants also performing the secondary task made nearly twice that many. The authors concluded that this task
relies heavily on working memory, and similar conclusions have been drawn
about other problem-solving tasks through the use of dual task paradigms (Howe,
Rabinowitz, & Powell, 1998; Logie, Gilhooly, & Wynn, 1994).

The final method that has been used to examine the relationship between
working memory and problem solving is statistical association. In an article
provocatively titled "Reasoning ability is (little more than) working-memory capacity?" Patrick Kyllonen and Raymond Christal (1990) reported data showing
that people who have a large working memory capacity also score well on tests
of reasoning, whereas those with small working memory capacity score poorly.
They reported four studies, each with 400 or more people tested. Reasoning
ability was tested with a total of 15 tests across the four experiments. Sample
problems are shown in Table 10.7.

Table 10.7   ***Sample Questions from Kyllonen and Christal's (1990) Study***

Test Name	Sample Question
Arithmetic reasoning	Pat put in a total of 16.5 hours on a job during 5 days of the past week. How long is Pat's average workday?
Number sets	Select the set that doesn't fit: 234 567 357 678
Necessary arithmetic operations	Chairs priced at $40 each are being sold in lots of four at 85% of the original price. How much would four chairs cost? 1. Divide and add 2. Multiply and multiply 3. Subtract and divide 4. Multiply and divide
Nonsense syllogisms	All trees are fish. All fish are horses. Therefore, all trees are horses. True or false?
Three-term series	Dick is better than Pete, John is worse than Pete. Who's best: Dick, John, or Pete?

The authors found a consistently high correlation (around .80 or .90 across experiments) between their measures of working memory and measures of reasoning ability. This strong relationship is consistent with the idea that effective reasoning and problem solving depend on working memory capacity (see also Carpenter, Just, & Shell, 1990; Engle, Tuholski, Laughlin, & Conway, 1999; Reber & Kotovsky, 1997).

Thus far, our discussion of how nonexperts can be better problem solvers has focused on working memory, so the advice really boils down to this: "If you want to be a good problem solver, have a good working memory." But working memory capacity does not feel as if it is under our control. You can increase that amount of information you can keep in working memory by studying a particular domain. Thus, you can increase your working memory capacity for chess positions by learning a lot about chess, but that is tantamount to committing yourself to becoming an expert. Is there no simpler way to improve one's problem solving?

Richard Catrambone (1994; 1995; 1996; 1998; Catrambone & Holyoak, 1990) has been investigating one possibility: encouraging people to set subgoals. Catrambone noted that people often are poor at solving problems that differ in even minor ways from example problems, a fact that we have already discussed. In particular, people tend to memorize a series of steps that depend on the surface features of the problem (Chi et al., 1981; Larkin et al., 1980; Ross, 1987, 1989). Therefore, if the surface features of the problem change, the memorized solution is of no use because the solution steps were tied to the surface features (Reed, Ackinclose, & Voss, 1990). Catrambone suggested that people should be taught to form subgoals as they solve problems. Setting subgoals is effective because problems within a domain are likely to share a subgoal, even if the steps to achieve that subgoal vary. For example, in physics problems of the sort used by Chi et al. (1981), people should be taught the subgoal of first determining which of the physical laws is applicable to the problem; that subgoal will always be useful, although achieving that subgoal will vary from problem to problem.

Unfortunately, trying to teach people subgoals explicitly is not very effective. For one thing, people like to see examples when they are trying to solve problems, not just abstract solution procedures (Cheng, Holyoak, Nisbett, & Oliver, 1986; LeFevre & Dixon, 1986). For another thing, when people have tried to teach people subgoals directly, it simply hasn't worked very well (e.g., Reed & Bolstad, 1991). Catrambone (1996) tried a different method. He showed participants example problems and applied labels to groups of steps, with the idea that people would chunk these steps together into a subgoal. For example, participants saw the following problem:

> *A judge noticed that some of the 219 lawyers at City Hall owned more than one briefcase. She counted the number of briefcases each lawyer owned and found that 180 of the lawyers owned exactly one briefcase, 17 owned two briefcases, 13 owned three briefcases, and 9 owned four briefcases. Use the Poisson distribution to determine the probability of a randomly chosen lawyer at City Hall owning exactly two briefcases.*

Catrambone had participants study this solution:

$$E(X) = \frac{1(180) + 2(17) + 3(13) + 4(9)}{219} = \frac{\boxed{\text{Total number of briefcases owned}}}{219} = \frac{289}{219}$$

$$P(X = x) = \frac{[(e^{-\lambda})(\lambda^x)]}{x!}$$

$$P(X = 2) = \frac{[(2.718^{-1.32})(1.32^2)]}{2!} = \frac{(.27)(1.74)}{2} = .235$$

There were two conditions in this experiment, and the critical difference between them was whether they saw the information labeling one of the steps ("Total number of briefcases owned/219"). It's in the box in the equation to indicate that half of the participants saw it, and half didn't.

Catrambone hypothesized that participants in the two conditions would develop different representations of the solution, as shown in Table 10.8.

Note the important difference in the hypothetical representation: In one, part of the solution procedure includes that one should find the total number of objects as part of the solution.

At transfer, all participants saw a different problem:

> *Over the course of the summer, a group of five kids used to walk along the beach each day collecting seashells. We know that on Day 1 Joe found four shells, on Day 2 Sue found two shells, on Day 3 Mary found five shells, on Day 4 Roger*

Table 10.8 **Hypothetical Representations of the Solutions for Catrambone's (1996) Lawyer and Briefcase Problem**

No Label	Label
Goal: find λ.	Goal: find λ.
Method	Method
1. Multiply each category (e. g.,. owning exactly zero briefcases, etc.) by it observed frequency.	1. Goal: Find total number of briefcases. Method: a. Multiply each category by its observed frequency. b. Sum the results to obtain the total number of briefcases.
2. Sum the results.	2. Divide the total number of briefcases by the total number of lawyers to obtain the average number of briefcases per lawyer.
3. Divide the sum by the total number of lawyers to obtain the average number of briefcases per lawyer.	

found three shells, and on Day 5 Bill found six shells. Use the Poisson distribution to determine the probability of a randomly chosen kid finding three shells on a particular day.

Note that this problem is similar, but it requires finding a total frequency in a different way: You have to add a set of simple frequencies instead of having to multiply categories (zero, one, two, or three briefcases) by the observed frequency. Thus, finding the total is simpler in this problem, but people might not know how to deal with it if they didn't understand that part of the solution procedure is to find the total number of objects. Indeed, Catrambone (1995;1996) found that participants who had seen the subgoal as part of the solution procedure during training were about twice as likely to solve this new problem as participants who did not see the subgoal as part of the solution.

In sum, making people better at solving problems is not easy. Although some progress has been made, it appears that the best advice is still "practice, practice, practice."

STAND-ON-ONE-FOOT QUESTIONS

12. *How do experts differ from novices?*
13. *What is the definition of practice?*
14. *Other than practice, what makes someone good at solving problems?*

QUESTIONS THAT REQUIRE TWO FEET

15. *Does practice guarantee expertise?*
16. *Do you think working memory capacity is an important limitation in insight problems?*
17. *Based on everything you've read in this chapter, what is the best advice you would give to, say, a high school student learning geometry who wants to know the best way to learn to solve problems in that domain.*

KEY TERMS

problem solving
problem space
problem state
operator
brute force search
combinatorial
  explosion
heuristic

hill climbing
working backward
means–ends analysis
General Problem Solver
verbal protocol
problem behavior graph
surface similarity
structural similarity

insight problem
functional fixedness
set effects
restructuring
practice
ten-year rule
isomorph
dual task paradigm

11

Language

Dixon was alive again. Consciousness was upon him before he could get out of the way; not for him the slow gracious wandering from the halls of sleep, but a summary, forcible ejection. He lay sprawled, too wicked to move, spewed up like a broken spider crab on the tarry shingle of the morning. The light did him harm, but not as much as looking at things did; he resolved, having done it once, never to move his eyeballs again. A dusty thudding in his head made the scene before him beat like a pulse. His mouth had been used as a latrine by some small creature of the night, and then as its mausoleum. During the night, too, he'd somehow been on a cross-country run and then been expertly beaten up by secret police. He felt bad.

—*Lucky Jim*, Kingsley Amis, 1953, p. 64

In this chapter, we discuss in some detail why we should be amazed by our ability to understand this paragraph from *Lucky Jim*, and we try to unravel some of the processes that make the feat possible.

First, note what your experience is when you read a paragraph or listen to someone speak. You feel that you read or hear words, not individual letters or sounds. Of course it must be the case that you do read individual letters—how else could you differentiate *dead* and *bead*—but you must do so with such speed that the process is not open to awareness. As we'll see, the process of differentiating individual speech sounds is even more difficult than identifying letters during reading.

Identifying letters to form words seems difficult enough, but the problem is still more complicated. For example, did you stumble over the word *light* in the paragraph? Presumably you did not pause to wonder whether it referred to brightness, or lack of weight, or a joyous mood. It seems difficult enough to find the right word in memory amid the clutter of the approximately 60,000 words we know; what do you do when the word you need to find in memory has more than one meaning?

We can also note that even if the mind successfully retrieved the meanings of all of the words, there is still great ambiguity in a simple pile of words. Take the simplest sentence of the paragraph, "He felt bad." Interpreting those three words depends critically on word order, the importance of which becomes obvious if one changes the word order. "He bad felt" sounds as though one is calling someone a piece of felt cloth of poor quality. "Felt he bad" gives the same sense of someone enduring negative sensations, but it has an interrogative note, and sounds as though it were uttered by Yoda. And how do you know that "He felt bad" was not an imprecation of the manner in which Dixon feels things? Sure, he feels, but he's not very good at it. The longer sentences in the paragraph are all the more open to confusion. Word order is not the proper way to think about this factor, of course; what we're really talking about is grammar, and we'll discuss in this chapter how strings of words are interpreted to signify meanings.

Finally, we might consider the larger context of the paragraph. Even if one understands an individual sentence, the meaning of that sentence often is lost if it is not put in the context of the surrounding sentences. Does Amis really want you to know that Dixon has a bad taste in his mouth and that it hurts to move his eyes? Yes, but the author wants you to know those things as a way of communicating that Dixon is awaking with a historic hangover. Amis's purpose probably was achieved—you likely made this inference—although a hangover is never mentioned. How did you know it? There must be some process by which successive sentences are put together into broader ideas and themes, and indeed this process is so successful that one can draw new inferences from these ideas.

Our goals in this chapter are straightforward. First we will discuss in more detail, **What is language and what makes language processing difficult?** Our analysis of the Amis paragraph gives you a sense of the kinds of problems the mind faces in trying to decode language. Language appears to be full of ambiguities—words have multiple meanings, sentences can be interpreted in more than one way—so why is it that other people's speech and the text we read rarely seems ambiguous? In the second part of the chapter we ask, **"How are these ambiguities resolved?"** As we'll see, a key idea is the use of multiple sources of information at the same time. A word may be ambiguous in isolation, but if one recruits other sources of information—such as the sentence the word is in or the conversational context—that usually helps to resolve the ambiguity.

In the final part of this chapter we consider language in the broader context of other types of cognition: **How are language and thought related?** In particular, we take up two questions that have been of intense interest to psychologists and the public. First, can animals be taught the rudiments of language? We've all seen popular television programs in which great apes appear to be communicating with humans via sign language. Just how effective are the apes at communicating? Second, we look exclusively at humans to consider whether the particular words and grammar of our language influence the way we think. It sometimes appears that we think by talking to ourselves; does that mean that the selection of words available to us ultimately proscribes certain types of thought? As we'll see, the answer to both questions in this section have less glamour than one might hope. Apes may have some rudimentary linguistic ability, but their skills have been exaggerated in the popular press. Second, the particular language you speak may have some modest effect on how you think. Early studies indicated little or no effect of language on thought, but these studies may have selected tasks in which such effects were very unlikely to appear.

Before we approach the upper reaches of linguistic usage, however, we will follow the example of grade schools, and begin at the beginning, with the definition of language.

➤ WHAT IS LANGUAGE, AND WHAT MAKES LANGUAGE PROCESSING DIFFICULT?

➤ *PREVIEW* We begin by defining language. This task proves more difficult than one would imagine (the definition is more than simply "communication"), but a definition is crucial to let us know for what we are trying to account. Next, we consider the problems in accounting for how language is perceived. It turns out that there are ambiguities at every level of language: Sentences can be ambiguous, words can be ambiguous, even the very sounds that compose individual words can be ambiguous. In this section we simply describe these problems, and in the next section we discuss how they are resolved. Finally, we close this section by examining what is known about the structure of our language, or grammar. This topic is vital because it shows us just how complex language is and lets psychologists know exactly what they are trying to explain.

What Is Language?

We've begun several previous chapters by defining terms: attention, working memory, and so on. Language proves more difficult to define, and there is not complete agreement as to how it should be defined. There are different characteristics that one can impute to language (or not) that change its character, and these characteristics change what we take to be our assignment in accounting for how language is used. Nevertheless, the following properties usually are deemed critical in its definition (Clark & Clark, 1977):

- **Communicative:** Languages permit communication between individuals.
- **Arbitrary:** The relationship between the elements in the language and their meaning is arbitrary. There is no special reason that the word *chair* must have the referent that it does. It would be perfectly acceptable for the utterance *table* to have the referent that *chair* now does. The word *big* doesn't have to be in some sense bigger than the word *miniscule*. Arbitrariness is a key feature of symbols. A set of sounds stands for a particular meaning, but which sounds stand for which meaning is arbitrary.
- **Structured:** Language is structured, meaning that the pattern of symbols is not arbitrary. It makes a difference whether you say, "The boy ran from the angry dog," "The dog ran from the angry boy," or "Boy the from dog ran angry."
- **Generative:** The basic units of language (words) can be used to build a limitless number of meanings.
- **Dynamic:** Language is not static. It is changing constantly as new words are added and as the rules of grammar (slowly and subtly) change.

These characteristics are important because they give us information about what we are trying to account for when we try to understand how people use language. For example, consider generativity. You may recall from chapter 1 that this property was behind one of the important criticisms Noam Chomsky leveled at B. F. Skinner's behavioristic account of language. Skinner argued that the principles of operant and classical conditioning could account for how children learn language. Chomsky argued that they could not because language is generative; behaviorist principles can account for whether one is more likely to repeat an action taken before, but a distinctive property of language is that we almost never say the same thing twice. In essence Chomsky was saying that Skinner's theory was bound to miss the mark because Skinner failed to appreciate what language is. That is why psychologists are eager to define language; it's a mistake we don't want to make again.

Language is almost always considered at multiple levels of analysis. The lowest level is an analysis of the sounds that make up words. (Throughout the chapter we refer to spoken language, with the understanding that similar analyses would apply to languages that use gesture, such as American Sign Language.) The next level is the words themselves. One level higher, words are combined into sentences, and at the highest level, sentences are combined into a story or text. Each level of analysis brings different problems. Let's look at those levels in turn.

PHONEMES.   Individual speech sounds are called **phonemes.** Phonemes roughly correspond to letters of the alphabet, but some letters must do double duty. For example, *a* is pronounced differently in *baby* and in *back; th* is pronounced differently in *thin* and *then;* these are different phonemes. In all, there are about 46 phonemes in English—the exact count varies among experts—and something like 200 phonemes worldwide. Table 11.1 shows a standard taxonomy of phonemes found in English.

The 46 English phonemes are combined in various ways to produce all of the approximately 600,000 words in the English language.

Why is the perception of phonemes difficult? After all, there are only 46 sounds to be perceived and categorized. In visual perception, you might have to identify anything out in the world. It seems that if someone utters the word *boot* you would simply perceive the three phonemes that compose that word (*b, u, t*), string them together, and thereby hear the word. Even though people can perceive phonemes quite rapidly in accelerated speech—perhaps as many as 50 phonemes per second (Foulke & Sticht, 1969)—it doesn't seem that the problem should be that tough because there are only 46 possible things to hear.

Table 11.1   Standard Taxonomy of Phonemes in English

Consonants				Vowels		Diphthongs	
p	pill	θ	thigh	i	beet	ay	bite
b	bill	ð	thy	ɪ	bit	æw	about
m	mill	š	shallow	e	bait	ɔy	boy
t	till	ž	measure	ɛ	bet		
ɖ	dill	č	chip	æ	bat		
n	nil	ǰ	gyp	u	boot		
k	kill	l	lip	ʊ	put		
g	gill	r	rip	ʌ	but		
ŋ	sing	y	yet	o	boat		
f	fill	w	wet	ɔ	bought		
v	vat	ʍ	whet	a	pot		
s	sip	h	hat	ə	sofa		
z	zip			i	marry		

Source: Clark & Clark (1977).

The first difficulty is that individual speakers produce phonemes quite differently. Different people simply have different ways of pronouncing phonemes. These differences can be quite large if one compares speakers from different regions of the United States. For example, New Englanders are famous for dropping *r*s except those at the beginning of a word (e.g., "Pahk the cah in Hahvahd Yahd," meaning "Park the car in Harvard yard"). Such accents are occasions for comic moments in films that are not very funny, but the variation in phoneme pronunciation becomes still more extreme among nonnative speakers of English. In many cases, these speakers are equipped with a different set of phonemes than the 46 that English-speakers use. When infants babble, they use all the 200 phonemes found worldwide, but by the age of 1 year, the sounds they produce are already whittled down to the phonemes of their native tongue (Blake & de Boysson-Bardies, 1992; Brown, 1958). In one well-known example, adult Japanese speakers do not differentiate between the sounds *l* and *r*. These two phonemes are similar in many respects, but they differ in the position of the tongue when they are pronounced. In Japanese, the sounds *r* and *l* are interchangeable, so Japanese speakers do not differentiate them. Therefore, it is not trivial for a Japanese speaker learning English as an adult to produce *l*s and *r*s reliably.

Despite substantial variations in how speakers produce phonemes, listeners are able to understand their speech; you have doubtless heard English spoken by native speakers of Russian, Chinese, Arabic, and so on. Nevertheless, it is true that native speakers of English make more errors in perceiving speech generated by nonnative speakers of English, and the extent to which they make errors depends on the strength of the speaker's accent (Schmid & Yeni-Komshian, 1999).

Another difficulty of phoneme perception is that phoneme production varies not only between speakers but within an individual speaker. It is not the case that you have a stockpile of phonemes that you string together like beads to form words. If that were true, a phoneme would sound the same regardless of the word in which it appeared, but an individual phoneme is indeed affected by the phonemes that surround it. For example, if you say the word "tulip" slowly, you'll notice that you round your lips before the "t" sound. Why? Because your lips need to be rounded to properly say the upcoming "u" sound. Rounding your lips early doesn't affect the "t" sound, so you may as well round them early. This phenomenon of making one movement in a way that anticipates future movements is coarticulation. Coarticulation refers to executing a movement in a way that anticipates a future movement or is influenced by a past movement. When you say the word tulip, you round your lips in preparation for the *u* sound *before* you've uttered the *t* sound. You don't simply utter each phoneme in the order it appears (e.g., utter the *t,* then round the lips to utter the *u* and so on. The result of these anticipatory movements is that phoneme production is somewhat sloppy, irregular, and variable from word to word. Why is it, then, that we don't hear other people's pronunciation as sounding sloppy and irregular? We take up the answer in the next section, but first we consider still more confusing problems as we discuss the perception of words.

WORDS.   When you hear someone speaking, your perception is that the person utters discrete words. By discrete, I mean that it seems that there are small pauses between words, small bits of dead air. That turns out not to be true. When people speak, they produce a continuous stream of phonemes. For this reason, researchers sometimes call speech a speech stream, to emphasize its continuous nature. To convince yourself that this is true, recall the last time you heard someone speak a language you do not understand. It is impossible to tell where the breaks are between words.

The fact is that the segmentation of phonemes into words is subject to error. A rich source of such errors is misheard song lyrics. Most of us have had the humiliating experience of mentioning an interesting song lyric to a friend, only to discover we had been mishearing the lyric all along. Some examples appear in Table 11.2.

How are we able to segment phonemes into words? Why do we seldom mishear spoken words but make more errors when words are sung?

Even if you hear the word correctly, many words have multiple meanings. If I say "I really like hot dogs," do I mean that I like frankfurters, or that I like athletes who show off? How do you access the correct meaning?

SENTENCES.   Suppose that all of the problems we've discussed so far have been resolved, and perceiving words (and their constituent phonemes) is effortless. Can one therefore understand sentences? Unfortunately, the problems are just beginning.

It seems clear enough that the order in which the words are perceived is a crucial determinant of the meaning of the sentence; drawing words from a sack yields meaningless word strings, not sentences (e.g., "Wish John he jumped had

Table 11.2. Examples of Misheard Song Lyrics From Edwards (1995, 1996, 1997)

Misheard Lyric	Actual Lyric	Song and Artist
Until the sun comes up on a sentimental cup full of lard.	Until the sun comes up over Santa Monica Boulevard.	Sheryl Crow, "All I Wanna Do"
Sometimes my mom plays tricks on me.	Sometimes my mind plays tricks on me.	Green Day, "Basket Case"
I want that gown.	I won't back down.	Tom Petty, "I Won't Back Down"
'Scuse me, while I kiss this guy.	'Scuse me, while I kiss the sky.	Jimi Hendrix, "Purple Haze"
There's a wino down the road / I should have stolen Oreos.	And as we wind on down the road / Our shadows taller than our souls.	Led Zeppelin, "Stairway to Heaven"
Alex the seal.	Our lips our sealed.	The Go-Go's, "Our Lips Are Sealed"
I've got a naked pate.	I've got a new complaint.	Nirvana, "Heart-Shaped Box"
The girl with colitis goes by.	The girl with kaleidoscope eyes.	The Beatles, "Lucy in the Sky With Diamonds"

higher"). Even small changes in word order can dramatically change the meaning of sentences: Compare "John wished he had jumped higher" to "He wished John had jumped higher." The reversal of two words completely changes the meaning.

The preceding examples emphasize the importance of word order (which is the heart of syntax, which we'll discuss later). The problem of ambiguity in sentences goes deeper, however. Consider the sentence, "Time flies like an arrow." The meaning seems unambiguous, yet there are at least five grammatically correct interpretations. Note that in interpretations 2 through 5, *flies* refers to a type of insect.

1. *Time moves quickly, as an arrow does.*
2. *Assess the pace of flies as you would assess the pace of an arrow.*
3. *Assess the pace of flies in the same way that an arrow would assess the pace of flies.*
4. *A particular variety of flies (time flies) adore arrows.*
5. *Assess the pace of flies, but only those that resemble an arrow.*

Despite the fact that there are five possible interpretations of the sentence, few people perceive the ambiguity, and most perceive the intended meaning (interpretation 1).

What is the process by which the mind assesses word order, so that the difference between "Hit John with the big bat" and "John hit with the big bat" is appreciated, and chooses one among many interpretations of an ambiguous sentence such as "Time flies like an arrow?"

TEXTS.   When psychologists refer to a **text**, they typically mean a group of related sentences forming a paragraph or a group of related paragraphs. One of the most notable (and frequently studied) phenomena of text comprehension is that people make inferences when they read a text. For example, consider this rather mundane text:

> I went to the store to buy a CD but I didn't see anything I liked. Next I went to the Mall to buy a shirt, but I didn't have much cash. Then I bought some lunch and on the way home I ran into a friend. We talked on the corner for a while, and then I went home.

Did I bring anything home? Your answer probably is "no," but the paragraph never states explicitly whether I did. I could have bought a CD I didn't care for that much. I could have purchased the shirt with a credit card (or shoplifted it). I might have brought my lunch home with me; the paragraph never said where I ate the lunch.

These points seem silly, but their very silliness drives home an important point: Most people reading this text probably would make the same inferences you made. Nevertheless, the reason we make these inferences is far from obvious. What is it about a text that leads you to make an inference? You probably didn't infer that I wept when I found I didn't have the money for the shirt. Why not? That's not stated in the text, but neither is the fact that I came home without the shirt, and you probably were happy to make that inference. What inferences are important enough that our cognitive system makes them (often outside of awareness), and what aspects of a text lead us to make inferences?

Grammar

Thus far, this section has contained a great many questions and almost no answers. Answers to these questions begin with a discussion of grammar. Grammar does not refer to diagramming sentences as you did in school. **Grammar** is a set of rules that describes the legal sentences that can be constructed in a language. We begin with grammar because it tells us what people do when they produce and perceive sentences.

If our goal is to describe the set of rules that allows the production of grammatical sentences, we must define what makes a sentence grammatical. One can't use the rules found in a grammar book. We're trying to find out what rules are in people's minds as they produce and perceive sentences, and those need not correspond to the rules of "accepted" grammar that appear in books. One option might be to follow some people around and note what they say; from what they say we can divine the rules they used to generate these sentences. That's not a bad idea, but what people say is not a clear window into the rules that produce sentences. Sentences often have stops and starts and "ums" because people lose their train of thought, forget a word and start the sentence over again, and so on. Thus a friend might say "Have you gone to that new . . . uh . . . not the taco place, but it's the one with the, you know where John used to work, but across the street from there?" You probably wouldn't protest if you heard this sentence in causal conversation, but both you and the person who produced it would agree that it is not grammatical. (The next time you're in a group of people, take note of how often sentences are ungrammatical.)

For these reasons, Noam Chomsky (1957, 1965) argued persuasively that a distinction should be made between **competence** and **performance.** Competence is people's knowledge of grammar; performance is the way people actually talk. Competence is our pristine, pure knowledge of how we think sentences should be produced. Performance is the way we actually produce them once this knowledge has passed through the vagaries of an imperfect memory, the social pressures of conversation, and the other factors that influence sentence production. How, then, can you know what people's competence is when you can't judge competence from performance? Chomsky suggested having people read a sentence and asking them whether it seems grammatical to them. Participants typically show good agreement when this method is used. For example, examine the following sentences and see which appear grammatical.

The dog ate the bone.
Dog ate.
The dog ate.
Ate bone the dog.
The bone ate the dog.
By the dog the bone was.

The dog the bone was eaten.

The bone was eaten by the dog.

The dog ate the bone?

Now we have a method by which to analyze grammar. So what are the rules by which sentences are generated? Early attempts to describe these rules by behaviorist psychologists treated sentences as chains of associated words; we'll call them **word-chain grammars.** A word-chain grammar proposes that grammatical sentences are constructed word by word, by selecting the next word in a sentence based on the associations of the rest of the words in the sentence. Hence, you might have the start of a sentence such as, "The boy took his baseball bat and hit the _____ ." Based on past associations, you might well guess that the next word is likely to be *ball*. The problem with word-chain grammars is that someone could end that sentence with the word *window, umpire,* or *squid,* and these sentences would still be grammatical. How can we explain the grammaticality of these weird sentences using the concept of associations?

Chomsky developed the famous sentence "Colorless green ideas sleep furiously" to demonstrate that a sentence composed of words that are very unlikely to follow one another can still be grammatical. This sentence, although odd, certainly passes our test of sounding grammatical, yet how often have we heard something green also described as colorless? How often have ideas been said to sleep? Probably never, yet we effortlessly understand the sentence.

One step that might seem to bring us closer to a correct grammar is to specify only what the next part of speech will be instead of trying to specify the next word. We're still dealing with word-chain grammars, so the next part of speech would be based on associations of the parts of speech of the words that have already appeared in the sentence. For example, we could specify that a noun will have to fill the space in the sentence about the baseball bat. Some researchers did develop such grammars, but they were ineffective. There are two problems with grammars that treat language as parts-of-speech chains. One problem is that there are still too many possible combinations. For example, the sentence "The boy took his baseball bat and hit the _____ " could be completed by a noun (*ball*), but the next word could also be an adjective (*smelly ball*) or an adverb (*very smelly ball*). Nevertheless, the fact that one could make a lot of choices in creating sentences does not seem insurmountable. It points to a more complicated device to generate the proper chain of words but does not indicate that developing a grammar is impossible.

Chomsky pointed out another problem that is fatal to word-chain grammars: Languages have dependencies in them that can span many words and can be embedded within one another. Here's what that means. A word dependency is a situation in which uttering one word commits the speaker to uttering another word (or type of word) later in the sentence. For example, once you utter a singular (or plural) subject of a sentence, the verb must agree in number, wherever the verb later appears in the sentence (e.g. "The little *dogs,* whose master was the nastiest, most foul-mouthed monster who had ever simultaneously threatened me with litigation and tried to romance me, *were* nevertheless quite loving to me"). Despite all the intervening words (and there is no telling how many or few intervening words there will be), one must be sure that the subject and verb agree in number. There are other word dependencies in English. If you use the word *either,* then you will later use the word *or.* If you use the word *at,* then you will use a noun or a gerund (the *-ing* form of a verb that serves as a noun, e.g., *walking*).

The second problem is that these dependencies can be combined and embedded within one another. For example, you can start with, "Either Dan or Bobbie will go" and then embed another clause, forming, "Either Dan or Bobbie will go, or Karen and Jon will go." The options for embedding are endless, and each way in which these dependencies might be embedded requires a different mechanism within a word chaining device to properly generate the word chain. You can generate an infinite number of such embedded sentences, but an infinitely complex word-chain generator is not an option.

The solution is to abandon linear chains and switch to a grammar that represents sentences as hierarchies. In particular, people have turned to grammars in which each node of the hierarchy is a phrase. These are called **phrase structure grammars.** An example of a phrase structure is shown in Figure 11.1.

The advantage of phrase structure grammar is that it specifies a limited number of sentence parts and a limited number of ways in which these sentence parts can be combined. Nevertheless, the system offers great flexibility in creating sentences. Here is a partial list of sentence parts:

Sentence = noun phrase + verb phrase
Verb phrase = verb + noun phrase

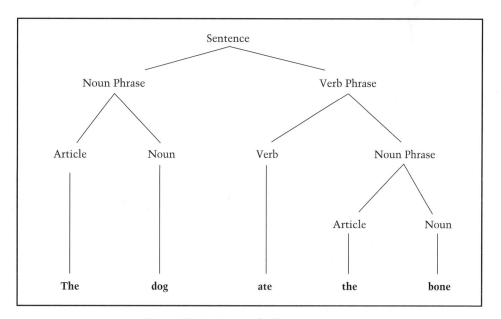

Figure 11.1. *A sample phrase structure.*

Noun phrase = noun
Noun phrase = adjective + noun
Noun phrase = article + noun
Verb = auxiliary + verb

Note one way in which we have greatly simplified our grammar: *Noun phrase* has been defined just once, but it appears within other phrases. Thus a noun phrase is part of a sentence, and it is also part of a verb phrase (as shown in Figure 11.1). A word-chaining grammar would have needed to duplicate the machinery of generating noun phrases for the two different functions they serve. In a phrase structure grammar, phrases are treated as interchangeable parts, and phrases can be joined into the hierarchies representing sentences as needed.

Phrase structures can handily account for the embedding problem that arises when forms such as "either . . . or" are used. We can define phrases like this:

Sentence = noun phrase + verb phrase
Sentence = "either" sentence "or" sentence
Sentence = sentence "and" sentence
Sentence = "if" sentence "then" sentence

This definition allows **recursion.** In this case recursion is a symbol that has the same symbol embedded within it as part of the definition; for example, "sentence" may be part of the definition of another "sentence." Let's take the form *Sentence = "Either" sentence "or" sentence,* but to make the example clear, we'll add subscripts like this: *Sentence$_1$ = "Either" sentence$_2$ "or" sentence$_3$.* To generate *sentence$_1$* we need to define *sentence$_2$* and *sentence$_3$*, so we go to our list of phrases and decide that we'll define *sentence$_2$* using the phrase *Sentence = "if" sentence "then" sentence.* Now we have *Sentence$_1$ = "Either" (Sentence$_2$ = "if" sentence$_4$ "then" sentence$_5$) "or" sentence$_3$.* Next we'll define *sentence$_5$* as *noun phrase + verb phrase.* The final sentence definition is *Sentence$_1$ = "Either" (Sentence$_2$ = "if" sentence$_4$ "then" sentence$_5$) "or" (sentence$_3$ = noun phrase + verb phrase),* which sounds more complicated than it really is.

> Either if Dan relaxes now then he works later, or I will conclude that he doesn't intend to work at all.

Thus, by defining a limited number of phrases and a limited number of ways that they can be combined but allowing these parts to be interchangeable and to be embedded within one another, we end up with a very powerful grammar.

An important feature of the grammar is that it can account for some of the ambiguities of language. As you know, there are occasions in which the meaning of a sentence is unclear. Steve Pinker (1994) provided this example from a television guide:

Tonight's program discusses stress, exercise, nutrition, and sex with Celtic forward Scott Wedman, Dr. Ruth Westheimer, and Dick Cavett.

Two possible phrase structure trees are consistent with this sentence; the difference between these two trees is shown in Figure 11.2.

The hierarchy on the left is consistent with the interpretation that there are many topics to be discussed with Dick Cavett, one of them being sex. The hierarchy on the right is consistent with the interpretation that one of the topics to be discussed is having sex with Dick Cavett. There is nothing in the sentence to tell you which interpretation is correct—the sentence is ambiguous—because the sentence can be parsed into more than one phrase structure hierarchy. Let me emphasize that this property of phrase structure grammars is good. Some sentences are ambiguous, so our grammar must have a way to account for the ambiguity. (Naturally, the ambiguity of such sentences may be resolved by background knowledge such as the likelihood of various topics being discussed on television.)

As helpful as phrase structure grammars are, Chomsky (1957) pointed out that they cannot give a complete account of how we interpret language. He provided the now-classic example of the sentence "Visiting relatives can be a nuisance." This sentence is ambiguous; it can be interpreted as "Going to visit one's relatives can be a nuisance" or "Relatives who are visiting can be a nuisance." Despite this ambiguity of meaning, the phrase structure for both interpretations is the same. Why, then, is the sentence ambiguous?

Chomsky argued that ambiguous sentences such as these constituted evidence for two different levels of representation. One is **deep structure.** Deep structure refers to the representation of a sentence constructed according to a basic set of phrase structure rules. One can take the deep structure of a sentence, apply transformations to it, and obtain a different phrase structure hierarchy. This final phrase structure hierarchy is called the **surface structure,** which

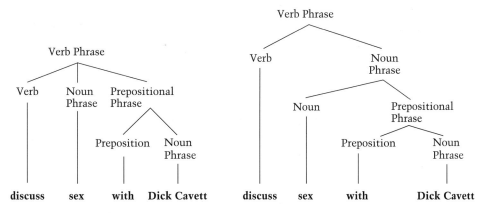

Figure 11.2. *Two possible phrase structures corresponding to the same sentence, illustrating one source of ambiguity in sentences.*

yields the order in which words will be uttered. The idea, then, is that one might start with the deep structure "Dan hit the ball" but then apply a transformation to the deep structure that yields different surface structures: "Dan hit the ball" or "The ball was hit by Dan" or "Dan hit what?"

A single deep structure can be transformed in different ways, leading to different surface structures. Similarly, transformations of different deep structures can lead to the same surface structure. That is the account provided for sentences that have only one phrase structure but are nevertheless ambiguous. Thus, one might start with the deep structure corresponding to "Relatives visiting someone can be a nuisance" or the deep structure "To visit relatives can be a nuisance." Although the deep structures are different, when the proper transformations are applied to each, they yield an identical surface structure.

The distinction between surface and deep structures has changed over the years, particularly in terms of the transformations that change deep structures into surface structures (see Gernsbacher, 1994, for different alternatives). Nevertheless, the differentiation of surface and deep structure is still useful.

To summarize, we have identified a number of ambiguities in language that make the cognitive system's job formidable. There are ambiguities at every level of analysis: in phonemes, in words, in sentences, and in groups of sentences or texts. At the same time, the analysis of language provided by linguists offers a helpful starting point. It suggests a way that the language comprehension system might be organized. In the next section we discuss how these ambiguities are resolved.

STAND-ON-ONE-FOOT QUESTIONS

1. What is language?
2. Why is the perception of phonemes difficult?
3. What's the difference between competence and performance?
4. What is wrong with word-chain grammars?

QUESTIONS THAT REQUIRE TWO FEET

5. I've argued here that structure is important in language, but it seems that sometimes structure is not so important. For example, if a child said to you, "You, me, cookie, go now, hurry," you would know what the child meant even though this is not a grammatical utterance. How is that possible?

6. Can you make any guesses as to why song lyrics in particular are easily misheard? (Hint: Look at that the actual lyrics in Table 11.2 and imagine a friend saying them to you during a conversation.)

➤ HOW ARE AMBIGUITIES RESOLVED?

> ➤ PREVIEW In the previous section we discussed ambiguities in language at four levels of analysis. In this section we discuss how these ambiguities are resolved. Ambiguous phonemes are identified through the use of higher-level context and through mechanisms that are somewhat forgiving of slight mispronunciations. Words can be read in either of two ways: through a process that directly matches spelling to the word in memory or through a process that translates the spelling into a sound pattern, which is then matched to the word's sound in memory. Sentences also are disambiguated through higher-level contextual information, and a similar mechanism may be at work that helps to make inferences in longer texts.

In this section we discuss how ambiguities are resolved, allowing effective perception of language. Just as we described the difficulties of language level by level, we'll discuss the proposed solutions to these problems level by level.

We said that the perception of phonemes is difficult because there is so much variability in how they are produced, both across different speakers (because of accents, for example) and even within speakers because of coarticulation. However, other factors help listeners makes sense of this noisy input. First, the surrounding context helps to disambiguate phonemes that are pronounced sloppily. Richard Warren (1970) showed that listeners can not only adjust for phonemes that are poorly pronounced but can adjust when phonemes are missing altogether. In one experiment, participants heard this sentence: "The state governors met with their respective leg*slatures convening in the capital city."

Participants heard this sentence on a tape, and a cough was spliced into the sentence where you see the "*," replacing the phoneme corresponding to the letter *i*. Remarkably, not only did everyone understood the sentence, but almost none of the participants perceived that any part of the sentence was missing. In another experiment (Warren & Warren, 1970; see also Warren & Sherman, 1974), participants heard several sentences:

It was found that the *eel was on the axle.
It was found that the *eel was on the shoe.
It was found that the *eel was on the orange.
It was found that the *eel was on the table.

Once again, the "*" indicates the location in which a phoneme was replaced by a cough spliced into the tape. Participants heard different phonemes depending on the context. In the first sentence they heard *wheel,* in the second they heard *heel,* in the third *peel,* and in the fourth *meal.* People were not consciously contemplating what sound was missing and then making a guess as to what they should have heard; they believed that they heard the complete word. This demonstration is all the more remarkable because the information that clarified the missing phoneme occurred four words later. This phenomenon is called the **phoneme restoration effect:** a missing phoneme is restored by the context and is never consciously identified as missing. If you think about your own experience, it seems believable that participants didn't notice that one phoneme was replaced by a cough; someone might cough while you are sitting in a lecture hall listening to a speaker, and it doesn't disrupt your perception of the talk.

A second source of disambiguating information comes from vision. You may have noticed that if you are listening to someone whose speech is difficult to understand (because of a thick accent, for example, or because they speak softly), you find yourself watching the person's mouth carefully as he or she talks. When I was in college I had an English professor who was very shy, and his lecturing style was to look toward the floor and mumble. Although the class was small and the auditorium was large, we all sat in the front row and stared at his mouth, straining to get all possible information to help us catch his words.

The use of vision in the perception of speech is at the root of the **McGurk effect,** named for one of its discoverers (MacDonald & McGurk, 1978; McGurk & MacDonald, 1976). In this effect, one watches a videotape of someone pronouncing "pa pa pa" repeatedly. However, the soundtrack has been dubbed with someone pronouncing "na na na" repeatedly. The participant perceives the person on the videotape to be saying "ma ma ma." (Other sets of phonemes yield similar effects.) Participants fuse the two differing sources of information into a sound that best fits that auditory and visual pattern.

Still another factor that aids in our perception of phonemes is **categorical perception.** *Categorical perception* refers to the fact that we do not perceive slight differences in phonemes; phonemes can vary along certain dimensions with no cost in their perceivability. Let me explain what that means. The phonemes *p* and *b* are produced in a similar way; the lips are initially closed, and then opened, releasing air. When *b* is pronounced, the vocal cords vibrate simultaneously with the expulsion of air, whereas when *p* is pronounced there is a short delay between the expulsion of air and when the vocal cords begin to vibrate. That delay (called voice onset time) is the only difference between *b* and *p*, so listeners must be alert for the length of the voice onset time. One would imagine that when voice onset time is very short it will sound like *p*, when it is long it will sound like *b*, and when it is of medium length, it will sound like something between *p* and *b*. That's not what happens, however. The utterances are categorized as *b* or *p*; you never hear something as a mushy, between-*p*-and-*b* sound.

Alvin Liberman and his associates (Liberman, Harris, Hoffman, & Griffith, 1957) conducted the landmark study on this phenomenon. They programmed a computer to synthesize speech and could therefore precisely separate in time the sound simulating the rush of air from the sound simulating voicing. They varied voice onset time between –150 ms (i.e., voicing starting before the rush of air) to +150 ms. Their results were systematic. Up to a value of about 10 ms, everyone agreed the sound was *b* and above a value of 40 ms everyone agreed it was *p*. If the voice onset time was between 10 and 40 ms, people might hear it as *b* or *p* (the likelihood varied between people), but the interesting finding was that if it sounded like *b* with a 20-ms voice onset time, that *b* sounded perfectly well formed, just as good as a *b* with a –10 ms voice onset time. The point is that the auditory system seems to place each speech stimulus into a category, and once the stimulus is categorized, it becomes a perfectly good example of the category. The advantage for speech perception is obvious. It doesn't matter if a phoneme is produced somewhat sloppily as long as it is closer to the target phoneme than to another phoneme.

We've listed three ways in which the auditory system can disambiguate phonemes. What have researchers said about how these sources of information are put together? Can we be more specific about the mechanism by which phonemes are perceived?

Alvin Liberman and his colleagues (Liberman, Cooper, & Shankweiler, 1967; Liberman & Mattingly, 1985) proposed a **motor theory of speech perception.** The core of this theory is that speech perception shares processes with speech production or relies on knowledge about how speech is produced. For example, the phonemes at the start of the word *put* and at the end of word *top* are different. They are produced differently because of the phonemic context— that is, because of coarticulation—but they don't sound different to the listener. Liberman would argue that the speaker does not intend for these sounds to be different, and the listener knows that. The speech perception processes are closely tied to speech production mechanisms, making it easy to infer what the speaker wanted to produce and thereby undoing the effects of coarticulation. The speech perception processes can account for coarticulatory effects and therefore perceive what the speaker intended to produce (well-formed *p*s), rather than the sloppy phonemes that were actually produced.

This motor theory holds that speech perception is the product of a rather specialized module that is specifically designed to perceive phonemes and "clean up" the sloppy ones. However, other evidence calls that interpretation into doubt. First, categorical perception occurs not only for speech but for non-speech sounds such as chirps and bleats (Pastore, Li, & Layer, 1990). Furthermore, categorical perception occurs not only in humans but in other animals including chinchillas, quail, and chimpanzees (Kuhl, 1989; Moody, Stebbins, & May, 1990), and crickets show categorical perception of pure tones (Wyttenback, May, & Hoy, 1996). Thus, categorical perception may not be an adaptation that is specific to human linguistic abilities but rather may be an accidental property of the way our (and other species') auditory system is designed. (If you're wondering, it's not hard to test the perception of *b* versus *p* in a nonhuman. Simply teach it via operant conditioning that it should press a button upon hearing a *b* to get a reward and that pressing the button when a *p* is heard earns no reward. Then start playing speech sounds with varied voice onset times and see when the animal presses the button. My first week in graduate school I met a woman who had kept a chinchilla from one of these studies. I was impressed.)

Other researchers have developed phoneme perception theories that do not invoke special mechanisms of perception (Marslen-Wilson & Warren, 1994; Marslen-Wilson, 1987; Massaro, 1989; Massaro & Oden, 1995; McClelland & Elman, 1986).

Words

We have said that there are mechanisms that help our perceptual systems make sense of poorly pronounced phonemes: The context of a sentence helps us infer what missing phoneme would be appropriate, and categorical perception lets us hear a phoneme correctly as long as it's close to the intended phoneme. Does that mean that recognizing words is a snap? No.

Most researchers believe that words are recognized through a matching process in which a spoken word is compared with a mental dictionary. This mental dictionary is called a **lexicon,** and it contains representations of all of the words you know. It does not contain meanings but contains the pronunciation, spelling, and part of speech for each word. The lexical entry would have a pointer to another place where the meaning would be stored. A sample lexical entry is, as follows:

> Pronunciation: blæk
> Spelling: black
> Part of speech: adjective
> Meaning pointer: → {this directs the system to another location where the meaning is stored}

When someone is speaking and pronounces a string of phonemes, the phoneme string is compared with the pronunciations of the words in the lexicon. If the phoneme string matches an entry, the word has been identified, and the cognitive system has access to the other properties of the word, including the spelling, part of speech, and meaning. Of course, the matching process must be incredibly rapid to keep up with naturally occurring speech. How might the matching process work? One way that psycholinguists have sought to better understand this process is to examine the conditions under which it fails. How resistant is the system to poor input (i.e., mispronounced words)?

The straightforward way to address this question is to let people listen to some words—some correctly pronounced and some mispronounced—and see what gets access to the lexicon. If a word is mispronounced but still gets access to the lexicon, then clearly the mispronunciation was not important to the matching process. But how do you know whether the cognitive system has gained access to the lexicon? Researchers have capitalized on the idea that entry to the lexicon gains access to all components of the lexicon; if you hear *blæk*, then the other information in the lexical entry becomes active, such as the spelling *black*. Researchers can therefore measure access to the lexicon via **cross-modal priming.** In this experimental paradigm the participant listens to spoken words and periodically sees a word appear on a computer screen. The participant is to make a **lexical decision** on the word on the screen, which simply means to decide whether it is a word; sometimes it is a real word (e.g., *black*), and sometimes it is a nonword (e.g., *blarb*). The idea is that if the word on the screen is the same as a word you just heard, it is primed. **Priming** changes a word to a more active state, resulting in easier processing. For example, a participant might hear, "The man considered retiling his kitchen using black and white checkerboard tiles." Just after the word *black* is uttered, the word *black* appears on the screen. Suppose another participant also sees *black* on the screen, but the sentence he or she heard didn't mention the word *black* and instead mentioned rough and smooth tiles. The person who heard the word *black* should be faster in deciding that the printed word *black* is a real word than the person who did not hear the word. If you hear the word, you gain access to the lexicon, and all the information in the lexicon is available, and because the spelling is readily available, you're a bit faster in deciding that the letter string is a real word— that's priming. It's called cross-modality priming because the first word is auditory and the second is visual, so there are two modalities in which the word is presented.

The way the method would be used, then, is to compare lexical decision times to the letter string *black* when you hear *black* (i.e., properly pronounced) and when you hear the word mispronounced (e.g., *blab*). Do you still gain access to the lexicon (as measured by priming) when the word is mispronounced? More specifically, what kinds of mispronunciation blocks access to the lexicon, and what sort of mispronunciations don't affect the matching process?

Surprisingly enough, initial research indicated that the lexicon was fairly picky about how things are pronounced. William Marslen-Wilson and his associates (Marslen-Wilson, Moss, & van Halen, 1996; Marslen-Wilson & Zwitserlood, 1989) used a slightly different version of cross-modal priming in which the prime and the target word are related in meaning instead of being identical (e.g., hear *honey* and see *bee*). They found no cross-modal priming at all when the primed word was changed (e.g., *noney* instead of *honey*). They found that access to the lexicon was blocked even when the changed phoneme was quite similar to the correct phoneme (e.g., *task* changed to *dask*) or when the changed phoneme was the final sound in the word, not the initial sound (e.g., *apricot* changed to *apricod*).

These results seem surprising. How could the lexical system be so choosy about pronunciation, given that the input to the system is so frequently degraded, either by ambient noise, or because the speaker has an accent, or has something in their mouth, or some other factor? A further experiment by Garth Gaskell and Marslen-Wilson (1996; see also Gaskell & Marslen-Wilson, 1998) clarified the conditions under which degraded input blocks access to the lexicon. They looked more carefully at the kind of mispronunciations used in the experiment. Some mispronunciations occur naturally because of the positions of the articulators (e.g., the tongue and lips) as different phonemes are pronounced; in other words, some mispronunciations can occur easily because of coarticulation. Other mispronunciations would be unlikely to occur. For example, in saying "pine bench" a natural mispronunciation would be "pime bench" because the position of the articulators is similar for *m* and *b* (note that you close your lips to pronounce them). So if you position the articulators for the *b* a bit early, that could result in your saying "pime" instead of "pine." An unnatural mispronunciation would be to say "pime cupboard" because the place of articulation is quite different for *m* and *c*.

The experimenters used four types of stimuli, shown in the Table 11.3, representing conditions in which there was a mispronunciation (or not) and whether the mispronunciation was a natural one.

When the changed phoneme was a natural one, participants still were able to access the lexicon. When the change was unnatural, however, they didn't get lexical access, even though the change was a small one.

What does this result indicate about lexical access? In the previous section we pointed out that there is variability in how phonemes are produced, which means there is variability in how words are pronounced. How does the language system deal with that variability? The traditional approach was to treat the variability as noise, or static. There is an ideal way to pronounce a word, according to this view, and any deviation from that ideal simply means that the word is poorly pronounced and therefore less likely to be identified. The Gaskell and Marslen-Wilson results indicate that this view is unlikely to be correct because not all mispronunciations are treated equally; they are not all treated as noise.

Another approach would be to have the stored version of the word account for the variation in pronunciations. For example, instead of having the required sound pattern be the entire word, the required sound pattern could consist of a smaller set of the key features of the word. Variations in pronunciation that still had the key features would be tolerated, but if the key features were disturbed or absent, the word would not be recognized (Lahiri & Marslen-Wilson, 1991).

Still another approach would be to assume that there is a single, fully specified version of the word, but there are also inferential processes that make guesses about what some phonemes probably should have been. An example of such a model is the TRACE model of James McClelland and Jeffrey Elman (1986). This is a connectionist network model, a type of model we introduced in chapter 7. The model has nodes that may become active. The nodes are connected by links, along which activation may be passed to other nodes or may inhibit the activity of other nodes.

As shown in Figure 11.3, there are three layers of nodes. The bottommost layer represents acoustic features. We haven't discussed acoustic features, but they are the building blocks of phonemes. The next layer represents phonemes. A particular pattern of active acoustic features is connected to an individual phoneme, so if all those features are active, the node for the phoneme becomes quite active, and if one or two features are missing the phoneme still is active, but less so. The third layer of nodes represents words. A particular pattern of phoneme nodes is connected to an individual word node, so if the right

Table 11.3. ***Stimuli Used in Gaskell and Marslen-Wilson's (1996) Experiment***

Sentence Type	Changed	Unchanged
Natural change	Pime bench	Pine bench
Unnatural change	Pime cupboard	Pine cupboard

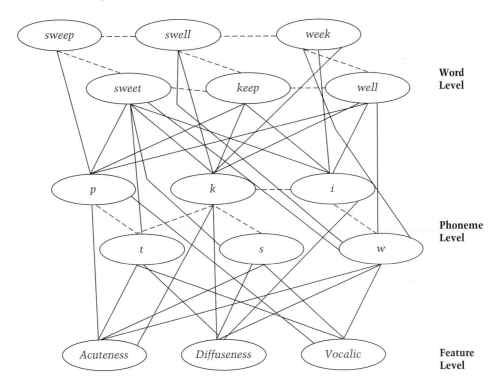

Figure 11.3. *A very simplified version of McClelland and Elman's (1986) TRACE model. The lines indicate links between nodes; to keep the figure simple, only some of the links are shown. The solid lines are excitatory connections, and the dotted lines are inhibitory. Note that the links within a level are inhibitory (again, not all links are shown) because more than one word is not pronounced; if the word is more likely to be* sweep, *then it is less likely to be* sweet, *and* sweet *should be inhibited. The links between levels are excitatory, and they are bidirectional. If the phonemes* s, w, *and* i *are active, that will activate the words that are consistent with those phonemes (e.g.,* sweet *and* sweep); *the word activations will activate phonemes that are consistent with those words (*p *and* t).*

phonemes are active they pass their activation to the word node, making the word active. An important feature of the model is that there are connections not only from the lower-level layers going up but also going in the other direction. Thus, suppose one heard the phonemes *swi* (corresponding to the letters *swee*). The activation of those phonemes would propagate activation upward to the word level, activating words that start with that sound (e.g., *sweet* and *sweep*). The activation of those words would in turn propagate activity downward in the model, leading to activity of the phonemes *t* and *p*. Thus, the TRACE model includes processes that could compensate for poorly pronounced or missing phonemes.

All findings we have discussed thus far have concerned the comprehension of spoken words. What about reading written words? A popular class of models are **dual route models of reading** (Baron & Strawson, 1976; Behrmann & Bub, 1992; Coltheart, Curtis, Atkins, & Haller, 1993; Coltheart & Rastle, 1994;

BOX 11.1. FUNCTIONAL IMAGING
OF SINGLE WORD PROCESSING

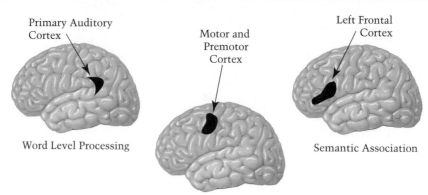

Primary Auditory Cortex

Motor and Premotor Cortex

Left Frontal Cortex

Word Level Processing

Semantic Association

Motor Programming of Articulation

Our discussion in the text has focused on lexical access in reading. Much work using functional imaging has focused on the different contributions of brain structures to processes strictly within auditory processing.

In some of the seminal studies using positron emission tomography, Steve Petersen and his colleagues (Petersen et al., 1988) sought to examine processes related to word perception and production. Recall that effective use of brain imaging requires control conditions that are tightly matched to the experimental condition. Here are the three conditions Petersen used:

Control Task	Experimental Task	Critical Component
View fixation cross	Hear or see words	Automatic word-level processing
Hear or see words	Repeat words	Motor programming of articulation
Repeat words	Generate verbs associated with words	Semantic association

Thus, participants performed four tasks: looking at a fixation cross, passively hearing (or seeing) words, repeating words that they saw or heard, or generating an appropriate verb to go with a word they saw or heard (e.g., seeing *cake*, saying *eat*). The tasks were set up so that Experimental task – Control task = Critical component. Petersen could subtract the activations from the control task from the experimental task to yield activations associated with one critical component of single-word processing.

The figures above show the activations resulting from the subtractions. As you can see, presentation of the words leads to automatic processing in the appropriate sensory areas: primary visual cortex for visual presentation and primary auditory cortex (or more broadly, activity around the sylvian fissure) for auditory

(Continued)

presentation. The activity associated specifically with programming the articulators to repeat a word is isolated in motor areas: primary motor, premotor, and supplementary motor cortices and cerebellum. When participants must access the meaning of words, activation is observed in left frontal cortex (working memory), anterior cingulate (attention), and right cerebellum (the function of which is not understood). In this original study Petersen et al. did not observe activation in temporal lobe, which is where most researchers thought word meanings are stored, but subsequent studies observed activation of the temporal lobe when the lexicon is accessed.

This study was one of the first to show the power of functional imaging to localize cognitive processes. It is a model of thoughtful task analysis that leads to carefully controlled conditions and subsequent clear patterns of activation.

Forster & Chambers, 1973; Paap & Noel, 1991; for an approach to reading that is not dual route, see Seidenberg & McClelland, 1989). These models contend that there are two mechanisms for reading. One route uses a direct lexicon lookup procedure based on the word's spelling. Earlier in this chapter we said that the lexicon includes information about spelling, and this route simply matches the written word to the spelling entries in the lexicon. The second route uses a translation procedure that converts the written letters to a sound and then matches the sound to the auditory entry in the lexicon; after the written input has been converted to sound, recognizing the written word is similar to recognizing a spoken word.

This dual route model neatly accounts for several findings that are otherwise difficult to accommodate. When you see words like *slint* or *papperine,* you can read them aloud, if you so desire. How? These aren't real words, so you have no lexical entry for them. This ability seems to require postulating that readers know a set of rules that convert letters and groups of letters into phonemes—call them letter-to-phoneme rules. On the other hand, this set of rules cannot completely account for reading because readers also successfully read so-called exception words such as *colonel* and *pint* whose pronunciation is not in line with the letter-to-phoneme rules. The dual route model proposes that these words are not handled by the letter-to-phoneme translation processes. If they were, you would pronounce *colonel* as *kahlownell* and *pint* would rhyme with *hint.* Instead, you use the spelling of these words to establish that they are in the lexicon. The spelling also lets you gain access to the lexical entry for the word, and once you've gained access to the word's lexical entry, you have access to the word's pronunciation.

Thus the dual route model can easily account for our ability to read nonwords (e.g., *slint*), which uses the letter-to-phoneme route, irregular words (e.g., *pint*), which uses the spelling-lookup route, and regular words (e.g., *cake*), which might use either route. But do we really need two routes? Can we find more compelling evidence that these routes are truly separate?

One form of evidence comes from different types of dyslexia. You are probably aware that dyslexia is a problem in reading. **Acquired dyslexia** is a reading problem in an adult that is caused by brain damage (e.g., as from a stroke or removal of a brain tumor) in people who were normal readers before the injury. There are two types of acquired dyslexia. In **surface dyslexia** the reading of non-words (and regular words) is preserved, but the patient has difficulty reading irregular words. Hence, the patient could read *nurse* or *glebe* but might read *glove* as rhyming with *cove* and *flood* as rhyming with *mood* (Marshall & Newcombe, 1973). An extreme case of this disorder, patient K.T. (McCarthy & Warrington, 1986) could read irregular words correctly only about 47% of the time, even if they were quite common (i.e., that appeared quite frequently in the language), but could read regular words accurately 100% of the time. The clear interpretation within the dual route model is that the letter-to-phoneme rules are intact in this patient, but there is selective damage to the spelling-lookup route.

An altogether different type of dyslexia is observed in other patients. These patients have selective difficulty in reading nonwords. They can correctly read irregular words (e.g., *yacht*) and regular words (e.g., *cup*) but they cannot read nonwords. This pattern of reading abilities is called **phonological dyslexia** (Beauvois & Derouesne, 1979). One extremely impaired patient could read regular words correctly with 90% accuracy even when they were long (e.g., *satirical*) but could not read even simple nonwords aloud (e.g., *nust*). Even more incredibly, the patient could name individual letters successfully, but he could not say which sound they made, although he could repeat the sound if it were given to him (Funnell, 1983).

We have been discussing acquired dyslexia, which strikes an accomplished reader as a result of brain damage. A second type of dyslexia, **developmental dyslexia,** is abnormal development of reading processes in children. A number of reading researchers have argued that developmental dyslexia takes one of two patterns, corresponding closely to the surface or phonological dyslexia one sees in acquired dyslexia (Harris & Coltheart, 1986; Marshall, 1984).

The dual route model also accounts for some particular patterns of data in normal adult readers. For example, suppose I gave you a **lexical decision task.** In this task you see a string of letters and must say whether the letter string forms a word; for example, you might see *wolt* or *beep.* Now suppose you saw the word *koat* or *phocks.* Both have pronunciations that match real words (*coat* and *fox*), but they are not words. What should the dual route model predict? Response times to these nonwords should be slower than to nonwords whose pronunciation does not match real words. The response times should be slower because the two routes will conflict as to the correct answer. The letters-to-phonemes route identifies the sound pattern as matching a word in the lexicon, whereas the spelling-lookup route does not identify a word in the lexicon with this spelling. This expected pattern of response times has been verified (Rubenstein, Lewis, & Rubenstein, 1971).

The dual route model also predicts that normal readers, when reading aloud, should be slower in reading exception words such as *yacht* than reading nonexception words such as *round.* Exception words generate two conflicting readings of *yacht:* the correct pronunciation derived from the pronunciation entry in the lexicon (which was accessed via the spelling-lookup route) and an incorrect pronunciation derived from the letter-to-phoneme rules that would sound something like *yatcht,* rhyming with *patched.* There is no conflict for regular words such as *round*, however, because both routes produce the same sound. The data are more or less consistent with the prediction (Paap & Noel, 1991; Seidenberg, Waters, Barnes, & Tanenhaus, 1984; Taraban & McClelland, 1987), but the effect seems small or nonexistent if one examines irregular words that are very common in the language and that participants therefore are likely to have a great deal of experience reading.

Sentences

Although we just finished discussing the processing of words, we must immediately reconsider how the lexicon is accessed in the context of sentences because once we have words grouped in a sentence, we can ask whether access to the lexicon is biased by the context of the sentence. To take a classic example (Swinney, 1979), consider these two sentences, each containing the word *bugs*.

> The room was filthy, and there were *bugs* in the corner, according to my friend.
> The embassy was not secure, and there were *bugs* in the corner, according to my friend.

Had you read each sentence in isolation, you probably would have been aware of only one meaning of the word *bugs*. We can ask whether our introspection matches what our cognitive system is actually doing. Does the beginning of the sentence bias access to the lexicon, so that the meaning of *bugs* that is appropriate to the context is accessed and the other meaning is not accessed?

Early research indicated that both meanings are accessed but that the meaning inappropriate to the context is suppressed rapidly. More recent research indicates that that conclusion is not wholly right, but I'll describe that first study because it is important to understand the method it used. David Swinney (1979) presented participants with sentences such as the "bugs" sentences auditorily. As they listened, they also had to perform a lexical decision task to words that periodically appeared on a computer screen. The critical word appeared on the screen right after participants heard the word "bugs." The lexical decision was to be made to the word *spy, ant,* or *sew. Sew* is related to neither meaning of *bug*, so you wouldn't expect people to respond especially quickly to it, but *spy* and *ant* are related to the separate meanings of the word *bugs*, so if one meaning of *bugs* has been accessed in the lexicon, you would expect that the participant could verify a related word quickly. So if you present *bugs* in the dirty room sentence, you expect people to respond quickly to *ant;* do they also respond quickly to *spy?* If they do, that indicates that both meanings of *bugs* are accessed from the lexicon, even though the sentence clearly indicates that only one meaning is appropriate.

Swinney reported that both word meanings are accessed; there was an advantage in recognizing the word *ant* or the word *spy*, and the advantage was there for either sentence. But when Swinney changed the experiment by probing for lexical access not immediately after *bugs* but four words later, he observed facilitation only for the context-appropriate meaning; if participants heard the dirty room sentence and saw *spy* on the screen at the end of the sentence, they showed no priming when they identified *spy* as a word. Swinney concluded that both meanings of a word are accessed but that the context of the sentence usually makes one meaning of the word clearly inappropriate, and that inappropriate meaning is suppressed quickly.

However, further work indicated that a strong biasing context could affect access to the lexicon, resulting in only the appropriate meaning being retrieved. Greg Simpson and Merilee Kreuger (1991) had participants read sentences aloud in which the last word was a homophone. The sentences biased the homophone toward the dominant (i.e., more common) meaning or toward the subordinate (i.e., less common) meaning, or did not bias the interpretation, as follows:

Dominant: This has been a cold and rainy *spring.*
Subordinate: This is a broken and rusty old *spring.*
Ambiguous: This really is not a very good *spring.*

Participants were asked to read each sentence aloud. As they read the last word, another word appeared on the screen, and they were to read that word aloud as quickly as possible. The final word could be related to the dominant meaning (the season), the subordinate meaning (coil), or an unrelated word (e.g., *cow*). The assumption was that it would be easier to read a word if a semantically related word was activated recently. The unrelated word therefore provides a baseline for how quickly each participant can read words. If the biasing context doesn't affect lexical access, then people should be faster in reading words related to either the dominant or subordinate meaning because both meanings are activated, no matter how the sentence biases your interpretation. The results showed that the context did matter.

When the biasing context matched the final to-be-read word, participants were faster in reading it (compared to their time in reading the completely unrelated word). If the biasing context did not match the final to-be-read word, there was no advantage in reading time and therefore presumably no lexical access for that meaning of the word. The delay between the end of the sentence (when the lexicon would be accessed for the homophone) and the presentation of the to-be-read word had no effect on the pattern of results.

The reasons for the difference between these results and Swinney's are not entirely clear. One possibility is that the experiments differed in the strength of the biasing context. It may be that the context must be strong enough to restrict lexical access. Another possibility is that the results depend on the task. Swinney's task is really two tasks: Participants must always be watching the screen as they listen to the sentences, so they must divide attention. The division of attention may water down the biasing effect of the context. In any event, it does appear that lexical access can be affected by context, at least under some conditions.

Suppose that the perception of phonemes and of words has proceeded apace, and one is attempting to understand how these words combine to form

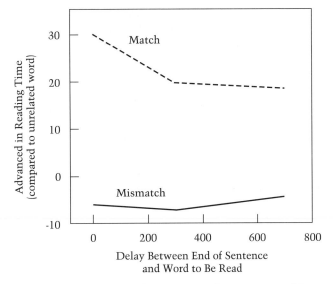

Figure 11.4. *Results of the experiment by Simpson and Krue-*
ger (1991). When the biasing context matched
the final word, priming was observed, but no
priming was observed when it did not. Priming
is shown as a difference score; it's the degree to
which people could read the last word faster
than a control word. Note that the delay be-
tween the end of the sentence and the occur-
rence of the to-be-read word had no impact on
the amount of priming. These results indicate
that lexical access is biased by context.

a sentence. As we mentioned earlier, it is obviously not sufficient to simply
perceive words; the sentence "I'd rather die than swim" has very different
meaning from "I'd rather swim than die," and the difference between those sentences clearly is not a difference of words but of the arrangement of words.
We said earlier that sentences are represented in terms of phrase structures.
Thus much of the debate centers on how listeners take the word-by-word input
of speech and build the appropriate hierarchical phrase structure representation for each sentence. For example, consider this sentence: "The horse raced
past the barn fell."

What? Even after rereading it, you still may not understand what this
sentence means. Here's a rephrasing that makes it clearer: "The horse that was
raced past the barn is the one that fell." Even if you understood the meaning
without the rephrasing, you probably felt jarred when you came to the word *fell*.
This sentence is called a **garden path sentence.** A garden path sentence is one
in which your cognitive system builds a phrase structure, but later in the sentence it becomes clear that something must be wrong with the phrase structure as built. The cognitive system is led down the garden path, so to say, by
a pattern of words that indicates one structure but actually requires another

BOX 11.2. FUNCTIONAL ACTIVATION OF SYNTACTIC PROCESSING

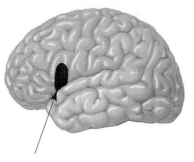 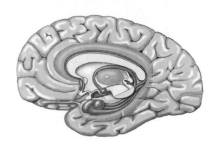

Broca's area

What part of the brain is important for parsing grammar? Lesion studies going back to the classic work of Broca in the late 19th century implicate an area in the lateral inferior frontal lobe, just anterior to the primary motor strip. This area is called Broca's area, in honor of Broca's contribution. The classic Broca's aphasic patient who has damage restricted to this area shows grammar-related deficits in production and comprehension of speech. When speaking, a patient with Broca's aphasia shows what is called telegraphic speech, omitting articles and function words, often omitting tense, and in general showing sparse use of grammar. Here is an example from Gardner (1977):

> INTERVIEWER: What was your work before you entered the hospital?
> PATIENT: I'm a sig . . . no . . . man . . . uh, well, . . . again.
> INTERVIEWER: You were a signal man?
> PATIENT: . . . right.
> INTERVIEWER: Were you in the Coast Guard?
> PATIENT: No, er, yes, yes, . . . ship . . . Massachu . . . chusetts . . . Coastguard . . . years [holds up hand to indicate 19].
> INTERVIEWER: You were in the Coast Guard for nineteen years?
> PATIENT: Oh . . . boy . . . right . . . right
> INTERVIEWER: Why are you in the hospital?
> PATIENT: [patient points to paralyzed arm] Arm no good [points to mouth] Speech . . . can't say . . . talk, you see.
> INTERVIEWER: What happened to make you lose your speech?
> PATIENT: Head, fall, Jesus Christ, me no good, str, str . . . oh Jesus . . . stroke.

This patient knows what he wants to say but has problems generating the sentences to say it. Patients with Broca's aphasia also have difficulty understanding complex syntactic structures, and they rely on context and meaning to help them

(Continued)

understand even simple syntax. For example, a Broca's aphasic patient would be able to understand "The boy hit the ball" because the meanings of *boy, hit,* and *ball* constrains who hit what. If the sentence were "The boy hit the girl" the patient might make errors because either the boy or the girl might do the hitting. Once embedded clauses are added (e.g., "The boy that the girl saw hit the dog"), a patient with Broca's aphasia would make many errors.

Functional imaging data support the importance of Broca's area. For example, in one study David Caplan and his associates (Caplan, Alpert, & Waters, 1998) had participants read sentences that varied only in their syntactic structure. Some sentences had a center-embedded relative clause ("The juice that the child spilled stained the rug"). Control sentences conveyed the same meaning, but with right-branching relative clauses ("The child spilled the juice that stained the rug"). Participants were to read the sentences for meaning; some were plausible and some were not, and they made a plausibility judgment about each sentence. Behavioral studies have shown that sentences with center-embedded clauses are more difficult to process (e.g., they take longer to read).

The researchers subtracted the activation associated with the simpler sentences from the activation associated with the syntactically more complex sentences and found a strong activation restricted to part of Broca's area as well as activation in cingulate gyrus (probably caused by increased attentional demands of the more complex sentences). Work is continuing to further elucidate the various subprocesses that must contribute to a complex function such as syntax comprehension.

---

structure. Let us call the psychological mechanism that derives phrase structures from sentences the sentence parser. The sentence parser assumes that *raced* is the main verb of the sentence. This assumption need not be true; why, then, doesn't the sentence parser wait until all of the evidence is in? For whatever reason, the parser doesn't. It takes gambles. Most of the time the gambles are good ones, and sentence processing proceeds smoothly. Occasionally, it makes a mistake and needs to tear apart the phrase structure representation it had been building and start over again.

This simple example points the way to some of the important dimensions on which models of sentence processing differ. First we might ask what cues the sentence parser uses to derive an interpretation. Second, we might ask when the parser commits to an interpretation. Clearly it had committed itself to a particular interpretation of the ongoing sentence before it reached the last word (*fell*). Does it have to assign a place to each word as it comes in? Does it have a buffer of three or four words so that it can suspend judgment on a particular word until it gets more information? Third, we might ask whether the parser is influenced by surrounding context. Suppose you saw this pair of sentences:

THALIA: Did the horse standing by the pond fall, or was it the one that Warren raced past the barn?

DEXTER: The horse raced past the barn fell.

Or perhaps the parser is sensitive to the semantics of the words that it is parsing. For example, suppose the sentence had been, "The horse led past the barn fell."

"Led" typically is not an active verb for horses. Horses are led; they don't lead others. Would that make any difference at all in how people interpret the sentence, perhaps making them less likely to traipse down the garden path? Let's look at some of the cues the parser uses to build phrase structures.

Key words provide an important cue to the correct phrase structure organization. For example, the word *a* indicates that a noun phrase follows. The words *who, which,* and *that* indicate a relative clause. One source of support for the importance of key words comes from studies in which the key words are omitted. Jerry Fodor and Merrill Garrett (1967) presented participants with one of two variants of a sentence; one had the key words and the other did not, as follows:

The car that the man whom the dog bit drove crashed.
The car the man the dog bit drove crashed.

Both sentences contain relative clauses, but in the second sentence the relative pronouns have been removed. Participants were to listen to one of these sentences and paraphrase it to show that they understood it; participants were faster and more accurate in paraphrasing sentences that did have the relative pronouns present. Presumably the relative pronouns are cues that there is a relative clause in the sentence (see also Hakes & Cairns, 1970; Hakes & Foss, 1970).

Another cue the parser uses is word order; more specifically, the parser assumes that sentences will be active. People are faster in determining the meaning of a sentence if it is in the active voice ("Bill hit Mary") than in the passive voice ("Mary was hit by Bill"; Slobin, 1966).

There are many sentences in which word order and key words are not enough to go on, however. When a new word is perceived, it's not clear how it should be parsed. Lyn Frazier (1978, cited in McKoon & Ratcliff, 1998) proposed a rule that the parser might use in such cases: the **principle of minimal attachment.** The idea is that the parser is biased to add new words and phrases to a node that already exists on the hierarchy rather than creating a new node. In a classic study examining this proposal, Keith Rayner and his associates (Rayner, Carlson, & Frazier, 1983) showed participants two similar sentences that differed in their phrase structures.

The spy saw the cop with binoculars but the cop didn't see him.
The spy saw the cop with a revolver but the cop didn't see him.

The relevant part of the phrase structure for each sentence is shown in Figure 11.5.

Note that in the sentence on the left, *binoculars* is part of the verb phrase started by *saw,* whereas in the sentence on the right, *revolver* requires that a new node be generated to represent the noun phrase. Rayner and his associates

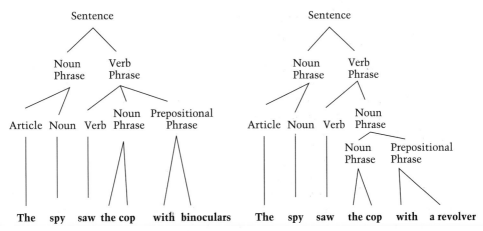

Figure 11.5. *Phrase structures for the key parts of the sentences in the experiment by Rayner et al. (1983). Note that the hierarchical structure is more complex for the phrase on the right.*

recorded participants' eye movements while they read these (and similar) sentences and found that reading times were longer when minimal attachment was violated, and the increased time resulted from locations of the violation; participants' eyes dwelled on those locations longer.

Until the mid-1990s, most researchers thought that the types of cues we've been discussing—key words, word order, and minimal attachment—pretty much accounted for how sentences were parsed. Note that all these cues are syntactic cues; they concern syntax, and the semantics or meaning of the sentence plays no role in parsing it. This conclusion was based on studies that used a variant of the "spy with binoculars" study. Fernanda Ferreira & Charles Clifton (1986) used sentences like the following:

The defendant examined by the lawyer shocked the jury.

The evidence examined by the lawyer shocked the jury.

In the first sentence *examined* could be the main verb, and the fact that it is a participle is clear only once the word *by* has been read. In the second sentence, *examined* couldn't be the main verb because the evidence could not examine something; *examined* must be a participle. Nevertheless, you get the same garden path eye movements seen in the "spy with binoculars" study. The conclusion was that semantic content does not help constrain the way a sentence is parsed (see also Mitchell, Corley, & Garnham, 1992; Rayner, Garrod, & Perfetti, 1992).

More recent studies call that conclusion into doubt (Altmann, Garnham, & Dennis, 1992; Altmann, Garnham, & Henstra, 1994; Britt, 1994; Britt, Perfetti, Garrod, & Rayner, 1992). For example, Gerry Altmann and Mark Steedman (1988) provided participants with a strong semantic context to bias the interpretation of the key phrase:

Noun phrase context: A burglar broke into a bank carrying some dynamite. He planned to blow open a safe. Once inside he saw that there was a safe *which had a new lock* and a safe *which had an old lock.*

Verb phrase context: A burglar broke into a bank carrying some dynamite. He planned to blow open a safe. Once inside he saw that there was a safe *which had a new lock* and a strongbox *which had an old lock.*

Noun phrase target: The burglar blew open the safe with the new lock and made off with the loot.

Verb phrase target: The burglar blew open the safe with the dynamite and made off with the loot.

The experimenters generated stimulus materials that could bias a reader toward a noun phrase interpretation or toward a verb phrase interpretation. Then the target sentence could contain a noun phrase or a verb phrase (as in the spy/binoculars study).

Normally you would expect strong garden path effects for the target sentence when the "old lock" version was presented, and indeed a prior experiment with a neutral context showed that such effects were obtained. In this experiment, however, the effects were moderated by the biasing context: people read the critical phrase more quickly when the context had biased them to expect it.

Whether semantics plays a role in parsing remains unclear. Although this study indicated that semantics did influence parsing, other studies demonstrate different results. Some studies (e.g., Boland & Boehm-Jernigan, 1998; MacDonald, Pearlmutter, & Seidenberg, 1994; Trueswell, Tanenhaus, & Garnsey, 1994) indicated that the parsing system is sensitive to frequency information. In other words, if a verb is most often used in one syntactic context, the parser assumes that context is being used until other evidence disconfirms that assumption. For example *examined* may be used more often as a main verb than as a past participle.

There is evidence that semantic information in the sentence helps parse it only when there is no reliable information about the syntactic role a word typically plays. That is, if it is not clear whether *examined* is usually a main verb or a participle, then the noun preceding it might be evaluated for its meaning to see whether that can help parse *examined*. If *examined* is almost always a main verb (and seldom a participle) the parser just bulls ahead, assuming that it's a main verb, as usual (Boland, 1997; Spivey & Tanenhaus, 1998).

Another factor in the construction of alternative syntactic representations is the person's working memory capacity. There is much evidence that the size of a person's working memory is correlated with how quickly and accurately the person can parse complex sentences (King & Just, 1991) and with how many interpretations of an ambiguous sentence he or she can maintain simultaneously (MacDonald, Just, & Carpenter, 1992; Miyake, Carpenter, & Just, 1994).

Texts

A text is a group of connected sentences forming a paragraph or paragraphs. We started our discussion of sentences by noting that a sentence is much more than a group of words. Likewise, a text is more than a group of sentences. We will discuss two key aspects of text comprehension: making inferences about texts and seeking coherence within texts.

Much of what we understand to be true in a text is never explicitly stated but rather is inferred. Here's an example:

Billy walked slowly to the front of the room. The teacher waited for him.

How old is Billy? Is Billy a student? Why is he walking slowly? In a text that is just two sentences long, you probably infer that Billy is young, that he's walking slowly because he's reluctant to face the teacher, and in turn you've inferred that he's reluctant to face the teacher because he's done something wrong. You know these facts although they are never stated because you apply background knowledge to your understanding of the text.

The second aspect of text comprehension that we will discuss is the active effort to make texts coherent. We do not passively record the meanings of the sentences given; we tie them together so that they make sense. The fact that we struggle to integrate sentences in a text so that they make sense together can be appreciated simply. Imagine your reaction if I presented this text:

Billy walked slowly to the front of the room. The teacher waited for him. The crowd roared as the Americans won the gold.

The final sentence seems out of place, as though it belongs in some other story. Our response to a sentence that doesn't make sense is to search long-term memory for information that might make the text sensible. Suppose that earlier in the story you had been told that Billy's father is on the Olympic hockey team and that Billy had been caught listening to the game on a contraband radio, despite his teacher's stern warning not to do so. If you search long-term memory and find that information, the final sentence becomes comprehensible.

When do we make inferences? When do we recruit background knowledge to help us make sense of a text? To address these questions we need first to consider how texts are represented. Most researchers (e.g., Fletcher & Chrysler, 1990; Glenberg & Langston, 1992; Schmalhofer & Glavanov, 1986) agree that there are three levels of representation in text processing, as first suggested by Teun van Dijk and Walter Kintsch (1983): a surface code, a textbase, and a situation model. The **surface code** represents the exact wording and syntax of the sentences. The **textbase** represents the ideas of the text in a format called propositions, but it does not preserve the particular wording and syntax. If you make inferences as you read the text, those inferences are stored in the textbase as well. The **situation model** refers to still deeper knowledge, corresponding to an integration of the knowledge provided by the text and prior knowledge. Figure 11.6 shows the textbase and situation model representations corresponding to a text.

We have already discussed the components of the surface code—wording and syntax—but the components of the textbase and situation model take a different form. The basic unit of textbases and situation models is the proposition. We discussed propositions in the context of visual imagery, when we

Textbase:

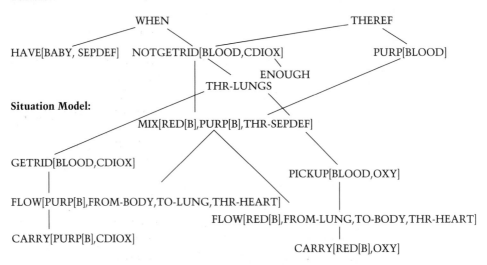

Note. The situation model consists of an inference (the MIX proposition) and several previous knowledge nodes.

Figure 11.6. *Constraint satisfaction network.*

compared visual images with verbal representations (propositions). A **proposition** is the most basic unit of meaning that has a truth value. Propositions have the syntax *relation(argument)*. A relational term can be a verb, adjective, or conjunction. The arguments are nouns. For example, the proposition *red(car)* represents the idea that a particular car is red. The proposition *gave(boy, girl, ball)* represents the idea that the boy gave the ball to the girl.

How do we know that the surface code, textbase, and situation model are separate in the mind? A commonly used technique is to have participants read a text and then take a recognition test for different types of sentences. For example, participants might read this text (adapted from Reder, 1982, who used only a subset of the probe questions described here).

> The heir to a large hamburger chain was in trouble. He had married a lovely young woman who had seemed to love him. Now he worried that she had been after his money after all. He sensed that she was not attracted to him. Perhaps he consumed too much beer and french fries. No, he couldn't give up the fries. Not only were they delicious, he got them for free.

Later, participants could be asked whether the following sentences were part of the story:

> The heir married a lovely young woman who had seemed to love him (verbatim sentence).
> The heir had the feeling that the woman did not find him good-looking (paraphrase).

The heir got his french fries from his family's hamburger chain (plausible inference based on the situation model).

The heir was careful to eat only healthful food (false statement).

Participants are to say whether the sentence presented appeared in the story. One can estimate the contributions of different representations to performance on the recognition test. For example, to the extent that people are accurate in rejecting paraphrases and accepting verbatim sentences, they must be using a memory of the surface code. If they accept paraphrases but reject inferences, that is a measure of their reliance on the textbase representation, and if they accept inferences but reject false statements, that indicates a reliance on the situation model.

Most studies show that participants' reliance on different representations changes over time. If they are tested soon after reading the text, participants rely on the surface code (i.e., they remember what they have read almost word for word). However, if there is a delay, participants come to rely more on the textbase (i.e., they remember the meaning of what they read, but they are not very accurate in remembering the exact words used to convey the information).

Factors besides time contribute to the detail of the surface code, the textbase, and the situational model. Rolf Zwaan (1994) examined whether the genre of the writing influenced how people read text. He provided a short

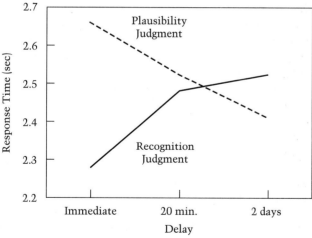

Figure 11.7. *Data from Reder (1982). The data show response times to make recognition judgments (this sentence appeared in the story) and plausibility judgments (this sentence describes something plausible, given the story). Shown here are data from plausible sentences. Note that plausible judgments initially are slower, but the pattern reverses as time passes, indicating that participants initially rely on the surface code to make judgments but later rely on the textbase.*

text for participants to read and told them that it was either a passage from a novel or a clipping from a newspaper story.

Participants' memory for the text varied depending on the genre they thought the text was from. If they thought they were reading a newspaper story, participants didn't remember much about the specific words and phrases used in the story (i.e., the surface code) and instead remembered the broadest outline of the story (situation model). The reverse is true if they believed they were reading part of a novel. This finding is certainly sensible: When you read a novel, you expect that the style is important, whereas for a newspaper story you're concerned mostly with the facts. Other work indicates that people remember different aspects of a text depending on the perspective they are encouraged to take when reading it (Baillet & Keenan, 1986; Lee-Sammons & Whitney, 1991) or their goals in reading it (Aaronson & Ferres, 1986; Noordman, Vonk, & Kempff, 1992).

These differences in memory that appear with changes in time or perspective of the reader are taken as evidence that the surface code, textbase, and situation model are separate. How and when are the textbase and situation model constructed? According to the most influential models of reading (Just & Carpenter, 1992; Kintsch, 1988), the textbase and situation models are built in parallel as one comprehends the surface code. If that's true, that means that one makes inferences as one reads. Again, remember that these inferences are generated automatically, not consciously considered and weighed.

There has been debate about the type of inferences people draw. Most researchers agree that inferences are drawn when information is missing from the text. If the text says, "Jennifer drove the nail," there is no information provided about what she used to drive it. One's background knowledge about nails would lead to the inference that Jennifer used a hammer. In Kintsch's (1988) model, the inference is made this way. A word or set of words from the text would enter working memory and then activate related concepts in long-term memory. This activation would cycle between working memory and long-term memory several times in such a way that concepts with strong activations become more active and those with weak activations become less active. After this process, concepts from long-term memory that are strongly related to concepts in the text become strongly activated; that is, reading about someone driving a nail results in the concept *hammer* becoming active because it is so closely related to *nail* and *to drive*.

The number of inferences that could be generated from even a brief, simple text is almost unlimited. One can make inferences about a character's motivation, why they did what they did, things they might have done that were not in the text, things they didn't do, and so on. The cognitive resources to generate inferences are assumed to be limited, so a limited number of inferences must be drawn. What sorts of inferences might be drawn?

Most theorists agree that inferences are drawn to enhance the coherence of a text. Thus, an inference becomes necessary when some incoherence is noted. The disagreement between researchers arises over what sorts of representations readers (or listeners) seek to make coherent. For example, suppose you saw this sentence: "The collie rushed at Rebecca, who cowered because she was afraid of the big dog." In this case, there is little doubt that a reader would use the knowledge in memory that a collie is a type of dog and that in this sentence *collie* and *dog* refer to the same entity. Gail McKoon and Roger Ratcliff (1992) claimed that the only inferences people make are ones that are necessary to maintain coherence within a sentence or across two sentences.

McKoon and Ratcliff (1992) tested this hypothesis by providing readers with two short paragraphs to read. The first paragraph introduced a goal (e.g., killing the president) and a subordinate goal (using a rifle). The second paragraph took one of three forms. In the control condition, the goal and the subordinate goal were achieved. In the try-again condition the subordinate goal could not be met, so the character tried to meet the goal a second time. In the substitution condition the subordinate goal could not be met, but the character abandoned it, substituting a new subordinate goal. The texts are as follows:

Introduction paragraph:	The crowd's cheers alerted the onlookers to the president's arrival. The assassin wanted to kill the president. He reached for his high-powered rifle. He lifted the gun to his shoulder to peer through its scope.
Control condition:	The assassin hit the president with the first shot from his rifle. Then he started to run toward the west. The searing sun blinded his eyes.
Try-again condition:	The scope fell off as he lifted the rifle. He lay prone to draw a sight without the scope. The searing sun blinded his eyes.
Substitution condition:	The scope fell off as he lifted the rifle. So he reached for his hand grenades. The searing sun blinded his eyes.

Participants read the stories one sentence at a time. After the last sentence a word appeared on the screen, and they were to say whether that word had appeared in the story. One test word was *kill*, which was relevant to the goal set up in the first paragraph. If people make inferences as they read to make a text globally coherent, then they would need to access the general goal of killing the president in the substitution condition; the participant should be puzzled as to why the character is reaching for the hand grenades, but the participant will recall from long-term memory that the goal is to kill the president, and the hand grenade sentence will make sense. Because they have just accessed this memory, it should be easy for these participants to verify that *kill* was in the text. In the control condition, the character has a new goal (escape), so participants should be slower to verify that *kill* was in the sentence.

McKoon and Ratcliff made a different prediction, however. They maintained that readers do not make inferences to maintain global coherence. Rather, they argued that readers make inferences only to make sentences coherent, so they predicted that there should be no difference between the three conditions in time to verify that *kill* was in the text. The data showed that McKoon and Ratcliff's prediction was verified.

The data included verification times for the word *rifle*. These times were faster overall, which is not surprising given that participants read this word more recently. Verification times were fastest in the try-again condition, the only condition in which the subordinate goal of using the rifle was maintained until the end of the story. This result shows that the word verification method McKoon and Ratcliff used is sensitive enough to detect participant's inferences. The important conclusion is from the verification times for *kill*, which indicate that participants may not seek global coherence as they read.

McKoon and Ratcliff claimed that the methods other researchers have used to test whether readers draw inferences are inaccurate because these methods really test whether people draw inferences during the test, not while the person is reading. For example, I might have you read a short story about someone visiting a restaurant and then later ask you, "Did you read that the person ate his or her food?" If you say, "Yes, the story said that," how can I know whether you inferred that fact as you read the story or whether you infer it when I ask the question the next day?

Other researchers posit that there are higher-level memory representations that cause people to draw inferences across much broader segments of text than a sentence or two; these researchers argue that as one reads, one builds a textbase or situation model, and if these representations are self-contradictory or are missing pieces that are easily filled by knowledge in long-term memory, then inferences will be made (Albrecht & O'Brien, 1993; Graesser, Singer, & Trabasso, 1994; Hess, Foss, & Carroll, 1995; Singer, Graesser, & Trabasso, 1994).

In one experiment, Edward O'Brien and Jason Albrecht (1992) measured reading times as participants read a paragraph. A sentence in the paragraph was made to be either consistent or inconsistent with an earlier sentence. Here is an example of the sort of paragraph they used:

> As Kim stood (inside/outside) the health club she felt a little sluggish. [Workouts always made her feel better. Today she was particularly looking forward to the exercise class because it had been a long, hard day at work. Her boss had just been fired and she had to fill in for him on top of her own work.] *She decided to go outside and stretch her legs a little.* She was getting anxious to start and was glad when she saw the instructor go in the door of the club. Kim really liked her instructor. Her enthusiasm and energy were contagious.

In the first sentence, half of the participants read that Kim was inside the club and half that she was outside. The critical sentence is in italics, and you can see that this sentence describes her as going outside. This sentence makes sense if Kim was described in the first sentence as being inside, but not if she was described as being outside. The experimenters also manipulated how far apart this potentially conflicting information was in the story. In the sample paragraph there are three sentences between the two conflicting sentences. Those three intervening sentences were omitted for some participants. Thus, there were two independent variables in this experiment: whether the initial information conflicted with the crucial sentence and whether this initial information appeared one sentence before the crucial sentence or three sentences before the crucial sentence. Figure 11.8 shows reading times for the crucial sentence. Participants are always faster in reading the crucial sentence when it is consistent with the information presented earlier. It is presumed that reading

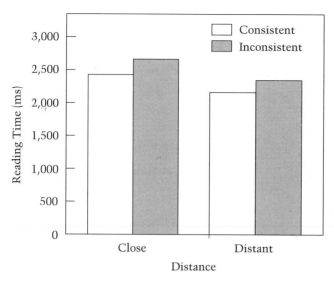

Figure 11.8. *Results from O'Brien and Albrecht's (1992) study indicating that participants compare information in new sentences with information from prior sentences. Participants were slower to read a sentence that was inconsistent with an old sentence, even if the conflicting sentence was distant from the one they were reading.*

times are longer because participants are struggling to make sense of the conflicting information.

It is also important that the advantage for the consistent version is maintained even when three sentences separate the initial and the test sentence. McKoon and Ratcliff's theory would also predict slower reading times in the close condition because the information in the test sentence conflicts with information presented just one sentence earlier. Their theory would not predict the observed difference in the distant condition, however. O'Brien and Albrecht argued that participants maintain a situation model as they read, and new information is integrated in the model as it comes in. If the reader has been told that Kim is outside and later is told that she *goes* outside (implying that she is not already outside), the inconsistency is detected and is reflected in the slower reading times as the participant tries to make sense of the conflicting information.

We've discussed two studies that examine when readers make inferences, and these studies conflict. Indeed, the most recent research indicates that the answer to the question, "What sort of inferences are made?" is not going to be a simple one. It is possible that the longevity of inferences may vary: Some inferences are made and discarded, whereas others are maintained (e.g., Millis & Just, 1994). It is also likely that making inferences depends on working memory, so there may be substantial individual differences in the number of inferences made, depending on the reader's working memory capacity (Whitney, Ritchie, & Clark, 1991); for a review of the literature on inferences, see Graesser, Millis, and Zwaan (1997).

STAND-ON-ONE-FOOT QUESTIONS

7. *What factors help in the perception of phonemes?*
8. *What are the two routes to the lexicon in reading according to dual route theories?*
9. *What is a garden path sentence, and why are they important?*
10. *What causes people to draw inferences from texts?*

QUESTIONS THAT REQUIRE TWO FEET

11. *Given what you know about lexical access, describe what happens when someone tells a pun.*
12. *What do you think would happen to a text if the writer ensured that you did not have to draw any inferences? Would the text seem especially well written and clear?*
13. *Suppose you and I are planning a hike. I look out the window, where I see it is pouring rain. I turn to you and say "This is ideal weather." What does this example tell you about sentence processing?*

➤ HOW ARE LANGUAGE AND THOUGHT RELATED?

> ➤ PREVIEW In this section we examine the relationship of language and thought. We focus on two particular issues within this broad topic. First, we consider whether nonhuman primates can acquire language. This question is of interest because their ability to do so (or lack thereof) provides important information about the cognitive abilities of apes. As we'll see, the linguistic abilities of apes are limited, indicating that although they are good at many tasks, using linguistic symbols and acquiring grammar is not something at which they excel. Second, we examine the relationship of language and thought. Languages differ in the concepts they make explicit; some languages offer succinct words and phrases to express a particular concept, whereas expressing the same concept in another language might be considerably more clumsy. Does that mean that thought about the concept is more efficient in the first language? To date, the answer is that the advantage is small if it exists at all, but we'll also discuss reasons that this question may not have been examined in the best way.

To this point we have focused on language as an independent system. We have treated language as though it were disconnected from the other topics in this book: memory, problem solving, reasoning, and so on. In one way—a trivial way—we know that language influences thought because different words lead to different thoughts. We can also safely draw the trivial conclusion that different thoughts lead you to utter different words. The deeper question is whether there is a more intimate relationship between language and thought. For example, are certain types of thought dependent on having the words to express them? Can we use linguistic abilities as a measure of one's abilities to think in particular ways? In this section, we take up these questions.

Ape Language

As you no doubt know, several human researchers have undertaken to teach language to nonhuman primates (e.g., chimps, gorillas, bonobos). Why did they do so? The obvious answer—that it would be cool to talk to apes—is accurate, but it is not sufficient motivation. Most researchers are interested in these language projects because they tell us something interesting about the cognitive capabilities of nonhuman primates. In this chapter we've discussed some of the complexities of the grammatical structure of language. Are nonhuman primates able to master these complexities?

Notice that this goal is very different from the goal of being able to communicate with a chimp. If you simply want to be able to know something about what a chimp wants to do (i.e., you want it to be able to make requests) and you want to be able to give it commands, that is a different undertaking from teaching the chimp language. To keep the distinction clear in our minds, we can return to the definition of language that we discussed earlier in the chapter, and we can contrast that with simple communication. We said that language is communicative, arbitrary, structured, generative, and dynamic (again, recognizing that the exact criteria are not universally recognized). Most animal communication systems have only the first of these properties. In the wild, chimps use a series of grunts and howls to communicate specific meanings—danger from a snake, for example—but these communicative signals are not arbitrary. They are fixed in their meaning and seem to be part of the animal's genetic inheritance. The same is true of the communication systems of honeybees (which communicate about food sources), birds (whose song often signals ownership of territory), or other nonhuman animals.

Some researchers of ape language have commented that as some humans discover greater and greater linguistic abilities in primates, other humans scurry off to redefine language, effectively "raising the bar" to ensure that we are the only species that can *really* use language (see the exchange between Kako, 1999, and Shanker, Savage-Rumbaugh, & Taylor, 1999). Having read this far in the chapter, you should be able to appreciate that the insistence on the use of grammar is not an arbitrary requirement but is essential to a definition of language.

So just how well do nonhuman primates do? The upshot is "not all that well." We begin by describing briefly the better known of these projects, and I summarize the claims made by the researchers about their pupils' achievements. Then we take up the criticisms that have been leveled at this work.

The early attempts to teach language to primates were doomed to fail because the researchers tried to teach chimps vocal speech. The chimp's vocal tract and articulators are unsuited to form the sounds properly. Asking chimps to produce vocal speech is like asking humans to flap their arms and fly; our arms aren't suited to make us airborne, and the chimp vocal tract is not suited to allow the clear pronunciation needed for vocal speech.

In the 1960s several projects were initiated that solved that problem. Beatrice and Allen Gardner (Gardner & Gardner, 1967a, 1967b, 1975; Gardner, Gardner, & Van Cantfort, 1989) raised a chimp, Washoe, in the manner of a human infant, with exposure to toys, play areas, and activities. More importantly, the Gardners spoke American Sign Language (ASL) to Washoe, and used only ASL in her presence. Furthermore, the Gardners actively taught ASL to Washoe. They molded her hands into the correct shape for signs and rewarded her for signing correctly. This process of actively teaching the language to the chimp and actively teaching it how to articulate the words of the language was adopted by other researchers. Herb Terrace and his associates (Terrace, Petitto, Sanders, & Bever, 1979) also used ASL to train a chimp that they named Nim Chimpsky (a play on the name of linguist Noam Chomsky). Still another researcher who sought to use ASL is Francine Patterson (1978, 1981), who taught a gorilla, Koko. Koko may be the best-known nonhuman "speaker" because she seems to have been the most widely covered in popular press. There were even references to Koko in two different episodes of the TV show *Seinfeld*. (If that's not "making it" I don't know what is.)

David Premack (1971, 1976a, 1976b) took quite a different approach. He trained a chimp, Sarah, to communicate by placing metal-backed chips on a magnetic board. The chips symbolized nouns (*chocolate, dish, Sarah*), verbs (*is, give, insert*), concepts (*same, if–then*), and adjectives (*red, yellow*). The chips were arbitrary in their appearance, meaning that the chip corresponding to the concept *chocolate* did not look like a piece of chocolate. Somewhat similar in spirit is the approach taken by Sue Savage-Rumbaugh and her colleagues (Savage-Rumbaugh et al., 1983; Savage-Rumbaugh, Romski, Sevcik, & Pate, 1983; Savage-Rumbaugh, Rumbaugh, & Boysen, 1978; Savage-Rumbaugh, Rumbaugh, Smith, & Lawson, 1980). They taught a chimp, Lana, and later a bonobo, Kanzi (Savage-Rumbaugh, Shanker, & Taylor, 1998), a language they called "Yerkish," named for the Yerkes primate center where they worked and Lana lived. Lana had 24-hour access to a computer keyboard on which were printed arbitrary symbols, each symbol standing for a concept. Lana could punch the keys to form "sentences." The symbols on the keys she pressed were echoed on a screen, and Yerkish communication from a trainer could appear on the screen. An advantage of having the utterance echoed on a screen was that it reduced the working memory requirements for the speaker; the length of an utterance would not be artificially limited simply because the speaker could not keep a long utterance in mind.

These primates had an opportunity to learn at least two aspects of language that, if they learned them, would represent a remarkable achievement. The first thing they might learn is the symbolic nature of words. We would like to establish what sort of knowledge they have. Can they use the symbol for chocolate in many different contexts, indicating that perhaps they know the abstract relationship between the word and the referent, or do they simply know that they are often given chocolate when they push a key with a particular symbol? The latter may not be very different from what a pigeon can learn. This question concerns the property of language we have called arbitrariness, the notion that a word is a symbol.

A second question we can ask about primate language is whether they understand how to use syntax. As we've discussed, humans are very sensitive to syntax, even to simple aspects of word order. For example, "water bird" is a bird that lives on or near water, whereas "bird water" refers to a particular type of water that is for birds. Can primates appreciate the difference between the two?

The claims made for the learning of primates in these studies ranges from modest to modestly spectacular. The most spectacular of these claims has been made by Patterson about the gorilla Koko, but we won't be discussing Koko. The claims include what is easily the largest vocabulary among the primate speakers, well-formed syntax, spontaneous signing (i.e., not simply signing in response to a request to sign), and, most amazingly, puns, jokes, and cunning lies. The problem is that Patterson has not published in scientific journals for a number of years, meaning that her claims must be taken at her word. No scientist expects to be believed without a critical review of his or her work by knowledgeable peers. Unfortunately, the most interesting claims about primate language must go unchecked.

Many of the other claims fall in a second group, and these claims are considerably less grand. Washoe acquired 132 signs, Nim acquired 125, and estimates from other groups are in this range. There are some problems with these data, however. The researchers on the Washoe project may well have been too optimistic (or generous) in how they coded signs. One problem is that chimps have a limited repertoire of signs that they perform in the wild, without ever being taught. One is a reaching gesture with palm up, which indicates that they want something. Another is to shake the hand, which indicates hurrying. The lion's share of the two-word combinations recorded on the Wahsoe project involved the words *hurry, please, come,* and *more.* Thus about half of the two-word combinations arguably involved signs that were not taught to Washoe. Jane Goodall, upon visiting the Nim Chimpsky project, remarked that she recognized all of Nim's "signs" as gestures that chimps perform in the wild (Pinker, 1994). These data bear on our assessment of whether the ape's language has the characteristic of arbitrariness. This appears to be less of a problem in studies using truly arbitrary symbols for communication instead of hand gestures.

How can we be sure that any of the primates are really using words as symbols? That's another important aspect of arbitrariness. In an operant conditioning paradigm a rat might press a lever for food and receive a reward, but we wouldn't call bar pressing the use of a symbol. When a primate is trained to execute a gesture and receives a food reward or praise for doing so, how does that differ from the bar-pressing rat?

In one experiment, Savage-Rumbaugh and her colleagues (Savage-Rumbaugh et al., 1983) had two chimps engage in a conversation. The first observed a trainer hide a food item in a container. The first then pressed the key on a keyboard with the symbol for the food item, thereby telling the second chimp (who never saw the food) what item was hidden. The second chimp was then to request that specific food item, and if it did so correctly, the two split the food.

This result sounds fairly impressive as an example of two chimps communicating, but does it show that chimps are using words as symbols? Robert

Epstein and his colleagues didn't think so (Epstein, Lanza, & Skinner, 1980). They got the same behavior from pigeons, named Jack and Jill. They had adjoining cages with a transparent wall between them. Jack pecked a key labeled "WHAT COLOR?" That was a cue for Jill to look behind a curtain where there were three lights—red, green, and yellow—that were not visible to Jack. After ascertaining which light was illuminated, Jill pecked one of three keys—*R*, *G*, or *Y*—which Jack could see. Jack then pecked a key labeled "THANK YOU," whereupon Jill was given a food reward. Jack then pecked one of three keys indicating which light was illuminated and received his own reward. Thus, we can conclude that pigeons can use symbolic language, or we can conclude that we need more stringent tests of the symbolic use of language.

What would be a satisfactory demonstration of the use of words as symbols? The key property one would look for is transfer to a novel testing situation. Once you know the referent for the word *chocolate* you can use that word in all sorts of situations: You can request chocolate, you can describe chocolate, you can comment on chocolate. On the other hand, if you've learned something in a rote manner, as an operantly conditioned response, the behavior you've learned is inflexible or is generalizable in predictable and limited ways. Primates in these language studies receive many practice trials and are drilled in the use of these signs and nevertheless speak about a fairly limited range of topics, most of which are requests for things. That said, it's true that at least in some cases they combine signs in ways that they have not been taught to do (Terrace et al., 1979), which indicates at least some rudimentary use of words that they have learned as symbols.

There are a few celebrated examples of seeming spontaneity in ape language. One was an instance in which Washoe was near a swan on a pond and the trainer asked, "What that?" Washoe responded, "Water bird," thus appearing to coin a new term for an as-yet unnamed object. However, Washoe might have simply been commenting that water was visible, and so was a bird.

What about grammar? Recall that one of the characteristics defining language is that it is structured. Also recall that ignoring the importance of grammar in language is a serious mistake; grammar is at the very heart of what makes language language. The upshot of primate grammar is that they just don't get it, except in the most rudimentary form. The best analysis of chimp grammar comes from Terrace and his colleagues' analysis of Nim's "sentences." They found that he did seem to understand some basic ideas about word order; for example, he put *more* before another word (*chocolate, tickle*) far more than by chance. However, analysis of videotapes indicated that Nim's sentences often were full or partial imitations of something his trainer had just finished saying. Finally, one must take note of the mind-cracking sameness of primate utterances. Here are the top 10 (in order) four-word "sentences" uttered by Nim:

> Eat drink, eat drink
> Eat Nim eat Nim
> Banana Nim banana Nim
> Drink Nim drink Nim

Banana eat me Nim

Banana me eat banana

Banana me Nim me

Grape eat Nim eat

Nim eat Nim eat

Play me Nim play

Nim's longest utterance, at 16 words, was "Give orange me give eat orange me eat orange give me eat orange give me you."

The final word on nonhuman primate language is this: It's not close (at all) to the language humans use. We began this section by noting that the question of whether primates can use language would be interesting because it would tell us something about their mental capabilities. It seems likely to me that there is some use of words as symbols in the speech of primates and probably some nonrandom ordering of the symbols, showing some primitive understanding of grammar. But the main question posed has been answered: Apes cannot learn language or much of anything like language.

Ironically, the opposite conclusion seems to have taken hold in the public imagination, at least the public with which I have contact. People seem to be under the impression that some apes have been taught to speak to us in a Dr. Doolittle sort of scenario. This "fact" is most often trotted out to humble us, the human species, for being so arrogant as to think that we are special, when in fact other animals have the capability of language, thus proving that we are not that different from other species. Some of the researchers on these projects have reached conclusions in this vein.

As Steve Pinker (1994) eloquently pointed out, the very comparison shows remarkable human arrogance. Why pick language as the metric by which we evaluate whether we are the same as other species? That's a contest humans can't lose, and indeed have not lost, whatever the popular press accounts may say. Why not compare chimps with humans in terms of the ability to climb trees? Why not compare our memories with those of seed-caching birds such as corvids, who can remember thousands of locations in which they've hidden seeds? Why not compare our perceptual abilities with that of honeybees, who can perceive ultraviolet light? My point is that humans are unique, but so is every other species. Each species has abilities and failings. The claim that we should compare our linguistic abilities with those of apes to evaluate their worth is scientifically empty.

Language and Thought

There is little doubt that how and what we think affects what we say and that what we say affects how we think. But is there a deeper relationship between language and thought? It is not the case that each language has the same set of words representing a given number of concepts and that languages differ only in the sound of these words. Languages differ in the concepts for which words exist, and in some languages particular aspects of a concept are highlighted by the grammar of the language. Do such differences across languages mean that the speakers of these different languages actually *think* differently?

The idea that language molds thoughts and molds our perception of reality was advanced by linguist Edward Sapir, who wrote,

> We see and hear and otherwise experience very largely as we do because the language habits of our community predispose certain choices of interpretation. (Sapir, 1956)

This perspective was carried on by one of Sapir's students, a businessman and amateur linguist, Benjamin Whorf (1956). Their position became know as the **Sapir–Whorf hypothesis** or sometimes simply the **Whorfian hypothesis.** The strongest version of the Whorfian hypothesis is that thought is so intimately tied to language that it may be impossible to express the thoughts generated in one language in another language. This strong position has few adherents. It is generally accepted that all languages are flexible enough and powerful enough to express the ideas of other languages. The difference may be one of convenience. For example, the Kiriwina language of New Guinea has a word, *mokita,* which means "truth that everyone knows but no one speaks about." Americans surely are familiar with this concept and can express it, but it is simpler to express in Kiriwina.

The weak version of the Whorfian hypothesis has received more careful investigation. The weak version states that the language that one speaks favors some thought processes over others; it's not that your language makes some thoughts impossible, but rather that the language you speak biases you to think in certain ways. This weak version has been tested carefully in a few domains. The conclusion is that there is little evidence favoring the Whorfian hypothesis, even in its weak form, but I also think it's fair to say that researchers have not selected the best tasks to investigate this issue and that better evidence supporting the Whorfian hypothesis may yet be forthcoming.

One myth about the Whorfian hypothesis should be laid to rest: It is not true that Eskimo languages have a large number of ways to refer to the concept *snow*. Whorf mentions this possible example and claims that there are three words for snow in "Eskimo." The example has been picked up in popular culture and exaggerated to mythic status (Martin, 1986). English has a fair number of words for snow—*snow, slush, sleet, powder*—and may not have any fewer than Inuit languages (Pinker, 1994).

Much of the early systematic work on the Whorfian hypothesis was conducted on color naming. One of the original studies was conducted by Roger Brown and Eric Lenneberg (1954). They selected color naming because colors have properties that are objectively describable (wavelength), but different languages divide the color spectrum into different numbers of hues. In their experiment, Brown and Lenneberg showed one group of participants a set of colors. Some were agreed upon as readily namable and these colors were considered codable (i.e., linguistically codable). A second group of participants were then asked to view colors (both codable and not) and were later given a recognition test. Memory was somewhat better for codable colors than noncodable ones, providing weak evidence for the Whorfian hypothesis; the way that participants named colors seemed to affect their memory for them.

Later research painted a different picture, however. Eleanor Rosch (then E. R. Heider, 1972), whose work we discussed in the chapter on categorization, actually examined the color memory of people who speak different languages. Most notably, she went to New Guinea and tested speakers of Dani, a language that has but two color terms: *mola* for lighter colors such as white, yellow, and orange, and *mili* for darker colors such as black, purple, and blue. Rosch had participants perform two tasks. First, she presented people with 40 color chips and asked them to name them. On this task the Dani and English speakers performed quite differently. The Dani agreed with each other on very light colors (all *mola*) and very dark colors (all *mili*), but there was disagreement in the midrange because individual participants had individual perceptions of the location of the dividing line between mola and mili. English speakers showed much greater agreement on how to categorize colors.

Rosch also administered a recognition task. The Whorfian hypothesis might lead one to expect that the Dani would easily confuse all *mola* colors, but that's not what happened. Although their scores were lower overall than English speakers, the Dani made the same sorts of mistakes English speakers did, and their performance was best on the same chips on which English speakers excelled (the "reddest" red, for example).

In a follow-up experiment, Rosch and Donald Oliver (Heider & Oliver, 1972) administered a recognition test to both Dani and English speakers in which they were to remember a color chip and then select it from two choices. The crucial comparison was whether the two choices crossed a color line. Sometimes the two chips were similar but one would be called green by most people and the other blue. Other times the two choices were equally similar (i.e., the same difference in wavelength) but both would be called blue. Participants performed equally well when the two choices were on the same side or different sides of the color line, and that was true for both Dani and English speakers.

These two experiments provide strong evidence against the Whorfian hypothesis, at least in the domain of color naming. Several recent experiments by Ian Davies and his colleagues largely confirm these results, although their data contain some elements consistent with a weak effect of language on thought. Davies and Greville Corbett (1997) examined speakers of English, Russian, and Setswana, which is spoken in Botswana. Russian has two terms for blue (roughly corresponding to light blue and dark blue), whereas the Setswana use a single term that encompasses both blue and green. The experimenters gave participants 65 color chips and asked them to put the chips into groups as they saw fit. Surprisingly, the speakers of different languages generated groupings that were quite similar. The Setswana speakers tended to put more green chips with blue, as expected, but the Russian speakers did not tend to separate the light and dark blue chips. In a follow-up experiment, Davies and colleagues (Davies, Sowden, Jerrett, Jerrett, & Corbett, 1998) repeated the experiment but dictated to participants the number of categories they should create (between 2 and 12). They predicted that there would be greater agreement among Setswana speakers when he dictated a small number of groups, because Setswana has only six color names, and greater agreement among the English and Russian speakers when he dictated a large number of groups, because those languages have 11 or 12 color names, respectively. As Davies put it, "The most striking feature of the results was the marked similarity of the [color] groups chosen across the three language groups" (1998, p. 433). However, there were small, reliable differences in expected direction predicted by the Whorfian hypothesis. A third study using a task where participants were to select the least similar in a triad of colors yielded similar results: There was marked similarity across languages, but the differences, small though they were, were consistent with the Whorfian hypothesis (Davies et al., 1998).

A notable feature of the research on the effect of language on color naming is how particularly badly suited this domain seems for studying the question at hand. Color perception is deeply seated in the physiology of the visual system, beginning with the cones in the retina (de Valois & de Valois, 1993). It appears to be a system that will not show any flexibility, whatever one's language is; language would be molded to the inflexible physiology of vision, not the other way around.

The consistency of color perception around the world was emphasized in a different way by linguists Brent Berlin and Paul Kay (1969), who surveyed the color names of 98 languages and noted that although languages vary in the number of color terms (from a low of 2, as in Dani, to a high of 12, as in Russian), there is a remarkable consistency in the way that languages slice up the color spectrum. If there are only two color terms, those terms correspond to black and white. If there are three, red is added. Fourth and fifth are yellow and green. Sixth and seventh are blue and brown. Eighth through eleventh is a horse race between purple, pink, orange, and gray. The researchers presumed that the salience of these different colors is a function of the physiology of the nervous system.

So a single-sentence summary of the research on the Whorfian hypothesis might be this: There is little evidence supporting the Whorfian hypothesis, but color perception probably is a bad domain in which to look for evidence. An equally bad domain is counterfactual reasoning, which was launched in a book by Alfred Bloom (1981). Bloom noted that Mandarin Chinese (henceforth, we'll simply call it Chinese) has no subjunctive tense. The subjunctive tense is used in English and other languages to signal that the speaker is going to make a false supposition to consider what would happen were the supposition true. For example, one could say, "If Dennis were to fly, he would get there faster." The use of "were to" and the use of the past tense in the main clause signals to the listener that this is a counterfactual.

Chinese does not have a subjunctive tense. Instead, there is only the "if–then" construction. If the supposition is obviously false, then one constructs counterfactuals using a normal "if–then" sentence: "If I am a member of the Rolling Stones, I will retire before I embarrass myself." The listener understands that I am not a member of the Rolling Stones and am instead offering advice about what they should do. On the other hand, if the listener cannot be expected to know that the supposition is false, the speaker must explicitly state that it is false: "Mrs. Wong not know English. If Mrs. Wong know English, she then can read the *New York Times*" (Au, 1983, p. 157).

Bloom hypothesized that Chinese speakers would have a hard time understanding counterfactual statements because it is not as straightforward to express them in their language, compared to English. In several experiments, Bloom had participants read a story in English (participants in the United States) or Chinese (participants in Taiwan or Hong Kong). In one story, an explorer sees a group of aborigines boiling a pot of water, then throwing a dead human in the pot, and later eagerly drinking the broth. The observer cannot speak the native language and so does not know that the dead person was a revered leader of the group who died in an accident, that they believe that by drinking the broth they will ingest some of his laudable characteristics, and that the aborigines are friendly. The key question at the end of the story is what the explorer knew. Bloom reported that 98% of the English speakers understood the counterfactual nature of the story and reported that the explorer didn't know that the aborigines were friendly, and so on, whereas only 7% of the Chinese speakers interpreted the story counterfactually. Bloom interpreted these results as showing that it is difficult for Chinese speakers to think counterfactually because their language makes it cumbersome to express that thought.

Terry Au (1983, 1984) showed in a series of studies that this conclusion was wrong. She attributed Bloom's results to poor translations of the Chinese. The Chinese was too much a word-for-word translation and therefore not idiomatic. Many languages sound odd if they are translated word for word. Au provided better, idiomatic translations of the stories, and reported that her Chinese participants showed marvelous understanding of counterfactuals, just as English speakers did. In a further study, Au had Chinese–English bilinguals translate the stories from Chinese into English, but using unidiomatic English. When those stories were used, only 52% of the English speakers understood the counterfactual nature of the story.

Like the color naming enterprise, this topic—counterfactuals—seems to have been a bad domain in which to examine the Whorfian hypothesis. As Au pointed out, it would be strange indeed to propose that all Chinese speakers cannot understand counterfactuals very well. Does that mean that Chinese people seldom feel regret? After all, regret requires that one consider a counterfactual ("If I had done X, things would have turned out better").

More recent work has provided better, if limited, evidence for the Whorfian hypothesis. Irene Miura and associates have investigated the learning of place values among children who speak different languages. Place values refers to learning the base-10 system of numbers. Children must learn that after the number 9, one puts a 1 in a tens place and starts over again at 0 in the ones place to form the number 10. In Japanese, Korean, and Chinese, place values are explicit in the names of numbers. For example, 26 is called "two-ten six" and 38 is "three-ten eight." In English, however, place values are much more obscure. The value of 10 is designated by the ending -*teen* in 13–19 but by the ending -*ty* in numbers 20–99. Furthermore, there are special names for 11 and 12.

Irene Miura and her colleagues (Miura, 1987; Miura, Kim, Chang, & Okamoto, 1988; Miura & Okamoto, 1989; Miura et al., 1993, 1994). Miura showed that Chinese-, Korean-, and Japanese-speaking children are better than their counterparts who speak English, French, or Swedish in understanding place values in multidigit numbers. In one experiment (Miura et al., 1994) children were shown numbers and were asked to use cubes to show the amount that the number represented. These included individual cubes and groups of 10 cubes stuck together, and the Asian children were more likely than the Western children to use these groups of 10. However, further research (Saxton & Towse, 1998) indicated that these effects are largely ameliorated if each child is shown a practice trial in which the use of the tens unit is demonstrated.

In other work consistent with the Whorfian hypothesis, Shi Zhang and Bernd Schmitt (1998) examined the mental representation of classifiers within Chinese. Classifiers are words that are used with numbers or determiners (*this, that, the*) to form noun phrases. For example, whereas English speakers would say "One bed," Chinese speakers say "yi zhang chuang." *Yi* means "one" and *chuang* means bed. *Zhang* is a classifer used for long, flat objects such as beds, tables, desks, and photographs. There are classifiers for many different categories of objects in Chinese, as shown in Table 11.4.

As you can see from the table, classifiers typically refer to the perceptual qualities of objects.

Zhang and Schmitt examined whether the use of these classifiers has any impact on the representation of these objects in the memories of Chinese speakers. The experimenters simply presented pairs of words to English speakers and Chinese speakers and asked them to rate the similarity of the words. They found that the Chinese speakers consistently rated words as more similar if they shared a classifier. (The classifier was not mentioned in the experiment, of course.) So this experiment indicates that Chinese speakers think that a snake is more similar to a river (for example) than English speakers do, and that is true presumably because these two words take the same classifier. A second experiment asked participants to recall words, and the Chinese speakers tended to remember words in clusters, each cluster corresponding to a classifier. In a final experiment, Zhang and Schmitt asked participants to view and rate photographs of objects. Participants were to evaluate the photographs for possible use in advertisements. Although the photographs had no text, some of the objects depicted would take the classifer *ba* which is used for graspable objects. Furthermore, half of the participants saw photos showing a hand grasping the object, and half saw a photo without the hand. Chinese speakers rated photographs as more appropriate for an advertisement if the hand was present in the photographs of objects that take the classifer *ba*. One might think that this effect resulted from the nature of the objects; if it's a graspable object, then naturally an advertisement should show someone grasping it. But Zhang and Schmitt also tested Japanese speakers whose language also takes classifiers, but not the same set as Chinese. Japanese speakers showed no preference for photographs with or without the hand.

In sum, the evidence favoring the Whorfian hypothesis is not substantial, but it does exist. (See also Naigles & Terrazas, 1998, for an interesting example.) The study of language and thought got off on the wrong foot in two ways. First, the Whorfian hypothesis was stated too strongly. It is clearly not the case that some thoughts are impossible in other languages or even that some people are unlikely to think in certain ways simply because their language makes the

Table 11.4 **Glossary of the Classifiers and Stimuli Objects and Products Used in the Studies**

Classifier[a]	Character[b]	Study[c]	Semantic Features[d]	Objects and Products[e] (total = 60)
ba[3]	把	1. 3	Can be grasped with a hand	Door key, hack, ruler, pliers, brush, cane, umbrella, broom
ding[3]	頂	1, 2	Top	Hat, mosquito net, tent, palanquin
duo[3]	朵	1, 2	Amorphous	Mushroom, flame, cloud, spray
geng[1]	根	1, 2	Root or root-like thing	Sausage, nail, stick, chewing gum, match, braid
ke[1]	顆	1, 2	Bead-like item	Tooth, star, pearl, heart
kou[3]	口	1	Openings	Vat, coffin
jia[4]	架	1	Wooden frame-like	Airplane, swing
jie[2]	節	1	A cut section, between joints	Battery, railroad car
mien[4]	面	1, 2	Surface	Flag, wall, mirror, drum
mei[2]	枚	1, 2	Round piece	Rubber stamp, ring, political buttons, stamp
pian[4]	片	1, 2	Slice	Meat, snowflake, tablet, tree leaf
shan[4]	扇	1	Fan-like	Window, divider
tiao[2]	條	1, 2, 3	Strip, for long and slender things, often bendable	Snake, river, soap bar, road, boat, fish, pants, cord, rope, cable
zuo[4]	座	1	Seat or seat-like things	House, bell, temple, mountain

[a]Classifiers are given in pinyin, the standard transliteration used for Chinese characters.   [b]Chinese characters.   [c]Studies in which the classifier effect is tested.   [d]The perceptual and conceptual features that each classfier depicts.   [e]Stimuli products and objects used in the studies.

expression of those thoughts a bit awkward. Earl Hunt and Franca Agnoli (1991) emphasized this point in their review of this topic, and they suggested that the right dependent measure is not whether a speaker of a language can have a thought but rather whether there is a processing cost to having a particular type of thought for a speaker of a particular language. That is the metric we usually use in language research, and indeed throughout cognitive psychology. For example, people certainly can process the sentence, "The spy saw the cop with a revolver but the cop didn't see him." What's interesting is that there is a small cost of processing that sentence relative to similar sentences. Thus, it's wrong to look for catastrophic failures across languages; we're not going to see them. What we might see is small biases in the desired way to process, or slight costs to processing in certain ways, that are associated with a particular language.

The second problem with this literature is that it started off with a couple of bad ideas. Color naming was a badly chosen research topic for reasons already named, and so was counterfactual reasoning. These two failures discouraged researchers from pursuing the Whorfian hypothesis, but more recent work indicates that there may well be some interesting effects of language and thought along the lines that Whorf suggested.

STAND-ON-ONE-FOOT QUESTIONS

14. *What key features of language would you want to evaluate in the use of language by apes?*
15. *In the final analysis, can apes use language?*
16. *Why were the initial tests of the Whorfian hypothesis ill suited to test the question?*
17. *Is some version of the Whorfian hypothesis likely to be correct?*

QUESTION THAT REQUIRES TWO FEET

18. *If the Whorfian hypothesis is correct, what does that imply about people who can speak more than one language?*

KEY TERMS

phonemes
speech stream
text
grammar
competence
performance
word-chain
    grammars
phrase structure
    grammars
recursion
deep structure
surface structure

phoneme restoration
    effect
McGurk effect
categorical perception
motor theory of speech
    perception
lexicon
cross-modal priming
lexical decision
priming
dual route models
    of reading
acquired dyslexia

surface dyslexia
phonological dyslexia
developmental dyslexia
lexical decision task
garden path sentence
principle of minimal
    attachment
surface code
textbase
situation model
proposition
Sapir–Whorf hypothesis
Whorfian hypothesis

Appendix

➤ ## SIGNAL DETECTION THEORY

In some areas of cognitive psychology, we conduct experiments in which participants are asked to detect faint signals amidst a background of noise. For example, the participant might be asked to watch a computer monitor, on which a very faint light occasionally appears. Such tasks occur in the some professions as well. Radar and sonar operators try to detect signals indicative of ships or planes amidst background noise. Doctors try to detect the sound of a heart murmur amidst the other sounds of the body. Radiologists try to detect visual signals indicative of abnormalities amidst a noisy background on an x-ray image.

How can we evaluate whether someone is effective or ineffective at detecting such signals? Take the simple example of detecting a faint visual signal. On each trial of such an experiment, the participant must either say "yes" or "no," meaning the signal was or was not present. In addition, the signal really was or wasn't there. It's therefore easy to evaluate the participant's accuracy. Actual signals of possible outcomes on each trial are shown below.

		Actual Signal	
		Present	Absent
Participant's decision	Present	Hit	False alarm
	Absent	Miss	Correct rejection

Obviously hits and correct rejections represent accurate decisions. Misses and false alarms represent inaccurate decisions.

The problem is that there are really two factors that go into your decision. One is your **sensitivity**—just how good you are at detecting signals—and the other is your **bias**. Your bias represents your criterion for saying that you see a signal. For example, I may say, "Whatever you do, don't miss any signals!" In this situation, you'll be very liberal in saying that you see a signal. On the other hand, I may say "Whatever you do, don't say that you see a signal when there is not really one there!" Obviously under those instructions, you'll be much more conservative in saying that you see a signal. Note that whether I'm conservative or liberal in calling out "I see it!" has nothing to do with my absolute sensitivity in seeing a signal.

Signal detection theory allows you to separate sensitivity and bias. The easist way to understand how it works is to examine the graphic below.

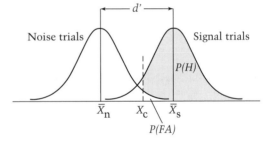

Suppose that the horizontal axis represents the intensity of the signal that you perceive. You can think of it as the amount of activity in your visual cortex, if you like. The vertical axis is the frequency of a particular type of trial (high means very frequent, low means very infrequent).

There are two distributions, labeled "noise trials" and "signal trials." "Noise" means background noise—the flicker of the computer monitor, for example. "Signal" really represents the signal *and* the background noise; thus, for most signal trials there is more signal intensity than for most noise trials. The distributions overlap in this example. That's because the perceived intensity of the signal or the background noise can vary from trial to trial, so sometimes it happens that a (noise) trial is perceived as more intense than a (signal + noise) trial. Although the distributions overlap, their averages (or means, labeled by the X with the bar over it) are separate. Their averages are in the center of the distributions.

The distance between the averages is labeled d' (said "d-prime"). This is a measure of the participant's sensitivity; it's their absolute ability to differentiate between the noise and the (signal + noise). Here's another way to think about it. Suppose that the task were to detect the sound of someone shouting "HEY" (signal) amidst the background noise of a silent classroom during a final examination. In that case the intensity of the noise would be very low, and the intensity of the signal would be very high. The (noise) distribution would be far to the left, and the (signal + noise) distribution would be far to the right, so the distance between them (d') would be large. On the other hand, if the signal were the sound of someone talking, and the background noise was a loud rock concert, the two distributions would be very close together, and d' would be small.

The participant will also set a criterion for how intense a signal must be before they will decide that it is so intense that it must contain the signal. That criterion is shown in the figure as X_c. Any stimulus of greater intensity than that will be called signal and any stimulus of lesser intensity will be called no signal. If the two distributions were really far apart (as in the clap in the examination example), you could put the criterion anywhere between these distributions and you'd never make a mistake, because everything above the criterion is indeed a clap (signal) and everything below the criterion is indeed noise (no clap). When the distributions overlap, however, you're going to make some incorrect decisions.

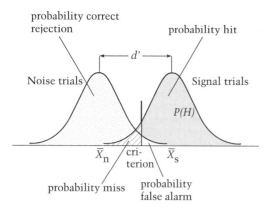

The correct and the incorrect decisions can be viewed on this new graph and related to the table above. Consider first what happens when the perceived intensity of the signal is above the criterion. The participant is going to say "signal present." Most of the time, that will be true: as shown by the shaded region of the signal distribution, most of the trials where the participants say "signal" are trials where the signal is present. Note, however, that one tail of the noise distribution is above the criterion, so there is some chance that a trial above the intensity criterion will actually be a noise trial. That's a false alarm, where the participant says "signal" but there was only noise present.

We can analyze the other decision the same way. When the participant says "no signal" (i.e., noise) most of the time that decision is correct; it's a correct rejection. But some the "signal" trials have so little intensity that they fall below the criterion. When that happens, the trial is a "miss." The participant calls it a "no signal" trial because the intensity was below criterion, but the signal was actually present.

Note that the proportion of hits, misses, false alarms and correct rejections will change as the criterion moves to the right or left. Again, the criterion might change as the participant changes his or her estimates of how important it is to gain certain accurate judgments or to avoid certain inaccurate ones.

The graph shows you the two values the experimenter really wants to know: the d' or absolute accuracy the participant brings to the task, and the participant's criterion in making the judgments. I've pointed out that the participant's sensitivity and criterion shape the number of hits, misses, false alarms, and correct rejections. The technique in signal detection analysis is basically to work backwards from the way we've described it. The experimenter takes the participant's performance (hits, misses, false alarms, correct rejections) as shown in the table above, and uses those values to infer the sensitivity and bias. We won't go into the mathematical procedures of how that's done.

Thus, in the end, one can take the participant's performance and tease apart the two factors that contribute to his or her decision: the sensitivity and the criterion they bring to the detection task.

➤ ## STATISTICAL SIGNIFICANCE

Suppose I said to you "Look at this coin. Looks normal, right? It's actually a trick coin. Even though it has a heads side and a tails side, it comes up heads every time it's tossed." You inspect it, and it does indeed seem to be a normal coin. Your friend tosses it and it comes up heads. Are you convinced that it's a trick coin?

Probably not, or at least, you shouldn't be. After all, a regular coin comes up heads half the time. Maybe the coin came up heads by chance. What would we do to get a better test of the coin? Toss it more. How many heads in a row would you need to see before you were willing to accept that this was a trick coin? Three? Ten?

There are three steps to note about our thinking here. First, when we say "I'd have to see the coin come up heads three times in a row to be convinced that it's a trick coin," we are acknowledging that the outcome we expect (heads) can occur by chance, and therefore we want to see an outcome that is unlikely to come up by chance—the coin comes up heads three times in a row, for example—before we are convinced. That is the core idea of statistical significance. There is some outcome that we expect, but we know that outcome could occur by chance; therefore, we look for an outcome that is so improbable, we figure it could not have occurred by chance.

The second step in our thinking is to note how rare an event would have to be before we are willing to accept it as improbable. Have a look at the table below, which shows the odds of tossing a fair coin a given number of times and having it come up heads each time.

Number of tosses	Approximate probability of all heads
1	.5
2	.25
3	.125
4	.063
5	.031
6	.016
7	.008
8	.004
9	.002
10	.001

In psychology, the standard cutoff is a probability of .05. If you know the odds of something occurring by chance, and then observe a deviation from chance that would only occur with a probability of .05, then you conclude that that deviation from chance is so large that there are forces other than chance at work; in other words, this must be a trick coin. Thus in the coin example, we'd want to see five heads in a row, to take us to a probability smaller than .05 before we'd be convinced that the coin is unfair.

The third step to note is that we need to know the odds of the event occurring by chance. We're trying to evaluate whether the coin is unfair, but we can only call it unfair if we know what happens when the coin is fair. In the case of the coin that's easy because it's defined by the nature of the coin—it should be heads half the time. For other questions, it's not quite as obvious. For example, suppose we develop a tonic that is supposed to make you feel more energetic. How could we evaluate whether it works? We could give the tonic to someone each day and see whether or not he feels energetic. But giving it to just one person is rather like tossing the coin only one time; it's too easy for the one person to feel energetic by chance. We could give the tonic to ten people and see how many of them feel energetic. But what are the odds of feeling energetic by chance, i.e., without the tonic? In the case of the coin, we know what should happen by chance. In the case of the tonic, we can't really predict what happens by chance, so we need to observe what happens by chance. In other words, we need a second group of people who don't get the tonic, but whose energy level we measure. Then we can compare the self-rated energy levels of people who do and do not get the tonic. Then we can ask the question, "Are the energy ratings of the tonic-drinkers higher than the ratings of the no-tonic-drinkers?"

Suppose that we find that the tonic-drinkers' energy ratings are indeed higher than the non-tonic drinkers. Isn't it possible that they are a little higher just due to chance? Absolutely. In the case of the coin we demanded that the coin came up heads a lot before we were willing to accept it as a trick coin: there needed to be an extreme difference between what we observed (lots of heads) and what would be expected by chance (half heads). The same principle applies to the tonic example. Not just any difference between the groups will do. The difference between the groups needs to be extreme enough that we think it was very unlikely to have occurred by chance. It's easy to calculate the relevant odds for the coin. It's more complicated for the tonic example, but the principle is the same. Statistical significance refers to observing a difference between two groups that is so large that we conclude it is very unlikely to have occurred by chance.

Answers

Answers to Questions in Chapter 1

1. The first assumption is about what questions should be addressed first. The second type of assumption is something you believe, which may or may not be true, that colors your view of a cognitive process even before you start to study it.

2. For much of this century a lot of psychologists (especially American psychologists) assumed that any theory of the mind could describe only the environment and people's behaviors. These psychologists were called behaviorists. They assumed that because observation is a critical part of the scientific method, and you can't observe thought directly, thought cannot be part of a scientific theory. This assumption seems quite solid, but it overlooks the possibility that you can propose ways in which thoughts lead to behaviors. In other words, you can make thoughts indirectly observable if you specify what sort of thoughts lead to what sort of behaviors. That is the approach that cognitive psychologists have used.

3. People believed it probably wouldn't work because that would mean that human behavior was deterministic, which they could not believe was true.

4. They were interested primarily in the origin of knowledge: Was knowledge largely innate, or was it acquired through experience? Other psychological questions were addressed during the Renaissance (e.g., learning and perception) but usually in service of the larger question of the origin of knowledge.

5. Initially, psychologists sought to explain the contents of consciousness. Behaviorism changed the goal of the discipline to explaining behavior.

6. I would say people don't hold it much at all, given the belief in extrasensory perception (ESP), astrology, and the like. ESP and astrology are exactly the sort of explanations we're talking about; they are unobservable explanations for worldly events. You *could* gather evidence for or against these phenomena (and there is a great deal of evidence indicating that they

are not real), but true believers always have an answer, such as "If you try to gather evidence about it, the ESP goes away" or "Astrology works, but not perfectly every time—it describes only general tendencies of what will happen." Thus, in the end you can gather evidence about these phenomena, yet many people are perfectly happy to accept them as explanations for things that happen.

7. I think they should, but not in the sense in which introspectionists use them. A great deal of work in cognitive and social psychology has shown that people's introspections on how and why they do things are not always accurate (Nisbett & Wilson, 1977), but on the other hand, there are times when people's descriptions of how they solve problems can be informative. But most importantly, introspections should be part of the data that are to be explained (Marr, 1982). If you are developing a theory of vision, for example, it would be a rather empty theory if it did not explain why that hill over there looks really steep, even though it's actually not all that steep. Our introspective experience is part of mental life, and it is worthy of explanation.

8. New data indicated that behaviorism was not completely successful in accounting for animal behavior (e.g., fixed action patterns, critical periods) and for some aspects of human behavior (e.g., language, apparent strategies in memory retrieval).

9. The heart of the information processing paradigm is the comparison of the brain to a computer. Both process information, in that both take in information, represent it symbolically, manipulate the symbols with different processes, refer to memory, and produce an output. Another important part of the information processing paradigm is that information processing occurs in discrete stages, as shown in the "What is your hometown?" example.

10. Partly by reference to other disciplines. They argued that neuroscience and artificial intelligence researchers used abstract representations in their work with no apparent loss of rigor. They were also successful in arguing that certain problems (e.g., accounting for human ability in language) seemed to require such representations for an adequate explanation.

11. The answer is very likely to be "yes." On one hand, you could point to the fact that children seem to reach developmental milestones at around the same time: rolling over, crawling, first steps, first words, etc. But the critical period idea suggests that if those crucial time windows are missed, it will be difficult to learn the skill later, and the fact that most kids learn them at around the same age doesn't speak to that issue. There are only a few examples of kids who, because of severe deprivation, seemed not to have the chance to learn to speak, for example, and these cases seem to support the idea of a critical period for language (Itard, 1962).

Other data based on larger numbers of children support the idea of a critical period for language. Children appear to be "programmed" to learn language, learning vocabulary at the unbelievable rate of an average of 9 words per day between the ages of 2 and 9. You may know someone who was raised bilingually. You'll note that kids can pick up two languages almost as quickly as one (research confirms this observation). This is true only when you're quite young. Once you're older (and taking a foreign language in school, for example) it is much harder to learn another language.

12. To be honest, I don't even have a very good guess as to the ratio of failures to successes, but I'm confident that the ratio is very low. I bring this question up simply to emphasize that your mind is constantly performing remarkable cognitive feats that you are not aware of. That's part of the point of the "What's your home town?" analysis: to show that even cognitive processes that appear very simple actually are quite complex when you consider them in information-processing terms. One of the ways cognitive psychologists think about this point is to consider what it would take to get a computer to perform the same function. Viewed in that light, it becomes clear that cognitive processes that are quite easy for us—recognizing objects, reaching for things—are extremely complex.

13. Yes, absolutely. That is how cognitive psychologists often approach these problems. As I mentioned in that discussion, cognitive psychologists typically work on just one problem (e.g., memory) rather than trying to figure out how the entire cognitive system works because just one component of the system is dauntingly complicated. If you're trying to figure out how memory works, you could approach it just the same way that we did in the "What is your hometown?" example. You could figure that memory starts with some information coming in from the environment (e.g., someone says "I just saw a quincunx"),

and the end product of the memory search is that you conclude that you don't know what a quincunx is. How do you determine that you don't know that? Do you check every single part of your memory, or do you check for a while, and then quit? Wait a minute—what does it mean to "check" memory? How might memories be organized such that you can "check" them? And off you go. . . .

Answers to Questions in Chapter 2

1. Size and distance, shape and orientation, and light source, reflectance and shadow.

2. You would think that the answer would relate to familiar size. You would assume that the car will be the normal size for a car, so if it looks small it's probably a regular-sized car but far away. To a point, that's true. As we'll see in the next section, however, familiar size only helps a little bit in disambiguating size and distance.

3. No. The earth is much bigger than the moon, so you'd have to move farther away from the earth than the surface of the moon for it to work, or you'd have to move your thumb closer to your eye.

4. Objects can be identified by their edges; edges usually can be identified by lines. Perkins's laws are guidelines to interpreting the visible two-dimensional arrangement of lines into the three-dimensional shape of objects.

5. Surfaces are uniformly colored, gradual changes in luminance usually are caused by shadow, light sources are above the visual scene, and surface lightness is interpreted depending on the ratios of lightness of areas that are next to one another in the same plane.

6. They show the importance of binocular parallax in depth perception. People perceive depth in these displays even though there are no cues to depth except binocular parallax and even though the correspondence problem seems impossibly complex; the two images must be matched up in the left and right retinas so the disparity can be evaluated, but the matching seems very difficult in these stimuli. Nevertheless, people perceive depth, which perhaps indicates that our visual systems are good at evaluating binocular parallax.

7. The most important difference concerns what one assumes is in the environment and what one thinks is in the mind. The computational point of view assumes that the visual cues in the environment are basically lines; the environment is viewed as an impoverished source of visual information, so a fair amount of computation is necessary for this impoverished input to be made into something sensible.

According to the ecological point of view, on the other hand, the environment is a wonderfully rich source of information. The psychologist's first job is to discover what these sources of information are and which ones humans use in vision. Once we do a good job of describing the environment, they believe, the job of describing how the mind uses this information will be much easier.

8. Because the day was brilliantly clear, there was no atmospheric perspective. With that cue to distance gone, it looked oddly like a model.

9. Get low. Strangers may seem scary to toddlers not only because they are strange but also because they appear so big. People (including toddlers) focus on faces, so get your face down to the eyeheight of the toddler.

10. One set of theories says the representation is object centered, meaning that the parts of the objects are located relative to one another. The other set of theories holds that they are viewer centered, meaning that there would be several representations for each object, one for each point of view.

11. There is evidence in both monkeys and humans that different parts of the brain support tasks demanding "what" knowledge and "how" knowledge, namely temporal lobe for "what" and parietal lobe for "how." The second type of evidence comes from humans with intact brains. It is possible to fool the "what" system with visual illusions, but the "how" system is not fooled by these illusions.

Answers to Questions in Chapter 3

1. It seems that people can, but it is actually difficult to be certain because it is always possible that people switch attention rapidly between tasks rather than truly dividing attention.

2. Adding a second task may change the way in which the first task is performed. The attentional requirements of a task do not remain constant irrespective of the secondary task. In other words, different secondary tasks interact with the same primary tasks in different ways.

3. No. Structural explanations claim that interference between tasks occurs because of competition for mental structures (e.g., working memory), whereas attentional explanations claim that interference occurs because of competition for attentional resources.

4. It could be that music with words takes more attention to listen to, but I think another explanation is more likely. It may be that these people cannot help but process the words semantically. Semantic processing of spoken (or sung) words may be automatic.

Processing the meaning of the sung words interferes with processing the words that are read. Thus, it's not that music with words takes more attention to listen to; rather, the words are processed whether you want them to be or not, and that interferes with reading.

5. A multiple resources model. The comedian apparently thought that there should be no interference between vision (looking for the house number) and audition (listening to the music). The fact is that we do find the music distracting. As described in the text, even though there is certainly less interference when different modalities are used, there is still some common demand, so people try to minimize the interference.

6. You might guess that because driving is automatic, it doesn't make much difference whether you're talking on a cellular phone; there should be attention to spare while driving. In fact, heavy use of cellular phones (more than 50 min per month) is a risk factor for accidents (Violanti & Marshall, 1996). But you would expect that the expertise of the driver would be a factor, and that seems to be true. Using cellular phones while driving is a greater risk for less experienced drivers, apparently because they are more likely to glance away from the road (usually to dial) for long periods of time and at risky moments when attention to the road is crucial (Wikman, Nieminen, & Summala, 1998).

7. The evidence indicates that it's early. A number of studies indicated that the filter might be late, but in those cases it appears that participants might not have been attending solely to the material they were told to attend to; they seem to have been occasionally "sampling" the other channel. Some proposed that the filter is "movable," but this probably means that there is a fixed filter (which is early) and that you can choose to allocate more or less attention to other sources. For example, you can listen to your friend at a party closely and try to ignore other conversations at a party, or you can listen to your friend and simultaneously try to monitor the party around you to see whether anyone is talking about anything interesting.

8. It selects objects for further processing, not locations in space.

9. In a disjunctive search the target differs from the distractors on just one feature (e.g., color), and the search is easy; in fact, it occurs automatically, meaning that all the elements in the field are evaluated simultaneously, and the subject experiences pop-out. In a conjunctive search, the target is defined by the conjunction of two features (color and shape), and visual search is difficult; the search progresses serially, not in parallel.

10. At the start of the chapter we noted that it is crucial to be able to monitor the environment for things that are not currently attended to see whether attention should be refocused. The heroine apparently is not processing unattended sounds very carefully. Again, it seems as if the filter is early, so to detect the scuffling sound as threatening (and not caused by a tree limb scraping the house, for example), she might need to be focusing attention away from her shower periodically, but the situation she thinks she's in (showering safe at home) does not warrant frequent sampling of the environment for threatening sounds. You may have noticed the same phenomenon. If you are talking to a friend in your living room at noon, you may not notice the scratching noise of a squirrel on the roof because you have chosen not to allocate much attention to your surroundings. However, a very similar noise may enter awareness if you are talking to your friend while walking down a dark, deserted street at night in a strange New York City neighborhood because you have allocated more attention to monitoring your surroundings.

11. Any situation in which two objects are intertwined (i.e., spatially overlap) and you successfully attend to just one indicates that you are directing attention to an object, not a location. Another example would be looking at your reflection in the glass of a picture frame and successfully ignoring the picture.

12. Stimuli that appear suddenly in the periphery, either sights or sounds, capture attention. Still, whether they capture attention seems to depend on the mental set of the person. For example, if you're walking down a city street, sounds and sights appear all the time, and they don't seem to attract attention. It may be that stimuli appearing in the periphery capture attention only if they are infrequent. The details of this phenomenon are not well understood.

13. The reason you get ironic effects is that the monitoring process does not demand attentional resources. If you have limited attentional resources (e.g., you're distracted, tired, or stressed), the operating process, which demands attention, will not operate very effectively. The operating process is the one that finds suitable distractions. Therefore, the monitoring process, which doesn't demand attention, searches for the "forbidden" mental contents, which is enough to *put* the forbidden mental contents into awareness. Thus the heart of ironic effects lies in the differing attentional demands of the operating and monitoring process.

14. As you know from reading this chapter, trying *not* to think about something is pretty ineffective. The best strategy would be to tell your friend to go ahead and think about his girlfriend all he wants, perhaps even to the point of forcing himself to think about her. It's hard to predict when thoughts of the girlfriend will subside, but they will do so faster with this technique than by trying not to think about her.

15. Car alarms have a terrible bias: They go off not only for robbers, but for people nudging the car as they walk by, cats jumping on the hood, and sometimes a bystander taking a deep breath nearby. They are like a radar operator who constantly says, "I see a ship!" Car alarms are completely ineffective because they rely on the idea that people will go running to investigate when they hear a car alarm. No one does because they go off all the time, just as you would ignore the radar operator who kept claiming to see ships all the time.

16. This is a vigilance task at its worst. These people must watch radar scopes for missiles that never come, yet if they miss the missile on the scope, the results are catastrophic. I would make the shifts of these workers as short as possible (because sensitivity in vigilance tasks declines rapidly).

Answers to Questions in Chapter 4

1. The partial report procedure allows a more accurate estimate than the whole report procedure of how much information people can apprehend with a brief exposure. In partial report, participants are exposed to stimuli and immediately thereafter are given a cue as to which stimuli to report. Because the cue is given after the stimuli have disappeared, the participant cannot know which stimuli he or she will be asked to report, so the percentage of stimuli successfully reported may be taken as a fair estimate of all the stimuli that are reportable. The whole report procedure underestimates the span of apprehension because participants forget some of the stimuli apprehended even as they are reporting others; the partial report procedure avoids that problem.

2. Visual or iconic memory has a large capacity (as many as 15 items or more, depending on conditions), it fades quickly (anywhere from 0.25 to 2.0 s, depending on conditions), and it can be masked, meaning you can knock the contents of sensory memory out by presenting new stimuli. Echoic memory has similar characteristics, although it is shorter lived (0.25 s).

3. It is difficult to give a simple answer to this question. *Precategorical* means that information residing in iconic memory does not contain semantic information. Cueing by semantic content in the partial report procedure doesn't seem to work. On the other hand, effects such as the flanker effect indicate that there may be some semantic information in iconic memory. In the final analysis, it may be that there is no absolute distinction between presence or absence of semantic information in iconic memory.

4. Films typically are shot at 24 frames per second, meaning that each frame of the film would appear for about 42 ms. The shutter of a typical film projector is not open continuously: It is closed more than it is open, so when you watch a film you are looking at a black screen more than you are looking at the movie. Iconic memory carries you over these intervals and makes the visual experience continuous even though the visual stimulation is not.

You may come up with your own examples, but I can tell you about one time I actually used iconic memory. In my old apartment, I didn't have a phone by the bed. If it rang in the middle of the night I had to walk out to the kitchen to answer it. I didn't feel like turning on the light because it was too bright, but I didn't want to crash into furniture on the way to the phone either. I used iconic memory by flipping the lights on for just a moment. That gave me a tachistoscopic flash of the room, and I could read iconic memory to avoid the furniture on the way to the phone.

5. This question wasn't quite fair because there isn't enough information in the chapter to answer it. You'll notice that retinal afterimages have fuzzy edges; they don't carry much detail. That's because of nystagmus: Your eye is constantly jiggling a little bit. The fact is that retinal cells tire really fast—in about 5 s—and if your eye weren't jiggling all the time, when you held something in a steady gaze, the object would disappear after about 5 s because the retinal neurons would quit. Thus, when you stare at something (like the reversed Jesus) you are tiring the retinal cells, but your eyes are jiggling, so the neurons corresponding to the edge of the picture are alternately being stimulated by white or black as they jiggle on and off the figure. That's why the edge is blurry. For the same reason, the splotches and imperfections in the middle of the figure are blurred over.

6. Material may be coded acoustically (in terms of sound), semantically (in terms of meaning), of visuospatially (in terms of visual appearance).

7. Forgetting occurs because of proactive interference, retroactive interference, and decay. Proactive interference is the forgetting of new material caused by having learned material earlier. Retroactive interference is the forgetting of previously learned material caused by learning new material. Decay is the spontaneous loss of previously learned material.

8. Not really. That is people's performance on the digit span task, it's true, but it is more accurate to say that the capacity of primary memory depends on how the participant codes the material and how the participant views the content of the material. The code is important because an acoustic code has a capacity of about 2 s of material. The capacity in the

semantic and visuospatial codes depends on the participant's ability to chunk the material.

9. Although this measure can prevent proactive interference from material during the experiment, you can't rule out the possibility of proactive interference from processing just before the experiment. You have no way of knowing what people were doing before they began the experiment, so if some percentage of the participants had just finished studying or thinking about materials similar to those used in the experiment right before they walked in, that could account for the apparent decay effects reported in the experiment. This objection probably is impossible to overcome, and Baddeley and Scott's experiment seems to do about as good a job as possible of ruling out possible proactive interference effects.

10. The best plan is to space your studying so that there are breaks between study sessions. If you can't do that, at least try to study dissimilar subjects back to back because interference is greater when the subjects are similar.

11. *Primary memory* is a generic term that is not tied to any particular theory. *Short-term memory* is a term from a particular theory, the modal model. (Short-term memory was proposed to code material exclusively acoustically, to lose material exclusively through decay, etc.) *Working memory* is also a term from a particular theory, Baddeley's working memory model. In popular culture *short-term memory* has taken on the generic meaning in the generic sense. Among psychologists, *short-term memory* usually has the more specific meaning tied to the modal model. However, psychologists do use the term *long-term memory* in the generic sense.

12. The phonological loop is composed of the phonological store, which is the site where 2 s of acoustic material can be stored. The articulatory control process allows one to write acoustic information to the phonological loop through subvocal rehearsal.

13. Working memory capacity correlates with reading comprehension scores. Working memory capacity also correlates with scores on standardized intelligence tests. Finally, normal aging leads to the decline of a range of cognitive capabilities. At least some of this decline appears to be rooted in a decline in working memory.

14. This irrelevant verbiage gains obligatory access to the phonological loop, which is where I'm trying to keep the instructions she just gave me. A nod and a smile would be better.

15. Such patients exist, and their long-term memory is surprisingly good. Remember, the phonological loop is not the only pathway to long-term memory, as evidenced by the fact that you can still encode and rehearse things under articulatory suppression. But they are probably impaired at learning vocabulary. Their vocabulary doesn't seem impaired, probably because they have had a lot of practice, but they are impaired in learning vocabulary words in a new language, where the main thing to be learned is the sound of the unfamiliar word (Baddeley, Papagno, & Vallar, 1988).

Answers to Questions in Chapter 5

1. Emotion has an impact, but naturally we remember many things that are not emotional, so it seems likely that this factor affects memory in a limited number of circumstances. Depth of processing—the extent to which material is considered in terms of its meaning—has a profound impact on encoding.

2. Depth of processing predicts that the extent to which a memory is encoded depends solely on the depth of processing during encoding. It turns out that the match between encoding and retrieval processes also is important. The other problem concerns the levels of processing theory. The theory is not detailed enough to differentiate two different tasks that are shallow.

3. Clearly, the best advice you can offer is to process the material deeply. That means that you have to think about what the material *means.* The best way to do that is to think up questions with which to test yourself. Thinking up your own questions has the added advantage of getting you to try to think of what your professor is likely to ask. Regarding remembering names at a party, the advice is more or less the same. If you want to remember names, you have to actually think about the person's name. Most people who don't remember names (including me—I'm horrible) simply don't pay much attention when they first hear the name.

4. Before you give an explanation, verify that this is true. When someone tells me they remember little of their wedding day, I have to curb the desire to narrow my eyes and cock my head in a mask of police-inquisitor suspicion. "Oh really," I want to say. "You don't remember getting dressed that morning? You don't remember the kiss-the-bride part?" One of the first things you learn as a psychologist is that your own experiences and intuitions (and those of your wedding-amnesic friends) can be a terrific source of hypotheses about the human mind, but you shouldn't believe something based on subjective experience alone. Psychology books are full of things that many people believe that are false. (For starters, most people believe in ESP.)

To my knowledge, no one has examined in true experiment whether high emotion can lead to a failure of memory. Let's suppose for a moment that it were true. It might be that emotionality has what is called an inverted-U effect on memory. That means that when emotional levels are low, a bit more emotion improves memory, but that when emotion levels are high, more emotion harms memory. This inverted-U relationship is found in certain types of physical performance tasks, so it might be observed for memory, but this is speculation.

5. I think advertisements that are well remembered are processed more deeply. The Kit-Kat song is pretty catchy. It could also work out that advertisements that are repeated a lot may become more memorable, despite the result of the Craik and Watkins (1973) experiment. You can think of each repetition of a commercial as another opportunity for you to encode the material deeply. Even if you ignore the ad the first 20 times you see it, perhaps on the 21st viewing you'll note that the advertised car really does have more leg room, by golly.

6. It reduces what you have to remember by allowing you to chunk, it guides your interpretation of details through the activation of schemas, and it makes unusual things stand out.

7. It ought to be. You can test this hypothesis easily enough. If you're a baseball fan (for example), watch a game (or part of a game) with a nonfan and later see who remembers more of the game.

8. It's easy to guess at what the schemas for these "types" of people would be. Librarians are typically women, they are spinsters, they have glasses and wear their hair in a bun, and they are not a lot of fun. Engineers are male, have little sense of humor and mediocre interpersonal skills, and they wear out-of-date clothes and pocket protectors. It is a sobering thought that our minds may be designed in such a way that we automatically categorize objects (including people) and abstract out schemas (stereotypes) to fit the categories. Naturally, the fact that we *know* these stereotypes does not mean that we have to act in accordance with them.

9. Here's one way you could do it. There are three main effects of prior knowledge on encoding: It reduces what you have to remember, it guides your interpretation of details, and it makes unusual things stand out. You could chunk those three main points into one image. Take a tour *guide* (complete with map, camera, and foreign phrase translation book) and *reduce* him in size. Then put him with a tour group of regular-sized people who are sitting so that he *stands out.* Silly, yes, but bizarre images are effective for memory.

10. It would make deep processing easier. Recall that deep processing involves connecting new information to information that you already know. If you have more prior knowledge, it will be easier to connect the new information to things you already know.

11. Consolidation is a hypothetical process by which memories become more stable and less susceptible to disruption. The evidence consistent with consolidation is that patients with retrograde amnesia show a temporal gradient to their memory loss, indicating that older memories have become more resistant to injury. The other important evidence is that patients with anterograde amnesia always have some retrograde amnesia too (which is also temporally graded), indicating that loss of the consolidation process caused by injury causes an inability to form new memories and disrupts the ongoing consolidation of memories that had been encoded before the injury.

12. If consolidation occurs at night one way to disrupt memory would be to prevent people from sleeping. Memory is indeed disrupted if you prevent people from sleeping. Thus, even if you feel as if you're a night owl, you're probably better off studying during the day before a big test rather than studying late into the night.

13. Based on the consolidation evidence, some researchers have suggested that it is more appropriate to think of three types of memory: working memory, long-term memory, and an intermediate memory. Intermediate-term memory describes the state of memories that are not fully consolidated. The basic distinction is that secondary memories are represented by changes in the physical structure of the brain—new branches between neurons—whereas intermediate-term memories are represented by changes in the way the existing network communicates.

Instead of proposing another memory system like intermediate-term memory, one could propose some process within secondary memory that acts like a rehearser that happens outside of awareness. Somewhere outside of consciousness, all memories are continually rehearsed and therefore become stronger and more stable. Again, such a process mostly would be overwhelmed by forgetting, but it might account for how consolidation works.

Answers to Questions in Chapter 6

1. Free recall, cued recall, recognition, and savings in relearning are the four measures. They differ in sensitivity in that one measure of memory may indicate that some information has been forgotten, but another measure may show that some part of the memory remains in the storehouse.

2. The most important factor at retrieval is the cues that are provided. Cues that more closely match how the material was encoded are more likely to lead to successful retrieval. Thus, if the measure provides more cues, one of the cues is likely to be helpful.

3. The cues are more important, as shown by the recognition failure of recallable words effect.

4. Prior knowledge tells us what usually happens in similar situations. We can use that in two ways. First, we may try harder to retrieve a bit of information because we know from prior knowledge that the event must have happened (as when we struggle to remember the type of cake served at a child's birthday party because we know from prior knowledge that cake must have been served). Second, we may mistake knowledge from prior experience for retrieval of a particular event. For example, we may mistakenly believe that cake was served at a particular child's birthday party because the serving of cake is so consistent with our prior experience of children's birthday parties.

5. He or she might come up with something, but it would be mostly a reconstruction. This date was not picked arbitrarily. In February 1987 Ronald Reagan challenged reporters at a press conference to remember what they were doing August 8, 1985. The reporters were silent. Reagan was trying to make the point that it is hard to remember the events of a specific day 19 months ago, and in a way he was right. Your memory is not designed to answer questions of this sort because it is not indexed according to date. It is indexed by events. If I went to the Metropolitan Museum of Art that day, I may (or may not) be able to recover that fact, but if I did, it would require lots of reasoning about where I was on August 8. However, if you simply ask, "Have you ever been to the Metropolitan Museum of Art," my answer would be immediate and confident. Cues to the same event can be either very effective or very ineffective in leading you to remember the event.

6. This seems like a straightforward case of recognition failure of a recallable stimulus. Suppose you are walking down the street in your hometown. If someone stopped you and said, "Can you tell me what Peter, that guy in the room down the hall, looks like?" You'd say, "Sure," and you would be able to generate a mental image of Peter and describe him—in short, you recall his face. But when you're walking down the street, you fail to recognize his face. His face is in a context different from the one in which you learned it, just as the word *CHAIR* alone is in a different context from the one in which you learned it if you saw it in the presence of the word *glue*.

7. Decay theory and interference theory. There is little support for decay theory, but it is very difficult or impossible to disprove. There is more evidence supporting a role for interference in forgetting, especially for a process of unlearning.

8. This proposal is impossible to disprove, but it is viewed as quite unlikely by memory researchers. The standard observations in support of the idea (hypnosis, Penfield's stimulation studies) are more likely to be reconstructions than real memories.

9. Probably, but it seems to happen very infrequently. It's difficult to obtain convincing evidence of repression because it is always possible that the memory is inaccurate, that the person did not truly forget the event, although they think they did, or that the loss of the memory was caused by a normal forgetting process, not repression. Although repression may occur, many memory researchers believe it has been overdiagnosed in the last 10 years because of the use of hypnosis and guided imagery techniques, which are known to generate false memories.

10. Interference is the big enemy in trying to learn new material. As you've seen, interference can be proactive or retroactive, so long bouts of studying pay diminishing returns. The more you try to learn in a single session, the more difficult learning becomes because of proactive interference and the more likely you are to forget the material studied earlier because of retroactive interference. Therefore, short, frequent study sessions, broken up by other activities, are the most efficient.

11. This is a classic case of source confusion. Initially, you remember the event itself, but with repeated tellings of the story you get confused about whether you're remembering the actual events or the events as told to you by family members.

Answers to Questions in Chapter 7

1. The classical view proposes that objects are categorized by comparing the object to a list of necessary and sufficient properties that an object must have to fit a category. Hence, the description of an uncle is "brother of a parent." If someone is the brother of a parent, he is an uncle because he meets the necessary and sufficient conditions for uncledom. The data indicating that the classical view is either wrong or incomplete concerned participants' ratings of typicality of category exemplars (and other typicality effects). No exemplar of a category should seem more or less typical if one is using a list of necessary and sufficient conditions to put things into a category. Either an object meets the category requirements or it doesn't, and an object is therefore either a member of the category or not. Because this seems not to be the case (at least for some categories some of the time) the classical view must be either incorrect or incomplete.

2. Typicality can be measured by asking participants to rate typicality. When asked to verify whether an exemplar is a member of a category (e.g., a dalmatian is a dog), participants are quicker to do so for typical category members. People tend to put more typical exemplars of a category first in a sentence. If a typical instance of a category has a property, people are more willing to guess that this property extends to other members of the category.

3. Prototype theory and exemplar theory both propose that new exemplars are categorized by evaluating the similarity of the exemplar to memory representations; if it is similar, it is deemed to be a member of the category. The difference is that the exemplar theory proposes that each exemplar of a category is stored in memory, whereas the prototype theory proposes that a prototype is abstracted from the many exemplars one sees, and that the prototype is stored.

4. It appears that both types of categorization occur. Studies in the 1980s indicated that at times people categorize based on rules, even if similarity dictated a different categorization. The job now is to determine when one type of categorization is used and when the other is used.

5. This theory seems to require an endlessly large memory store. How big would memory have to be for me to store every instance of a car I look at as a new car? And every dog, and every chair, and so on? This problem has not been overlooked by categorization researchers. One easy solution that some models have taken is to set a criterion for similarity for an individual exemplar to be stored. If the exemplar that you're looking at is similar to an exemplar already in memory, then there is no need to store it again (although the fact that you've seen this exemplar again may be stored). This saves you from having 10 million exemplars of your mother stored in memory.

6. The newspapers use the word *grandma* for shock value. Why is it shocking? It's the tension between the classical, rule-driven meaning of *grandma* and the prototypical grandma. Anyone who is female and the parent of a parent is a grandma. That's the classical categorization definition. The prototypical features of a grandma include much more, such as being sweet, baking cookies, knitting, and sitting quietly at home. Therefore, it's exciting when a grandma does something vigorous or outrageous.

7. First, your memory shows an excellent addressing system in that it can retrieve material very quickly, despite the great volume of material it potentially has available. Second, if the desired information is not in memory, the system makes available information that is either close in meaning or relevant because it may allow you to make an inference that allows you to answer the question that was not in memory.

8. Advantages: It allows the retrieval of object properties, it allows content-addressable storage, typicality is a natural outgrowth of the model, the model creates defaults, and it's resistant to faulty input. Disadvantages: The model has not always been very specific, and it appears that activation spreads to an unreasonable degree.

9. The chief difference is one of representation. In a model with a local representation, a concept is represented by the activity of a single node. In a model with a distributed representation, a concept is represented by the pattern of activation across multiple nodes.

10. You may recall that early empiricist philosophers placed a great deal of emphasis on associations; the building of associations was at the heart of intelligent behavior. Spreading activation models have association at their heart. The links between nodes are nothing more than associations. These models represent an advance over earlier associationist ideas, however, because they are more precise in their predictions. Regarding consciousness, the associationist nature of the model leads to a natural prediction about consciousness. Because activity passes between the nodes in the model, *something* is always active in the network. One could say that whatever is active is what is in consciousness, so the ebb and flow of activity in the model represents the flow of consciousness.

11. This question is a bit unfair because my hunch is that you would probably say "distributed," and I think the real answer is that neither is very realistic in any important way. On the surface the distributed models seem to look more like networks of neurons. For one thing, we are pretty confident that a concept is not represented in a single neuron, and the local representation appears to claim just that, if you take a single node in the network to be a single neuron. But models using the distributed representation still only use hundreds or thousands of "neurons" to represent processes that surely require millions of neurons in the brain. Thus, I would say that neither model is especially realistic in terms of biological plausibility; both are useful as models of cognitive processes. Other researchers have worked hard to develop models that take neuroanatomy and neurophysiology quite seriously (e.g., Granger, Wiebe, Taketani, & Lynch, 1996; Levy, 1996), but we haven't discussed those models here.

12. There are a great many of these unbalanced association pairs, where a strong association (salt–pepper)

doesn't go the other way (pepper–salt). Some researchers have argued that this means that each node should be connected by *two* links, one for each direction. The link from *salt* to *pepper* would be strong, but the link from *pepper* to *salt* would be weak.

13. Most cognitive psychologists agree that the critical feature is different processes and representations that operate on them. Most of the evidence thus far has been evidence that hypothetical memory systems are separate in terms of the brain structures that support them. Many researchers are willing to bet that anatomic separability goes hand in hand with cognitive differences, but it has been difficult to prove that these anatomically separate systems are also cognitively separate.

14. The proposal that memory systems are separate grew out of the attempt to explain why amnesic patients are able to learn some tasks normally. Initially researchers proposed that there was some memory process that was damaged in amnesia but that certain tasks didn't require that process—those were the tasks that amnesic patients could learn. No one could figure out what that process might be, however, so researchers began to consider the idea that some types of memory were intact in amnesia because they were supported by a separate memory system.

15. At least five: systems supporting declarative memory, repetition priming, motor skill learning, classical conditioning, and emotional conditioning. In fact, some have suggested further fractionation of some of these systems (Keane, Gabrieli, Fennema, Growdon, & Corkin, 1991; Schacter, 1990).

16. This possibility has not been studied very carefully, but it seems likely that these various memory systems might all affect behavior simultaneously. For example, when you're learning a new sport, you often acquire information about how to play it declaratively, and there are also motor skill processes contributing. For example, suppose you were an experienced tennis player and started playing squash for the first time. A squash coach might tell you that your stroke looked too much like a tennis stroke: You kept our wrist locked instead of whipping it, as a squash player would. In this case, the motor skill system is producing behavior consistent with its experience (squash movement), and the declarative system is trying to influence the movement based on the coach's instruction (a declarative memory). I think most researchers would agree that these systems may well influence one another directly and that more than one may influence behavior (as in the tennis and squash example), but how this works has not been examined in any detail.

17. The tennis and squash example is a good one. I think another example can be found whenever you are afraid of something but try to control your fear. Suppose I am afraid of snakes but I want to overcome my fear and hold a small python to impress the friends I'm with. The emotional conditioning system might be telling me to drop the snake and run, whereas the declarative system would be calling up memories that show that this small snake poses no real threat and that I should hang on to it.

Answers to Questions in Chapter 8

1. The imageless thought controversy concerned whether it was possible to have thoughts that were not accompanied by images. This debate occurred in the late 19th century and was important because psychologists using introspection examined their own mental images as they solved a problem as a way of learning about thought. If thought could proceed in the absence of images, it meant that at least some thoughts were not open to examination using this method.

2. Paivio pointed out that psychologists were willing to accept verbal reports about purported verbal experience from participants. In other words, when a participant said that he or she remembered some words, the experimenter believed it. Even though there was no assurance that the participant really remembered the words per se, the experimenter used these reports to infer what the cognitive representations were that allowed the participant to remember. Paivio argued that experimenters should be just as willing to accept verbal reports of visual imagery and to use these reports to make inferences about cognitive processes that allow the participant to remember.

3. The two key results were that mentally rotating an object a greater distance took more time and that mentally rotating an object in depth was not harder than rotating it in the picture plane. This result was important because it was the first study that offered a clear way to study how images are transformed. It was also important because the data were very orderly, which implied that a single (perhaps simple) process underlies mental rotation.

4. One problem is that it's hard for me to rate my imagery ability because I don't have anything to which I might compare it. I may think my images are quite distinct and bright, whereas in reality they are pale compared to yours. Indeed, in one study Jeffrey Walczyk (1995) correlated participants' ratings of their images with the actual accuracy of the images and found correlations within an individual but not across individuals. That essentially means that I know how clear one of my images is relative to my typical image ("this is a good one" or "this one isn't one of my clearer images"), but I have no idea how my images stack up to yours.

5. This question has been studied frequently, and researchers have found that bizarreness helps (Campos, Perez, & Gonzalez, 1997; McDaniel et al., 1995; Sharpe & Markham, 1992; Worthen, 1997, but see Ironsmith & Lutz, 1996; Wollen, Weber, & Lowry, 1972). Why bizarreness helps is not really known. It is always possible that a bit more effort must be put into bizarre images or that they are more distinctive (but see McDaniel et al., 1995). The bizarreness effect was mentioned by the Greeks, but the precise reasons for the memory advantage of bizarre images is still unknown.

6. It depends on the event and on what you're doing, but when one listens to a sporting event, one often engages mental imagery to understand what is happening in the game. For example, if you heard the announcer at a baseball game say, "It's a line drive straight up center field, but the runner at first is going anyway. The ball is caught, and the centerfielder is throwing it back to first to try to tag him up. It's going to be close, but now the runner at third is trying for home." If you're a fan, you're very likely to generate a visual image of this action. We've reviewed data showing that imagery interferes with visual tasks. Thus, listening to a sporting event that encourages you to visualize the action may not be a great idea if you are performing a task that is visually demanding, such as driving a car or using power tools.

7. Images might be an epiphenomenon, the results of experiments consistent with the idea that people use images may result from demand characteristics, and the results of imagery experiments can be explained by models of cognition that use propositions alone.

8. Propositions are relational; images do not describe a particular relationship. Propositions have syntax; images do not. Propositions have a truth value; images do not. Propositions are abstract; images are specific. Propositions are not spatial; images are inherently spatial.

9. They showed that demand characteristics are not a factor in imagery experiments. They proposed more specific imagery theories so that more specific predictions could be tested. And, most importantly, they collected lots of data in a variety of paradigms that were easy to account for with an imagery theory but were increasingly difficult to account for with a theory that used only propositions.

10. To account for this effect, you just need to make two assumptions: Details are embedded in larger features, and you can have only a limited number of features active in working memory at one time. For example, suppose you are imaging a rabbit. The representation might look like the figure below.

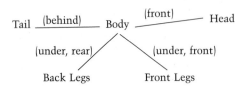

Now suppose you are asked whether a rabbit has a pink nose. You need more information about the head. This information is embedded in the "head" representation, so you unpack the "head" representation to get more details about it, yielding the representation below.

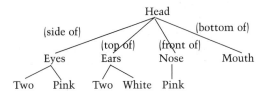

All the information about the head (including the information about the pink nose) cannot be included when one initially images a rabbit because of working memory limitations. When the question about the nose is asked, the representation is abandoned and another is generated that includes more details about the head. The creation of this new representation leads to the epiphenomenal feeling of zooming in.

11. Psychologists distrust participants' introspections because in other areas of psychology participants' introspections are wrong at least as often as they are right. First, for many cognitive processes participants have no introspections at all; no one knows how their perceptual processes or motor control processes work. So what reason is there to think that for this particular cognitive function (answering certain types of questions about rabbits' noses and the like) you have reliable introspections? Second, people's intropsections often are wrong. For example, participants who are comparing different brands of a product show a bias to select the product on the far right if they are arranged in a line. When asked whether such a factor might have influenced their behavior, however, almost all participants denied it, "usually with a worried glance at the interviewer suggesting that they were dealing with a madman" (Nisbett & Wilson, 1977, p. 244). People's introspections are fine as sources for hypotheses, but they are not trustworthy as data.

12. Images must be generated and maintained. Then they can be inspected and transformed.

13. Visual imagery concerns what objects look like (e.g., their color, their basic shape). Spatial imagery concerns objects' locations (e.g., where objects are in a scene) and spatial transformations of objects in imagery (e.g., mental rotation). Visual imagery is in the ventral visual pathway (the temporal lobe) and spatial imagery is in the dorsal visual pathway (the parietal lobe).

14. The key result was discovered as follows. Participants were asked to image multipart objects using a grid as a guide for the shape of the object. Xs appeared in the grids as they were imaging them. The response time to say whether the Xs would be on the objects, depended on the location of the Xs, such that if the Xs were on parts of the object that would be imaged first, response times were short. If the Xs were on parts of the object that would be imaged later, response times were longer. This result was interpreted as showing that when the Xs appeared, participants were still creating the image. They created it part by part, and as soon as they imaged the part where the X was, they could answer the question as to whether the X covered the part.

15. Imagery does seem to have some properties in common with Baddeley's visuospatial sketchpad. Imagery is limited in how much it can contain, you can increase its capacity through chunking, and it seems to have dissociable visual and spatial aspects. These are all characteristics of Baddeley's visuospatial sketchpad.

16. We've briefly mentioned that imagery might aid perception. If you're imaging an object it is easier to perceive an object that matches your image, but that situation may be rare in the real world. Imagery may play an important role in certain types of problem solving. For example, a Nobel prize–winning physicist has said that he often thought of physics problems not in terms of formal proofs but in terms of imaginary physical models of the systems (Feynman & Leighton, 1985). For a brief review of other reports of the importance of imagery in scientific problem solving, see Shepard and Cooper (1982). For a more detailed discussion of the uses of imagery in creativity, see Finke (1996).

17. This broad characterization (or caricature) is not bad. One can think in terms of a rather simple model: low level perceptual processes can write to a screen of limited spatial extent; this screen is the location of visual experience (i.e., where we have the awareness of seeing something). What is written to the screen gets stored in memory in a secondary memory representation. This secondary memory representation is a visual image. We also have the ability to take this representation and write its contents back on the screen. That is visual imagery. Hence, perception = low-level processes → screen → secondary memory, whereas imagery = secondary memory → screen.

Answers to Questions in Chapter 9

1. Rational models are those in which decisions are internally consistent, that is, in which your decisions don't conflict with one another. Normative models of decision making propose a criterion by which choices can be compared and a best choice can be selected.

2. They are similar because they are both criteria that could be used in normative theories of decision making. They differ in that expected value is based solely on the financial return that can be expected from a particular choice, whereas expected utility considers the value a person places on the return and the likelihood that the return will be obtained.

3. Their choices do not show transitivity, and their choices change depending on the problem frame.

4. I doubt it. Utility theory might help in explaining why people play lotteries because the utility of the huge prize is so much greater than the utility of the small amount needed to play. (Although the expected value of a lottery is so abysmally bad, it's still difficult to understand why people play.) That is not true of typical casino games, where the amount bet and the payoff are not very different. Why, then, do people gamble at casinos? As you would guess, the reasons are doubtless many and complex, but a large part of the reason probably results from people believing that they have special knowledge that gives them an edge over the house, if not consistently, than at least at particular moments of play. If you would like to see a cornucopia of these (useless) methods, there are many for sale via the World Wide Web.

5. Suppose you said, "You're walking down the street in Washington, DC, and you want to by a soda. You see a sign on a pushcart ahead indicating that sodas cost 75 cents, but you see a pushcart across the street where they cost 70 cents. Would you cross the street to save a nickel?" It's safe to say that some people who would refuse the bet would nevertheless cross the street (incurring a very small risk of being killed) to save a nickel.

6. Representativeness: An event is judged to be more likely to belong to a category if it has the features of the category that are deemed important.

    Availability: The likelihood of an event is assumed to be proportional to the ease with which examples of the event can be brought to mind.

    Anchoring and adjustment: The person starts with some initial probability value (anchor) by doing

a partial calculation of the problem or by using a probability statement in the problem and then adjusts that initial estimate upward or downward based on other information in the problem.

7. Sample size information, which is important in judging how consistent or stable a probability is. People ignore base rate information (information about the frequency or likelihood of an event in a population) if they get any other information that helps them evaluate a particular event. Although that is not information per se, people also ignore the possibility of regression to the mean, a statistical phenomenon that should enter into their judgments of probability of future events.

8. Gigerenzer argues that people's cognitive systems are biased to use frequencies of events, not probabilities of events. By giving participants problems that describe probabilities, we give them information that is in a format that their cognitive systems cannot readily use.

9. Suppose that people who read lie detector test results are 80% accurate in detecting liars. (I don't think that they are, but let's ignore that for the moment.) Suppose now that I am an employer, and I know that some of my employees are stealing from the company and I want to know who is stealing. I want all of my employees to submit to a lie detector test. Employee 1 walks in and claims not to have stolen, but the operator of the lie detector equipment says that Employee 1 is lying. What are the chances that Employee 1 has stolen from the company? The fact is that we don't know what the chances are. To figure that out, we would need some base rate information. If 95% of the people in the company aren't stealing, then the chances that this person is stealing is only 40%. When you're administering a lie detector test, you almost never know what the base rate of lying is, and because the lie detector test is imperfect, base rate information is essential to tell you the chances that any one person is lying.

10. The coach's improved record probably is regression to the mean. The team typically wins about half its games, so it is back to its typical level of play. New coaches' records often are compared to their predecessor's final year, but that's not a fair comparison because no one gets fired when they have an average year; they get fired when they have a bad year, and one would expect some improvement the next year because of regression to the mean.

11. When planning a project, one probably considers the different components of the project and estimates the time it will take to perform each component. These estimates might be accurate, but people seldom take into account the odds that something will go wrong. They fail to account for that because the probability of any one thing going wrong is quite low, but there are so many potential things that could go wrong, in aggregate the odds of a problem may be fairly high. People use the total time and fail to adjust adequately.

12. Deductive reasoning allows one to state that a conclusion must be true, given the premises. Inductive reasoning only allows one to say that a conclusion is more or less likely, given the premises.

13. No, familiarity does not seem to be the critical feature. Keep in mind that people can perform well on the problem even if it concerns unfamiliar material (such as tattoos and cassava), and they sometimes don't perform well even if it concerns familiar material (such as what sort of food and drink go together well). The ideas of permission and precaution schemas seem to better describe participants' performance in these tasks.

14. Syntactic models propose that people reason by manipulating the premises with a set of rules. These rules allow conclusions to be drawn from the premises. Semantic models propose that people evaluate the truth of conclusions by determining whether the conclusion is true under all conditions in which the premises are true.

15. Case-based reasoning seems somewhat less interesting than other forms of reasoning, perhaps because it seems as if it is hardly reasoning at all. Nevertheless, it seems likely that we often remember courses of action that we pursued in that past that worked out well. When you see that the time is 10:50 and you know that you have a class in 10 minutes, is it really necessary to reason about your next course of action, or can you rely on your memory of similar situations to guide you? This question is not settled, but my money is on memory.

16. For both conditional statements and syllogisms, the content of the problem is a very important factor in problem difficulty. Such results indicate that prior experience is likely to be very important in solving these problems. Prior experience may be important in that it suggests possible solutions (as in case-based reasoning models), or it may be important because it suggests how to interpret the meaning of problems (as in semantic reasoning models).

17. No. To draw such a conclusion would actually be a to commit a logical fallacy:

People don't reason on the Wason card selection task.
The Wason card selection task is a reasoning task.
Therefore, people don't reason on all reasoning tasks.

Answers to Questions in Chapter 10

1. Heuristics are needed to select operators; most problem spaces are too large for you to try a brute force search, and if the problem is unfamiliar you need some way to reduce the search space.

2. Hill climbing, working backward, and means–ends analysis.

3. First, identify the difference between your current state and the goal state. Second, search for an operator that addresses the largest difference between your current state and goal state. Third, if you cannot apply that operator, set as a subgoal to reach a state where you can apply that operator. Continue until there is no difference between your current state and the goal state.

4. Yes, means–ends analysis would work. You'd initially set as a goal to reach the highest hill. You would first set an operator of moving toward the top of the hill. If you hit an obstacle to moving toward the top of the highest hill (e.g., you were at the top of a small hill, or you faced a wall), you would set as a subgoal to get to a state in which you would again be able to move toward the top of the hill (e.g., to go downhill briefly).

5. Chess has the larger problem space because it has more pieces, and each piece can move in more ways. You could reduce the problem space of chess or checkers by reducing the number of pieces or restricting the options for how the pieces move.

6. The average person is probably like me, and I wouldn't know what to do beyond a brute force method (trying combinations of 0-0-1, then 0-0-2, and so on). The truth is I don't really know what a professional safecracker would do (all safecrackers are cordially invited to write me to let me know), but it seems clear that working backward won't help because you don't know what the goal state is. Hill climbing can't work for the same reason: You don't know what the goal is, so you don't know what constitutes moving toward the goal. Means–ends analysis seems closest because it seems that you'd want to set subgoals that would get you closer to the goal. One possible subgoal might be determining that you have the first number right by feeling a bearing fall in the lock, for example.

7. Background knowledge makes it more likely that you will see the deep structure of the problem, not just the surface features. Background knowledge may also yield automatization of some of the operators, which frees working memory to work on higher-level strategies to address the problem.

8. The key problem appears to be in noticing that an analogy is appropriate in the first place. When people know that an analogy is available they can usually (but not always) map from the familiar problem to the new problem. Unfortunately, people are too easily distracted by the surface features of a problem rather than the deep features, which means that they often fail to use analogies.

9. In both cases, you inappropriately apply past knowledge to a new problem. In functional fixedness, you use an object in a way that you have used it in the past; in a set effect, you apply a problem-solving procedure that you have used in the past.

10. This technique is called incubation, and although it sounds plausible, the evidence that it works is far from overwhelming (Goldman, Wolters, & Winograd, 1992; Smith & Blankenship, 1991). It seems plausible because the impasse may be caused by functional fixedness or set effects: You keep retrieving the same nonworkable ideas time after time. If you leave the problem, it seems possible that you would represent the problem differently upon your return and avoid the impasse.

11. Creativity, although a topic of great intrinsic interest, has been notoriously difficult for psychologists to study. A big part of the problem is that it is hard to study; you can't simply say to someone, "Okay, I've got my equipment all set, the video camera is on, go ahead and be creative NOW!" Nevertheless, we can look at creative behaviors retrospectively and see that they have some of the characteristics of insight problems, chiefly that they reformulate components that we are familiar with and make new, greater wholes from the components. The brilliance of a concept such as Ebay is in both its familiarity (it's a garage sale opportunity to find treasure in someone else's junk) and its exploitation of new technology (you can search through the junk at computer speed). Other times creativity consists of seeing underlying similarities where others had not seen them. The operating system of the Macintosh computer is a creative product because it creates an analogy to a desktop, a concept that noncomputer users were familiar with and that was readily applicable to computer use. The analogy was so compelling that it became the standard in the personal computer industry.

12. Experts have more domain knowledge than novices, and their knowledge is better organized; better in this case means that it is organized according to deep structure, which makes the knowledge more readily applicable to new problems. Experts may well use different procedures in solving problems, but there is no strong evidence supporting that conjecture yet.

13. Practice is not merely engaging in the activity. Deliberate practice implies engaging in the activity to improve proficiency, which means that the person must be motivated, the task must be at the correct level to encourage improvement, there must be immediate corrective feedback, and there must be repetition.

14. A large working memory capacity will make someone a good problem solver, and proficiency in setting subgoals may also be a helpful problem-solving strategy.

15. On the face of it, we almost never see an expert who has not engaged in a great deal of practice. The caveat is that all the data are correlational; the person who did all that practicing did so because he or she wanted to practice a great deal. So perhaps people who practice a lot are destined to become experts, but if you just took a person at random, made them practice the violin 6 hours a day for 10 years, you'd end up with a good violinist but not an expert. In other words, the correlational nature of the evidence may lead us to conclude that practice is a necessary condition for expertise, but it may not be a sufficient condition.

16. I don't think it is. In most insight problems (e.g., the candle problem, the radiation problem) one is not struggling to juggle in mind all the different elements of the problem. Rather, the difficulty is restructuring the problem space, and that is not especially demanding of working memory.

17. The first and best advice is simply to practice. The next best advice is to look for the deep structure of problems. Try to avoid simply applying formulas as a series of steps, as though it were a recipe. Instead, try to understand what those steps are doing—in other words, try to understand the subgoals that each step or group of steps is achieving.

Answers to Questions in Chapter 11

1. Definitions of language differ, but most of them include these characteristics of language: language is *communicative*; the relationship between elements in the language and their meaning is *arbitrary*; the pattern of elements is *structured*; language is *generative*, meaning that the basic elements can be combined in an infinite number of ways; and language is *dynamic*, meaning it is always evolving.

2. Because phonemes are produced differently by different speakers (because of accents, for example), and they are produced differently by individual speakers when the phonemes are in different contexts (a phenomenon called coarticulation).

3. Competence is people's knowledge of grammar (i.e., the rules they use to produce sentences). Performance refers to the sentences people actually produce. Competence is not the same as performance because the sentences people actually produce (performance) are influenced not only by their knowledge of grammar (competence) but by other cognitive factors (e.g., working memory limitations) or social factors (e.g., the desire to stop talking when interrupted).

4. They can't capture certain key properties of the way we produce sentences. For example, they cannot explain why we accept as grammatical sentences that string together words that we never hear together, such as "Color green ideas sleep furiously." Also, the machinery of word-chain grammars cannot produce sentences with remote dependencies (e.g., "either . . . or") with other grammatical structures embedded within them.

5. It's possible because the context and your background knowledge limit the number of interpretations you will entertain as being possible. You know that the child is saying (roughly), "Let's go get a cookie now," and is unlikely to be saying, "You, me, and the cookie should all leave now" because of your past experience with children. Imagine now that the kid says, "Abe, Sarah kick now," you don't know whether Abe kicked Sarah or Sarah kicked Abe because background knowledge doesn't help.

6. One reason song lyrics are difficult to understand is that they are often quite odd (e.g., " 'Scuse me, while I kiss the sky"). There is simply no telling what the words are going to be. People do use information about what is likely to have been said to understand speech. At the same time, predictability clearly is not the only source of information you use because you are perfectly able to understand the strangest string of words when they are uttered slowly and clearly. But if other cues are degraded (e.g., the phonemes are slurred and they are uttered as many instruments play), the cues of what the words are likely to mean may be all the more important.

7. We can use high-level meaning information to fill in phonemes that are severely degraded (phoneme restoration effect), we perceive phonemes that are slightly degraded as being normal phonemes (categorical perception), and we use visual information to supplement auditory information (McGurk effect).

8. One route is a direct matching process between the spelling of the word and the lexical entry spelling. The other route translates the spelling of the word into a sound and matches this sound to the sound entries in the lexicon.

9. A garden path sentence is one that seems to make no sense toward the end of the sentence because the grammar seems wrong. This occurs because the listener was parsing a sentence and toward the end of the sentence a word was perceived that made it clear that the ongoing parsing scheme was incorrect. Garden path sentences are important because errors in parsing are helpful in determining how parsing is

performed and because they show us that the mind parses sentences as words are perceived; the mind does not wait for the sentence to be completed before it starts parsing.

10. People appear to draw inferences when the text they are reading has some information that is missing or inconsistent. The chief debate is over how the cognitive system recognizes that information is missing. Most researchers think that texts are compared with information from long-term memory and with the text itself to find inconsistencies (in one of my favorite examples, Madame Bovary's eyes change color during the course of the novel) or missing information (e.g., simple inferences from long-term memory such as that nails are usually driven by hammers).

11. Under normal circumstances, the context of a sentence biases lexical access so that only the appropriate meaning of an ambiguous word becomes active. In the case of a pun, both meanings become active and enter awareness. Note that a simple dual interpretation is not enough for humor (e.g., "This is not a very good spring" is not funny). There must be something about the context that makes both meanings potentially applicable, as when a waitress told my table that the only dessert left was pudding whereupon an acquaintance countered, "You're pudding me on." (The rest of us hid behind our menus.)

12. The text would be criminally boring. The text "Billy walked slowly to the front of the room. The teacher waited for him" would turn into the following:

> Billy—he's a student in the class—he was walking toward the front of the room. By "front" of the room, I mean the place where the blackboard is, and the way all the students face when they're sitting. Anyway, he was walking on the floor; I mean he wasn't walking on top of the desks or anything. And he was walking slowly—not very slowly, to the point that it might take him an hour to reach the front of the room; just an average sort of slow. I think he was walking slowly because he was afraid. I can't be sure of that, because he didn't *say* so. . . .

This sort of demonstration indicates that not only can we draw inferences as we read texts, but doing so is a normal part of reading and saves a good deal of time.

13. This example indicates that sentence processing is sensitive to higher-level concerns. In this case, you would decode the meaning of the sentence, recognize that it was inappropriate given the context, and interpret it as sarcastic.

14. One feature you'd want to evaluate is the extent to which they seem to use words as abstract symbols and not simply as part of a stimulus–response pair. Roughly speaking, that's the difference between knowing that *apple* has the referent of the piece of fruit and being able to use the term *apple* in many different contexts and knowing that if you make a particular hand motion, you often get a piece of apple in return. The second thing you'd want to know is whether they have any appreciation of grammar. As described earlier in the chapter, grammar is central to language because it gives language its flexibility and power.

15. There seems to be some limited evidence for the use of words outside the context in which they were learned, which is evidence for understanding and using words as symbols. There is also evidence for some sensitivity to word order (e.g., using *more* before a noun, not after). As you would expect, it's hard to draw a firm line for which the near side definitely is language and the far side definitely is not. Apes can do some of the things that characterize language, and they do them in a rudimentary way. To my way of thinking, that's not really language.

16. Two paradigms gained attention. The first was testing of color perception and memory. This domain is so tightly tied to the physiology of the retina and other early visual processing centers that it is hard to believe that higher cognitive processes (such as language) could have much impact on it. The second domain was counterfactual reasoning, and the Whorfian hypothesis was stated in such an extreme form (Mandarin Chinese speakers can't think counterfactually) that it would have been a stunning, incomprehensible surprise if it had been correct.

17. It seems likely that it is. We discussed several examples of recent success in testing the Whorfian hypothesis toward the end of this section (e.g., the study using Chinese classifiers). If we adopt the version of the Whorfian hypothesis suggested by Hunt and Agnoli (1991), then we merely need to see a cost to processing imposed by a particular language. We might expect those costs arise at least occasionally.

18. They should be smarter, on average, than people who speak one language. If certain types of cognition are easier in one language than another, then bilinguals have more types of cognition at their disposal than people who speak just one language. At this point there is no conclusive evidence that being bilingual makes you any smarter than being monolingual (Okoh, 1980; Hakuta, 1986).

Glossary

Accessible Refers to a memory that can be accessed via the cues available at the time of the test.

Acoustic confusion effect Errors in primary memory based on sound (e.g., thinking one heard *g* instead of *d*). The presence of such errors indicates that participants use an acoustic code in primary memory on the task.

Acquired dyslexia A reading problem caused by brain damage in adults who were normal readers before the injury.

Activation The level of energy or excitement of a node, indicating that the concept the node represents is more accessible for use by the cognitive system.

Addressing system Scheme to organize memories in which each memory is given a unique address that can be used to look it up.

Agnosia A deficit of vision caused by brain damage in which the patient can appreciate shapes but cannot identify objects based on visual cues alone.

Algorithm A formula that can be applied to choice situations. It has the advantage of producing consistent outcomes, but algorithms may be complex and difficult to compute. Algorithms often are compared to heuristics.

Anatomic dissociation Evidence that two different tasks are supported by different parts of the brain.

Anchoring and adjustment A heuristic used to estimate probabilities in which the person starts with some initial probability value (anchor) by doing a partial calculation of the problem or by using a probability statement in the problem and then adjusting that initial estimate upward or downward based on other information in the problem.

Anterograde amnesia The loss of ability to learn new material after some insult to the brain.

Articulatory control process The process that allows one to enter information into the phonological store; it is literally the process of talking to yourself.

Articulatory suppression Refers to demanding that participants keep the articulatory system busy with nonsense during encoding (usually by saying "thethethethe" or something similar), thereby ensuring that they will not code stimuli in the phonological store.

Atmosphere A situation in which two premises of a syllogism are both either positive or negative or use the same quantifier. People are biased to accept as valid a conclusion that maintains the atmosphere.

Atmospheric perspective A cue to depth. Objects in the distance look less distinct because they are viewed through more dust and water particles in the air that scatter light.

Attention The mechanism for continued cognitive processing. All sensory information receives some cognitive processing; attention ensures continued cognitive processing.

Auditory suffix effect An extra word presented at the end of a list of to-be-remembered words impairs memory for the last word on the list, even if participants are told to ignore the extra word. It was initially thought to occur by knocking the last word out of echoic memory, but this effect probably occurs in the phonological loop.

Automatic process A process that takes few or no attentional resources and that happens without intention, given the right set of stimuli in the environment.

Availability A heuristic in which the likelihood of an event is evaluated by the ease with which examples of the event can be called to mind.

Available A memory can be said to be available if it is in principle recoverable (given the right set of cues), even if it cannot be accessed via the cues present at a given time.

Base rate The frequency of an event in the general population. When judging the likelihood that an event occurred, people tend to ignore the base rate if they are given any other information about the event.

Basic level category Category that is the most inclusive (i.e., the broadest) of which members still share most of their features.

Behavioral dissociation   Evidence that two tasks are affected differently by an independent variable (e.g., declarative memories are much affected by the passage of time, but motor skills are not).

Behaviorism   An approach to psychology that claims that the appropriate subject matter of psychology is behavior, not mental processes. It also emphasizes that psychologists should focus on that which is observable (i.e., stimuli in the environment and people's overt behaviors).

Bias   In signal detection theory, a measure of the participant's bias to either report or not report the presence of a signal. Bias is measured independently of the participant's actual ability to detect signals.

Binocular parallax   The disparity in retinal location of the same image for the two eyes.

Binocularly   Viewed with two eyes.

Bottom-up processing   Processing that starts with unprocessed sensory information and builds toward more conceptual representations.

British Museum algorithm   An algorithm that uses very simple processes to derive conclusions. Important in Braine's natural logic theory of deductive reasoning.

Brute force search   A problem-solving strategy in which all possible answers are examined until the correct solution is found.

Case-based reasoning theories   Theories proposing that we reason by remembering similar problems (cases) that we have encountered in the past.

Categorical perception   Refers to the fact that people do not perceive slight variations in how phonemes are pronounced. Phonemes can vary along certain dimensions with no cost in their perceivability.

Category   A group of objects that have something in common.

Central executive   The cognitive supervisor and scheduler, which integrates information from different sources and decides on strategies to be used in tasks and allocates attention.

Chunk   A unit of knowledge that can be decomposed into smaller units of knowledge. Similarly, smaller units of knowledge can be combined ("chunked") into a single unit of knowledge (e.g., chunking the numbers 1, 9, 0, and 0 into a unit to represent the year 1900).

Circular theory   A theory that uses term A to define term B but then also uses term B to define term A, leaving unclear what terms A and B mean.

Classical conditioning   A training procedure that produces a conditioned reflex.

Classical view of categorization   The view that concepts are represented as lists of necessary and sufficient properties.

Cognitive economy   The principle of designing a cognitive system in a way that conserves resources (e.g., memory storage space).

Combinatorial explosion   The phenomenon in which the number of states in the problem space increases very rapidly, even with modest increases in the number of attributes of the problem that might be changed. For example, if one tries to look four moves ahead in a chess game instead of two moves ahead, the number of states in the problem much more than doubles.

Competence   People's knowledge of grammar, that is, the rules that they use to construct sentences. Competence is contrasted with **Performance,** which refers to the way that people actually talk. Performance is influenced not only by the rules of grammar but by lapses of memory and other factors that make the sentences people utter less grammatical than their competence indicates.

Computational approach   The dominant approach discussed throughout the book, it assumes that the information provided by the environment is impoverished and that the cognitive system must do a lot of computation to derive the richness of environment.

Concepts   The mental representation that allows one to generalize about objects in a category.

Conclusion   A statement of fact derived by logical processes. One may confidently propose that a conclusion is true or false within a problem based on its logical relation to the premises. Whether the conclusion is true in the real world depends on the truth or falseness of the premises.

Concreteness or abstractness   A characteristic of words. Concrete words refer to real objects in the word (e.g., *pencil, train*). Abstract words do not (e.g., *intellect, miracle*). It is much easier to generate images associated with concrete words than abstract words, which was important in early studies showing the influence of imagery on memory.

Conditional statements   A logical form composed of three statements. The first premise states, "If condition *p* is met, then *q* follows." The second premise states whether *p* or *q* is true. The third is a conclusion about *p* or *q*.

Conditioned reflex   A reflex that is learned (i.e., that is the product of experience).

Conditioned response   In classical conditioning, the response elicited by a conditioned stimulus after training. It is usually similar but not identical to the unconditioned stimulus.

Conditioned stimulus   In classical conditioning, a stimulus that before training does not elicit a consistent response. During training, its presentation is paired with the unconditioned stimulus.

Conjunctive search In a visual search task, a search in which the target differs from the distractors on two features, for example, the target is large and red and although some of the distractors are large and some are red, none of the distractors are both large and red. It requires a conjunction of two features (largeness and redness) to identify the target.

Consolidation A hypothetical process by which memories become more stable over time, even if they are not rehearsed.

Construction Similar to the idea of reconstruction. Reconstruction is the process by which memories are recalled. Construction is a particular memory that feels to the participant like a real memory but has no basis in fact.

Content-addressable storage Scheme by which to organize memories in which the content of the memory itself serves as the storage address.

Contention scheduling The process by which the relative importance of two tasks is weighed if executing the tasks simultaneously is not possible.

Context Information about the time and place in which a memory was encoded.

Context effect The idea that memory will be better if the physical environment at encoding matches the physical environment at retrieval.

Continuous task A task in which there is no obvious beginning and ending to each trial; there is a continuous stream of stimuli and responses (e.g., a pursuit tracking task. Compare with **Discrete task.**

Convergence A cue to distance. As an object gets closer, an observer crosses his or her eyes more to keep the image of the object on the center of the fovea of each eye. The extent to which the eyes are crossed can be used as a cue to distance.

Conversational implicature The tendency for people to treat the language of logic as though it has the same meaning as everyday language.

Conversion error An error in dealing with a syllogism in which a person reverses one of the premises. For example the premise reads "All *A*s are *B*s" and the participant believes that it is also true that "All *B*s are *A*s."

Correspondence problem To use binocular parallax as a cue to depth, one must match up the left and right retinal images. The correspondence problem refers to the difficulty of doing that if the images in the retina contain many possible matches.

Critical features Features of objects that don't change as the object undergoes various transformations (e.g., gets larger or rotates in space).

Critical period A window of opportunity during which a particular type of learning will be easy for

the organism. If the critical period is missed, however, the learning will be difficult or even impossible.

Cross-modal priming A method of measuring access to the lexicon. In the most frequently used version of cross-modal priming, the participant listens to words and periodically must make a lexical decision about a letter string that appears on a computer screen as quickly as possible. Response times are shorter if the spoken word matches the letter string.

Cued recall A way of testing memory in which the experimenter provides the participant the time and place in which the memory was encoded as well as some hint about the content of the to-be-remembered material (e.g., "Tell me the words I read to you an hour ago. One of them was something to eat.").

Cues Some information from the environment (or that the participant is able to generate) as a starting point for retrieval.

Decay theory Refers to the hypothesis that forgetting results (at least in part) from the spontaneous decomposition of memories over time.

Decision making A situation in which a person is presented with two or more explicit courses of action, with the requirement that he or she select just one.

Declarative memory Memory for facts and events, often called "knowing that" memory.

Deductive reasoning Problems to which one can apply formal logic and derive an objectively correct solution.

Deep processing Thinking about the meaning of stimulus materials at encoding.

Deep structure In language, the deep structure is the representation of a sentence constructed according to a basic set of phrase structure rules, without any transformations applied to the resulting representation. If transformations are applied, the sentence might be turned into a question or be phrased in the passive voice, for example.

Default value A characteristic that is a part of a schema that is assumed to be true in the absence of other information. For example, unless one is told otherwise, one assumes that a dog is furry; furriness is a default characteristic for dogs.

Demand characteristics Anything about the way the experiment is conducted that signals to the participant what the desired, appropriate, or expected behavior is.

Depth of processing A description of how one thinks about material at encoding. *Depth* refers to the degree of semantic involvement (that is, the word's meaning).

Deterministic The view that all acts (including human acts) have antecedent causes in the physical world.

Developmental dyslexia An abnormal development of reading processes in children.

Dichotic listening Task in which participants listen to material on headphones, and each earpiece plays a different message. Participants are to attend to just one message and must **Shadow** that message to show that they are doing so. The dichotic listening task often is used to study how much the unattended material is processed.

Digit span task Participants hear a list of digits read to them, one digit per second, and must immediately recite the list in the correct order. This task has been used to measure primary memory capacity since the turn of the century.

Direct measure A measure in which one infers something about cognition by directly querying the participant about his or her cognitive processing. For example, a free recall measure directly asks the participant how much of some material they can remember.

Discrete task A task in which each trial has a discrete beginning and ending (e.g., a simple response time task). Compare with **continuous task.**

Disjunctive search In a visual search task, a search in which the target differs from the distractors on just one feature (e.g., the target is larger than the distractors or the target is the only stimulus that has a horizontal line in it).

Distractor Items that appear on a visual search experiment trial that are not the target item that the participant is to find. Also used in recognition memory experiments to denote incorrect responses. Synonyms of *distractor* are *foil* and *lure.*

Distributed representation A representational scheme in which a concept is distributed across multiple units.

Dual-coding hypothesis Paivio's proposal that concepts can be encoded verbally, in terms of mental images, or both.

Dual route models of reading Models that posit two mechanisms for reading. One route uses a direct matchup of the spelling and entries in the lexicon, and the other translates the letters into sounds and then matches the sound to the auditory entry in the lexicon.

Dual task paradigm A method of examining the attentional demands of a task. The target task is performed alone and in the presence of a secondary task; if the target task requires little or no attention, performance should not deteriorate when the secondary task is added.

Early filter A theory proposing that attention acts as a filter early in the processing stream. Implies that all sensory stimuli are analyzed for their physical characteristics, but only those that are attended to are analyzed for their semantic characteristics.

Echoic memory Name given to the auditory variety of sensory memory.

Ecological approach Emphasizes that the environment has rich sources of information in it and that the computations the visual system needs to perform are probably not that extensive.

Elaborative rehearsal A type of encoding in which new material is related to material one already knows.

Emotional conditioning Classical conditioning in which the unconditioned response is an emotion.

Empiricist The view that most of human knowledge is acquired over one's lifetime through experience.

Epiphenomenon A phenomenon that is not related to the function of a system. Some researchers argued that images are an epiphenomenon; the sensation of "seeing" an image is real, but that doesn't mean that the sensation has anything to do with the actual cognitive task being performed.

Episodic memory Memory that is associated with a particular time and place, with a this-happened-to-me feeling.

Exemplar An instance of a category.

Exemplar model Model of categorization that maintains that all exemplars are stored in memory, and categorization judgments are made by judging the similarity of the new exemplar to all the old exemplars of a category.

Expected utility A normative theory of choice in which the best choice is the one that offers the reward with the greatest personal value to the individual, not necessarily the greatest financial reward. The theory allows that in some situations, it may be more valuable to an individual to be very likely to get a modest reward rather than to have a small probability to get a large reward.

Expected value A normative theory of choice in which the best choice is the one that offers that largest financial payoff.

Eyeheight The height of the observer's eyes from the ground. Can be used as a cue to object size.

Familiar size Using one's knowledge of the typical size of an object as a cue to the likely size and distance of an object. For example, if a child appears larger than an adult, it is likely that the child is closer to the observer.

Feature singleton An object that has a feature that no other stimulus in the field has.

Fixed-action patterns Complex behaviors in which an animal engages despite very limited opportunities for practice or reward. Usually taken as evidence for innate or inborn learning.

Flanker effect   Stimuli (usually words) that appear to the sides of a target and that participants are instructed to ignore, which nevertheless affect participants' behavior.

Flanker task   A task in which the participant is asked to respond to one stimulus (typically it's a word to be read) while ignoring a stimulus that appears nearby (the flanker). The typical result is that the to-be-ignored stimulus influences performance.

Flashbulb memories   A very rich, very detailed memory that is encoded when something that is emotionally intense happens.

Focus gambling   When trying to learn a new category, using the strategy of generating a narrow hypothesis about the necessary and sufficient properties that define a category.

Foil   See **Distractor.**

Free recall   A way of testing memory in which the experimenter provides no cues other than the time and place in which the memory was encoded (e.g., "Tell me the words I read to you an hour ago").

Functionalism   A school of psychology in the late 19th century that held that the functions of mental processes were paramount and that psychologists should therefore focus on describing the function of thought processes.

Galvanic skin response   An indirect measure of nervousness that measures how much moisture (perspiration) is on the participant's palms.

Garden path sentence   A sentence in which the cognitive system initially builds one phrase structure as the sentence is perceived, but later in the sentence it becomes clear that this in-progress phrase structure is incorrect.

General Problem Solver   An artificial intelligence program that uses the means–ends analysis heuristic. The General Problem Solver has been successful in solving a variety of problems.

Generalize   Usually applied to categories, it means to use information gathered from one exemplar to a different exemplar of the same category. For example, if you learn that a specific dog likes to have its stomach rubbed, you may generalize that knowledge to other dogs and assume that they too like to have their stomachs rubbed.

Generative   A property of systems that can produce new, novel output. Language is generative, meaning you can produce and understand completely novel utterances. Generativity seemed difficult to achieve with behaviorist accounts of language, which seemed successful in predicting the likelihood that one would repeat an action, not in describing how a novel action could be generated.

Good continuation   Points that can be interpreted connecting a straight or smoothly curving line will be interpreted that way rather than as connecting sharply angled lines.

Graceful degradation   A property of a model (of memory or of another cognitive process) whereby if the model is partially damaged it is able to continue functioning, although not as accurately. The human brain often shows graceful degradation; if it is damaged, cognitive processes often are compromised, but can still partially function.

Grammar   A set of rules that describes the legal sentences that can be constructed in a language.

GSR   See *galvanic skin response.*

Hemispatial neglect   A deficit of attention caused by brain damage in which a patient ignores the half of the visual world opposite the brain damage.

Heuristics   Simple cognitive rules that are easy to apply and that usually yield acceptable decisions but can lead to errors.

Hierarchical theory   Theory of memory organization in which concepts are organized in a taxonomic hierarchy (e.g., *animal* is above *bird*, which is above *canary*) and characteristic properties are stored at each level.

Hill climbing   A heuristic in which one searches for an operator that will take you to a state in the problem space that appears to be closer to the goal than you are now.

Homunculus   A small person inside the head who performs cognitive functions such as looking at images on a screen. Proposing a homunculus explains nothing, and no one would ever do it on purpose; accusing someone of having a homunculus in his or her model is a scathing criticism.

Iconic memory   Name given to the visual variety of sensory memory.

Illusory correlation   People have a bias to judge that two events or characteristics of an event go together if people had a prior belief that they go together or if they are natural associates. Illusory correlation is related to the availability heuristic because you judge that two things are correlated if you can think of many instances in which the two things co-occurred.

Image   A representation of knowledge that includes spatial information. Images often are called quasi-pictorial, meaning that they have some of the important qualities of pictures but are not themselves pictures.

Image inspection   Processes engaged to better know the visual characteristics of an image.

Imageless thought controversy.   Debate over whether it is possible to have thoughts that are not accompanied by images. This debate occurred in the late 19th century and was critical to the introspectionist program because they studied imagery as a window into thought processes. If some thought was not accompanied by images, it was not clear how it could be studied.

Imagens   Term for representations that support mental images in Paivio's dual-coding hypothesis.

Incidental memory test   A memory test in which the participants are not expressly told that their memory will be tested later.

Indirect measure   A measure in which you infer something about cognition based on performance. For example, a priming measure does not query participants as to whether they remember having seen particular words presented earlier. Instead, participants are asked to identify briefly presented words to see whether they are more successful in doing so with the words that were presented earlier.

Inductive reasoning   Reasoning that allows one to say that a conclusion is more or less likely to be true but does not allow one to say that a conclusion must be true.

Insight problem   A problem in which the solver feels that the answer comes all at once, in an "Aha!" moment of illumination.

Intentional memory test   A memory test in which the participants are told that their memory will be tested later.

Interference theory   The theory that much or most of forgetting results from retrieval failure caused by interference of other learned material.

Introspectionism   A method of studying the mind that became nearly synonymous with structuralism. The method entails observing one's thought processes, but it was deemed important that a more experienced introspectionist train a novice in the method. Researchers using introspection were almost always structuralists, seeking to use introspection to describe the basic components of consciousness.

Intrusion   On a memory test, material that is appropriate to another context is inappropriately produced as a response in the wrong context.

Inverse optics problem   The problem of recovering three-dimensional shape from a two-dimensional projection, like the projection on the retina.

Isomorph   A problem with a different surface story that has a problem space of the same size, number of branches, and minimum solution path as a target problem.

Landmark   Task used to test monkeys' ability to appreciate spatial relations.

Late filter   A theory proposing that attention acts as a filter late in the processing stream. Implies that all sensory stimuli are analyzed for their physical characteristics and their meaning, but only those that are attended to enter awareness.

Levels of processing framework   A framework for understanding memory that proposes that the most important factor determining whether something will be remembered is the depth of processing.

Lexicon   The mental dictionary, which has information stored about all of the words a person knows. The lexicon stores the pronunciation, spelling and part of speech of each word and has a pointer to another location in which the meaning is stored.

Light source, reflectance, and shadow indeterminacy Refers to the fact that the amount of light hitting the retina from an object depends on the light source, the reflectance of the object, and whether the object is in shadow.

Likelihood principle   Suggestion that among the many ways of interpreting an ambiguous visual stimulus, the visual system will interpret it as the stimulus that is most likely to occur in the world.

Limited attention   Continued cognitive processing cannot occur for all available sensory stimuli; simply put, you can't pay attention to everything simultaneously.

Linear perspective   A cue to depth. Parallel lines converge in the distance, so the closer they are to converging, the farther away the location.

Links   Representation of the relationship between concepts. In the hierarchical model the links are labeled (e.g., "has this property"), whereas in spreading activation models the links simply pass activation from one node to another.

Local contrast   Dependence of the perceived surface lightness on the ratios of lightness of areas that are next to one another and are in the same plane.

Local representation   A representational scheme in which a concept has a single location (e.g., it is represented in one node in a semantic network).

Logogens   Term for verbal representation in Paivio's dual-coding hypothesis.

Loss aversion   The unpleasantness of a loss is larger than the pleasantness of a similar-sized gain.

Luminance   The amount of light your eye receives.

Lure   See **Distractor.**

Maintenance rehearsal   A type of encoding in which one repeats new material over and over to oneself.

Mask   An array of tiny random black and white squares or a stimulus of randomly oriented squiggles and lines. A mask is used to knock another stimulus out of iconic memory. *Mask* can also be used as a verb (e.g. "The second stimulus masked the first.").

McGurk effect   An effect showing that both visual and auditory information are used in phoneme perception.

Means–ends analysis   A problem-solving heuristic that uses a set of rules about when to work forward or backward and when and how to set subgoals.

Mediated priming   Priming that goes through two links, not just one. For example, if *lion* primes *stripes* it is probably because the priming was mediated through *tiger* (i.e., *lion* primes *tiger*, which primes *stripes*).

Mental model   A semantic representation corresponding to a possible configuration of the world. Mental models are the heart of Johnson-Laird's mental models theory of deductive reasoning.

Mnemonic   An aid to memory. Mnemonics usually require that you memorize a simple word or set of words. This memorized material then provides cues to the more-difficult-to-memorize material that you want to remember.

Modal model   A model composed of the most common features of models of short-term memory in the early 1970s. The modal model turned out to be incorrect in many details.

Monitoring process   In Wegner's model of mental control, the monitoring process searches for mental contents that are inconsistent with desired thoughts. The purpose is to serve as a warning system that mental control is failing. This process does not require attentional resources.

Monocularly   Viewed with one eye.

Motor theory of speech perception   A theory positing that speech perception shares processes with or relies on knowledge about how speech is produced.

Multiple resources   A theory of attention in which attention is thought to be composed of a number of pools of attention, each dedicated to a different type of task.

Multiply determined   Term used to emphasize that most behaviors have many factors that influence them. For example, a decision of whether to enter a restaurant may depend on who you're with, your memory of your last trip to the restaurant, how crowded it is, how hungry you are, how much money you have, and other factors.

Nativist   The view that much of human knowledge is innate.

Nodes   Representation of concepts in hierarchical and spreading activation theories.

Nondeterministic   The view that at least some acts have antecedent causes outside the physical world.

Nonmatching to sample   Visual recognition task administered to monkeys to test their ability to recognize objects.

Normative theories   A theory of choice that describes a set of rules by which some choices are better than others and one choice can be said to be optimal.

Object-centered representation   A mental representation of what an object looks like relative to the object itself. The representation can support recognition of the object when it is viewed from any perspective.

Obligatory access   Refers to the fact that verbal information (but not all sounds) appear to be entered into the phonological loop by its mere presence, even if the participant does not want it to enter.

Occam's razor   The principle that parsimony is important in evaluating scientific theories. Specifically, if two theories account for data equally well, the simpler theory is to be preferred.

Occlusion   A cue to depth. An object that occludes another is closer.

Operant conditioning   Learning whereby the animal (or person) makes a response that has consequences (e.g., reward or punishment). These consequences change the probability that the response will be made again.

Operating process   In Wegner's model of mental control, the operating process seeks mental contents that are consistent with desired thoughts. For example, if one is trying not to think of a white bear, the operating process seeks distractions from that thought. This process requires attentional resources.

Operator   A process one can apply to a problem to change to a different state in the problem space.

Parallel search   A visual search in which all of the stimuli in a field are evaluated simultaneously. One can tell that a search is parallel if adding extra distractors to the search does not increase the participant's response time. Participants usually experience popout with parallel searches.

Parsimonious   A theory is parsimonious if it is the simplest theory possible that accounts for all of the data. The noun is *parsimony*.

Parsing paradox   For some ambiguous figures, it seems impossible to identify the figure without knowing what its parts are, but its parts cannot be identified unless one knows what the figure is.

Partial report procedure   Developed by Sperling to examine iconic memory, it's a procedure whereby participants are shown an array of stimuli (usually letters or numbers) very briefly and then are given a cue telling them which subset of the stimuli to report. This method showed that participants perceive most of the stimuli in a complex array.

Performance   The grammaticality of the sentences that people utter. Performance is influenced not only by the grammatical rules people know (**competence**) but by other factors such as lapses of memory and social considerations such as interruptions.

Perkins's laws   A set of rules describing how to interpret configurations of line intersections as parts of three-dimensional objects.

Permastore   A hypothetical state of memory from which memories are not forgotten.

Phoneme restoration effect   Phonemes that are poorly produced are "restored" by higher-level processes so that the perceiver believes that the missing phoneme actually was present. The system can infer what the missing phoneme should have been based on the context.

Phonemes   Individual speech sounds.

Phonological dyslexia   A pattern of reading difficulty in which the person has difficulty reading nonwords (e.g., *slint*) but can read irregular words (e.g., *yacht*).

Phonological loop   The part of the working memory model in which auditory information is stored.

Phonological store   The part of the phonological loop that can store about 2 s of auditory information.

Phrase structure grammars   A grammar that represents sentences hierarchically, with each node of the hierarchy corresponding to a phrase structure.

Pictorial cues   Cues to distance that can be used in two-dimensional pictures.

Picture theory of imagery   The experience of visual imagery is created by activating a memory representation. This memory representation was created by viewing objects in the real world.

Pop out   A phenomenon in a task in which you are searching for a target among distractors. Subjectively, it feels to the participant as if visual search is unnecessary because the target simply pops out and is instantly recognizable. Objectively, there is very little cost to visual search time if extra distractors are added to the task.

Practice   In developing expertise, practice is defined as activity designed to improve skill (as opposed to play or performance) and therefore must include corrective feedback and repetition and must be at the appropriate level of difficulty.

Pragmatic reasoning schemas   Sets of rules defined in relation to goals that can be used to evaluate situations such as permissions or obligations. A key aspect of pragmatic reasoning schemas is that they encourage conclusions that are practical in the real world, as opposed to formal logic, which can lead to conclusions that are technically correct but not useful.

Preattentively   Refers to processing that occurs whether attention is applied to the stimulus or not.

Premise   A statement of fact taken to be true for the purposes of a logical problem.

Primacy effect   Refers to the fact that memory for items at the beginning of a list is good (relative to that for items in the middle of the list).

Primary memory   Hypothetical buffer in which information may be held briefly. Contrast with **Secondary memory.**

Priming   The facilitation or bias of later processing of a stimulus caused by prior exposure to the stimulus. Usually taken to mean that the representation of the word is in an active state, resulting in easier processing. A word can be primed if a person has seen or heard the word recently or if a word close in meaning has been perceived recently.

Principle of minimal attachment   The principle that as the cognitive system parses sentences it is biased to build phrase structures in such a way that it adds new words to existing nodes in the phrase structure hierararchy rather than creating new nodes.

Principle of truth   Proposal in Johnson-Laird's model of deductive reasoning that people tend to construct models representing only what is true, not what is false.

Prior beliefs   Real-world knowledge that can influence people's evaluation of a syllogism. They are more likely to accept as true a syllogism with a conclusion that they know is true and to reject a syllogism with a conclusion that they know is false.

Proactive interference   Earlier learning interferes with new learning.

Probabilistic view of categorization   Category membership is proposed to be a matter of probability. Prototype and exemplar models fall within the probabilistic view.

Problem   In the study of problem solving, a problem is any situation in which a person has a goal and that goal is not yet accomplished.

Problem behavior graph   A representation of the problem space as the participant solved (or attempted to solve) a problem. Problem behavior graphs typically are derived from verbal protocols.

Problem frame   The particular way a problem is described. Several problems may offer the same core set of payoffs and probabilities of payoffs, but the problems could vary in terms of how they are described.

Problem space   All possible configurations that a problem can take.

Problem state   A particular configuration of the elements of the problem.

Procedural memory   Memory for skills, often called "knowing how" memory.

Process   A process manipulates representations in some way. For example, a computer might have a process for addition to add numbers. The mind might have a process that maintains the activity of a representation in primary memory, thus keeping it in consciousness.

Proposition   A verbal representation of knowledge. It is the most basic unit of meaning that has a truth value.

Prototype   A prototype has all of the features that are characteristic of a category.

Psychic budget   How we mentally categorize money we have spent or are considering spending.

Psychological refractory period   A period of time after one response is executed during which a second response cannot be selected.

Random dot stereograms   Special stimuli with no cues to depth except binocular parallax.

Rational   In the context of decision making, rational choices are ones that are internally consistent (e.g., that show transitivity).

Rational analysis models of reasoning   Models based on the idea that people may answer reasoning problems based on their assessment of the costs and benefits of particular answers.

Recency effect   Refers to the fact that memory for items at the end of a list is quite good in a task demanding immediate free recall.

Recognition   Method of testing memory in which the experimenter presents the participants with the to-be-remembered material along with other material that was not initially encoded (distractors). The participant must select the to-be-remembered items from among these other items.

Recognition failure of recallable words   The effect in which words that were not recognized are nevertheless recalled successfully on a later test.

Reconstruction   The idea that memories are not simply pulled out of the storehouse; rather, they are interpreted in terms of prior knowledge to reconstruct what *probably* happened.

Recursion   A process can be recursive if it calls on itself to get its job done. A definition of something is recursive if the definition contains the thing defined. For example, one definition of a sentence is "two sentences joined by the word 'and.' "

Reflex   An automatic action by the body that occurs when a particular stimulus is perceived in the environment.

Regression to the mean   Statistical phenomenon by which extremely high or low scores on any measure are likely to move toward the mean if they are taken a second time.

Relative height   A cue to depth. Objects that are higher in the picture plane are farther away.

Repetition priming   Effect in which performance of a task is biased by ones having seen the same words or pictures sometime earlier.

Representation   A symbol for an entity or concept in the real world. For example, a computer might use a binary code 011 to represent the concept 8.

Representativeness   A heuristic that leads you to judge the probability of an event as more likely to belong to a category if it has the features of the category that you deem important.

Repression   The active forgetting of an episode that would be too painful or threatening to the self to be remembered.

Response competition   A source of interference whereby an old response already in memory interferes with a new response that you're trying to learn.

Response selection   A hypothetical stage of processing in which a response to a stimulus is selected (e.g., to push a button), but the actual preparation of the motor act (e.g., finger movement) is not yet complete.

Response to stimulus interval   The time after the participant has responded but before the next stimulus has appeared.

Retroactive interference   Later learning interferes with earlier learning.

Retrograde amnesia   The loss of memories encoded before an insult to the brain.

Sample size   The number of things in a group that you are evaluating. People mistakenly ignore sample size in judging the reliability or consistency of a measure.

Sapir–Whorf hypothesis   Synonymous with **Whorfian hypothesis.**

Satisfice   To select the first choice that is satisfactory (i.e., above some threshold) rather than evaluating every choice and selecting the best of those. Psychologists believe that people must satisfice most of the time because there are usually too many choices to allow evaluation of all of them.

Savings in relearning   A way of testing memory in which the participant learns some material (e.g., a list of words) to a criterion (e.g., can recite the list twice without error). After a delay, the participant must relearn the list to criterion again. If the participant can reach criterion in fewer trials the second time, he or she has shown savings in relearning.

Schema   A memory representation containing general information about an object or an event. It contains information representative of a type of event rather than of a single event.

Script   A type of schema that describes a series of events.

Second-order isomorphism   Term used by Shepard and Chipman (1970) to describe the relationship of pictures and mental images. They suggested that the parts of images have the same functional relationship to one another that the parts of pictures have to one another.

Secondary memory   Repository for memories. Contrast with **primary memory.**

Selective   The assumption that one is able to disburse the limited resource of attention as desired.

Semantic memory   Memories that are not associated with a particular time and place or with a feeling that the memory happened to you. Semantic memories cover world knowledge (e.g., "frogs are green").

Semantic models of reasoning   Models based on the idea that a conclusion is true if it can be shown to be true under all conditions in which the premises are true.

Semantic network   Name given to all the nodes and links in a spreading activation model.

Semantic priming   Effect in which performance of a task is biased by having seen semantically related words or pictures viewed earlier.

Sensitivity   In signal detection theory, a measure of the participant's absolute ability to detect a signal. Sensitivity is measured independently of any bias the participant might have to report or not report signals. Also, the ability of a test to detect memories that are in the storehouse.

Sensory memory   General term referring to sensory buffers that can hold much information, but only for a second or so.

Serial position   The position of a word (or other stimulus) in a list, usually of to-be-remembered stimuli.

Serial search   A visual search in which each stimulus in a field is evaluated one at a time. One can tell that a search is serial if adding extra distractors to the search increases the participant's response time. Participants do not experience popout with serial searches.

Set effects   In problem solving, a set effect occurs when a particular problem-solving procedure is applied because it has been effective in the past, even if it is not appropriate to the current problem.

Shadow   In a dichotic listening task, participants listen to material on headphones, and each earpiece plays a different message. Participants are to attend to just one message and must shadow that message to show that they are doing so. Shadowing means repeating the to-be-attended message aloud as they hear it.

Shallow processing   Thinking about the surface characteristics of stimulus materials (that is, what they look like, sound like, and so on).

Shape and orientation indeterminacy   Refers to the fact that shape and orientation are indeterminate from a two-dimensional projection (e.g., such as a coin that looks like an ellipse if it is turned).

Short-term memory   A particular theory of primary memory. Short-term memory usually is accorded a duration of 30 s (if the material is not rehearsed) and a capacity of about five chunks of information.

Signal detection theory   A method of analyzing data that provides separate measures of **sensitivity** and **bias.**

Situation model   A level of representation in text processing. The situation model refers to deep knowledge of a text that represents an integration of information from the text and knowledge the reader had before reading the text.

Size and distance indeterminacy   Refers to the fact that the size of an object on the retina is determined by the actual size of the object and by the distance of the object from the observer.

Source   The information about the context in which something was learned (e.g., from whom one heard it, where one read it).

Span of apprehension   The amount of information that can enter consciousness at once.

Spatial imagery   Imagery that emphasizes where objects or parts of objects are located. Spatial imagery can be contrasted with visual imagery, which emphasizes what things look like.

Speech stream   A term used to refer to spoken speech that emphasizes its continuous nature. Although we perceive speech to be composed of individual words (and therefore to have short breaks between the words), speech sounds are produced fairly continuously.

Spontaneous recovery   The sudden uncovering a memory that was thought to be forgotten.

Spreading activation model   A model in which memory is conceived of as a network of nodes connected by links, and activation spreads from node to node via the links.

Stereopsis   A cue to distance that depends on the fact that our two eyes get slightly different views of objects.

Strength view of memory   The idea that memories vary in how strongly they are represented, and more strongly represented memories are easier to retrieve.

Structural explanation An explanation for the limitation of performing multiple cognitive tasks simultaneously that emphasizes limitations in cognitive structures (e.g., working memory) rather than attentional resources.

Structural similarity Refers to whether two problems share content that allows them to be solved by the same strategy (e.g., if problems can both be solved by Newton's second law, they share structural similarity, even if one involves a falling body and the other an inclined plane).

Structuralism A school of psychology in the late 19th century, the goal of which was to describe the structures that make up thought. Researchers often used the introspective method.

Subordinate level category Defined as a category that is one level less inclusive than the basic level category.

Successive scanning When trying to learn a new category, using the strategy of formulating a hypothesis and making selections based on that hypothesis until it is disconfirmed.

Sunk costs An investment (e.g., of money, time, emotion) that is irretrievably spent and should not affect current decisions about spending but nevertheless often does.

Superordinate level category Defined as a category that is one level more inclusive than the basic level category.

Supposition Something that one supposes to be true to evaluate the consequences of its being true. Suppositions are important in some theories of deductive reasoning.

Surface code A level of representation in text processing. The surface code refers to the exact wording and syntax of sentences.

Surface dyslexia A pattern of reading difficulty in which the person has difficulty reading irregular words (e.g., *yacht*) but can read nonwords (e.g., *slint*).

Surface similarity Refers to whether two problems share similar elements (e.g., if both problems entail inclined planes, the problems have surface similarity even if very different strategies are necessary to solve them).

Surface structure In language, the order in which words are uttered in a sentence. The surface structure is the product of the **deep structure** plus any transformations that are applied to the deep structure.

Syllogism A logical form composed of three statements of fact: two premises and a conclusion.

Syntactic models of reasoning Models proposing that humans reason by accepting premises and then applying a set of processes that manipulate the premises in an effort to evaluate a given conclusion or derive a conclusion.

Tacit knowledge In the imagery debate, tacit knowledge is a participant's knowledge of how objects in the real world move. It was suggested by some that participants used this tacit knowledge to simulate real-world movement and thereby produce results in imagery experiments that match real-world phenomena.

Target Term used in visual search experiments for the item that the participant is expected to find. Also used in recognition memory experiments to denote the correct response.

Template A viewer-centered representation. A simple template matching theory of object recognition says that you compare what you see to templates stored in memory.

Temporal gradient Refers to a characteristic of anterograde amnesia; memories of more recent events are more impaired than memories of events that happened a longer time ago.

Ten-year rule The phenomenon that experts in almost all fields are seldom able to compete at the very highest levels with less than a decade of intense practice.

Text A group of related sentences forming a paragraph or a group of related paragraphs.

Textbase A level of representation in text processing. The textbase represents the ideas of the text but does not preserve the particular wording and syntax.

Texture gradient A cue to depth. A field is assumed to have a uniform texture gradient, so if more detail is visible in part of the field, it is assumed to be closer.

Top-down processing Processing in which conceptual knowledge influences the processing or interpretation of lower-level perceptual processes.

Transfer appropriate processing The idea that memory will be better to the extent that the cognitive processes used at encoding match the cognitive processes used at retrieval.

Transitivity If a relationship holds between the first and second of three elements and it holds between the second and third, it should hold between the first and third. If choices were rational, there would be transitivity of preference between choices. However, transitivity does not always hold.

Typicality The fact that some members of a category are viewed as better (i.e., more typical) exemplars than others (e.g., a golden retriever is a typical dog, whereas a chihuahua is not).

Unconditioned response In classical conditioning, the response to an unconditioned stimulus (e.g., salivation).

Unconditioned stimulus In classical conditioning, a stimulus that leads to a consistent response from the animal before any training begins (e.g., food).

Unlearning The process of learning new material actively causes the forgetting of old material.

Verbal protocol A method of gathering data in problem-solving (or other) experiments. The participant is asked to solve a problem and to simultaneously describe his or her thoughts. These descriptions are assumed to bear some relationship to the cognitive processes that actually support solving the problem and so can be used as a window into these processes.

Viewer-centered representation A mental representation of what an object looks like relative to the observer.

Vigilance The ability to maintain attention to a task in which stimuli appear infrequently.

Visual afterimages If you stare at a stable visual scene for 30 s or so, a visual afterimage appears when you then look at a blank field such as a white wall. The visual afterimage is opposite in color to the image and is caused by cells in the retina becoming "fatigued" from the consistent stimulation.

Visual angle A measure of the apparent size of things on the retina.

Visual imagery Sometimes *visual imagery* refers to any imagery in the visual modality. It also has a more specialized meaning, referring to imagery tasks that emphasize what things look like. Visual imagery can be contrasted with spatial imagery, which emphasizes where things are located.

Visuospatial sketchpad A buffer on which visual or spatial information can be manipulated and briefly stored. It is thought to be similar to and perhaps synonymous with visual imagery.

What/how hypothesis Alternative to the what/where hypothesis, this proposal holds that the visual system segregates analysis of what objects are (object recognition and location) and how to manipulate them (visual information dedicated to the motor system).

What/where hypothesis Hypothesis that the visual system segregates analysis of what objects are (object recognition) and where they are (spatial location).

Whorfian hypothesis The idea that language influences thought. The strong version of the hypothesis holds that certain thoughts are impossible to entertain in certain languages. The weaker version holds that it may be easier to entertain certain thoughts in certain languages.

Word-chain grammars A proposal that people construct sentences by chaining one word after another, according to a set of rules about what words would be admissible next in the chain or what words are highly associated with words already in the sentence.

Word length effect The finding that participants can remember more words if the words can be said quickly.

Working backward A problem-solving heuristic in which one begins at the goal state of the problem and tries to work back to the starting state.

Working memory Specific theory of primary memory proposed by Baddeley & Hitch (1974), it has three parts: a phonological loop, a visuospatial sketchpad, and a central executive. Working memory is proposed to be a workspace for cognitive processes, not simply a short-term storage device.

References

Aaronson, D., & Ferres, S. (1986). Reading strategies for children and adults: A quantitative model. *Psychological Review, 93*(1), 89–112.

Adamson, R. E. (1952). Functional fixedness as related to problem solving: A repetition of three experiments. *Journal of Experimental Psychology, 44,* 288–291.

Adelson, E. H. (1998). Illusions and demos [Online]. Available: http://www-bcs.mit.edu/persci/high/gallery/checker-shadow_illusion.html

Ahn, W.-K., & Graham, L. M. (1999). The impact of necessity and sufficiency in the Wason four-card selection task. *Psychological Science, 10*(3), 237–242.

Albert, M. L., Butters, N., & Levin, J. (1979). Memory for remote events in chronic alcoholics and alcoholic Korsakoff patients. In H. Begleiter & M. Kissen (Eds.), *Alcohol intoxication and withdrawal.* New York: Plenum.

Albrecht, J. E., & O'Brien, E. J. (1993). Updating a mental model: Maintaining both local and global coherence. *Journal of Experimental Psychology: Learning, Memory, and Cognition, 19*(5), 1061–1070.

Alivisatos, B., & Petrides, M. (1997). Functional activation of the human brain during mental rotation. *Neuropsychologia, 35*(2), 111–118.

Allen, S. W., & Brooks, L. R. (1991). Specializing the operation of an explicit rule. *Journal of Experimental Psychology: General, 120*(1), 3–19.

Almor, A., & Sloman, S. A. (1996). Is deontic reasoning special? *Psychological Review, 103*(2), 374–380.

Alpert, J. L., Brown, L. S., Ceci, S. J., Courtois, C. A., Loftus, E. G., & Ornstein, P. A. (1996). *Working group on investigation of memories of childhood abuse: Final report.* Washington, DC: American Psychological Association.

Altmann, G. T., Garnham, A., & Dennis, Y. (1992). Avoiding the garden path: Eye movements in context. *Journal of Memory & Language, 31*(5), 685–712.

Altmann, G. T. M., Garnham, A., & Henstra, J.-A. (1994). Effects of syntax in human sentence parsing: Evidence against a structure-based proposal mechanism. *Journal of Experimental Psychology: Learning, Memory, and Cognition, 20*(1), 209–216.

Altmann, G., & Steedman, M. (1988). Interaction with context during human sentence processing. *Cognition, 30*(3), 191–238.

Alvarez, P., & Squire, L. R. (1994). Memory consolidation and the medial temporal lobe: A simple network model. *Proceedings of the National Academy of Sciences of the United States of America, 91*(15), 7041–7045.

Anderson, J. R. (1976). *Language, memory, and thought.* Mahwah, NJ: Erlbaum.

Anderson, J. R. (1978). Arguments concerning representations for mental imagery. *Psychological Review, 85,* 249–277.

Anderson, J. R. (1983). A spreading activation theory of memory. *Journal of Verbal Learning & Verbal Behavior, 22*(3), 261–295.

Anderson, J. R. (1993). *Rules of the mind.* Mahwah, NJ: Erlbaum.

Anderson, M. C., Bjork, R. A., & Bjork, E. L. (1994). Remembering can cause forgetting: Retrieval dynamics in long-term memory. *Journal of Experimental Psychology: Learning, Memory, and Cognition, 20,* 1063–1081.

Anderson, M. C., & Spellman, B. A. (1995). On the status of inhibitory mechanisms in cognition: Memory retrieval as a model case. *Psychological Review, 102*(1), 68–100.

Anderson, R. C., & Pichert, J. W. (1978). Recall of previously unrecallable information following a shift in perspective. *Journal of Verbal Learning & Verbal Behavior, 17*(1), 1–12.

Atkinson, R. C., & Shiffrin, R. M. (1968). Human memory: A proposed system and its control processes. In K. W. Spence & J. T. Spence (Eds.), *The psychology of learning and motivation* (Vol. 2). New York: Academic Press.

Attneave, F., & Curlee, T. E. (1983). Locational representation in imagery: A moving spot task. *Journal of Experimental Psychology: Human Perception and Performance, 9*(1), 20–30.

Au, T. K. (1983). Chinese and English counterfactuals: The Sapir–Whorf hypothesis revisited. *Cognition, 15*(1–3), 155–187.

Au, T. K. (1984). Counterfactuals: In reply to Alfred Bloom. *Cognition, 17*(3), 289–302.

Averbach, E., & Sperling, G. (1961). Short term storage of information in vision. In C. Cherry (Ed.), *Information theory.* London: Butterworths.

Ayres, T. J., Jonides, J., Reitman, J. S., Egan, J. C., & Howard, D. A. (1979). Differing suffix effects for the same physical suffix. *Journal of Experimental Psychology: Human Learning and Memory, 5,* 315–321.

Baddeley, A. (1986). *Working memory.* Oxford, UK: Clarendon Press/Oxford University Press.

Baddeley, A. (1996). Exploring the central executive. *Quarterly Journal of Experimental Psychology: Human Experimental Psychology, 49A,* 5–28.

Baddeley, A., Gathercole, S., & Papagno, C. (1998). The phonological loop as a language learning device. *Psychological Review, 105*(1), 158–173.

Baddeley, A. D. (1966). The capacity for generating information by randomization. *Quarterly Journal of Experimental Psychology, 18*(2), 119–129.

Baddeley, A. D., Grant, W., Wight, E., & Thomson, N. (1975). Imagery and visual working memory. In P. M. A. Rabbitt & S. Dornic (Eds.), *Attention and performance V* (pp. 205–217). London: Academic Press.

Baddeley, A. D., & Hitch, G. J. (1974). Working memory. In G. Bower (Ed.), *The psychology of learning and motivation* (Vol. 8). New York: Academic Press.

Baddeley, A. D., Lewis, V., & Vallar, G. (1984). Exploring the articulatory loop. *Quarterly Journal of Experimental Psychology: Human Experimental Psychology, 36A*(2), 233–252.

Baddeley, A., & Lieberman, K. (1980). Spatial working memory. In R. Nickerson (Ed.), *Attention and performance VIII* (pp. 521–539). Mahwah, NJ: Erlbaum.

Baddeley, A. D., Papagno, C., & Vallar, G. (1988). When long-term learning depends on short-term storage. *Journal of Memory & Language, 27*(5), 586–595.

Baddeley, A. D., & Scott, D. (1971). Short term forgetting in the absence of proactive interference. *Quarterly Journal of Experimental Psychology, 23*, 275–283.

Baddeley, A. D., Thomson, N., & Buchanan, M. (1975). Word length and the structure of short-term memory. *Journal of Verbal Learning & Verbal Behavior, 14*(6), 575–589.

Bahrick, H. P. (1984). Semantic memory content in permastore: Fifty years of memory for Spanish learned in school. *Journal of Experimental Psychology: General, 113*(1), 1–29.

Baillet, S. D., & Keenan, J. M. (1986). The role of encoding and retrieval processes in the recall of text. *Discourse Processes, 9*(3), 247–268.

Baizer, J. S., Kralj-Hans, I., & Glickstein, M. (1999). Cerebellar lesions and prism adaptation in Macaque monkeys. *Journal of Neurophysiology, 81*(4), 1960–1965.

Banks, W. P., & Barber, G. (1977). Color information in iconic memory. *Psychological Review, 84*(6), 536–546.

Barclay, J. R., Bransford, J. D., Franks, J. J., McCarrel, N. S., & Nitsch, K. (1974). Comprehension and semantic flexibility. *Journal of Verbal Learning & Verbal Behavior, 13*(4), 471–481.

Bar-Hillel, M., & Fischhoff, B. (1981). When do base rates affect predictions? *Journal of Personality & Social Psychology, 41*(4), 671–680.

Barnes, J. M., & Underwood, B. J. (1959). "Fate" of first-list associations in transfer theory. *Journal of Experimental Psychology, 58*, 97–105.

Baron, J., & Strawson, C. (1976). Use of orthographic and word-specific knowledge in reading words aloud. *Journal of Experimental Psychology: Human Perception and Performance, 2*(3), 386–393.

Barrouillet, P. (1996). Transitive inferences from set-inclusion relations and working memory. *Journal of Experimental Psychology: Learning, Memory, and Cognition, 22*(6), 1408–1422.

Bartlett, F. C. (1932). *Remembering: A study in experimental and social psychology.* Cambridge, UK: Cambridge University Press.

Basok, M. (1990). Transfer of domain-specific problem-solving procedures. *Journal of Experimental Psychology: Learning, Memory, and Cognition, 16*(3), 522–533.

Basok, M., & Holyoak, K. J. (1989). Interdomain transfer between isomorphic topics in algebra and physics. *Journal of Experimental Psychology: Learning, Memory, and Cognition, 15*(1), 153–166.

Bass, E., & Davis, L. (1988). *The courage to heal: A guide for women survivors of child sexual abuse.* New York: Perennial Library/Harper & Row.

Basso, A., Spinnler, H., Vallar, G., & Zanobio, M. E. (1982). Left hemisphere damage and selective impairment of auditory verbal short-term memory: A case study. *Neuropsychologia, 20*, 263–274.

Battig, W. F., & Montague, W. E. (1969). Category norms of verbal items in 56 categories: A replication and extension of the Connecticut category norms. *Journal of Experimental Psychology, 80*(3, Pt. 2), 1–46.

Baylis, G. C., & Driver, J. (1993). Visual attention and objects: Evidence for hierarchical coding of location. *Journal of Experimental Psychology: Human Perception and Performance, 19*(3), 451–470.

Beauvois, M. F., & Derouesne, J. (1979). Phonological alexia: Three dissociations. *Journal of Neurology, Neurosurgery, and Psychiatry, 42*, 1115–1124.

Bechara, A., Damasio, A. R., Damasio, H., & Anderson, S. W. (1994). Insensitivity to future consequences following damage to human prefrontal cortex. *Cognition, 50*(1–3), 7–15.

Bedard, J., & Chi, M. T. (1992). Expertise. *Current Directions in Psychological Science, 1*(4), 135–139.

Beech, J. R., & Allport, D. A. (1978). Visualization of compound scenes. *Perception, 7*(2), 129–138.

Begg, I., & Harris, G. (1982). On the interpretation of syllogisms. *Journal of Verbal Learning & Verbal Behavior, 21*(5), 595–620.

Behrmann, M., & Bub, D. (1992). Surface dyslexia and dysgraphia: Dual routes, single lexicon. *Cognitive Neuropsychology, 9*(3), 209–251.

Berlin, B., & Kay, P. (1969). *Basic color terms: Their universality and evolution.* Berkeley: University of California Press.

Bertamini, M., Yang, T. L., & Proffitt, D. R. (1998). Relative size perception at a distance is best at eye level. *Perception & Psychophysics, 60*(4), 673–682.

Biederman, I. (1981). On the semantics of a glance at a scene. In M. Kubovy & J. Pomerantz (Eds.), *Perceptual organization.* Mahwah, NJ: Erlbaum.

Biederman, I. (1987). Recognition-by-components: A theory of human image understanding. *Psychological Review, 94*(2), 115–117.

Bisiach, E., & Luzzatti, C. (1978). Unilateral neglect of representational space. *Cortex, 14*(1), 129–133.

Blake, J., & de Boysson-Bardies, B. (1992). Patterns in babbling: A cross-linguistic study. *Journal of Child Language, 19*(1), 51–74.

Bloom, A. H. (1981). *The linguistic shaping of thought: A study in the impact of language on thinking in China and the West.* Mahwah, NJ: Erlbaum.

Bloom, B. S. (1985). Generalizations about talent development. In B. S. Bloom (Ed.), *Developing talent in young people* (pp. 507–549). New York: Ballantine.

Boland, J. E. (1997). Resolving syntactic category ambiguities in discourse context: Probabilistic and discourse constraints. *Journal of Memory & Language, 36*(4), 588–615.

Boland, J. E., & Boehm-Jernigan, H. (1998). Lexical constraints and prepositional phrase attachment. *Journal of Memory & Language, 39*(4), 684–719.

Bolhuis, J. J., & Honey, R. C. (1998). Imprinting, learning and development: From behaviour to brain and back. *Trends in Neurosciences, 21*(7), 306–311.

Bontempi, B., Laurent-Demir, C., Destrade, C., & Jaffard, R. (1999). Time-dependent reorganization of brain circuitry underlying long-term memory storage. *Nature, 400*(6745), 671–675.

Bouchard, T. J., & McGue, M. (1981). Familial studies of intelligence: A review. *Science, 212*(4498), 1055–1059.

Bousfield, W. A. (1953). The occurrence of clustering in the recall of randomly arranged associates. *Journal of General Psychology, 49*, 229–240.

Bower, G. H. (1972). Mental imagery and associative learning. In L. Gregg (Ed.), *Cognition in learning and memory.* New York: Wiley.

Bower, G. H., Black, J. B., & Turner, T. J. (1979). Scripts in memory for text. *Cognitive Psychology, 11*(2), 177–220.

Bower, G. H., & Springston, F. (1970). Pauses as recoding points in letter series. *Journal of Experimental Psychology, 83*, 421–430.

Bowers, K. S., Regehr, G., Balthazard, C., & Parker, K. (1990). Intuition in the context of discovery. *Cognitive Psychology, 22*(1), 72–110.

Bradshaw, G. L., & Anderson, J. R. (1982). Elaborative encoding as an explanation of levels of processing. *Journal of Verbal Learning & Verbal Behavior, 21*(2), 165–174.

Braine, M. D. S. (1990). The "natural logic" aproach to reasoning. In W. F. Overton (Ed.), *Reasoning, necessity, and logic: Developmental perspectives* (pp. 133–157). Mahwah, NJ: Erlbaum.

Braine, M. D. S., & O'Brien, D. P. (1998). The theory of mental-propositional logic: Description and illustration. In M. D. S. Braine & D. P. O'Brien (Eds.), *Mental logic* (pp. 79–89). Mahwah, NJ: Erlbaum.

Braine, M. D. S., Reiser, B. J., & Rumain, B. (1984). Some empirical justification for a theory of natural propositional logic. In G. H. Bower (Ed.), *The psychology of learning and motivation: Advances in research and theory* (Vol. 18). New York: Academic Press.

Braine, M. D. S., & Rumain, B. (1983). Logical reasoning. In J. H. Flavell & E. M. Markman (Eds.), *Handbook of child psychology* (Vol. III, pp. 263–340). New York: Wiley.

Brandon, S., Boakes, J., Glaser, D., & Green, R. (1998). Recovered memories of childhood sexual abuse. *British Journal of Psychiatry, 172*, 296–307.

Brandt, S. A., & Stark, L. W. (1997). Spontaneous eye movements during visual imagery reflect the content of the visual scene. *Journal of Cognitive Neuroscience, 9*(1), 27–38.

Bransford, J. D., & Johnson, M. K. (1972). Contextual prerequisites for understanding: Some investigations fo comprehension

and recall. *Journal of Verbal Learning and Verbal Behavior, 11*, 717–726.

Breitmeyer, B. G., & Ganz, L. (1976). Implications of sustained and transient channels for theories of visual pattern masking, saccadic suppression, and information processing. *Psychological Review, 83*(1), 1–36.

Brewer, J. B., Zhao, Z., Desmond, J. E., Glover, G. H., & Gabrieli, J. D. E. (1998). Making memories: Brain activity that predicts how well visual experience will be remembered. *Science, 281*(5380), 1185–1187.

Britt, M. A. (1994). The interaction of referential ambiguity and argument structure in the parsing of prepositional phrases. *Journal of Memory & Language, 33*(2), 251–283.

Britt, M. A., Perfetti, C. A., Garrod, S., & Rayner, K. (1992). Parsing in discourse: Context effects and their limits. *Journal of Memory & Language, 31*(3), 293–314.

Broadbent, D. E. (1958). *Perception and communication.* Oxford, UK: Oxford University Press.

Broadbent, D. E. (1982). Task combination and selective intake of information. *Acta Psychologica, 50*(3), 253–290.

Broerse, J., & Crassini, B. (1980). The influence of imagery ability on color aftereffects produced by physically present and imagined induction stimuli. *Perception and Psychophysics, 28*(6), 560–568.

Broerse, J., & Crassini, B. (1981). Misinterpretations of imagery-induced McCollough effects: A reply to Finke. *Perception and Psychophysics, 30*(1), 96–98.

Brooks, L. R. (1968). Spatial and verbal components of the act of recall. *Canadian Journal of Psychology, 22*(5), 349–368.

Brown, J. (1958). Some tests of the decay theory of immediate memory. *Quarterly Journal of Experimental Psychology, 10*, 12–21.

Brown, R. (1958). *Words and things.* Glencoe, IL: Free Press.

Brown, R., & Kulik, J. (1977). Flashbulb memories. *Cognition, 5*(1), 73–99.

Brown, R., & McNeill, D. (1966). The "tip of the tongue" phenomenon. *Journal of Verbal Learning & Verbal Behavior, 5*(4), 325–337.

Brown, R. W., & Lenneberg, E. H. (1954). A study in language and cognition. *Journal of Abnormal & Social Psychology, 49*, 454–462.

Bruner, J. S., Goodnow, J. J., & Austin, G. A. (1956). *A study of thinking.* New York: Wiley.

Bryan, W. L., & Harter, N. (1897). Studies in the physiology and psychology of the telegraphic language. *Psychological Review, 4*(1), 27–53.

Buckner, R. L., Kelley, W. M., & Petersen, S. E. (1999). Frontal cortex contributes to human memory formation. *Nature Neuroscience, 2*(4), 311–314.

Buckner, R. L., & Petersen, S. E. (1996). What does neuroimaging tell us about the role of prefrontal cortex in memory retrieval? *Seminars in the Neurosciences, 8*, 47–55.

Bundesen, C., & Larsen, A. (1975). Visual transformation of size. *Journal of Experimental Psychology: Human Perception and Performance, 1*(3), 214–220.

Burke, A., Heuer, F., & Reisberg, D. (1992). Remembering emotional events. *Memory & Cognition, 20*(3), 277–290.

Buzsaki, G. (1989). Two-stage model of memory trace formation: A role for "noisy" brain states. *Neuroscience, 31*(3), 551–70.

Cahill, L., Haier, R. J., Falon, J., Alkire, M. T., Tang, C., Keator, D., Wu, J., & McGaugh, J. L. (1996). Amygdala activity at encoding correlated with long-term, free recall of emotional information. *Proceedings of the National Academy of Sciences, 93,* 8016–8021.

Cahill, L., & McGaugh, J. L. (1995). A novel demonstration of enhanced memory associated with emotional arousal. *Consciousness & Cognition: An International Journal, 4*(4), 410–421.

Calne, D. B. (1999). *Within reason: Rationality and human behavior.* New York: Pantheon.

Campos, A., Perez, M. J., & Gonzalez, M. A. (1997). The interactiveness of paired images is affected by bizarreness and image vividness. *Imagination, Cognition & Personality, 16*(3), 301–307.

Caplan, D., Alpert, N., & Waters, G. (1998). Effects of syntactic structure and propositional number on patterns of regional cerebral blood flow. *Journal of Cognitive Neuroscience, 10*(4), 541–552.

Caramazza, A., & Shelton, J. R. (1998). Domain-specific knowledge systems in the brain: The animate–inanimate distinction. *Journal of Cognitive Neuroscience, 10*(1), 1–34.

Carlson, B. W. (1990). Anchoring and adjustment in judgments under risk. *Journal of Experimental Psychology: Learning, Memory, and Cognition, 16*(4), 665–676.

Carpenter, P. A., Just, M. A., & Shell, P. (1990). What one intelligence test measures: A theoretical account of the processing in the Raven Progressive Matrices Test. *Psychological Review, 97*(3), 404–431.

Catrambone, R. (1994). Improving examples to improve transfer to novel problems. *Memory & Cognition, 22*(5), 606–615.

Catrambone, R. (1995). Aiding subgoal learning: Effects on transfer. *Journal of Educational Psychology, 87*(1), 5–17.

Catrambone, R. (1996). Generalizing solution procedures learned from examples. *Journal of Experimental Psychology: Learning, Memory, and Cognition, 22*(4), 1020–1031.

Catrambone, R. (1998). The subgoal learning model: Creating better examples so that students can solve novel problems. *Journal of Experimental Psychology: General, 127*(4), 355–376.

Catrambone, R., & Holyoak, K. J. (1990). Learning subgoals and methods for solving probability problems. *Memory & Cognition, 18*(6), 593–603.

Cave, C. B., & Kosslyn, S. M. (1993). The role of parts and spatial relations in object identification. *Perception, 22*(2), 229–248.

Ceci, S. J., & Liker, J. K. (1986). A day at the races: A study of IQ, expertise, and cognitive complexity. *Journal of Experimental Psychology: General, 115*(3), 255–266.

Cermak, L. S., & Butters, N. (1972). The role of interference and encoding in the short-term memory deficits of Korsakoff patients. *Neuropsychologia, 10,* 89–96.

Chapman, G. B., & Bornstein, B. H. (1996). The more you ask for, the more you get: Anchoring in personal injury verdicts. *Applied Cognitive Psychology, 10*(6), 519–540.

Charlot, V., Tzourio, N., Zilbovicius, M., Mazoyer, B. M., & Denis, M. (1992). Different mental imagery abilities result in different regional cerebral blood flow activation patterns during cognitive tasks. *Neuropsychologia, 30*(6), 565–580.

Chase, W. G., & Simon, H. A. (1973). Perception in chess. *Cognitive Psychology, 4*(1), 55–81.

Chater, N. (1996). Reconciling simplicity and likelihood principles in perceptual organization. *Psychological Review, 103*(3), 566–581.

Chater, N., & Oaksford, M. (1999). The probability heuristics model of syllogistic reasoning. *Cognitive Psychology, 38*(2), 191–258.

Chen, W., Kato, T., Zhu, X. H., Ogawa, S., Tank, D. W., & Ugurbil, K. (1998). Human primary visual cortex and lateral geniculate nucleus activation during visual imagery. *Neuroreport, 9,* 3669–3674.

Chen, Z. (1995). Analogical transfer: From schematic pictures to problem solving. *Memory & Cognition, 23*(2), 255–269.

Cheng, P. W., & Holyoak, K. J. (1985). Pragmatic reasoning schemas. *Cognitive Psychology, 17*(4), 391–416.

Cheng, P. W., & Holyoak, K. J. (1989). On the natural selection of reasoning theories. *Cognition, 33*(3), 285–313.

Cheng, P. W., Holyoak, K. J., Nisbett, R. E., & Oliver, L. M. (1986). Pragmatic versus syntactic approaches to training deductive reasoning. *Cognitive Psychology, 18*(3), 293–328.

Cherry, E. C. (1953). Some experiments on the recognition of speech, with one and with two ears. *Journal of the Acoustical Society of America, 25,* 975–979.

Cherubini, P., Garnham, A., & Oakhill, J. (1998). Can any ostrich fly? Some new data on belief bias in syllogistic reasoning. *Cognition, 69*(2), 179–218.

Chi, M. T. H., Feltovich, P., & Glaser, R. (1981). Categorization and representation of physics problems by experts and novices. *Cognitive Science, 5,* 121–152.

Chomsky, N. (1957). *Syntactic structures.* The Hague: Mouton.

Chomsky, N. (1959). A review of B. F. Skinner's *Verbal behavior. Language, 35,* 26–58.

Chomsky, N. (1965). *Aspects of the theory of syntax.* Cambridge, MA: MIT Press.

Clark, H. H., & Clark, E. V. (1977). *Psychology and language: An introduction to psycholinguistics.* New York: Harcourt, Brace, Jovanovich.

Clarke, H. M. (1911). Conscious attitudes. *American Journal of Psychology, 22*(2), 214–249.

Clarke, V. J., & Lamberts, K. (1997). Strategy shifts and expertise in solving transformation rule problems. *Thinking & Reasoning, 3*(4), 271–290.

Cohen, N. J., & Squire, L. R. (1980). Preserved learning and pattern-analyzing skill in amnesia: Dissociation of knowing how and knowing that. *Science, 210,* 207–210.

Colle, H. A., & Welsh, A. (1976). Acoustic masking in primary memory. *Journal of Verbal Learning & Verbal Behavior, 15*(1), 17–31.

Collins, A. M., & Loftus, E. F. (1975). A spreading-activation theory of semantic processing. *Psychological Review, 82*(6), 407–428.

Collins, A. M., & Quillian, M. R. (1969). Retrieval time from semantic memory. *Journal of Verbal Learning & Verbal Behavior, 8*(2), 240–247.

Collins, A. M., & Quillian, M. R. (1972). How to make a language user. In E. Tulving & W. Donaldson (Eds.), *Organization of memory* (pp. 309–351). New York: Academic Press.

Coltheart, M., Curtis, B., Atkins, P., & Haller, M. (1993). Models of reading aloud: Dual-route and parallel distributed-processing approaches. *Psychological Review, 100*(4), 589–608.

Coltheart, M., & Rastle, K. (1994). Serial processing in reading aloud: Evidence for dual-route models of reading. *Journal of Experimental Psychology: Human Perception and Performance, 20*(6), 1197–1211.

Conrad, C. (1972). Cognitive economy in semantic memory. *Journal of Experimental Psychology, 92*(2), 149–154.

Conrad, R. (1964). Acoustic confusions in immediate memory. *British Journal of Psychology, 55*(1), 75–84.

Cooper, E. H., & Pantle, A. J. (1967). The total-time hypothesis in verbal learning. *Psychological Bulletin, 68,* 221–234.

Cooper, L. A. (1975). Mental rotation of random two-dimensional shapes. *Cognitive Psychology, 7*(1), 20–43.

Cooper, L. A. (1976). Demonstration of a mental analog of an external rotation. *Perception and Psychophysics, 19*(4), 296–302.

Cooper, L. A., Schacter, D. L., Ballesteros, S., & Moore, C. (1992). Priming and recognition of transformed three-dimensional objects: Effects of size and reflection. *Journal of Experimental Psychology: Learning, Memory, and Cognition, 18,* 43–57.

Cooper, L. A., & Shepard, R. N. (1975). Mental transformation in the identification of left and right hands. *Journal of Experimental Psychology: Human Perception and Performance, 1*(1), 48–56.

Corkin, S. (1968). Acquisition of motor skill after bilateral medial temporal lobe excision. *Neuropsychologia, 6,* 255–265.

Corkin, S. (1984). Lasting consequences of bilateral medial temporal lobectomy: Clinical course and experimental findings in H. M. *Seminars in Neurology, 4,* 252–262.

Cornoldi, C., Cortesi, A., & Preti, D. (1991). Individual differences in the capacity limitations of visuospatial short-term memory: Research on sighted and totally congenitally blind people. *Memory & Cognition, 19*(5), 459–468.

Corteen, R. S., & Wood, B. (1972). Autonomic responses to shock-associated words in an unattended channel. *Journal of Experimental Psychology, 94*(3), 308–313.

Cosmides, L. (1989). The logic of social exchange: Has natural selection shaped how humans reason? Studies with the Wason selection task. *Cognition, 31*(3), 187–276.

Cosmides, L., & Tooby, J. (1992). Cognitive adaptations for social exchange. In J. Barkow, L. Cosmides, & J. Tooby (Eds.), *The adapted mind: Evolutionary psychology and the generation of culture* (pp. 163–228). New York: Oxford University Press.

Cosmides, L., & Tooby, J. (1994). Beyond intuition and instinct blindness: Toward an evolutionarily rigorous cognitive science. *Cognition, 50*(1–3), 41–77.

Cosmides, L., & Tooby, J. (1996). Are humans good intuitive statisticians after all? Rethinking some conclusions from the literature on judgment under uncertainty. *Cognition, 58*(1), 1–73.

Cosmides, L., & Tooby, J. (2000). The cognitive neuroscience of social reasoning. In M. Gazzaniga (Ed.), *The cognitive neurosciences* (2nd ed., pp. 1259–1270). Cambridge, MA: MIT Press.

Cowan, N. (1987). Auditory sensory storage in relation to the growth of sensation and acoustic information extraction. *Journal of Experimental Psychology: Human Perception and Performance, 13*(2), 204–215.

Cowan, N. (1995). *Attention and memory: An integrated framework.* New York: Oxford University Press.

Craik, F. I., & Lockhart, R. S. (1972). Levels of processing: A framework for memory research. *Journal of Verbal Learning and Verbal Behavior, 11,* 671–684.

Craik, F. I., & Tulving, E. (1975). Depth of processing and the retention of words in episodic memory. *Journal of Experimental Psychology: General, 104*(3), 268–294.

Craik, F. I., & Watkins, M. J. (1973). The role of rehearsal in short-term memory. *Journal of Verbal Learning & Verbal Behavior, 12*(6), 599–607.

Craver-Lemley, C., & Reeves, A. (1992). How visual imagery interferes with vision. *Psychological Review, 99*(4), 633–649.

Crowder, R. G. (1967). Prefix effects in immediate memory. *Canadian Journal of Psychology, 21*(5), 450–461.

Daneman, M., & Carpenter, P. A. (1980). Individual differences in working memory and reading. *Journal of Verbal Learning & Verbal Behavior, 19*(4), 450–466.

Daugman, J. (1990). Brain metaphor and brain theory. In E. Schwartz (Ed.), *Computational neuroscience.* Cambridge, MA: MIT Press.

Davies, I. R. L., & Corbett, G. G. (1997). A cross-cultural study of colour grouping: Evidence for weak linguistic relativity. *British Journal of Psychology, 88*(3), 493–517.

Davies, I. R. L., Sowden, P. T., Jerrett, D. T., Jerrett, T., & Corbett, G. G. (1998). A cross-cultural study of English and Setswana speakers on a colour triads task: A test of the Sapir–Whorf hypothesis. *British Journal of Psychology, 89*(1), 1–15.

Davis, H. L., Hoch, S. J., & Ragsdale, E. E. (1986). An anchoring and adjustment model of spousal predictions. *Journal of Consumer Research, 13*(1), 25–37.

Dawson, M. E., & Schell, A. M. (1982). Electrodermal responses to attended and nonattended significant stimuli during dichotic listening. *Journal of Experimental Psychology: Human Perception and Performance, 8*(2), 315–324.

De Groot, A. D. (1946/1978). *Thought and choice in chess.* The Hague: Mouton.

de Valois, R. L., & de Valois, K. K. (1993). A multi-stage color model. *Vision Research, 33*(8), 1053–1065.

Denis, M., & Carfantan, M. (1985). People's knowledge about images. *Cognition, 20*(1), 49–60.

Descartes, R. (1664/1972). *Traite de L'homme* [Treatise on man] (T. Hall, Trans.). Cambridge, MA: Harvard University Press.

Deutsch, J. A., & Deutsch, D. (1963). Attention: Some theoretical considerations. *Psychological Review, 70,* 51–61.

di Lollo, V. (1980). Temporal integration in visual memory. *Journal of Experimental Psychology: General, 109*, 75–97.

Dickstein, L. S. (1975). Effects of instructions and premise order on errors in syllogistic reasoning. *Journal of Experimental Psychology: Human Learning & Memory, 1*(4), 376–384.

Dickstein, L. S. (1976). Differential difficulty of categorical syllogisms. *Bulletin of the Psychonomic Society, 8*(4), 330–332.

Dickstein, L. S. (1978). The effect of figure on syllogistic reasoning. *Memory & Cognition, 6*(1), 76–83.

Dinges, D. F., Whitehouse, W. G., Orne, E. C., Powell, J. W., Orne, M. T., & Erdelyi, M. H. (1992). Evaluating hypnotic memory enhancement (hypermnesia and reminiscence) using multitrial forced recall. *Journal of Experimental Psychology: Learning, Memory, and Cognition, 18*, 1139–1147.

Donnelly, C. M., & McDaniel, M. A. (1993). Use of analogy in learning scientific concepts. *Journal of Experimental Psychology: Learning, Memory, and Cognition, 19*(4), 975–987.

Dooling, D. J., & Christiaansen, R. E. (1977). Episodic and semantic aspects of memory for prose. *Journal of Experimental Psychology: Human Learning and Memory, 3*, 428–436.

Driver, J., & Spence, C. J. (1994). Spatial synergies between auditory and visual attention. In C. M. M. Umilta (Ed.), *Attention and performance 15: Conscious and nonconscious information processing.* Attention and performance series (pp. 311–331). Cambridge, MA: MIT Press.

Duncker, K. (1945). On problem-solving. *Psychological Monographs, 5*, 113.

Durso, F. T., Rea, C. B., & Dayton, T. (1994). Graph-theoretic confirmation of restructuring during insight. *Psychological Science, 5*(2), 94–98.

Eddy, D. M. (1982). Probabilistic reasoning in clinical medicine: Problems and opportunities. In D. Kahneman, P. Slovic, & A. Tversky (Eds.), *Judgment under uncertainty: Heuristics and biases.* Cambridge, UK: Cambridge University Press.

Edwards, G. (1995). *Scuse me . . . while I kiss this guy: And other misheard song lyrics.* New York: Fireside.

Edwards, G. (1996). *He's got the whole world in his pants: And more misheard song lyrics.* New York: Fireside.

Edwards, G. (1997). *When a man loves a walnut: And even more misheard song lyrics.* New York: Fireside.

Efron, R. (1970a). Effect of stimulus duration on perceptual onset and offset latencies. *Perception and Psychophysics, 8*(4), 231–234.

Efron, R. (1970b). The relationship between the duration of a stimulus and the duration of a perception. *Neuropsychologia, 8*(1), 37–55.

Eich, E. (1984). Memory for unattended events: Remembering with and without awareness. *Memory & Cognition, 12*(2), 105–111.

Eich, E., & Macaulay, D. (2000). Are real moods required to reveal mood-congruent and mood-dependent memory? *Psychological Science, 11*, 244–248.

Engle, R. W., Tuholski, S. W., Laughlin, J. E., & Conway, A. R. A. (1999). Working memory, short-term memory, and general fluid intelligence: A latent-variable approach. *Journal of Experimental Psychology: General, 128*(3), 309–331.

Enns, J. T., & Rensink, R. A. (1991). Preattentive recovery of three-dimensional orientation from line drawings. *Psychological Review, 98*(3), 335–351.

Epstein, R., & Kanwisher, N. (1998). A cortical representation of the local visual environment. *Nature, 392*(6676), 598–601.

Epstein, R., Lanza, R. P., & Skinner, B. F. (1980). Symbolic communication between two pigeons *(Columba livia domestica). Science, 207*(4430), 543–545.

Epstein, W. (1965). Nonrelational judgments of size and distance. *American Journal of Psychology, 78*, 120–123.

Erdelyi, M. H. (1994). Hypnotic hypermnesia: The empty set of hypermnesia. *International Journal of Clinical and Experimental Hypnosis, 42*, 379–390.

Ericsson, K. A. (1996). The acquisition of expert performance: An introduction to some of the issues. In K. A. Ericsson (Ed.), *The road to excellence: The acquisition of expert performance in the arts and sciences, sports, and games* (pp. 1–50). Mahwah, NJ: Erlbaum.

Ericsson, K. A., Krampe, R. T., & Tesch-Roemer, C. (1993). The role of deliberate practice in the acquisition of expert performance. *Psychological Review, 100*(3), 363–406.

Ericsson, K. A., & Simon, H. A. (1993). *Protocol analysis: Verbal reports as data* (Rev. ed.). Cambridge, MA: MIT Press.

Ernst, G. W., & Newell, A. (1969). *GPS: A case study in the generality of problem solving.* New York: Academic Press.

Estes, W. K. (1994). *Classification and cognition.* New York: Oxford University Press.

Estes, W. K., Campbell, J. A., Hatsopoulos, N., & Hurwitz, J. B. (1989). Base-rate effects in category learning: A comparison of parallel network and memory storage–retrieval models. *Journal of Experimental Psychology: Learning, Memory, and Cognition, 15*(4), 556–571.

Evans, J. S. B. T., Barston, J. L., & Pollard, P. (1983). On the conflict between logic and belief in syllogistic reasoning. *Memory & Cognition, 11*(3), 295–306.

Evans, J. S. B. T., Handley, S. J., Harper, C. N. J., & Johnson-Laird, P. N. (1999). Reasoning about necessity and possibility: A test of the mental model theory of deduction. *Journal of Experimental Psychology, 25*, 1495–1513.

Evans, J. S. B. T., Newstead, S. E., & Byrne, R. M. J. (1993). *Human reasoning: The psychology of deduction.* Mahwah, NJ: Erlbaum.

Falmagne, R. J. (1990). Language and the acquisition of logical knowledge. In W. F. Overton (Ed.), *Reasoning, necessity, and logic: Developmental perspectives. The Jean Piaget symposium series* (pp. 111–131). Mahwah, NJ: Erlbaum.

Farah, M. J. (1985). Psychophysical evidence for a shared representational medium for mental images and percepts. *Journal of Experimental Psychology: General, 114*(1), 91–103.

Farah, M. J. (1990). *Visual agnosia: Disorders of object recognition and what they tell us about normal vision.* Cambridge, MA: MIT Press.

Farah, M. J., Hammond, K. M., Levine, D. N., & Calvanio, R. (1988). Visual and spatial mental imagery: Dissociable systems of representation. *Cognitive Psychology, 20*(4), 439–462.

Farah, M. J., Soso, M. J., & Dasheiff, R. M. (1992). Visual angle of the mind's eye before and after unilateral occipital lobectomy. *Journal of Experimental Psychology: Human Perception and Performance, 18*(1), 241–246.

Fechner, G. T. (1860). *Elements of psychophysics.* Leipzig: Breitkopf & Hartel.

Femina, D. D., Yeager, C. A., & Lewis, D. O. (1990). Child abuse: Adolescent recods vs. adult recall. *Child Abuse and Neglect, 14,* 227–231.

Fernandez, A., & Glenberg, A. M. (1985). Changing environmental context does not reliably affect memory. *Memory & Cognition, 13*(4), 333–345.

Fernberger, S. W. (1921). A preliminary study of the range of visual apprehension. *American Journal of Psychology, 32,* 121–133.

Ferreira, F., & Clifton, C. (1986). The independence of syntactic processing. *Journal of Memory & Language, 25*(3), 348–368.

Fetz, E. E., & Cheney, P. D. (1980). Postspike facilitation of forelimb muscle activity by primate corticomotoneuronal cells. *Journal of Neurophysiology, 44,* 751–772.

Feynman, R. P., & Leighton, R. (1985). *"Surely you're joking, Mr. Feynman!": Adventures of a curious character.* New York: Bantam.

Finke, R. A. (1980). Levels of equivalence in imagery and perception. *Psychological Review, 87*(2), 113–132.

Finke, R. A. (1981). Interpretations of imagery-induced McCollough effects. *Perception and Psychophysics, 30*(1), 94–95.

Finke, R. A. (1996). Imagery, creativity, and emergent structure. *Consciousness & Cognition: An International Journal, 5*(3), 381–393.

Finke, R. A., Pinker, S., & Farah, M. J. (1989). Reinterpreting visual patterns in mental imagery. *Cognitive Science, 13*(1), 51–78.

Finke, R. A., & Shepard, R. N. (1986). Visual functions of mental imagery. In K. R. Boff & L. Kaufman (Eds.), *Handbook of perception and human performance* (Vol. 2, pp. 1–55). New York: Wiley.

Fletcher, C. R., & Chrysler, S. T. (1990). Surface forms, textbases, and situation models: Recognition memory for three types of textual information. *Discourse Processes, 13*(2), 175–190.

Fletcher, P. C., Frith, C. D., Baker, S. C., Shallice, T., Frackowiak, R. S., & Dolan, R. J. (1995). The mind's eye: Precuneus activation in memory-related imagery. *Neuroimage, 2,* 195–200.

Flexser, A. J., & Tulving, E. (1978). Retrieval independence in recognition and recall. *Psychological Review, 85*(3), 153–171.

Fodor, J. A., & Garrett, M. (1967). Some syntactic determinants of sentential complexity. *Perception and Psychophysics, 2*(7), 289–296.

Fodor, J. D. (1995). Comprehending sentence structure. In L. R. Gleitman & M. Liberman (Eds.), *An invitation to cognitive science* (Vol. 1, pp. 209–246). Cambridge, MA: MIT Press.

Forster, K. I., & Chambers, S. M. (1973). Lexical access and naming time. *Journal of Verbal Learning & Verbal Behavior, 12*(6), 627–635.

Foulke, E., & Sticht, T. G. (1969). Review of research on the intelligibility and comprehension of accelerated speech. *Psychological Bulletin, 72*(1), 50–62.

Frederickson, R. (1992). *Repressed memories: A journey to recovery from sexual abuse.* New York: Parkside.

Freyd, J. J. (1987). Dynamic mental representation. *Psychological Review, 94,* 427–438.

Freyd, J. J., & Finke, R. A. (1984). Representational momentum. *Journal of Experimental Psychology: Learning, Memory, and Cognition, 10*(1), 126–132.

Funnell, E. (1983). Phonological processes in reading: New evidence from acquired dyslexia. *British Journal of Psychology, 74*(2), 159–180.

Gabrieli, J. D. E. (1998). Cognitive neuroscience of human memory. *Annual Review of Psychology, 49,* 87–115.

Gallistel, C. R. (1990). *The organization of learning.* Cambridge, MA: MIT Press.

Galton, F. (1883). *Inquiries into human faculty and its development.* London: Macmillan.

Gardner, B. T., & Gardner, R. A. (1967a). Teaching sign language to a chimpanzee: II. Demonstrations. *Psychonomic Bulletin, 1*(2), 36.

Gardner, B. T., & Gardner, R. A. (1975). Evidence for sentence constitutents in the early utterances of child and chimpanzee. *Journal of Experimental Psychology: General, 104*(3), 244–267.

Gardner, H. (1976). *The Shattered Mind.* New York: Vintage.

Gardner, H. (1985). *The mind's new science: A history of the cognitive revolution.* New York: Basic Books.

Gardner, R. A., & Gardner, B. T. (1967b). Teaching sign language to a chimpanzee: I. Methodology and preliminary results. *Psychonomic Bulletin, 1*(2), 36.

Gardner, R. A., Gardner, B. T., & Van Cantfort, T. E. (Eds.). (1989). *Teaching sign language to chimpanzees.* Albany: State University of New York Press.

Garry, M., Manning, C. G., Loftus, E. F., & Sherman, S. J. (1996). Imagination inflation: Imagining a childhood event inflates confidence that it occurred. *Psychonomic Bulletin & Review, 3*(2), 208–214.

Gaskell, M. G., & Marslen-Wilson, W. D. (1996). Phonological variation and inference in lexical access. *Journal of Experimental Psychology: Human Perception and Performance, 22*(1), 144–158.

Gaskell, M. G., & Marslen-Wilson, W. D. (1998). Mechanisms of phonological inference in speech perception. *Journal of Experimental Psychology: Human Perception and Performance, 24*(2), 380–396.

Gauthier, I., Tarr, M. J., Anderson, A. W., Skudlarski, P., & Gore, J. C. (1999). Activation of the middle fusiform "face area" increases with expertise in recognizing novel objects. *Nature Neuroscience, 2*(6), 568–573.

Gebauer, G., & Laming, D. (1997). Rational choices in Wason's selection task. *Psychological Research, 60*(4), 284–293.

Georgopoulos, A. P., Lurito, J. T., Petrides, M., Schwartz, A. B., & Massey, J. T. (1989). Mental rotation of the neuronal population vector. *Science, 243*(4888), 234–236.

Gernsbacher, M. A. (Ed.). (1994). *Handbook of psycholinguistics.* San Diego: Academic Press.

Gerrig, R. J. (1989). Suspense in the absence of uncertainty. *Journal of Memory & Language, 28*(6), 633–648.

Gershberg, F. B., & Shimamura, A. P. (1995). Impaired use of organizational strategies in free recall following frontal lobe damage. *Neuropsychologia, 33*(10), 1305–1333.

Ghez, C., Gordon, J., Ghilardi, M. F., & Sainburg, R. (1995). Contributions of vision and proprioception to accuracy in limb movements. In M. S. Gazzaniga (Ed.), *The cognitive neurosciences* (pp. 549–564). Cambridge, MA: MIT Press.

Gibson, B. S., & Jiang, Y. (1998). Surprise! An unexpected color singleton does not capture attention in visual search. *Psychological Science, 9*(3), 176–182.

Gibson, J. J. (1979). *The ecological approach to visual perception.* Boston: Houghton Mifflin.

Gick, M. L., & Holyoak, K. J. (1980). Analogical problem solving. *Cognitive Psychology, 12*(3), 306–355.

Gick, M. L., & Holyoak, K. J. (1983). Schema induction and analogical transfer. *Cognitive Psychology, 15*(1), 1–38.

Gigerenzer, G. (1992). How to make cognitive illusions disappear: Beyond "Heuristics and Biases." *European review of social psychology, 2,* 83–115.

Gigerenzer, G., Hell, W., & Blank, H. (1988). Presentation and content: The use of base rates as a continuous variable. *Journal of Experimental Psychology: Human Perception and Performance, 14,* 513–525.

Gigerenzer, G., & Hoffrage, U. (1995). How to improve Bayesian reasoning without instruction: Frequency formats. *Psychological Review, 102*(4), 684–704.

Gigerenzer, G., Hoffrage, U., & Kleinboelting, H. (1991). Probabilistic mental models: A Brunswikian theory of confidence. *Psychological Review, 98*(4), 506–528.

Gigerenzer, G., & Hug, K. (1992). Domain-specific reasoning: Social contracts, cheating, and perspective change. *Cognition, 43*(2), 127–171.

Gigerenzer, G., & Todd, P. M. (1999). Fast and frugal heuristics: The adaptive toolbox. In G. Gigerenzer, P. Todd, & the ABC Research Group (Eds.), *Simple heuristics that make us smart. Evolution and cognition* (pp. 3–34). New York: Oxford University Press.

Gilchrist, A. L. (1997). Perceived lightness depends on perceived spatial arrangement. In I. Rock (Ed.), *Indirect perception* (pp. 351–356). Cambridge, MA: MIT Press.

Gilhooly, K. J., Logie, R. H., Wetherick, N. E., & Wynn, V. (1993). Working memory and strategies in syllogistic-reasoning tasks. *Memory & Cognition, 21*(1), 115–124.

Glanville, A. D., & Dallenbach, K. M. (1929). The range of attention. *American Journal of Psychology, 41,* 207–236.

Glanzer, M., & Cunitz, A. R. (1966). Two storage mechanisms in free recall. *Journal of Verbal Learning & Verbal Behavior, 5*(4), 351–360.

Glenberg, A. M., & Langston, W. E. (1992). Comprehension of illustrated text: Pictures help to build mental models. *Journal of Memory & Language, 31*(2), 129–151.

Gluck, M. A., & Bower, G. H. (1988). From conditioning to category learning: An adaptive network model. *Journal of Experimental Psychology: General, 117*(3), 227–247.

Glucksberg, S., & Cowen, G. N. (1970). Memory for nonattended auditory material. *Cognitive Psychology, 1*(2), 149–156.

Gobet, F., & Simon, H. A. (1996). The roles of recognition processes and look-ahead search in time-constrained expert problem solving: Evidence from grand-master–level chess. *Psychological Science, 7*(1), 52–55.

Gobet, F., & Simon, H. A. (1998). Expert chess memory: Revisiting the chunking hypothesis. *Memory, 6*(3), 225–255.

Godden, D. R., & Baddeley, A. D. (1975). Context-dependent memory in two natural environments: On land and underwater. *British Journal of Psychology, 66*(3), 325–331.

Goel, V., Gold, B., Kapur, S., & Houle, S. (1997). The seats of reason? An imaging study of deductive and inductive reasoning. *NeuroReport, 8,* 1305–1310.

Goel, V., Gold, B., Kapur, S., & Houle, S. (1998). Neuroanatomical correlates of human reasoning. *Journal of Cognitive Neuroscience, 10*(3), 293–302.

Goldman, W. P., Wolters, N. C., & Winograd, E. (1992). A demonstration of incubation in anagram problem solving. *Bulletin of the Psychonomic Society, 30*(1), 36–38.

Goldston, D. B., Hinrichs, J. V., & Richman, C. L. (1985). Subjects' expectations, individual variability, and the scanning of mental images. *Memory & Cognition, 13*(4), 365–370.

Goodale, M. A., & Milner, A. D. (1992). Separate pathways for vision and action. *Trends in Neurosciences, 15,* 20–25.

Gopher, D., Brickner, M., & Navon, D. (1982). Different difficulty manipulations interact differently with task emphasis: Evidence for multiple resources. *Journal of Experimental Psychology: Human Perception and Performance, 8*(1), 146–157.

Gordon, P. C., & Meyer, D. E. (1987). Control of serial order in rapidly spoken syllable sequences. *Journal of Memory and Language, 26,* 300–321.

Graesser, A. C., Millis, K. K., & Zwaan, R. A. (1997). Discourse comprehension. *Annual Review of Psychology, 48,* 163–189.

Graesser, A. C., Singer, M., & Trabasso, T. (1994). Constructing inferences during narrative text comprehension. *Psychological Review, 101*(3), 371–395.

Graf, P., & Schacter, D. L. (1985). Implicit and explicit memory for new associations in normal and amnesic subjects. *Journal of Experimental Psychology: Learning, Memory, & Cognition, 11,* 501–518.

Graf, P., Shimamura, A. P., & Squire, L. R. (1985). Priming across modalities and priming across category levels: Extending the domain of preserved function in amnesia. *Journal of Experimental Psychology: Learning, Memory, and Cognition, 11*(2), 386–396.

Granger, R., Wiebe, S. P., Taketani, M., & Lynch, G. (1996). Distinct memory circuits composing the hippocampal region. *Hippocampus, 6*(6), 567–578.

Greeno, J. G. (1974). Hobbits and orcs: Acquisition of a sequential concept. *Cognitive Psychology, 6*(2), 270–292.

Griggs, R. A. (1984). Memory cueing and instructional effects on Wason's selection task. *Current Psychological Research & Reviews, 3*(4), 3–10.

Griggs, R. A., & Cox, J. R. (1982). The elusive thematic-materials effect in Wason's selection task. *British Journal of Psychology, 73*(3), 407–420.

Gudjonsson, G. H. (1997). Accusations by adults of child sexual abuse: A survey of members of the British False Memory Society (BFMS). *Applied Cognitive Psychology, 11,* 3–18.

Gustin, W. C. (1985). The development of exceptional research mathematicians. In B. S. Bloom (Ed.), *Developing talent in young people* (pp. 270–331). New York: Ballantine.

Haber, R. N. (1983). The impending demise of the icon: A critique of the concept of iconic storage in visual information processing. *Behavioral & Brain Sciences, 6*(1), 1–54.

Haffenden, A. M., & Goodale, M. A. (1998). The effect of pictorial illusion on prehension and perception. *Journal of Cognitive Neuroscience, 10*(1), 122–136.

Hakes, D. T., & Cairns, H. S. (1970). Sentence comprehension and relative pronouns. *Perception and Psychophysics, 8*(1), 5–8.

Hakes, D. T., & Foss, D. J. (1970). Decision processes during sentence comprehension: Effects of surface structure reconsidered. *Perception and Psychophysics, 8*(6), 413–416.

Hakuta, K. (1986). *Mirror of language.* New York: Basic Books.

Hamilton, D. L., & Gifford, R. K. (1976). Illusory correlation in interpersonal perception: A cognitive basis of stereotypic judgments. *Journal of Experimental Social Psychology, 12*(4), 392–407.

Hamilton, D. L., Stroessner, S. J., & Mackie, D. M. (1993). The influence of affect on stereotyping: The case of illusory correlations. In D. M. Mackie & D. L. Hamilton (Eds.), *Affect, cognition, and stereotyping: Interactive processes in group perception* (pp. 39–61). San Diego: Academic Press.

Hampton, J. A. (1995). Testing the prototype theory of concepts. *Journal of Memory & Language, 34*(5), 686–708.

Harris, M., & Coltheart, M. (1986). *Language processing in children and adults.* London: Routledge & Kegan Paul.

Hart, J. T. (1965). Memory and the feeling-of-knowing experience. *Journal of Educational Psychology, 56*, 208–216.

Hart, J. T. (1967). Memory and the memory-monitoring process. *Journal of Verbal Learning & Verbal Behavior, 6*(5), 685–691.

Hartley, A. A. (1977). Mental measurement in the magnitude estimation of length. *Journal of Experimental Psychology: Human Perception and Performance, 3*(4), 622–628.

Hassebrock, F., Johnson, P. E., Bullemer, P., Fox, P. W., & Moller, J. H. (1993). When less is more: Representation and selective memory in expert problem solving. *American Journal of Psychology, 106*(2), 155–189.

Hayes, J. R. (1981). *The complete problem solver.* Philadelphia: Franklin Institute Press.

Hayman, C. A., Macdonald, C. A., & Tulving, E. (1993). The role of repetition and associative interference in new semantic learning in amnesia: A case experiment. *Journal of Cognitive Neuroscience, 5*(4), 375–389.

Hebb, D. O. (1949). *The organization of behavior.* New York: Wiley.

Hebb, D. O. (1968). Concerning imagery. *Psychological Review, 75*, 466–477.

Heider, E. R. (1972). Universals in color naming and memory. *Journal of Experimental Psychology, 93*(1), 10–20.

Heider, E. R., & Oliver, D. C. (1972). The structure of the color space in naming and memory for two languages. *Cognitive Psychology, 3*(2), 337–354.

Helmholtz, H. L. F. von. (1910/1962). *Treatise on physiological optics* (J. P. Southall, Trans., Vol. 3). New York: Dover.

Hess, D. J., Foss, D. J., & Carroll, P. (1995). Effects of global and local context on lexical processing during language comprehension. *Journal of Experimental Psychology: General, 124*(1), 62–82.

Hess, E. H. (1958). "Imprinting" in animals. *Scientific American, 198*, 81–90.

Hintzman, D. L. (1992). Mathematical constraints and the Tulving–Wiseman law. *Psychological Review, 99*(3), 536–542.

Hirst, W., & et al. (1980). Dividing attention without alternation or automaticity. *Journal of Experimental Psychology: General, 109*(1), 98–117.

Hoffman, D. D., & Richards, W. A. (1984). Parts of recognition. *Cognition, 18*(1–3), 65–96.

Holyoak, K. J., & Koh, K. (1987). Surface and structural similarity in analogical transfer. *Memory & Cognition, 15*(4), 332–340.

Holyoak, K. J., & Thagard, P. R. (1989). A computational model of analogical problem solving. In S. O. A. Vosniadou (Ed.), *Similarity and analogical reasoning* (pp. 242–266). New York: Cambridge University Press.

Howe, M. L., Rabinowitz, F. M., & Powell, T. L. (1998). Individual differences in working memory and reasoning–remembering relationships in solving class-inclusion problems. *Memory & Cognition, 26*(5), 1089–1101.

Hubel, D. H., & Wiesel, T. N. (1979). Brain mechanisms of vision. *Scientific American, 241*(3), 150–162.

Huber, J., Payne, J. W., & Puto, C. (1982). Adding asymmetrically dominated alternatives: Violations of regularity and the similarity hypothesis. *Journal of Consumer Research, 9*, 90–98.

Hull, C. (1920). Quantitative aspects of the evolution of concepts. *Psychological Monographs (Whole no. 123).*

Hunt, E., & Agnoli, F. (1991). The Whorfian hypothesis: A cognitive psychology perspective. *Psychological Review, 98*(3), 377–389.

Huppert, F. A., & Piercy, M. (1978). Dissociation between learning and remembering in organic amnesia. *Nature, 275*(5678), 317–318.

Hyde, T. S., & Jenkins, J. J. (1973). Recall for words as a function of semantic, graphic, and syntactic orienting tasks. *Journal of Verbal Learning & Verbal Behavior, 12*(5), 471–480.

Intons-Peterson, M. J. (1981). Constructing and using unusual and common images. *Journal of Experimental Psychology: Human Learning & Memory, 7*(2), 133–144.

Intons-Peterson, M. J. (1983). Imagery paradigms: How vulnerable are they to experimenters' expectations? *Journal of Experimental Psychology: Human Perception and Performance, 9*(3), 394–412.

Ironsmith, M., & Lutz, J. (1996). The effects of bizarreness and self-generation on mnemonic imagery. *Journal of Mental Imagery, 20*(3–4), 113–126.

Irwin, D. E. (1993). Perceiving an integrated visual world. In D. Meyer & S. Kornblum (Eds.), *Attention and performance XIV: Synergies in experimental psychology, artificial intelligence, and cognitive neuroscience* (pp. 121–142). Cambridge, MA: MIT Press.

Irwin, D. E., Yantis, S., & Jonides, J. (1983). Evidence against visual integration across saccadic eye movements. *Perception and Psychophysics, 34*(1), 49–57.

Itard, J.-M. G. (1962). *The wild boy of Aveyron.* New York: Appleton-Century-Crofts.

Izquierdo, I., & Medina, J. H. (1997). Memory formation: The sequence of biochemical events in the hippocampus and its connection to activity in other brain structures. *Neurobiology of Learning & Memory, 68,* 285–316.

Jacobs, J. (1887). Experiments in prehension. *Mind, 12,* 75–79.

James, W. (1890). *Principles of psychology.* New York: Holt.

Jameson, D. (1985). Opponent-colors theory in light of physiological findings. In D. Ottoson & S. Zeki (Eds.), *Central and peripheral mechanisms of color vision* (pp. 8–102). New York: Macmillan.

Jeannerod, M. (1994).The representing brain: Neural correlates of motor intention and imagery. *Behavioral and Brain Sciences, 17,* 187–245.

Jevons, W. S. (1871). The power of numerical discrimination. *Nature, 3,* 281–282.

Johnson, K. E., & Mervis, C. B. (1997). Effects of varying levels of expertise on the basic level of categorization. *Journal of Experimental Psychology: General, 126*(3), 248–277.

Johnson, M. K., & Hasher, L. (1987). Human learning and memory. *Annual Review of Psychology, 38,* 631–668.

Johnson-Laird, P. N. (1999). Deductive reasoning. *Annual Review of Psychology, 50,* 109–135.

Johnson-Laird, P. N., & Bara, B. G. (1984). Syllogistic inference. *Cognition, 16*(1), 1–61.

Johnson-Laird, P. N., & Byrne, R. M. (1989). Only reasoning. *Journal of Memory & Language, 28*(3), 313–330.

Johnson-Laird, P. N., & Byrne, R. M. (1991). *Deduction.* Mahwah, NJ: Erlbaum.

Johnson-Laird, P. N., Byrne, R. M., & Schaeken, W. (1992). Propositional reasoning by model. *Psychological Review, 99*(3), 418–439.

Johnson-Laird, P. N., Legrenzi, P., & Legrenzi, M. S. (1972). Reasoning and a sense of reality. *British Journal of Psychology, 63*(3), 395–400.

Johnson-Laird, P. N., & Savary, F. (1999). Illusory inferences: A novel class of erroneous deductions. *Cognition, 71*(3), 191–229.

Johnston, W. A., & Heinz, S. P. (1978). Flexibility and capacity demands of attention. *Journal of Experimental Psychology: General, 107*(4), 420–435.

Jolicoeur, P. (1990). Identification of disoriented objects: A dual systems theory. *Mind and Language, 5,* 387–410.

Jolicoeur, P., & Kosslyn, S. M. (1985). Demand characteristics in image scanning experiments. *Journal of Mental Imagery, 9*(2), 41–49.

Jonides, J. (1980). Voluntary versus automatic control over the mind's eye's movement. In J. B. Long & A. D. Baddeley (Eds.), *Attention and performance IX* (pp. 187–203). Mahwah, NJ: Erlbaum.

Julesz, B. (1971). *Foundations of cyclopean perception.* Chicago: University of Chicago Press.

Just, M. A., & Carpenter, P. A. (1980). A theory of reading: From eye fixations to comprehension. *Psychological Review, 87*(4), 329–354.

Just, M. A., & Carpenter, P. A. (1992). A capacity theory of comprehension: Individual differences in working memory. *Psychological Review, 99*(1), 122–149.

Kahneman, D. (1968). Method, findings, and theory in studies of visual masking. *Psychological Bulletin, 70*(6, Pt. 1), 404–425.

Kahneman, D. (1973). *Attention and effort.* New York: Prentice Hall.

Kahneman, D., Knetsch, J. L., & Thaler, R. (1990). Experimental tests of the endowment effect and the Coase theorem. *Journal of Political Economy, 98,* 1325–1348.

Kahneman, D., & Tversky, A. (1973). On the psychology of prediction. *Psychological Review, 80*(4), 237–251.

Kahneman, D., & Tversky, A. (1996). On the reality of cognitive illusions. *Psychological Review, 103*(3), 582–591.

Kako, E. (1999). Elements of syntax in the systems of three language-trained animals. *Animal Learning and Behavior, 27,* 1–14.

Kaplan, C. A., & Simon, H. A. (1990). In search of insight. *Cognitive Psychology, 22*(3), 374–419.

Keane, M. (1987). On retrieving analogues when solving problems. *Quarterly Journal of Experimental Psychology: Human Experimental Psychology, 39*(1-A), 29–41.

Keane, M. M., Gabrieli, J. D. E., Fennema, A. C., Growdon, J. H., & Corkin, S. (1991). Evidence for a dissociation between perceptual and conceptual priming in Alzheimer's disease. *Behavioral Neuroscience, 105,* 326–342.

Kelly, M. H., Bock, J. K., & Keil, F. C. (1986). Prototypicality in a linguistic context: Effects on sentence structure. *Journal of Memory & Language, 25*(1), 59–74.

Keppel, G., & Underwood, B. J. (1962). Proactive inhibition in short-term retention of single items. *Journal of Verbal Learning & Verbal Behavior, 1*(3), 153–161.

Kerr, N. H. (1987). Locational representation in imagery: The third dimension. *Memory & Cognition, 15*(6), 521–530.

Kihlstrom, J. F. (1983). Instructed forgetting: Hypnotic and nonhypnotic. *Journal of Experimental Psychology: General, 112,* 73–79.

King, J., & Just, M. A. (1991). Individual differences in syntactic processing: The role of working memory. *Journal of Memory & Language, 30*(5), 580–602.

Kintsch, W. (1988). The role of knowledge in discourse comprehension: A construction integration model. *Psychological Review, 95*(2), 163–182.

Kirby, K. N. (1994). Probabilities and utilities of fictional outcomes in Wason's four-card selection task. *Cognition, 51,* 1–28.

Knoblich, G., Ohlsson, S., Haider, H., & Rhemius, D. (1999). Constraint relaxation and chunk decomposition in insight problem solving. *Journal of Experimental Psychology: Learning, Memory, and Cognition, 25*(6), 1534–1536.

Koelega, H. S., Brinkman, J.-A., Hendriks, L., & Verbaten, M. N. (1989). Processing demands, effort, and individual differences in four different vigilance tasks. *Human Factors, 31*(1), 45–62.

Kohler, W. (1929). *Gestalt psychology.* New York: Liveright.

Kolodner, J. L. (1992). An introduction to case-based reasoning. *Artificial Intelligence Review, 6*(1), 3–34.

Kolodner, J. L. (1994). From natural language understanding to case-based reasoning and beyond: A perspective on the cognitive model that ties it all together. In R. C. L. E. Schank (Ed.), *Beliefs, reasoning, and decision making: Psycho-logic in honor of Bob Abelson* (pp. 55–110). Mahwah, NJ: Erlbaum.

Kosslyn, S. M. (1973). Scanning visual images: Some structural implications. *Perception and Psychophysics, 14*(1), 90–94.

Kosslyn, S. M. (1975). Information representation in visual images. *Cognitive Psychology, 7*(3), 341–370.

Kosslyn, S. M. (1976). Using imagery to retrieve semantic information: A developmental study. *Child Development, 47*(2), 434–444.

Kosslyn, S. M. (1978). Measuring the visual angle of the mind's eye. *Cognitive Psychology, 10*(3), 356–389.

Kosslyn, S. M. (1980). *Image and mind.* Cambridge, MA: Harvard University Press.

Kosslyn, S. M. (1994). *Image and brain: The resolution of the imagery debate.* Cambridge, MA: MIT Press.

Kosslyn, S. M. (1995). Mental imagery. In S. M. Kosslyn (Ed.), *Visual cognition: An invitation to cognitive science* (Vol. 2, pp. 267–296). Cambridge, MA: MIT Press.

Kosslyn, S. M., Alpert, N. M., Thompson, W. L., Maljkovic, V., Weise, S. B., Chabris, C. F., Hamilton, S. E., Rauch, S. L., & Buonanno, F. S. (1993). Visual mental imagery activates topographically organized visual cortex: PET investigations. *Journal of Cognitive Neuroscience, 5*(3), 263–287.

Kosslyn, S. M., Ball, T. M., & Reiser, B. J. (1978). Visual images preserve metric spatial information: Evidence from studies of image scanning. *Journal of Experimental Psychology: Human Perception and Performance, 4*(1), 47–60.

Kosslyn, S. M., Cave, C. B., Provost, D. A., & von Gierke, S. M. (1988). Sequential processes in image generation. *Cognitive Psychology, 20*(3), 319–343.

Kosslyn, S. M., Flynn, R. A., Amsterdam, J. B., & Wang, G. (1990). Components of high-level vision: A cognitive neuroscience analysis and accounts of neurological syndromes. *Cognition, 34*(3), 203–277.

Kosslyn, S. M., & Schwartz, S. P. (1977). A stimulation of visual imagery. *Cognitive Science, 1*, 265–295.

Kosslyn, S. M., Sukel, K. M., & Bly, B. M. (1999). Squinting with the mind's eye: Effects of stimulus resolution on imaginal and perceptual comparisons. *Memory and Cognition, 27*, 276–287.

Kosslyn, S. M., Thompson, W. L., & Alpert, N. M. (1997). Neural systems shared by visual imagery and visual perception: A positron emission tomography study. *Neuroimage, 6*, 320–334.

Kosslyn, S. M., Thompson, W. L., Kim, I. J., & Alpert, N. M. (1995). Topographical representations of mental images in primary visual cortex. *Nature, 378*(6556), 496–498.

Kosslyn, S. M., Thompson, W. L., Kim, I. J., Rauch, S. L., & Alpert, N. M. (1996). Individual differences in cerebral blood flow in Area 17 predict the time to evaluate visualized letters. *Journal of Cognitive Neuroscience, 8*(1), 78–82.

Kotovsky, K., Hayes, J. R., & Simon, H. A. (1985). Why are some problems hard? Evidence from Tower of Hanoi. *Cognitive Psychology, 17*(2), 248–294.

Kotovsky, K., & Simon, H. A. (1990). What makes some problems really hard: Explorations in the problem space of difficulty. *Cognitive Psychology, 22*(2), 143–183.

Krosnick, J. A., Li, F., & Lehman, D. R. (1990). Conversational conventions, order of information acquisition, and the effect of base rates and individuating information on social judgments. *Journal of Personality & Social Psychology, 59*(6), 1140–1152.

Kubovy, M. (1983). Mental imagery majestically transforming cognitive psychology. *Contemporary Psychology, 28*, 661–664.

Kubovy, M., Cohen, D. J., & Hollier, J. (1999). Feature integration that routinely occurs without focal attention. *Psychonomic Bulletin & Review, 6*, 183–203.

Kuhl, P. K. (1989). On babies, birds, modules, and mechanisms: A comparative approach to the acquisition of vocal communication. In R. Dooling & S. H. Hulse (Eds.), *The comparative psychology of audition: Perceiving complex sounds* (pp. 379–419). Mahwah, NJ: Erlbaum.

Kunen, S., & May, J. G. (1980). Spatial frequency content of visual imagery. *Perception and Psychophysics, 28*(6), 555–559.

Kunen, S., & May, J. G. (1981). Imagery-induced McCollough effects: Real or imagined? *Perception and Psychophysics, 30*(1), 99–100.

Kwak, H.-W., Dagenbach, D., & Egeth, H. (1991) Further evidence for a time-independent shift of the focus of attention. *Perception and Psychophysics, 49*(5), 473–480.

Kyllonen, P. C., & Christal, R. E. (1990). Reasoning ability is (little more than) working-memory capacity? *Intelligence, 14*(4), 389–433.

Lahiri, A., & Marslen-Wilson, W. (1991). The mental representation of lexical form: A phonological approach to the recognition lexicon. *Cognition, 38*(3), 245–294.

Laming, D. (1996). On the analysis of irrational data selection: A critique of Oaksford and Chater (1994). *Psychological Review, 103*(2), 364–373.

Larkin, J., McDermott, J., Simon, D. P., & Simon, H. A. (1980). Expert and novice performance in solving physics problems. *Science, 208*(4450), 1335–1342.

Larrick, R. P. (1993). Motivational factors in decision theories: The role of self-protection. *Psychological Bulletin, 113*(3), 440–450.

Le Bihan, D., Turner, R., Zeffiro, T. A., Cuenod, C. A., Jezzard, P., & Bonnerot, V. (1993). Activation of human primary visual cortex during visual recall: A magnetic resonance imaging study. *Proceedings of the National Academy of Sciences of the United States of America, 90*, 11802–11805.

Leake, D. B. (1998). Case-based reasoning. In W. Bechtel & G. Graham (Eds.), *A companion to cognitive science.* Malden, MA: Blackwell.

Lee-Sammons, W. H., & Whitney, P. (1991). Reading perspectives and memory for text: An individual differences analysis. *Journal of Experimental Psychology: Learning, Memory, and Cognition, 17*(6), 1074–1081.

LeFevre, J.-A., & Dixon, P. (1986). Do written instructions need examples? *Cognition & Instruction, 3*(1), 1–30.

Leopold, R. L., & Dillon, H. (1963). Psycho-anatomy of a disaster: A long term study of post-traumatic neuroses in survivors of a marine explosion. *American Journal of Psychiatry, 119*, 913–921.

Lesgold, A. M. (1984). Acquiring expertise. In J. R. Anderson & S. M. Kosslyn (Eds.), *Tutorials in learning and memory: Essays in in honor of Gordon Bower.* New York: Freeman.

Levine, D. N., Warach, J., & Farah, M. J. (1985). Two visual systems in mental imagery: Dissociation of "what" and "where" in imagery disorders due to bilateral posterior cerebral lesions. *Neurology, 35*(7), 1010–1018.

Levy, W. B. (1996). A sequence predicting CA3 is a flexible associator that learns and uses context to solve hippocampal-like tasks. *Hippocampus, 6*(6), 579–590.

Lewandowsky, S., & Li, S.-C. (1995). Catastrophic interference in neural networks: Causes, solutions, and data. In F. N. Dempster & C. J. Brainerd (Ed.), *Interference and inhibition in cognition* (pp. 329–361). San Diego: Academic Press.

Lewis, C., & Keren, G. (1999). On the difficulties underlying Bayesian reasoning: A comment on Gigerenzer and Hoffrage. *Psychological Review, 106*(2), 411–416.

Lezak, M. D. (1995). *Neuropsychological assessment.* New York: Oxford University Press.

Liberman, A. M., Cooper, F. S., & Shankweiler, D. P. (1967). *Human performance in low signal tasks.* Ann Arbor, MI: University of Michigan.

Liberman, A. M., Harris, K. S., Hoffman, H. S., & Griffith, B. C. (1957). The discrimination of speech sounds within and across phoneme boundaries. *Journal of Experimental Psychology, 54*, 358–368.

Liberman, A. M., & Mattingly, I. G. (1985). The motor theory of speech perception revised. *Cognition, 21*(1), 1–36.

Light, L. L., & Carter-Sobell, L. (1970). Effects of changed semantic context on recognition memory. *Journal of Verbal Learning and Verbal Behavior, 9*, 1–11.

Loftus, E. F., & Loftus, G. R. (1980). On the permanence of stored information in the human brain. *American Psychologist, 35*(5), 409–420.

Loftus, G. R. (1983). The continuing persistence of the icon. *Behavioral and Brain Sciences, 6*, 28.

Logan, G. D. (1988). Toward an instance theory of automatization. *Psychological Review, 95*(4), 492–527.

Logie, R. H., Gilhooly, K. J., & Wynn, V. (1994). Counting on working memory in arithmetic problem solving. *Memory & Cognition, 22*(4), 395–410.

Lopes, L. A. (1991). The rhetoric of irrationality. *Theory & Psychology, 1*(1), 65–82.

Lotze, M., Montoya, P., Erb, M., Huelsmann, E., Flor, H., Klose, U., Birbaumer, N., & Grodd, W. (1999). Activation of cortical and cerebellar motor areas during executed and imagined hand movements: An fMRI study. *Journal of Cognitive Neuroscience, 11*(5), 491–501.

Lu, Z. L., Williamson, S. J., & Kaufman, L. (1992). Behavioral lifetime of human auditory sensory memory predicted by physiological measures. *Science, 258*(5088), 1668–1670.

Luchins, A. S. (1942). Mechanization in problem solving: The effect of Einstellung. *Psychological Monographs*(6), 95.

Lynn, S. J., Lock, T. G., Myers, B., & Payne, D. G. (1997). Recalling the unrecallable: Should hypnosis be used to recover memories in psychotherapy? *Current Directions in Psychological Science, 6*, 79–83.

Lytle, R. A., & Lundy, R. M. (1988). Hypnosis and the recall of visually presented material: A failure to replicate Stager and Lundy. *International Journal of Clinical and Experimental Hypnosis, 36*, 327, 335.

MacDonald, J., & McGurk, H. (1978). Visual influences on speech perception processes. *Perception and Psychophysics, 24*(3), 253–257.

MacDonald, M. C., Just, M. A., & Carpenter, P. A. (1992). Working memory constraints on the processing of syntactic ambiguity. *Cognitive Psychology, 24*(1), 56–98.

MacDonald, M. C., Pearlmutter, N. J., & Seidenberg, M. S. (1994). The lexical nature of syntactic ambiguity resolution. *Psychological Review, 101*(4), 676–703.

Maltz, W., & Holman, B. (1986). *Incest and sexuality: A guide to understanding and healing.* New York: Free Press.

Manktelow, K. I., & Evans, J. S. (1979). Facilitation of reasoning by realism: Effect or non-effect? *British Journal of Psychology, 70*(4), 477–488.

Manktelow, K. I., & Over, D. E. (1990). Deontic thought and the selection task. In K. Gilhooly, M. Keane, R. Logie, & G. Erdos (Eds.), *Lines of thinking: Reflections on the psychology of thought* (Vol. 1). Chichester, UK: Wiley.

Manktelow, K. I., & Over, D. E. (1991). Social roles and utilities in reasoning with deontic conditionals. *Cognition, 39*(2), 85–105.

Marbe, K. (1901). *Experimentelle Untersuchungen uber die psycholgischen Grundlagen der sprachlicihen Analogiebildung.* Leipzig: Engellmann.

Maren, S., & Fanselow, M. S. (1996). The amygdala and fear conditioning: Has the nut been cracked? *Neuron, 16*, 237–240.

Mark, L. S. (1987). Eyeheight-scaled information about affordances: A study of sitting and stair climbing. *Journal of Experimental Psychology: Human Perception and Performance, 13*(3), 361–370.

Markman, A. B., & Dietrich, E. (2000). In defense of representation. *Cognitive Psychology, 40*, 138–171.

Marr, D. (1971). Simple memory: A theory for archicortex. *Philosophical Transactions of the Royal Society of London, Series B, 262*, 23–81.

Marr, D. (1982). *Vision.* San Francisco: W.H. Freeman.

Marshall, J. C. (1984). Toward a ratinal taxonomy of the developmental dyslexias. In R. N. Malatesha & H. A. Whitaker (Eds.), *Dyslexia: A global issue.* Dordrecht, the Netherlands: Martinus Nijhoff.

Marshall, J. C., & Newcombe, F. (1973). Patterns of paralexia: A psycholinguistic approach. *Journal of Psycholinguistic Research, 2*(3), 175–199.

Marslen-Wilson, W., Moss, H. E., & van Halen, S. (1996). Perceptual distance and competition in lexical access. *Journal of Experimental Psychology: Human Perception and Performance, 22*(6), 1376–1392.

Marslen-Wilson, W., & Warren, P. (1994). Levels of perceptual representation and process in lexical access: Words, phonemes, and features. *Psychological Review, 101*(4), 653–675.

Marslen-Wilson, W., & Zwitserlood, P. (1989). Accessing spoken words: The importance of word onsets. *Journal of Experimental Psychology: Human Perception and Performance, 15*(3), 576–585.

Marslen-Wilson, W. D. (1987). Functional parallelism in spoken word-recognition. *Cognition, 25*(1–2), 71–102.

Martin, A., Haxby, J. V., Lalonde, F. M., Wiggs, C. L., & Ungerleider, L. G. (1995). Discrete cortical regions associated with knowledge of color and knowledge of action. *Science, 270*(5233), 102–105.

Martin, A., Ungerleider, L. G., & Haxby, J. V. (2000). Category specificity and the brain. In M. S. Gazzaniga (Ed.), *The new cognitive neurosciences* (2nd ed., pp. 1023–1036). Cambridge, MA: MIT Press.

Martin, L. (1986). "Eskimo words for snow": A case study in the genesis and decay of an anthropological example. *American Anthropologist, 88*(2), 418–423.

Martin, T. A., Keating, J. G., Goodkin, H. P., Bastian, A. J., & Thach, W. T. (1996). Throwing while looking through prisms: I. Focal olivocerebellar lesions impair adaptation. *Brain, 119,* 1183–1198.

Massaro, D. W. (1970). Preperceptual auditory images. *Journal of Experimental Psychology, 85*(3), 411–417.

Massaro, D. W. (1989). Testing between the TRACE model and the fuzzy logical model of speech perception. *Cognitive Psychology, 21*(3), 398–421.

Massaro, D. W., & Loftus, G. R. (1996). Sensory and perceptual storage: Data and theory. In E. L. Bjork & R. A. Bjork (Eds.), *Memory. Handbook of perception and cognition* (2nd ed., pp. 67–99). San Diego: Academic Press.

Massaro, D. W., & Oden, G. C. (1995). Independence of lexical context and phonological information in speech perception. *Journal of Experimental Psychology: Learning, Memory, and Cognition, 21*(4), 1053–1064.

Mayes, A. R., Meudell, P., & Neary, D. (1980). Do amnesics adopt inefficient encoding strategies with faces and random shapes? *Neuropsychologia, 18*(Suppl. 4, 5), 527–540.

McBeath, M. K., Shaffer, D. M., & Kaiser, M. K. (1995). How baseball outfielders determine where to run to catch fly balls. *Science, 268*(5210), 569–573.

McCarthy, R. A., & Warrington, E. K. (1986). Phonological reading: Phenomena and paradoxes. *Cortex, 22*(3), 359–380.

McClelland, J. L. (1981). *Retrieving general and specific knowledge from stored knowledge of specifics.* Paper presented at the Third Annual Conference of the Cognitive Science Society, Berkeley, CA.

McClelland, J. L., & Elman, J. L. (1986). The TRACE model of speech perception. *Cognitive Psychology, 18*(1), 1–86.

McClelland, J. L., McNaughton, B. L., & O'Reilly, R. C. (1995). Why there are complementary learning systems in the hippocampus and neocortex: Insights from the successes and failures of connectionist models of learning and memory. *Psychological Review, 102*(3), 419–437.

McClelland, J. L., & Rumelhart, D. E. (1981). An interactive activation model of context effects in letter perception: I. An account of basic findings. *Psychological Review, 88*(5), 375–407.

McCloskey, M., & Cohen, N. J. (1989). Catastrphic interference in connectionist networks: The sequential learning problem. In G. H. Bower (Ed.), *The psychology of learning and motivation: Advances in research and theory, 24* (pp. 109–165). San Diego: Academic Press.

McCloskey, M., Wible, C. G., & Cohen, N. J. (1988). Is there a special flashbulb-memory mechanism? *Journal of Experimental Psychology: General, 117*(2), 171–181.

McConkey, K. M., Labelle, L., Bibb, B. C., & Bryant, R. A. (1990). Hypnosis and suggested pseudomemory: The relevance of test context. *Australian Journal of Psychology, 42,* 197–205.

McConnell, A. R., Sherman, S. J., & Hamilton, D. L. (1994). Illusory correlation in the perception of groups: An extension of the distinctiveness-based account. *Journal of Personality & Social Psychology, 67*(3), 414–429.

McDaniel, M. A., Einstein, G. O., DeLosh, E. L., May, C. P., & Brady, P. (1995). The bizarreness effect: It's not surprising, it's complex. *Journal of Experimental Psychology: Learning, Memory, and Cognition, 21*(2), 422–435.

McGurk, H., & MacDonald, J. (1976). Hearing lips and seeing voices. *Nature, 264,* 746–748.

McKoon, G., & Ratcliff, R. (1992). Inference during reading. *Psychological Review, 99*(3), 440–466.

McKoon, G., & Ratcliff, R. (1998). Memory-based language processing: Psycholinguistic research in the 1990s. *Annual Review of Psychology, 49,* 25–42.

McKoon, G., Ratcliff, R., & Dell, G. S. (1986). A critical evaluation of the semantic–episodic distinction. *Journal of Experimental Psychology: Learning, Memory, and Cognition, 12*(2), 295–306.

McNamara, T. P. (1992). Priming and constraints it places on theories of memory and retrieval. *Psychological Review, 99*(4), 650–662.

McNamara, T. P. (1994). Priming and theories of memory: A reply to Ratcliff and McKoon. *Psychological Review, 101*(1), 185–187.

McNamara, T. P., & Healy, A. F. (1988). Semantic, phonological, and mediated priming in reading and lexical decisions. *Journal of Experimental Psychology: Learning, Memory, and Cognition, 14*(3), 398–409.

McNeil, J. E., & Warrington, E. K. (1993). Prosopagnosia: A face-specific disorder. *Quarterly Journal of Experimental Psychology: Human Experimental Psychology, 46A*(1), 1–10.

Medin, D. L., & Schaffer, M. M. (1978). Context theory of classification learning. *Psychological Review, 85,* 207–238.

Mellet, E., Tzourio, N., Denis, M., & Mazoyer, B. (1995). A positron emission tomography study of visual and mental spatial exploration. *Journal of Cognitive Neuroscience, 7*(4), 433–445.

Mellet, E., Tzourio, N., Denis, M., & Mazoyer, B. (1998). Cortical anatomy of mental imagery of concrete nouns based on their dictionary definition. *Neuroreport: An International Journal for the Rapid Communication of Research in Neuroscience, 9*(5), 803–808.

Melton, A. W., & Irwin, J. M. (1940). The influence of degree of interpolated learning on retroactive inhibition and the overt transfer of specific responses. *American Journal of Psychology, 53,* 173–203.

Merikle, P. M. (1980). Selection from visual persistence by perceptual groups and category membership. *Journal of Experimental Psychology: General, 109*(3), 279–295.

Metcalfe, J. (1986a). Feeling of knowing in memory and problem solving. *Journal of Experimental Psychology: Learning, Memory, and Cognition, 12*(2), 288–294.

Metcalfe, J. (1986b). Premonitions of insight predict impending error. *Journal of Experimental Psychology: Learning, Memory, and Cognition, 12*(4), 623–634.

Metcalfe, J., & Wiebe, D. (1987). Intuition in insight and non-insight problem solving. *Memory & Cognition, 15*(3), 238–246.

Meyer, D. E., & Schvaneveldt, R. W. (1971). Facilitation in recognizing pairs of words: Evidence of a dependence between retrieval operations. *Journal of Experimental Psychology, 90*(2), 227–234.

Miller, G. A. (1956). The magical number seven, plus or minus two: Some limits on our capacity for processing information. *Psychological Review, 63,* 81–97.

Millis, K. K., & Just, M. A. (1994). The influence of connectives on sentence comprehension. *Journal of Memory & Language, 33*(1), 128–147.

Milner, B. (1971). Interhemispheric differences in the localization of psychological processes in man. *British Medical Bulletin, 27,* 272–277.

Mitchell, D. B., & Richman, C. L. (1980). Confirmed reservations: Mental travel. *Journal of Experimental Psychology: Human Perception and Performance, 6*(1), 58–66.

Mitchell, D. C., Corley, M. M., & Garnham, A. (1992). Effects of context in human sentence parsing: Evidence against a discourse-based proposal mechanism. *Journal of Experimental Psychology: Learning, Memory, and Cognition, 18*(1), 69–88.

Miura, I. T. (1987). Mathematics achievement as a function of language. *Journal of Educational Psychology, 79*(1), 79–82.

Miura, I. T., Kim, C. C., Chang, C.-M., & Okamoto, Y. (1988). Effects of language characteristics on children's cognitive representation of number: Cross-national comparisons. *Child Development, 59*(6), 1445–1450.

Miura, I. T., & Okamoto, Y. (1989). Comparisons of U.S. and Japanese first graders' cognitive representation of number and understanding of place value. *Journal of Educational Psychology, 81*(1), 109–114.

Miura, I. T., Okamoto, Y., Kim, C. C., Chang, C.-M., Steere, M., & Fayol, M. (1994). Comparisons of children's cognitive representation of number: China, France, Japan, Korea, Sweden, and the United States. *International Journal of Behavioral Development, 17*(3), 401–411.

Miura, I. T., Okamoto, Y., Kim, C. C., Steere, M. et al. (1993). First graders' cognitive representation of number and understanding of place value: Cross-national comparisons: France, Japan, Korea, Sweden, and the United States. *Journal of Educational Psychology, 85*(1), 24–30.

Miyake, A., Carpenter, P. A., & Just, M. A. (1994). A capacity approach to syntactic comprehension disorders: Making normal adults perform like aphasic patients. *Cognitive Neuropsychology, 11*(6), 671–717.

Monsaas, J. A. (1985). Learning to be a world-class tennis player. In B. S. Bloom (Ed.), *Developing talent in young people* (pp. 211–269). New York: Ballantine.

Moody, D. B., Stebbins, W. C., & May, B. J. (1990). Auditory perception of communication signals by Japanese monkeys. In W. C. Stebbins & M. A. Berkley (Eds.), *Comparative perception* (Vol. 2, pp. 311–343). New York: Wiley.

Moray, N. (1959). Attention in dichotic listening: Affective cues and the influence of instructions. *Quarterly Journal of Experimental Psychology, 11,* 56–60.

Moray, N. (1967). Where is capacity limited? A survey and a model. *Acta Psychologica, 27,* 84–92.

Morris, C. D., Bransford, J. D., & Franks, J. J. (1977). Levels of processing versus transfer appropriate processing. *Journal of Verbal Learning & Verbal Behavior, 16*(5), 519–533.

Morton, J. (1969). Interaction of information in word recognition. *Psychological Review, 76*(2), 165–178.

Munger, M. P., Solberg, J. L, & Horrocks, K. K. (1999). The relation between mental rotation and representational momentum. *Journal of Experimental Psychology: Learning, Memory, and Cognition, 25,* 1557–1568.

Murdock, B. B. (1974). *Human memory: Theory and data.* Mahwah, NJ: Erlbaum.

Naigles, L. R., & Terrazas, P. (1998). Motion-verb generalizations in English and Spanish: Influences of language and syntax. *Psychological Science, 9,* 363–369.

Navon, D., & Gopher, D. (1979). On the economy of the human-processing system. *Psychological Review, 86*(3), 214–255.

Neath, I., Surprenant, A. M., & Crowder, R. G. (1993). The context-dependent stimulus suffix effect. *Journal of Experimental Psychology: Learning, Memory, and Cognition, 19*(3), 698–703.

Neisser, U. (1967). *Cognitive psychology.* New York: Appleton-Century-Crofts.

Neisser, U. (1972). Changing conceptions of imagery. In P. W. Sheehan (Ed.), *The function and nature of Imagery.* New York: Academic Press.

Neisser, U. (1984). Interpreting Harry Bahrick's discovery: What confers immunity against forgetting? *Journal of Experimental Psychology: General, 113*(1), 32–35.

Neisser, U., & Becklen, R. (1975). Selective looking: Attending to visually specified events. *Cognitive Psychology, 7*(4), 480–494.

Nelson, K. (1974). Concept, word, and sentence: Interrelations in acquisition and development. *Psychological Review, 81*(4), 267–285.

Nelson, T. O. (1978). Detecting small amounts of information in memory: Savings for nonrecognized items. *Journal of Experimental Psychology: Human Learning & Memory, 4*(5), 453–468.

Newell, A. (1990). *Unified theories of cognition.* Cambridge, MA: Harvard University Press.

Newell, A., & Simon, H. A. (1956). The logic theory machine: A complex information processing system. *IRE Transactions on Information Theory, IT-2,* 61–79.

Newell, A., & Simon, H. A. (1972). *Human problem solving.* Englewood Cliffs, NJ: Prentice Hall.

Newell, A., Shaw, J. C., & Simon, H. A. (1962). The process of creative thinking. In H. E. Gruber, G. Terell, & M. Wertheimer (Eds.), *Contemporary approaches to creative thinking.* New York: Atherton.

Newell, A. M., & Rosenbloom, P. S. (1981). Mechanisms of skill acquisition and the law of practice. In J. R. Anderson (Ed.), *Cognitive skills and their acquisition* (pp. 1–55). Mahwah, NJ: Erlbaum.

Newstead, S. E., & Griggs, R. A. (1983). Drawing inferences from quantified statements: A study of the square of opposition.

Journal of Verbal Learning & Verbal Behavior, 22(5), 535–546.

Newstead, S. E., Pollard, P., & Evans, J. S. (1992). The source of belief bias effects in syllogistic reasoning. *Cognition, 45*(3), 257–284.

Nickerson, R. S., & Adams, M. J. (1979). Long-term memory for a common object. *Cognitive Psychology, 11*(3), 287–307.

Nisbett, R. E., & Ross, L. (1980). *Human inference: Strategies and shortcomings of human judgment.* Englewood Cliffs, NJ: Prentice Hall.

Nisbett, R. E., & Wilson, T. D. (1977). Telling more than we can know: Verbal reports on mental processes. *Psychological Review, 84*(3), 231–259.

Nissen, M. J., & Bullemer, P. (1987). Attentional requirements of learning: Evidence from performance measures. *Cognitive Psychology, 19*, 1–32.

Noordman, L. G., Vonk, W., & Kempff, H. J. (1992). Causal inferences during the reading of expository texts. *Journal of Memory & Language, 31*(5), 573–590.

Norman, D. (1970). Introduction: Models of human memory. In D. Norman (Ed.), *Models of human memory* (pp. 1–15). New York: Academic Press.

Norman, D. A. (1968). Toward a theory of memory and attention. *Psychological Review, 75*(6), 522–536.

Norman, D. A. (1981). Categorization of action slips. *Psychological Review, 88*(1), 1–15.

Norman, D. A., & Bobrow, D. G. (1975). On data-limited and resource-limited processes. *Cognitive Psychology, 7*(1), 44–64.

Norman, D. A., & Shallice, T. (1986). Attention to action: Willed and automatic control of behavior. In R. J. Davidson, G. E. Schwarts, & D. Shapiro (Eds.), *Consciousness and self-regulation. Advances in research and theory* (Vol. 4, pp. 1–18). New York: Plenum.

Nosofsky, R. M., Kruschke, J. K., & McKinley, S. C. (1992). Combining exemplar-based category representations and connectionist learning rules. *Journal of Experimental Psychology: Learning, Memory, and Cognition, 18*(2), 211–233.

Novick, L. R., & Holyoak, K. J. (1991). Mathematical problem solving by analogy. *Journal of Experimental Psychology: Learning, Memory, and Cognition, 17*(3), 398–415.

Oakhill, J. V., & Johnson-Laird, P. N. (1985). The effects of belief on the spontaneous production of syllogistic conclusions. *Quarterly Journal of Experimental Psychology: Human Experimental Psychology, 37A*(4), 553–569.

Oakhill, J., Johnson-Laird, P. N., & Garnham, A. (1989). Believability and syllogistic reasoning. *Cognition, 31*(2), 117–140.

Oaksford, M., & Chater, N. (1996). Rational explanation of the selection task. *Psychological Review, 103*(2), 381–391.

Oberauer, K., Wilhelm, O., & Diaz, R. R. (1999). Bayesian rationality for the Wason selection task? A test of optimal data selection theory. *Thinking & Reasoning, 5*(2), 115–144.

Oberly, H. S. (1924). The range for visual attention, cognition and apprehension. *American Journal of Psychology, 35*, 332–352.

O'Brien, E. J., & Albrecht, J. E. (1992). Comprehension strategies in the development of a mental model. *Journal of Experimental Psychology: Learning, Memory, and Cognition, 18*(4), 777–784.

O'Craven, K. M., Downing, P. E., & Kanwisher, N. (1999). fMRI evidence for objects as the units of attentional selection. *Nature, 401*(6753), 584–587.

O'Keefe, J., & Nadel, L. (1978). *The hippocampus and the cognitive map.* Oxford, UK: Oxford University Press.

Okoh, N. (1980). Bilingualism and divergent thinking among Nigerian and Welsh school children. *Journal of Social Psychology, 110*(2), 163–170.

Osherson, D., Perani, D., Cappa, S., Schnur, T., Grassi, F., & Fazio, F. (1998). Distinct brain loci in deductive versus probabilistic reasoning. *Neuropsychologia, 36*(4), 369–376.

Osman, A., & Moore, C. M. (1993). The locus of dual-task interference: Psychological refractory effects on movement-related brain potentials. *Journal of Experimental Psychology: Human Perception and Performance, 19*(6), 1292–1312.

Owen, A. M. (1997). Cognitive planning humans: Neuropsychological, neuroanatomical and neuropharmacological perspecives. *Progress in Neurobiology, 53*, 431–450.

Paap, K. R., & Noel, R. W. (1991). Dual-route models of print to sound: Still a good horse race. *Psychological Research, 53*(1), 13–24.

Paillard, J. (1991). Motor and representational framing of space. In J. Paillard (Ed.), *Brain and space* (pp. 163–182). Oxford, UK: Oxford University Press.

Paivio, A. (1963). Learning of adjective–noun paired associates as a function of adjective–noun word order and noun abstractness. *Canadian Journal of Psychology, 17*(4), 370–379.

Paivio, A. (1965). Abstractness, imagery, and meaningfulness in paired-associate learning. *Journal of Verbal Learning & Verbal Behavior, 4*(1), 32–38.

Paivio, A. (1971). *Imagery and verbal processes.* New York: Holt, Rinehart & Winston.

Paivio, A. (1975). Imagery and synchronic thinking. *Canadian Psychological Review, 16*(3), 147–163.

Paivio, A. (1986). *Mental representations.* Oxford, UK: Oxford University Press.

Paivio, A. (1991). *Images in mind: The evolution of a theory.* London: Harvester Wheatsheaf.

Paivio, A., & Foth, D. (1970). Imaginal and verbal mediators and noun concreteness in paired-associate learning: The elusive interaction. *Journal of Verbal Learning & Verbal Behavior, 9*(4), 384–390.

Paivio, A., Smythe, P. C., & Yuille, J. C. (1968). Imagery versus meaningfulness of nouns in paired-associate learning. *Canadian Journal of Psychology, 22*(6), 427–441.

Palm, K. M., & Gibson, P. (1998). Recovered memories of childhood sexual abuse: Clinicians' practices and beliefs. *Professional Psychology—Research & Practice, 29*, 257–261.

Palmer, S. E. (1975). The effects of contextual scenes on the identification of objects. *Memory & Cognition, 3*, 519–526.

Parasuraman, R., & Davies, D. R. (1977). A taxonomic analysis of vigilance perfromance. In R. R. Mackie (Ed.), *Vigilance: Theory, operational performance, and physiological correlates* (pp. 559–574). New York: Plenum.

Parsons, L. M. (1987a). Imagined spatial transformation of one's body. *Journal of Experimental Psychology: General, 116*(2), 172–191.

Parsons, L. M. (1987b). Imagined spatial transformations of one's hands and feet. *Cognitive Psychology, 19*(2), 178–241.

Pashler, H. (1988). Cross-dimensional interaction and texture segregation. *Perception and Psychophysics, 43*(4), 307–318.

Pashler, H. E. (1998). *The psychology of attention.* Cambridge, MA: MIT Press.

Pashler, H., Carrier, M., & Hoffman, J. (1993). Saccadic eye movements and dual-task interference. *Quarterly Journal of Experimental Psychology: Human Experimental Psychology, 46A*(1), 51–82.

Pastore, R. E., Li, X.-F., & Layer, J. K. (1990). Categorical perception of nonspeech chirps and bleats. *Perception and Psychophysics, 48*(2), 151–156.

Patel, V. L., & Groen, G. J. (1991). The general and specific nature of medical expertise: A critical look. In K. A. Ericsson & J. Smith (Eds.), *Toward a general theory of expertise* (pp. 93–125). Cambridge, UK: Cambridge University Press.

Patterson, F. G. (1978). The gesture of a gorilla: Language acquisition in another pongid. *Brain & Language, 5*(1), 72–97.

Patterson, F. G. (1981). Can an ape create a sentence? Some affirmative evidence. *Science, 211*(86–87).

Paulesu, E., Frith, C. D., & Frackowiak, R. S. (1993). The neural correlates of the verbal component of working memory. *Nature, 362*(6418), 342–345.

Pavlides, C., Miyashita, E., & Asanuma, H. (1993). Projection from the sensory to the motor cortex is important in learning motor skills in the monkey. *Journal of Neurophysiology, 70,* 733–741.

Penfield, W. (1959). *Speech and brain mechanisms.* Princeton, NJ: Princeton University Press.

Perkins, D. N. (1972). Visual discrimination between rectangular and nonrectangular parallelopipeds. *Perception and Psychophysics, 12*(5), 396–400.

Petersen, S. E., Fox, P. T., Posner, M. I., Mintun, M., & Raichle, M. E. (1988). Positron emission tomographic studies of the cortical anatomy of single-word processing. *Nature, 331*(6157), 585–589.

Peterson, L., & Peterson, M. J. (1959). Short-term retention of individual verbal items. *Journal of Experimental Psychology, 58,* 193–198.

Phelps, R. M., & Shanteau, J. (1978). Livestock judges: How much information can an expert use? *Organizational Behavior and Human Performance, 21,* 209–219.

Phillips, L. H., Wynn, V., Gilhooly, K. J., Della Sala, S., & Logie, R. H. (1999). The role of memory in the Tower of London task. *Memory, 7*(2), 209–231.

Piatelli-Palmarini, M. (1994). *Inevitable illusions: How mistakes of reason rule our minds.* New York: Wiley.

Pinker, S. (1994). *The language instinct.* New York: William Morrow.

Pinker, S., & Prince, A. (1988). On language and connectionism: Analysis of a parallel distributed processing model of language acquisition. *Cognition, 28*(1–2), 73–193.

Plous, S. (1989). Thinking the unthinkable: The effects of anchoring on likelihood estimates of nuclear war. *Journal of Applied Social Psychology, 19*(1), 67–91.

Podgorny, P., & Shepard, R. N. (1978). Functional representations common to visual perception and imagination. *Journal of Experimental Psychology: Human Perception and Performance, 4*(1), 21–35.

Polk, T. A., & Newell, A. (1995). Deduction as verbal reasoning. *Psychological Review, 102*(3), 533–566.

Pomerantz, J. R., & Kubovy, M. (1986). Theoretical approaches to perceptual organization: Simplicity and likelihood principles. In K. R. Boff & L. Kaufman (Eds.), *Handbook of perception and human performance* (Vol. 2, pp. 1–46). New York: Wiley.

Posner, M. I., Goldsmith, R., & Welton, K. E., Jr. (1967). Perceived distance and the classification of distorted patterns. *Journal of Experimental Psychology, 73*(1), 28–38.

Posner, M. I., & Keele, S. W. (1968). On the genesis of abstract ideas. *Journal of Experimental Psychology, 77*(3, Pt. 1), 353–363.

Posner, M. I., & Keele, S. W. (1970). Retention of abstract ideas. *Journal of Experimental Psychology, 83*(2, Pt. 1), 304–308.

Posner, M. I., & Snyder, C. R. (1975). Attention and cognitive control. In R. L. Solso (Ed.), *Information processing and cognition: The Loyola symposium.* Mahwah, NJ: Erlbaum.

Posner, M. I., Snyder, C. R., & Davidson, B. J. (1980). Attention and the detection of signals. *Journal of Experimental Psychology: General, 109*(2), 160–174.

Prabhakaran, V., Smith, J. A. L., Desmond, J. E., Glover, G. H., & Gabrieli, J. D. (1997). Neural substrates of fluid reasoning: An fMRI study of neocortical activation during performance of the Raven's Progressive Matrices Test. *Cognitive Psychology, 33*(1), 43–63.

Premack, D. (1971). Language in chimpanzee? *Science, 172*(3985), 808–822.

Premack, D. (1976a). *Intelligence in ape and man.* Mahwah, NJ: Erlbaum.

Premack, D. (1976b). Language and intelligence in ape and man. *American Scientist, 64*(6), 674–683.

Priest, A. G., & Lindsay, R. O. (1992). New light on novice–expert differences in physics problem solving. *British Journal of Psychology, 83*(3), 389–405.

Proffitt, D. R., Bhalla, M., Gossweiler, R., & Midgett, J. (1995). Perceiving geographical slant. *Psychonomic Bulletin & Review, 2*(4), 409–428.

Pylyshyn, Z. W. (1973). What the mind's eye tells the mind's brain: A critique of mental imagery. *Psychological Bulletin, 80*(1), 1–24.

Pylyshyn, Z. W. (1981). The imagery debate: Analogue media versus tacit knowledge. *Psychological Review, 88*(1), 16–45.

Pynoos, R. S., & Nader, K. (1989). Children's memories and proximity to violence. *Journal of the American Academy of Child and Adolescent Psychiatry, 28,* 236–241.

Ratcliff, R., & McKoon, G. (1988). A retrieval theory of priming in memory. *Psychological Review, 95*(3), 385–408.

Ratcliff, R., & McKoon, G. (1994). Retrieving information from memory: Spreading-activation theories versus compound-cue theories. *Psychological Review, 101*(1), 177–184.

Rauch, S. L., Savage, C. R., Brown, H. D., Curran, T., Alpert, N. M., Kendrick, A., Fischman, A. J., & Kosslyn, S. M. (1995). A PET investigation of implicit and explicit sequence learning. *Human Brain Mapping, 3*(4), 271–286.

Raven, J. C. (1976). *Standard progressive matrices: Sets A, B, C, D & E.* Oxford, UK: Oxford University Press.

Rayner, K., Carlson, M., & Frazier, L. (1983). The interaction of syntax and semantics during sentence processing: Eye movements in the analysis of semantically biased sentences. *Journal of Verbal Learning & Verbal Behavior, 22*(3), 358–374.

Rayner, K., Garrod, S., & Perfetti, C. A. (1992). Discourse influences during parsing are delayed. *Cognition, 45*(2), 109–139.

Rayner, K., & Pollatsek, A. (1983). Is visual information integrated across saccades? *Perception and Psychophysics, 34*(1), 39–48.

Reber, A. S. (1999). *The new gambler's Bible.* New York: Crown.

Reber, P. J., & Kotovsky, K. (1997). Implicit learning in problem solving: The role of working memory capacity. *Journal of Experimental Psychology: General, 126*(2), 178–203.

Reder, L. M. (1982). Plausibility judgments versus fact retrieval: Alternative strategies for sentence verification. *Psychological Review, 89*(3), 250–280.

Reed, S. K. (1974). Structural descriptions and the limitations of visual images. *Memory & Cognition, 2*(2), 329–336.

Reed, S. K., Ackinclose, C. C., & Voss, A. A. (1990). Selecting analogous problems: Similarity versus inclusiveness. *Memory & Cognition, 18*(1), 83–98.

Reed, S. K., & Bolstad, C. A. (1991). Use of examples and procedures in problem solving. *Journal of Experimental Psychology: Learning, Memory, and Cognition, 17*(4), 753–766.

Register, P. A., & Kihlstrom, J. F. (1987). Hypnotic effects on hypermnesia. *International Journal of Clinical and Experimental Hypnosis, 35,* 155–170.

Reich, S. S., & Ruth, P. (1982). Wason's selection task: Verification, falsification and matching. *British Journal of Psychology, 73*(3), 395–405.

Reisberg, D. (Ed.). (1992). *Auditory imagery.* Mahwah, NJ: Erlbaum.

Reitman, J. S. (1971). Mechanisms of forgetting in short-term memory. *Cognitive Psychology, 2*(2), 185–195.

Revlis, R. (1975). Two models of syllogistic reasoning: Feature selection and conversion. *Journal of Verbal Learning & Verbal Behavior, 14*(2), 180–195.

Richardson-Klavehn, A., & Bjork, R. A. (1988). Measures of memory. *Annual Review of Psychology, 39,* 475–543.

Richman, C. L., Mitchell, D. B., & Reznick, J. S. (1979). Mental travel: Some reservations. *Journal of Experimental Psychology: Human Perception and Performance, 5*(1), 13–18.

Rips, L. J. (1975). Inductive judgments about natural categories. *Journal of Verbal Learning & Verbal Behavior, 14*(6), 665–681.

Rips, L. J. (1989). Similarity, typicality, and categorization. In S. O. A. Vosniadou (Ed.), *Similarity and analogical reasoning* (pp. 21–59). New York: Cambridge University Press.

Rips, L. J. (1994). *The psychology of proof: Deductive reasoning in human thinking.* Cambridge, MA: MIT Press.

Rips, L. J., Shoben, E. J., & Smith, E. E. (1973). Semantic distance and the verification of semantic relations. *Journal of Verbal Learning & Verbal Behavior, 12*(1), 1–20.

Rist, R. S. (1989). Schema creation in programming. *Cognitive Science, 13*(3), 389–414.

Robins, S., & Mayer, R. E. (1993). Schema training in analogical reasoning. *Journal of Educational Psychology, 85*(3), 529–538.

Roediger, H. L. III, Wheeler, A., & Rajaram, S. Remembering, knowing, and reconstructing the past. In D. L. Medin (Ed.), *The psychology of learning and motivation: Advances in research and theory, 30* (pp. 97–134).

Rogers, S. (1996). The horizon-ratio relation as information for relative size in pictures. *Perception and Psychophysics, 58*(1), 142–152.

Roland, P. E., Eriksson, L., Stone-Elander, S., & Widen, L. (1987). Does mental activity change the oxidative metabolism of the brain? *Journal of Neuroscience, 7,* 2373–2389.

Rosch, E. H. (1973). On the internal structure of perceptual and semantic categories. In T. E. Moore (Ed.), *Cognitive development and the acquisition of language* (pp. 111–144). New York: Academic Press.

Rosch, E., Mervis, C. B., Gray, W. D., Johnson, D. M., & Boyes-Braem, P. (1976). Basic objects in natural categories. *Cognitive Psychology, 8*(3), 382–439.

Rosch, E., & Mervis, C. B. (1975). Family resemblances: Studies in the internal structure of categories. *Cognitive Psychology, 7*(4), 573–605.

Rosenthal, R. (1976). *Experimenter effects in behavioral research.* (Enlarged ed). New York: Irvington.

Rosner, S. R., & Hayes, D. S. (1977). A developmental study of category item production. *Child Development, 48*(3), 1062–1065.

Ross, B. H. (1987). This is like that: The use of earlier problems and the separation of similarity effects. *Journal of Experimental Psychology: Learning, Memory, and Cognition, 13*(4), 629–639.

Ross, B. H. (1989). Distinguishing types of superficial similarities: Different effects on the access and use of earlier problems. *Journal of Experimental Psychology: Learning, Memory, and Cognition, 15*(3), 456–468.

Ross, B. H., & Kennedy, P. T. (1990). Generalizing from the use of earlier examples in problem solving. *Journal of Experimental Psychology: Learning, Memory, and Cognition, 16*(1), 42–55.

Rubenstein, H., Lewis, S. S., & Rubenstein, M. A. (1971). Evidence for phonemic recoding in visual word recognition. *Journal of Verbal Learning & Verbal Behavior, 10*(6), 645–657.

Rubin, D. C., & Kozin, M. (1984). Vivid memories. *Cognition, 16*(1), 81–95.

Rumelhart, D. E., Hinton, G. E., & McClelland, J. L. (1986). A general framework for parallel distributed processing. In D. E. Rumelhart, J. L. McClelland, & the PDP Research Group (Eds.), *Parallel distributed processing, Volume 1: Foundations* (pp. 45–76). Cambridge, MA: MIT Press.

Rumelhart, D. E., & McClelland, J. L. (1987). Learning the past tenses of English verbs: Implicit rules or parallel distributed processing? In B. MacWhinney (Ed.), *Mechanisms of language aquisition* (pp. 195–248). Mahwah, NJ: Erlbaum.

Rundus, D., & Atkinson, R. C. (1970). Rehearsal processes in free recall: A procedure for direct observation. *Journal of Verbal Learning & Verbal Behavior, 9*(1), 99–105.

Sabbah, P., Simond, G., Levrier, O., Habib, M., Trabaud, V., Murayama, N., Mazoyer, B. M., Briant, J. F., Raybaud, C., & Salamon, G. (1995). Functional magnetic resonance imaging at 1.5 T during sensorimotor and cognitive task. *European Neurology, 35*(3), 131–136.

Sagar, H. A., & Schofield, J. W. (1980). Racial and behavioral cues in Black and White children's perceptions of ambiguously aggressive acts. *Journal of Personality & Social Psychology, 39*(4), 590–598.

Sagar, H. J., Sullivan, E. V., Gabrieli, J. D. E., Corkin, S., & Growdon, J. H. (1988). Temporal ordering and short-term memory deficits in Parkinson's disease. *Brain, 111,* 525–539.

Sagi, D., & Julesz, B. (1985). Fast noninertial shifts of attention. *Spatial Vision, 2,* 141–149.

Sakamoto, T., Arissian, K., & Asanuma, H. (1989). Functional role of the sensory cortex in learning motor skills in cats. *Brain Research, 503,* 258–264.

Salthouse, T. A. (1984). The skill of typing. *Scientific American, 250*(2), 128–135.

Salthouse, T. A. (1992). Reasoning and spatial abilities. In F. I. M. Craik & T. A. Salthouse (Eds.), *The handbook of aging and cognition* (pp. 167–211). Mahwah, NJ: Erlbaum.

Salthouse, T. A. (1993). Influence of working memory on adult age differences in matrix reasoning. *British Journal of Psychology, 84,* 171–199.

Salthouse, T. A. (1996). The processing-speed theory of adult age differences in cognition. *Psychological Review, 103,* 403–428.

Sapir, E. (1956). *Culture, language and personality.* Los Angeles: University of California Press.

Saufley, W. H., Otaka, S. R., & Bavaresco, J. L. (1985). Context effects: Classroom tests and context independence. *Memory & Cognition, 13*(6), 522–528.

Savage-Rumbaugh, E. S., Pate, J. L., Lawson, J., Smith, S. T., & Rosenbaum, S. (1983). Can a chimpanzee make a statement? *Journal of Experimental Psychology: General, 112*(4), 457–492.

Savage-Rumbaugh, E. S., Romski, M. A., Sevcik, R., & Pate, J. L. (1983). Assessing symbol usage versus symbol competency. *Journal of Experimental Psychology: General, 112*(4), 508–512.

Savage-Rumbaugh, E. S., Rumbaugh, D. M., & Boysen, S. (1978). Symbolic communication between two chimpanzees *(Pan troglodytes)*. *Science, 201*(4356), 641–644.

Savage-Rumbaugh, E. S., Rumbaugh, D. M., Smith, S. T., & Lawson, J. (1980). Reference: The linguistic essential. *Science, 210*(4472), 922–925.

Savage-Rumbaugh, S., Shanker, S. G., & Taylor, T. J. (1998). *Apes, language, and the human mind.* New York: Oxford University Press.

Saxton, M., & Towse, J. N. (1998). Linguistic relativity: The case of place value in multi-digit numbers. *Journal of Experimental Child Psychology, 69*(1), 66–79.

Schacter, D. L. (1990). Perceptual representation systems and implicit memory: Toward a resolution of the multiple memory systems debate. *Annals of the New York Academy of Sciences, 608,* 543–571.

Schacter, D. L. (1996). *Searching for memory.* New York: Basic Books.

Schacter, D. L., Chiu, C. Y. P., & Ochsner, K. N. (1993). Implicit memory: A selective review. *Annual Review of Neuroscience, 16,* 159–182.

Schacter, D. L., & Tulving, E. (1994). What are the memory systems of 1994? In D. L. Schacter & E. Tulving (Eds.), *Memory systems 1994* (pp. 1–38). Cambridge, MA: MIT Press.

Schank, R. C., & Abelson, R. P. (1977). *Scripts, plans, goals, and understanding.* Mahwah, NJ: Erlbaum.

Scheerer, M. (1963). Problem-solving. *Scientific American, 208*(4), 118–128.

Schellenberg, E. G., Iverson, P., & McKinnon, M. C. (1999). Name that tune: Identifying popular recordings from brief excerpts. *Psychonomic Bulletin & Review, 6,* 641–646.

Schmalhofer, F., & Glavanov, D. (1986). Three components of understanding a programmer's manual: Verbatim, propositional, and situational representations. *Journal of Memory & Language, 25*(3), 279–294.

Schmid, P. M., & Yeni-Komshian, G. H. (1999). The effects of speaker accent and target predictability on perception of mispronunciations. *Journal of Speech Language & Hearing Research, 42*(1), 56–64.

Schmidtke, V., & Heuer, H. (1997). Task integration as a factor in secondary-task effects on sequence learning. *Psychological Research, 60*(1–2), 53–71.

Schneider, W., & Shiffrin, R. M. (1977). Controlled and automatic human information processing: I. Detection, search, and attention. *Psychological Review, 84*(1), 1–66.

Schooler, J. W. (1994). Seeking the core: The issues and evidence surrounding recovered accounts of sexual trauma. *Consciousness & Cognition: An International Journal, 3*(3–4), 452–469.

Schooler, J. W., Bendiksen, M., & Ambadar, Z. (1997). Taking the middle line: Can we accommodate both fabricated and recovered memories of sexual abuse? In M. A. Conway (Ed.), *Recovered memories and false memories. Debates in psychology* (pp. 251–292). Oxford, UK: Oxford University Press.

Schwarz, N., Strack, F., Hilton, D. J., & Naderer, G. (1991). Base rates, representativeness, and the logic of conversation: The contextual relevance of "irrelevant" information. *Social Cognition, 9*(1), 67–84.

See, J. E., Howe, S. R., Warm, J. S., & Dember, W. N. (1995). Meta-analysis of the sensitivity decrement in vigilance. *Psychological Bulletin, 117*(2), 230–249.

Seidenberg, M. S., & McClelland, J. L. (1989). A distributed, developmental model of word recognition and naming. *Psychological Review, 96*(4), 523–568.

Seidenberg, M. S., Waters, G. S., Barnes, M. A., & Tanenhaus, M. K. (1984). When does irregular spelling or pronunciation influence word recognition? *Journal of Verbal Learning & Verbal Behavior, 23,* 383–404.

Sekuler, R., & Nash, D. (1972). Speed of size scaling in human vision. *Psychonomic Science, 27*(2), 93–94.

Shaffer, W. O., & LaBerge, D. (1979). Automatic semantic processing of unattended words. *Journal of Verbal Learning & Verbal Behavior, 18*(4), 413–426.

Shafir, E., & Tversky, A. (1995). Decision making. In E. E. Smith & D. N. Osherson (Eds.), *Thinking* (Vol. 3, pp. 77–100). Cambridge, MA: MIT Press.

Shallice, T. (1982). Specific impairments of planning. *Philosophical Transactions of the Royal Society of London, 298,* 199–209.

Shallice, T., & Evans, M. E. (1978). The involvement of the frontal lobes in cognitive estimation. *Cortex, 14*(2), 294–303.

Shanker, S. G., Savage-Rumbaugh, E. S., Taylor, T. J. (1999). Kanzi: A new beginning. *Animal Learning and Behavior, 27,* 24–25.

Shanks, D. R., & St. John, M. F. (1994). Characteristics of dissociable human learning systems. *Behavioral & Brain Sciences, 17*(3), 367–447.

Sharpe, L., & Markham, R. (1992). The effect of the distinctiveness of bizarre imagery on immediate and delayed recall. *Journal of Mental Imagery, 16*(3–4), 211–220.

Shepard, R. N. (1967). Recognition memory for words, sentences, and pictures. *Journal of Verbal Learning & Verbal Behavior, 6*(1), 156–163.

Shepard, R. N., & Chipman, S. (1970). Second-order isomorphism of internal representations: Shapes of states. *Cognitive Psychology, 1,* 1–17.

Shepard, R. N., & Cooper, L. A. (1986). *Mental images and their transformations.* Cambridge, MA: MIT Press.

Shepard, R. N., & Feng, C. (1972). A chronometric study of mental paper folding. *Cognitive Psychology, 3*(2), 228–243.

Shepard, R. N., & Metzler, J. (1971). Mental rotation of three-dimensional objects. *Science, 171*(3972), 701–703.

Sherry, D. F., & Schacter, D. L. (1987). The evolution of multiple memory systems. *Psychological Review, 94,* 439–454.

Shiffrin, R. M., & Schneider, W. (1977). Controlled and automatic human information processing: II. Perceptual learning, automatic attending and a general theory. *Psychological Review, 84*(2), 127–190.

Shih, S.-I., & Sperling, G. (1996). Is there feature-based attentional selection in visual search? *Journal of Experimental Psychology: Human Perception and Performance, 22*(3), 758–779.

Shulman, H. G. (1972). Semantic confusion errors in short-term memory. *Journal of Verbal Learning & Verbal Behavior, 11*(2), 221–227.

Simon, D. P., & Simon, H. A. (1978). Individual differences in solving physics problems. In R. Siegler (Ed.), *Children's thinking: What develops?* Mahwah, NJ: Erlbaum.

Simon, H. A. (1957). *Models of man: Social and rational.* New York: Wiley.

Simon, H. A. (1974). How big is a chunk? *Science, 183*(4124), 482–488.

Simon, H. A., & Chase, W. G. (1973). Skill in chess. *American Scientist, 61*(4), 394–403.

Simon, H. A., & Gilmartin, K. (1973). A simulation of memory for chess positions. *Cognitive Psychology, 5*(1), 29–46.

Simpson, G. B., & Kreuger, M. A. (1991). Selective access of homograph meanings in sentence context. *Journal of Memory & Language, 30*(6), 627–643.

Singer, M., Graesser, A. C., & Trabasso, T. (1994). Minimal or global inference during reading. *Journal of Memory & Language, 33*(4), 421–441.

Skinner, B. F. (1938). *The behavior of organisms: An experimental analysis.* New York: Appleton-Century-Crofts.

Skinner, B. F. (1957). *Verbal behavior.* New York: Appleton-Century-Crofts.

Skinner, B. F. (1984). *The shaping of a behaviorist.* New York: New York University Press.

Slobin, D. I. (1966). Grammatical transformations and sentence comprehension in childhood and adulthood. *Journal of Verbal Learning & Verbal Behavior, 5*(3), 219–227.

Sloman, S. A. (1998). Categorical inference is not a tree: The myth of inheritance hierarchies. *Cognitive Psychology, 35,* 1–33.

Sloman, S. A., & Rumelhart, D. E. (1992). Reducing interference in distributed memories through episodic gating. In A. F. Healy, S. M. Kosslyn, & R. M. Shiffrin (Eds.), *Essays in honor of William K. Estes* (Vol. 1, pp. 227–248). Mahwah, NJ: Erlbaum.

Smith, E. E., & Medin, D. L. (1981). *Categories and concepts.* Cambridge, MA: Harvard University Press.

Smith, E. E., Patalano, A. L., & Jonides, J. (1998). Alternative strategies of categorization. *Cognition, 65*(2–3), 167–196.

Smith, E. E., Shoben, E. J., & Rips, L. J. (1974). Structure and process in semantic memory: A featural model for semantic decisions. *Psychological Review, 81*(3), 214–241.

Smith, E. E., & Sloman, S. A. (1994). Similarity- versus rule-based categorization. *Memory & Cognition, 22*(4), 377–386.

Smith, J. D., & Minda, J. P. (2000). Thirty categorization results in search of a model. *Journal of Experimental Psychology: Learning, Memory, and Cognition, 26,* 3–27.

Smith, S. M., & Blankenship, S. E. (1991). Incubation and the persistence of fixation in problem solving. *American Journal of Psychology, 104*(1), 61–87.

Smith, S. M., Glenberg, A., & Bjork, R. A. (1978). Environmental context and human memory. *Memory & Cognition, 6*(4), 342–353.

Sosniak, L. A. (1985). Learning to be a concert pianist. In B. S. Bloom (Ed.), *Developing talent in young people* (pp. 19–67). New York: Ballantine.

Spelke, E., Hirst, W., & Neisser, U. (1976). Skills of divided attention. *Cognition, 4*(3), 215–230.

Spencer, R. M., & Weisberg, R. W. (1986). Context-dependent effects on analogical transfer. *Memory & Cognition, 14*(5), 442–449.

Sperling, G. (1960). The information available in brief visual presentation. *Psychological Monographs, 74*(11, Whole no. 498).

Sperling, G., & Melchner, M. J. (1978). The attention operating characteristic: Example from visual search. *Science, 202,* 315–318.

Sperling, G., & Weichselgartner, E. (1995). Episodic theory of the dynamics of spatial attention. *Psychological Review, 102*(3), 503–532.

Spivey, M. J., & Tanenhaus, M. K. (1998). Syntactic ambiguity resolution in discourse: Modeling the effects of referential context and lexical frequency. *Journal of Experimental Psychology: Learning, Memory, and Cognition, 24*(6), 1521–1543.

Squire, L. R. (1987). *Memory and brain.* New York: Oxford University Press.

Squire, L. R. (1992). Memory and the hippocampus: A synthesis from findings with rats, monkeys, and humans. *Psychological Review, 99,* 195–231.

Squire, L. R., & Cohen, N. (1979). Memory and amnesia: Resistance to disruption develops for years after learning. *Behavioral & Neural Biology, 25*(1), 115–125.

Squire, L. R., Slater, P. C., & Chace, P. M. (1975). Retrograde amnesia: Temporal gradient in very long term memory following electroconvulsive therapy. *Science, 187*(4171), 77–79.

Stark, L., & Ellis, S. (1981). Scanpaths revisited: Cognitive models direct active looking. In D. Fisher, R. Monty, & J. Senders (Eds.), *Cognition and visual perception* (pp. 193–226). Mahwah, NJ: Erlbaum.

Sternberg, R. J., & Davidson, J. E. (1995). *The nature of insight.* Cambridge, MA: MIT Press.

Stroop, J. R. (1935). Studies of interference in serial verbal reactions. *Journal of Experimental Psychology, 18*, 643–662.

Swinney, D. A. (1979). Lexical access during sentence comprehension: (Re)consideration of context effects. *Journal of Verbal Learning & Verbal Behavior, 18*(6), 645–659.

Takeuchi, A. H., & Hulse, S. H. (1993). Absolute pitch. *Psychological Bulletin, 113*(2), 345–361.

Tanaka, J. W., & Taylor, M. (1991). Object categories and expertise: Is the basic level in the eye of the beholder? *Cognitive Psychology, 23*(3), 457–482.

Taraban, R., & McClelland, J. L. (1987). Conspiracy effects in word pronunciation. *Journal of Memory & Language, 26*(6), 608–631.

Tarr, M. J. (1995). Rotating objects to recognize them: A case study on the role of viewpoint dependency in the recognition of three-dimensional objects. *Psychonomic Bulletin & Review, 2*(1), 55–82.

Tarr, M. J., & Pinker, S. (1990). When does human object recognition use a viewer-centered reference frame? *Psychological Science, 1*, 253–256.

Terrace, H. S., Petitto, L. A., Sanders, R. J., & Bever, T. G. (1979). Can an ape create a sentence? *Science, 206*(4421), 891–902.

Tetlock, P. E. (1991). An alternative metaphor in the study of judgment and choice: People as politicians. *Theory & Psychology, 1*(4), 451–475.

Tetlock, P. E. (1992). The impact of accountability on judgment and choice; Toward a social contingency model. *Advances in Experimental Social Psychology, 25*, 331–376.

Thaler, R. (1980). Toward a positive theory of consumer choice. *Journal of Economic Behavior and Organization, 1*, 39–60.

Theeuwes, J., & Burger, R. (1998). Attentional control during visual search: The effect of irrelevant singletons. *Journal of Experimental Psychology: Human Perception and Performance, 24*(5), 1342–1353.

Thomas, J. C. (1974). An analysis of behavior in the hobbits–orcs problem. *Cognitive Psychology, 6*(2), 257–269.

Thompson, A. L., & Klatzky, R. L. (1978). Studies of visual synthesis: Integration of fragments into forms. *Journal of Experimental Psychology: Human Perception and Performance, 4*(2), 244–263.

Thompson, R. F. (1986). The neurobiology of learning and memory. *Science, 223*, 941–947.

Thorndike, E. L. (1911). *Animal intelligence* (Vol. 2). New York: Macmillan.

Tinbergen, N. (1952). The curious behavior of the stickleback. *Scientific American, 182*, 22–26.

Titchener, E. B. (1909). *Experimental psychology of the thought-processes.* New York: Macmillan.

Tranel, D., Bechara, A., & Damasio, A. R. (2000). Decision making and the somatic marker hypothesis. In M. Gazzaniga (Ed.), *The Cognitive neurosciences* (2nd ed., pp. 1259–1270). Cambridge, MA: MIT Press.

Treisman, A., & Gormican, S. (1988). Feature analysis in early vision: Evidence from search asymmetries. *Psychological Review, 95*(1), 15–48.

Trueswell, J. C., Tanenhaus, M. K., & Garnsey, S. M. (1994). Semantic influences on parsing: Use of thematic role information in syntactic ambiguity resolution. *Journal of Memory & Language, 33*(3), 285–318.

Tulving, E. (1967). The effects of presentation and recall of material in free-recall learning. *Journal of Verbal Learning & Verbal Behavior, 6*(2), 175–184.

Tulving, E. (1968). When is recall higher than recognition? *Psychonomic Science, 10*(2), 53–54.

Tulving, E. (1972). Episodic and semantic memory. In E. Tulving & W. Donaldson (Ed.), *Organization and memory.* New York: Academic Press.

Tulving, E. (1983). *Elements of episodic memory.* Oxford, UK: Oxford University Press.

Tulving, E. (1986). Episodic and semantic memory: Where should we go from here? *Behavioral & Brain Sciences, 9*(3), 573–577.

Tulving, E., & Pearlstone, Z. (1966). Availability versus accessibility of information in memory for words. *Journal of Verbal Learning & Verbal Behavior, 5*, 381–391.

Tulving, E., Schacter, D. L., McLachlan, D. R., & Moscovitch, M. (1988). Priming of semantic autobiographical knowledge: A case study of retrograde amnesia. *Brain & Cognition, 8*(1), 3–20.

Tulving, E., Schacter, D. L., & Stark, H. A. (1982). Priming effects in word-fragment completion are independent of recognition memory. *Journal of Experimental Psychology: Learning, Memory, and Cognition, 8*(4), 336–342.

Tulving, E., & Thomson, D. M. (1973). Encoding specificity and retrieval processes in episodic memory. *Psychological Review, 80*, 359–380.

Tulving, E., & Wiseman, S. (1975). Relation between recognition and recognition failure of recallable words. *Bulletin of the Psychonomic Society, 6*(1), 79–82.

Turner, M. L., & Engle, R. W. (1989). Is working memory capacity task dependent? *Journal of Memory & Language, 28*(2), 127–154.

Turvey, M. T. (1973). On peripheral and central processes in vision: Inferences from an information-processing analysis of masking with patterned stimuli. *Psychological Review, 80*(1), 1–52.

Tversky, A. (1969). Intransitivity of preferences. *Psychological Review, 76*(1), 31–48.

Tversky, A. (1977). Features of similarity. *Psychological Review, 84*(4), 327–352.

Tversky, A., & Kahneman, D. (1973). Availability: A heuristic for judging frequency and probability. *Cognitive Psychology, 5*(2), 207–232.

Tversky, A., & Kahneman, D. (1974). Judgment under uncertainty: Heuristics and biases. *Science, 185*(4157), 1124–1131.

Tversky, A., & Kahneman, D. (1981). The framing of decisions and the psychology of choice. *Science, 211*(4481), 453–458.

Tversky, A., & Kahneman, D. (1983). Extensional versus intuitive reasoning: The conjunction fallacy in probability judgment. *Psychological Review, 90*(4), 293–315.

Tversky, A., & Kahneman, D. (1986). Judgment under uncertainty: Heuristics and biases. In H. R. Arkes & K. R. Hammond (Eds.), *Judgment and decision making: An interdisciplinary reader* (pp. 38–55). Cambridge, UK: Cambridge University Press.

Tversky, A., Sattath, S., & Slovic, P. (1988). Contingent weighting in judgment and choice. *Psychological Review, 95*(3), 371–384.

Tversky, A., & Simonson, I. (1993). Context-dependent preferences. *Management Science, 39,* 1179–1189.

Tversky, A., Slovic, P., & Kahneman, D. (1990). The causes of preference reversal. *American Economic Review, 80,* 204–217.

Ullman, S., & Basri, R. (1991). Recognition by linear combinations of models. *IEEE Transactions on Pattern Analysis and Machine Intelligence, 13,* 992–1006.

Underwood, B. J. (1951). Studies of distributed practice: II. Learning and retention of paired-adjective lists with two levels of intra-list similarity. *Journal of Experimental Psychology, 42,* 153–161.

Underwood, B. J., & Goad, D. (1951). Studies of distributed practice: I. The influence of intra-list similarity in serial learning. *Journal of Experimental Psychology, 42,* 125–134.

Underwood, G. (1976). Semantic interference from unattended printed words. *British Journal of Psychology, 67*(3), 327–338.

Ungerleider, L., & Mishkin, M. (1982). Two cortical visual systems. In D. J. Ingle, M. A. Goodale, & R. J. W. Mansfield (Eds.), *Analysis of visual behavior* (pp. 549–586). Cambridge, MA: MIT Press.

Valentine, E. R. (1985). The effect of instructions on performance in the Wason selection task. *Current Psychological Research & Reviews, 4*(3), 214–223.

Vallar, G., & Baddeley, A. D. (1984). Phonological short-term store, phonological processing and sentence comprehension: A neuropsychological case study. *Cognitive Neuropsychology, 1*(2), 121–141.

van der Kamp, J., Savelsbergh, G., & Smeets, J. (1997). Multiple information sources in interceptive timing. *Human Movement Science, 16*(6), 787–821.

van Dijk, T., & Kintsch, W. (1983). *Strategies of discourse comprehension.* San Diego: Academic Press.

Vargha-Khadem, F., Gadian, D. G., Watkins, K. E., Connelly, A., Van Paesschen, W., & Mishkin, M. (1997). Differential effects of early hippocampal pathology on episodic and semantic memory. *Science, 277*(5324), 376–380.

Violanti, J. M., & Marshall, J. R. (1996). Cellular phones and traffic accidents: An epidemiological approach. *Accident Analysis & Prevention, 28*(2), 265–270.

von Neumann, J., & Morgenstern, O. (1944). *Theory of games and economic behavior.* Princeton, NJ: Princeton University Press.

Von Wright, J. M. (1968). Selection in visual immediate memory. *Quarterly Journal of Experimental Psychology, 20*(1), 62–68.

Wagner, A. D., Schacter, D. L., Rotte, M., Koutstaal, W., Maril, A., Dale, A. M., Rosen, B. R., & Buckner, R. L. (1998). Building memories: Remembering and forgetting of verbal experiences as predicted by brain activity. *Science, 281*(5380), 1188–1191.

Walczyk, J. J. (1995). Between- versus within-subjects assessments of image vividness. *Journal of Mental Imagery, 19*(1–2), 161–175.

Wallingford, R. (1975). Long distance running. In A. W. Tayler & F. Landry (Eds.), *The scientific aspects of sports training* (pp. 118–130). Springfield, IL: Charles C. Thomas.

Wardlaw, K. A., & Kroll, N. E. (1976). Autonomic responses to shock-associated words in a nonattended message: A failure to replicate. *Journal of Experimental Psychology: Human Perception and Performance, 2*(3), 357–360.

Warner, C. B., Juola, J. F., & Koshino, H. (1990). Voluntary allocation versus automatic capture of visual attention. *Perception and Psychophysics, 48*(3), 243–251.

Warren, R. M. (1970). Perceptual restoration of missing speech sounds. *Science, 167*(3917), 392–393.

Warren, R. M., & Sherman, G. L. (1974). Phonemic restorations based on subsequent context. *Perception and Psychophysics, 16*(1), 150–156.

Warren, R. M., & Warren, R. P. (1970). Auditory illusions and confusions. *Scientific American, 223*(6), 30–36.

Warren, W. H. (1984). Perceiving affordances: Visual guidance of stair climbing. *Journal of Experimental Psychology: Human Perception and Performance, 10*(5), 683–703.

Warrington, E. K., & Weiskrant, L. (1979). Conditioning in amnesic patients. *Neuropsychologia, 20,* 233–248.

Warrington, E., & Weiskrantz, L. (1968). New method of testing long-term retention with special reference to amnesic patients. *Nature, 217,* 972–974.

Wason, P. C. (1968). Reasoning about a rule. *Quarterly Journal of Experimental Psychology, 20*(3), 273–281.

Wason, P. C. (1969). Regression in reasoning? *British Journal of Psychology, 60*(4), 471–480.

Watkins, M. J., & Schiano, D. J. (1982). Chromatic imaging: An effect of mental colouring on recognition memory. *Canadian Journal of Psychology, 36*(2), 291–299.

Waugh, N. C., & Norman, D. A. (1965). Primary memory. *Psychological Review, 72*(2), 89–104.

Weber, R. J., & Harnish, R. (1974). Visual imagery for words: The Hebb Test. *Journal of Experimental Psychology, 102*(3), 409–414.

Wegner, D. M. (1994). Ironic processes of mental control. *Psychological Review, 101*(1), 34–52.

Wegner, D. M., & Erber, R. (1992). The hyperaccessibility of suppressed thoughts. *Journal of Personality & Social Psychology, 63*(6), 903–912.

Wegner, D. M., Schneider, D. J., Carter, S. R., & White, T. L. (1987). Paradoxical effects of thought suppression. *Journal of Personality & Social Psychology, 53*(1), 5–13.

Weiskrantz, L., & Warrington, E. K. (1979). Conditioning in amnesic patients. *Neuropsychologia, 17*(2), 187–194.

Welford, A. T. (1952). The "psychological refractory period" and the timing of high-speed performance: A review and a theory. *British Journal of Psychology, 43*, 2–19.

Welford, A. T. (1980). The single-channel hypothesis. In A. T. Welford (Ed.), *Reaction time* (pp. 215–252). New York: Academic Press.

Westheimer, G. (1988). Vision: Space and movment. In R. C. Atkinson, R. J. Herrnstein, G. Lindzey, & R. D. Luce (Eds.), *Steven's handbook of experimental psychology* (2nd ed., Vol. 1, pp. 165–194). New York: Wiley. •

Whitney, P., Ritchie, B. G., & Clark, M. B. (1991). Working-memory capacity and the use of elaborative inferences in text comprehension. *Discourse Processes, 14*(2), 133–145.

Whorf, B. L. (1956). *Language, thought, and reality: Selected writings.* Cambridge, MA: Technology Press of MIT.

Wickelgren, W. (1974). *How to solve problems.* San Francisco: W.H. Freeman.

Wickens, C. D. (1984). Processing resources in attention, dual task performance, and workload assessment. In R. Parasuraman & R. Davies (Eds.), *Varieties of attention* (pp. 63–102). New York: Academic Press.

Wickens, C. D. (1992). *Engineering psychology and human performance* (2nd ed.). New York: HarperCollins.

Wickens, D., Dalezman, R., Eggemeier, E., & Thomas, F. (1976). Multiple encoding of word attributes in memory. *Memory & Cognition, 4*, 307–310.

Wikman, A.-S., Nieminen, T., & Summala, H. (1998). Driving experience and time-sharing during in-car tasks on roads of different width. *Ergonomics, 41*(3), 358–372.

Wiley, J. (1998). Expertise as mental set: The effects of domain knowledge in creative problem solving. *Memory & Cognition, 26*(4), 716–730.

Williams, L. M. (1995). Recovered memories of abuse in women with documented child sexual victimization histories. *Journal of Traumatic Stress, 8*(4), 649–673.

Willingham, D. B. (1997). Systems of memory in the human brain. *Neuron, 18*, 5–8.

Willingham, D. B., Nissen, M. J., & Bullemer, P. (1989). On the development of procedural knowledge. *Journal of Experimental Psychology: Learning, Memory, and Cognition, 15*, 1047–1060.

Wittgenstein, L. (1953). *Philosophical investigations.* Oxford, UK: Blackwell.

Wollen, K. A., Weber, A., & Lowry, D. H. (1972). Bizarreness versus interaction of mental images as determinants of learning. *Cognitive Psychology, 3*(3), 518–523.

Wood, N., & Cowan, N. (1995). The cocktail party phenomenon revisited: How frequent are attention shifts to one's name in an irrelevant auditory channel? *Journal of Experimental Psychology: Learning, Memory, and Cognition, 21*(1), 255–260.

Wood, N. L., Stadler, M. A., & Cowan, N. (1997). Is there implicit memory without attention? A reexamination of task demands in Eich's (1984) procedure. *Memory & Cognition, 25*(6), 772–779.

Woodward, A. E., Bjork, R. A., & Jongeward, R. H. (1973). Recall and recognition as a function of primary rehearsal. *Journal of Verbal Learning & Verbal Behavior, 12*(6), 608–617.

Woodworth, R. (1938). *Experimental psychology.* New York: Henry Holt.

Woodworth, R. S., & Schlosberg, H. (1954). *Experimental psychology* (Rev. ed.). New York: Holt.

Woodworth, R. S., & Sells, S. B. (1935). An atmosphere effect in formal syllogistic reasoning. *Journal of Experimental Psychology, 18*, 451–460.

Worthen, J. B. (1997). Resiliency of bizarreness effects under varying conditions of verbal and imaginal elaboration and list composition. *Journal of Mental Imagery, 21*(1–2), 167–194.

Wraga, M. J. (1999a). The role of eye height in perceiving affordances and object dimensions. *Perception and Psychophysics, 61*, 490–507.

Wraga, M. J. (1999b). Using eye height in different postures to scale the heights of objects. *Journal of Experimental Psychology: Human Perception and Performance, 25*, 518–530.

Wright, C. E. (1990). Generalized motor programs: Reexamining claims of effector independence in writing. In M. Jeannerod (Ed.), *Attention and performance XIII: Motor representation and control* (pp. 294–320). Mahwah, NJ: Erlbaum.

Wundt, W. (1894). *Lectures on human and animal psychology* (S. E. Creigton and E. B. Tichener, Trans.). New York: Macmillan.

Wyttenbach, R. A., May, M. L., & Hoy, R. R. (1996). Categorical perception of sound frequency by crickets. *Science, 273*, 1542–1544.

Yachanin, S. A. (1986). Facilitation in Wason's selection task: Content and instructions. *Current Psychological Research & Reviews, 5*(1), 20–29.

Yantis, S. (1992). Multielement visual tracking: Attention and perceptual organization. *Cognitive Psychology, 24*(3), 295–340.

Zhang, S., & Schmitt, B. (1998). Language-dependent classification: The mental representation of classifiers in cognition, memory, and ad evaluations. *Journal of Experimental Psychology: Applied, 4*(4), 375–385.

Zwaan, R. A. (1994). Effect of genre expectations on text comprehension. *Journal of Experimental Psychology: Learning, Memory, and Cognition, 20*(4), 920–933.

CREDITS

Figure 1.7 From Havanastreet.com

Figure I.1 From BIOLOGICAL PSYCHOLOGY by Stephen B. Klein. Copyright © 1990 by Stephen B. Klein. Reprinted by permission of Prentice-Hall, Inc.

Figure I.2 From pp. 108 & 218 from COGNITIVE NEUROSCIENCE: The Biology of the Mind by Michael Gazzaniga, et al. Copyright © 1998 by the authors. Reprinted by permission of W. W. Norton & Company.

Photo I.1 Nina Leen/Time Life Syndication.

Figures I.3, I.4, I.6 From FUNDAMENTALS OF ANATOMY & PHYSIOLOGY 4th edition by Frederic H. Martini. Copyright © 1989 by Frederic H. Martini. Reprinted by permission of Prentice-Hall, Inc.

Figure I.5 Figure from p. 31 in THE HUMAN CENTRAL NERVOUS SYSTEM 3rd edition by R. Nieuwenhuys, J. Voogd and C. Van Huijzen. Copyright © 1988 by Springer-Verlag. Reprinted by permission.

Figure B2.1 Michael Tarr.

Figure 2.6 Reproduced from http://bcs.mit.edu/persci/high/gallery/checkershadowillusion.html. By permission of Ted Adelson, Massachusetts Institute of Technology

Photo 2.1 U.S. Army Photo.

Figure 2.7 Reprinted from "Perceived Lightness Depends on Perceived Spatial Arrangement" by A. L. Gilchrist, *Science*, 195, January 14, 1977. Copyright © 1977 by American Association for the Advancement of Science. Reprinted by permission.

Figure 2.8 From "Vision: Space and Movement" by G. Westheimer in STEVEN'S HANDBOOK OF EXPERIMENTAL PSYCHOLOGY 2nd edition, Volume I by Atkinson, et al. Copyright © 1988 by G. Westheimer. Reprinted by permission of John Wiley & Sons, Inc.

Photo 2.2 Jean-Francois Millet, French (1814–1875) The Gleaners, Oil on canvas, 83.8 × 111.8 cm La Reunion des Musees Nationaux, Louvre, Paris.

Photo 2.3 Zade Rosenthal/Kobal Collection.

Figure 2.17 From Havanastreet.com

Figure 2.18 Table from HUMAN INFORMATION PROCESSING: An Introduction to Psychology 2nd edition by Peter H. Lindsay and Donald A. Norman. Copyright © 1977 by Harcourt, Inc. Reproduced by permission of the publisher.

Figure 2.20 Figure 22, p. 139, Recognition-by-Components: A Theory of Human Image Understanding by I. Biederman. *Psychological Review*, 94(2), 1987.

Figure 2.21 Figure 2, p. 62 from "Rotating Objects to Recognize Them: A Case Study on the Role of Viewpoint Dependency in the Recognition of Three-Dimensional Objects" by M. J. Tarr, *Psychonomic Bulletin & Review*, 2(1), 1995. Copyright © 1991 by the Psychonomic Society, Inc. Reprinted with permission.

Figure 2.23 Figure 3 from "Perceiving Geographical Slant" by D. R. Profitt et al., *Psychonomic Bulletin & Review*, 2(4), 1995. Copyright © 1995 by the Psychonomic Society, Inc. Reprinted by permission.

Box 2.2 From "A Cortical Representation of the Local Visual Environment" by R. Epstein and N. Kanwisher in *Nature*. 392, 1998. Copyright © 1998 by Macmillan Magazines Limited. Reprinted by permission of *Nature*.

Figure 3.3 From "Task Integration as a Factor in Secondary-Task Effects on Sequence Learning" by V. Schmidtke and H. Heuer, *Psychological Research*, 60(1-2), 1992. Copyright © 1992 by Springer-Verlag. Reprinted by permission of the publisher.

Figure 3.6 Figure 1, p. 316 from "The Attention-Operating Characteristic: Example from Visual Search" by G. Sperling and M. J. Melchner, *Science*, 202, 1978. Copyright © 1978 by American Association for the Advancement of Science. Reprinted by permission.

Figure 3.7 & 3.8 Figure 2, p. 11 and figure 3, p. 12 from "Controlled and Automatic Human Processing: I. Detection, Search, and Attention" by Walter Schneider and Richard M. Shiffrin, *Psychological Review*, 1977, 84. Copyright © 1977 by the American Psychological Association. Reprinted with permission.

Figure 6.4 Graph from "Effects of Changed Semantic Context on Recognition Memory" by L. L. Light and L. Carter-Sobell, *Journal of Verbal Learning & Verbal Behavior*, 9, 1970. Copyright © 1970 by Academic Press, Inc. Reprinted by permission.

Figure 6.5 Figure from p. 155 in "Retrieval Independence in Recognition and Recall" by A. J. Flexser and E. Tulving, *Psychological Review*, 85, 1978. Copyright © 1978 by the American Psychological Association. Reprinted by permission.

Figure 6.6 Graph from "Facilitation in Recognizing Pairs of Words: Evidence of a Dependence Between Retrieval Operations" by D. Meyer and R. W. Schvaneveldt, *Journal of Experimental Psychology: General*, 90, 1971. Copyright © 1971 by the American Psychological Association. Reprinted by permission.

Figure 6.8 Figure from "On the Status of Inhibitory Mechanisms in Cognition: Memory Retrieval as a Model Case" by M. C. Anderson and B. A. Spellman, *Psychological Review*, 102(1), 1995. Copyright © 1995 by the American Psychological Association. Reprinted by permission.

Figure 6.9 & Figure 6.10 Figure 7, p. 17 and sample questions from the Appendix in "Semantic Memory Content in Permastore: Fifty Years of Memory for Spanish Learned in School" by H. P. Bahrick, *Journal of Experimental Psychology*, 113(1), 1984. Copyright © 1984 by the American Psychological Association. Reprinted by permission.

Box 6.2 Figure 1, p. 312 from "Frontal Cortex Contributes to Human Memory Formation" by R. L. Buckner, W. M. Kelly, and S. E. Peterson, *Nature Neuroscience*, 2(4), 1999. Copyright © 1999 by Macmillan Magazines Ltd. Reprinted by permission of *Nature*.

Table 6.3 Table from p. 635 in "Suspense in the Absence of Uncertainty" by R. J. Gerrig, *Journal of Memory & Language*, 28(6), 1989. Copyright © 1989 by Academic Press, Inc. Reprinted by permission.

Figure 7.2 Figure 1, p. 30 from "Perceived Distance and the Classification of Distorted Patterns" by M. E. Posner, R. Goldsmith, and K. E. Welton, Jr., *Journal of Experimental Psychology: General*, 73(1), 1967. Copyright © 1967 by the American Psychological Association. Reprinted by permission.

Figure 7.5 Figure from "Features of Similarity" by A. Tversky, *Psychological Review*, 84(4), 1977. Copyright © 1977 by American Psychological Association. Reprinted by permission.

Figure 7.8 Figure 10, p. 27 from PARALLEL DISTRIBUTED PROCESSING: EXPLORATIONS IN THE MICROSTRUCTURE OF COGNITION Volume I by David E. Rumelhart et al. Copyright © 1986 by the authors. Reprinted by permission of MIT Press.

Figure 7.11 Diagram from "What Does Neuroimaging Tell Us About the Role of Prefrontal Cortex in Memory Retrieval?" by R. L. Buckner and S. E. Petersen, *Seminars in the Neurosciences*, 8, 1996. Copyright © 1996 by Academic Press, Inc. Reprinted by permission.

Table 7.5 Figure 11, p. 27 from PARALLEL DISTRIBUTED PROCESSING: EXPLORATIONS IN THE MICROSTRUCTURE OF COGNITION Volume I by David E. Rumelhart et al. Copyright © 1986 by the authors. Reprinted by permission of MIT Press.

Box 7.1 From p. 1020 in THE COGNTIVE NEUROSCIENCES 2nd edition by Michael Gazzaniga. Copyright © 2000 by Michael Gazzaniga. Reprinted by permission of MIT Press.

Box 7.2 From p. 1026 in THE COGNITIVE NEUROSCIENCES 2nd edition by Michael Gazzaniga. Copyright © 2000 by Michael Gazzaniga. Reprinted by permission of MIT Press.

Figure 8.2 From p. 67 in MENTAL REPRESENTATIONS by A. Paivio. Copyright © 1986 by the author. Reprinted by permission of Oxford University Press.

Figure 8.5 Figure 2, p. 702 in "Mental Rotation of Three-Dimensional Objects" by R. N. Shepard and J. Metzler, *Science*, 171, 1971. Copyright © 1971 by the American Association for the Advancement of Science. Reprinted by permission.

Figure 8.6 Figure 1, p. 91 from "Scanning Visual Images: Some Structural Implications" by S. M. Kosslyn, *Perception & Psychophysics*, 49(5), 1991. Copyright © 1991 by the Psychonomic Society, Inc. Reprinted by permission.

Figure 8.11 Figure 1, p. 29 from Stephan A. Brandt and Lawrence W. Stark, "Spontaneous Eye Movements During Visual Imagery Reflect the Content of the Visual Scene," *Journal of Cognitive Neuroscience*, 9:1 (January, 1997). Copyright © 1997 by the Massachusetts Institute of Technology. Reprinted by permission.

Figure 8.12 Figure from "Mental Rotation of Random Two-Dimensional Shapes" by L. A. Cooper, *Cognitive Psychology*, 7(1), 1975. Copyright © 1975 by Academic Press, Inc. Reprinted by permission

Box 8.2 Figure 3, p. 328 from "Neural Systems Shared by Visual Imagery and Visual Perception: A Positron Emission Tomography Study" by S. M. Kosslyn, W. L. Thompson, and N. M. Alpert, *NeuroImage*, 6, 1997. Copyright © 1997 by Academic Press, Inc. Reprinted by permission.

Box 8.3 Figure 1, p. 234 in "Mental Rotation of the Neuronal Population Vector" by A. P. Georgopoulos, et al., *Science*, 243, 1989. Copyright © 1989 by the American Association for the Advancement of Science. Reprinted by permission.

Table 9.2 Table from p. 33 in "Intrasensitivity of Preferences" by A. Tversky, *Psychological Review*, 80(1), 1969. Copyright © 1969 by the American Psychological Association. Reprinted by permission.

Box 9.1 Figure from p. 1052 in THE COGNITIVE NEUROSCIENCES 2nd edition by Michael Gazzaniga. Copyright © 2000 by Michael Gazzaniga. Reprinted by permission of MIT Press.

Figure 10.8 Figure 1, p. 95 in "Graph-Theoretic Confirmation of Restructuring During Insight" by F. T. Durson, C. B. Rea, & T. Dayton, *Psychological Science*, 5(2), 1994. Copyright © 1994 by Blackwell Publishers, Inc. Reprinted by permission.

Figure 10.10 Adapted from figure 3, p. 173 of "When Less is More: Representation and Selective Memory in Expert Problem Solving" by Frank Hassebrock, Paul E. Johnson, Peter Bullemer, Paul W. Fox and James H. Moller, *American Journal of Psychology*, 106:2 (Summer 1993). Copyright © 1993 by the Board of Trustees of the University of Illinois. Used with the permission of the University of Illinois Press.

Figure 10.11 Figure 9, p. 379 from "The Role of Deliberate Practice in the Acquisition of Expert Performance" by K. A. Ericsson, R. T. Krampe, and C. Tesch-Roemer, *Psychological Review*, 100(3), July 1993. Copyright © 1993 by the American Psychological Association. Reprinted by permission.

Table 10.2 & Table 10.3 Tables from pp. 335 and 337 in "Surface and Structural Similarity in Analogical Transfer" by K. J. Holyoak and K. Koh, *Memory &*

Cognition, 15(4), 1987. Copyright © 1987 by the Psychonomic Society, Inc. Reprinted by permission.

Table 10.7 Table from "Reasoning Ability is (Little More Than) Working-Memory Capacity" by P. C. Kyllonen and R. E. Christal, *Intelligence*, vol. 14, no. 4, 1990. Copyright © 1990 by Elsevier Science. By permission of Elsevier Science.

Table 10.8 From pp. 1021–1022 in "Generalizing Solution Procedures Learned From Examples" by R. Catrambone, *Journal of Experimental Psychology: Learning, Memory & Cognition*, 22(4), 1996. Copyright © 1996 by the Psychonomic Society, Inc. Reprinted by permission.

Figure 11.7 Graph from "Plausibility Judgements versus Fact Retrieval: Alternative Strategies for Sentence Verification" by L. M. Reder, *Psychological Review*, 89(3), 1982. Copyright © 1982 by American Psychological Association. Reprinted by permission.

Figure 11.8 Graph from "Comprehension Strategies in the Development of Mental Mode" by E. J. O'Brien and J. E. Albrecht, *Journal of Experimental Psychology: Learning, Memory & Cognition*, 18(4), 1992. Copyright © 1992 by American Psychological Association. Reprinted by permission.

Table 11.1 Chart from p. 179 IN PSYCHOLOGY AND LANGUAGE: An Introduction to Psycholinguistics by Eve V. Clark and Herbert H. Clark. Copyright © 1977 by Harcourt, Inc. Reprinted by permission of the publisher.

Table 11.4 Table 1, p. 378 from "Language-Dependent Classification: The Mental Representation of Classifiers in Cognition, Memory and Ad Evaluations" by S. Zhang and B. Schmitt, *Journal of Experimental Psychology: Applied*, 4(4), 1998. Copyright © 1998 by American Psychological Association. Reprinted by permission.

Author Index

SUBJECT INDEX